Cost
Accounting
and
Control

CECIL GILLESPIE, M.B.A.

Certified Public Accountant
Professor of Accounting
Northwestern University

Cost
Accounting
and
Control

PRENTICE-HALL, INC. · 1957

Englewood Cliffs, N.J.

PREFACE

This book deals with cost accounting, cost control, and costs for use in business planning. It emphasizes current practice in cost accounting and related fields, and will be useful to business managers and to accountants who construct costs and interpret them for use in running a business.

The first half of the book treats uses and classifications of cost, job order costing, process costing, and joint-product and by-product costing. The second half covers cost control, which includes standard costs, and costs for use in business planning. The chapters on costs for business planning cover budgeting, cost-volume-profit relationships, problems of alternative choice and costs for special purposes, and distribution costs. A final chapter is devoted to cost planning (cost system design) and costs for government contracts. The subject matter of the second half is particularly timely in view of the importance of the cost accountant as a member of the management team.

Special attention is paid to reports for management and to managerial uses of cost accounting. In many chapters, reports to management are presented in the beginning and the cost accounting technique follows. Through this approach, the reader can see the use of a technique before he gets into the details of the technique. To reduce complicated techniques to simple elements, a judicious use is made of visual aids in the way of line diagrams and charts.

Coverage of the reports is realistic and complete. The early chapters are concerned with a small business in which cost accounting requirements are relatively simple. The next section of the book is concerned with a somewhat larger business in which the management must rely upon a fairly comprehensive cost accounting system in order to make decisions. A large company having both distribution problems and manufacturing problems is the basis for the later chapters. Although the companies described are necessarily hypothetical, they are typical of numerous actual ones. The use of a series of concrete situations developed from simple to complex makes the book both logical and practical.

In the matter of techniques, the subjects of process costs and the analysis of variances in standard costs systems have received proper shares of text and problems. Because the author believes that these subjects are important, interesting, and of more than average difficulty, he has given them exhaustive treatment.

Questions are included at the end of each chapter to test the reader's knowledge of and appreciation for the theory structure which has been developed in the book. Discussion questions are provided to call the reader's attention to debatable points of theory. In these questions, costs for various intended uses by management are emphasized. In addition, the book includes a set of relatively easy problems and a set of relatively difficult problems. The two sets parallel the coverage of the book. Their purpose is to help the reader acquire mastery of cost accounting techniques and facility in solving cost problems which arise in business planning.

Two appendices are provided for the reader who wants to see "how the whole plan ties together":

I. A complete set of cost control reports for a manufacturing business; and

II. A complete budget for a manufacturing business.

A third appendix is an annotated bibliography of the most significant articles on distribution costs, presented because of the relatively recent development of this field of cost accounting.

The author has received many helpful suggestions from his colleagues and from teachers at other universities. Professor Virgil Boyd and Mr. Edward Rennhack of Northwestern University composed some of the exercises and problems, and gave constructive comment on the text. Professor Arthur E. Carlson of the School of Business and Public Administration at Washington University, Professor Philip T. Meyers of the School of Business Administration at the University of Minnesota and Professor W. A. Howe, Head of the Department of Accounting at Temple University, have read the entire manuscript and given the author the benefit of their skill and experience.

CECIL GILLESPIE

Chicago, Illinois

TABLE OF CONTENTS

Function. Organization for physical control: Personnel. Managerial information. Accounts. Forms. *Accounting Procedure.* Procedure for receipts. Procedures for issues. Physical inventories. Adjustment of book inventories to physical inventory. Summary of materials transactions.

I. Materials Classification. Meaning of materials classification; Need for formal classification. Direct materials; Indirect materials and operating supplies. Some materials may be either direct or indirect; Advantage of direct charging. Maintenance supplies and repair parts. Some elements in laid-down cost. Material losses. Materials overhead: Materials storage and handling expense. *II. Quantity Control.* Meaning of quantity control. Tying cost accounting to product engineering and production control. *III. Materials Prices in Cost Accounting.* Prices used in cost accounting. Effect of method of pricing upon inventory valuation and profits. Last-in, first-out method. Cost or market, whichever lower.

Function. Organization. Managerial information. Direct labor, indirect labor defined. Forms. *Procedure.* Administrative and selling payroll. F.I.C.A. tax—company's share. Posting general journal totals at the end of the month. Recording indirect labor. Summary.

Hidden labor losses. *I. Classification of Labor.* Labor classes defined. Entries for payroll taxes, reserves, and insurance. Fringe benefits. Labor overhead in the larger sense. *II. Labor Costing Under Incentive Pay Plans.* Weekly labor report under piece-work plan; Control of allowances. Forms for piece-rate wage plan. Piece-work payroll. Quantity control in piece-rate wage payment plan. Labor costing under various incentive wage payment plans.

Expense items. Purchased services; Building and machinery expense. *I. Classification of Factory Expense for Control in a Small Factory.* Factory expense defined: Classification by (a) object and (b) varia-

PART FOUR: COST PLANNING

APPENDICES

CONTENTS

22. ... Final Analyse ...

PART FOUR: COST PLANNING

23. Cost Planning ...

APPENDICES

Cost
Accounting
and
Control

Part One

COST ACCOUNTING

THE FIELD OF COST ACCOUNTING

Cost accounting is a set of procedures for determining the cost of a product and of the various activities involved in its manufacture and sale, and for planning and measuring performance. Cost accounting is distinguished from financial accounting in that the former focuses attention upon individual products and relatively minute groups of activities, whereas the latter takes the view exemplified by monthly balance sheets and statements of profits.

Although cost accounting is sometimes considered a management tool of larger businesses, actually formal cost accounting may be equally indispensable in smaller concerns. A relatively small company (having, say, 80 employees) may be manufacturing a line of products which, all told, involves thousands of parts, some purchased and some manufactured in the factory, which contains a variety of productive machinery. In such a factory, the possibility of arriving at product costs by intuition to provide a factor for setting up the selling price list is very small indeed.

Similarly, the possibility of getting a good measure of operating labor performance of the people who run the cutting machines, welding equipment, drill presses, lathes, planers, and other equipment without the records that are the foundation of a cost system is small. The machine shop foreman may know which operators are consistent producers, but top management will have no good way to determine whether shop performance is satisfactory and, if not, where the trouble lies.

Measurement of operating performance on materials is another factor for which a cost system would be useful. In the absence of a good cost system, a machinist might spoil a piece of material after spending labor and machine time on it, then get another piece of material and start again, all without a supervisor knowing about it. Or the operators might be using a great deal more material than is actually needed for the product turned out. Numerous other examples of the need for formal cost accounting in even relatively small concerns could, of course, be given.

Cost accounting is often used in the marketing end of a business as well

3

as in the manufacturing end. Certain phases of the marketing activity, notably finished goods warehousing and delivery to customer by truck, are an extension of the kind of cost accounting that is operated in the factory proper. The actual determination of warehousing and delivery costs may be more complicated than the determination of costs on the factory assembly line, but the need for those costs may be as great as the need for manufacturing costs. In measuring the clerical activities found in the order department, cost accounting is also finding application, particularly in large organizations.

Cost accounting is used in marketing departments not only for the measurement of performance, but also as a tool in planning. In a typical situation, many options are available to the marketing executive in the way of methods of sale, territorial coverage, and so forth. It is very useful for such an executive to know what would be the probable cost and profit of each of several alternatives before he makes his decisions.

This book deals with cost accounting for both small and large businesses and for both manufacturing and marketing activities. The illustrative reports are based upon ones designed for and used in actual businesses, although the company names are fictitious. The reports and cost accounting methods used by smaller companies are presented in the early chapters, and reports and methods of larger companies in the later chapters.

In this chapter, there will be presented first a simple cost formula—the formula for cost of product—with example of how product cost is put together. Next, the managerial uses of costs will be discussed in some detail, followed by a description of the accounting and cost accounting organization in a typical manufacturing company.

Structure of product costs in the Benson and West Manufacturing Company. The Benson and West Manufacturing Company manufactures four products of an assembly nature, from materials bought outside. Illustrative costs of three of the products are set out on page 5. Note that these costs include (a) the cost of materials bought outside, (b) the cost of the labor expended upon the materials to convert them to finished product, and (c) a charge for factory expense, often described as the "overhead of the factory."

The formula for cost of product is:

$$\text{Materials}$$
$$+$$
$$\text{Labor}$$
$$=$$
$$\text{Prime Cost}$$

$$+$$
$$\text{Factory Expense}$$
$$=$$
$$\text{Factory Cost}$$

+

Selling and Administrative Expense

=

Cost to Make and Sell

+

Profit or

−

Loss

=

Selling Price

Product Costs (Illustrative)
Total Costs and Unit Costs of Selected Production Orders
February, 19—

	Product A		Product B		Product C	
Particulars	*Total Amount*	*Per Product Unit*	*Total Amount*	*Per Product Unit*	*Total Amount*	*Per Product Unit*
Production order no.	102		101		103	
Quantity..................	600		300		600	
Date completed............	Feb. 13, 19—		Feb. 12, 19—		Feb. 13, 19—	
Materials.................	$ 936.00	$1.56	$ 348.00	$1.16	$ 984.00	$1.64
Labor.....................	956.00	1.60	664.50	2.215	1,303.00	2.17
Factory expense...........	577.50	.96	405.00	1.35	795.00	1.33
Factory cost..............	$2,469.50	$4.12	$1,417.50	$4.725	$3,082.00	$5.14

Figure 1-1

Note that in Figure 1-1 a *unit cost* of each lot of product is shown. Unit product cost is total factory cost for the lot divided by number of units produced. The cost accountant compiles the cost of *each* lot of product (that is, each production order) and computes the unit product cost when a lot of product is completed. The unit costs shown in Figure 1-1 are:

Product A................. $4.12
Product B.................   4.725
Product C.................   5.14

The unit costs are likely to be more useful to the management than the total costs of the lots. In fact, where different lots of production involve different quantities produced (which is probably the usual situation), it is obviously necessary to reduce the total costs of the lots to a per unit basis to make the costs comparable.

Managerial uses of costs. Managerial uses of costs may be classified: (1) *Measurement of performance*. Measurement of performance by cost accounting methods consists fundamentally in comparing the current cost of manufacturing a product or performing a service or carrying out a function with some previously determined cost. The latter cost may be one that was actually achieved in the recent past, or it may be an estimate of what the cost should be under good performance. In a well-organized cost system, periodic reports are prepared to show the performance of supervisors at all levels. Thus, each factory foreman would receive reports covering the activities for which he is responsible, and the factory superintendent would receive a set of reports showing the performance of his foremen.

In the same way, the supervisors in charge of various marketing activities (selling, order department, warehousing, and delivery) would receive reports on their own activities, and the sales manager would likewise receive reports on the performance of those supervisors. The structure of reports is built up along the lines of responsibility. In general, supervisors at the lower levels receive frequent, detailed reports on their own activities, and supervisors at the upper levels receive less frequent summary reports on the performance of supervisors under them.

Study of the sets of management reports in this book will show that the need for formal cost accounting reports for the measurement of performance tends to increase up to a certain point as the size of the organization increases. The John Benson business, used for illustrative purposes in the early chapters, requires relatively few reports because the number of employees is small and John Benson did a great deal of his supervision of manufacturing operations on the basis of first-hand observation. The Benson and West Manufacturing Company, on the other hand, which is the basis for illustrations in the later chapters requires a more elaborate structure of reports. This company employs many more people than the predecessor organization, and it operates through several levels of supervisors. The top management of Benson and West has relatively little opportunity for first-hand observation of manufacturing operations and must, of necessity, receive regular reports on the performance of its supervisory staff.

(2) *Inventory valuation and control.* Cost accounting is likely to play a fundamental role in valuation of inventories in a manufacturing concern. The mechanics of valuing inventories tends to be more complicated in a manufacturing concern than in a mercantile concern. Whereas in a mercantile concern there is only the *merchandise* inventory to consider, in manufacturing concerns there are likely to be three inventories: (a) materials, the substance from which the manufactured product is produced; (b) work in process, which is the manufactured product in various stages of completion at inventory date; and (c) finished goods, which is manufactured goods ready for sale. The valuation of finished goods involves the combination of materials, labor, and factory expense in proper proportions for each of the products in the inventory, as indicated in the table, "Product Costs (Illustrative)" on page 5.

The valuation of work in process follows the same pattern as for finished goods, but it is complicated by the fact that various stages of completion may be represented among the goods on the production floors at inventory date. One lot of product may be half completed as to labor, while another may be only one-fourth completed. It would be expected that this difference would be reflected in the values at which the lots would be carried in the inventory.

The two general methods of setting up inventories in a manufacturing concern (physical inventory and book inventory) are explained and illustrated in Chapter 3. As the name suggests, the physical inventory method involves counting the items in inventory, pricing them appropriately for the stage of completion, and finally extending quantities and prices to determine values. The book inventory method involves the operation of inventory control accounts in such manner that the balances of the accounts are the inventory valuations required for statement purposes.

Complete cost accounting systems are likely to incorporate book inventories from which the financial statements may be prepared. In fact, it is often said that one of the advantages of a complete cost system is that it makes possible the preparation of monthly financial statements without the trouble and expense of taking monthly physical inventories. This advantage is often a very real one. The author thinks of cases where monthly statements without the need for monthly physical inventories were one of the main reasons for installing a cost system.

Inventory control (as distinguished from inventory valuation) involves keeping the quantities of various inventory items in line with sales. If the quantities are too small, sales may be lost or production may stop. If the quantities are too large, too much working capital is tied up in inventories and the necessity for scaling down inventories one way or another may arise. In some factories, the detailed quantity information on inventories provided by the cost system may be used for production control purposes. In the Benson and West Manufacturing Company, for instance, the detailed inventory records kept by the inventory clerks in the accounting department are used by the planning and production control clerks in the performance of their duties. If the inventory records were not available in the accounting department, some other means would have to be provided to keep the production control clerks informed as to quantities of various materials on hand, the quantities of each product in process, and the quantities of each product in finished goods stores.

(3) *Use in setting selling prices.* The Benson and West Manufacturing Company manufactures (a) certain staple products on which it has a great deal of competition product for product and (b) certain made-to-order goods produced according to customer specifications. The sales manager prices the staple products on the basis of the prices he thinks his competitors are

charging for the same items. He uses product *costs* to determine on what products he is making the greatest gross profit (or in some cases, taking a loss).

On the custom products, the sales manager is called upon to give *bids* to prospective customers. When a salesman turns up an inquiry for a bid on a certain quantity of specified goods, the cost accountant estimates the cost of the job, reviewing his figures with the industrial engineer and the factory superintendent. The sales manager then sets the bid, with knowledge of the estimated cost of the job. This is not to say, of course, that the sales manager simply adds a percentage to the estimated cost to cover selling and administrative expense and profit. He is influenced by his knowledge of the market in general, the customer in particular, and the volume requirements of the Benson and West Manufacturing Company. The estimated cost is useful to him in that it shows him what he must sell for to make a profit. It prevents him from selling the job at a loss without knowing it.

(4) *Use in budgeting.* The controller of the Benson and West Manufacturing Company prepares a number of budgets for certain periods in advance, including budget statement of profits, budget cost of plant improvements, budget of cash receipts and disbursements, and so forth. (A complete illustrative budget for the company is presented in Appendix II. Its use and method of construction are explained in Chapters 23-25.) These budgets, of course, reflect the plans of the management for future period(s) and they indicate the expected results of those plans. They are the means of getting the sales manager, the factory superintendent, and the treasurer into agreement as to a program that can be sold, manufactured, and financed. The *manufacturing cost* schedules of the complete budget are prepared for the controller by the cost accountant.

(5) *Use in planning changes in products, plant, or methods of production or distribution.* The *comparative costs* used in planning changes in products, plant, or methods of distribution (mentioned above) are constructed partly of cost accounting information and partly of other information. Comparative costs are explained and illustrated in Chapters 27-29.

Organization: Relationship of cost accountant to other executives in the business. The organization of cost accounting varies somewhat among companies. In a small company, one cost man may do all the *cost bookkeeping* and operate the *cost controls* to determine whether expenditures have been excessive. He may do whatever *cost analysis* he thinks is necessary to answer the manager's question as to why the costs are high this month, and he may make the *cost comparisons* which are useful to the manager in making his decisions regarding various changes. (The four terms in italics are descriptive terms; definitions appear at the end of this chapter.)

In larger organizations, there is likely to be a supervising cost accountant, cost clerks and ledger clerks, and cost analysts. Figure 1-2 on page

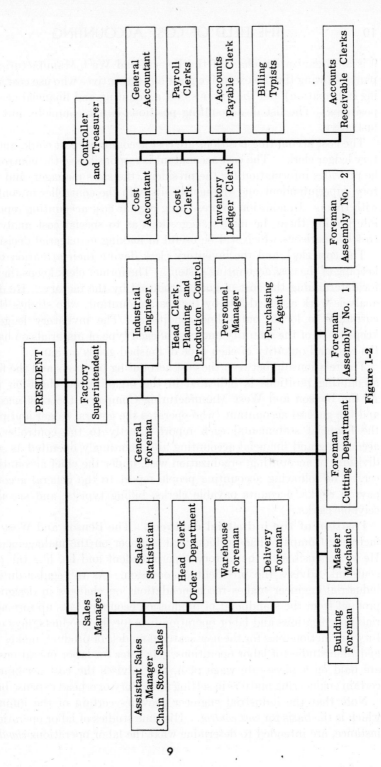

ORGANIZATION CHART

BENSON AND WEST MANUFACTURING COMPANY

Figure 1-2

9

9 is an organization chart of the Benson and West Manufacturing Company, showing the top executive positions (executives who use cost accounting information) and the various cost accounting and financial accounting positions. The list of accounting positions is not complete, but it is illustrative.

The cost accounting positions are cost accountant, cost clerk, and inventory ledger clerk.   The cost accountant is responsible to the controller, but he provides information for the president, the sales manager, and the factory superintendent and frequently sits with the controller in conferences with them.   In addition to presenting regular cost accounting reports and interpreting them, he makes suggestions as to special cost analyses and cost comparisons which will be useful in making managerial decisions.

The cost clerk and the inventory clerk devote their attention to bookkeeping of the cost accounting system.   The former clerk keeps the records for determining the cost of goods produced by the factory.   He does the analysis work assigned him by the cost accountant, who studies the costs currently to locate out-of-line conditions.   The inventory ledger clerk keeps track of the quantity and cost of each type of materials on hand and the cost and quantity of each type of finished goods on hand.

The relationship between the cost accounting positions and the financial accounting positions is indicated in the organization chart on page 9. At the Benson and West Manufacturing Company, the cost accountant and the general accountant (who operates the general ledger and prepares the financial statements) each report directly to the controller.   Cost accounting and financial accounting are accordingly operated as separate divisions of accounting, organization wise, under the chief accounting officer.   The following accounting people report to the general accountant: payroll clerks, accounts payable clerks, billing typists, and accounts receivable clerks.

Position of the industrial engineer.   The Benson and West Manufacturing Company has an industrial engineer on the management staff. He is responsible to the factory superintendent and he, like the cost accountant, advises the president on occasion.   As to regular duties, the industrial engineer makes recommendations on changes in design of the product from the standpoint of production economy, sets up formal materials specifications and labor operation lists for the products, lays out factory production lines for the new seasonal models of product, makes motion and time studies of labor operations, sets rates for labor operations which are paid on a piece-rate wage plan, and advises the cost accountant on certain engineering matters in setting up factory overhead expense budgets.

Note that the industrial engineer provides certain of the information which is the basis for *cost control*.   His time studies of labor operations, for instance, are intended to determine what the labor operations *should* cost.

His piece rates or other estimated labor costs are accordingly used by the cost accountant for control purposes. His studies of materials allowances are similarly used by the cost accountant for cost control purposes.

Summary: Cost accounting and its components. The general term *cost accounting* includes:

Cost accounting proper, or *cost bookkeeping*, which involves the recording of costs according to pre-arranged classifications. Usually, cost bookkeeping does not operate entirely separately from the financial accounting system, but rather as an extension or subdivision of it.

Cost *control*, which is the determination of whether the current costs are out of line with what is regarded as a satisfactory performance.

Cost *analysis*, which involves determining why costs are out of line and who is responsible. Cost analysis often proceeds from cost control. In practice, the cost control routines and reports should indicate that costs in a certain area are excessive, and analysis would be undertaken to determine why the costs are excessive and who is responsible.

Cost *comparison*, which is the comparison of the cost of alternate products, activities, methods, or areas in the field of production or distribution. Cost comparisons answer the question "What would be the effect on costs if we changed such and such?" Sometimes the management is considering a change in the product or in the method of manufacture, or a change in the method or area of distribution, or a change in type or capacity of equipment. Cost comparisons would be made as one of the factors in the decision as to whether the change should be made.

Cost *planning* is, strictly speaking, cost system or procedure planning. It involves determining what regular management reports are necessary, what cost records and cost controls must be set up and maintained to produce the reports, and to some extent what cost accounts must be included in the classifications to make analysis possible. In this last connection, note that although it is not possible to include all accounts necessary to answer all possible questions, it is possible to anticipate some of the information that the analyst will need to do his work.

QUESTIONS

1-1. (a) What is meant by unit product cost?
(b) Give mathematical formulas for determining unit product cost.

1-2. Discuss briefly the managerial uses of unit costs.

1-3. The general term *cost accounting* is usually considered to include several distinct but related record-keeping or managerial activities. Name them and describe them briefly.

1-4. It is said that some phases of cost control involve the work of the industrial engineer and some phases involve the cost accountant. Discuss this statement and name forms of cost control with which the industrial engineer is directly concerned, and forms with which the cost accountant is directly concerned.

1-5. The president of the company tells you, the cost accountant, that he thinks the cost of a certain product that the company makes is "too high." What might be meant by this statement? Describe information that you might set up to assist him in determining whether the cost is too high, and in what respects.

Chapter 2

TYPES OF COST SYSTEM; COST UNITS AND CLASSIFICATIONS

It is now desirable to describe briefly the various types of cost system and methods of classifying costs. The reader will become aware that there is no one cost system which is the format for all types and sizes of business and that there is likewise no one method of classifying costs for all purposes.

Even two companies in the same line of business are not likely to have exactly the same cost system and classifications. Because cost accounting is a management tool fitted to the requirements of the specific users, a cost system and cost classifications are likely to be custom made. Cost planning involves careful survey of company reports, organization, products, and plant.

Types of cost system. Basically, there are two types of cost system: job order and process. A *job order cost system* may be used where specific order production control is in operation. In such a cost system, the cost clerk receives a copy of each production order, and he sets up a cost sheet for each production order. The cost sheet is used to compile the cost of the production order as work is done. The cost per unit of product is accordingly an average cost for a specific order.

An example of the use of a job order cost system occurs in printing plants. In such a plant, a cost sheet is set up for each job, to compile the costs incurred in the composing room, the press room, the bindery, and other departments involved. In these cases, most of the jobs or orders are different, and the management wants to know the cost performance on each job.

Other examples are found in connection with building construction and ship construction. In building construction where one company does the the entire job, cost sheet(s) are used to compile separately excavation, foundation, structural steel, brick laying, carpenter work, electrical work, roofing, painting, and perhaps other classifications for each job.

In ship construction, costs of a single ship may be compiled on job orders which are decided upon by the engineers, estimators, and cost people when the ship is being designed. It is necessary to set up job orders to provide logical integrated engineering units for estimating in the first place and to localize any excess spending which occurs in the actual building.   The job orders are numbered in a logical scheme and listed in a formal "Job Order Book for Hull No.—." Copies of the job order book are provided for the engineers, estimators, cost people, and the shipyard purchasing and accounting people who issue purchase orders, job tickets, and requisitions. There may be 500 or more job orders for compiling the cost of a ship.   One group of job orders will be set up, for instance, for hull and machinery, which will include orders for boilers, propulsion machinery, electric generators, air conditioning machinery, and so on.

An *assembly cost* is a type of job cost.   As the name indicates, it may be used in assembly plants, where various parts are manufactured in certain departments, later to be put together to make major product units.   In an automobile plant, for instance, parts such as wheels, frames, axles, motors, generators, and so forth will be made in separate departments and later assembled into automobiles on an assembly line.   In a factory which produces large cameras for the graphic arts industries, parts are made in various departments for assembly into the rear case assembly, the glass screen mechanism, the front case and bellows, and other assemblies which are, in turn, put together to make the complete camera.

In an assembly cost system, there are *parts* cost sheets and *assembly* cost sheets.   The former are used to compile the cost of parts.   In an automobile plant, there would be parts cost sheets for wheels, frames, axles, and all the other parts manufactured by the company.   A parts cost sheet would be used to compile the cost of materials, labor, and factory expense chargeable to a specified quantity of a particular part.

Assembly cost sheets would be used to compile the cost of the finished assembly.   They show the costs of the parts and the cost of the labor and expense required to assemble the parts.

A *process cost system* is used where it is not possible or not desirable to identify successive jobs or lots of production for cost accumulating purposes.   In a process cost system, costs and production units are accumulated *period by period*.   At the end of each period (often one month) cost per unit of goods produced is determined as an average unit cost for the period.

For example, in the manufacture of pig iron, once a blast furnace is put into operation, it operates continuously for a long period of time if there is no lack of orders for iron.   Iron ore, limestone, and coke are charged into the furnace at intervals, and molten iron is tapped at the base of the furnace.   In this case, it is not possible to identify successive lots of input because they merge in the furnace.   An account is set up either for the product "pig iron" or for the department "blast furnace," and it is charged for the cost of iron ore, limestone, coke, labor, and expense used during the month.   Likewise, a record is kept of tons of pig iron tapped from the furnace during the month.   At the end of the month, the cost of pig iron produced is computed as total debits to the account divided by tons produced.

Other examples of factories that use process costs are breweries, cement mills, and flour mills.   In each of these cases, the unit product cost is an average for a period.   Note that in addition to the unit product cost, it is customary in process industries to compute *unit conversion* costs period by period.   A unit conversion cost for a department is labor plus expense divided by units for which the department is given credit.   Unit conversion cost, which specifically excludes materials, is used as an index of performance within the department.   It can also be used to construct unit product costs, since the appropriate unit materials costs plus unit conversion costs would equal total unit product cost.

The example of process costs given above (pig iron manufacture) illustrates single stage process costing.   Only one department or stage is involved.   A more complicated form of process costing is *multiple stage* process costing.   As the name suggests, production passes from one stage or department to another in succession.   Thus, a steel mill might comprise the blast furnace department, which produces pig iron, the open hearth department, which converts iron into steel in the form of ingots, and the rolling mill, which rolls the ingots into blooms or other shapes.

A complete explanation of process costing, both single stage and multiple stage, is presented in Chapters 13 and 14.

Operation costing is a type of process costing.   The focal point is an operation or a group of closely related operations.   Setting up an operation cost system involves identifying specific measurable operations being performed repetitively for significant periods and selecting work units or cost units for measuring the production which comes out of each operation.   A unit conversion cost is computed for each operation by dividing cost by work units or cost units produced.

To illustrate the construction of operation costs, in a factory that produces covered wire of various types, there may be the following departments: wire mill, in which copper rod is drawn to bare copper wire; braiding and twisting department, in which strands of bare copper wire are twisted (and multiple covered wires braided); the covering department, which covers bare wire with fabric insulator; and the enameling department, which covers bare wire with insulator.   These are departments.   Now, in the wire mill the operations recognized for costing purposes might be heavy drawing, medium drawing, and fine drawing.   The larger sizes of wire go through the first operation; the medium sizes go through the first and second; and the fine sizes go through all three operations.   Number of pounds of wire drawn is compiled for each operation, and unit conversion cost for each operation is determined monthly.

In the sewing room of a work garment plant, 30 or 40 operations might be set up. The cost of serging, say, might be determined per foot of piece goods serged, making buttonholes might be determined per dozen button-holes, and so on.

A *class cost* is a cost for a period for a specified group of products.* It is an average cost for the period. In a foundry, all castings up to 10 pounds in weight may be costed in one class, all castings 11 pounds to 20 pounds in in another class, all castings 21 pounds to 30 pounds in a third class. Or several classes might be recognized for castings in each weight group. Class 1-10A would be simple castings; Class 1-10B would be intricate cast-ings; and so on.

In the operation of class costs, the cost of each class and the pounds pro-duced (in this example) for each class would be compiled. At the end of each period, a cost per pound would be determined for each class.

Cost units: Purposes. A cost unit is a unit of measurement in terms of which costs are expressed. Cost units may be *sales* units—that is, units used by the manufacturer and his customer for the negotiation of sale of the product.

Such units are found in all complete cost sytems because one of the aims of cost accounting is to provide a product cost basis (or factor) for selling prices. For this purpose, the cost units must be sales units. In some cases the product sales unit is the major unit found in the cost system. (In the simple system illustrated in Chapter 4, the basic cost unit is such a unit.)

In some cases, cost units are essentially *production* units or *work* units. These units represent an attempt to measure as accurately as possible the amount of work turned out of a process or operation. Thus, *feet* may be the cost unit for serging work garments in the sewing room of a garment plant, and *number* of *buttons* sewed may be the cost unit for the button sew-ing operation. Note that these production cost units as *statistical units* would themselves be useful for measuring performance in the sewing room.

In a coaster wagon factory, the following cost units are used (among others): *Each* (for the completed wagons), *each* (for such subassemblies as the front bolster assembly, the rear bolster assembly), *pounds* of sheet steel (for the shearing operation), pieces punched (for the punch press opera-tions, square feet painted (for the painting operation.)

Cost units that are production units have another use. After the whole structure of such cost units has been set up for a factory, they may be put together to arrive at the final unit product cost. Thus, in a factory which manufactures bare copper wire, the cost per pound of fine gauge might be arrived at by the formula: copper cost per pound of finished product plus cost per pound for the heavy drawing operation (labor and expense) plus cost per pound for the medium drawing operation plus cost per pound for the fine operation.

* John Neuner, *Cost Accounting Principles and Practice* (Homewood, Ill.: Richard D. Irwin, Inc., 1952), p. 6.

Cost units: Summary of types. In most cost systems a number of different cost units are used. Cost units may have to be selected for finished product, parts, processes, operations, and services (as where a factory produces its own power). It is necessary that the units be very carefully selected and that these units be satisfactory measures of work turned out, since they are to be used for the measurement of performance as well as for the construction of final product costs for selling price purposes. They should be meaningful to the factory supervisor for the first purpose and to the product cost estimator for the second purpose. One of the most important factors in the success of a cost system is the skill and care with which the cost units are selected.

Cost units may be stated in terms of:

(1) *Units or pieces*, where there are not significant differences in size or weight among the various units or pieces.

(2) *Weighted units*, as where there are significant differences in size or weight such as would invalidate the use of simple units or pieces for the measurement of performance. Thus, in a work garment plant dozens packed might be a suitable cost unit for all garments packed regardless of style or size. In a radio factory, on the other hand, units packed might not be a satisfactory measure of work done in the packing room because of difference in models handled. It might be decided to use weighted units, counting a table model as 1 and a console model as 2, and so forth.

(3) *Commercial units of measure* intended to recognize the physical nature of the product, such as pounds, tons, gallons, barrels, feet, yards, cubic feet, and cubic yards.

(4) *Area* (such as square feet for painting or electro-plating).

(5) *Standard time*. In some cases none of the above units will fit because of the peculiarity of the operating situation. Instead of measuring output for costing purposes in terms of physical units of goods handled, the cost man measures production in terms of the amount of time it should have taken to do the work. Thus in a sheet rolling mill (steel), the roller may work on several orders at the same time, putting through a few sheets of one order and then a few sheets of another. It may not be feasible to keep track of the amount of time spent on each order as the orders go through, or even to keep track of the tonnage at the rolls. When the mill is getting "warmed up" some sheet "handles" readily and some does not. It may be feasible, however, at the end of each day's run, to determine the amount allowable according to the engineer's estimates. This time would be stated in terms of "standard hours." Thus at the end of the day, it may be found that the mill produced 7.6 standard hours in 8 actual hours.

Cost classifications. The beginning student in cost accounting may have the idea that costs are recorded according to a single classification which serves all purposes. This impression might be gained by looking at a set of journals and cost sheets in a cost system. It might seem that after the columnar journals have been set up and the transactions recorded in the proper columns, which are in turn posted to accounts, that would be the end of the cost accounting. As a matter of fact, the systems man does attempt to anticipate the various uses which will be made of cost accounting data when he sets up the classifications of accounts. In spite of the care which he takes, however, it is usually necessary after the original recording of transactions to re-assemble the recorded data in various ways for various purposes. If the systems man has done a good job of arranging the basic classifications, it should be possible to get out the costs that are required for the various purposes.

It is not possible to explain in this chapter all the uses of cost accounting and the classifications that would serve each use. The relationship of use to the nature of the classification will develop as the chapters unfold. It *is desirable* at this point, however, to state that there are different classifications for different purposes, and to indicate what some of the classifications are.

Some of the classifications of cost illustrated in this text are:

(1) *By function or operation.* A classification of expense accounts by major function of the business is included in the general ledger classification of John Benson on page 25. Note that accounts are provided for administration, selling, manufacturing, and financing. In a set of warehouse accounts, accounts might be provided for putting goods into stock, taking goods out of stock, assembling orders, and packing. In a wire mill, accounts might be provided for heavy drawing, medium drawing, and fine drawing.

(2) *By element.* This is a classification of manufacturing costs into accounts for materials, labor, and factory expense (Chapter 3).

(3) *Into direct and indirect groups.* The terms *direct* and *indirect* are defined with reference to the cost units which have been selected. A direct cost is one which can be allocated to the cost unit. Thus, where the product unit is the cost unit (as it is in Chapter 4), a direct material is one identified with the product and considered feasible to measure in terms of product units. An indirect material would be one which it is not considered feasible to measure in terms of product units. Labor may be similarly classified where the product unit is considered the cost unit. Finally, purchased services (for example, power bought outside and professional engineers' fees) and fixed charges on plant (for example, depreciation, insurance, and taxes) may be classified as direct or indirect with regard to products. A tabular summary of the concept of direct and indirect costs with reference to products appears on page 19.

(4) *By object* (nature of the goods or services used). The classification of factory expenses in Chapter 9 includes groups of accounts for each of the following: labor (separate account for each major indirect labor occupa-

tion), operating supplies, maintenance supplies and repair parts, purchased services, travel, and fixed charges (separate accounts for depreciation, insurance, and taxes).

Classification of Costs: Direct and Indirect
As Regards Products (Job Order System)

Materials	*Labor*	*Purchased Service; Fixed Charges on Plant**
(See Page 101 for complete classification and examples)	(See Page 160 for complete classification and examples)	(See Page 176 for complete classification and examples)
Direct materials	*Direct labor*	*Direct service; fixed charges*
Materials identified with specific product, which can be measured and charged to cost sheets.	Labor identified with specific product, which can be measured and charged to cost sheets.	Service; fixed charges identified with specific product, which can be measured and charged to cost sheets.
Indirect materials	*Indirect labor*	*Indirect service; fixed charges*
(a) Materials identified with specific product, which it is *not* considered feasible to measure and charge to cost sheets.	(a) Labor identified with specific product, which it is *not* considered feasible to measure and charge to cost sheets.	(a) Service; fixed charges identified with specific product, which it is *not* considered feasible to measure and charge to cost sheets.
(b) Materials used for the benefit of production in general, and not reasonably identifiable with specific product.	(b) Labor used for the benefit of production in general, and not reasonably identifiable with specific product	(b) Service; fixed charges used for the benefit of production in general, and not reasonably identifiable with specific product.

* Examples of fixed charges on plant are depreciation, insurance, and taxes.

Figure 2-1

(5) *Fixed and variable* (Chapter 9). For purposes of control, it is useful to classify expenses according to whether they are *fixed* (expected to remain at same amount within the normal range of volume for the business), variable (expected to change more or less directly with changes in volume), or semivariable (expected to change with changes in volume, but in "steps" rather than directly). Illustration of classification of accounts according to general variability appears in Chapter 9.

(6) *By responsibility* (Chapter 12). In some factories a number of departments are in operation, each having its own supervisor who is responsible for the control of certain expenses used to operate the department. In such cases, it is necessary to classify expenses by department to measure the supervisor's spending performance.

Time when costing is done. In practice certain costing is done *before* production takes place (predetermined costs) and certain costing is done as and after production takes place (historical costing). The illustration of job order cost accounting in Chapter 4 is an example of historical costing, since the unit costs are computed on the cost sheets after the jobs are finished.   On the other hand, the standard product costs described in Chapter 17 are an example of predetermined costs, since the product costs for a manufacturing season are set up before the beginning of the season.   The reader will observe that certain uses of costs *require* that they be predetermined costs.   This is the case, for instance, where they are used in setting up price lists or catalog prices.

Work orders.   The various types of work orders found in manufacturing concerns which are closely related to the cost accounting system are described below.   In some cases, the issuance of a work order starts a cycle of cost accounting operations.

Production Orders.   These are orders issued by the planning or production control people instructing (and authorizing) a foreman to produce specified goods.   The orders will state among other details (a) what is to be produced, (b) when it is required, and (c) to whom it is to be delivered (for instance, some other department or the finished goods warehouse).

Production orders are primarily a part of the scheduling mechanism whereby materials, labor, and production facilities are coordinated and put into relationship to sales and finished goods inventories.   Note that there is a definite relationship between the production control system and the cost accounting system.   Where a job order cost system is in operation, the cost clerk receives a copy of each production order, and he sets up a cost sheet for each of them.   As the job is worked on in the factory, he charges the cost sheet with the materials and labor used.   When the job is finished, he applies factory expense to the cost sheet and finally determines the cost of completed job.

Other types of work orders in which the cost accountant is interested are:

Betterment Orders.   These orders are issued by a planning group in the factory office, instructing responsible supervisors to proceed with specified work in respect to plant which will increase its value.   Betterments involve either (a) adding new machines and buildings to the existing plant or (b) improving the existing machines and buildings.

The cost accountant receives a copy of each betterment order, and he sets up a *betterment order cost sheet* on which he compiles the cost of the job as it is being done.   When the job is completed, he totals the charges to the cost sheet and thus determines the cost at which the asset should be set up in the general books.   If the betterment order cost sheets are few in number, they may be kept in the work in process ledger, along with the production order cost sheets.   In that case, when a betterment order cost sheet is completed and removed from the work in process ledger, the entry is debit Plant account and credit Work in Process.

Repair Orders.   These are orders issued by a planning group, instructing responsible supervisors to proceed with specified repair work, that is, work which is intended to keep the plant in day-to-day operating efficiency.

The cost of repair work (unlike the cost of betterment work) is charged in the ordinary cost bookkeeping to Factory Expense. Often the management desires to have reports on the cost of repair jobs, however, and the cost accountant may be instructed to set up cost sheets for repair orders for the purpose of such reporting. Some companies have a rule that if the estimated cost of a repair is above a specified amount, a repair order cost sheet shall be maintained by the cost accountant, and the cost of the job reported to the management.

Standing Orders. These are instructions to and authority for incurring factory expense necessary to operate a department or carry out some operating function. Note that standing orders are not work orders in the sense that the above named orders are. Standing orders are likely to be issued when a new classification of expense accounts is set up or when the classification of expense accounts is revised. The order will specify *standing order numbers* to be charged when expense is incurred. Standing order numbers are *expense account* numbers.

QUESTIONS

2-1. Distinguish the following types of cost systems:
(a) Job
(b) Assembly costs
(c) Process
(d) Operation
(e) Class cost

2-2. (a) Explain what is meant by a cost unit. Differentiate from "unit cost."
(b) Explain four types of cost units.
(c) Why is it essential that cost units be selected or developed carefully?

2-3. What cost units would be developed for:
(a) Manufacturers
(b) Traders
(c) Institutions—hospitals, schools, etc.

2-4. In setting up the classification of cost accounts for a small manufacturing business, the factory expense accounts might be set up according to object or nature of the goods or services used. Aside from classification by object, what bases of classification can you name?

Name or describe briefly each of six bases and explain why each classification would be useful.

2-5. Explain what is meant by (a) historical costs and (b) predetermined costs. Explain why particular uses of costs may require one or the other.

2-6. What is your understanding of the terms "direct material" and "indirect material"?

2-7. Explain the primary use and the relationship to the cost accounting system of each of the following orders:
(a) Production order
(b) Standing order
(c) Betterment order
(d) Repair order

PROBLEMS

2-1. The Aldora Lamp Company manufactures two styles of lamps—a table lamp and a floor lamp—from materials and parts purchased outside.

A table lamp consists of the following materials and parts:

1 base (wood) unpainted................	$2.00
1 shade (plastic) unpainted	1.00
1 socket with switch....................	.80
6 feet electric cord.....................	1.20
Paint.................................	.30

A floor lamp consists of the following materials and parts:

1 base (iron)..........................	$4.00
1 shade (plastic) unpainted.............	1.00
1 socket with switch....................	.80
11 feet electric cord...................	2.20
Paint.................................	.20

Each style of lamp is assembled by *assemblers* who are paid $1.50 per hour and decorated by *painters* who are paid $2 per hour. An assembler can put together a table lamp in 20 minutes and a floor lamp in 30 minutes. A painter can paint the base and stencil the shade of a table lamp in 45 minutes and stencil the shade of a floor lamp in 15 minutes. The iron bases of floor lamps are not painted.

Factory expense is applied to floor lamps and table lamps by means of a calculated rate per labor hour. Factory expense for a month is $2,000, and the total labor time of assemblers and painters is 2,000 hours.

You are required to set out in detail the cost per unit of a table lamp and the cost of a floor lamp. Show a separate total for each *element* of cost. Include factory expense in the cost of each lamp at the rate of $1.00 per labor hour.

2-2. The Warrington Manufacturing Company manufactures automatic washing machines in several models. Before a new model is put into production, the cost department computes a *predetermined* cost, working from the blueprints, and using expected prices and quantities.

Using the following information, you are asked to:

1. Lay out an estimate sheet according to your own ideas. You may use columnar analysis paper.

2. Enter all available information relating to the cost of the proposed model.

Only one copy need be prepared, but it is assumed that copies would be sent to (1) factory superintendent, (2) engineering department, and (3) sales manager.

MATERIALS: List of materials (parts) required and expected prices:

Symbol	Descriptive Name	Used by Department	Expected Price Each
A-10	Transmission	Assembly	$12.00
A-20	Base and frame	Assembly	9.00
A-30	Motor	Assembly	12.00
A-40	Timer	Assembly	3.00
A-50	Tub	Assembly	6.00
A-60	Door and scale	Test and pack	2.00
A-70	Cabinet	Assembly	3.00
P-10	Paint	Painting	3.00
C-10	Crate	Test and pack	2.00

(One washer requires one of each of the above items)

LABOR: Operation list:

Symbol	Description	Performed in Department	Expected Average Time (One washer) (in hundredths)
A-1	Attach transmission to base	Assembly	.90 hours
A-2	Attach motor to base	Assembly	.30 hours
A-3	Attach timer to transmission	Assembly	.25 hours
A-4	Attach tub, cabinet, and door to frame	Assembly	.30 hours
P-1	Paint	Painting	.50 hours
T-1	Test	Test and pack	.30 hours
T-2	Pack	Test and pack	.45 hours

(One washer requires a single performance of each of the above operations)

LABOR: Rates:

Department	Expected Rate
Assembly, all.................	$1.50
Painting.....................	1.60
Testing......................	1.60
Packing......................	1.50

FACTORY EXPENSE: Rates (to be applied to hours):

Department	Expected Rate
Assembly.....................	$1.00
Painting.....................	1.50
Testing and packing...........	1.20

INVENTORIES AND MANUFACTURING COSTS

Account classification for a small manufacturing concern. This chapter and the following one describe the accounts, statements, and cost records kept by a small manufacturing business. (The name John Benson is fictitious.) The business manufactures a simple assembly product (designated Product E in these chapters) from materials and parts bought outside. Materials are received in a receiving room and stored in the raw materials storeroom until needed. Then, the materials are drawn out of stores and used in the assembly department to make Product E. The finished goods are placed in finished goods warehouse when completed, and stored there until they. are sold. When the product is sold, it is taken out of stock, packed, and shipped to the customer.

Mr. Benson manages the business himself, devoting full time to its administration. He has a bookkeeper-clerk who does all the office work. There are two salesmen who call on the trade, spending most of their time away from the company offices. The office is used mostly by Mr. Benson and the bookkeeper-clerk, and it has desk space for the two salesmen.

In the factory proper (raw materials storeroom and assembly department), there are usually about 30 workmen. There is also a warehouseman in the finished goods warehouse, and a packer and shipping clerk in the shipping room.

The account classification (Figure 3-1) includes an account for each of the three inventories:

A/c 5 Materials Inventory, in which is recorded the value of materials in the raw materials storeroom at a particular time.

A/c 6 Work in Process, in which is recorded materials, labor, and factory expense expended upon the product in the assembly department as of inventory date. Note that at an inventory date, the goods in the assembly department are likely to be in various stages of completion. The inventory value of each unit of goods includes the materials, labor, and factory expense applied to the unit through the last operation performed on the unit.

A/c 7 Finished Goods, in which is recorded the cost of the finished goods in the finished goods warehouse at inventory date.

The classification also includes among others, the following accounts:

A/c 60 Cost of Goods Sold, which is a summary account, used only at the end of the month to show cost of goods shipped out during the month.

A/c 70 Purchases of Materials.

A/c 81 Direct Labor, which is the labor of workmen who put the product together in the assembly department.

A/c 82 Factory Expense, which includes all labor and expense incurred to maintain the raw materials storeroom and the assembly department ready for operation.

JOHN BENSON, MANUFACTURER

Classification of Accounts

ASSETS:

1. Cash
2. Accounts Receivable
5. Materials Inventory
6. Work in Process Inventory
7. Finished Goods Inventory
11. Prepaid Rent
12. Prepaid Insurance
20. Machinery and Equipment
20R. Reserve for Depreciation—Machinery and Equipment

LIABILITIES:

31. Vouchers Payable
32. Accrued Taxes

NET WORTH:

40. John Benson, Capital
41. John Benson, Drawing

INCOME AND EXPENSE:

50. Sales
60. Cost of Goods Sold
70. Purchases of Materials
81. Direct Labor
82. Factory Expense
83. Selling and Shipping Expense
84. Administrative Expense
90. Purchase Discounts

Figure 3-1

Some of the types of expenses commonly included in Factory Expense are:

Indirect labor—(supervision, factory clerks, janitors, etc.)
Factory supplies and repair parts

JOHN BENSON FACTORY

INVENTORIES AND MANUFACTURING COSTS

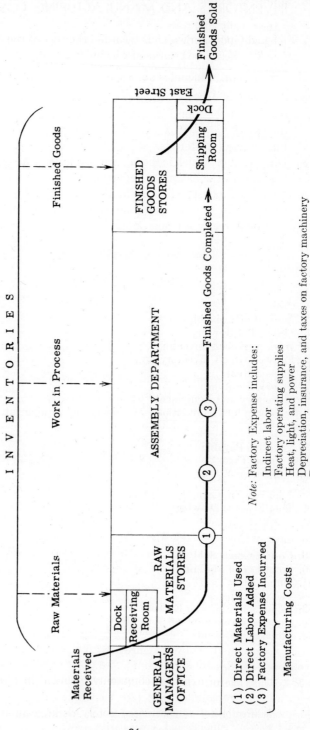

Figure 3-2

Heat, light, and power
Freight on materials
Depreciation—Machinery and equipment
Insurance—Machinery and equipment
Taxes—Machinery and equipment
Rent on factory

A/c 83 Selling and Shipping Expense, which comprises the costs of the selling and shipping activities, including labor and expense incurred in the finished goods warehouse and the shipping room.

A/c 84 Administrative Expense, which includes the salary of the proprietor-manager and the bookkeeper-clerk, together with all office supplies and services used for the general administration of the business.

(The above definitions are preliminary in nature. More precise definitions are presented in later chapters.)

Location of inventories in factory. The diagram on page 26 shows the location of the three inventories in the Benson factory: materials, work in process, and finished goods. It is presented at this point to assist the reader to visualize the flow of materials through the raw materials storeroom into the assembly department and the flow of finished goods from the assembly department to the finished goods warehouse.

Statements. Financial statements for John Benson are illustrated on pages 28 and 29. The following comments are intended to distinguish the statements of a small manufacturing concern from those of a trading concern, with which the reader is already familiar.

The Balance Sheet (Figure 3-3) shows the financial condition of the business as of December 31, 19__. The three inventories shown among the current assets (raw materials, work in process, and finished goods) are inventories as of that date.

The Statement of Profits (Figure 3-4) covers a one-month period (December, 19__). This statement shows a single amount for cost of goods sold ($17,780), the details of which are set out in a supporting statement, the Statement of Cost of Goods Manufactured and Sold.

The Statement of Cost of Goods Manufactured and Sold (Figure 3-5) covers a period of one month. It summarizes the elements of cost which have been discussed previously, namely materials used ($11,110), direct labor used ($9,272), and factory expense used ($3,965). The total of these three elements used ($24,347) is factory cost. The next section of the statement is headed "Deduct-Increase in Work in Process." In this case, the closing inventory of work in process ($3,502) is greater than the opening inventory ($3,285) by the amount of $217. It is apparent then that of the $24,347 of factory cost, $217 went to increase the work in process inventory and the remainder ($24,130) went out of the factory and into finished goods warehouse as completed goods manufactured. This latter amount is described as Cost of Goods Manufactured on the statement.

Proceeding to the next section, headed "Deduct-Increase in Finished Goods," note that the closing inventory ($12,350) is greater than the opening inventory ($6,000) by $6,350. Therefore, we conclude that of the $24,130 of completed goods manufactured which went into the finished goods warehouse during the month, $6,350 went to increase the finished goods inventory and the remainder ($17,780) went out of the warehouse as cost of goods sold.

Note that, if the inventories discussed above had *decreased*, the decrease in work in process inventory would have been added to factory cost to arrive at cost of goods manufactured. Similarly, the decrease in finished goods inventory would have been added to cost of goods manufactured to arrive at cost of goods sold.

JOHN BENSON

Balance Sheet—December 31, 19__			Exhibit I
Assets			
CURRENT ASSETS:			
Cash....................................		$ 9,176.00	
Accounts receivable......................		16,000.00	
Inventories—			
Raw materials........................	$ 6,490.00		
Work in process......................	3,502.00		
Finished goods.......................	12,350.00	22,342.00	
Total current assets..................			$47,518.00
PREPAID EXPENSES:			
Prepaid rent...........................		$ 1,547.00	
Prepaid insurance......................		229.17	1,776.17
FIXED ASSETS:			
Machinery and equipment..............		$10,000.00	
Less—Reserve for depreciation..........		513.37	
Total fixed assets.....................			9,486.63
Total assets......................			$58,780.80
Liabilities and Net Worth			
CURRENT LIABILITIES:			
Accounts payable (or vouchers payable).....		$18,200.00	
Accrued taxes...........................		70.00	
Total current liabilities................			$18,270.00
NET WORTH:			
John Benson, capital.....................		$37,688.80	
Add—Profit for December, 19__ (Exhibit II)		2,822.00	
Total net worth......................			40,510.80
Total liabilities and net worth........			$58,780.80

Figure 3-3

Exhibit II

JOHN BENSON

**Statement of Profits
for the Month of December, 19__**

Sales		$24,000.00
Less—Cost of goods sold (Exhibit III)		17,780.00
Gross profit		$ 6,220.00
Less—Selling and administrative expense:		
Selling and shipping expense	$ 2,000.00	
Administrative expense	1,420.00	3,420.00
Net income		$ 2,800.00
Add—Purchase discounts		22.00
Net profit (Exhibit I)		$ 2,822.00

Figure 3-4

Exhibit III

JOHN BENSON

**Statement of Cost of Goods Manufactured and Sold
for the Month of December, 19__**

Materials:		
Inventory, December 1, 19__	$ 3,300.00	
Add—Purchases	14,300.00	
Total	$17,600.00	
Deduct—Inventory, December 31, 19__	6,490.00	
Cost of materials used		$11,110.00
Direct labor		9,272.00
Prime cost		$20,382.00
Factory expense		3,965.00
Total factory cost		$24,347.00
Deduct—Increase in work in process:		
Inventory, December 31, 19__	$ 3,502.00	
Inventory, December 1, 19__	3,285.00	217.00
Cost of goods manufactured		$24,130.00
Deduct—increase in finished goods:		
Inventory, December 31, 19__	$12,350.00	
Inventory, December 1, 19__	6,000.00	6,350.00
Cost of goods sold (Exhibit II)		$17,780.00

Figure 3-5

Methods of recording manufacturing inventories and determining cost of goods sold.   There are two methods of recording inventories and determining cost of goods sold, in manufacturing concerns.   The first method is the physical inventory method, by which physical inventories of materials, work in process, and finished goods are extended into cost values and recorded (a) on the worksheet from which statements are prepared and (b) in the general ledger, by means of a journal entry.

The reader is familiar with the recording of physical inventories and determination of cost of goods sold in mercantile concerns.   The principle is the same for manufacturing concerns as for mercantile concerns.   When closing inventories are recorded, the effect is to deduct them from (opening inventories plus current costs) to determine cost of goods sold.

The second method is the book inventory method.   By this method, cost of goods completed and cost of goods sold are compiled from basic records on a day-to-day basis as jobs are completed and as goods are shipped out. Under this method, total cost of goods manufactured and total cost of goods sold are recorded in inventory accounts in such manner as to leave balances which represent inventories on hand.

The use of both methods is illustrated in the following sections.   The business of John Benson for the month of December, 19— is used as the basis for each illustration and accordingly, the same set of statements (Figures 3-3 to 3-5) would be produced under either method.

I. PHYSICAL INVENTORY METHOD

Bookkeeping Steps Listed:

The steps of procedure under the physical inventory method are:

(1) During the month, compile transactions on a day-to-day basis. Take a trial balance of the general ledger at the end of the month.

(2) At the end of the month, take physical inventories, record them on a worksheet which starts with the trial balance, prepared in (1), complete the worksheet, and prepare the statements from the worksheet.

(3) Record the inventories in the books and close the books.

The worksheet and closing entries are illustrated in the following sections.

Worksheet; Recording the inventories; Preparing statements. The worksheet prepared at the end of the month appears on page 32.   The first two money columns are for the trial balance at the end of the month after all journals have been posted, but before adjustments.

The following adjusting entry appears in the Adjustments columns:

Factory expense...........................	$911.00	
Reserve for depreciation—Machinery and equipment...........................		$ 46.67
Prepaid insurance.......................		20.83
Accrued taxes..........................		70.00
Prepaid rent...........................		773.50
To record the following charges to factory expense for the month:		
Depreciation on machinery and equipment	$ 46.67	
Insurance expired.......................	20.83	
Taxes accrued..........................	70.00	
Rent expired...........................	773.50	
Total............................	$911.00	

This entry illustrates typical factory expense charges that might be recorded by monthly adjusting entries.

The remaining columns on the worksheet are set up with direct reference to the statements which are to be prepared. The worksheet provides pairs of columns for statement of cost of goods manufactured and sold, statement of profits, and balance sheet, respectively.

Note that purchases of materials, $14,300, direct labor, $9,272, and factory expense, $3,965 are all carried from the debit column of Trial Balance to the debit column of Statement of Cost of Goods Manufactured and Sold (since they represent the elements of manufacturing cost).

The recording of inventories directly in the Cost of Goods Manufactured and Sold columns (instead of in the Adjustment columns) might be puzzling to the student until the logic of so doing is explained. The *opening* inventories (Materials, $3,300, Work in Process, $3,285, and Finished Goods, $6,000) are simply carried from the Trial Balance debit column to the Cost of Goods Manufactured and Sold debit column. The closing inventories, arrived at through physical count, appear at the bottom of the worksheet as "supplementary data." They are entered in the credit column of Statement of Cost of Goods Manufactured and Sold. (Materials, $6,490; Work in Process, $3,502; Finished Goods, $12,350.) The balance of Cost of Goods Manufactured and Sold columns is cost of goods sold. The two columns now contain all the amounts necessary for calculating cost of goods sold: Opening inventories (now in debit position in the Statement columns) plus material, labor, and factory expense (also in debit column) minus closing inventories. (The subtraction has been accomplished by putting the closing inventories in the credit column.)

The calculated balance of Cost of Goods Manufactured and Sold column is $17,780. It is entered in the credit column of Cost of Goods Manufactured and Sold and the debit column of Statement of Profits and labeled (in the Particulars column) "Cost of Goods Sold."

The worksheet is completed in the usual manner, except that the following points should be remembered: The three *closing* inventories are recorded

JOHN BENSON

Worksheet, December 31, 19___
(Physical Inventory Method)

Particulars	Unadjusted Trial Balance December 31, 19___ Debits	Credits	Adjustments Debits	Credits	Adjusted Trial Balance Debits	Credits	Statement of Cost of Goods Manufactured and Sold Debits	Credits	Statement of Profits Debits	Credits	Balance Sheet Debits	Credits
Cash	$ 9,176.00				$ 9,176.00						$ 9,176.00	
Accounts receivable	16,000.00				16,000.00						16,000.00	
Materials inventory	3,300.00(a)				3,300.00		(a)$ 3,300.00	$ 6,490.00(b)			6,490.00	
Work in process inventory	3,285.00(a)				3,285.00		(a) 3,285.00	3,502.00(b)			3,502.00	
Finished goods inventory	6,000.00(a)				6,000.00		(a) 6,000.00	12,350.00(b)			12,350.00	
Prepaid rent	2,320.50			(1)$773.50	1,547.00						1,547.00	
Prepaid insurance	250.00			(1) 20.83	229.17						229.17	
Machinery and equipment	10,000.00				10,000.00						10,000.00	
Reserve for depreciation—Machinery and equipment		$ 466.70		(1) 46.67		$ 513.37						$ 513.37
Vouchers payable		18,200.00				18,200.00						18,200.00
Accrued taxes				(1) 70.00		70.00						70.00
John Benson, capital		37,688.80				37,688.80						37,688.80
Sales		24,000.00				24,000.00				$24,000.00		
Purchases of material	14,300.00				14,300.00		14,300.00					
Direct labor	9,272.00				9,272.00		9,272.00					
Factory expense	3,054.00		(1)$911.00		3,965.00		3,965.00					
Selling and shipping expense	2,000.00				2,000.00				$ 2,000.00			
Administrative expense	1,420.00				1,420.00				1,420.00			
Purchase discounts		22.00				22.00				22.00		
	$80,377.50	$80,377.50	$911.00	$911.00	$80,494.17	$80,494.17						
Cost of goods sold								17,780.00	17,780.00			
							$40,122.00	$40,122.00				
Net profit									2,822.00			2,822.00
									$24,022.00	$24,022.00	$59,294.17	$59,294.17

(a) These inventories are opening inventories (December 1, 19___)

(b) Closing inventories (December 31, 19___) are:

Materials	$ 6,490.00
Work in process	3,502.00
Finished goods	12,350.00

Figure 3-6

32

in the debit column of Balance Sheet (because they are current assets on balance sheet date), as well as in the credit column of Cost of Goods Manufactured and Sold columns, as stated above.   Also, selling and shipping expense and administrative expense are carried to Statement of Profits debit column.   They are *not* part of the cost of manufacturing goods, and they must accordingly be shown in the Statement of Profits columns.

The statements illustrated on pages 28–29 are prepared from the worksheet (page 32).

Recording the inventories and closing the books. The closing entries shown below are prepared from the worksheet (page 32).

Entry (a) is prepared from the Cost of Goods Manufactured and Sold columns.   It closes the opening inventory accounts, purchases, labor, and expense accounts and sets up the closing inventories and cost of goods sold. The balancing figure of this entry, cost of goods sold ($17,780), of course agrees with the cost of goods sold figure on the worksheet and on the Statement of Cost of Goods Manufactured and Sold.   Cost of goods sold equals opening inventories plus materials, labor, and factory expense minus closing inventories.

Entry (b) is prepared from the Statement of Profits columns of the worksheet.   It closes Cost of Goods Sold and the income and expense

(a)

Cost of goods sold............................	$17,780.00	
Materials inventory...........................	6,490.00	
Work in process inventory...................	3,502.00	
Finished goods inventory....................	12,350.00	
Materials inventory......................		$ 3,300.00
Work in process inventory..............		3,285.00
Finished goods inventory...............		6,000.00
Purchases of materials..................		14,300.00
Direct labor...........................		9,272.00
Factory expense........................		3,965.00

To close the opening inventories, purchases, labor, and expense accounts, and to record the closing inventory accounts and cost of goods sold

(b)

Sales.......................................	$24,000.00	
Purchase discounts.........................	22.00	
Cost of goods sold......................		$17,780.00
Selling and shipping expense............		2,000.00
Administrative expense.................		1,420.00
Profit and loss........................		2,822.00

To close the above accounts to Profit and Loss

(c)

Profit and loss.............................	$ 2,822.00	
John Benson—Capital..................		$ 2,822.00

To close profit for period to capital account

Figure 3-7

accounts which appear on the Statement of Profits to the Profit and Loss account. The balancing figure of this entry, net profit $2,822.00, agrees with the profit figure per the worksheet.

Entry (c) closes the profit for the period to the capital account.

II. BOOK INVENTORY METHOD

The chart on page 35 illustrates the book inventory method of determining cost of goods sold. Under this method separate inventory accounts are maintained for materials, work in process, and finished goods, respectively, but they are not operated in the same manner as under the physical inventory method.

Note that cost value flows through the three inventory accounts in a manner analogous to the movement of materials through the factory. The movement in each case is indicated in the chart. The *entries* by which the flow is recorded [numbered (1) and (6) through (10) in the chart] are known as *transfer* entries. The name is appropriate, since they do record the transfer of materials into the raw materials storeroom and from there into the assembly department; also the transfer of finished goods from the assembly department to the finished goods warehouse, and from there to the customer (not illustrated). Note that the complete entry for cost of goods shipped out [(10) in the chart] is a debit to Cost of Goods Sold and a credit to Finished Goods Inventory account.

Under the book inventory method, Materials Inventory account is charged at the end of the month for materials purchased and credited for materials used during the month. The balance of the account ($6,490) represents closing inventory of materials. It represents the total cost value of the materials in the raw materials storeroom at the end of the month.

Work in Process account is charged at the end of the month for materials used, labor used, and factory expense used during the month. It is credited for the total cost of goods completed during the month. Cost of goods manufactured is compiled during the month by keeping track of materials, labor, and expense applicable to each lot of production worked upon. The cost of goods manufactured amount then is the total cost of all the lots of production completed and transferred to the finished goods warehouse. The balance of the Work in Process account at the end of the month ($3,502) represents the cost value of the partly finished goods still in the assembly department at that date.

Finished Goods account is charged at the end of the month for the total cost of goods completed during the month and credited for the total cost of goods shipped out of the finished goods warehouse during the month. This requires keeping track of the cost of the particular items in stores, identifying the goods shipped out, and compiling the total cost of those goods.

INVENTORY CONTROL ACCOUNTS FOR MANUFACTURING COMPANY

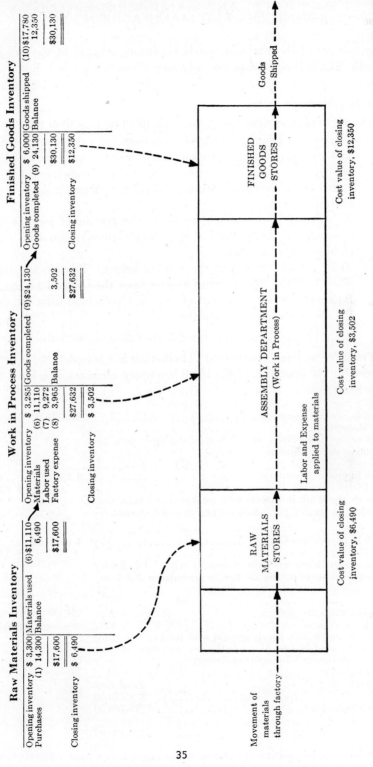

Raw Materials Inventory

Opening inventory	$ 3,300	Materials used	(6)$11,110
(1) 14,300		Balance	6,490
	$17,600		$17,600
Closing inventory	$ 6,490		

Work in Process Inventory

Opening inventory	$ 3,285	Goods completed	(9)$24,130
Materials (6)	11,110		
Labor used (7)	9,272		
Factory expense (8)	3,965	Balance	3,502
	$27,632		$27,632
Closing inventory	$ 3,502		

Finished Goods Inventory

Opening inventory	$ 6,000	Goods shipped	(10)$17,780
Goods completed (9)	24,130	Balance	12,350
	$30,130		$30,130
Closing inventory	$12,350		

Movement of
materials
through factory ----

| RAW
MATERIALS
STORES | ASSEMBLY DEPARTMENT
(Work in Process)

Labor and Expense
applied to materials | FINISHED
GOODS
STORES | Goods
Shipped |

Cost value of closing
inventory, $6,490

Cost value of closing
inventory, $3,502

Cost value of closing
inventory, $12,350

Figure 3-8

35

The balance of the Finished Goods Inventory account at the end of the month ($12,350) represents the cost value of finished goods in stores at that date.

Bookkeeping Steps Listed:

The steps of procedure under the book inventory method are:

(1) During the month, compile transactions on a day-to-day basis (as under the physical inventory method), and also keep track of (a) cost of materials used, (b) cost of finished goods completed and transferred to finished goods stores, and (c) cost of goods shipped out to customers.

(2) At the end of the month, complete the posting of journals to the accounts (as under physical inventory method); also draft transfer entries and record them.

(3) Take a trial balance of the general ledger. Prepare the Balance Sheet and the Statement of Profits from the General Ledger Trial Balance and the Statement of Cost of Goods Sold from the data in the three inventory accounts.

Steps (2) and (3) are illustrated in the following sections.

Transfer entries illustrated.   Following is a complete set of transfer entries for the operation of the three inventory accounts on a book inventory basis:

(6)*

Work in process inventory................................	$11,110.00	
Materials..		$11,110.00

To record total direct materials used during month, per summary of requisitions

(7)

Work in process inventory................................	$ 9,272.00	
Direct labor...		$ 9,272.00

To charge Work in Process with total of direct labor used during the month, per balance of Direct Labor account

(8)

Work in process inventory................................	$ 3,965.00	
Factory expense..		$ 3,965.00

To charge Work in Process account with total factory expense incurred during the month per balance of Factory Expense account

(9)

Finished goods inventory................................	$24,130.00	
Work in process inventory..............................		$24,130.00

To charge Finished Goods account with total cost of goods manufactured during the month, per summary of cost sheets of completed production orders:

Production Order No.	Total Cost
51....................................	$ 4,370.00
52....................................	19,760.00
Total..........................	$24,130.00

* The entry numbers (6)-(10) are keyed to the chart on page 35 and a companion chart in Chapter 4.

(10)

Cost of goods sold......................................	$17,780.00	
Finished goods inventory.............................		$17,780.00
To charge Cost of Goods Sold account for total cost of goods shipped during month, per summary of invoices		

General ledger trial balance. A worksheet illustrating the complete set of transfer entries appears on page 38. In practice, the entries would be posted to the accounts in the general ledger. The worksheet illustration is presented in this chapter, instead of the complete set of accounts, to save space. The General Ledger Trial Balance appears below.

JOHN BENSON

Trial Balance after Transfer Entries, December 31, 19__

	Debits	Credits
Cash.................................	$ 9,176.00	
Accounts receivable....................	16,000.00	
Materials inventory....................	6,490.00	
Work in process inventory..............	3,502.00	
Finished goods inventory...............	12,350.00	
Prepaid rent..........................	1,547.00	
Prepaid insurance.....................	229.17	
Machinery and equipment..............	10,000.00	
Reserve for depreciation—Machinery and equipment...........................		$ 513.37
Vouchers payable......................		18,200.00
Accrued taxes.........................		70.00
John Benson, capital...................		37,688.80
Sales.................................		24,000.00
Cost of goods sold.....................	17,780.00	
Selling and shipping expense...........	2,000.00	
Administrative expense.................	1,420.00	
Purchase discounts....................		22.00
	$80,494.17	$80,494.17

Figure 3-9

It is possible to prepare a Balance Sheet and a Statement of Profits from this Trial Balance. It is not possible to prepare a Statement of Cost of Goods manufactured and Sold from this trial Balance because the Trial Balance does not show such details as cost of materials, labor, or expense used, or cost of goods completed.

Statements. The Balance Sheet (page 28) and the Statement of Profits (page 29) are prepared from the General Ledger Trial Balance above. The Statement of Goods Manufactured and Sold (page 29) is prepared directly from the inventory accounts, which are illustrated on page 39.

JOHN BENSON

Worksheet, December 31, 19___
(Book Inventory Method)

	Trial Balance Before Transfer Entries December 31, 19___		Transfer Entries for Month		Trial Balance After Transfer Entries		Statement of Profits		Balance Sheet	
	Debits	Credits	Debits	Credits	Debits	Credits	Debits	Credits	Debits	Credits
Cash	$ 9,176.00				$ 9,176.00				$ 9,176.00	
Accounts receivable	16,000.00				16,000.00				16,000.00	
Materials inventory	17,600.00			(6)$11,110.00	6,490.00				6,490.00	
Work in process inventory	3,285.00		(6)$11,110.00 (7) 9,272.00 (8) 3,965.00	(9) 24,130.00	3,502.00				3,502.00	
Finished goods inventory	6,000.00		(9) 24,130.00	(10) 17,780.00	12,350.00				12,350.00	
Prepaid rent	1,547.00				1,547.00				1,547.00	
Prepaid insurance	229.17				229.17				229.17	
Machinery and equipment	10,000.00				10,000.00				10,000.00	
Reserve for depreciation—Machinery and equipment		$ 513.37				$ 513.37				$ 513.37
Vouchers payable		18,200.00				18,200.00				18,200.00
Accrued taxes		70.00				70.00				70.00
John Benson, capital		37,688.80				37,688.80				37,688.80
Sales		24,000.00				24,000.00		$24,000.00		
Direct labor	9,272.00			(7) 9,272.00						
Factory expense	3,965.00			(8) 3,965.00						
Selling and shipping expense	2,000.00				2,000.00		$ 2,000.00			
Administrative expense	1,420.00				1,420.00		1,420.00			
Purchase discounts		22.00				22.00		22.00		
	$80,494.17	$80,494.17								
Cost of goods sold			(10) 17,780.00		17,780.00		17,780.00			
Net profit							2,822.00			2,822.00
			$66,257.00	$66,257.00	$80,494.17	$80,494.17	$24,022.00	$24,022.00	$59,294.17	$59,294.17

Figure 3-10

38

INVENTORY ACCOUNTS

Raw Materials Inventory

Inventory, December 1, 19__	$ 3,300	Materials used	(6)	$11,110
Purchases	14,300	Balance		6,490
	$17,600			$17,600
Inventory, December 31, 19__	$ 6,490			

Work in Process Inventory

Inventory, December 1, 19__		$ 3,285	Goods completed	(9)	$24,130
Materials	(6)	11,110			
Labor	(7)	9,272			
Factory expense	(8)	3,965	Balance		3,502
		$27,632			$27,632
Inventory, December 31, 19__		$ 3,502			

Finished Goods Inventory

Inventory, December 1, 19—		$ 6,000	Goods shipped	(10)	$17,780
Goods completed	(9)	24,130	Balance		12,350
		$30,130			$30,130
Inventory, December 31, 19__		$12,350			

Figure 3-11

Closing entries. Closing entries which would be made under the book inventory method are:

(a)

Sales............................	$24,000.00	
Purchase discounts................	22.00	
Cost of goods sold.............		$17,780.00
Selling and shipping expense.....		2,000.00
Administrative expense..........		1,420.00
Profit and loss................		2,822.00

To close the above accounts to Profit and Loss

(b)

Profit and loss....................	$ 2,822.00	
John Benson, capital...........		$ 2,822.00

To close profit and loss for period to capital account

Figure 3-12

QUESTIONS

3-1. What inventory accounts are likely to be kept for a manufacturing concern? Name and describe three **inventories**.

3-2. On the basis of Chapter 3, define direct materials, indirect materials, and factory expense. Give examples of items that might be charged to factory expense.

3-3. Give the mathematical formulas upon which the Statement of Cost of Goods Manufactured and Sold in Chapter 3 is based.

3-4. In general, what are the two methods of recording manufacturing inventories and determining cost of goods sold? Describe concisely.

3-5. The Kenilworth Company uses the physical inventory method of determining cost of goods sold. Following are entries without explanations or amounts, in simple journal entry form. You are asked to write a one-sentence explanation for each entry and state what special journal (if any) might be used for transactions of the type:

(a) Purchases of materials
    Accounts payable—trade
(b) Machinery and equipment
    Accounts payable—others
(c) Accounts payable
    Direct labor
    Factory expense
    Selling and shipping expense
    Administrative expense
      Purchases discounts
      Cash

(d) Accounts receivable
    Sales
(e) Cash
    Accounts receivable
(f) Factory expense
    Reserve for depreciation—
      Machinery and equipment
    Prepaid insurance
    Accrued taxes
    Prepaid rent

3-6. State a rule which expresses the method of handling the opening inventories and the closing inventories on the worksheet in Figure 3-6.

3-7. The Wilmette Company uses the book inventory method of determining cost of goods sold. Following are entries without explanations or amounts, in simple journal entry form. You are asked to write a one-sentence explanation for each entry and state what special journal (if any) might be used for transactions of the type:

(a) Factory expense
    Reserve for depreciation—
      Machinery and equipment
    Prepaid insurance
    Accrued taxes
    Prepaid rent
(b) Work in process inventory
    Materials

(c) Work in process inventory
    Direct labor
(d) Work in process inventory
    Factory expense
(e) Finished goods inventory
    Work in process inventory
(f) Cost of goods sold
    Finished goods inventory

EXERCISES

3-1. The trial balance of John Fisher, a manufacturer, for January 31, 19__ appears on the worksheet form in the Workbook. Adjustment data for the month ending that date are:

(1) Estimated depreciation on machinery and equipment $ 200.00
(2) Estimated depreciation on general office furniture
     and fixtures. 50.00
(3) Insurance expired on machinery. 15.00
(4) Closing inventories, determined by physical count:
     Raw materials. 2,000.00
     Work in process. 3,000.00
     Finished goods. 4,000.00

Required:

(a) Prepare worksheet, using the blank form provided.

(b) Prepare a balance sheet, statement of profits, and statement of cost of goods manufactured and sold.

3-2. Perpetual inventory control accounts and certain other manufacturing cost accounts are presented in the Workbook. Required to post transfer entries as of the end of January, to the accounts provided:

(1)	Materials used	$ 7,000.00
(2)	Direct labor	as shown
(3)	Factory expense	as shown
(4)	Cost of goods completed	26,615.00
(5)	Cost of goods sold	25,615.00

After completing your solution, compare the data shown in the accounts with the items shown in the Statement of Cost of Goods Manufactured and Sold columns of the worksheet in your solution to Exercise 3-1.

PROBLEMS

3-1. From the following information, prepare:

(1) Worksheet, January 31, 19__
(2) Balance Sheet, January 31, 19__
(3) Statement of Profits, Month of January, 19__
(4) Statement of Cost of Goods Manufactured and Sold, Month of January, 19__

R. W. HANSON

Trial Balance, January 31, 19__

	Debits	Credits
Cash	$ 1,300.00	
Accounts receivable	800.00	
Raw materials inventory	2,000.00	
Work in process inventory	3,000.00	
Finished goods inventory	4,000.00	
Land	10,000.00	
Building	40,000.00	
Reserve for depreciation—Building		$ 4,000.00
Machinery	30,000.00	
Reserve for depreciation—Machinery		5,000.00
Accounts payable		3,000.00
R. W. Hanson, capital		80,500.00
R. W. Hanson, drawing	600.00	
Sales		8,000.00
Purchases of materials	4,000.00	
Direct labor	2,000.00	
Indirect labor	500.00	
Factory supplies used	600.00	
Power	300.00	
Depreciation expense—Building	200.00	
Depreciation expense—Machinery	100.00	
Selling expense	600.00	
Administrative expense	500.00	
	$100,500.00	$100,500.00

Inventory, January 31, 19__:

Raw materials	$2,500.00
Work in process	3,500.00
Finished goods	4,500.00

3-2. Assume that R. W. Hanson uses a book inventory system of determining cost of goods sold, instead of a physical inventory system as in Problem 3-1.

The Trial Balance Before Transfer Entries for January 31, 19__ follows:

Accounts	Debits	Credits
Cash..............................	$ 1,300.00	
Accounts receivable.................	800.00	
Raw materials inventory*.............	6,000.00	
Work in process inventory............	3,000.00	
Finished goods inventory.............	4,000.00	
Land..............................	10,000.00	
Building...........................	40,000.00	
Reserve for depreciation—Building.....		$ 4,000.00
Machinery.........................	30,000.00	
Reserve for depreciation—Machinery...		5,000.00
Vouchers payable....................		3,000.00
R. W. Hanson, capital...............		80,500.00
R. W. Hanson, drawing..............	600.00	
Sales..............................		8,000.00
Direct labor.......................	2,000.00	
Indirect labor......................	500.00	
Factory supplies used................	600.00	
Power.............................	300.00	
Depreciation expense—Building........	200.00	
Depreciation expense—Machinery......	100.00	
Selling expense......................	600.00	
Administrative expense...............	500.00	
	$100,500.00	$100,500.00

* Opening inventory, $2,000 plus purchases, $4,000.

Data for transfer entries:

(1) Materials used, per summary of requisitions, $3,500.
(2) Direct labor, per trial balance.
(3) Factory expense incurred, per trial balance.
(4) Cost of goods completed, per summary of cost sheets, $6,700.
(5) Cost of goods sold, per summary of costed invoices, $6,200.

Required:

(1) Draft transfer entries in simple journal entry form.
(2) Set up worksheet with the following pairs of money columns:
   Trial Balance Before Transfer Entries
   Transfer Entries for Month
   Statement of Profits
   Balance Sheet

Post the transfer entries to the worksheet and complete the worksheet. The profit by this method should be the same as the profit determined by physical inventory method in Problem 3-1.

(3) Set up T accounts for:
   Materials Inventory
   Work in Process Inventory
   Finished Goods Inventory
   Cost of Goods Sold

Enter the opening inventories, post the transfer entries drafted in (1), and balance the inventory accounts.

3-3. This problem is based upon physical inventory method of determining cost of goods sold.

Using (a) William Wright's Trial Balance Before Adjustments and (b) physical inventories and other adjustment data, prepare:

(1) Worksheet, providing pairs of columns for Trial Balance Before Adjustments, *Adjustments*, Cost of Goods Manufactured and Sold, Statement of Profits, and Balance Sheet.

(2) Closing entries.

WILLIAM WRIGHT

Trial Balance Before Adjustments, December 31, 19__

Accounts	Debits	Credits
Cash	$ 2,850.00	
Accounts receivable	8,540.00	
Material inventory	3,000.00	
Work in process inventory	4,000.00	
Finished goods inventory	2,000.00	
Prepaid insurance	650.00	
Land	10,000.00	
Building	50,000.00	
Reserve for depreciation—Building		$ 5,000.00
Machinery	20,000.00	
Reserve for depreciation—Machinery		2,000.00
Accounts payable		2,345.00
Notes payable		1,650.00
William Wright, capital		92,595.00
Sales		32,000.00
Purchases of materials	10,500.00	
Direct labor	10,000.00	
Factory expense	4,500.00	
Selling and shipping expense	6,400.00	
Administrative expense	3,250.00	
Sales discounts	120.00	
Purchases discounts		220.00
	$135,810.00	$135,810.00

ADJUSTMENT DATA:

(a) Physical inventories, December 31, 19__:

Materials	$4,500.00
Work in process	6,000.00
Finished goods	1,000.00

(b) Other data:

Accrued direct labor, December 31	$ 200.00
Charges to factory expense—	
(1) Indirect labor	100.00
(2) Insurance expired during month	300.00
(3) Depreciation on building for month	500.00
(4) Depreciation on machinery for month	400.00

3-4. This problem is based upon the book inventory method of determining cost of goods sold.

Using (a) William Wright's Trial Balance After Adjustments (but before transfer entries) and (b) data for transfer entries, prepare:

(1) *Complete* set of transfer entries in simple journal form, beginning with materials used.
(2) T accounts for Materials Inventory, Work in Process Inventory, Finished Goods Inventory, and Cost of Goods Sold. Post to these inventory accounts (a) opening inventory balances (see trial balance) and (b) transfer entries. Balance the inventory accounts to show closing inventories.
(3) Trial balance as it would appear after transfer entries are posted.
(4) Closing entries.

WILLIAM WRIGHT

Trial Balance After Adjustments (but Before Transfer Entries)

December 31, 19__

Accounts	Debits	Credits
Cash	$ 2,850.00	
Accounts receivable	8,540.00	
Materials inventory*	13,500.00	
Work in process inventory (December 1, 19__)	4,000.00	
Finished goods inventory (December 1, 19__)	2,000.00	
Prepaid insurance	350.00	
Land	10,000.00	
Building	50,000.00	
Reserve for depreciation—Building		$ 5,500.00
Machinery	20,000.00	
Reserve for depreciation—Machinery		2,400.00
Accounts payable		2,345.00
Notes payable		1,650.00
Accrued wages		300.00
William Wright, capital		92,595.00
Sales		32,000.00
Direct labor	10,200.00	
Factory expense	5,800.00	
Selling and shipping	6,400.00	
Administrative expense	3,250.00	
Sales discounts	120.00	
Purchases discounts		220.00
	$137,010.00	$137,010.00

* Opening inventory, $3,000 plus purchases $10,500.

DATA FOR CERTAIN TRANSFER ENTRIES (AT COST)

Materials used	$ 9,000.00
Cost of goods completed	23,000.00
Cost of goods sold	24,000.00

3-5. Prepare the following statements for William Wright:
(1) Balance Sheet, December 31, 19__
(2) Statement of Profits for December, 19__
(3) Statement of Cost of Goods Manufactured and Sold for December, 19__.

You may use either:

(a) Your worksheet solution to Problem 3-3, reflecting the assumption that cost of goods manufactured and sold are determined through the use of physical inventories.

(b) Your solution to Problem 3-4 (Parts 2 and 3), reflecting the assumption that cost of goods manufactured and sold are determined through the use of book inventories.

Chapter 4 ∼∼∼∼∼∼∼∼∼∼∼∼∼∼∼∼∼∼∼∼∼∼∼∼∼∼∼∼∼∼∼∼∼∼∼

RECORDS FOR THE SMALL MANUFACTURING BUSINESS: OUTLINE OF JOB ORDER COST SYSTEM

Journals for the small manufacturing business. The following journals are used to record the transactions of John Benson, whose business is described in Chapter 3:

> Voucher register
> Cash disbursements journal
> General journal
> Sales journal
> Cash receipts journal

The voucher register and the cash disbursements journal are the journals used for the operation of the voucher system, which is described in the first part of this chapter. As will be seen, the voucher register is used to set up the liability for purchases of materials and services (such as power) supplied by an outside concern, and the liability for payroll when it is made up at the end of the payroll period. The voucher register is accordingly the book of original entry for charges to Materials Inventory, Direct Labor, and Factory Expense accounts, among others.

The general journal is used to record, among other entries, end-of-the-month adjustments for depreciation, insurance expired, rent expired, and taxes accrued, and also the transfer entries described in the previous chapter (page 36).

The sales journal is a conventional one with which the reader is familiar except that it provides, in addition to the usual column for sales value of shipments to customers, a column for cost value of each shipment. The cash receipts journal is conventional. It is included in this chapter to complete the illustration of a set of journals for a small manufacturing business.

The voucher system. The voucher system is a verification and approval procedure for purchase invoices and other current liabilities. Under this system, a *voucher* is written for a purchase invoice, or for a group of purchase invoices from one creditor, to be paid with one check. The essential point is that there is separation of the verification and approval procedure, on the one hand, and the cash disbursing procedure on the other hand. Ideally, the verification and approval work is done by one person or group of people and the disbursing by another person. The disbursing cashier would not be permitted to issue a check except on receipt of a properly approved voucher.

	ACCOUNTS PAYABLE VOUCHER				VOUCHER NO. _____1_____
					CHECK NO. _____
PAYABLE TO	*Herman Manufacturing Co.*				DATE PAID _____
	113 Ardmore Street				
	Lincoln, Illinois				

DATE	MEMO	ACCT. NO.	DETAIL	INVOICE AMOUNT
12/1/-	*Materials*			*1 00 00*

EXPLANATION:			TOTAL	
			DISC. %	
			NET	

AUDITED	APPROVED	ENTERED	DATE ENTERED
C.J.R.	*L.T.Y.*	*F.S.L.*	*12/3/-*

FORM 601-15 U.S.A.

Form courtesy Wilson Jones Company

Figure 4-1

A voucher form is illustrated above. This form is a ready-printed stationer's form which provides for entry of name and address of the creditor, amount of the check, description of the invoice(s) covered by the voucher, together with the dates of the invoices, discount percentages and amounts, and the initials of the employees who perform the various steps of verification, approval, and entry.

In the verification procedure, it is usual (say, in the case of receipts of materials) to compare the vendor's invoice with the office copy of the purchase order and the receiving report. The object, of course, is to determine that the materials described on the invoice were actually ordered and that they were actually received. Prices shown by the invoice are checked against the purchase order or against quotations or price lists and the extensions (quantity × price) and additions are re-calculated. The voucher is signed by someone who has authority to approve vouchers for payment. (This procedure is discussed in more detail in Chapter 5, "Accounting for Materials.")

It should be emphasized at this point that a voucher is written for every invoice or similar evidence of liability, whether for purchase of materials, payroll, or expense, or for expenditure for plant, and whether the invoice is to be paid immediately or at the end of a credit period. This fact will be understood when it is considered that the disbursing cashier may not issue a check except on receipt of a properly approved voucher. A voucher must be issued for an invoice even though it is paid the same day it is received.

Uses of copies of the voucher: Elimination of the accounts payable ledger. Frequently, a number of copies are made of each voucher. The original voucher is sent to the creditor with the check. It serves as a remittance advice, showing the creditor exactly which of his invoices are covered by the check. Use of vouchers as remittance advices is good practice, particularly when there are numerous transactions between a buyer and a seller. Sometimes certain of the invoices are not paid in full on due date because some of the material has been returned to the vendor (or for some other reason). Indicating just what a check does cover will help the vendor keep his records straight. This point is really to the mutual advantage of both vendor and customer, because it may eliminate disagreements as to balances and the possible need for later reconciliations of accounts between them.

One copy of the voucher may be filed by serial number. The serial number file will be useful for "look-up" purposes when the serial number of the voucher is known. It also provides a control against loss of vouchers or delay in processing. This control is effected by scanning the file occasionally to determine that the numbers of the vouchers in file form an unbroken series and, if not, investigating any missing numbers.

Another copy of the voucher may be filed alphabetically by creditor's name, say with invoices, copies of purchase orders, and receiving reports attached. The alphabetical file would be useful in determining the volume of purchases from each creditor. It would also be useful in answering questions about prices and specifications of the materials bought from particular suppliers.

In many cases, the accounts payable ledger is dispensed with when a voucher system is operated. A file of unpaid vouchers can be operated to provide current information on the amount owed each creditor. The procedure would involve writing vouchers as soon as invoices are verified and approved, and filing the vouchers in the unpaid voucher file. On due date vouchers would be pulled from the unpaid voucher file, the check would be written, and the office copies of the vouchers filed in the paid vouchers file. The unpaid voucher file would accordingly show the amount due at any time. (Note that the *voucher register* may also be operated to show currently what vouchers are unpaid. This procedure is explained in the section on the voucher register, which follows.)

It should be noted at this point that the voucher system works best when the company pays specific invoices as they become due, rather than round amounts on account. The accounts payable system is better designed for recording payments of round amounts on account—and carrying running balances—than the voucher system.

Entries for vouchers issued and vouchers paid. As far as journal entries are concerned, the voucher system involves only two steps: (1) when the voucher is issued, entering it in the voucher register and (2) when the voucher is paid, entering the check in the cash disbursements journal.

The following entries (in simple journal entry form) are illustrative:

(1) Purchase of materials

Voucher register:
Dr. Materials inventory...................	$ 900.00	
Cr. Vouchers payable...................		$ 900.00

Cash disbursements journal (when paid):
Dr. Vouchers payable...................	$ 900.00	
Cr. Cash...............................		$ 900.00

(2) Payroll, total $2,861.00

Voucher register:
Dr. Direct labor.........................	$2,316.00	
Factory expense (indirect labor)...........	370.00	
Selling and shipping expense (shipping labor)	175.00	
Cr. Vouchers payable.................		$2,861.00

Cash disbursements journal (payroll paid):
Dr. Vouchers payable...................	$2,861.00	
Cr. Cash............................		$2,861.00

(3) Power bill, $115.00

Voucher register:
Dr. Factory expense......................	$ 115.00	
Cr. Vouchers payable...................		$ 115.00

Cash disbursements journal (when paid):
Dr. Vouchers payable...................	$ 115.00	
Cr. Cash..............................		$ 115.00

Note that all vouchers are credited to Vouchers Payable account when they are issued. All checks are debited to Vouchers Payable account when they are issued.

Voucher register. This register (page 50) comprises a debit column for each of the major classes of outlay: Materials, Direct Labor, Factory Expense, Selling and Shipping Expense, and Administrative Expense, and a credit column for Vouchers Payable. It also provides a Miscellaneous Accounts, Debit section for items for which no special column is provided.

The register form provides a line for each disbursement voucher issued during the month. The illustration shows the entries for materials purchased, $900 (Dec. 8), payroll, $2,861 (Dec. 6), and electric power, $115 (Dec. 27), among other entries.

The only posting made from the voucher register illustrated is the end-of-the-month posting of column totals (except for the items in the Miscellane-

Voucher Register

Date	Issued To	Particulars	Vo. No.	Check No.	Date (Paid)	Vouchers Payable, Credit	Materials Inventory, Debit	Direct Labor, Debit	Factory Expense, Debit	Selling & Shipping Expense, Debit	Administrative Expense, Debit	Misc. Name	Misc. No.	Misc. Amount
19—										$	$			$
Dec. 3	Hermann Manufacturing Company	Materials	1	1	2/6	$11,000 00	$11,000 00	$	$					
6	Payroll—factory; shipping	Payroll for week	2			2,861 00		2,316 00	370 00	175 00				
8	Hermann Manufacturing Company	Materials	3	2	2/8	2,200 00	2,200 00							
8	Judson Mill Supply Company	Factory supplies	4	3	2/13	900 00			900 00					
13	Payroll—factory; shipping	Payroll for week	5	4	2/19	2,895 00		2,335 00	390 00	170 00				
19	Norton and Company	Repair service	6	5	2/20	450 00			450 00					
20	Payroll—factory; shipping	Payroll for week	7			2,840 00		2,300 00	360 00	180 00				
—	Various	Miscellaneous	8-10	6-8		1,129 00			109 00	800 00	220 00			
23	McCoskey Company	Purchase machinery	11	9	2/27	2,000 00						Machinery	20	2,000 00
27	Payroll—factory; shipping	Payroll for week	12	10	2/27	2,856 00		2,321 00	360 00	175 00				
27	Commonwealth Company	Electric power	13	11	2/27	115 00			115 00					
27	Dickinson Company	Materials	14	12	2/27	1,100 00	1,100 00							
27	Payroll—office, selling	Payroll for month	15			1,700 00				500 00	1,200 00			
						$32,046 00	$14,300 00	$9,272 00	$3,054 00	$2,000 00	$1,420 00			$2,000 00

Figure 4-2

ous Accounts, Debit section, which are posted individually).   The posting
is:

Materials inventory............	$14,300.00
Direct labor..................	9,272.00
Factory expense...............	3,054.00
Selling and shipping expense.....	2,000.00
Administrative expense.........	1,420.00
Machinery and equipment.......	2,000.00
Vouchers payable............	$32,046.00

Cash disbursements journal.   All cash disbursements are entered
in this journal below.   (Note that all disbursement *vouchers* are entered
in the voucher register before the check is drawn.   The disbursement is
then recorded in the cash disbursements journal.)

The cash disbursements journal provides columns for Vouchers Payable
Debit, Purchase Discount Credit, and Cash Credit.   There are no postings
from this journal during the month.   At the end of the month, the column
totals are posted directly to the general ledger by the following debit and
credits:

Vouchers payable..............	$16,846.00
Purchase discount...........	$ 22.00
Cash......................	16,824.00

Note that when a check is entered in the cash disbursements journal a
reference entry is also made in the voucher register.   In that register, check
number and date are entered in the Paid column.   Any voucher then
which does not show a check number is an unpaid voucher.

Cash Disbursements Journal

Month of __December, 19__

Date		Name	Check No.	Vo. No.	Vouchers Payable, Debit	Purchase Discount, Credit	Cash, Credit
19—							
Dec.	6	Payroll.......................	1	2	$ 2,861 00		$ 2,861 00
	8	Judson Mill Supply Company.....	2	4	900 00		900 00
	13	Payroll.......................	3	5	2,895 00		2,895 00
	19	Norton & Company	4	6	450 00		450 00
	20	Payroll.......................	5	7	2,840 00		2,840 00
	—	Various.....................	6-8	8-10	1,129 00		1,129 00
	27	Payroll.......................	9	12	2,856 00		2,856 00
	27	Commonwealth Company........	10	13	115 00		115 00
	27	Dickinson Company.............	11	14	1,100 00	$ 22 00	1,078 00
	27	Payroll (Office).................	12	15	1,700 00		1,700 00
					$16,846 00	$ 22 00	$16,824 00

Figure 4-3

Proof of unpaid vouchers. The reader is familiar with certain book-keeping proofs which are made in connection with subsidiary ledgers at the end of each month. If an accounts receivable ledger is operated, for instance, it is customary to prove that ledger by listing the balances at the end of the month and comparing the total of such balances with the balance of the Accounts Receivable Control account.

The *unpaid vouchers* in a voucher system may be proved in a similar manner. The list of unpaid vouchers is made by copying off all the vouchers in the voucher register (page 50) for which no check number appears in the Paid column:

Unpaid Vouchers

December 31, 19__

Vo. No.	Date Issued	Issued To	Amount
a	11/28	Norton Company*..................	$ 3,000.00
1	12/3	Hermann Manufacturing Company...	11,000.00
3	12/8	Hermann Manufacturing Company...	2,200.00
11	12/23	McCoskey Company...............	2,000.00
		Agrees with balance of Vouchers Payable a/c	$18,200.00

* This voucher appears on the voucher register page for November (not illustrated).

The total of unpaid vouchers, per the list, $18,200, should agree with the balance of Vouchers Payable account at the end of the month. Refer to the worksheet, page 32 ($18,200) or the worksheet, page 38.

General journal. This journal (page 53) is the conventional two-column general journal, with the addition of a special column for accumulating factory expense. Debits to factory expense are recorded in this column. The individual debits to factory expense illustrated in this journal would not be posted separately: a single total ($911) would be posted to the debit of Factory Expense account at the end of the month. All items in the Miscellaneous columns would, of course, be posted in detail.

Sales journal. The sales journal (page 54) is the same as might be used for a trading concern, except that the form provides a column for *cost* of each shipment, as well as the usual column for sales value (the amount for which the customer is billed). (Cost values are put on the office copies of sales invoices as explained later in this chapter.)

The amounts in the Sales Value column are posted individually to the customers accounts on a day-to-day basis. The total of the Sales Value column at the end of the month is posted directly from the sales journal page, by the following debit and credit:

Accounts receivable control account......	$24,000.00	
Sales.................................		$24,000.00

General Journal

Month of ___December,___ _19___

Date		Particulars	F	Miscellaneous		Factory Expense, Debit
				Debits	*Credits*	
19—						
Dec.	31	Factory expense..........................		$		$ 46 67
		Reserve for depreciation—Machinery and equipment.......................			46 67	
		To record depreciaton on factory machinery and equipment for month				
	31	Factory expense..........................				20 83
		Prepaid insurance....................			20 83	
		To record insurance expired on factory machinery and equipment for month				
	31	Factory expense..........................				70 00
		Accrued taxes........................			70 00	
		To record property taxes accrued on factory machinery and equipment for month				
	31	Factory expense..........................				773 50
		Prepaid rent.........................			773 50	
		Rent expired on factory space for month				
					$ 911 00	$ 911 00
		TRANSFER ENTRIES (6)				
Dec.	31	Work in process inventory.................		$11,110 00		
		Materials inventory...................			$11,110 00	
		Materials used during month, per summary of requisitions				
		(7)				
	31	Work in process.........................		9,272 00		
		Direct labor.........................			9,272 00	
		To close balance of direct labor account to work in process account				
		(8)				
	31	Work in process inventory		3,965 00		
		Factory expense......................			3,965 00	
		To close balance of factory expense account to work in process account (Balance consists of $3,054.00 from voucher register and $911.00 from the general journal.)				
		(9)				
	31	Finished goods inventory..................		24,130 00		
		Work in process inventory			24,130 00	
		Cost of goods manufactured for month, per summary of cost sheets of completed production orders				
		(10)				
	31	Cost of goods sold.......................		17,780 00		
		Finished goods inventory			17,780 00	
		Cost of goods sold for month, per summary of invoices				
				$66,257 00	$66,257 00	

Figure 4-4

As to the cost column: there is no posting of individual items. At the end of the month, the total of the cost column is journalized among the transfer entries (Entry No. 10) as a debit to Cost of Goods Sold account and a credit to Finished Goods account.

Cash receipts journal. The cash receipts journal below provides columns for General Ledger Credit, Accounts Receivable Credit, Sales Discount Debit, and Cash Debit. This journal is the same as would be used in a trading concern. The amounts in the Accounts Receivable Credit column are posted to the customers accounts on a day-by-day basis. The General Ledger Credit column is used for receipts of cash from sources other than customers' accounts. Column totals (except General Ledger Credit) are posted at the end of the month.

Sales Journal

Month of December, 19__

Date	Customers	Terms	Inv. No.	Sales Value	Cost
19__					
Dec. 2	Wilson Myers....................	2/10, n/30	81	$ 9,000 00	$ 6,000 00
10	John Rollins.....................	On account	82	6,000 00	4,370 00
18	Fred Fisher......................	2/10, n/30	83	9,000 00	7,410 00
				$24,000 00	$17,780 00
	End-of-month postings— Sales Value column is posted from this journal as follows: Dr. Accounts receivable control....... Cr. Sales..................... Cost total is entered in general journal. See general journal entry #10				$24,000 00	$24,000 00

Figure 4-5

Cash Receipts Journal

Month of December, 19__

Date	Account Credited	Explanation	General Ledger, Credit	Accounts Receivable, Credit	Sales Discount, Debit	Cash, Debit
19__						
Dec. 2	Lincoln Belden........	On account		$10,000 00		$10,000 00
22	John Rollins..........	On account		5,000 00		5,000 00
23	Wilson Myers.........	On account		5,000 00		5,000 00
				$20,000 00		$20,000 00

Figure 4-6

OUTLINE OF THE JOB ORDER COST SYSTEM

General description: Ledgers of the cost system. As was stated in Chapter 2, a job order cost system may be used where specific order production control is in operation. In such a cost system, the cost clerk receives a copy of each production order, and he sets up a cost sheet for each one. The cost sheet is used to compile the cost of the production order as work is done on it in the factory. The cost per unit of product is accordingly an average cost for a specific order.

Cost sheets are kept for convenience in a file or binder, called the work in process ledger. As materials and labor are used on a production order in the factory, the cost clerk posts appropriate charges to the cost sheet for the production order. When a production order is completed in the factory, the cost clerk pulls the cost sheet from the work in process ledger, totals the materials and labor charges, adds an amount for factory expense (as explained later in this chapter), and summarizes the three elements to arrive at the total cost of the order. At any moment, the work in process ledger comprises only the cost sheets of "open" or uncompleted production orders.

A Work in Process Control account is kept in the general ledger. It is charged and credited from various journals, as indicated in the previous sections of this chapter, and the balance of this control account at the end of the month represents the cost value of all production in process at that time.

At the end of the month, the cost clerk who does the current posting to cost sheets is expected to prove the open cost sheets against the balance of the Work in Process Control account. He does this by making a list of the open cost sheets and footing the list to show the total of all charges. The latter total should agree with the balance of the Work in Process Control account.

The work in process ledger and its control account are the heart of the job order cost system. The operation of cost sheets is explained and illustrated in this chapter, which contains an outline of a complete job order cost system. In addition to the work in process ledger, a complete job order cost system usually includes two other inventory ledgers: the materials ledger, which comprises a card or account for each class of materials carried in stores (introduced in Chapter 5, "Accounting for Materials") and the finished goods ledger, which comprises a card or account for each class of finished goods carried in the finished goods warehouse (Chapter 11).

The cost accounting cycle. When a cost accounting system is in operation, a certain sequence of bookkeeping steps is followed each month. These steps begin with the recording of materials issued from stores and end with the recording of total cost of the goods shipped out.

The steps in the *cost accounting cycle* (as the sequence is called) are diagrammed on page 59 and described as follows:

DAILY AND AT THE END OF THE MONTH:

(1) Issue *requisitions* for materials to be issued from materials stores, indicating among other particulars, description of the materials to be issued and number of the production order on which the goods are to be used.

Cost Sheet

*Production Order No.*___51____

*Date Promised*___Dec. 2, 19___

*Quantity and Description*___2,000 Units E___   *Date Started*___Nov. 27, 19___ .

*Made For*_____Stock_____   *Date Completed*___Dec. 2, 19___

		MATERIALS				LABOR		
Date	*Req. No.*	*Quantity*	*Symbol*	*Amount*		*Date*	*Hours*	*Amount*
19— Dec. 1	Balance*	2,000 yd.		$2,200|00		Balance* Dec. 1-2	500 500	$760|00 760|00

SUMMARY	*Amount*	
		Date 12/31/—
		Summarized By
Materials..........................	$2,200|00	
Labor.............................	1,520|00	J. R. H.
Factory expense—1,000 hours @ 65¢.....	650|00	
Total cost........................	$4,370|00	
Cost per unit......................	$2.185	

* These balances are the totals of postings to this cost sheet before Dec. 1.

Figure 4-7a

After the goods are issued from the storeroom, sort the requisitions according to production order numbers and post requisitions to cost sheets. Enter the total for each day in a summary, which will show the month's total at the end of the month. (The month's total is used as the basis for Step 6 in the chart.)

(2) Issue job tickets to keep track of the direct labor time which each employee spends on each production order. (Each job ticket shows, among other particulars, employee's name and number, hours worked, rate of pay, and number of the production order on which the man worked.) Multiply hours on each job by rate of wages to determine labor amount.

Sort the job tickets for each day by production order number and post labor dollars to the cost sheets. Enter each day's labor in a payroll. At the end of each pay period, record labor thus charged (through the voucher register) by a debit to Direct Labor and a credit to Vouchers Payable.

(3) During the month, keep track of factory expense incurred, compil-

Cost Sheet

Production Order No.____52____

Date Promised___Dec. 24, 19___

Quantity and Description____8,000 Units E____

Date Started____Dec. 3, 19___

Made For_____Stock_____

Date Completed ___Dec. 24, 19___

MATERIALS					LABOR		
Date	Req. No.	Quantity	Symbol	Amount	Date	Hours	Amount
19— Dec. 5	21	8,100	"e"	$ 8,910 00	Dec. 3-24	5,000	$7,600 00

SUMMARY	Amount	
Materials............................	$ 8,910 00	Date 12/31/—
Labor...............................	7,600 00	Summarized By
Factory expense: 5,000 hours @ 65¢......	3,250 00	J. R. H.
Total cost............................	$19,760 00	
Cost per unit.........................	$ 2.47	

Figure 4-7b

ing charges in the Factory Expense account. At the end of the month, determine a factory expense rate per hour by the formula:

$$\text{Factory expense (rate per hour)} = \frac{\text{Factory expense incurred during the month}}{\text{Direct labor hours worked during the month}} = \frac{\$3965}{6100} = \$.65$$

(There are a number of types of factory expense rates for applying factory expense to production orders. Use of a *direct labor hour* rate is assumed in this section. Other types of rate are explained and illustrated in Chapter 10.)

Apply the factory expense rate to the cost sheets for the month by multiplying hours posted to the cost sheets during the month by the rate. Post the resulting dollar amounts to the cost sheets. (This is done at the end of the month.) The total amount applied to cost sheets in this case would be 6100 hours × $.65 = $3965.

Cost Sheet

Production Order No.____53____

Date Promised____Dec. 30, 19__

Quantity and Description____2,000 Units E____

Date Started____Dec. 26, 19__

Made For____Stock____

Date Completed_____

MATERIALS					LABOR		
Date	Req. No.	Quantity	Symbol	Amount	Date	Hours	Amount
19__ Dec.	22	2,000		$2,200|00	Dec. 26-30	600	$912|00

SUMMARY	Amount	Summarized By Date____
Materials...........................		
Labor..............................		
Factory expense:		
600 hours @ 65¢ = $390.00..........		
Total cost.........................		
Cost per unit......................		

Figure 4-7c

(4) Summarize the cost sheets of all production orders completed during the month.

This is done by totaling the materials charges and the labor charges previously posted to the cost sheets, and then setting out a grand total of materials, labor, and expense for the production order. Determine *unit cost* by the formula:

Total cost of the production order ÷ number of units produced = unit cost

(5) Determine cost of goods shipped. This may be done by using the office copy of each invoice sent to customers for goods shipped to them. The cost of the particular goods shipped on each invoice may be entered on the office copy of the invoice, by referring to the cost sheet for the production order on which the goods were produced, or by some other method. (This procedure is known as "costing the invoices.")

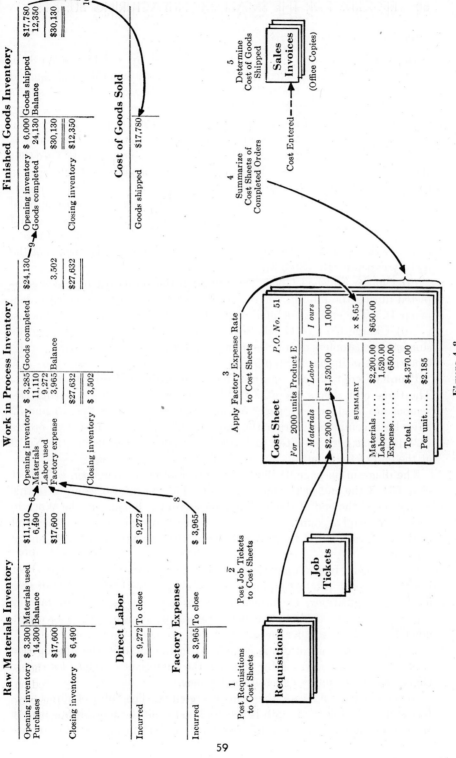

Figure 4-8

AT THE END OF THE MONTH:

(6) Record the total of direct materials used by a debit to Work in Process ($11,110) and a credit to Materials. Note that the total charged to Work in Process is the total of requisitions charged to the cost sheets during the month (Step 1).

(7) Charge Work in process account with the total direct labor incurred during the month ($9,272) (per the Direct Labor account). The entry is debit Work in Process ($9,272) and credit Direct Labor account. Note that the total charge to Work in Process is the total of job tickets charged to cost sheets during the month (Step 2).

(8) Charge Work in Process account with total factory expense applied to cost sheets ($3,965). The entry is debit Work in Process ($3,965) and credit Factory Expense. Note that the total charge to Work in Process agrees with the sum of the amounts applied to cost sheets by means of the factory expense rate (Step 3).

(9) Charge Finished Goods account with the total cost of goods completed during the month, per the total of cost sheets of completed orders (Step 4). The entry is debit Finished Goods and credit Work in Process.

(10) Charge Cost of Goods Sold account with the total cost of goods shipped to customers during the month, per total of the cost entries on the office copies of invoices (Step 5).

Proof of cost sheets against Work in Process Control account. The three cost sheets operated by the John Benson business during December are illustrated on pages 56-58. Note that Orders Nos. 51 and 52 have been completed during the month. The total of these two orders ($24,130) has been credited to Work in Process by Journal Entry No. 9 at the end of the month.

The diagram on page 61 illustrates the proof of the one open cost sheet (No. 53) at the end of the month. Note that the total of charges to this cost sheet at the end of the month agrees with the balance of the Work in Process Control account. If there were several open cost sheets, the total of the charges to all of them should agree with the balance of the Control account.

Summary. In the operation of a job order cost system, a cost sheet is set up for each production order. Cost sheets are charged for materials used per requisitions, for direct labor per job tickets, and for factory expense by means of factory expense rate(s) which are applied to direct labor hours or some other factor which is represented on all cost sheets.

When a production order is completed in the factory, the appropriate cost sheet is summarized by totaling the materials charges, the labor charges, and the factory expense applications.

Accumulating totals for the control accounts: The total of direct materials used during the month is accumulated from the requisitions and at the end of the month, that total is debited to Work in Process Control ac-

ANALYSIS OF CHARGES TO COST SHEETS SHOWING PROOF
OF OPEN COST SHEET AT END OF MONTH

Work in Process Control Account

Opening inventory (Order #51)		$ 3,285	Completed:		
Materials	GJ	11,110	Order #51	$ 4,370	
Labor	GJ	9,272	Order #52	19,760	$24,130
Factory expense	{ VR { GJ	3,965	Balance		3,502
		$27,632			$27,632
Closing inventory		$ 3,502			

*Agrees
with*

CHARGES TO COST SHEETS

Particulars	Order #51 (Fig. 4-7a)	Order #52 (Fig. 4-7b)	Order #53 (Fig. 4-7c)	Total Charges
Opening inventory:				
Materials................	$2,200.00	$	$	$
Labor: 500 hours........	760.00			
Expense: 500 hours @ 65¢..	325.00			
Total...................	$3,285.00			3,285.00
Charges during month:				
Materials................		8,910.00	2,200.00	11,110.00
Labor....................	760.00	7,600.00	912.00	9,272.00
Expense.................	325.00	3,250.00	390.00	3,965.00
Total charges...........	$4,370.00	$19,760.00	$3,502.00	$27,632.00
	Completed	Completed		

Note: The total of charges to Order #53 ($3,502.00), open at the end of the month,
agrees with the balance of Work in Process Control account.

Figure 4-9

count and credited to Materials Control account. The total of direct
labor used during the month is accumulated in the voucher register, and it is
posted to the Direct Labor account at the end of the month, as a debit.
The debit balance is transferred to Work in Process Control account by a
debit to that account and a credit to Direct Labor account.

The total of factory expense incurred during the month appears as a
debit balance in Factory Expense account at the end of the month.   The
factory expense rate illustrated in this chapter was calculated on the basis of
that factory expense balance.   The balance of Factory Expense account is
closed to Work in Process Control account by a debit to the latter account
and a credit to Factory Expense.

The total of completed cost sheets is accumulated during the month.   At
the end of the month, the total cost of production orders completed is

credited to Work in Process Control account and debited to Finished Goods Control account.

At the end of the month, the total of charges to open cost sheets is proved against the Work in Process Control account by totaling the charges on each open cost sheet, listing the open cost sheets and their balances, then comparing the total of the list with the balance of the control account. Any difference between the control accounts and the total of the cost sheets must be investigated and corrected.

QUESTIONS

4-1. Name the journals which you might find in the cost system of a small manufacturing business. Name the ledgers which are a part of the cost system.

4-2. In what way might the voucher register system be expected to save clerical time over the purchase journal system?

4-3. Name the types of transactions which are recorded in the voucher register.

4-4. How is the sales journal illustrated in Chapter 4 different from one which might be used by a wholesaling company?

4-5. Describe the proof of unpaid vouchers. What is it intended to prove?

4-6. What is meant by the "cost accounting cycle"? Name the steps performed during the month. Name the steps performed at the end of the month.

4-7. Enumerate the most important items shown on cost sheets of a job order cost system.

EXERCISES

4-1. The Evanston Manufacturing Company operates a job order cost system, using the following journals which are set out in the Workbook:

(a) Voucher register
(b) Cash disbursements journal
(c) Sales journal
(d) Cash receipts journal
(e) General journal

Required:

(1) Enter the transactions in the following list in the appropriate journals. Also enter all required transfer entries as of the end of the month. Use the account names shown in the classification, Exercise 4-2.
(2) Foot and cross-foot the journals at the end of the month.

Transactions for February
(Numbers are dates)

(2) Received materials (and the invoice) from Chicago Steel Company, 2/10, n/30, $1,000.
(3) Sold finished goods (costing $1,200) out of stock for $2,000 to Stewart Brewster & Co., 2/10, n/30.
(5) Borrowed cash from bank on 90-day loan, $4,000.
(6) Factory payroll for week vouchered and paid:

Direct labor	$800.00
Indirect labor (charge Factory Expense)	600.00

(9) Received factory supplies and repair parts from Central Tool Company, $250. (Charge Factory Expense.)

(10) Received invoice for machine repair service from Brigham Repair Service, $80.   (Charge Factory Expense.)
(11) Paid Chicago Steel Company invoice of February 2, taking the discount.
(12) Received cash from Stewart Brewster & Co., for invoice of February 3, less discount.
(13) Factory payroll for week vouchered and paid:

Direct labor................................ $700.00
Indirect labor.............................. 600.00

(16) Vouchered and paid salesmen's traveling expenses, $400.
(17) Paid Central Tool Company invoice of February 9.
(18) Received and paid bill for advertising from Taylor Advertising Agency, $600.
(20) Factory payroll for week vouchered and paid:

Direct labor................................ $850.00
Indirect labor.............................. 600.00

(23) Sold finished goods (costing $1,600) out of stock to Wayne & Co. for $3,000, 2/10, n/30.
(27) Factory payroll for week vouchered (but not paid):

Direct labor................................ $800.00
Indirect labor.............................. 600.00

(27) Administrative and selling payroll for month vouchered (but not paid):

Administrative salaries...................... $600.00
Selling salaries............................. 900.00

(27) Electric power bill for month received from Edison Co., $200.
(27) Fixed charges against factory for month:

Depreciation............................... $300.00
Insurance.................................. 70.00
Taxes...................................... 200.00
Rent on factory building (credit Prepaid Rent).. 500.00

(27) Materials used during the month, per summary of requisitions, $800.
(27) Cost of goods completed during month, per summary of cost sheets, $5,000.

4-2. (a) The following accounts for the Evanston Manufacturing Company are provided in the Workbook. Post all of the journals in your solution to Exercise 4-1 to these accounts. Enter complete references in posting.

GENERAL LEDGER

1 Cash
7 Accounts Receivable
11 Materials Inventory
12 Work in Process Inventory
13 Finished Goods Inventory
21 Prepaid Insurance
22 Prepaid Rent
30 Machinery (no data given)
30R Reserve for Depreciation
40 Vouchers Payable
41 Bank Loan
42 Accrued Taxes
50 Sales

GENERAL LEDGER

60 Cost of Goods Sold
71 Direct Labor
72 Factory Expense
73 Selling and Shipping Expense
74 Administrative Expense
81 Purchase Discount
82 Sales Discount

CUSTOMERS LEDGER

Stewart Brewster & Co.
Wayne & Company

(b) Prove the balance of Vouchers Payable account.

4-3. A table listing production orders, materials requisitions, and job tickets issued, also factory expense invoices or accruals and production orders completed for the Dodd Company, appears herewith. Four cost sheets and the Work in Process Control account are provided in the Workbook.

Required:

(1) Post the cost sheets, using all given data and rates which can be derived from the table. Note that in practice the cost sheets might be posted directly from requisitions and job tickets, instead of from a summary of them. (Use a direct labor hour rate for applying factory expense.)
(2) Make all necessary postings to the Work in Process account, entering also the initials of the journal from which the postings came. Post the Work in Process account *from totals calculated from the table.*
(3) Prove sum balance of postings to open cost sheets at end of the week. For the purposes of this problem, assume a one-week accounting period.

PROBLEMS

4-1. The Hollis Company wants a purchase and payment system that will provide for formal approval of every invoice before it is recorded as a liability. There is to be organizational separation of (a) verification and approval of invoices from (b) cash disbursing. The treasurer suggests that it might be possible to eliminate the accounts payable ledger, since the company almost always pays specific invoices within their credit periods, rather than round amounts on account.

Required:

(1) Rule up forms for voucher register, general journal, and check register.
(2) Set up T accounts for the list of accounts.
(3) Enter the transactions in the journals.
(4) Post the journals to the accounts.
(5) As of the end of the month, prepare a list of unpaid vouchers. Prove the total of the unpaid vouchers against the balance of the Vouchers Payable account.

Start with Voucher No. 101 and Check No. 51. Use transaction numbers as dates. For end-of-the-month posting, use date of January 31.

Transactions for January
(Numbers are dates)

(1) Purchased materials, $1,000 from Morgan & Co., terms 2/10, n/30.
(2) Opened petty cash fund, $100.
(3) Paid the voucher to Morgan & Co. (transaction 1) less discount.
(4) Made the entries for the weekly payroll paid at the end of the week: Direct Labor, $200; Selling Expense, $400; and Delivery Expense, $200.
(5) Received the electric light bill for $30 from Edison Co. and paid it the same day (Charge Factory Expense).
(6) Bought office equipment from Piedmont Company for $800 and issued voucher.
(7) Made arrangement to handle payment for office equipment (transaction 6) with a note. Issued the note.
(8) Replenished petty cash fund. Petty cash payments chargeable to the following accounts have been made: Factory Expense, $30; Selling Expense, $20; Delivery Expense, $10.
(9) Purchased materials, $200, from Norton & Co., terms cash. Paid the invoice immediately.

DODD COMPANY

Requisitions, Job Tickets, Expense Invoices, Expense Accruals, Etc.

Week of January 2, 19___

Date	Production Orders Issued		Direct Materials Requisitions			Direct Labor Job Tickets			Factory Expense Invoices or Accruals		Production Orders Completed Job No.
	Job No.	Product	Req. No.	Job No.	Amount	Job No.	Hours	Amount	Amount	Description	
Jan. 2	21	100 Units Product R	31	21	$285 00	21	40	$60 00	$150 00	Rent	
3	22	50 Units Product S	32	22	165 00	21	20	30 00			
						22	20	20 00			
4	23	25 Units Product T	33	23	120 00	21	10	15 00			
						22	10	15 00			
						23	20	30 00			
5	24	10 Units Product U	34	24	80 00	21	10	15 00			
						22	20	30 00			
						23	10	15 00			
						24	10	15 00			
6			35	22	50 00	21	30	45 00	50 00	Depreciation	21
			36	23	20 00	22	20	30 00	20 00	Insurance	22
						23	10	15 00	40 00	Taxes	
						24	10	15 00	40 00	Power	

(10) Purchased materials, $500, from Smith Company, terms 2/10, n/30.

(11) Returned $200 defective materials to Smith Company.

(12) Received bill for insurance premium from Northwestern Insurance Company, $360 for 12-month policy.

(13) Purchased office supplies, $40, on credit from Lincoln Stationery Co.

(14) Paid the note in transaction 7.

Accounts

11. Cash in Bank	62. Notes Payable
12. Petty Cash	71. Direct Labor
16. Materials Inventory	91. Factory Expense
21. Office Supplies Inventory	92. Selling Expense
22. Prepaid Insurance	93. Delivery Expense
31. Office Equipment	99. Purchase Discounts
61. Vouchers Payable	

4-2. The Douglas Manufacturing Company operates a job order cost system, using (among others) the following accounts in the general ledger.

1. Cash	30. Sales
2. Accounts Receivable	40. Cost of Goods Sold
4. Materials Inventory	50. Direct Labor
5. Work in Process Inventory	60. Factory Expense
6. Finished Goods Inventory	71. Selling and Shipping Expense
10. Machinery	72. Administrative Expense
10R. Reserve for Depreciation	81. Purchase Discount
21. Vouchers Payable	82. Sales Discount

The company operates a voucher register similar to that on page 50, a cash disbursements journal (page 51), a sales journal (page 54), a cash receipts journal (page 54), and a general journal (page 53).

Required:

(1) Rule up journal forms similar to those shown on the pages listed in the previous paragraph, omitting the cash receipts journal.

(2) Enter the following transactions in the journals. Foot and cross-foot the journals.

Transactions for January
(Numbers are dates)

(1) Bought materials from Jones & Co. for $1,000, terms 2/10, n/30.

(2) Bought factory expense supplies for immediate use from Lincoln Supply Co. for $200, terms 2/10, n/30.

(5) Vouchered and paid the factory payroll: Direct labor, $300; indirect labor, $200.

(6) Paid Jones & Co. for the materials in (1), taking the discount.

(7) Paid Lincoln Supply Co. for the supplies in (2), taking the discount.

(8) Vouchered and paid the bill for power from Edison Co., $150.

(9) Sold manufactured product as follows:
To Bell & Co., Sales value, $800; cost, $600.
To Howell & Co., Sales value, $1,000; cost, $700.

(31) Estimated depreciation on machinery for one month, $50.

(31) Direct materials used during the month, $900.

(31) Direct labor applied to production orders during month: see balance of Direct Labor account.

(31) Factory expense applied to production orders during month: see balance of Factory Expense account.

(31) Cost of production orders completed during the month, $1,800.

(31) Cost of goods sold during the month per sales journal as shown in transaction (9), $1,300.

4-3 (*continuation of* **4-2**). Set up T accounts for the following accounts in the list in Problem 4-2: 1, 2, 4, 5, 6, 21, 30, 40, 50, 60, 81, omitting the remaining accounts. Post the following opening balances:

> #4 Materials inventory, $300.
> #5 Work in process inventory, $400.
> #6 Finished goods inventory, $500.

Required:

Using your solution to Problem 4-2, post the journals to the T accounts.

4-4. The trial balance of J. W. Austin for January 31, 19— before transfer entries appears:

Accounts	Debits	Credits
Cash.................................	$ 800.00	
Accounts receivable....................	1,200.00	
Raw materials inventory (including purchases for month)........	1,000.00	
Finished goods inventory...............	2,000.00	
Building and machinery................	22,000.00	
Vouchers payable......................		$ 3,600.00
J. W. Austin, capital...................		21,900.00
Sales.................................		3,000.00
Direct labor..........................	600.00	
Factory expense......................	600.00	
Selling and administrative expense........	300.00	
	$28,500.00	$28,500.00

There was no work in process on January 1, but 4 jobs (numbered 101-104) were started. Summaries kept in the accounting department showed the following information:

(1) Materials used per summary of requisitions:

Job No.	Amount
101.................	$100.00
102.................	200.00
103.................	300.00
104.................	200.00
Total.............	$800.00

(2) Direct labor used, per summary of job tickets:

Job No.	Amount
101.................	$ 50.00
102.................	100.00
103.................	200.00
104.................	250.00
	$600.00

(3) Factory expense is applied to jobs on the basis of direct labor expended on the jobs. Since total factory expense was $600 and total direct labor $600, it was decided to apply factory expense to jobs at the rate of 100% of direct labor.

(4) Jobs 101 and 102 were completed during the month.

(5) Cost of goods shipped out, per summary of costed invoices, $1,800.

Required:

(1) Set up T accounts for the following ledger accounts:

Raw Materials Inventory
Work in Process Inventory Control
Finished Goods Inventory
Cost of Goods Sold

Post the opening balances to Raw Materials Inventory account and Finished Goods Inventory account.

(2) Set up T accounts for a work in process ledger or cost ledger. Provide separate accounts for Job No. 101, Job No. 102, Job No. 103, and Job No. 104.

(3) Post charges for materials, labor, and factory expense to the accounts for the four jobs in the work in process ledger.

(4) Draft transfer entries affecting the accounts in (a) and post to the T accounts. Balance the three inventory accounts.

(5) Show how you would prove the work in process ledger against its control account.

Chapter 5

ACCOUNTING FOR MATERIALS

Function. The function of accounting for materials in a job order cost system includes:

(a) Keeping track of the quantity and value of each type of material on hand,

(b) Determining the quantity and cost of materials used on job orders processed in the factory and materials used otherwise, and

(c) Summarizing the value of materials received and value of materials used period by period, to provide totals for financial and operating statements.

The first function—keeping track of each type of material on hand—is often accomplished by setting up a card or account for each type of material. *Receipts* of materials are added to the proper card, *issues* from materials stores are deducted, and the current balances are entered. The running balances are useful not only for accounting purposes, as will be explained in this chapter, but often for materials control and production control purposes as well. They may be used, for instance, to show when additional purchases should be made to avoid running out of materials. And they may be used by the person who issues production orders. Obviously, he would need to know whether materials are on hand or coming before issuing a production order.

The second function—determining the cost of materials used in each job —is part of the task of keeping the job cost record (or cost sheet) on which the costs of *all* elements are compiled. The third function—summarizing— involves the operation of special journals for compiling periodic totals.

Organization for physical control: Personnel. Physical control of materials refers to storage, handling, and protection of materials through the use of proper facilities and personnel. Physical control is necessary in the first place to safeguard the materials against waste, theft, and unrecorded operating losses. It is also necessary for the proper operation of the cost system. In the absence of proper physical control, it is possible for materials to be released without *any* record being made. The inventory cards or accounts would not show the true balances on hand, and the cost sheets would not show the correct costs.

In the Benson Manufacturing Company factory, good physical control is maintained through the use of a materials storeroom, shown in the diagram on page 178. Raw materials from suppliers are received at the receiving dock and unpacked in the receiving room. Here each shipment is checked for quantity and condition. The materials are counted, or weighed or otherwise measured, and a receiving report is written. They are then placed in the bins and other receptacles, and they are released by the store-keeper only upon receipt of a properly signed requisition.

Some of the personnel directly concerned with materials control are in-dicated in the organization chart below. They include the materials

ORGANIZATION CHART (Partial)

BENSON AND WEST MANUFACTURING COMPANY

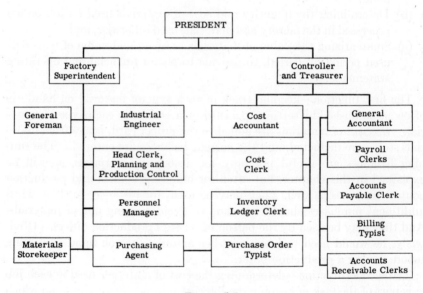

Figure 5-1

ledger clerk, who posts receipts and issues to the materials accounts (and who also does the posting to cost sheets and finished goods accounts), the storekeeper, and the purchase order typist. These people spend all or part of their time on the materials control function. In addition, other people are concerned in an incidental way with writing primary papers such as requisitions, disbursement vouchers for payment of suppliers, and so forth.

Managerial information. A job order cost system would provide the following items of managerial information, useful for the control of materials:

(1) *Quantity of each material on hand for current reference.* As indicated above, this information is useful in the performance of the purchasing and production control functions.

(2) *Periodic inventory reports,* showing value of each class of materials on hand at a particular inventory date. Such reports are issued monthly to support the balance sheet. They are used to show how much working capital is tied up in each class of inventory. When inventory turnover changes significantly, the management may study increases and decreases in particular classes to determine which ones are involved. In some cases, inventories might be increased in anticipation of increased production and sales. Or the inventory might be increased in anticipation of a tight materials supply situation or rising materials prices. In other cases, an increase might mean simply that the production control people failed to coordinate inventories and sales properly, and that the situation must be corrected.

In some industries, the product may be made of a relatively small number of speculative raw materials. Examples are products made of copper, wool, and cotton. Materials may comprise a large part of total cost of the product. In such cases, the management will watch the investment in materials carefully not only to keep the investment at a reasonable figure, but also to give consideration to the possibility of speculative profits or losses.

(3) *Comparisons of current actual materials cost in production with estimated material cost or with past actual costs.* In job shops which take work on a bid basis, actual materials costs (per product unit and total) of completed jobs are compared with estimated costs. The latter costs are often set out in complete detail as to items, quantities, and prices by the planners and estimators. Then, if there is a significant difference between the actual materials cost and the estimated materials cost in a completed job, the cost man will make comparisons to locate the causes. He may compare materials used, item for item, per the cost sheet with materials specified, per the estimate. He can thus determine whether, for instance, more material was used than was indicated in the estimate, or whether the prices paid were greater than the estimate. In such shops, the cost sheet may provide a Description column under materials in which the items charged to the job may be identified.

In analyzing materials costs on completed jobs, the cost man may find that performance in the factory was unsatisfactory, for which the foreman was responsible, or that prices were higher than expected. Or he may conclude on investigation, that the estimate was faulty in the first place, or that something is wrong with the cost bookkeeping. He may find, for instance, that two pieces of a certain material were charged to the job when, in the nature of the job, only one could possibly appear in the finished job.

Upon investigation, he may find that one of them was charged to the wrong job.

Note that cost record-keeping of itself will not correct unsatisfactory conditions and situations, but it does provide the basis for locating and correcting such conditions. Cost *analysis*, of the type indicated in the previous paragraph, may be necessary to locate causes and responsibilities.

In some businesses, the control of materials waste (produced inevitably in the nature of the materials and the processing) and spoilage (which is due to faulty work) are important. Sometimes, it is so important that specific record-keeping and control are necessary. Separate accounting for waste and spoilage is described in Chapter 6.

Current specification and price information. This information is usually required as a supplement to job order costs. The management is likely to ask more or less constantly, such questions as "What were the specifications on that last shipment of ½″ rolled steel we got from Morgan?" and "What is the current price of 2″ casing?" Although the first question might be considered an "engineering" question and the second a "purchasing department" question, in a small business, they are likely to be answered by the accounting department. The accounting department may keep a file of purchase invoices by vendor, to which lookups may be made, or it may keep formal records of materials specifications and materials prices. In some cases, the accounting department may make regular reports of prices of important materials to the management, along with the monthly cost records.

Accounts. The following accounts relating to materials are kept in a job order cost system:

(1) Materials Control account, which is the control account for the materials ledger. It is charged at the end of the month for the total of materials received during the month and credited for the total of materials used during the month. The balance of the account represents the value of materials in inventory at the end of the month.

The Materials Control account is supported by the materials ledger, which comprises a card or account for each class of material carried in the materials storeroom. These accounts are charged for materials received currently as they are received and credited currently for materials used. Running balances represent materials on hand. At the end of the month, the sum of the balances of the Materials Ledger accounts agree with the balance of Materials Ledger Control account.

(2) Materials in Process Control account, which is the control account for the materials section of the job order cost sheets. It is charged at the end of the month for the total of direct materials charged to the cost sheets, and credited for the total materials on the cost sheets of jobs completed during the month. The balance of materials in process at the end of the month represents the value of materials in the uncompleted product units

in the factory. This account and the Labor in Process and Factory Expense in Process accounts to be explained in later chapters take the place of the single Work in Process account explained in Chapter 4.

REQUISITION FOR EACH KIND OF MATERIAL

PURCHASE ORDER NO.

PURCHASE REQUISITION

REQUISITION NUMBER 46

PURCHASING DEP'T. PLEASE ORDER FOR DEP'T Store DATE Jan. 27 19—

DELIVER TO Store NOTIFY Fred Lewis FOR USE ON —

ON HAND 2,500 ONE MONTH USAGE 5,000 CHARGE NO. Materials DATE WANTED immed.

REMARKS

	QUANTITY	DESCRIPTION OF MATERIAL	PRICE
1	5,000	Material "a"	
5			

APPROVED ____ FINAL APPROVED F. S. Lawler SUPERINTENDENT SIGNED Fred Lewis

Form courtesy Wilson Jones Company

Figure 5-2

At the end of the month, materials charges on the open cost sheets are proved against the balance of the Materials in Process Control account. This is done by making a list of the totals of the materials charges to those cost sheets and comparing the grand total of the list with the balance of the Materials in Process Control account.

FROM Benson Manufacturing Company
22 East Street, Chicago, Ill.

PURCHASE ORDER

NO. 42

DATE January 28 19—

CONDITIONS
1. PLACE ABOVE NUMBER ON INVOICE PACKAGES AND CORRESPONDENCE.
2. ACKNOWLEDGE ORDER AND STATE WHEN YOU WILL SHIP.
3. NO CHARGE ALLOWED FOR PACKING OR CARTAGE.

TO Walton Company
835 West Milton Street, Chicago

PLEASE ENTER OUR ORDER AS FOLLOWS:- SHIP VIA Your truck

QUANTITY	DESCRIPTION	PRICE	PER	AMOUNT
5,000	Material "a"	52	each	2,600 00

BY

FORM 601-11 WJ U.S.A.

Form courtesy Wilson Jones Company

Figure 5-3

Forms. Typical forms used in recording materials received and issued in a job order cost system are:

Purchase requisition, which is a written request to the purchasing department to purchase specified materials or services. Where the goods are

FORM 605-05 WJ U.S.A.
PURCHASING & ACCOUNTING DEPT.

RECEIVING RECORD

No. 51

Feb. 1 19–

From Walton Company — Rec'd by Reed

Via: Truck — Frt. & Exp. Chgs.

Hauled by — Charges

Quantity	Unit	Description of Material	Purchase Order	Charge
5,000	each	Material "a"	42	Materials

Del'd to Dept. No. Store — Signed by Joe Reed

Form courtesy Wilson Jones Company

Figure 5-4

regularly kept in the material storeroom, the purchase requisition may be issued by the materials ledger clerk. This clerk would issue such a requisition for particular materials when the balance on hand as shown by the Materials Ledger account falls below a prescribed minimum. Or for special materials and services, purchase requisitions might be issued by a

ACCOUNTS PAYABLE VOUCHER

VOUCHER NO. 111

CHECK NO.

DATE PAID

PAYABLE TO Walton Company
835 West Milton Street
Chicago, Illinois

DATE	MEMO	ACCT. NO.	DETAIL	INVOICE AMOUNT
1/28/-	Materials			2,600.00

EXPLANATION: — TOTAL — DISC. % — NET

AUDITED	APPROVED	ENTERED	DATE ENTERED
R.J.L.	S.T.Y.	R.O.J.	2/1/-

FORM 601-15 WJ U.S.A.

Form courtesy Wilson Jones Company

Figure 5-5

foreman or other supervisor or the office manager. The original form goes to the purchasing department; copy is retained by the person issuing.

Purchase order, used by the purchasing department to order materials or services from suppliers. Details such as quantity and description of the item(s), date delivery expected, and method of shipment and routing may be shown. Original goes to supplier and a copy is retained by the purchasing department for follow-up purposes and for use in verification of the supplier's invoice. In some cases, a copy is sent to receiving department to notify them that goods are coming. A serial number copy is retained by the purchasing department for control purposes.

Receiving report, written by the storekeeper or the receiving clerk to provide a record of the receipt of materials. Among other particulars, it shows quantity and description of the materials, apparent condition of the goods, name and address of the supplier, and method of shipment. The original goes to the purchasing department; a copy goes to the person who requested the goods; and a copy is retained by the receiving department.

Bill of lading, or other transportation bill.

Supplier's invoice, a form showing quantities, prices, and amounts for materials received. It is the source of entries in the materials accounts and other records.

Disbursement voucher. This form is a remittance advice describing the items covered by a check sent to a supplier. A copy is filed alphabetically with suppliers invoice, receiving report, and copy of purchased order attached. A control copy is filed by serial number.

Materials account, illustrated on page 78.

Requisition (page 82) which is instruction to (and authority for) the storekeeper to release specified materials from the storeroom. A requisition may be written by a foreman who requires the materials for his department or by the production control clerk who wrote the production order on which the materials are to be used.

Sometimes bills of materials are used, instead of requisitions, for the release of materials to production. A bill of materials is a list of all the materials required for a production order, showing the quantity of each material allowed for the production order. In some cases, the materials are actually issued all at one time, when the production order is to be started. Where it is possible to do this, a good control over quantities of material used can be obtained at the source, that is, at the point of issue. If the production floor requires more material than the original allotment provided by the bill of materials, a special requisition must be written and signed by the foreman.

ACCOUNTING PROCEDURE

Procedure for receipts. The procedure for recording receipt of materials begins at the point where the office copy of the purchase order, the receiving report and the purchase invoice are matched (and found to be in agreement) and the disbursement voucher is written. Then the steps are:

(1) Enter the purchase invoice in the appropriate account(s) of the materials ledger.

(2) Enter the voucher in the voucher register.

(3) At the end of the month, post the total of the Materials column of the voucher register to the Materials Inventory Control account in the general ledger.

These steps are explained in detail in the following sections.

1. *Enter the Invoice in the Materials Ledger.* The materials ledger comprises an account for each type of materials carried in the materials storeroom. Each account in turn comprises a separate section for "received," "issued," and "balance." Under date of February 1, each account shows the quantity and value of a particular item in the storeroom on that inventory date. The sum of the three balances ($1,250 + $754 ÷ $1,312 = $3,316) agree with the opening balance of the Materials Inventory Control account.

Entry of the invoice includes date, receiving report number, quantity, price each, and total amount ($2,600). New balance amount is computed: previous new balance ($1,250) + this receipt ($2,600) = new balance ($3,850). New balance *quantity* (7,500) is computed by the same formula.

The Materials Ledger account form illustrated on page 000, which shows both quantity and value information, is one of several types that might be used. Other types of account form provide for (1) quantity only (which would be useful for purchasing and production control purposes) and (2) values only (which would be useful for financial accounting purposes).

2. *Enter the Voucher in the Voucher Register.* The illustration shows how to make the entry for a voucher for materials put into the storeroom. Note that the entry is a debit to Materials Inventory Control account and a credit to Vouchers Payable.

There are also entries for:

Voucher No. 114, Eastern and Western Railroad Co. $800, which is charged to Factory Expense Account Number 562, Freight on Materials. To save space, only one freight entry is shown on the voucher register for the month. In practice, there might be an entry for each day on which materials are received, since it is the usual practice to pay freight bills immediately.

The illustrated method of recording freight on materials—charging it to the Factory Expense account by that name—is the simplest of several

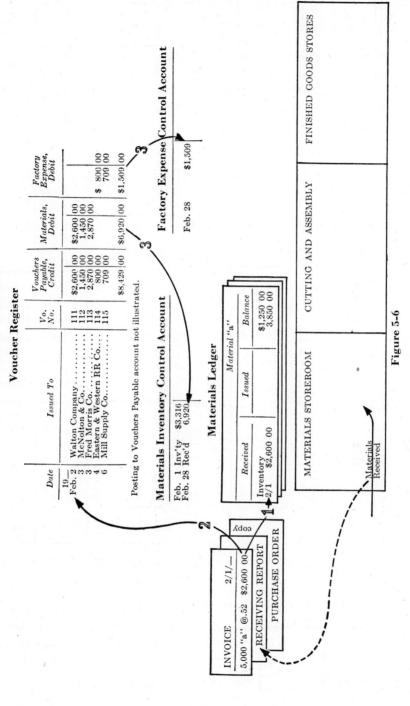

MATERIALS RECEIPTS

Figure 5-6

MATERIALS LEDGER ACCOUNTS

Illustrating Entry of Materials Received

Materials Account

Description _____ Materials "a"

		Received					Issued				Balance	
Date 19__	Rec. Report	Quantity	Price	Amount	Date 19__	Req. No.	Quantity	Price	Amount	Quantity	Amount
Feb. 1	Inven 51	tory 5,000	$ 50 52	$ 2,600 00				$	$	2,500 7,500	$1,250 00 3,850 00

Materials Account

Description _____ Materials "b"

		Received					Issued				Balance	
Date 19__	Rec. Report	Quantity	Price	Amount	Date 19__	Req. No.	Quantity	Price	Amount	Quantity	Amount
Feb. 1 3	Inven 52	tory 2,500	$ 58 58	$ 1,450 00				$	$	1,300 3,800	$ 754 00 2,204 00

Materials Account

Description _____ Materials "c"

		Received					Issued				Balance	
Date 19__	Rec. Report	Quantity	Price	Amount	Date 19__	Req. No.	Quantity	Price	Amount	Quantity	Amount
Feb. 1 3	Inven 53	tory 3,500	$ 82 82	$ 2,870 00				$	$	1,600 5,100	$1,312 00 4,182 00

1

Enter Invoice in the Materials Ledger

78

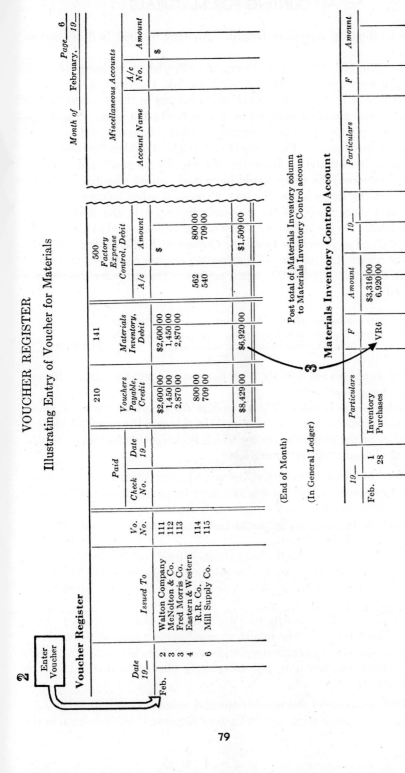

VOUCHER REGISTER

Illustrating Entry of Voucher for Materials

Month of __February,__ 19__   Page __6__

Voucher Register

Date 19—	Issued To	Vo. No.	Paid — Check No.	Paid — Date 19—	210 Vouchers Payable, Credit	141 Materials Inventory, Debit	500 Factory Expense Control, Debit — A/c	500 Factory Expense Control, Debit — Amount	Miscellaneous Accounts — Account Name	Miscellaneous Accounts — A/c No.	Miscellaneous Accounts — Amount
Feb. 2	Walton Company	111			$2,600|00	$2,600|00		$			$
3	McNolton & Co.	112			1,450|00	1,450|00					
3	Fred Morris Co.	113			2,870|00	2,870|00					
4	Eastern & Western R.R. Co.	114			800|00		562	800|00			
6	Mill Supply Co.	115			709|00		540	709|00			
					$8,429|00	$6,920|00		$1,509|00			

(End of Month)

(In General Ledger)

Post total of Materials Inventory column to Materials Inventory Control account

Materials Inventory Control Account

19—	Particulars	F	Amount	19—	Particulars	F	Amount
Feb. 1	Inventory		$3,316|00				$
28	Purchases	VR6	6,920|00				

Figure 5-8

79

possible methods of recording freight. Another method is described in Chapter 6.

Voucher No. 115, Mill Supply Company, $709, which is charged to Factory Expense account No. 540, Indirect Materials, Factory Operating Supplies and Repair Parts. These goods were not put in the storeroom when received, as the materials covered by vouchers 111-113 were. The goods from Mill Supply Company were turned over to the foreman who requested that they be purchased. The charge to Account 540 makes the item an expense charge immediately. If, on the other hand, the goods had been put into the storeroom, the entry would have been similar to entries 111-113.

Note that the items in the Factory Expense Control column would be posted on a daily basis, to the accounts indicated in the A/c column. These accounts are in the factory expense ledger (illustrated in Chapter 9).

3. *Post Total of Materials Inventory Column at End of Month.* At the end of the month, the columns in the voucher register are footed and cross-footed to determine that debits equal credits. The entry for the register illustrated is:

> Dr. Materials inventory control account......... $6,920.00
> Dr. Factory expense control account............ 1,509.00
>   Cr. Vouchers payable account................ $8,429.00

The totals are posted directly from the voucher register page to the accounts in the general ledger.

Procedures for issues. The procedure for recording issues of materials to production orders is as follows. (In this case the requisitions show the number of the production order which is chargeable for the materials. Such materials are "direct" materials.)

(1) Price and extend the requisitions and enter them in the materials ledger accounts. (This step and the remaining ones are explained in the following sections.)

(2) Sort the requisitions by production order number and enter requisitions on the cost sheets.

(3) Enter requisitions in the requisition journal, or (if they are numerous) enter the day's total of requisitions in the journal. The requisition journal is the book of original entry for issues of materials from the storeroom.

(4) At the end of the month, foot and cross-foot the requisition journal, and post totals for the month to accounts in the general ledger.

The procedure for materials requisitions to be charged to standing orders (Factory Expense accounts), not completely illustrated in the chart on page 87, is:

(1) Price and extend the requisitions and enter in materials ledger.

(2) Enter the requisitions in the Factory Expense Control column of the

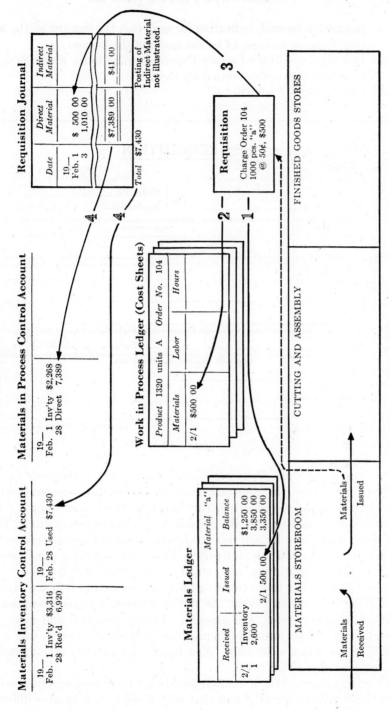

MATERIALS ISSUES

Figure 5-9

requisition journal, indicating for each one, the number of the Factory Expense account to be charged and the amount.

(3) Post the items in the Factory Expense column to the accounts in the factory expense ledger, on a daily basis.

(4) Same as Step 4, above.

ORIGINAL This copy to be sent to Stock Record when goods have been delivered to Department Ordering.

REQUISITION

From *Assembly* Dept. Date *Feb. 1, 19—*

Wanted ______ For { Order No. *104* / Replacement / Equipment }

QUANTITY	DESCRIPTION
1,000	*Material "a"*

FORM 601-02 U.S.A.

Requisitions for articles not carried must be approved by Works Mgr. before purchase is made.

Approved ______ Signed *J. Brown*

FOREMAN WILL NOT USE THIS SPACE

Purchase Order No ______

Ordered From ______

Form courtesy Wilson Jones Company

Figure 5-10

1. *Price and Extend Materials Requisitions: Enter in Materials Ledger.* In some procedures, these operations are performed as two separate steps. In the one illustrated (page 84), they are performed concurrently. The combined operation is: Sort the requisitions by materials account. Take the requisitions in order and refer each requisition to the appropriate materials account to find the cost price. Enter the cost price (for Material "a," 50¢) on the requisition, and extend the requisition (1,000 pieces "a" @ 50¢ = $500). After thus extending the requisition, enter it in the Materials Ledger account, as shown. In the illustration, note date, requisition number, quantity, price, and amount. Finally, compute and enter the new balance. The formula is: previous balance ($3,850) – this issue ($500) = new balance ($3,350). New balance for quantity is computed in the same manner as for value.

In pricing requisitions, it is often found that there were several receipts of a single type of material and that each receipt came in at a different price. The question arises what price shall be used in pricing the requisition at hand. There are several methods of pricing in common use. The one which is known as first-in, first-out pricing is illustrated on page 84. It operates on the assumption that the goods on hand first were the ones which were used first, and that several successive lots would be exhausted successively.

In the Materials Ledger account illustrated, note that the 2,500 units on hand in the opening inventory (Feb. 1) were valued at 50¢ per piece. The 1,000 pieces received the same day cost 52¢ per unit. When Requisition No. 31 for 1,000 pieces was received, it was priced at the oldest price, 50¢ per piece.

When Requisition No. 32 for 2,000 pieces was received, it was found upon reference to Materials "a" account that there were only 1,500 pieces left of the original inventory priced at 50¢. The requisition was, therefore, as priced:

1,500 pieces @ 50¢ = $750 (this exhausted the 2,500 units in opening inventory).
500 pieces @ 52¢ = $260 (priced from the materials received February 1).

Other methods of pricing materials issues are illustrated in the following chapter.

2. *Enter Direct Materials Requisitions on Cost Sheets.* Where the number of direct requisitions is large, the requisitions are sorted by production order number to facilitate posting and posted to the cost sheets. In the illustration on page 85, it is assumed that there were only nine requisitions during the month. They were simply random posted as they came through. The illustration shows the posting of all of them. Note that date, requisition number, symbol, and cost amount are posted.

3. *Enter Requisitions in Requisition Journal.* The illustration on page 87 shows the entry of materials requisitions chargeable to production order cost sheets (in the first column, headed "Materials in Process, Debit") and materials requisitions chargeable to standing orders (in the second column, headed "Factory Expense Control, Debit"). Both types are entered in the third column ("Materials Credit").

Items in the Factory Expense column are posted to the accounts indicated in the "F" column, on a daily basis.

4. *Post Totals of Requisition Journal at End of Month.* At the end of the month the columns of the requisition journal are footed and cross-footed. The totals are posted to general ledger accounts as follows:

Dr. Materials in process control account (for direct materials).. $7,389.00
Dr. Factory expense control account for (indirect materials)... 41.00
Cr. Materials.. $7,430.00

5. *Prove Materials Ledger.* At the end of each month, the sum of the balances of the accounts in the materials ledger is proved against the balance of the Materials Ledger Control account. This is done as a test of the

MATERIALS LEDGER ACCOUNT

Illustrating Entry of Requisition

Description _____ Materials "a"

Price and extend requisition; enter in materials ledger

Materials Account

	Received					Issued				Balance	
Date 19__	Rec. Report	Quan-tity	Price	Amount	Date 19__	Req. No.	Quan-tity	Price	Amount	Quan-tity	Amount
Feb. 1	Inventory		$	$				$	$		
1	51	5,000	50 52	2,600 00	Feb. 1	31	1,000	50	500 00	2,500	$1,250 00
					3	32	1,500	50	750 00	7,500	3,850 00
							500	52	260 00	6,500	3,350 00
										4,500	2,340 00

Figure 5-11

84

Cost Sheet   *No.* __104__

Quantity and Description _____ 1,320 Units   Product A _____

Made For _____

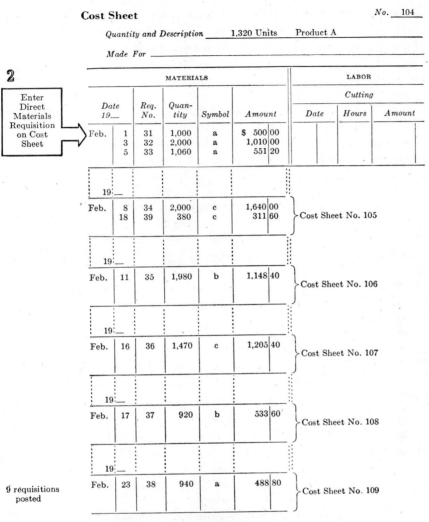

Figure 5-12

Total posting to cost sheets: $7,389.00
Agrees with total charge to Materials in Process account
  at end of month from requisition journal (Figure 5-13)

accuracy of posting and computing balances in the ledger and as proof that all the media represented in the balance of the control account were actually posted to subsidiary accounts. The illustrations on pages 88 and 89 show this proof. Note that the sum of the balances in the subsidiary materials ledger is $2,806 and that the balance of the control account is the same amount.

Physical inventories. The trial balance proof of the materials ledger discussed in the previous section is a proof of the clerical accuracy of entries in the materials ledger. It is not intended to prove that the quantity of goods shown in the materials ledger account is actually in the storeroom. If all the paper work has been done completely and correctly, and if the physical control over materials has operated perfectly, the balance in the storeroom will be the same as the balances in the accounts. The chances of perfect agreement are so slight, however, that it is necessary to take physical inventories occasionally and compare physical count with book balance to determine to what extent the book inventories are "off." (It is not necessary, however, to take physical inventory as frequently as *every month* for the sole purpose of getting financial statements. The book inventories will serve to produce financial statements.)

Physical inventory can be done on a round-the-calendar basis. One or more inventory checkers regularly employed can count the items in certain designated bins or other storage spaces each day and send their counts to the accounting department where the materials ledger accounts are adjusted as required. The aim would be so to schedule the inventory crews that the whole inventory would be checked say twice a year. Round-the-calendar checking would support the contention that where perpetual inventories are operated it is not necessary to shut down the plant to take a physical inventory.

In some cases, it may be desired to take the entire physical inventory at one time (several successive days). This might be the case in a seasonal business where the plant is normally shut down at a certain time each year. In such cases, the following physical inventory procedure might be used, employing two separate crews, one of which checks the other:

(1) The first counting crew is provided with a quantity of cards that can be sealed in envelopes. These envelopes are equipped with eyelets and strings so that they can be fastened onto bins or receptacles of items counted. The first crew counts goods, enters identifying descriptions, codes, and counts on the cards, inserts the cards in the envelopes and fastens the envelopes onto the receptacles.

(2) The inventory supervisor inspects the storeroom spaces to see that all of the bins or receptacles have been counted—that nothing has been missed.

(3) The second counting crew is dispatched over the area of the storeroom previously covered by the first crew. It makes the second count of the items and records it on the envelopes, together with identifying description and codes.

(4) The envelopes are removed from the bins or receptacles and taken to the office where the cards are removed. The count shown on each card is compared with the count shown on the envelopes from which it is removed. Where there is a discrepancy, the item is counted again to establish a figure which can be accepted.

(5) The accepted counts are entered on inventory sheets, which are

Requisition Journal

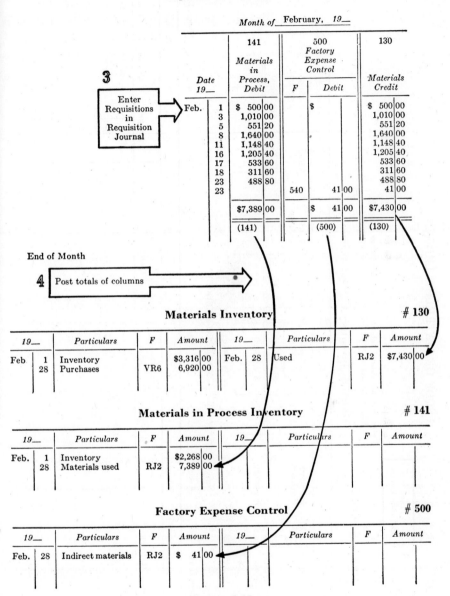

Month of February, 19__

3 Enter Requisitions in Requisition Journal

Date 19__		141 Materials in Process, Debit	500 Factory Expense Control F	Debit	130 Materials Credit
Feb.	1	$ 500 00	$		$ 500 00
	3	1,010 00			1,010 00
	5	551 20			551 20
	8	1,640 00			1,640 00
	11	1,148 40			1,148 40
	16	1,205 40			1,205 40
	17	533 60			533 60
	18	311 60			311 60
	23	488 80			488 80
	23		540	41 00	41 00
		$7,389 00	$	41 00	$7,430 00
		(141)	(500)		(130)

End of Month

4 Post totals of columns

Materials Inventory # 130

19__		Particulars	F	Amount	19__		Particulars	F	Amount
Feb	1	Inventory		$3,316 00	Feb.	28	Used	RJ2	$7,430 00
	28	Purchases	VR6	6,920 00					

Materials in Process Inventory # 141

19__		Particulars	F	Amount	19__		Particulars	F	Amount
Feb.	1	Inventory		$2,268 00					
	28	Materials used	RJ2	7,389 00					

Factory Expense Control # 500

19__		Particulars	F	Amount	19__		Particulars	F	Amount
Feb.	28	Indirect materials	RJ2	$ 41 00					

Figure 5-13

PROOF OF MATERIALS LEDGER

Prove Materials Ledger

(In General Ledger)

Determine that sum of balances of materials ledger accounts ($2,806.00) agrees with balance of Control account.

Materials Inventory Control Account

19—		F	Amount	19—		F	Amount
Feb. 1	Inventory	VR6	$ 3,316.00	Feb. 28	Used	RJ2	$ 7,430.00
28	Purchases		6,920.00		Balance		2,806.00
			$10,236.00				$10,236.00
Mar. 1	Inventory		$ 2,806.00				

MATERIALS LEDGER

Materials Account

Description Materials "a"

	Received					Issued				Balance	
Date 19—	Rec. Report	Quantity	Price	Amount	Date 19—	Req. No.	Quantity	Price	Amount	Quantity	Amount
Feb. 1	Inventory							$		2,500	$1,250 00
1	51	5,000	$ 50 52	$ 2,600 00						7,500	3,850 00
					Feb. 1	31	1,000	50	500 00	6,500	3,350 00
					3	32	1,500	50	750 00	4,500	2,340 00
					5	33	500	52	260 00	3,440	1,788 80
					23	38	1,060	52	551 20	2,500	1,300 00
							940	52	488 80		

Figure 5-11a

Materials Account

Description Materials "b"

Received					Issued					Balance	
Date 19__	Rec. Report	Quantity	Price	Amount	Date 19__	Req. No.	Quantity	Price	Amount	Quantity	Amount
Feb. 1		Inventory	$					$	$	1,300	$ 754 00
3	52	2,500	58	$ 1,450 00						3,800	2,204 00
					Feb. 11	35	1,980	58	1,148 40	1,820	1,055 60
					11	37	920	58	533 60	900	522 00

Materials Account

Description Materials "c"

Received					Issued					Balance	
Date 19__	Rec. Report	Quantity	Price	Amount	Date 19__	Req. No.	Quantity	Price	Amount	Quantity	Amount
Feb. 1		Inventory	$					$	$	1,600	$1,312 00
3	52	3,500	82	$ 2,870 00						5,100	4,182 00
					Feb. 8	34	2,000	82	1,640 00	3,100	2,542 00
					16	36	1,470	82	1,205 40	1,630	1,336 60
					18	39	380	82	311 60	1,250	1,025 00
					24	40	50	82	41 00	1,200	984 00

Trial Balance of Materials Ledger:

Materials "a".........................	$1,300.00
Materials "b".........................	522.00
Materials "c".........................	984.00
Total, agrees with Control...........	$2,806.00

Figure 5-14b

printed with the two identical extension columns, side by side. The right-hand extension column is detachable from the body of the sheet along a perforated line. Both the main sheet and the detachable column bear the same serial number (preprinted), which makes it possible to match a detached column with its main sheet.

(6) The inventory sheets are priced and extended a first time, and the extensions are entered in the right-hand column, which is then detached from the main sheet and filed away by the supervisor.

(7) The inventory sheets are then redistributed to the calculating machine operators, who re-extend them and enter the new extensions on the main sheets.

(8) The detached columns are then matched with the main sheets and the two sets of extensions compared. Where there is a discrepancy, the extension is recalculated.

(9) The final extensions are compared with the balances shown by the perpetual inventory accounts.

(10) The inventory sheets are compared with the materials inventory accounts to locate differences.

Adjustment of book inventories to physical inventory. When there is a discrepancy between the physical inventory amounts and perpetual inventory balances, the perpetual inventory balances are adjusted to agree with the physical inventory. The adjustments may, of course, be plus or minus. The net total of the adjustments in the subsidiary accounts is recorded in the general ledger so that the Materials Control account will agree with the sum of the balances in the materials ledger.

Thus if, as a net amount, the accounts in the materials ledger have been reduced to agree with physical inventory, the following entry would be recorded in the general journal and posted to the general ledger:

Inventory over and short account (Factory expense).. $xxx
    Materials control account...................... $xxx
    To record the net difference between physical inventory and book inventory.

Summary of materials transactions. The entries for the issue of a *direct material* are diagrammed and explained in the previous pages. The accounting paper is a requisition. It is credited to the materials ledger account for the particular materials described and charged to the cost sheet for the job on which the materials were used. It is entered in the requisition journal from which, at the end of the month, a total of direct materials used is debited to Materials in Process Control account and credited to Materials Control account.

The entry for the issue of an *indirect material* out of the materials storeroom (not illustrated) is likewise made from a requisition. It is credited to a materials ledger account and entered in the Indirect Materials column of the requisition journal from which it is posted to the appropriate account in the factory expense ledger. The total of indirect materials drawn from raw materials stores as shown by the requisition journal is debited to Factory Expense Control account and credited to Raw Materials Control account.

The entry for purchase of factory supplies to be used immediately is made from the purchase invoice or from a disbursement voucher. It is recorded in the voucher register in the Factory Expense, Debit column and the Vouchers Payable, Credit column. The individual debit is posted from that journal to the appropriate account in the factory expense ledger. At the end of the month, the totals of Factory Expense, Debit column and Vouchers Payable, Credit column are posted to those accounts in the general ledger.

Material issued to a production order, found to be excess and returned to the materials storeroom, is recorded on a materials credit slip or a requisition marked "credit." It is debited to the materials ledger account for the particular material and credited to the cost sheet for the production order which was charged for the original issue. It is then entered in the Direct Materials column of the requisition journal in red. When that column is totaled at the end of the month, the red entry is subtracted from the sum of the black entries and the balance representing *net materials issued* is debited to Materials in Process Control account and credited to Materials Control account. The effect of the entry for the credit slip actually is to credit Materials in Process Control account and debit Materials Control account.

QUESTIONS

5-1. Describe briefly the function of accounting for materials in a job order cost accounting system.

5-2. In a typical small industrial company, what employees are directly involved in the physical control of materials? What employees are directly involved in the accounting work for purchase, receipt, and issue of materials?

5-3. Describe some items of managerial information useful for the control of materials, which would be provided by a job order cost accounting system.

5-4. (a) Describe the debits and credits to Materials Control account and indicate the source of each debit and credit. What does the balance of the account represent? What subsidiary ledger supports the Material Control account? How do you prove the postings to that ledger?

(b) Describe the debit(s) to Materials in Process Control account and indicate the source of each. What subsidiary ledger supports the Materials in Process Control account?

(c) What debit(s) to Factory Expense Control account are mentioned and illustrated in Chapter 5? What subsidiary ledger supports the Factory Expense Control account?

5-5. Name the basic forms used in accounting for materials in a job order cost system.

5-6. (a) Describe the main features of a plan for taking physical inventory in a manufacturing plant.

(b) Is it necessary to take physical inventory in a factory in which a complete cost accounting system (with perpetual inventory accounts) is operated?

EXERCISES

5-1. The materials ledger of the Brunswick Manufacturing Company appears in the Workbook along with certain other forms. The invoices for materials received for the month of February have been posted by the materials ledger clerk to the accounts, but they have not been entered in any other records. The requisitions for materials issued have likewise been posted to the materials ledger accounts, but they have not been entered in any other records.

Required:

(1) Complete all entries required for materials received.
(2) Complete all entries required for materials issued.
Note that requisitions for indirect materials (indicated "SO" in the materials ledger accounts) are to be entered in the Factory Expense column of the requisition journal and posted as described on page 83.
(3) Foot and cross-foot the journals and post them to the general ledger accounts, on the assumption that there are no other transactions for the month. Enter closing balances in the general ledger accounts.
(4) Prepare trial balances of each of the following ledgers, and indicate whether each of them agrees with its control accounts:

Materials ledger
Work in process ledger (materials columns)
Factory expense ledger

Use the journal, ledger, and trial balance forms provided. Detach from the Workbook, fasten them securely together, and submit.

5-2. For the following transactions, set out this information in columnar arrangement: (a) what basic accounting paper is used for the original writing of the transaction, (b) what subsidiary ledger account (if any) would be debited, (c) what subsidiary ledger account (if any) would be credited, (d) what special journal would be used for summarizing the particular type of transaction, and (e) general ledger accounts affected. (Give debit and credit for each transaction). (Use blank in Workbook.)

(a) Purchased materials for stores, $800. See sample solution on the following page.
   (1) Issued materials from stores, to be charged to Production Order No. 201, $200.
   (2) Issued materials from stores, to be charged to a factory expense account, $50.
   (3) Purchase factory supplies to be used immediately, $85.
   (4) Some of the materials issued to Production Order No. 201 (Transaction 1) were found to be excess. They were returned to stores. Cost value, $60. Use a requisition as a materials credit slip.
   (5) Some materials in the storeroom were found to be defective. They were returned by the storekeeper to the supplier, $40. Use a debit memo to supplier.
   (6) Several of the materials accounts in the materials ledger show balances less than the balances disclosed in the physical inventory. (Adjustment?) Use requisition form marked "inventory over and *short.*" Amount, $38.

5-2 (*continued*)

Trans- action No.	(a) Basic Accounting Paper Used to Record Trans- action	(b) (c) Subsidiary Ledger (if any)		(d) Special Journal Used for Summa- rizing the Type of Transaction	(e) General Ledger Accounts Affected (Give debit and credit for each transaction)		
		Account Debited	Account Credited		Account Names	Debits	Credits
(a)	Invoice	Materials ledger account	None (no creditors ledger is kept)	Voucher register	Materials inventory Vouchers payable	$800|00	$800|00

5-3. Using the "fill-in" forms in the Workbook, make all entries required for the following transactions:

(1) Opening inventory of materials (January 1, 19___):

    Materials A: 200 units @ $1.25...................... $ 250.00

(2) Opening inventory of work in process:

    P.O. No. 101 for 10 units of Item X:
    Materials...................................... $ 100.00
    Labor... 200.00
    Factory expense, 100 hours in Department No. 1
      ($100.00 in control account)

(3) Production orders issued during the month:

    P.O. No. 102 for 50 units of Item Y
    P.O. No. 103 for 100 units of Item Z

(4) Materials purchased:

    Jan. 3, Marshall & Co., 400 units A @ $1.50........... $ 600.00
      (Receiving Report No. 13)
    Jan. 4, Wilton & Co., 600 units B @ $2.00............. 1,200.00
      (Receiving Report No. 14)
    Jan. 5, Norden & Co., 500 units C @ $3.00............ 1,500.00
      (Receiving Report No. 15)

(5) Materials used on production orders:

    Jan. 4, P.O. No. 101—100 units A (Requisition No. 8)
    Jan. 5, P.O. No. 102—200 units B (Requisition No. 9)
    Jan. 19, P.O. No. 103—100 units C (Requisition No. 10)

(6) Indirect materials drawn from materials stores:

    January 16, 50 units B (Requisition 11)

Assume that there are no other transactions for materials during the month. Foot the journals and post to control accounts. Prepare a trial balance of the materials ledger and prove against the balance of the related control account.

PROBLEMS

5-1. (a) Assume that the A Company operates no special journals. Draft entries for January in simple journal entry form for the following transactions. Indicate what subsidiary ledgers would be affected and indicate whether the entry in the subsidiary ledger account would be a debit or a credit. Use transaction numbers as dates.)

(1) Receive and store 1,000 pieces of Material X @ 40¢ from the Sherwood Company.
(2) On Requisition No. 81, issue 400 pieces of Materials X for use on Production Order No. 206.
(6) On Requisition No. 82, issue 100 pieces of Material X for use to repair factory machinery.
(7) Receive and store 600 pieces of Material X @ 50¢ from the Sherwood Company.
(8) Issue 600 pieces of Material X for use on Production Order No. 207.

(9) 50 pieces of Material X issued on Requisition No. 81, drawn for Production Order No. 206, were returned to materials store. Make the entry at the cost price at which it was originally issued. Material Credit Slip No. 21.

(10) Return 40 pieces of Material X (out of the 50 received January 9). This material was found to be defective. Issue Debit Memo No. 11 charging the Sherwood Company.

(11) Purchase factory maintenance supplies to be used immediately, $80.

(b) Set up a columnar illustration of a materials ledger account for Material X and post all the entries for part (a) which affect that account. Show all details usually found in a materials ledger account.

5-2. A recap of materials receipts, issues from storerooms, returns to storeroom, and returns to vendors for the month of January, 19— appears on the following page.

Required:

(1) Using columnar analysis paper, set up three materials accounts like Figure 5-11 (Material A, Material B, and Material C, respectively) and three cost sheets like Figure 5-12 (Job No. 10, Job No. 11, and Job No. 12, respectively).

(2) Enter all transactions (shown in the recap) in the materials accounts and in the cost sheets. A credit entry on the cost sheets may be entered in red or in black, followed by an asterisk. On the materials ledger, enter returns to storeroom in the "Received" section.

5-3. Following is a list of account balances from the general ledger of Fred Lincoln, Manufacturer, as of January 31, 19—. Inventories are taken by physical count and recorded by journal entry at the end of the month. The list of account balances reflects all adjusting entries except inventories.

Accounts payable............................	$14,000.00
Accounts receivable.........................	32,000.00
Accrued labor...............................	2,000.00
Accrued taxes...............................	800.00
Administrative expense......................	800.00
Advertising expense.........................	400.00
Building....................................	12,000.00
Cash..	12,000.00
Depreciation on building....................	200.00
Depreciation on machinery...................	400.00
Direct labor................................	8,000.00
Finished goods inventory (January 1)........	6,000.00
Insurance expense...........................	600.00
Interest expense............................	500.00
Interest income.............................	700.00
Land..	10,000.00
Fred Lincoln, capital.......................	78,800.00
Machinery...................................	24,000.00
Prepaid advertising.........................	1,600.00
Prepaid insurance...........................	1,200.00
Purchases of materials......................	12,000.00
Raw materials inventory (January 1).........	2,000.00
Reserve for bad debts.......................	800.00
Reserve for depreciation—Building...........	1,200.00
Reserve for depreciation—Machinery.........	2,400.00
Sales.......................................	30,000.00
Selling expense.............................	1,200.00

5-2 (continued)

THE McNAIR COMPANY

Recap of Materials Receipts, Issues from Storeroom, Returns to Storeroom, and Returns to Vendors

Month of January, 19__

I. RECEIPTS FROM VENDORS

Date	Voucher No.	Material	Quantity	Price	Vendor
Jan. 1	51	A	100	$2.00	Brown
2	52	B	200	3.00	Smith
3	53	C	300	4.00	Wilson
4	54	B	100	3.50	Smith
5	55	A	50	2.10	Brown

II. ISSUES FROM STOREROOM

Requisition No.	Job No.	Material	Quantity
80	10	A	30
81	11	B	50
82	12	C	100

III. RETURNS TO STOREROOM

Credit Slip	Job No.	Material	Quantity
C 5	10	A	10
C 6	11	B	5

IV. RETURNS TO VENDORS

Date	Voucher No.	Material	Quantity	Vendor
Jan. 1				
2				
3	51	A	5	Brown
4				Smith

96

Taxes expense............................	800.00
Work in process inventory (January 1).......	5,000.00

Inventories, January 31, 19— are:

Raw materials..........................	$ 3,000.00
Work in process........................	4,000.00
Finished goods.........................	8,000.00

Required:

(1) Set up worksheet for financial statements.
(2) Prepare:
    (a) Balance Sheet
    (b) Statement of Profits
    (c) Statement of Cost of Goods Manufactured and Sold
(3) Draft closing entries.

MATERIALS CLASSIFICATION, QUANTITY
CONTROL, AND PRICING

Chapter 5 explained and illustrated accounting procedures for the receipt of materials into stores and the issue of materials out of stores. It was devoted to the mechanics of keeping track of materials on hand and compiling charges to cost sheets for direct materials used and to factory expense accounts for indirect materials used. The present chapter deals partly with mechanics and partly with policy matters with which the cost accountant and the executive who uses costs should be familiar.

The first part of this chapter is devoted to materials classification—classification for purchasing, inventory, and issuing purposes, and classifications for recording the use or other disposition of materials. It will be seen that setting up a classification of accounts for materials may be a complicated project but, when properly done, a rewarding one, particularly in a large business.

Materials quantity control—concerned with means of safeguarding the accuracy of materials quantities for accounting and cost accounting purposes—is presented next. This section illustrates what is meant by "tying the quantities through" in a cost system and explains why sound quantity control is absolutely essential to the successful operation of a cost system.

The final section discusses materials pricing, which is concerned with the mechanics of pricing requisitions and inventories by various methods (first-in, first-out; average; replacement; standard) and the effect of pricing upon the costs intended for various uses. The method of pricing in use obviously has an effect upon costs, whether used for the measurement of performance, or as a factor in setting selling prices, or for inventory valuation and profit determination. It is important therefore that careful consideration be given to pricing policies by both the cost accountant who is responsible for setting up the costs and the management people who use them.

I. MATERIALS CLASSIFICATION

Meaning of materials classification; Need for formal classification. In general, a classification is a listing of items according to certain characteristics common to all the items.   In regard to materials, a classification is a listing according to such features as composition, size, use, and so forth.   In small businesses where few different types of materials are handled, there may be no formal classification of materials.   Requests for purchase are issued to the purchasing department, and purchase orders are issued to the suppliers on the basis of specifications which someone remembers, or looks up on old invoices.   Materials ledger accounts are added to the materials ledger as new types of items come into the storeroom.   Likewise, charges to accounts are made according to memory or according to a check to see what account was charged the last time a similar item was received or used.

In larger businesses in which numerous different items are handled, it is often desirable to set up formal written classification of materials for use in purchasing, storing, issuing, and accounting for materials.   The basic classifications relating to materials are:

(1) Classification according to physical, chemical, optical, or other characteristics recognized and stated by the people who designed the products and laid out the production lines.   Thus, in the manufacture of desks, a materials classification of this type lists the various woods, glues, stains, varnishes, and waxes, and the hardware items to be used in the various models.   It would show quality specifications, sizes, and other similar information necessary for positive identification of an item in the storeroom and in the records.   Some companies incorporate their formal materials classifications in catalogs distributed within the company organization.

Materials classifications of the type described above may be used as a control first of all so that no greater number of materials items, or qualities, sizes, or shapes, are bought and stored than absolutely necessary to make the product and maintain the plant.   Some companies have been able to reduce the investment in inventories significantly by instituting formal classification plans.   In making the survey of materials being bought and stored on the one hand and materials specifications actually needed on the other, it was found that far more varieties were carried than were needed.

After a classification is set up it is used by various factory and accounting people to determine the exact specifications for purchasing, or issuing from stores, or recording in the accounts.   Often, the items in the materials classification are given code numbers.   These code numbers make positive identification possible, and they are often used in accounting forms and records instead of lengthy descriptive names.

(2) Classification according to (a) use and (b) accounts to be charged for

the use or loss of materials (See page 101).   Such classification is intended
to aid in charging materials to production order cost sheets on the one hand
or to factory expense accounts on the other.   This classification includes
not only the invoice cost of the materials proper but also such items of laid-
down cost as freight-in and, further, materials purchasing, storage, and handling expense.   The latter items are sometimes referred to as "materials
overhead."   It is discussed in the following sections, under the headings:

> Direct materials
> Indirect materials and operating supplies
> Maintenance supplies; repair parts
> Laid-down cost; freight on materials
> Materials losses
> Materials overhead: materials storage and handling expense

Direct materials; Indirect materials and operating supplies.   A
direct material is one which (a) is identified with a particular product and
(b) is feasible to measure and charge to the cost sheets for particular
production orders.*   Lumber used to make custom desks is an example of
direct material.   It is identified with the product, and it would seem to be
feasible to measure the quantity of lumber used in a particular production
order and to charge the cost sheet for the order.

Indirect material is identified with particular units of product, but which
it is not considered feasible to measure and charge to the cost sheets of specific production orders.   In some garment manufacturing factories, thread
is treated as an indirect material.   It is identified with particular products,
clearly enough, but in some factories it is not considered feasible to measure
the amount of thread used in the garments of a particular order and to keep
track of it separately for cost accounting purposes.

As to accounting entries, direct materials are charged to cost sheets (and
in total to Materials in Process account) and indirect materials are charged
to standing orders (and in total to Factory Expense Control account).

In addition to indirect materials, which actually go into the product,
there are certain physical goods, known as factory *operating supplies*, which
are used as and when production takes place but which do not actually go
into the product.   Tissue paper and chalk used in the cutting room of a garment factory are examples.

Operating supplies are charged to an appropriate factory expense account, as used.   Sometimes a single factory expense account is used for indirect materials and factory operating supplies.   Note that, from an expense control standpoint, it would be expected that indirect materials and
operating supplies would vary to some degree with volume of operations.

---

* In this chapter, direct material and indirect material are defined and illustrated with
reference to the *product unit* as the cost unit.   In general, a material is defined as direct
or indirect with reference to the specific cost unit, being direct if it is allocable to the
selected cost unit.   Various examples of cost units are presented in Chapter 2.

Some materials may be either direct or indirect; Advantage of direct charging. It is obvious that materials such as lumber in custom desks would likely be treated as direct materials. Others, such as thread in a garment plant and glue in a furniture factory, would be treated as direct or indirect, depending upon whether the management considered it feasible to measure the amount that goes into particular production orders and to do the clerical work of recording the charges.

CLASSIFICATION OF MATERIALS: DIRECT AND INDIRECT
as Regards Products (Job Order System)

Direct-Materials
Materials identified with specific product, which can be measured and charged to cost sheets.

Indirect materials and operating supplies;
maintenance supplies and repair parts
Indirect materials: identified with specific product, which it is *not* considered feasible to measure and charge to cost sheets.
Operating supplies: physical goods used as and when production takes place, but which do not actually go into the product.
Maintenance supplies and repair parts: physical goods used to keep the building, machinery, or other facilities in a state of readiness for occupancy or use.

Material losses
Losses of material units or weight between materials receipt and product output
- Waste
- Spoilage
- Scrap
- Shrinkage in process (heat loss, chemical change, etc.)
- Inventory shortage

Materials overhead

Figure 6-1

In practice, the bill of materials which specifies *all* the materials necessary to make the product may be used in making the decision about what materials will be treated as direct materials and what ones indirect. Some materials will be clearly direct; they can be measured and charged to cost sheets. Other materials listed on the bill of materials will be considered not significant enough from a dollar standpoint to warrant the expenses of direct charging. They may be classified as indirect materials for cost accounting purposes. All such materials will thenceforth be charged to standing orders as and when drawn from stores.

Handling a material as a direct material is known as *direct* charging; handling it as an indirect material is known as *indirect* charging. The advantage of direct charging is increased accuracy of the unit cost. It is expected that the tedious process of measurement in terms of specific production orders will result in more accurate unit product costs than the procedure of passing the material through the factory expense accounts and thence to the cost sheets by way of more or less arbitrary expense rates.

Maintenance supplies and repair parts. In all factories certain physical goods are used to keep the building, machinery, and other facilities in a state of readiness for occupancy or use. These goods do not actually go into the product in a physical sense, and use of them is not expected necessarily to vary with volume of production. Examples may be grouped:

(1) Maintenance supplies, such as lubricating oils, electric light bulbs and fluorescent tubes, sweeping compound and other janitors' supplies. Under the definition in the above paragraph, coal for heating the building would be also included.

(2) Repair parts for factory machinery and repair items for the building.

All these items are usually charged to factory expense, as are indirect materials. In many factories, however, separate subsidiary expense accounts or standing orders are set up for (a) indirect materials and operating supplies and (b) maintenance supplies and repair parts. This is desirable where significant amounts of the various classes of goods are used. As stated above, indirect materials and operating supplies would be expected to vary to some extent with volume of production. Maintenance supplies and repair parts, on the other hand, would not necessarily vary with volume of production. The management might decide to let certain repairs and maintenance go during periods of peak production and to make good during periods of low production. What would be considered reasonable must be decided by the management on the basis of advice by qualified maintenance people. In some cases, it may be necessary to set up several specific accounts under indirect materials and factory operating supplies and several under maintenance and repairs to make it possible for the management to exercise proper control. There might be a separate account for needles, for instance, and one for coal.

In probably the great majority of cases an item will be clearly either operating or maintenance at the point of use. In some cases, it might be debatable whether the item is an operating supply or a maintenance supply. It can be argued, for instance, that oil is needed to operate a machine and it is also needed to maintain it in a state of readiness to operate. There is some justification for either position, and yet it is not feasible to separate each charge for oil into operating on the one hand and maintenance on the other. In cases where it seems possible for successive accounting people to have different interpretations, the desirability for consistency becomes apparent. This is accomplished by maintaining a formal account manual which describes the items chargeable to each expense account.

Some elements in laid-down cost. Laid-down cost is the cost of materials at the buyer's plant as distinguished from say the price quoted at the seller's plant. In cost accounting, questions arise as to the proper handling of various elements of laid-down cost beyond invoice prices f.o.b. the supplier's factory. Some of the items may involve significant amounts, as compared to invoice price, and the method of handling is therefore important to the managers who use costs in making decisions.

Some of the elements of laid-down cost and considerations related to them, are:

Invoice cost; purchase discounts. There are two schools of thought on the matter of taking invoice cost and any related purchase discount into cost:

(1) Charge Materials Inventory account (and consequently the cost sheets, when materials are used) for the *gross* invoice price of materials. The voucher register on page 79 illustrates a charge to Materials Inventory account for gross invoice price. If a purchase discount is taken when a voucher is paid, the discount is recorded in the cash disbursements journal.

(2) Charge Materials Inventory account for the *net* invoice price of the materials. To illustrate, assume that the invoice shows gross amount of $1,000, subject to a discount of 2 per cent for payment within 10 days. The entry in the voucher register would be debit Materials and credit Vouchers Payable for $980. If the voucher is paid within the discount period, the entry in the cash disbursements journal is debit Vouchers Payable and credit Cash for $980. If the voucher is paid after the discount period has expired, the entry is debit Vouchers Payable $980, debit Purchase Discounts Lost $20, and credit Cash $1,000.

Note that the factory is charged for the gross invoice price consistently (under Method 1) or the net invoice cost consistently (under Method 2). Under either method, the charge to the factory would not fluctuate simply because the treasurer's office took, or failed to take, a discount.

The second method (charging the factory for the net cost of materials) would seem to be more reasonable than the first method. Financing the business (and paying vouchers within the discount period) is the responsibility of the treasurer rather than the factory superintendent. For multiple item invoices, however, the method would involve allocating the discount on an invoice to the various items on the invoice. Charging invoices at net would entail more clerical work than charging the factory for gross invoice cost of the items.

Freight on materials may be recorded by either of two general methods:

(1) *Direct charging.* Charge the materials account of the particular item received for the freight (along with the invoice amount as illustrated in Figure 6-2). Where a single freight bill covers a single in-shipment of materials, this method of accounting is relatively simple. In the usual procedure of verifying freight bills for payment, the freight bills are matched with the invoices or the receiving reports. This is done in an effort to assure that no freight bills are paid for goods which were not actually received. It follows that it is a simple matter to enter the invoice *and* the

freight bill in the Materials Ledger account, and then to enter vouchers for each of them in the voucher register. In Figure 6-2, note that the freight bill ($100) is entered in the Received section of the Materials account and also in the Materials column of the voucher register. The issue price of materials "a" including freight for the lot indicated is 54¢ per unit.

Under this method, prices used for pricing requisitions and crediting materials accounts would include freight as well as invoice cost. This method technically constitutes "direct charging" of freight on materials, since it fits the definition of measuring the item and charging it to the cost sheet.

Where the freight bill covers a joint shipment of a number of items, however, the direct charging method is not likely to be simple. The freight bill would have to be split among a number of materials accounts. This might involve problems of selecting proper bases and considerably more clerical effort than the indirect charging method, which does not involve splitting freight bills.

The advantage of direct charging of freight is the one stated earlier in the chapter: increased accuracy in unit product costs.

(2) *Indirect charging.* Charge each freight bill to the freight on materials account through the voucher register, as illustrated on page 79, Voucher #114. When this is done, the freight becomes part of the factory expense total which is applied to cost sheets by means of factory expense rates, as explained in Chapter 10.

Import duties, like freight on materials, should be charged to the materials account where it is clerically feasible to split the charges among the appropriate materials accounts.

Material losses. Material losses may be classified as follows:

Spoilage—defective portions of regular production, having a value recoverable only through reprocessing.

Waste—that portion of basic raw material lost in processing, having no recovery value.

Scrap—the incidental residue from certain types of manufacture, recoverable without further processing.

Shrinkage—loss in which units of input disappear in processing, through vaporization or other chemical or physical change. In this case, the total of measurable and measured output is less than the total of input.

Inventory loss—shortage in inventory, disclosed by comparison of physical inventory with book inventory.

It should be noted that the definitions of waste, spoilage, and scrap vary with trade usage from industry to industry. The definitions given here appear in Greer, "Accounting for Joint Products and By-Products," *N.A.C.A. Bulletin*, August 15, 1936, quoting Fox, N.A.C.A. April 1, 1934.

The first four losses are discussed in the following sections. Inventory losses were discussed in the previous chapter.

DIRECT CHARGING OF FREIGHT ON MATERIALS

Voucher Register

Month of __February__ 19__

Date	Issued To	Vo. No.	Paid		Vouchers Payable, Credit	Materials Inventory, Debit	Factory Expense Control, Debit	
			Check No.	Date			A/c	Amount
Feb. 2	Walton Company	111			$2,600 00	$2,600 00		
2	Eastern and Western R.R. Co.	112			100 00	100 00		

Materials Account

Description _____ Materials "a"

Date	RECEIVED				ISSUED					BALANCE	
	Rec. Report	Quan-tity	Price	Amount	Date	Req. No.	Quan-tity	Price	Amount	Quan-tity	Amount
Feb. 1	Inventory									2,500	$1,250 00
2	51	5,000 Freight	$ 50 54	$ {2,600 00 100 00}						7,500	3,950 00

Issue price, including freight, 54¢

Figure 6-2

Spoilage. Spoilage is the result of faulty work. Depending upon the nature of the industry and the particular circumstances, spoiled work may be:

(1) Removed from production and destroyed.
(2) Repaired and sold as ordinary production (firsts) or as seconds.

In any case, the management wants a quantity control over spoilage so that it may be assumed that all spoilage is being reported by the inspectors. (Quantity controls are explained on pages 109-111.) It also wants to know the cost of any repair work done, sales proceeds from spoilage, and the loss on spoilage.

The methods of disposition named above are discussed in the following paragraphs.

(1) Removed from production and destroyed. In some cases, spoiled work may not be salable and has to be destroyed. An example may occur in a pattern shop which manufactures wooden patterns for use in foundries. (The pattern is actually a wooden model of a part to be cast in metal in the foundry.) Where a job is done to customer's copy and specifications, as in this case, there would be no market for spoiled work. The spoiled pattern may have almost no salvage value. When spoiled jobs are pulled from production, Work in Process account is credited for the cost of the job to point of spoilage and a Spoiled Work Expense account is charged.

(2) Repaired and sold as ordinary production (firsts) or as seconds. In some job shops, it is possible to repair damaged jobs and sell them either as ordinary production (firsts) or as seconds. In a shop manufacturing dies for use in punch presses and other related equipment, this may be possible. In this case, the repair cost may be charged to the cost sheet on which the costs of the original operations are compiled. The repair charges may be identified by a symbol of some kind so that they can be located in any later cost analysis of the job.

Waste and Scrap. Waste and scrap are physical substances yielded more or less inevitably, rather than as a result of faulty operation. Waste has no recovery value. Scrap *has* recovery value, without further processing.

Waste may be produced in the manufacture of pig iron. In the production operation, iron ore, limestone, and coke are charged into a blast furnace. Pig iron is tapped from the base of the furnace as the prime product. Slag is likewise tapped from the furnace, and if it has no value (as is sometimes the case), the slag is waste.

Scrap is commonly produced in shearing and cutting operations. In the garment industry, a certain amount of scrap material is produced in the cutting room when bolts of materials are cut according to patterns for garments. In the manufacture of coaster wagons from sheet steel, scrap materials are produced in the shearing department where sheets of steel are sheared into blanks for the punch press department. Scrap is also produced in the punch press department where the blanks are punched into the shape of wheels, body parts, and so on.

In a manufacturing business in which waste or scrap are produced the management wants to know:

(1) How much (in quantitative units) was produced, in comparison with input. Although a certain amount of waste or scrap is inevitable, it is possible that excessive amounts of materials have been used and *all* the difference between quantity input and quantity output reported as waste or scrap. Any increase in the proportion of waste or scrap to good production would be subject to question.

(2) The sales value of the scrap produced or sold.

(3) The effect of production of scrap on the unit cost of ordinary product, resulting from any credit to cost of the ordinary product for the sales of scrap.

Part II of this chapter describes quantity controls, which are the means of reconciling input, output, and spoilage, waste, or scrap quantities as a proof of quantities reported.

Shrinkage. As indicated above, shrinkage is loss in which units of input disappear in processing, through vaporization or other chemical or physical change. In this case, the total of measurable and measured output is less than the total of input. In the smelting of iron ore, for instance, the weight of iron and slag tapped at the base of the blast furnace is less than the weight of iron ore, limestone, and coke. This shrinkage is caused by burning up a certain part of the input during the smelting process. Illustrations of process cost situations in which shrinkage occurs appear in Chapter 14, "Process Costs."

Materials overhead: materials storage and handling expense. Materials purchasing, storage, and handling expense includes the following items:

Labor of purchasing department people
Purchasing department office expense
Labor of receiving clerk and storekeepers
Supplies used in the storeroom
Electric light and heat used in the storeroom
Rent of storeroom space (also the cost of refrigeration where the material requires it)
Depreciation, insurance, and taxes on storeroom equipment

In the interest of equitable costing (that is, charging each job for the benefit which it receives), the cost of materials chargeable to a job would be not only the laid-down cost of the materials but the cost of the materials up to the point where the materials go onto the job. Such a charge as the latter would include the cost of purchasing, storing, and handling the materials. In some cases, materials overhead is a significant item of cost. In a steel mill or steel fabricating shop, it may be considerable because of the bulk and weight of the materials. In some manufacturing plants (tobacco, for instance) materials overhead is significant partly because of the length of time the material is aged in storage.

In general, there are two methods of getting materials overhead onto the cost of production orders or jobs done. The simplest method is to charge the various materials overhead items to the general factory expense accounts as they are incurred and apply them to cost sheets by means of the general factory expense rates. Actually, this method implies no special treatment: materials overhead goes the way of all other factory expense. This method is explained in Chapter 10 and used throughout the remaining chapters on the job order cost system. It is also used in the job order cost practice set.

A more specialized method of accounting involves the use of a separate overhead rate for materials overhead. In a printing plant, for instance, a separate rate per pound for paper storage and handling may be charged to printing jobs. Jobs done for customers who supply their own paper as well as jobs done for other customers, would thus be charged for paper handling. The steps may be outlined:

(1) Set up a separate materials overhead expense account for the above named objects. Compile materials storage and expense currently in this account.

(2) Compute a rate for the application of storage and handling expense to cost sheets for product produced. Such a rate might be based upon value or weight of materials handled. Formulas are:

(a) Rate based upon value of materials handled:

$$\text{Materials storage and handling expense rate} = \frac{\text{Materials storage and handling expense}}{\text{Value of materials issued to production}}$$

This rate is a per cent.

(b) Rate based upon weight of materials handled:

$$\text{Materials storage and handling expense rate} = \frac{\text{Materials storage and handling expense}}{\text{Weight of materials issued to production}}$$

This would be a rate per pound or other unit.

(3) Apply the rate to cost sheets. Rate (a) would be applied as a per cent of materials cost shown on the cost sheets, or rate (b) would be applied as an amount per pound (say) of materials posted to the cost sheet.

It should be stated that although purchasing department labor and expense must be mentioned as items of materials overhead, they are frequently simply charged to factory expense. Materials storage and handling, on the other hand, are more likely to receive special attention.

II. QUANTITY CONTROL

Meaning of quantity control. Quantity control is the recording, reconciliation, and verification of quantitative data to insure its accuracy. Stated simply, it is the combination of features in a cost accounting system which are designed to insure that the quantity figures used in that system are correct. It may seem perfectly obvious to the layman that the "numbers" used in a cost system "have to be right." The full implication of quantity control as an integrated set of features is not so obvious. Quantity control is really a tying-through of quantities from the time the materials come in until the time the finished goods go out.

The diagram below illustrates certain features of a job order cost accounting system whose operation constitutes quantity control. (Dollar columns have been omitted from the forms to focus attention on the flow of quantities.) Quantity control features suggested by the illustration are:

QUANTITY CONTROL

(Job Order Cost System)

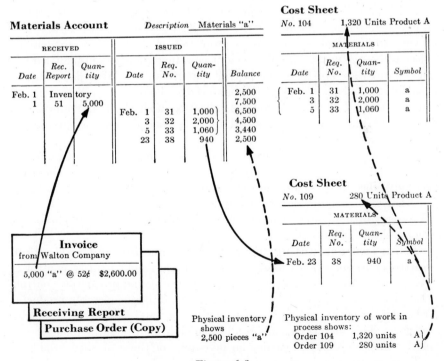

Figure 6-3

(1) Matching invoice, receiving report, and purchase order to determine that they are in agreement (that is, to determine that 5,000 units *is* the correct quantity).

(2) Recording quantities received (5,000) and quantities issued (various) in the materials ledger account and verifying the balance on hand (2,500) by physical count.

(3) Charging quantities of materials used to cost sheets (various) and analyzing materials charges on each order (not illustrated) to determine whether use of materials was excessive.

(4) Tally of units of product produced by an inspector or counter to determine that the full quantity called for on each production order actually came out of production as (a) good product or (b) scrap. For scrap produced, the inspector is required to issue a scrap report to the accounting department. Here quantities of output can be reconciled with quantities of input.

(5) Verification of production orders (No. 104 and No. 109) and product units in process periodically by physical count.

Quantity control is intended to provide safeguards at a number of points. In the first place, it is a safeguard of the accuracy of the unit product costs computed by the cost department. Note that if the quantities on which unit costs are based are wrong, the unit costs are wrong. Quantity control is intended to insure the accuracy of quantities used by the cost clerk.

Quantity control is a means of protection against excess payment of piece-rate wage payments. When a piece-rate wage payment plan is used, the quantities reported to the payroll department for labor payment are usually checked against quantities produced as shown in the production and cost records. Likewise, it provides indication of shortages in materials on hand that may have been caused by loss, theft, unauthorized use, or unauthorized shipment out.

Where quantity control is carried all the way through to billing of completed jobs, as it can be in job printing, it is a safeguard that customers are actually billed for all quantities run and shipped.

Other examples of quantity controls appear in Chapter 13 and 14 on "Process Costing," and Chapter 15 covering among other topics, accounting for shrinkage.

Tying cost accounting to product engineering and production control. In some job shops, one of the features of quantity control is the tying of cost accounting to product engineering and production control. Consider the factory that manufactures a line of large assembly products, from certain parts manufactured in the factory and certain parts bought outside. This factory assembles all large end-product units upon receipt of customer's order. It carries no inventory of those finished products.

There are standard end-product assemblies in the catalog and price lists, but there are numerous optional features as well, many of which are made or bought outside when a customer orders them.   The product is technical in that only an engineer or production man experienced in the business can identify the parts or materials and state in what subassembly they are used. A large portion of the orders call for certain optional parts for replacement on end-product assemblies purchased by the customer previously.   There are 400 or 500 parts in a typical end-product assembly.

In this factory, the engineering department designs the product and makes drawings for all parts manufactured in the factory.   It also makes up a standard bill of material for each part, listing all the materials that are required for the part.   All major assemblies, subassemblies, and parts are classified in a formal classification plan (page 99), as are all major materials.   The minor items such as nuts and bolts (known as general stock items) are not formally classified.   A numbering plan has been adopted for these classifications, and all engineering blueprints, all production control records, all product cost records, and all end-products and parts price lists are organized and filed according to the same classification and numbering plan.

The tie-in between engineering and production control on the one hand and cost accounting and cost control on the other hand begins when the customer's order is received.   First of all, the engineering department does an "engineering editing" of the order to determine exactly what products (and sometimes parts) the customer is ordering.   The engineering department writes the code numbers of assemblies (and optional parts) on the order, so that all clerks who handle the order—from production control to billing and costing the shipment—will know exactly what product or part is meant.   When the order goes to the production control department, that department issues production orders—assembly orders and parts orders— and the supporting bills of materials.   The cost clerk receives a copy of each production order and each bill of materials.

A very effective quantity control is operated for materials.   As each requisition charged to a parts order or assembly order comes to the cost clerk, he checks it against the bill of materials to determine whether the item requisitioned is actually allowed or excess.   Sometimes a workman spoils a piece of material and requisitions a second one.   The cost clerk prepares weekly reports on all excess pieces of materials drawn, showing the value and the person responsible.   Also, the positive identification of parts facilitates pricing the shipments to determine that the customer is charged the correct amount, and costing each shipment to arrive at the correct cost of sales.

III.   MATERIALS PRICES IN COST ACCOUNTING

Prices used in cost accounting.   The following sections of this chapter discuss several methods of materials pricing used in cost accounting and explain the significance of prices upon costs intended to be used for various purposes. Prices to be considered are:

(1) First-in, first out
(2) Weighted average
(3) Replacement
(4) Standard

The uses to be considered are those named in Chapter 1, namely: (a) costs as a factor in setting selling prices, (b) measurement of performance, and (c) inventory valuation and profit determination. It will be seen that different methods of pricing produce different results in the matter of unit costs and inventory values. For this reason, the manager who uses the costs should be familiar with the pricing policy being followed and with the effect of the price policy upon costs.

First-in, First-out. Under this method of pricing (introduced in Chapter 5), it is assumed that the first materials received were the first used. In pricing requisitions and crediting the materials ledger accounts, the prices paid for the various lots of materials received are applied in succession. The illustrative materials ledger account on page 113 shows how requisitions are priced on this basis. Two lots are indicated in the Received section—the 2.500 units on hand in the opening inventory which priced at $.50 per unit, and the 5,000 units received on the first day of the month at a cost of $.65 per unit.

The first requisition (No. 31 for 1,000 units) was priced at $.50, since the 1,000 units were assumed to come from the opening inventory. (That left 1,500 units of the 2,500 units purchased at $.50). The second requisition (No. 32) was for 2,000 units. This requisition was priced as:

1,500 units @ 50¢..............	$ 750.00
500 units @ 65¢..............	325.00
2,000 units.....................	$1,075.00

The quantity of materials in the opening inventory (the $.50 items) is now exhausted, and the remaining requisitions are priced at $.65 per unit.

Weighted Average. A weighted average price for a particular type or class of material is an average for the receipts of a period determined by dividing dollars by quantities. Thus, if there were 2,500 units of a material in inventory February 1 at $.50 and 5,000 units were received at $.65 February 1, an average price could be computed:

February 1, inventory	2,500 units @ $.50............	$1,250.00
February 1, purchase	5,000 units @ $.65............	3,250.00
	7,500 units..................	$4,500.00

The average price is $4,500 ÷ 7,500 = $.60 per unit.

The $.60 price would be used for all issues recorded until the next receipt,

COMPARISON OF PRICING OF REQUISITIONS
FIRST-IN, FIRST-OUT; AVERAGE

(a) First-in, first-out:

Materials Account Description _Materials "a"_

Date 19__		RECEIVED				ISSUED				BALANCE	
		Rec. Report	Quan-tity	Price	Amount	Req. No.	Quan-tity	Price	Amount	Quan-tity	Amount
Feb.	1 1	Inventory 51	5,000	$ 50 65	$3,250 00			$		2,500 7,500 6,500	$1,250 00 4,500 00 4,000 00
	1					31	1,000	50	$ 500 00		
	3					32	{ 1,500 500	50 65	750 00 325 00	4,500	2,925 00
	5					33	1,060	65	325 00 689 00	3,440	2,236 00
	23					38	940	65	611 00	2,500	1,625 00

(b) Average

Materials Account Description _Materials "a"_

Date 19__		RECEIVED				ISSUED				BALANCE	
		Rec. Report	Quan-tity	Price	Amount	Req. No.	Quan-tity	Price	Amount	Quan-tity	Amount
Feb.	1 1	Inventory 51	5,000	$ 50 65	$3,250 00			$		2,500 7,500 6,500	$1,250 00 4,500 00 3,900 00
	1					31	1,000	60	$ 600 00		
	3					32	2,000	60	1,200 00	4,500	2,700 00
	5					33	1,060	60	636 00	3,440	2,064 00
	23					38	940	60	564 00	2,500	1,500 00

Figure 6-4

when a new average price is computed. This pricing operation is illustrated in the materials account on page 113. A newly computed price is entered in the Price column under Issued, on the same line as the entry for the purchase.

In some cases, the average price of a material is computed *at the end of the month,* to comprise opening inventory and all purchases of that material recorded during the month. This method of computing average prices would make it necessary to hold the requisitions until the end of the month for pricing and extending. An illustration of this method appears in Chapter 13.

Replacement Prices. Replacement price of a particular material is the price that would have to be paid to buy that material on the current date. To illustrate the distinction between actual prices and replacement prices, assume:

<pre>
Purchased 1,000 yds. "a" @ $.60 on January 3 . . . . $ 600.00
Purchased 2,000 yds. "a" @ $.55 on January 18 . . . .   1,100.00
Used 500 yds. on January 20 on a job which was shipped
   out same day.
Inventory, January 31 . . . .   2,500 yds.
Replacement price, January 31 . . . . $.50 per yd.
</pre>

Under first-in, first-out pricing, the job which was worked and shipped January 20 would be charged for materials @ $.60, whereas under replacement prices, it would be charged for materials @ $.55, assuming that the replacement price is the same on January 20 as it was on January 18.

As to closing inventory values, under first-in, first-out, the calculation would be:

<pre>
Purchases:
   January 3, 1,000 yds. @ $.60 . . . . $ 600.00
   January 18, 2,000 yds. @ .55 . . . .   1,100.00
                                                    _____
   Total $1,700.00
   Used January 20, 500 yds. @ $.60 . . . .   300.00
                                                    _____
   Inventory, January 31, 2,500 yds. $1,400.00
</pre>

Under the replacement price method, the inventory would be valued for balance sheet purposes, 2,500 yds. @ $.50 = $1,250. Valuing the inventory at replacement would involve taking a loss on balance sheet date of $1.50, compared with FIFO valuation.

In this illustration, it appears that replacement prices are being applied on a *daily* basis. In practice, where the replacement price basis is used, the replacement price at the beginning of a month may be used for the entire month to simplify the bookkeeping. At the beginning of a month, the inventory would be revalued to reflect replacement prices on that date, and the same replacement prices would be used for costing purposes throughout the month.

Replacement pricing is sometimes used in industries where:

(1) Basic raw materials (such as copper or cotton) are used in the product.
(2) Material cost is a significant part of total product cost.
(3) The investment in materials (including materials in process and materials in finished goods) is significant.
(4) Changes in raw materials prices can be sudden and of considerable magnitude.
(5) Selling prices of the finished product tend to move with the replacement price of materials (that is, customers of the manufacturer expect a reduction in selling price of the manufactured product when the market quotation on raw material goes down).

Standard Prices. Standard prices are frequently used in *standard cost systems.* The standard prices set at the beginning of the period are used in the predetermined product costs likewise set up at the beginning of the year. The need for getting out price lists or catalog prices suggests the need for doing some predetermined costing involving such prices. Standard cost systems are discussed in Chapter 17.

In some systems, standard prices are used to value materials inventories and to charge work in process used. (This method is explained in Chapter 17.) The standard price of a material is a price set at the beginning of the year, representing the average expected price to be paid for the material during the year. When this method of pricing is used, materials inventory is charged for the *standard* value of the materials on an invoice received, vouchers payable is credited for the actual value (the amount due the creditor), and a price variance account is charged or credited for the difference. Charges to Work in Process are valued at the standard price, and the value of materials in inventory is accordingly the quantity in stock, extended at the standard price.

Effect of method of pricing upon inventory valuation and profits. *
As illustrated above, the method of pricing materials affects costs on the cost sheets, which may be used for (a) the measurement of performance or (b) consideration as a factor in setting selling prices. The method of pricing also affects the valuation of inventory and the measurement of profits. Thus, three different inventory pricing methods might produce three different sets of inventory and profits figures:

	First-In, First-Out		Last-In, First-Out		Weighted Average	
	First Period	Second Period	First Period	Second Period	First Period	Second Period
Gross profit.....	$3,670.00	$2,004.00	$3,070.00	$2,454.00	$3,527.62	$2,223.12
Net profit.......	1,870.00	304.00	1,270.00	754.00	1,727.62	523.12
Closing inventory	3,150.00	900.00	2,550.00	750.00	3,007.62	976.74

* This section is patterned after the Hanson Leather Company case in Clarence Nickerson, *Cost Accounting Text, Problems, and Cases,* published by McGraw-Hill Book Company, Inc., 1954, pp. 50-52. Used by permission of the publisher.

These figures are taken from the following statements which appear at the end of this chapter: (a) Comparative Statement of Profits (1) First-in, First-out Pricing, (2) Last-in, First-out Pricing, and (3) Weighted Average Pricing; (b) Purchases and Sales for Two Periods; and (c) Calculation of Inventories for Two Periods. In preparing these figures, the perpetual inventory account illustration (one month) on page 113 was used as the starting point and purchases by quarters with sales by quarters were added to make up a full two-year history. In the assumed purchases, prices are *rising* the first year and *falling* the second year.

From the above recap, it can be seen that closing inventory and profits were greater during the first year under first-in, first-out pricing than under either of the other methods. In this period of rising prices, the closing inventory in first-in, first-out pricing will be extended at the latest (higher) prices, in last-in, first-out at the earliest (lower) prices, and in weighted average pricing at an average of the higher and lower prices.

During the second year, closing inventory and profits were less under first-in, first-out pricing than under weighted average pricing. In this period of falling prices, the closing inventory in first-in, first-out pricing will be extended at the latest (lower) prices and in weighted average pricing will be extended at an average of the higher and lower prices. The second period inventory is smaller and profits are greater under last-in, first-out pricing than under either of the other methods of pricing. Note (in Figure 6-7) that the closing inventory is priced at $.50 per unit, which is less than the price used under either of the other methods.

Figure 6-7 (page 120) illustrates how an inventory is priced under last-in, first-out when the quantity in the inventory changes from inventory date to inventory date. The opening inventory of the first period is priced at $.50 per unit. The closing inventory for the first period is greater than the opening inventory by 2,000 units and that addition is priced at the first quarter purchase price, $.65 per unit. The inventory at the end of the second period is down to 1,500 units (which is less than the inventory with which the system was started), and is priced at $.50 per unit.

Last-in, first-out method. A discussion of the basic concept of LIFO, the reasons for adopting it in an actual case, and the effect of valuation of inventories at LIFO upon profits follows:

The last-in, first-out, or LIFO, method of valuing inventories was adopted by (General Electric Company) effective January 1, 1955. This method is based upon the concept that a continuing quantity of inventory is necessary for the operation of a business. By maintaining this quantity of inventory at a constant price level, the higher costs of current replacements during price increases are matched against current selling prices. As a result, earnings more nearly reflect the effect of current costs.

Costs of materials, especially copper, showed substantial increases during 1955, and future rises in costs of materials seemed probable. In addition, the employee program developed in 1955 provides for wage increases over a five-year period.

The LIFO method was adopted because of the desirability of reflecting these increasing costs in the computation of current earnings.

In general, except for tungsten stocks, the first-in, first-out, or FIFO, method was used for inventories prior to 1955. A simplified comparison of the two methods during periods of rising costs may be made as follows:

	Former method: FIFO	*Present method:* LIFO
Used for valuing inventory:	Higher current costs	Lower earlier costs
Charged against income:	Lower earlier costs	Higher current costs

During periods of rising costs the LIFO method results in lower inventory valuations. By matching higher current costs against current income, LIFO also results in lower income during periods of cost inflation. During periods of declining prices, the reverse is true.*

Cost or market, whichever lower. In some cases, an inventory valuation method known as *cost or market, whichever lower* is used for balance sheet purposes and for the measurement of profits. The term itself suggests that actual cost will be used for inventory valuation purposes if it is less than market price (replacement price on balance sheet date); otherwise, market price will be used. To illustrate, refer to Materials "a" account (first-in, first-out cost pricing) on page 113. According to this account, the cost value of Materials "a" on hand at the end of February is 2,500 units @ $.65 = $1,625. If market price on that date is $.70, the cost value shown in the account will be used for balance sheet and measurement of profits purposes. If market price on that date is $.60, however, that price will be used and the inventory value will be shown at 2,500 units @ $.60 = $1,500. In the latter case, the effect of the pricing method would be to reduce profits by $1,625 (inventory at cost per materials ledger) less $1,500 (inventory stated at market) or $125. This method of pricing provides for a loss at the period-end when market price is less than cost price.

In the previous paragraph, the principle of *cost or market, whichever lower* is stated in terms of a single material—Material "a." How is the principle applied to an inventory of diverse items, a typical situation? Research Bulletin 43 of the American Institute of Accountants states:

Depending upon the character and composition of the inventory, the rule of *cost or market, whichever is lower* may properly be applied either directly to each item or to the total of the inventory (or, in some cases, to the total of the components of each major category). The method should be that which most clearly reflects periodic income.

* 1955 Annual Report, General Electric Company, page 22.

Comparative Statement of Profits, Two Periods

(1) First-in, First-out Pricing, (2) Last-in, First-out Pricing, and (3) Weighted Average Pricing

Particulars	First-In, First-Out		Last-In, First-Out		Weighted Average		Source: Figure
	First Period	Second Period	First Period	Second Period	First Period	Second Period	
Sales...........................	$18,900.00	$13,944.00	$18,900.00	$13,944.00	$18,900.00	$13,944.00	6-6
Less, cost of goods sold:							
Opening inventory.............	$ 1,250.00	$ 3,150.00	$ 1,250.00	$ 2,550.00	$ 1,250.00	$ 3,007.62	6-6
Purchases....................	17,130.00	9,690.00	17,130.00	9,690.00	17,130.00	9,690.00	
	$18,380.00	$12,840.00	$18,380.00	$12,240.00	$18,380.00	$12,697.62	
Less closing inventory........	3,150.00	900.00	2,550.00	750.00	3,007.62	976.74	6-7
Cost of goods sold............	$15,230.00	$11,940.00	$15,830.00	$11,490.00	$15,372.38	$11,720.88	
Gross profit..................	$ 3,670.00	$ 2,004.00	$ 3,070.00	$ 2,454.00	$ 3,527.62	$ 2,223.12	
Less, Administrative and Selling Expense							
Administrative Expense........	$ 800.00	$ 800.00	$ 800.00	$ 800.00	$ 800.00	$ 800.00	
Selling Expense..............	1,000.00	900.00	1,000.00	900.00	1,000.00	900.00	
Total expense................	$ 1,800.00	$ 1,700.00	$ 1,800.00	$ 1,700.00	$ 1,800.00	$ 1,700.00	
Net profit...................	$ 1,870.00	$ 304.00	$ 1,270.00	$ 754.00	$ 1,727.62	$ 523.12	

Figure 6-5

Purchases and Sales for Two Periods, by Quarters

	Purchases			Sales		
	Quantity	Price	Amount	Quantity	Price	Amount
First Period						
Opening inventory............	2,500	$.50	$ 1,250.00			
First quarter................	5,000	.65	3,250.00	5,000	$.78	$ 3,900.00
Second quarter..............	6,000	.68	4,080.00	5,000	.816	4,080.00
Third quarter................	8,000	.70	5,600.00	7,000	.84	5,880.00
Fourth quarter...............	6,000	.70	4,200.00	6,000	.84	5,040.00
Total four quarters.........	25,000		$17,130.00	23,000		$18,900.00
Opening inventory plus purchases...	27,500	Av. .66836	18,380.00			
Closing inventory............	4,500					
Second Period						
Opening inventory............	4,500					
First quarter................	3,000	$.68	$ 2,040.00	4,000	$.816	$ 3,264.00
Second quarter..............	4,000	.65	2,600.00	4,000	.78	3,120.00
Third quarter................	5,000	.65	3,250.00	6,000	.78	4,680.00
Fourth quarter...............	3,000	.60	1,800.00	4,000	.72	2,880.00
Total four quarters.........	15,000		$ 9,690.00	18,000		$13,944.00
Opening inventory plus purchases...	19,500					
Closing inventory............	1,500					

Figure 6-6

Calculation of Inventories for Two Periods

(1) First-in, First-out Pricing, (2) Last-in, First-out Pricing, and (3) Weighted Average Pricing

	First Period			Second Period		
	Quantity	Price	Amount	Quantity	Price	Amount
First-in, first-out						
Opening inventory	2,500	$.50	$1,250.00	4,500	$.70	$ 3,150.00
Closing inventory	4,500	.70	3,150.00	1,500	.60	900.00
Last-in, first-out						
Opening inventory	2,500	.50	1,250.00	4,500	.566	2,550.00
Closing inventory	4,500	.566	2,550.00	1,500	.50	750.00
Weighted average						
Opening inventory	2,500	.50	1,250.00	4,500	.66836	3,007.62
Closing inventory	4,500	.66836	3,007.62			
Closing inventory—last-in, first-out (first period) is calculated:						
Opening inventory, as above	2,500	.50	$1,250.00			
Addition to inventory	2,000	.65	1,300.00			
	4,500	.566	$2,550.00			
Closing inventory—weighted average (second period) is calculated:						
Opening inventory, as above				4,500	$.66836	$ 3,007.62
Total purchases, second period				15,000		9,690.00
Total opening inventory plus purchases				19,500		$12,697.62
Average, $12,697.28 ÷ 19,500					.65116	
Closing inventory				1,500	.65116	976.74

Figure 6-7

Discussion:

11. The purpose of reducing inventory to *market* is to reflect fairly the income of the period. The most common practice is to apply the *lower of cost or market* rule separately to each item of the inventory. However, if there is only one end product category, the cost utility of the total stock—the inventory in its entirety—may have the greatest significance for accounting purposes. Accordingly, the reduction of individual items to *market* may not always lead to the most useful result if the utility of the total inventory to the business is not below its cost. This might be the case if selling prices are not affected by temporary or small fluctuations in current costs or purchase or manufacture. Similarly, where more than one major product or operational category exists, the application of the *cost or market, whichever lower* rule to the total of the items included in such major categories may result in the most useful determination of income.*

The question arises as to how to record a reduction in value from cost per books to a lower "cost or market, whichever lower" value. Assume that the total cost of an inventory per the control account of the inventory ledger is $50,000 and that the cost or market, whichever lower value is $48,000. The reduction of $2,000 is recorded by a debit to Profit and Loss account and a credit to Reserve for Inventory Valuation. On the balance sheet the reserve would be deducted from the inventory to show a net value of $48,000. It would not be necessary (or desirable) to adjust the individual accounts in the inventory ledger.

REVIEW QUESTIONS

6-1. (a) What is meant by the term "materials classification"?

(b) What materials classifications might be useful to a medium-size or large business?

(c) Why might it be desirable to set up the classification in formal fashion?

6-2. (a) What is a direct material, an indirect material?

(b) Distinguish indirect materials from operating supplies and maintenance supplies.

(c) Explain the steps for recording the issue of materials classified respectively, as indirect materials, operating supplies, and maintenance supplies.

(d) What is meant by direct charging of a material? What is the advantage of direct charging?

(e) What means are taken in an accounting department to secure consistent uniformity in treating direct charges and indirect charges?

6-3. What is meant by direct charging and indirect charging of freight on materials? What entries are made in each case?

6-4. Discuss methods of: (a) compiling materials storage and handling expense, and (b) applying it to product.

6-5. (a) What is meant by quantity control in connection with accounting for materials in goods produced and sold?

(b) Give examples of quantity controls built into a cost accounting system.

(c) State a number of reasons why effective quantity control is necessary in a cost accounting system.

* American Institute of Accountants, Committee on Accounting Procedure, Accounting Research Bulletin No. 43, "Restatement and Revision of Accounting Research Bulletins," New York, 1953, page 32. (Supersedes Bulletins Nos. 1-42, 1939-1953.)

6-6. (a) Name several methods of pricing materials used in cost accounting. (b) Discuss the effect of materials pricing policy upon costs intended for various purposes.

6-7. (a) Might there be any reasons for including materials in product costs at current replacement prices of those materials, when the costs are to be used as a factor in setting selling prices?

(b) Might there be any reasons for valuing materials in inventories at replacement prices instead of, say, actual prices on a first-in, first-out basis?

DISCUSSION QUESTIONS

6-8. Why is the distinction among direct materials, indirect materials, operating supplies, maintenance supplies, and repair parts important for (a) control purposes and (b) allocation purposes?

6-9. Is any material always direct? Is any material always indirect?

6-10. The Nelson Company produces sewing boxes and other small products made of wood. The cost system is fundamentally a job order system. The cost accountant has asked the industrial engineer to calculate an allowance for glue per product unit for each style of product. The cost accountant uses this estimate (multiplied by the number of product units on a production order) for charging the cost sheets for glue. He likewise credits a glue account and charges Materials in Process for the total amounts of glue allowed at the estimated figures.

At physical inventory time, a physical inventory is taken of glue in the storeroom. The balance of the glue account is adjusted to the physical inventory with a contra-debit or credit to Factory Expense.

Is this procedure satisfactory for (a) cost accounting purposes and (b) financial accounting purposes?

6-11. The Winston-Salem Company buys leaf tobacco for making cigarettes. Each shipment is sorted into grades and stored for later use in manufacture. The cost of each shipment is allocated among the grades on the basis of selling prices of the grades. In some instances, selling prices change significantly after the cost of a shipment has been allocated.

The cost accountant asks whether he should re-allocate cost as and when selling price changes. What is your opinion?

6-12. The Lingonfelter Company has received a request for price quotation on 1,000 units of a special product. This product would be made from Material M of which the company has a large supply, bought at various times and at various prices.

The estimator asks what materials price should be used in making up the estimate on which the bid is to be based. The sales manager says that the lowest price should be used, so that he can be "more sure to get the order." The treasurer says that the highest price should be used, so that the inventory valuation remaining after the order has been manufactured will be as low as possible.

What is your opinion?

6-13. The Bowen Company manufactures brick, using clay which it mines and pays for on a royalty basis. The contract calls for a payment of $.10 a ton, with a minimum payment of $6,000 a year.

In 19-7, the company mined and used 40,000 tons of clay, and in 19-8, it mined and used 80,000 tons. What price per ton of clay should be used in costs calculated for various purposes?

6-14. The Ives Company manufactures wooden desks. Indicate by letter for each item whether it is likely to be direct material (D), indirect material (I), or either direct or indirect (E):

(a) Wood
(b) Stain for finishing
(c) Glue
(d) Screws
(e) Repair parts for factory machinery
(f) Printed forms for factory

EXERCISES

6-1. Following is a summary of receipts and issues of Material AA for the month of January:

	Receipts				Issues	
Date	Receiving Report No.	Quantity	Total Cost	Date	Requisition No.	Quantity
Jan. 1	Inventory	300	$ 900.00	Jan. 2	435	200
5	108	300	1,200.00	6	452	200
20	126	300	1,500.00	7	460	200

Required:

(a) Using the blank inventory account forms provided in the Workbook, enter all the above information in the account, assuming first-in, first-out pricing.

(b) Same as (a), but assume average pricing, with a new average price after each receipt.

6-2. Using the form provided in the Workbook, set out the information in columnar arrangement: (a) what basic accounting paper is used for the original writing of the transaction, (b) what subsidiary ledger account (if any) would be debited, (c) what subsidiary ledger account (if any) would be credited, (d) what specialized journal would be used for summarizing the particular type of transaction, and (e) general ledger accounts affected.

For form of your answer, see Sample Transaction and Sample Answer in Exercise 5-2.

(1) Issued materials from stores to be used on Production Order 201 and recorded as a direct cost of the order, $160.

(2) Issued materials from stores to be used on Production Orders 201, 204, 205 and possibly some others, and recorded as indirect materials, $40.

(3) Received from L.&N. Railroad Company a bill for freight on materials, to be recorded by "direct charging" to the materials account, $68.

(4) Received from L.&N. Railroad Company a bill for freight on materials, to be recorded by "indirect charging," $35.

(5) Assume that our company stores materials in a separate small building and that the management decides to record costs of storage and handling in a Materials Storage and Handling Expense account in the general ledger. Transactions:

(a) Labor of storekeeper, $440 (original paper: time report)
(b) Rent expense payable, $300
(c) Depreciation of storeroom equipment, $80 (original paper: depreciation schedule)

PROBLEMS

6-1. The A Company operates no special journals. Draft entries for January in simple journal entry form for the following transactions. Indicate what subsidiary ledger(s) would be affected and indicate whether the entry in the subsidiary ledger account would be a debit or a credit. (Use transaction numbers as dates.)

(1) Purchase several types of goods (from a mill supply company) to be used immediately as follows:

On Production Order No. 206	$300.00
As indirect materials	80.00
As operating supplies	60.00
As maintenance supplies	45.00
As repair parts	180.00
Total purchase	$665.00

(2) Receive and store raw materials from Woolsey Supply Co., $100, 2% 10 days, net 30 days (200 pcs. R @ $.50).

(4) Pay the invoice from Woolsey Supply Co.

Note: Make entries (2) and (4) two ways to illustrate two methods of handling the purchase discount.

(5) Receive and store raw materials from Northern Manufacturing Company 5,000 lbs. T @ $.40.

(7) Voucher the payroll for materials receiving clerks and storekeepers, $600 for the month. (*Note:* The A Company records materials storage and handling expense separately from other factory expense and applies it to cost sheets by means of a separate overhead rate.)

(8) Voucher the rent on the materials storeroom, $400 for the month.

(9) Depreciation on storeroom equipment, $100 for the month.

(10) Receive and store raw materials from Northern Manufacturing Company 10,000 lbs. T @ $.46.

(11) Use 400 lbs. T on Production Order No. 615 (Price materials @ average).

(12) Assume that an actual materials overhead rate per pound is calculated at the end of the month.

  (a) Calculate the rate assuming that 22,000 lbs. of materials were issued during the month.

  (b) Draft the entry to close the balance of materials storage and handling expense to Materials in Process account.

6-2. The following transactions of the Phillips Manufacturing Company relate to materials (use transaction numbers as dates):

(2) Received the following materials from Simpson Company:

100 units "a" @ $2.50	$250.00
200 units "b" @ 3.00	600.00
Total	$850.00

(*Note:* The Phillips Manufacturing Company operates a voucher system for recording payables.)

(2) Received and paid the freight bill covering the shipment from Simpson Company, $30. Freight is to be recorded as a direct charge to the materials accounts, in this case on the basis of units received.

(3) Received from Boston Company: f.o.b. our warehouse:

200 units "c" @ $4.00................$800.00

(4) Received from Folts & Co., machine repair parts $60. (Charge these repair parts to expense immediately on receipt.)

(5) Purchased printed forms for use in factory, $20.

(6) The following materials were drawn from stores:

Requisition No.	Production Order No.	Description
501	101	50 units "a"
502	102	25 units "b"
503	103	40 units "c"

(7) 10 units "c," which were drawn on Requisition No. 503, were defective, and were returned to the storeroom by the foreman, who signed a stores return slip for the return.

(8) The storekeeper returned the 10 units "c" to Boston Co. for credit.

(31) Machine repair parts on hand, $20.

Required:

(1) Draft simple entries in general journal form to record the above transactions in the general ledger accounts. State the name of a special journal in which each entry might be recorded.

(2) Set up "T" accounts and post the entries.

6-3. The London Company operates a warehouse for the storage of raw materials. The costs of material storage and handling for one month are as follows:

LONDON COMPANY
Summary of Materials Warehouse and Handling Expense

Month of January, 19—

Labor:	
Foreman............................	$ 400.00
Receiving clerks.......................	1,200.00
Store keepers........................	2,400.00
Supplies used in warehouse.................	80.00
Repairs to equipment......................	40.00
Purchased services:	
Heat and light.........................	130.00
Fixed charges:	
Depreciation on equipment...............	60.00
Insurance on equipment..................	30.00
Taxes on equipment....................	45.00
Rent.................................	240.00
Total expense........................	$ 4,625.00

Operating Statistics

Pounds of materials issued from warehouse...	92,500
Value of materials issued from warehouse.....	$92,500.00

Required:

(1) Calculate several rates for allocation of materials warehouse and handling expense to jobs in the factory.

(2) Explain the condition under which you would use each type of rate.

6-4.

A COMPANY
Purchases and Sales for Two Periods, by Quarters

	Purchases			Sales		
	Quantity	Price	Amount	Quantity	Price	Amount
First Period						
Opening inventory.....	1,000	$6.35	$ 6,350.00			
First quarter........	500	6.00	$ 3,000.00	600	$ 9.00	$ 5,400.00
Second quarter.......	500	6.00	3,000.00	600	9.00	5,400.00
Third quarter........	600	7.00	4,200.00	700	10.50	7,350.00
Fourth quarter.......	700	7.00	4,900.00	650	10.50	6,825.00
Total, four quarters..	2,300		$15,100.00	2,550		$24,975.00
Opening inventory plus purchases.......	3,300					
Closing inventory......	750					
Second Period						
Opening inventory.....	750					
First quarter........	700	$6.17+	$ 4,325.00	700	$ 9.00	$ 6,300.00
Second quarter.......	700	6.00	4,200.00	700	9.00	6,300.00
Third quarter........	600	5.50	3,300.00	650	8.50	5,525.00
Fourth quarter.......	400	5.50	2,200.00	500	8.50	4,250.00
Total four quarters...	2,400		$14,025.00	2,550		$22,375.00
Opening inventory plus purchases.......	3,150					
Closing inventory......	600					

Expenses:	First Period	Second Period
Administrative.........	$1,000.00	$1,000.00
Selling................	2,000.00	1,800.00

The manager of the A Company asks you what effect the method of pricing inventories (as between first-in, first-out and weighted average) has upon the profits of two successive years. Using the following information, set up a Comparative Statement of Profits, Two Periods: (1) First-in. First-out Pricing and (2) Weighted Average Pricing.

Write a concise explanation of the difference in profits as between the two methods of pricing.

6-5. From the following data submit, in detail and in total, the value, at cost, of the closing inventory.

During a certain period, a plate-glass factory cast and rolled about 850,000 square feet of glass. The product, after cutting up in order to eliminate defects, was priced for sale as follows:

Size No.	Cents per square foot
1	28
2	24
3	22
4	20
5	14
6	5

Any product below No. 6 was returned to process and remelted.

As may be seen, the selling price for a given quality varied with the size, the largest perfect sheets selling for the highest price per square foot.

The total cost of materials, manufacture, grinding, polishing, cutting and sorting, including factory expense, was $120,807.

The inventories—in square feet—were:

Size No.	Opening	Closing
1	10,000	12,860
2		11,000
3	10,000	23,000
4		6,000
5		
6		2,000

The sales—at list selling prices—were:

Size No.	
1	$30,240.00
2	36,480.00
3	35,376.00
4	21,100.00
5	9,030.00
6	2,300.00

(American Institute of Certified Public Accountants)

Chapter 7

ACCOUNTING FOR LABOR

Function. Accounting for labor involves the obvious task of calculating the wages earned by each employee, the necessary F.I.C.A. tax and withholding tax deductions together with other deductions that may be a part of the pay plan, and the net pay due each employee. In a job order cost system, it also includes such cost accounting activities as distributing the labor costs to production orders and to factory expense accounts, and preparing reports on labor costs for the various products. These activities are basic. They provide the groundwork for *analysis*, which is a systematic attempt to get the costs down to units whose significance can be interpreted, and *control*, which consists in determining whether costs are excessive according to yardsticks which are set up.

The present chapter and the succeeding one are concerned with accounting for labor. They open the way for the discussion of analysis of labor costs which appears in Chapter 11 and control of labor costs which is presented in Chapter 18. Accounting for labor can be fairly complicated, particularly in large organizations, partly because of the need for maintaining strong internal check against overpayments or underpayments. In some companies, it includes the calculations and record-keeping of incentive wage payment plans which may range from simple to complex. Of recent years, accounting and cost accounting for labor have become increasingly important due to the legal requirements of social security and other legislation and the contractual requirements of employer and employee relationships.

Organization. In large organizations, separate clerks or groups of clerks may perform each of the functions named in the previous section. Thus, we may find the following organizational groups:

Employment department, which hires employees upon request of supervisors.

Timekeeping and (for piece work and other incentive plans) *production recording.* This activity may in turn be divided into:

(a) *Attendance timekeeping* which, as the name indicates, entails keeping track of the time each employee enters the premises at the beginning of each day or turn, the time he leaves, and the elapsed time. Attendance time is over-all time for the employee, day by day for the pay period.

(b) *Shop timekeeping*, which involves keeping a daily record of the time each employee spends on each job or other chargeable activity.

(c) *Production recording*—keeping count of each employee's production for piece work purposes. This may be done by the shop timekeeper.

Payroll proper, an activity involving the actual compiling of gross earnings, deductions, and net earnings due each employee, from information which comes in from Timekeeping and other sources. It usually also includes issuing the paycheck or pay envelope and keeping the F.I.C.A. tax and witholding tax records.

Labor cost accounting, which is the distribution of labor to cost sheets and accounts, mentioned above.

In addition to the above-named activities, the paymaster function—issuing the paychecks or pay envelopes produced by the payroll department—is technically a separate activity, recognized as such in the interest of good internal check. Sometimes the operation of pension records is a separate activity.

In the Benson Manufacturing Company, accounting for labor does not involve as many groups of people as in larger organizations. Attempt is made, however, to distribute various payroll functions among a number of people to secure good internal check.

Managerial information. With reference to labor cost, the management of the Benson Manufacturing Company wants to know the cost of labor expended on each production order by department (cutting department and assembly department) and also the cost of labor charged to the following factory expense accounts:

Indirect labor (supervision, factory clerical, storekeeper, and other indirect labor, as defined in the following section).
Overtime premium.
F.I.C.A. tax chargeable to the company.
Unemployment insurance expense.

To assist in the control of labor costs charged to production orders, the management desires labor cost per unit of product for each completed production order. Costs per unit for orders currently completed will be compared with the costs for previous orders. The management realizes that the previous costs do not necessarily represent what the product should cost under good performance, but no steps have been taken thus far to determine what the labor cost *should* be. If the average cost of a job completed today is not appreciably out of line with past costs, it is accepted without investigation. If it is out of line, the foreman is asked to explain it. In some cases, the cost man is asked to get the job time records and make an analysis by labor operation to see which operation was out of line. The management feels that when an incentive wage payment plan is installed in the assembly department, better control over labor performance will be secured.

The management also wants certain statistics, such as labor hours in each department (which is a primary index of the level of activity of the departments), the number of employees on the payroll of each department, the number hired, and the number dropped each week. After a piece rate wage payment is put into effect in the assembly department, the management will want to know the average wages earned per hour for employees on piece work. This figure is total gross wages paid the employees on piece work *divided by* actual hours worked. The average per hour is desired for the group and for each employee on piece work.

Direct labor, indirect labor defined. The previous paragraphs indicate that the management wants information regarding (1) labor chargeable to the job orders and (2) labor chargeable to various factory expense accounts. At this point, it is desirable to define the types of labor charges. The distinction between direct and indirect charges which applies to materials also applies to labor.

Direct labor is labor identified with particular products and considered feasible to measure and charge to specific production order cost sheets;* for example the labor of a sewing machine operator in a garment factory and the labor of a mechanic repairing automobiles in an automobile repair shop.

Indirect labor is labor identified with particular products but not considered feasible to measure and charge to specific production order cost sheets. For example, the labor of a sewing machine operator who makes belt loops for dungarees in a garment factory is handled as indirect labor when it is not considered feasible to keep track of the time spent making loops for the garments on each production order. Indirect labor is charged to factory expense.

Expense labor is labor expended for the benefit of production in general and not identified with particular products; for example, supervisory labor, factory clerical (factory payroll clerks, materials and finished goods ledger clerks, and the cost man), factory machine repairmen, materials handlers (often), janitors, and watchmen. The labor cost of these occupations is charged to factory expense.

In the forms and statements in Chapters 3 and 4, all labor which is not direct labor is charged to a single account (which, for the sake of a brief title, is called "Indirect Labor") in the factory expense ledger. In practice, if the amounts involved are significant, separate accounts should be kept for true indirect labor and for expense labor. Separate accounts may be set up

---

* This definition is based upon the assumption that the cost unit is the *product* unit. Cost units other than product units are possible. Recognizing this fact, direct labor would be defined as labor allocable to whatever cost unit is in use.

for various occupational groups within the expense labor category. They are likely to be useful to the manager since the possible degree of control varies with different occupational classes. True indirect labor can be expected to vary more or less directly with level of production. Repair labor may be expected to vary to some extent with level of production except for management decision to do certain repair work "off season."

Forms. The following forms (not all in a single system) are used in accounting for labor:

Attendance Time Card

Name George Nixon No. 31

Occupation Spreader Cutting

Week Ending Feb. 6 19_

Day & Date	MORNING		AFTERNOON		OVERTIME		Hours
	In	Out	In	Out	In	Out	
M — 1	8:00	12:00	1:00	5:00			8
T — 2	7:58	12:01	1:00	5:03			8
W — 3	8:00	12:00	1:00	5:00			8
Th — 4	8:00	12:02	1:00	5:02			8
F — 5	7:56	12:01	12:59	5:00			8
S — 6							
S							

Total clock hours   40

Overtime hours   —

Hourly wage rate $ 1.30

Figure 7-1

Attendance time cards—one for each employee—which provide a basic record of time entering the factory, time leaving the factory, and elapsed time each day. It is often used as the basis for entries on the payroll. Entries are usually made on these cards by means of attendance time clocks placed at the employees' entrance to the factory. Each employee pulls his card from a rack as he enters the factory, inserts it in the clock and stamps the time on the card, and then places his card in a second rack.

The cards remaining in the first rack during the day are the cards of absentees; from this rack a report of absentees may be made up. (See Figure 7-1.)

At the end of the day, each employee pulls his card out of the second rack on his way out of the factory, stamps the time on it, and puts it in the first rack. The recording operation is supervised by an attendance timekeeper or by a watchman to assure that the recording is done properly.

Job tickets, which provide a record of time spent on production orders (direct labor) and time chargeable to factory expense accounts. A separate ticket is issued for each job on which each man works each day, by the foreman or the shop timekeeper or the employee himself. Each ticket shows, among other things, employee number and name, production order number

Job Ticket

Name _George Nixon_   No. *31*

Dept. _Cutting_   Date _Feb. 1, 19—_

Customer _____   Order No. *104*

5:00 P	Finish	Operation No. _____
8:00 A	Start	
8:00	Elapsed	Rate $1.30 Amount $10.40

Figure 7-2

or standing order number (factory expense), starting time, finishing time, elapsed time, rate of wages, and extension (elapsed time *multiplied by* rate). (See Figure 7-2.)

Time may be stamped on the tickets by means of a job time recorder located conveniently within the shop. Start time is entered when the workman begins the job and finish time when he completes the job. At the end of the day, there should be tickets for each man to account for his total work time for the day. Total time for each man per his job tickets should agree with his total time for the day per attendance time card. The shop timekeeper may enter wage rates and extensions on job tickets before sending them to the office for processing.

Daily time reports, which may be used *instead* of job tickets and, if desired, to take the place of both attendance time cards and job tickets. When daily time reports are used, a single report is issued for each man for *all* his day's work. The report is headed with the man's name, number, and date.

Time spent on each job or each factory expense charge is entered on a separate line. The total time for the report should equal the day's total for the man. If attendance time cards are used, the daily total for each man per daily time report is compared with the attendance time per the attendance time report.

Daily Time Report			Date *Feb. 1, 19–*
In **8:00 A**	ATTENDANCE TIME	Name *George Nixon*	No. *31*
Out **12:00**			
In **1:00 P**		Department *Cutting*	
Out **5:00 P**		Elapsed-Day *8*	Hourly Rate *$1.30* · Amount *$10.40*
Finish **12:00**	JOB TIME	Employee No. *31* · Dept. No. *1*	Order or A/c No. *105*
Start **8:00 A**		Elapsed Time *4* · Hourly Rate *$1.30*	Amount *$5.20*
Finish **5:00 P**	JOB TIME	Employee No. *31* · Dept. No. *1*	Order or A/c No. *106*
Start **1:00 P**		Elapsed Time *4* · Hourly Rate *$1.30*	Amount *$5.20*
Finish	JOB TIME	Employee No. · Dept. No.	Order or A/c No.
Start		Elapsed Time · Hourly Rate	Amount
Finish	JOB TIME	Employee No. · Dept. No.	Order or A/c No.
Start		Elapsed Time · Hourly Rate	Amount

Figure 7-3

Note that the advantage of job tickets, described above (used under the proper conditions) is that they can be sorted by the cost man to facilitate taking off the totals for charging the cost sheets. This cannot be done, of course, with daily time reports, each of which comprises a number of charges. The advantage of the daily time reports, on the other hand, is that they require less repetitive writing (employee number, date, and rate, for instance).

Figure 7-3 shows a daily time report which combines a formal attendance time card with job tickets. The block at the top is actually the attendance time card and the blocks below are the job tickets. The employee receives a new daily time report each day as he enters the factory. He stamps the "in time" in the attendance time section and takes the card to the shop, where the first job time section is started. Each succeeding job time section is used as the employee works on successive jobs. At the end of the day, the employee stamps the "out" time in the attendance time section as he leaves the factory and turns the report over to the watchman.

The advantages of the type of daily time report shown in Figure 7-3 are: (1) The job time sections can be easily reconciled with the attendance time section because they are both on the same form, and (2) the job time sections can be separated on the perforated lines to provide sortable tickets.

Payroll, used for compiling wages due each employee for each period. One line is used for each employee, and columns are provided for hours worked each day, total hours for the week, gross earnings, various deductions, and net earnings. Separate columns are provided in the gross earnings sections for calculation of overtime. (See illustration on page 140.)

Employee's quarterly earnings record—one for each employee—used to compile quarterly and annual earnings and deductions. This form provides columns for hours worked, gross earnings, F.I.C.A. tax and withholding tax deducted, other deductions, and net pay week by week. It is used as a tax record, being the basis for reports to the Social Security Administration. (See illustration on page 145.)

This form is also used for internal wage administration purposes and, in certain respects, for the control of labor performance. Thus, it is used to determine who is entitled to paid vacations under the company policy in regard to length of service, and so on. Where a piece work wage plan is in operation, the earnings record for each employee is also a record of his performance over a period of time. It is particularly important in the case of new employees in their on-the-job-training period. At the Benson Manufacturing Company, periods of from several weeks to several months, depending upon the complexity of the operation, are required to bring an operator up to the desired proficiency and output. The earnings records are accordingly studied carefully by the management from week to week to see how each trainee is progressing. Records of experienced operators are are also studied to see how well they are maintaining their performance.

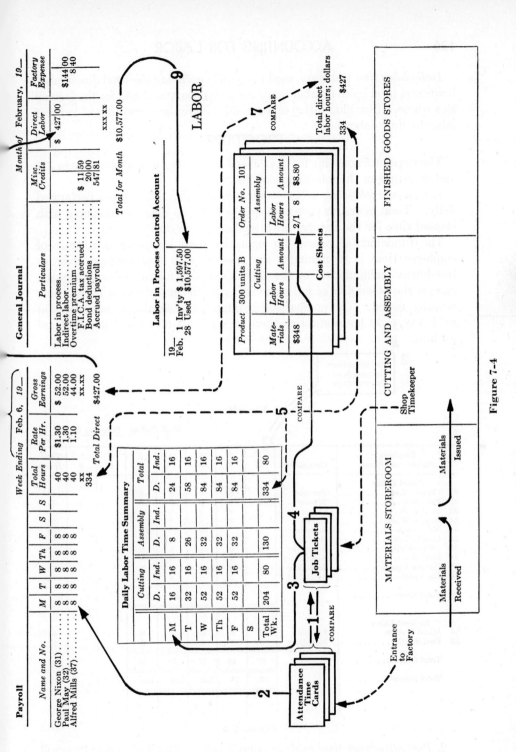

Figure 7-4

Daily labor time summary, used to compile each day the total direct labor hours and total indirect labor hours for each department and for the factory as a whole. (See illustration on page 137.) Note the percentage of indirect labor to direct labor.

PROCEDURE

The steps in accounting for payroll and labor cost are charted on page 135 and described in the following sections.

1. Compare job tickets with attendance time cards. This step is performed daily. Total hours for each employee per his job ticket is compared with elapsed time for the day per his attendance time card.

The fundamental reason for operating two independent records of employee time is to minimize the possibility of undiscovered error or fraudulent manipulation of the time records. It is also done to check against the possibility of failure to issue job tickets or loss of time tickets actually issued. The comparison is intended to establish that man did work, say, eight hours and that there are eight hours of job tickets on hand for him.

2 Post attendance time cards to payroll daily

Payroll

Week Ending February 6, 19___

Employee Number and Name	Occupation	1 M	2 T	3 W	4 Th	5 F	6 S	7 S	Total Hours
Direct Labor									
31 George Nixon	Spreader	8	8	8	8	8			40
32 Paul May	Marker	8	8	8	8	8			40
33 Fred York	Cutter		8	8	8	8			32
34 Norton Worth	Cutter		8	8	8	8			32
35 Nels Saxon	Bundler			10	10	10			30
36 Charles Lang	Bundler			10	10	10			30
37 Alfred Mills	Assembler	8	8	8	8	8			40
38 Fred Meek	Assembler		8	8	8	8			32
39 Gordon French	Assembler		8	8	8	8			32
40 Jay Upton	Assembler		2	8	8	8			26
Total direct		24	58	84	84	84			334
Indirect Labor									
51 Alfred Walton	Foreman	8	8	8	8	8			40
52 Fred Smith	Machinist	8	8	8	8	8			40
Total indirect		16	16	16	16	16			80
Total payroll		40	74	100	100	100			414

Figure 7-5

2. Post attendance time cards to payroll daily. The daily-posted payroll is used where a day-by-day time record is desired in the office. Attendance time cards are sent to the payroll clerk, who posts total hours for each employee to the proper column of the payroll. The cards are then returned to the rack for further time stamping. Note the posting of 8 hours for George Nixon, February 1 from the attendance time card (Figure 7-1) to the payroll (Figure 7-5). (To keep the illustration simple, it is assumed that certain employees work exclusively on direct labor and others work exclusively on indirect labor.)

Note that when this type of payroll is used, there are actually two attendance time records: the clock cards in the rack and the posted payroll record in the office. If the management does not want the daily posted record in the office, a payroll form *without* the daily hours columns can be used.

Daily Labor Time Summary

Month of__February,__19__

	Date	Cutting Department		Assembly Department		Total Plant	
		Direct	Indirect	Direct	Indirect	Direct	Indirect
	1	16	16	8		24	16
	2	32	16	26		58	16
	3	52	16	32		84	16
	4	52	16	32		84	16
	5	52	16	32		84	16
	6						
	Week	204	80	130		334	80
	8						
	9						

3 Enter daily total of job tickets →

Figure 7-6

Attendance time cards would be posted at the end of the week. Total hours for the week for each employee would be posted.

3. *Enter daily totals of job tickets in daily labor time summary.* The daily labor time summary shows hour totals for each department for (a) direct labor and (b) indirect labor. This step accordingly involves several operations, as follows: Separate the direct labor job tickets (those which show a production order number) from the indirect labor job tickets (those which show charge factory expense). Sort both groups by department. Total both groups by department and enter totals on the Daily Labor Time Summary. Enter totals for the factory in the two right-hand columns.

The Daily Labor Time Summary illustrated shows postings for the job tickets of February 1 (totaling 24 hours of direct labor time and 16 hours of indirect labor time) (Figure 7-6).

4. *Enter direct labor job tickets (labor hours and labor dollars) on cost sheets.*

COST SHEETS
ILLUSTRATING POSTING OF LABOR

4 | Enter direct labor job tickets on cost sheets

Cost Sheet

Production Order No. ___101___

Date Promised _____

Quantity and Description ___300 Units Product B___

Date Started _____

Made For _____

Date Completed ___Feb. 11,___ _19_

	MATERIALS					LABOR					
Date 19__	Req. No.	Quan- tity	Sym- bol	Amount	Cutting	nt	Assembly		Total		
							Hours	Amount	Hours	Amount	
Feb. 1	Balance			$348 00	Balance Feb. 1		225	$247 50	225	$247 50	
					2		8	8 30	8	8 80	
					3		26	28 60	26	28 60	
					4		32	35 20	32	35 20	
					5		32	35 20	32	35 20	
							32	35 20	32	35 20	
							143 00				

Enter total hours and dollars by dept. from job tickets

Cost Sheet

Production Order No. ___104___

Date Promised _____

Quantity and Description ___1,320 Units Product A___

Date Started _____

Made For _____

Date Completed _____

	MATERIALS					LABOR					
Date 19__	No.			ount	Date 19__	Cutting		Assembly		Total	
						Hours	Amount	Hours	Amount	Hours	Amount
Feb. 1	31	1,000	a		Feb. 1	16	$ 20 80			16	$ 20 80
3	32	2,000	a	1,010 00	2	32	44 80			32	44 80
5	33	1,060	a	551 20	3	52	72 80			52	72 80
					4	52	72 80			52	72 80
					5	52	72 80			52	72 80
						284 00					

Enter total hours and dollars by dept. from job tickets

At end of week:

5 | Prove direct labor hours: cost sheets: time summary payroll

Hours on Cost Sheets = Hours on Time Summary = Hours on Payroll
130 + 204 = 334   334   334
                      (Figure 7-6)   (Figure 7-5)

Figure 7-7

The job tickets were sorted by department in the previous operation, and they are in that order when received by the cost man for posting to the cost sheets. It is necessary only for him to sort them further by production order number, determine total hours and total dollars by department for each production order, and post.

Figure 7-7 shows postings to Production Order Numbers 101 and 104 for February 1, aggregating 24 hours of direct labor.

5. *At end of week, prove direct labor hours, indirect labor hours.* Direct labor hours on cost sheets (334) equal direct labor hours on the labor time summary (334) equal direct labor hours on the payroll (334).

This proof step is performed in an effort to bring to light any errors made in posting the direct labor job tickets to any of the three records. Note that it is done *before* the payroll clerk extends the payroll. It is desirable to locate and correct any mistakes in hours before extending those hours into dollars on the payroll.

Note also that the *indirect* labor hour total on the daily labor time summary (80) in Figure 7-6 agrees with the indirect labor hours total on the payroll.

6. *Compute and enter earnings, deductions, and net pay on payroll; overtime premium.* Total gross earnings for each employee is computed as follows:

(a) Multiply total clock hours per column (2) in the payroll (40, for George Nixon) by rate per hour ($1.30) to arrive at total straight time earnings ($52). Enter in column (4).

(b) If the employee worked any overtime during the week (that is, if in this case he worked more than 8 hours in any one day), compute overtime premium by the formula: overtime hours for the week (6 hours in all for Nels Saxon) *multiplied* by ½ the regular rate per hour (½ of $1.40 = $.70) equals $4.20. Enter in column (5).

(c) Straight time earnings ($42 for Nels Saxon) plus overtime premium ($4.20) equals total earnings ($46.20). Enter in column (6).

Note that this calculation of overtime premium gives effect to the rule of paying "time and a half for overtime" for all hours over eight each day. Note also that the overtime premium, that is, the *extra* cost of having the work done after 5 P.M., is segregated in a separate column so that the total amount can be charged to a special account for scrutiny by the management. In some cases, overtime premium is paid on the basis of hours over 40 for the week. This situation is not illustrated. Overtime premium would be calculated as excess of actual hours over 40 *multiplied by* ½ the hourly rate.

Next, deductions are entered on the payroll in columns (7), (8), and (9) and subtracted from total earnings [column (6)] to arrive at net pay [column (10)].

From the standpoint of the mechanics of record-keeping, there are two classes of deductions:

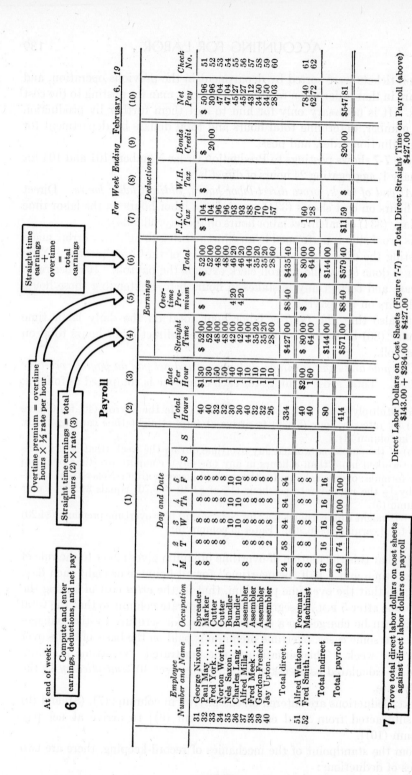

Direct Labor Dollars on Cost Sheets (Figure 7-7) = Total Direct Straight Time on Payroll (above) $427.00

$143.00 + $284.00 = $427.00

Figure 7-8

(a) *Office-controlled deductions*, for example, those computed directly by the payroll clerk from information kept by him; the F.I.C.A. tax deduction in column (7), which is computed in the illustration as 2 per cent of total earnings for each employee. Withholding tax, which would be another example, has been omitted from the illustration. In practice, the current rates and tables would be applied by the payroll clerk.

(b) *Field-controlled deductions*, those which originate outside the payroll department. Deductions from employees' wages for goods sold to them by the company is an example (not illustrated here). When the goods are sold to the employee, the sales slip is made out in the regular way, but the entry in the sales journal is a debit to Employees Accounts Receivable and a credit to Sales. A copy of the sales slip is sent to the payroll clerk who enters it in a deduction column headed "Employees Accounts Receivable." When the payroll is recorded in the general journal, Employees Accounts Receivable account is credited.

Sales slips come to the payroll clerk in batches. Each batch is accompanied by an adding machine tape which shows the amount of each ticket and the total of the batch. After the payroll clerk enters the tickets in the Employees Accounts Receivable column and totals the column, he proves the total against the total on the tape. Thus, the term, "field-controlled deduction" means that the outside office sets up the control against which the payroll clerk proves.

PROOF OF DEDUCTIONS AND NET EARNINGS. After all deductions have been entered and net earnings computed, gross earnings, deductions, and net earnings columns are footed. Proof of deductions and the net earnings column is:

> Total of gross earnings column ($579.40),
> Minus the sum of the totals of deductions columns
>   ($11.59 + $20.00 = $31.59),
> Equals the total of the net earnings column ($547.81).

This proof is applied to determine whether errors have been made in computing and entering net earnings.

7. *Prove total direct labor dollars on cost sheets against payroll.* This step involves listing the totals of labor charges to cost sheets made during the week and comparing the grand total with the comparable total on the payroll. Thus:

Charges to Production Order 101 during the week............ $143.00 ⎫ Figure 7-7
Charges to Production Order 104........................... 284.00 ⎭

Total charges, agreeing with payroll, direct labor [Column (4)] $427.00 Figure 7-8

Note that the total per payroll is *straight time pay*. It does not include overtime premium. The direct labor postings from job tickets to cost sheets are likewise straight time pay and do not include overtime premium.

(Overtime premium is charged to Factory Expense as illustrated in the following section.)

The reason for performing this proof is two-fold: It is an attempt to determine that no posting errors have been made to the payroll and the cost sheets from the job tickets. It is also an attempt to prove that the extensions (hours × rate) on the payroll and likewise the extensions on the job tickets (hours × rate) have been made correctly. If the totals of these two independent sets of extensions agree, it is taken as proof that the extensions were done correctly. If this proof of payroll against cost sheets were not made, some other method of proving extensions on payroll would have to be used (such as recomputing them on the payroll).

8. *Enter payroll for week in general journal.* The payroll for the week, illustrated on page 140 is entered in the general journal, as follows:

			Column of Payroll
Dr. Labor in process	$427.00		Column 4
Factory expense (Indirect labor a/c)	144.00		Column 4
Factory expense (Overtime premium a/c)	8.40		Column 5
Cr. F.I.C.A. Tax accrued		$ 11.59	Column 6
Bond deductions		20.00	Column 9
Accrued payroll		547.81	Column 10

The credits (in the Miscellaneous Accounts columns of the general journal) are posted immediately to their accounts in the general ledger. The debits to the factory expense ledger accounts are posted to those accounts immediately. The debit to Labor in Process, being in a column of its own, is not posted in detail, but is accumulated for the end-of-the-month posting.

Note that overtime premium is charged to an account of that name in the factory expense ledger. Thus, overtime premium is finally charged to Factory Expense. It will reach the cost sheets through factory expense rates, which are charged to the cost sheets as explained in Chapter 9. The assumption is that the overtime condition is a general one in the factory, and not caused by one particular job.

9. *Write disbursement voucher for payroll and enter in voucher register.* A disbursement voucher for the accrued payroll is written in favor of the paymaster and entered in the voucher register as illustrated in Figure 7-10 (Voucher No. 116). The entry in the voucher register is a debit to Accrued Payroll for $547.81 and a credit to Vouchers Payable for the same amount.

A single check is drawn for the net amount of the payroll. It is entered in the check register (not illustrated) and deposited in the Payroll account at the bank. This account is a special checking account used exclusively for payroll checks issued to the employees. (Note check numbers on the payroll. Payroll checks 51-62 were issued to cover this payroll.) The deposit of $547.81 in the Payroll account will cover the individual pay checks after they are cashed by the employees. After the individual pay-

8 — Enter payroll in general journal

General Journal

Month of _____ February ____ 19__

Date 19__	Particulars	Misc. A/c	Misc. Debits	Misc. Credits	142 Labor in Process, Debit — Amount	500 Factory Expense Control, Debit — A/c	500 Factory Expense Control, Debit — Amount	600 Selling and Shipping Expense Control, Debit — A/c	600 Selling and Shipping Expense Control, Debit — Amount	700 Administrative Expense Control, Debit — A/c	700 Administrative Expense Control, Debit — Amount
Feb. 6*	Labor in process...........		$	$	$427 00		$		$		$
	Indirect labor...........					510	$144 00				
	Overtime premium........					520	8 40				
	F.I.C.A. tax accrued...	222		11 59							
	Bond deductions........	223		20 00							
	Accrued payroll.......	221		547 81							
	Factory payroll for week										
27	Administrative salaries....									710	2,000 00
	Sales salaries...........							610	1,000 00		
	F.I.C.A. tax accrued...			60 00							
	Accrued payroll........			2,940 00							
	Administrative and selling payroll for month										
27	F.I.C.A. tax...........	222				531	250 74	631	20 00	731	40 00
	F.I.C.A. tax accrued...			310 74							
	Company's share of F.I.C.A. tax on payrolls										

* Entries for February 13, 20, and 27 omitted from this illustration.

Figure 7-9

143

Voucher Register

Month of ___February___ 19___

Date 19—	Issued To	Vo. No.	Paid Check No.	Paid Date	210 Vouchers Payable, Credit	141 Materials Inventory, Debit	500 Factory Expense Control, Debit A/c	Amount	Miscellaneous Accounts Account Name	A/c No.	Amount
Feb. 2	Walton Company	111	55	2/11/—	$2,600 00	$2,600 00		$			$
3	McNolton & Co.	112	56	2/11/—	1,450 00	1,450 00					
3	Fred Morris Co.	113	57	2/11/—	2,870 00						
4	Eastern & Western R.R. Co.	114			800 00		562	800 00			
6	Mill Supply Co.	115			709 00		540	709 00			
6	Factory Payroll	116	51	2/6/—	547 81				Accrued Payroll	220	547 81

9

Write disbursement voucher for payroll and enter in voucher register

Figure 7-10

roll checks are written, earnings and deductions are entered on employee's quarterly earnings records. (See illustration below.)

Administrative and selling payroll. The administrative and selling payroll is made out once a month, since the employees in those divisions are paid monthly. A payroll of the type illustrated on page 146 can be used for these divisions. Salaries are entered directly from a salary book

Employee's Quarterly Earnings Record

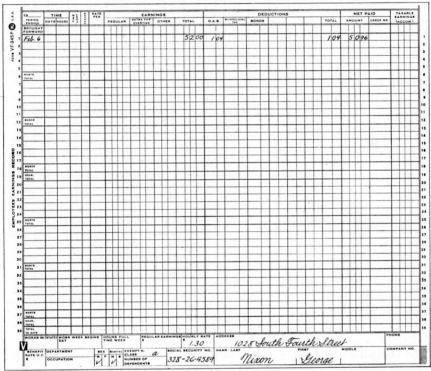

Form courtesy Wilson Jones Company

Figure 7-11

or other formal authorization record. Clock hours worked by hourly rated office and sales employees can be entered on this payroll from attendance time cards which are the same as those used for factory people.

The entry in the *general journal* for the administrative and selling payroll is illustrated on page 143. It comprises debits to Administrative Salaries and Sales Salaries, and credits to F.I.C.A. Tax Accrued and Accrued Payroll. This payroll is vouchered and paid in the same manner as the factory payroll.

F.I.C.A. tax—company's share. The employees' share of F.I.C.A. tax is deducted from the employees' pay on the payroll (as illustrated on page 140) and set up as a credit to F.I.C.A. Tax Accrued through the general journal (as illustrated on page 143). The *company* is liable for an amount of tax equal to the amount deducted from the employees' pay.

Salary Payroll

Form courtesy World Wide Press, Chicago

Figure 7-12

The company's share is recorded in the general journal at the end of the month by the following entry (illustrated on page 143):

Dr. Factory expense (F.I.C.A. tax expense a/c)	$250.74	(Factory payrolls)
Selling and shipping expense		
(F.I.C.A. tax expense a/c).............	20.00	(Selling and shipping payroll)
Administrative expense		
(F.I.C.A. tax expense a/c).............	40.00	(Administrative payroll)
Cr. Old age benefit tax accrued........	$310.74	

The company finally extinguishes the total accrual by paying the taxing authority, on a quarterly basis.

Posting general journal totals at the end of the month. Column totals are posted from the general journal at the end of the month. The following entry is illustrative:

Dr. Labor in process......................................	$10,577.00	
Factory expense control account........................	3,198.07	
Selling and shipping expense control account............	2,777.00	
Administrative expense control account.................	2,040.00	
Miscellaneous debits (total not posted).................	5,947.50	
Cr. Miscellaneous credits (total not posted)...........		$24,539.57

Recording indirect labor. In the accounting procedure illustrated in the previous pages, the following indirect labor accounts and expense labor accounts are kept:

(1) The indirect labor account proper, which is charged for indirect labor as defined on page 130 and also for expense labor, as defined on the same page. In practice, a number of accounts might be used in the indirect labor-expense labor group, but a single account is used in this chapter to reduce the amount of detail in the illustration.

(2) Overtime premium.

(3) F.I.C.A. tax.

(4) Workmen's insurance expense.

Note that in the payroll illustration, on page 140, all indirect labor and expense labor are segregated in a separate section of the roll. The total of such labor is accordingly charged to the Indirect Labor account through the general journal. Overtime premium is likewise charged to its own account through the general journal. Both of these charges originate in the payroll.

F.I.C.A. tax (company's share) and workmen's insurance expense are charged to accounts so named through the general journal, page 143.

Summary. Direct labor is labor which is identified with particular products, and which it is considered feasible to measure and charge to specific production order cost sheets. Indirect labor is labor which is identified with particular products, but which it is *not* considered feasible to measure and charge to specific production order cost sheets. Expense labor in a factory is labor which is expended for the benefit of production in general, and which is not identified with particular products. Indirect labor and expense labor in the factory are charged to factory expense.

In the illustrations in this chapter, the attendance time cards are the source forms for payroll, and the job tickets are the source forms for cost accounting. One attendance time card is used for each factory employee each week. One job ticket is issued for each job on which each man works each day (if the man is on direct labor) or for each charge to a factory expense account (if the man is on indirect labor or expense labor). Job tickets are reconciled with attendance time cards daily to determine that these two independent records of each employee's time agree. Total of job time for each man per the job tickets must agree with total for the man per the attendance time card.

The attendance time cards for direct labor people are recorded on the payroll, on which gross earnings, deductions, and net earnings for each person are calculated at the end of the pay period. The job tickets for direct labor people are sorted by department and entered on the daily labor time summary, then sorted by production order number and entered on the production order cost sheets.

After the payroll is completed at the end of the pay period, a general journal entry is made, debiting Labor in Process for total of direct labor charges for the period, debiting Factory Expense for overtime premium, crediting various deduction accounts for totals of amounts deducted from the employees' gross earnings, and crediting Accrued Payroll for total of net earnings due the employees.

A disbursement voucher is drawn for the latter amount and entered in the voucher register as a debit to Accrued Payroll and a credit to Vouchers Payable. Then a check is drawn in favor of the paymaster and recorded in the cash disbursements journal by a debit to Vouchers Payable and a credit to Cash in Bank. The paymaster deposits the check in a special payroll account at the bank and draws the individual checks for the employees against that payroll account.

In the payroll illustration on page 140, the time of indirect labor and expense labor people is carried in a separate section at the bottom of the payroll. When the general journal entry for payroll is made up, the total of indirect labor and expense labor in the factory is charged to Factory Expense.

A number of proof steps are described and illustrated in this chapter. They are performed in the order in which they appear in the procedure steps, to localize the amount of checking in case a failure to prove appears. As a final proof, the total of charges of direct labor to the cost sheets from the job tickets must agree with the total charge to Labor in Process control account which came from the payroll via the general journal.

QUESTIONS

7-1. Describe briefly the functions of accounting for labor in a job order cost accounting system.

7-2. Describe briefly a typical clerical organization for accounting for labor in a large manufacturing company.

7-3. Define and give examples of direct labor, indirect labor.

7-4. Describe briefly some of the types or items of managerial information concerning direct and indirect labor that the management of a manufacturing company might require.

7-5. Distinguish between an attendance time card, a job ticket, and a daily time report.

(b) Describe several timekeeping procedures that might be used in connection with a job order cost accounting system. Explain the advantages and disadvantages of each procedure.

7-6. In the payroll and labor cost procedure illustrated in Chapter 7, what feature or step is intended to prove that:

(a) the total hours worked by a man each day per job time tickets is correct?
(b) the direct labor hours for the week per the payroll have been correctly totaled?
(c) the straight time direct labor cost per the payroll has been correctly totaled?
(d) the extensions of hours and rates on the payroll have been made correctly?
(e) the deductions from outside (field-controlled deductions) have been taken up in the payroll?
(f) the deductions from gross pay have actually been made correctly on the payroll?

EXERCISES

7-1. The following basic forms of the Brunswick Manufacturing Company relating to labor are presented herewith:

(a) Attendance time cards for the week ending February 20, 19__
(b) Daily time reports for February 20, 19__ (Friday)

The following forms to be posted are provided in the Workbook:

(a) Payroll
(b) Production order cost sheets with certain materials and labor postings completed.

Required:

Using the forms provided, complete the accounting for labor for the week ending February 20:

(a) Compare total hours for each man for February 20 per daily time reports with total hours per the attendance time cards. (Write the comparison.)
(b) Post the daily time reports for February 20 to the cost sheets (total labor hours and total straight time labor dollars for the day to each order). Overtime premium is not to be charged to cost sheets.
(c) Post the attendance time cards (hours for each employee) for the week to the payroll.
(d) Prove total direct labor hours for week posted to cost sheets against total direct labor hours per payroll. (Write the comparison.)
(e) Complete the payroll. Pay time and a half for overtime. Calculate gross and net pay for each man, taking a 2 per cent F.I.C.A. tax deduction. Omit withholding tax (no data given).
(f) Prove direct labor dollars for the week posted to cost sheets against direct labor dollars on the payroll. (Write the comparison.)
(g) Draft general journal entries to record (1) the completed payroll and (2) company's share of F.I.C.A. tax.

Submit parts (a), (d), (f), and (g) on paper separate from your payroll form and cost sheet forms. Detach Payroll and Cost Sheets from the Workbook and submit.

7-2. Payrolls for Harrison Manufacturing Company, covering the complete month of January, are shown on pp 152-156. Note that the week ending February 3 is a split week: the labor for the first three days is chargeable to January while the labor for the last three days is chargeable to February.

Required:

(1) Compute the portion of the factory and shipping payroll for the week ending February 3 chargeable to January. Use the "fill-in" form in the Workbook: Accrued Factory and Shipping Payroll, January 28-31, 19__, inclusive.

Attendance Time Card (No. 101)

Name: Wilfred Lynn
Occupation: Assembler
Week Ending: February 20, _____ 19___

Day & Date	MORNING In	MORNING Out	AFTERNOON In	AFTERNOON Out	OVERTIME In	OVERTIME Out	Hours
M — 16	8:00	12:00	1:00	5:00			8
T — 17	7:58	12:01	1:00	5:03			8
W — 18	8:00	12:00	1:00	5:00			8
Th — 19	8:00	12:02	1:00	5:02			8
F — 20	7:56	12:01	12:59	5:00			8
S — 21							
S —							

Total Clock Hours	40
Overtime Hours	
Hourly Wage Rate	$1.50

Other Time Cards (Summary)

	101	102	103	104	105	111	112	113
Occupation	Assembler	Assembler	Assembler	Assembler	Assembler	Foreman	Clerk	Repairman
Week Ending	2/20/	2/20/	2/20/	2/20/	2/20/	2/20/	2/20/	2/20/
M — 16	8	8	8	8	8	8	8	8
T — 17	8	8	8	8	8	8	8	—
W — 18	8	10	8	8	8	8	—	—
Th — 19	8	8	10	—	8	8	—	—
F — 20	8	8	8	8	8	8	—	8
Total Clock Hours	40	42	42	32	40	40	16	16
Overtime Hours		2	2	—			—	—
Hourly Wage Rate	$1.50	$1.60	$1.50	$1.70	$1.50	$2.00	$1.25	$1.80

7-1

(2) Prepare a recap of factory and shipping payrolls for the month. Use the "fill-in" form in the Workbook. Charge overtime premiums paid on direct labor to Factory Expense. Charge all other overtime premiums to the same accounts as straight time labor.

(3) Draft a general journal entry to record a summary of all factory and shipping payrolls for January.

(4) Draft a general journal entry to record the salary payroll for the month, including the proper debit distribution. Assume that separate accounts are to be kept for Administrative Expense, Selling Expense, Shipping Expense, and Factory Expense.

(5) Draft a general journal entry to record the company's share of F.I.C.A. tax. The company's share is the same as total employees' share. Charge F.I.C.A. tax on direct labor to the Factory Expense account.

7-3. The following "fill-in" forms relating to payroll and labor costs are presented in the Workbook:

> Job tickets for January 5
> Payroll for week ending January 5
> Voucher register
> Cost sheets
> Departmental time summary for week ending January 5.
> In-process control accounts and certain other accounts.

7-1 (*continued*)

DAILY TIME REPORTS FOR FEBRUARY 20, 19__

Daily Time Report		No. 101	102	103	104	105
Name Wilfred Lynn	Rate Per Hour	$1.50	$1.60	$1.50	$1.70	$1.50
Occupation Assembler		Assem.	Assem.	Assem.	Assem.	Assem.
Date Feb. 20, 19__		2/20/__	2/20/__	2/20/__	2/20/__	2/20/__
12:00 Finish	Order No.	#41	#43	#42	#41	#42
8:00 A Start	Elapsed Time	4 hours	8 hours	2 hours	6 hours	8 hours
	Amount	$ 6.00	$12.80	$ 3.00	$10.20	$12.00
5:00 P Finish	Order No.	#42		#43	#43	
12:00 Start	Elapsed Time	4 hours		4 hours	2 hours	
	Amount	$ 6.00		$ 6.00	$ 3.40	
Finish	Order No.			#41		
Start	Elapsed Time			2 hours		
	Amount			$ 3.00		
Finish	Order No.					
Start	Elapsed Time					
	Amount					
Total Elapsed Time		8 hours	8 hours	8 hours	8 hours	8 hours
Total Amount		$12.00	$12.80	$12.00	$13.60	$12.00

Payroll

(Left-hand side)

No.	Name	Occupation	Hours 1 M	2 T	3 W	4 Th	5 F	6 S
10	Fred Nichols	Punch press operator	13.00	10.25	12.00	11.75	12.00	7.00
11	Joe Lucas	Assembling product	8	8	8	8	8	4
12	L. C. Lang	Painting product	8	8	10	8	8	
13	Thomas Jordan	Factory foreman	8	8	8	8	8	
14	Theodore Bell	Shipping clerk	8	8	8	8	8	
15	George Kellar	Packer (shipping)	8	8	8	8	8	4

(Right-hand side)

Department __Factory and Shipping__
Week Ending __January 6, 19—__

Total Hours	Rate per Hour	Total Straight Time Earnings	Overtime Premium Hours	Rate	Amount	Gross Earnings	Deductions Income Tax Withheld	F.I.C.A. Tax	Group Insurance	Net Earnings	Check No.
44	piece work av. $1.50	$ 66.00	4	$ .75	$3.00	$ 69.00	$	$1.38	$ .80	$ 66.82	
42	1.40	58.80	2	.70	1.40	60.20		1.20	.80	58.20	
40	=1.40	56.00				56.00		1.12	.80	54.08	
40	week	100.00				100.00		2.00	1.00	97.00	
40	1.70	68.00				68.00		1.36	.80	65.84	
44	1.30	57.20				57.20	$	1.14	.80	55.26	
		$406.00			$4.40	$419.40		$8.20	$5.00	$397.20	

7-2 (continued)

Payroll

(Left-hand side)

No.	Name	Occupation	Hours					
			8 M	9 T	10 W	11 Th	12 F	13 S
10	Fred Nichols..........	Punch press operator	{ 12.00	12.25	11.40	10.60	13.10	
11	Joe Lucas............	Assembling product	8	8	8	8	8	
12	L. C. Lang...........	Painting product	8	10	8	8	10	
13	Thomas Jordan.......	Factory foreman	8	8	8	8	8	
14	Theodore Bell........	Shipping clerk	8	8	8	8	8	
15	George Kellar........	Packer (shipping)	8	8	8	8	8	

(Right-hand side)

Department __Factory and Shipping__
Week Ending __January 13,__ 19__

	Total Hours	Rate per Hour	Total Straight Time Earnings	Overtime Premium			Gross Earnings	Deductions			Net Earnings	Check No.
				Hours	Rate	Amount		Income Tax Withheld	F.I.C.A. Tax	Group Insurance		
10	40	piece work	$ 59 35		$	$	$ 59 35	$	$1 19	$ 80	$ 57 36	
11	40	$ 1 40	56 00				56 00		1 12	80	54 08	
12	44	1 40	61 60	4	70	2 80	64 40		1 29	80	62 31	
13	40	week	100 00				100 00		2 00	1 00	97 00	
14	40	1 70	68 00				68 00		1 36	80	65 84	
15	40	1 30	52 00				52 00		1 04	80	50 16	
			$396 95			$2 80	$399 75	$	$8 00	$5 00	$386 75	

7-2 (continued)

Payroll

(Left-hand side)

No.	Name	Occupation	Hours 15 M	16 T	17 W	18 Th	19 F	20 S
10	Fred Nichols	Punch press operator	12.10	10.15	13.40	12.25	12.50	
11	Joe Lucas	Assembling product	8	8	8	8	8	4
12	L. C. Lang	Painting product	8	8	8	8	8	
13	Thomas Jordan	Factory foreman	8	8	8	8	8	
14	Theodore Bell	Shipping clerk	8	8	8	8	8	
15	George Kellar	Packer (shipping)	8	8	8	8	8	

(Right-hand side)

Department Factory and Shipping
Week Ending January 20, 19____

No.	Hours Total	Rate per Hour	Total Straight Time Earnings	Overtime Premium Hours	Rate	Amount	Gross Earnings	Income Tax Withheld	F.I.C.A. Tax	Group Insurance	Net Earnings	Check No.
10	40	piece work	$ 60 40		$	$	$ 60 40	$	$1 21	$ 80	$ 58 39	
11	40	$1 40	56 00				56 00		1 12	80	54 08	
12	44	1 40	61 60	4	70	2 80	64 40		1 29	80	62 31	
13	40	week	100 00				100 00		2 00	1 00	97 00	
14	40	1 70	68 00				68 00		1 36	80	65 84	
15	40	1 30	52 00				52 00		1 04	80	50 16	
			$398 00			$2 80	$400 80	$	$8 02	$5 00	$337 78	

154

Payroll

(Left-hand side)

Department Factory and Shipping
Week Ending January 27, 19___

No.	Name	Occupation	Hours 22 M	23 T	24 W	25 Th	26 F	27 S
10	Fred Nichols	Punch press operator	13.60	12.95	11.90	12.15	13.00	
11	Joe Lucas	Assembling product	8	8	8	8	8	
12	J. C. Lang	Painting product	8	8	8	8	8	
13	Thomas Jordan	Factory foreman	8	8	8	8	8	
14	Theodore Bell	Shipping clerk	8	8	8	8	8	
15	George Kellar	Packer (shipping)	8	8	8	8	8	

(Right-hand side)

	Hours Total	Rate per Hour	Total Straight Time Earnings	Overtime Premium Hours	Rate	Amount	Gross Earnings	Income Tax Withheld	F.I.C.A. Tax	Group Insurance	Net Earnings	Check No.
10	40	piece work	$ 63.60		$	$	$ 63.60	$	$1.27	$ .80	$ 61.53	
11	40	$1.40	56.00				56.00		1.12	.80	54.08	
12	40	1.40	56.00				56.00		1.12	.80	54.08	
13	40	week	100.00				100.00		2.00	1.00	97.00	
14	40	1.70	68.00				68.00		1.36	.80	65.84	
15	40	1.30	52.00				52.00		1.04	.80	50.16	
			$395.60		$	$	$395.60	$	$7.91	$5.00	$382.69	

7-2 (continued)

(Left-hand side)

Payroll

Department Factory and Shipping
Week Ending Feb. 3, 19___

No.	Name	Occupation	29 M	30 T	31 W	1 Th	2 F	3 S	Total Hours	Rate Per Hour	Total Straight Time Earnings
											$
10	Fred Nichols	Punch press operator	12.25	13.15	12.85				piece work	$	
11	Joe Lucas	Assembling product	8	8	8						
12	L. C. Lang	Painting product	8	8	10					1 40	
13	Thomas Jordan	Factory foreman	8	8	8					1 40	
14	Theodore Bell	Shipping clerk	8	8	8					we'ek 1 70	100 00
15	George Kellar	Packer (shipping)	8	8	8					1 30	

Salary Payroll

Department General Office and Sales
Month Ending January 31. 19___

No.	Name	Occupation	Gross Earnings	Income Tax Withheld	F.I.C.A. Tax	Group Insurance	Net Earnings	Check No.
101	William Norton	President	$1,000 00	$	$20 00	$ 3 00	$ 977 00	$
102	Fred Smith	Sales manager	750 00		15 00	2 00	733 00	
103	George Miller	Factory manager	750 00		15 00	2 00	733 00	
104	Upton Coulter	General accountant	700 00		14 00	2 00	684 00	
105	Stanley McMillan	Salesman	600 00		12 00	2 00	586 00	
106	Mary Cretchell	General office clerk	300 00		6 00	80	293 20	
			$4,100 00	$	$82 00	$11 80	$4,006 20	$

7-2 (continued)

Required:

(1) Make all entries directly on the "fill-in" forms necessary to record the job tickets for January 5.
(2) Complete the payroll and record it directly in the voucher register.
(3) Foot the voucher register and post the totals (assuming that there are no further transactions this month).
(4) Enter proofs of direct labor hours and direct labor dollars in the space provided.

PROBLEMS

7-1. The following transactions of the Phillips Manufacturing Company relate to labor. The Phillips Manufacturing Company records payroll entries directly into the voucher register (instead of setting up a payroll accrual in the general journal first). Make the required entries in simple general journal entry form:

(6) Factory and shipping payroll for week vouchered and paid.

Class	Hours	Amount
Direct labor	360	$570.00
Indirect labor	80	100.00
Shipping labor	60	80.00
Total	500	$750.00

(13) Factory and shipping payroll for week vouchered and paid:

Class	Hours	Amount
Direct labor	420	$615.00
Indirect labor	90	125.00
Shipping labor	60	80.00
Total	570	$820.00

(Entries for remaining weeks of month eliminated from problem.)

(31) General office and selling payroll for month vouchered and paid:

Administrative expense	$1,200.00
Selling expense	800.00
	$2,000.00

Required:

(1) Draft entries in simple general journal form to record the above information.
(2) Set up "T" accounts and post the entries.
Note: This problem calls for entries affecting general ledger accounts only. Supporting entries of direct labor hours and dollars on cost sheets, which would be included in a complete job order cost system, have not been made part of this problem.

7-2. Assume that the Alton Company operates no special journals. Draft entries for January in simple journal entry form for the following transactions. Indicate what subsidiary ledgers would be affected and indicate whether the entry in the subsidiary ledger account would be a debit or a credit.

(1) The payroll for the week totaled $500. A summary of the charges to cost sheets and standing orders showed:

P.O. No.	Amount
101	$ 80.00
102	20.00
103	100.00
104	60.00
105	140.00

S.O. No.	Amount
S. 1	$ 50.00
S. 2	10.00
S. 3	40.00

The above amounts are gross earnings. Deduct 2 per cent F.I.C.A. tax to arrive at net earnings, and make the entry for accrued payroll.

(2) Draft the entry for company's share of F.I.C.A. tax.

(3) Draft the entry for payment of the payroll.

CLASSIFICATION OF LABOR; CONTROL AND PRICING UNDER INCENTIVE WAGE PLANS

Hidden labor losses. In the absence of a proper classification of labor accounts and proper quantity controls for incentive pay plans hidden losses are likely to occur. Without a working set of accounts for direct labor (for example, production order cost sheets in Chapter 7), the manufacturer would not know the actual labor cost of his various products. Consequently, he would have no accounting basis for determining whether the work is being done efficiently, and he would have no accounting basis for making sound estimates on jobs to be done to customer's order on a bid basis.

If there is not a proper set of indirect labor accounts (and good timekeeping), the indirect labor complement in a factory is likely to build up faster than the management realizes. The same is true of fringe benefits to labor—although the impact of fringe benefits is sometimes more difficult to locate and to measure than the impact of that segment of indirect labor identified with specific occupations in the factory.

The importance of proper quantity controls under incentive pay plans is generally appreciated, although not all managements operate them. Such quantity controls involve verification of the reported quantities of production for which operators are paid. Without such controls, excess payments can be made. The amounts are then simply another hidden labor cost.

I. CLASSIFICATION OF LABOR

The general pattern of labor accounts presented in this chapter is similar to the pattern of materials accounts, presented in Chapter 6. Major classes of labor, considered from the standpoint of direct and indirect charges to product, are listed on page 160. The list includes, in addition to direct charges and indirect charges, labor losses and labor overhead.

Labor classes defined. Definitions of labor classes follow, with examples:

Direct Labor. Labor identified with particular products, which it is considered feasible to measure and charge to specific production order cost sheets. The labor of a cabinet maker working on desks in a furniture factory and the labor of a mechanic repairing automobiles would be direct labor.

Indirect Labor. (a) Labor identified with particular products, which it is not considered feasible to measure and charge to specific production order cost sheets; for example, the labor of a sewing machine operator making belt loops for dungarees in a garment factory is handled as indirect labor where it is not considered feasible to keep track of the time spent on the garments for *each* production order.

(b) Labor expended for the benefit of production in general and not identified with particular products; for example, supervisory labor, factory clerical (factory payroll clerks, materials and finished goods ledger clerks, and the cost man), factory machine repairmen, materials handlers (often), and janitors and watchmen.

CLASSIFICATION OF LABOR: DIRECT AND INDIRECT
(*As regards products: Job order cost system*)

Direct Labor:
  Labor identified with a specific product, which can be measured and charged to cost sheets.

Indirect Labor:
  Indirect labor proper: labor identified with a specific product, which it is not considered feasible to measure and charge to cost sheets.
  Expense labor: labor used for the benefit of production in general and not reasonably identified with a specific product:
    Supervisors
    Factory clerical
    Machine repairmen
    Materials handlers
    Janitors and watchmen

Labor Losses: Labor Allowances and Makeup (Incentive Pay)
  Payments made for time spent with no production or with substandard quantity:
    Waiting (no production)
    Machine delay (no production)
    Transfer (substandard quantity of production)
    Makeup to guarantee (substandard quantity)
    Labor re-operation (product repair: labor expended to correct faulty work)

Labor Overhead:
  Overtime premium and shift differential
  F.I.C.A. tax
  Workmen's insurance
  Provision for vacation pay
  Numerous other "fringe" benefits

Figure 8-1

Labor Losses. Allowances and makeup are frequently found in piece-work pay plans. Under a piece-work pay plan, an employee is paid a specified amount per unit (or piece) of product on which he performed a specified operation. A schedule of rates is in effect in which there may be a different rate per piece for each operation.

Typical allowances and makeup items which may be paid *in addition to* piece-work pay include waiting time and machine delay time. Where the employee is idle during working hours because of a lack of orders, he may be paid actual *waiting time* multiplied by the guaranteed rate per hour. Where the employee is idle during working hours because his machine is down for repairs, he may be paid actual *machine delay time* multiplied by the guaranteed rate per hour.

Another type of allowance may be paid where an employee is transferred from the operation for which he is trained and in which he is proficient to one for which he is not trained. The employee may be paid a *transfer* allowance to compensate him for loss of piece-work earnings, since the employee could not earn as much on piece work on a strange operation as he could on the operation for which he was trained. A frequent arrangement is to pay him the usual piece-work earnings on work actually accomplished in the new operation plus a transfer allowance equal to

[Actual hours worked × Earned rate per hour on the employees own job]
minus
[Piece-work earnings produced on the new operation].

The effect is to bring the employee's pay up to what it would probably be on his own operation.

Makeup to guarantee is an amount paid to employees who are guaranteed a specified average actual wage as a feature of an incentive wage pay plan. Assume a guaranteed rate of $1.25 per clock hour. If the employee earns $40 in piece work in 40 hours, the makeup to guarantee would be total guaranteed earnings (40 × $1.25 = $50) minus piece work earnings ($40) or $10.

Payments are sometimes made for *repairing faulty work*. Ordinarily, if an employee on piece work does an unsatisfactory job, the work inspector turns it back to him to be repaired (put into salable condition), and the employee is required to do repair work on his own time. He is, of course, paid the regular piece-work rate for the original performance of the operation. If the employee who did the faulty work cannot be identified, however, the product is turned over to some other employee who is paid actual time multiplied by a guaranteed rate for doing the repair job. The cost is charged to a Labor Re-operation account.

Labor Overhead. Overtime premium and shift differential are well-known examples of labor overhead. Overtime premium is a premium paid to an employee for working more than 8 hours in one day or 40 hours in one week. For example, an employee whose regular rate of pay is $1.50 per hour may be paid an overtime premium at the rate of ½ his regular rate or $.75 per hour. The premium is the extra $.75.

A shift differential is an extra amount paid over the day-shift rate for working the night shift. Thus, an employee regularly paid $1.50 for day-shift work may be paid $1.55 per hour for night-shift work, a differential of $.05 per hour.

F.I.C.A. Tax, vacation pay, and workmen's insurance expense are other examples of labor overhead. They are explained in the following section.

Entries for payroll taxes, reserves, and insurance. *F.I.C.A. Tax—company's share.*

The employees' share of F.I.C.A. tax is deducted from the employees' pay on the payroll (as illustrated in column 7 of the payroll on page 140) and set up as a credit to F.I.C.A. Tax Accrued through the general journal. The *company* is liable for an amount of tax equal to the amount deducted from the employees' pay. The company's share is recorded in the general journal at the end of the month by the following entry:

Dr. Factory expense (F.I.C.A. tax expense a/c) $250.74		(Factory payrolls)
Selling and shipping expense		
(F.I.C.A. tax expense a/c).............	20.00	(Selling and ship-ping payroll)
Administrative expense		
(F.I.C.A. tax expense a/c).............	40.00	(Administrative payroll)
Cr. F.I.C.A. tax accrued.............	$310.74	

Assuming that the company finally extinguishes the total accrual by paying the taxing authority, which it does on a monthly basis, the entry would be a debit to F.I.C.A. Tax Accrued and a credit to Cash.

Provision for Vacation Pay. The company gives all employees a vacation at the same time, by shutting down the factory during the first two weeks of July. All employees who have worked six months or more during the year preceding July 1 are paid two weeks vacation pay. The total expected cost of the vacation is spread over the working weeks by the following monthly entry:

Dr. Factory expense: provision for vacation pay......	$xxx	
Cr. Reserve for vacation pay.................		$xxx

Provision for vacation pay based upon the monthly payrolls. (The amount is approximately 2% of payroll.)

When the vacation pay is paid, the entry is:

Dr. Reserve for vacation pay......................	$xxx	
Cr. Cash.....................................		$xxx

This method of recording spreads the cost of the vacation over the working weeks and avoids charging a shutdown period with a labor cost when no work was done.

Workmen's Insurance. The entry to set up workmen's insurance expense expired is:

<pre>
Dr. Factory expense: Workmen's insurance.......... $xxx
    Cr. Prepaid workmen's insurance.............. $xxx
    To charge insurance to current operations, based
    upon payroll for the period.
</pre>

Fringe benefits. The term "fringe benefits" is a loose one referring to payments made to or for the benefit of employees over and above the common wages and salaries; for example, F.I.C.A. tax, workmen's insurance, and vacation pay, discussed above.

"Fringes" were hardly ever heard of in industry before the 1940's. That term sprang up in the labor relations shorthand of the World War II era to describe money costs and employment benefits that were on the periphery of, but actually outside, direct wage payments. It has persisted with all its looseness ever since. The result is that today it is used to cover all peripheral benefits or to denote only the non-statutory payments.*

Fisher and Chapman classify fringe benefits under the headings:†

(A) Premium for time worked
(B) Pay for time not worked
(C) Employee benefits (employer's contribution)
(D) Employees' activities

The list of 28 examples of fringe benefits compiled by them for use in a survey of a number of companies appears on page 164. In this survey, Fisher and Chapman found that the total cost of fringe payments per productive hour had reached the average of $.4099 by the beginning of 1953, for the companies surveyed.

Labor overhead in the larger sense. This general term applies to all the cost of labor above direct payments to the employee. The relationship of labor overhead to labor is roughly comparable to the relationship of materials overhead to materials. Labor overhead would include not only the cost of fringe benefits paid to or in behalf of the workman, but the cost of timekeeping and payroll, procurement (the employment department), employee welfare and industrial relations expense, and direct supervision. The dollar relationship of labor overhead to direct labor is important to the cost accountant because of the question of how to allocate the former to the product unit or other cost units in use. The allocation of overhead to products is discussed in Chapter 10.

---

* Austin Fisher and John F. Chapman, "Big Costs of Little Fringes," *Harvard Business Review*, Sept.-Oct., 1954, page 35. Quoted by permission of the publisher.

† *Ibid.*, page 37.

CLASSIFICATION OF FRINGE PAYMENTS*

A. *Premium for time worked*
  1. Overtime premium, including premium for Saturday, Sunday, and holiday worked.
  2. Shift premiums, P.M. and night.

B. *Pay for time not worked*
  1. Sick pay (paid for by company)
  2. Vacation pay
  3. Holiday pay (holidays not worked)
  4. Paid rest period
  5. Lunch period
  6. Jury pay allowance
  7. Voting pay allowance
  8. Pay for military service

C. *Employee benefits (employer's contribution)*
  1. Old age and unemployment compensation
  2. Workmen's compensation
  3. Pension plan
  4. Profit sharing
  5. Christmas bonus
  6. Group life
  7. Hospitalization
  8. Health and accident
  9. Surgical
  10. Death benefits
  11. Food cost subsidy
  12. Work shoes and clothing cost
  13. Payments to union representatives for time in grievances, negotiations, etc.
  14. Administrative cost of benefits
  15. Separation pay allowance

D. *Employees' activities*
  1. Service awards
  2. Athletics, recreation events
  3. Community activities, such as bowling, etc.

Figure 8-2

II. LABOR COSTING UNDER INCENTIVE PAY PLANS

Weekly labor report under piece-work plan; Control of allowances. Figure 8-3 shows a weekly labor report designed for the control of direct labor under a piece-rate wage payment plan which has special allowance features. Fundamentally, it shows the total amount of piece-work earnings and the total amount paid for each of the allowances, makeup, and overtime premium. The actual hours and all the dollar amounts are taken directly from column totals of the payroll. (The

* *Ibid.*, page 38.

method of calculating each allowance is illustrated on the payroll, page 168.)

The report illustrated provides an excellent control over direct labor. Each of the allowance accounts is a vital management index. Note the causes underlying these allowances:

> *Waiting time*—No work for the employee because of production control difficulties such as scheduling or dispatching.
> *Machine delay*—Machine breakdowns.
> *Transfer*—No regular workman was present for some particular operation, and the foreman had to shift an operator from some other position to get production moving. This may indicate excessive absenteeism or a short complement of trained people for critical operations.
> *Repair*—Faulty work.
> *Makeup to guarantee*—This represents one of the costs of training new employees up to the point of efficiency expected by the engineers who set the piece rates, or it may represent substandard performance of experienced employees. (In some factories, makeup for learners is separated from makeup for experienced employees on the report. The separation is made on the basis of the number of weeks the employee has been working.)
> *Overtime premium*—This is the premium paid for having work done after the regular quitting time, instead of during regular hours.

WEEKLY LABOR REPORT - ASSEMBLY DEPARTMENT

Week Ending February 6, 19--

Particulars	Amount	% to Total Piece Work Earned
Actual hours worked on piece work	130	x x
Piece work earned	$ 177 70	100.00%
Waiting time allowance	$ 2 00	
Machine delay allowance	2 00	
Transfer time allowance	2 00	
Repair allowance	1 00	
Makeup to guarantee	2 20	
Overtime premium	1 25	
Total allowances and makeup	$ 10 45	5.88%
Gross earnings	$ 188 15	
% of capacity worked	80%	
Average piece work earnings per actual hour	$ 1 44+	

Figure 8-3

Management likes to see that allowances are kept as small as possible. In Figure 8-3, the total allowances are over 5 per cent of total piece-work earnings. The percentage of allowances to total piece work produced is shown to give the manager a guide as to whether the allowances are increasing, when compared with volume of work done. Experience will tell the manager what a reasonable percentage would be.

Average piece-work earnings per hour is $1.44+. This average would be compared with the rate per hour paid nonpiece-rate workers (straight hourly rated employees) on the same type of work, either in this factory or in the other factories in the community. It is expected that the average for the former would be higher than the rate for the latter.

Per cent of capacity worked might be shown as an index of level of operations. A low percentage might indicate lack of orders, production control difficulties, operator absenteeism, or other factors which ought to be investigated.

JOB TICKET - PIECE WORK

Name Alfred Mills   No. 37

Department Assembly   Date Feb 1, 19—

	Finish	Job No.	Operation No.	Description
5:00 p		108	31	Assemble
8:00 a	Start	Quantity	Piece Rate	Amount
8:00	Elapsed	80	.12	$9.60

Figure 8-4

Forms for piece-rate wage plan. The special forms required to operate a piece-rate wage payment plan with allowances are:

Job ticket—piece work is a form providing, in addition to the usual items found on job tickets for hourly rated employees,

    (a) Operation no.
    (b) Description of operation
    (c) Quantity
    (d) Piece rate
    (e) Amount [(c) × (d)].

This form is illustrated in Figure 8-4.

Special allowance tickets (not illustrated), similar to job tickets, are used for recording the facts and the authorization at the source. These show the type of allowance intended, hours, rate of pay for the allowance, and any other facts required for the calculation. They must be approved by the foreman. The payroll clerk then records them in the proper column of the payroll, to the credit of the employee indicated.

A *piece-work payroll* is used for compiling (a) piece-work time and earnings and (b) allowance time and earnings. Operation of the piece-work payroll is described in the following section.

Piece-work payroll. The piece-work payroll illustrated on page 168 is used for employees in the assembly department. The pay plan specifies that each employee shall be paid the total of his piece rate earnings each week, except that each one is guaranteed $1 an hour. If an employee fails to earn sufficient piece work to yield an average of $1 per hour worked, the company will pay him the difference between his total piece-work earnings and guaranteed wages at the rate of $1 per hour. Such payment is known as *makeup to guarantee*.

The job ticket illustrated in Figure 8-4 provides spaces for recording pieces produced and piece rate as well as other typical information for use in a job order cost accounting system.

The payroll form provides two horizontal lines for each employee. The top line is used for hours worked on piece work and the bottom line for piece-work earnings. Both hours and earnings are posted daily from the job tickets. (The attendance time cards would not be posted to the payroll but would be used for verification of the job time and allowance time.) At the end of the week, total piece-work hours for each employee are entered in Column (2) and total piece-work earnings in Column (6).

Average rate per hour on piece work [Column (5)] is total piece-work earnings [Column (6)] divided by total hours worked on piece work [Column (2)]. Thus, for Alfred Mills, the earned rate per hour is $48.90 divided by 40 = $1.22+ per hour. The management expects that, at the end of the normal period for training, an average employee can earn about $1.25 per hour without extraordinary effort. As was indicated before, each employee's earned rate per hour is posted to his quarterly earnings record weekly, to provide a record of his progress.

Allowance hours and amounts for each employee are posted in total at the end of the week from the allowance slips. Note the entries for Luke Norton on line 5: 7 hours of allowance in Column (3) and $7 in Column (7).

Total hours for each employee are entered in Column (4). Total hours per payroll must agree with total hours per attendance time cards.

Overtime premium. Fred Meek (line 2 on the payroll) worked 2 hours overtime on Thursday and is entitled to overtime premium. (According to the pay plan in effect, overtime is paid for hours worked over 8 hours in any day, although the employee may not have worked 40 hours during the week.)

The formula for overtime premium, applied to Fred Meek, is:

Piece-Work Payroll

Department Assembly

Week Ending February 6, 19__

Line No.	*Employee Number and Name*	(1) *Piece Work Hours and Earnings By Day* 1 *M*	2 *T*	3 *W*	4 *Th*	5 *F*	6 *S*	7 *S*	(2) *Total Hours*	(3) *Hours on Allowance*	(4) *Total Hours*	(5) *Average Rate Per Hour: P.W.*	(6) *Earnings* *Piece Work*	(7) *Allowances*	(8) *Makeup to Guarantee*	(9) *Overtime Premium*	(10) *Total*
1	37 Alfred Mills........	8	8	8	8	8			40		40						
		9.60	10.20	9.40	9.90	9.80						$1 22+	$ 48 90	$	$	$	$ 48 90
2	38 Fred Meek.........		8	8	10	6			32		32						
			10.00	9.90	12.00	8.10						1 25	40 00			1 25	41 25
3	39 Gordon French.....		8	8	8	8			32		32						
			7.80	7.20	7.60	7.40						937+	30 00		2 00		32 00
4	40 Jay Upton.........		2	8	8	8			26		26						
			2.10	7.40	8.10	8.20						992+	25 80		20		26 00
5	41 Luke Norton......	8	8	6	6	5			33	7	40						
		8.80	7.20	6.60	5.40	5.00						1 00	33 00	7 00			40 00
	Totals..............	16	34	38	40	35			163	7	170						
		18.40	37.30	40.50	43.00	38.50							177 70	7 00	2 20	1 25	188 15

Deductions and net earnings columns not shown, same as Figure 7-8.

Figure 8-5

Overtime hours × ½ average rate, piece work plus allowance
2 × ½ of $1.25   = $1.25

Makeup to guarantee.   Any employee whose piece-work earnings plus allowances for the week are less than his actual hours multiplied by $1 is entitled to makeup, sufficient to raise his earnings to the rate of $1 per hour, according to the wage payment plan in effect.   Gordon French (line 3) earned only $30 total piece-work earnings for 32 hours work.   He is entitled to sufficient makeup to raise his earnings to 32 × $1 or $32.   Makeup of $2 is entered in the Makeup column (8).   Total earnings of $32 is then entered in Column (10).

Jay Upton (line 4) earned $25.80 for 26 hours work.   He is entitled to $.20 makeup to raise him to the $26 guaranteed.

Quantity control in piece-rate wage payment plan.   Where a piece-rate wage payment plan is used, it is necessary to operate quantity controls to safeguard the accuracy of the quantities of production reported for payment.   In some cases, this is done by keeping track of the number of pieces reported on job tickets and determining that the totals so reported do not exceed the quantity shown by the production order.   The basic idea is that, if the production order calls for 100 units of Product X and each unit of product requires five successive operations, no more than 100 units should be paid for in each operation.

Operation of the quantity control may involve routing the job tickets through the production control department.   This department may set up a tally for each production order providing (in the situation described above) a column for each operation.   Clerks would post quantities reported on job tickets to the proper tallies.   If the quantity reported exceeds the authorized quantity on a production order, the production clerk would report the excess to the foreman of the department where the error originated.   The foreman would take necessary steps to prevent recurrence of unsatisfactory reporting.

Note that where scrap occurs on the production line, the effect is to reduce the number of good units of production that will be produced on a production order.   Since it is the intention to pay piece-rate wages only for good units produced, the control record would have to be adjusted for scrap at the point where it occured.   Thus, if the production order called originally for 100 units, and 5 units were scrapped in process, net good units produced would be 95.   This would be the controlling quantity for piece-rate wage payment on that production order.

The clerical work required to operate a control as described above is considerable.   In some cases, modifications of the records or of the pay plan itself are worked out to simplify the record work.   In *group incentive* plans, for instance, all the operators in a group may be paid on the basis of production of the group, and individual production tallies would not be necessary.

Labor costing under various incentive wage payment plans. We saw in Chapter 6 that the method of pricing materials affects the structure of costs to be used for various purposes. A comparable situation exists with reference to wage payment plans. In setting up a wage payment plan, it is obviously necessary to determine how the mathematics of the plan are reflected in unit product costs as well as in the payment to an employee per clock hour worked. In a straight-day work plan (which, of course is not an incentive plan), the labor cost per unit of product turned out by an operator in eight hours decreases as the number of units increases, while the wage rate per hour remains constant. In a straight piece-work plan, the employee's earned rate per hour (average actual wage rate) increases as the number of units of product turned out in eight hours increases, whereas the labor cost per unit remains constant. In other incentive wage plans, the employee may be paid a bonus when he attains a stated level of output. In such plans, both the unit product cost and the employee's earned rate per hour may vary (although not directly) as units produced in eight hours increases. Several wage payment plans will be considered in the following paragraphs and two key figures for each plan—earned rate per hour and labor cost per unit of product—will be discussed.

As stated above, under *straight day work* (hourly rated), the employee's earned rate per hour [Column (2)] is constant, and the labor cost per unit of product [Column (4)] decreases directly as the number of units produced in eight hours increases. These facts are illustrated in the following table which (like all the other tables in this section) is concerned with the production of a single employee for an eight-hour day:

Straight Day Work (Hourly Rated)

(1)	(2)	(3)	(4)
			Labor
Quantity	Wage	Employee's	Cost Per Unit
Produced	Rate	Earnings	of Product
(pieces)	Per Hour	(8 hours)	(10 pcs./unit)
120	$1.80	$14.40	$1.20
160	1.80	14.40	.90
200	1.80	14.40	.72
240	1.80	14.40	.60
280	1.80	14.40	.52

Figure 8-6a

If costs are used to measure labor performance, a reduction in labor cost per unit could be regarded as an increase in labor efficiency. If costs are to be used as a factor in setting selling prices, on the other hand, the question arises "What labor cost might be included"? $1.20? $.52? Presumably the cost which represents the level of performance attainable by the average employee would be used.

Under *straight piece work*, the employee's earned rate per hour increases as the number of pieces produced in eight hours [Column (3)] increases, and the labor cost per unit of product [Column (4)] remains constant except for the effect of the legal minimum wage rate per hour.

Straight Piece Work

(1) Quantity Produced (pieces)	(2) Piece-Work Earnings ($.06/piece)	(3) Employee's Earned Rate Per Hour (8 hours)	(4) Labor Cost Per Unit of Product (10 pcs./unit)
120	$ 7.20	$1.00*	$.67
160	9.60	1.20	.60
200	12.00	1.50	.60
240	14.40	1.80	.60
280	16.80	2.10	.60

* Minimum wage rate per hour.

Figure 8-6b

Under one *standard time plan*, standard time allowance per unit of product is set for each operation by industrial engineering methods (as indicated in Chapter 18). In the operation of the wage payment plan, the total standard time produced by an employee is determined each day, as well as the actual (clock) time worked. The employee is paid either (a) standard time produced multiplied by base rate (say $1.80 per hour) or (b) actual hours multiplied by minimum rate ($1 per hour), whichever is greater. The earned rate per hour [Column (6)] increases directly as production, measured in standard hours, increases. The labor cost per unit [Column (7)] remains constant, except when the operator is paid at the minimum rate. This plan gives the same mathematical results as the straight piece-work plan illustrated above.

Standard Time Produced at Base Rate

(1) Quantity Produced (pieces)	(2) Standard Time Produced in Minutes (2 min./piece)	(3) Actual Time Worked in Minutes	(4) Standard Time Produced × Base Rate ($1.80/hour)	(5) Total Payment for Day	(6) Earned Rate Per Hour	(7) Labor Cost Per Unit of Product (10 pcs./unit)
120	240	480	$ 7.20	$ 8.00†	$1.00*	$.67
160	320	480	9.60	9.60	1.20	.60
200	400	480	12.00	12.00	1.50	.60
240	480	480	14.40	14.40	1.80	.60
280	560	480	16.80	16.80	2.10	.60

* Minimum rate.
† Actual hours @ minimum.

Figure 8-6c

Certain characteristics of the standard time plan should be noted. In the first place, where the standard time allowed for an operation or job is put on a job ticket before the job is started, the operator knows what time performance he is expected to achieve without further calculation. Also, after a day's work has been done, the operator's performance percentage for the day can be determined by dividing standard time produced by actual time worked. Thus, if an operator produces 280 pieces in a day, his

HALSEY PREMIUM WAGE RATE

(1) Quantity Produced	(2) Standard Time Produced, in Minutes (2 min./piece)	(3) Actual Time Taken in Minutes	(4) Pay at Operator's Regular Hourly Rate ($1.80)	(5) Value of Time Saved Minutes	(6) Value of Time Saved Amount	(7) Bonus (½ of Time Saved)	(8) Total Payment for Day	(9) Employee's Earned Rate Per Hour (8 Hours)	(10) Labor Cost Per Unit of Product (10 pcs./unit)
120	240	480	$14.40				$14.40	$1.80	$1.20
160	320	480	14.40				14.40	1.80	.90
200	400	480	14.40				14.40	1.80	.72
240	480	480	14.40				14.40	1.80	.60
280	560	480	14.40	80	$2.40	$1.20	15.60	1.95	.56

Figure 8-6d

EMERSON EFFICIENCY BONUS

(1) Quantity Produced	(2) Standard Time Produced, in Minutes (2 min./piece)	(3) Actual Time Taken, in Minutes	(4) Per Cent Efficiency (Standard ÷ Actual)	(5) Bonus Per Cent	(6) Base Pay for Day (8 Hours)	(7) Bonus Amount	(8) Total Payment for Day	(9) Employee's Earned Rate Per Hour (8 Hours)	(10) Labor Cost Per Unit of Product (10 pcs./unit)
120	240	480	66⅔%	0%	$14.40		$14.40	$1.80	$1.20
160	320	480	83⅓%	10%	14.40		14.40	1.80	.90
200	400	480	100%	20%	14.40	$1.44	15.84	1.98	.79
240	480	480	116%	20%	14.40	2.88	17.28	2.16	.72
280	560	480		20%	14.40	2.88	17.28	2.16	.62

Figure 8-6e

performance percentage is 560 (standard minutes) divided by 480 (actual minutes) = 116.6 per cent. Where the operator produces a number of different products, the calculation of performance percentage is based upon standard time produced for all products and actual clock time for the day. And finally, when it is necessary to change rates for the whole line of products, the change is likely to be reasonably simple. It is necessary only to set a new base rate to reflect the desired change, and to apply the new rate to the established standard times for the products.

The concept of "standard time produced @ base rate" comes up frequently (in fact, is fundamental) in standard cost systems. Standard cost systems are introduced in Chapter 17.

Two examples of standard time plans involving bonus are presented to show the effect of such a bonus upon product cost. Under the Halsey Premium Wage plan (page 172), the operator is paid a straight hourly rate basis until he meets standard (that is, when standard time produced in a day equals actual minutes worked for the day). Above that level, the operator is given a bonus of $\frac{1}{2}$ the time saved ($1.20 in the illustration). Note that the labor cost per unit [Column (10)] decreases directly with the increase in standard time produced for the day to the point where standard is reached (480 standard minutes = 480 actual minutes). The decrease in unit cost is slower after that point, since the time saving is shared between the company and the operator. (The percentage of sharing might vary from company to company.)

Under the Emerson Efficiency Bonus (page 172), a small bonus is given before standard is reached (67 per cent in this illustrative case), and the bonus percentage is increased as the efficiency percentage goes up. The bonus is applied to the base pay. Note that the labor cost per unit of product [Column (10)] decreases as the standard time produced in eight hours increases. It decreases directly until the point where bonus begins. Beyond that point, the decrease in unit product cost is not directly proportional to the increase in production.

The plans shown are four of numerous plans available. They are sufficient to illustrate that the cost accountant is interested in (a) what the employee can be expected to get out of a proposed plan, (b) what the company can be expected to get in the way of a reduction of labor cost, and (c) the expected labor cost per product unit.

REVIEW QUESTIONS

8-1. Define direct labor, indirect labor. Assume that the cost unit is the product unit.

8-2. What distinction is made between indirect labor proper and expense labor in this chapter? What accounts are set up for expense labor?

8-3. Give several examples of labor losses or labor allowances which may be found in connection with incentive wage payment plans. Explain each example and state how the loss factor is calculated for each of the examples.

8-4. Give several examples of labor overhead and explain each example, giving appropriate entries.

8-5. What are "fringe benefits"? Give some examples.

8-6. What is the particular significance of quantity controls in piece-rate wage payment plans?

8-7. How does the mathematics of the incentive wage payment affect costs in which the cost accountant is interested? Explain with reference to specific plans.

8-8. What is meant by "normal labor cost"?

DISCUSSION QUESTIONS

8-9. Discuss the methods of charging overtime premium to product and state the conditions under which each method could properly be used.

8-10. Discuss conditions under which each of the following job classifications might be direct labor:

Foreman
Production control clerk
Payroll clerk

Machine repairman
Janitor and watchman

8-11. The Wilton Company occasionally pays different wage rates per hour for the same quantity of work. In some cases, there are seniority rates, based upon length of service, for the same job classification. In some cases, a man of a higher job classification (and higher wage rate) is used because a man of the actual job classification required is not available when the job has to be done.

How would you deal with cases of different rates of pay for the same amount of work? (The company operates an historical job order cost system.)

8-12. In some incentive wage payment plans, the cost per unit of product goes up at a particular percentage of standard output because the workman is paid a bonus at that point. Recognizing the different uses that might be made of unit product costs, how would you handle the bonus situation?

EXERCISES

8-1. The piece-work payroll of the Bowman Manufacturing Company for the week ending February 7 shows the following information:

Employee Name and Number	Piece-Work Hours and Earnings by Day							Total Hours	Hours on Allowance	Total Hours
	1 M	2 T	3 W	4 Th	5 F	6 S	7 S			
George Johnson (1)	8	8	8	8	8			40		40
	11.80	12.10	12.05	11.00	11.05					
Lynn Ford (2)	8	8	6	8	8			38	(a) 2	40
	10.80	10.90	8.40	11.10	12.00					
Charles Norton (3)	8	8	8	5	8			37	(b) 3	40
	10.15	10.30	10.60	6.50	10.55					
John Land (4)	8	8	8	8	8			40		40
	9.90	9.40	8.85	10.05	9.80					
Nick Yost (5)	8	8	10	8	6			40		40
	12.30	11.90	15.00	12.00	8.80					

(a) waiting   (b) machine delay

Features of the pay plan are as follows:

(1) The plan is basically a piece-work plan with allowances for certain specified conditions beyond the operator's control.
(2) Guaranteed rate per hour on a weekly basis is $1.25. If an employee's piece-work earnings average less than $1.25 per hour on a straight clock-hour basis, the employee is paid makeup to guarantee sufficient to make up the difference.
(3) Allowances for waiting and machine delay are paid at guaranteed rate.
(4) Overtime premium is paid on all hours over eight hours each day at the rate of one-half the average rate per hour on piece work.

Required:

(a) Using the piece-work payroll provided in the Workbook post data from the table given herewith and complete the payroll.
(b) Prepare a Weekly Labor Report similar to that in Figure 8-3.

8-2. Using the blank form provided in the Workbook, record the following transactions, filling in the information called for in Columns (a)-(e):

(1) Draft the journal entry required for the payroll completed in Exercise 8-1. Although you were not required to deduct F.I.C.A. tax in Exercise 8-1, you are required to show it in Exercise 8-2.
(2) Draft the entry which would be made in the voucher register.
(3) Make the entry to record company's share of F.I.C.A. tax at 2 per cent.
(4) Make the entry to record workmen's insurance expired at ½ of 1 per cent.
(5) Make the entry to record provision for vacation pay at 2 per cent.

Only piece work is charged to Labor in Process. Allowances and makeup are charged to separate accounts in the general ledger. Overtime premium is charged to Factory Expense. (Assume that the company operates a factory expense ledger.) The basic paper for all transactions except (2) is a journal voucher.

PROBLEM

8-1. You have been asked to set up calculations illustrating the effect of various wage payment plans upon (a) the employee's earnings in an eight-hour day, and (b) the unit labor cost of Product A produced by an employee in an eight-hour day. The following information is available:

(1) Wage rate per hour, if employee is paid on an hourly wage basis, $1.00.
(2) Labor rate per piece of Part X, if employee is paid on a piece-work basis, $.03.
(3) Standard labor time allowed per piece of Part X, if employee is paid on a standard-time basis, 1.2 minutes.

Ten pieces of Part X are required for one unit of Product A.

Required:

Make the necessary calculations for each of three wage payment plans: straight hourly wage rate, straight piece rate, and standard time @ $1.50 per hour. Under each plan, the legal minimum rate is $1.00 per clock hour worked. Assume the following quantities of Part X produced per day: 120, 160, 200, 240, 280, 320.

~~~~~~

Chapter 9

FACTORY EXPENSE: ACCOUNTING
AND CONTROL

Expense items. Purchased services; Building and machinery expense. In addition to materials and labor, discussed in Chapters 5-8, a manufacturing business ordinarily requires such expense items as *purchased services* (for example, electric power and accountants' and engineers' fees) and building and machinery expense (for example, rent, or if the plant is owned, depreciation, insurance, and property taxes). These expense items may be classified as direct or indirect with reference to a selected cost unit, just as materials and labor may be classified.

Thus, assuming the cost unit is a product unit, building and machinery expense is:

Direct expense, if it is identified with a particular product and if it is considered feasible to measure it in terms of product units and charge the cost sheets of the product. (There are numerous cases where a building and all the machinery in it are used to produce a single product, perhaps for a single customer. Building and machinery expense in such cases is a direct expense of the product.)

Indirect expense, if it is used for the benefit of a number of products and if it cannot be readily identified with any particular product. This is the usual situation where a single factory and set of machinery is used to make a varied line of products.

Unused capacity loss, if the building and machinery are not used during a measured period and if depreciation, insurance, and taxes are considered a cost of idleness and not an expense of production. (The *unabsorbed expense* balance which is explained in this chapter is partly the cost of unused capacity, charged off to Profit and Loss at the end of the year.)

I. CLASSIFICATION OF FACTORY EXPENSE
FOR CONTROL IN A SMALL FACTORY

Factory expense defined: Classification by (a) object and (b) variability. Factory expense is the sum of the indirect elements of cost incurred to turn out a product: indirect materials, indirect labor, and indirect expense items such as purchased services and building and machinery expense, as described above.

An object classification is a classification according to the nature of the goods or services used. Most small manufacturing concerns use an object classification for recording factory expense. The following object classification is used by the Benson Manufacturing Company, whose factory is diagrammed on page 178. (Benson Manufacturing Company is successor to John Benson, Manufacturer, whose factory is diagrammed in Fig 3-2.)

BENSON MANUFACTURING COMPANY
Factory Expense Account Classification

Account No.	Account Name
510	Indirect labor
520	Overtime premium
531	F.I.C.A. tax expense
532	Workmen's insurance expense
540	Indirect materials, factory supplies, and repair parts
561	Heat, light, and power
562	Freight on materials
580	Unclassified factory expense
591	Depreciation—Machinery and equipment
592	Taxes—Machinery and equipment
599	Rent on factory

Figure 9-1

Note that accounts in the 510, 520, and 530 groups are related to labor. Accounts in the 540 group are comprised of indirect materials and supplies. Accounts in the 560 group are purchased services. Accounts in the 590 group include the building and equipment expenses, depreciation, insurance, taxes, and rent.

The number and assortment of accounts shown is probably the minimum on which a company like the Benson Manufacturing Company could operate satisfactorily. If additional accounts are desired, they can be added within the grouping indicated, since the numbering plan provides for orderly expansion. Under the indirect labor heading, for instance, a separate account could be provided for each important indirect labor occupation, such as supervision, factory clerical, repairmen, materials handlers, and janitors and watchmen. Under the 540 group, separate accounts could be added for lubricants, or printed forms, or repair parts, if desired. A similar expansion is possible for the purchased services group (560). The rule in general is that if a significant amount of money is spent for a particular object, an account can be set up for it. It is desirable to avoid having too many different objects in the same account, on the one hand, and too many separate object accounts with insignificant balances on the other hand.

Note also that the accounts in the classification are grouped roughly according to the nature and type of remedial action that can be taken to control the expense. At the bottom of the list are the fixed charges, about which almost nothing can be done as a short-run measure. At the top of the list are the labor items which it is at least theoretically possible for the manager to do something about. In the middle of the list are the goods and services the continuance and amounts of which are to some extent subject to managerial decision. Such objects as travel and technical society dues, for instance, are subject to a very considerable control by management. To some extent, certain repair and maintenance programs can be spread out, considering financial needs of the business as well as operating needs.

BENSON MANUFACTURING COMPANY

FACTORY

North Street

OFFICE	PARTS STORES	CUTTING DEPARTMENT	RAW MATERIALS STORES			East Street
			Receiving Room	Dock		
		ASSEMBLY DEPARTMENT	Shipping Room	Loading Dock		
For Future Occupancy			FINISHED GOODS STORES			

Figure 9-2

Managerial information. For the control of factory expense in a relatively small organization like the Benson Manufacturing Company, the management needs a monthly expense statement showing the actual expense incurred for each object. Comparisons with the actual expenses of previous months, or with a budget of expenses, should be provided to give the management a measuring stick for judging spending performance. In the latter case, the budget can be (a) a fixed budget, one set up at the beginning of a period on the basis of expected volume of operations for the period or (b) a flexible budget, one that is adjusted at the end of each month to reflect the actual volume of operations for the month. In making the adjustment, the variable items in the budget are scaled up or down as allowable for the actual level, and the fixed items are included unchanged.

The use of fixed budgets for the control of factory expense is illustrated in the present chapter. Flexible budgets for the control of expense are illustrated in Chapter 19.

Monthly factory expense statement; Control in a small factory.
The monthly factory expense statement for the Benson Manufacturing
Company provides an accounts column in which the expense account classi-
fication is shown, and also columns for (1) actual expense for the month,
(2) budget expense, and (3) increase or decrease of actual over budget.
An illustration appears below.

The budget is a fixed budget, based upon 8,000 hours of operation. Since
the actual hours (7,930) was only slightly less than budget, there should not
be much difference between actual expense and budget expense.   For
fixed expenses, most of which are placed at the bottom of the statement,
there should be no difference.   For the other expenses (which are called the
variable expenses), actual expense should be slightly less than budget
expense, if anything, since the actual volume of operations measured in
actual labor hours is less than the volume upon which the budget was based.

BENSON MANUFACTURING COMPANY
Factory Expense Statement—Month of February, 19—

Object Accounts	Actual Expense	Budget Expense	Excess (Saving*) over Budget
Hours..............................	7,930	8,000	
VARIABLE EXPENSE:			
Indirect labor......................	$1,951.60	$1,710.00	$241.60
Overtime premium...................	8.40		8.40
F.I.C.A. tax.......................	250.74	264.60	13.86*
Workmen's insurance................	242.46	235.00	7.46
Indirect materials, supplies, and			
repair parts......................	750.00	600.00	150.00
Heat, light, and power..............	99.43	190.00	90.57*
Freight on materials.................	800.00	600.00	200.00
Unclassified.......................	160.00	163.03	3.03*
Total variable expense...........	$4,262.63	$3,762.63	$500.00
FIXED EXPENSE:			
Depreciation—Machinery and equipment	$ 266.66	$ 266.66	$
Insurance—Machinery and equipment..	200.88	200.88	
Taxes—Machinery and equipment......	277.33	277.33	
Rent on building...................	1,492.50	1,492.50	
Total fixed expense..............	$2,237.37	$2,237.37	$
Total factory expense............	$6,500.00	$6,000.00	$500.00

Figure 9-3

Note that the actual expense of certain items is actually greater than the
budget expense.   Examples are indirect labor (which is $241.60 over the
budget) and indirect materials, supplies, and repair parts (over $150).
These expenses should be investigated by the manager to determine the
causes and correct them, if possible.   He would be likely to ask on what

occupation the excess indirect labor was spent and on what type of indirect materials, supplies, and repair part the excess in that group was spent.   To get the answer, the cost man would have to analyze the two accounts, the first named account by occupation and the second account by sub-object.

The manager can likely form a good opinion of whether an increase in an occupation or a sub-object was necessary. If it develops that an additional materials handler was added part time, the manager would know whether the addition was justified in view of what types of products were being processed. Likewise, it may appear that there has been a large increase in the charges for repair parts. The manager would be likely to know whether the increase is justified in the light of the number and type of repair jobs done.

Since the manager's inevitable first question in this company, as in all relatively small concerns, is "What did we spend the extra money for?" the cost man may decide to put a few more accounts in the expense ledger. He may decide to add an indirect labor account for each of the major occupations (supervision, factory clerical, repairmen, materials handlers, and janitors and watchmen). He may also decide to set up separate accounts for indirect materials and operating supplies (one account) maintenance supplies, and repair parts. The cost man will have to decide whether to do the extra work of recording required to keep the additional accounts or to do the analysis which will otherwise be required, by digging into the accounts after the end of the month, when the manager begins to ask questions.

II.   OPERATING THE FACTORY EXPENSE ACCOUNTS

Actual expense defined; Recording actual expenses.   Actual expense may be defined as expense incurred, recorded on the accrual basis. Actual expense is recorded *in detail* on a day-to-day basis in the accounts in the factory expense ledger and *by totals* at the end of the month in the Factory Expense Control account.   The monthly expense statement is prepared from the accounts in the expense ledger (and other information).

The journals from which factory expense accounts are posted are voucher register and requisition journal (Figure 9-4) and the general journal (Figure 9-5).

Voucher Register.   1. Enter disbursement vouchers in the voucher register, during the month.   For vouchers affecting Factory Expense, enter debits in the Factory Expense Control, Debit column, showing the amount and the factory expense ledger account number.   The vouchers shown represent respectively (114) freight on materials, (115) indirect materials and supplies delivered by the supplier to the custody of the foreman for immediate use, (117) factory rent, (118) electric power, and (119)

RECORDING ACTUAL FACTORY EXPENSES—I

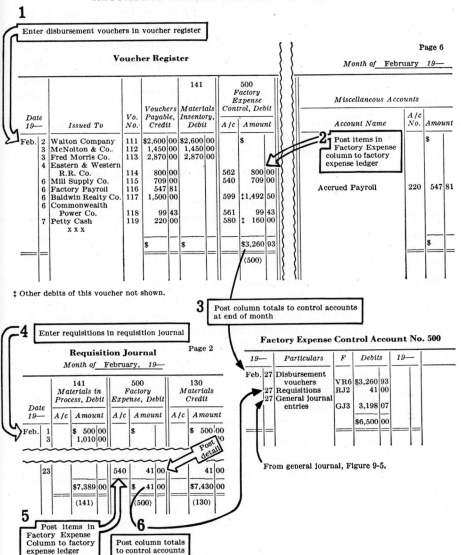

1 Enter disbursement vouchers in voucher register

Voucher Register

Page 6

Month of February 19—

Date 19—	Issued To	Vo. No.	Vouchers Payable, Credit	Materials Inventory, Debit (141)	Factory Expense Control, Debit (500) A/c	Factory Expense Control, Debit (500) Amount	Miscellaneous Accounts Account Name	A/c No.	Amount
Feb. 2	Walton Company	111	$2,600 00	$2,600 00		$			$
3	McNolton & Co.	112	1,450 00	1,450 00					
3	Fred Morris Co.	113	2,870 00	2,870 00					
4	Eastern & Western R.R. Co.	114	800 00		562	800 00			
6	Mill Supply Co.	115	709 00		540	709 00	Accrued Payroll	220	547 81
6	Factory Payroll	116	547 81						
6	Baldwin Realty Co.	117	1,500 00		599	‡1,492 50			
6	Commonwealth Power Co.	118	99 43		561	99 43			
7	Petty Cash	119	220 00		580	‡ 160 00			
	x x x								
			$	$		$3,260 93			$
						(500)			

2 Post items in Factory Expense column to factory expense ledger

‡ Other debits of this voucher not shown.

3 Post column totals to control accounts at end of month

4 Enter requisitions in requisition journal

Requisition Journal

Page 2

Month of February, 19—

Date 19—	Materials in Process, Debit (141) A/c	Materials in Process, Debit (141) Amount	Factory Expense, Debit (500) A/c	Factory Expense, Debit (500) Amount	Materials Credit (130) A/c	Materials Credit (130) Amount
Feb. 1		$ 500 00		$		$ 500 00
3		1,010 00				0
23			540	41 00		41 00
		$7,389 00		$ 41 00		$7,430 00
		(141)		(500)		(130)

Post detail

Factory Expense Control Account No. 500

19—	Particulars	F	Debits	19—
Feb. 27	Disbursement vouchers	VR6	$3,260 93	
27	Requisitions	RJ2	41 00	
27	General journal entries	GJ3	3,198 07	
			$6,500 00	

From general journal, Figure 9-5.

5 Post items in Factory Expense Column to factory expense ledger

6 Post column totals to control accounts

Figure 9-4

181

unclassified factory expense items. Enter credits in Voucher Payable Credit column.

2. Post the items in the Factory Expense Control, Debit column, to the accounts in the factory expense ledger day by day.

3. At the end of the month, foot and cross-foot the voucher register and *post the appropriate column totals to control accounts* in the general ledger. In the illustration, the total of the Factory Expense Control, Debit column ($3,260.93), is posted to the Factory Expense Control account in the general ledger.

Requisition Journal. 4. Enter requisitions for indirect materials in the requisition journal along with requisitions for direct materials, during the month. Enter the former in the Factory Expense, Debit column, showing both the amount of the requisition and the number of the factory expense account to be charged.

5. Post the items in the Factory Expense, Debit column, to the appropriate accounts in the factory expense ledger, day by day.

6. At the end of the month, foot and cross-foot the requisition journal and *post the column totals to the control accounts* in the general ledger. In the illustration, the total of Factory Expense, Debit column, is posted to the Factory Expense Control account in the general ledger.

General Journal. 7. Make journal entries for factory payrolls, during the month. (See entry for the payroll for the week ending February 6.) In making these entries, enter the charges to factory expense in the Factory Expense Control, Debit column, showing both the amounts and the account numbers. In the illustration, there is a charge for indirect labor and one for overtime premium.

8. Post the items in the Factory Expense Control, Debit column, to the appropriate accounts in the factory expense ledger, day by day.

9. Record the monthly adjusting entries which affect factory expense, at the end of the month. Enter the debits to factory expense accounts in the Factory Expense Control, Debit column, showing both amount and account number. The following entries appearing in the illustration are typical:

> F.I.C.A. tax accrued—company's share
> Workmen's insurance expense expired
> Depreciation on machinery and equipment
> Insurance on machinery and equipment
> Taxes on machinery and equipment

Post the debits from the journal to the accounts in the factory expense ledger.

10. Also at the end of the month, foot and cross-foot the columns of the general journal. *Post the total of the Factory Expense Control, Debit column, to the Factory Expense Control account in the general ledger.* In the illustration, the posting to the control account is $3,198.07.

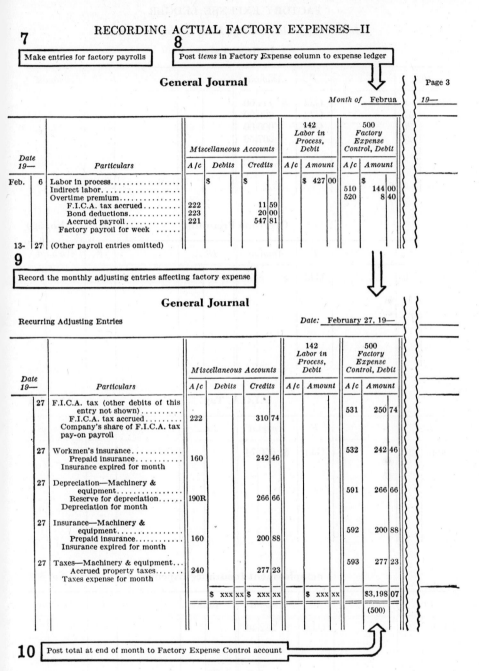

7 Make entries for factory payrolls

8 Post *items* in Factory Expense column to expense ledger

General Journal

Page 3

Month of ___Februa___   19—

Date 19—	Particulars	Miscellaneous Accounts			142 Labor in Process, Debit		500 Factory Expense Control, Debit	
		A/c	Debits	Credits	A/c	Amount	A/c	Amount
Feb. 6	Labor in process...............		$	$		$ 427 00		$
	Indirect labor.................						510	144 00
	Overtime premium.............						520	8 40
	F.I.C.A. tax accrued.........	222		11 59				
	Bond deductions.............	223		20 00				
	Accrued payroll.............	221		547 81				
	Factory payroll for week							
13- 27	(Other payroll entries omitted)							

9 Record the monthly adjusting entries affecting factory expense

General Journal

Recurring Adjusting Entries

Date: ___February 27, 19—___

Date 19—	Particulars	Miscellaneous Accounts			142 Labor in Process, Debit		500 Factory Expense Control, Debit	
		A/c	Debits	Credits	A/c	Amount	A/c	Amount
27	F.I.C.A. tax (other debits of this entry not shown).........						531	250 74
	F.I.C.A. tax accrued........	222		310 74				
	Company's share of F.I.C.A. tax pay-on payroll							
27	Workmen's insurance...........						532	242 46
	Prepaid insurance..........	160		242 46				
	Insurance expired for month							
27	Depreciation—Machinery & equipment...............						591	266 66
	Reserve for depreciation......	190R		266 66				
	Depreciation for month							
27	Insurance—Machinery & equipment...............						592	200 88
	Prepaid insurance...........	160		200 88				
	Insurance expired for month							
27	Taxes—Machinery & equipment...						593	277 23
	Accrued property taxes.......	240		277 23				
	Taxes expense for month							
			$ xxx xx	$ xxx xx		$ xxx xx		$3,198 07
								(500)

10 Post total at end of month to Factory Expense Control account

Figure 9-5

FACTORY EXPENSE LEDGER

(Illustratings Detail Postings Made During the Month)

Indirect Labor   No. 510

19__		F	Amount	19__		F	Amount
Feb.	6	GJ3	$ 144 00				
	13	GJ3	600 00				
	20	GJ3	600 00				
	27	GJ3	607 60				
			1,951 60				

Overtime Premium   No. 520

19__		F	Amount	19__		F	Amount
Feb.	6	GJ3	$ 8 40				

F.I.C.A. Tax   No. 531

19__		F	Amount	19__		F	Amount
Feb.	27	GJ3	$ 250 74				

Unemployment Insurance Expense   No. 532

19__		F	Amount	19__		F	Amount
Feb.	27	GJ3	$ 242 46				

Figure 9-6a

19__		F	Amount	19__		F	Amount
Feb. 6		VR6	$ 709 00				
27		RJ2	41 00				

Heat, Light, and Power   No. 561

19__		F	Amount	19__		F	Amount
Feb. 6		VR6	$ 99 43				

Freight on Materials   No. 562

19__		F	Amount	19__		F	Amount
Feb. 4		VR6	$ 800 00				

Unclassified Factory Expense   No. 580

19__		F	Amount	19__		F	Amount
Feb. 27		VR6	$ 160 00				

Figure 9-6b

Depreciation—Machinery and Equipment　　　　No. 591

19__			F	Amount		19__			F	Amount
Feb.	27		GJ3	$ 266 66						

Insurance—Machinery and Equipment　　　　No. 592

19__			F	Amount		19__			F	Amount
Feb.	27		GJ3	$ 200 88						

Taxes—Machinery and Equipment　　　　No. 593

19__			F	Amount		19__			F	Amount
Feb.	27		GJ3	$ 277 33						

Rent on Factory　　　　No. 599

19__			F	Amount		19__			F	Amount
Feb.	6		VR6	$1,492 50						

Figure 9-6c

No postings of items other than factory expense items are illustrated in Figures 9-4 and 9-5.   The items in the miscellaneous columns of the general journal would, of course, be posted in detail to the general ledger.

Postings to factory expense ledger accounts are illustrated on pages 184 to 186.

Trial Balance of the factory expense ledger is illustrated on this page. Note that the sum of the balances of subsidiary factory expense accounts ($6,500) agrees with the balance of the Factory Expense Control account, page 197.

BENSON MANUFACTURING COMPANY
Trial Balance—Factory Expense Ledger

February 28, 19—

No.	Account Name	Amount
510	Indirect labor	$1,951.60
520	Overtime premiums	8.40
531	F.I.C.A. tax	250.74
532	Unemployment insurance expense	242.46
540	Factory supplies, indirect materials, and repair parts	750.00
561	Heat, light, and power	99.43
562	Freight on materials	800.00
580	Unclassified factory expense	160.00
591	Depreciation—machinery and equipment	266.66
592	Insurance—machinery and equipment	200.88
593	Taxes—machinery and equipment	277.33
599	Rent on factory	1,492.50
	Total, per accounts	$6,500.00
	Agrees with control account number	500

Figure 9-7

III. EXPENSE APPLIED: ACTUAL BASIS AND NORMAL BASIS

The problem of how to apply expense to cost sheets; Factory expense rates.   Factory expense consists of items which by definition (a) are not identified with particular products or (b) cannot be measured with a reasonable amount of effort and charged to the cost sheets.   Since direct measurement in terms of product units is not possible or feasible, factory expense must be applied to cost sheets by more arbitrary means than direct measurement.   If a single product were produced, it might be feasible to divide the total expense for the month by the total number of units produced to arrive at an average expense cost per unit of product. There might be certain disadvantages to this method of applying expense, as will appear later in this chapter, but at least it would be the simplest method of applying expense to the units of a single product.

On the other hand, if several products are being manufactured, it must be recognized that some of the products may have received the benefit of more factory expense than have other products. It is necessary to select some quantitative factor common to all products and consequently all production orders, and to apply expense to cost sheets on the basis of that factor.

One of the factors common to all products and all orders is *direct labor hours*. It might be considered feasible to apply factory expense to jobs on the basis of the number of direct labor hours. This could be done by dividing factory expense for the month by direct labor hours for the month, and applying the resulting expense rate per hour to the direct labor hours posted to the cost sheets.

Expressed as a formula, the rate would be:

$$\text{Direct labor hour rate} = \frac{\text{Factory expense for month}}{\text{Direct labor hours for month}}$$

Using expense and hour figures for the Benson Manufacturing Company for February, the rate would be:

$$\text{Direct labor hour rate} = \frac{\$6,500.00}{7,930 \text{ hours}} = \$.8196+ \text{ per hour}$$

The direct labor hour rate is only one of a number of types of rate which might be used. One of the problems of the cost accountant is to select the rate or combination of rates which will apply factory expense equitably to the various products, that is, which will avoid penalizing one product to the advantage of some other product. A number of types are explained and illustrated in Chapter 10. Some factors to consider in selecting the proper type of rate are also discussed.

Actual rates and normal rates. An *actual* rate is one which is computed at the end of the month on the basis of actual factory expense and actual hours (in case of direct labor hour rate). The rate computed in the previous section is an actual rate. An actual rate is applied to the cost sheets for the month at the end of the month and, since expense and hours are likely to change from month to month, the actual expense rate is likely to be different month by month.

A *normal* rate is one which is computed at the beginning of a year on the basis of expected average expense per month for a full year and expected average hours per month for a full year.* A normal rate can be applied to the cost sheet for a production order as soon as the order is finished in the factory. And finally, the normal rate does not change from month to month as the actual rate usually does; the same normal rate is ordinarily used throughout the year.

Sections IV and V of this chapter illustrate and explain the accounting

---

* The term "normal rate" is used in this chapter to mean an *expected actual* rate for a coming one-year period; an average rate which anticipates the year's actual expense and actual hours. Other types of normal rate are explained in Chapter 11.

procedure for applying: (1) actual rates to cost sheets, (2) normal rates to cost sheets.

IV. EXPENSE APPLIED: ACTUAL BASIS

Procedure for actual basis. The procedure for (a) compiling actual expense and (b) applying expense to cost sheets by means of actual rates involves the following steps:

(1) to (10)—Compile actual factory expenses in the voucher register, the requisition journal, and the general journal during the month, and post totals to the Factory Expense Control account at the end of the month. This part of the procedure has been explained in the previous sections of this chapter.

(11)   At the end of the month, calculate the actual factory expense rate.

(12)   Apply actual expense rate to the hours which have been posted to the cost sheets during the month.

(13)   Make a general journal to record total factory expense applied.

11.   *Calculate Actual Expense Rate at End of Month.*   The formula is:

$$\frac{\text{Actual direct labor}}{\text{hour rate}} = \frac{\text{Actual factory expense per Factory Expense account}}{\text{Actual direct labor hours posted to cost sheets}}$$

The rate computed is:

$$\frac{\$6,500}{7,930 \text{ hours}} = \$.8196+ \text{ per hour}$$

The total actual hours could be obtained by recapping the totals of hours posted to the cost sheets during the month, or by using the total direct labor hours per the Daily Labor Time Summary, which shows the same total (7,930 direct labor hours).   The hour totals from both sources would have to be the same, since the hours on the cost sheets are totaled and proved against the Daily Labor Time Summary as a regular proof operation.

The actual factory expense rate would be expected to change from month to month in a seasonal business, as explained on page 191.

12. *Apply Actual Rate to Cost Sheets at End of Month.*   Under actual basis, all the cost sheets worked upon during the month are held until the end of the month.   Subtotals of hours worked during the month are then entered on the cost sheets.

Expense applied to a cost sheet equals actual hours worked during the month multiplied by actual rate for the month.   In the illustration on page 190, the amount applied in the summary section of the cost sheet for Production Order No. 104 is:

$$1,670 \text{ hours} \times \$.8196+ \text{ per hour} = \$1,368.73$$

APPLYING FACTORY EXPENSE TO COST SHEETS

(Actual Basis)

Cost Sheet

Produ~~~~er No. _____ 104

Date Rele~~~ Jan. 28, 19__

Date order completed

Quantity and Description _____ 1,320 Units Product A _____

Date Started _____

Made For _____

Date Completed _____ Feb. 12, 19__

MATERIALS				LABOR						
					Cutting		Assembly		Total	
Date 19__	Amount		Date 19__	Hours	Amount	Hours	Amount	Hours	Amount	
Feb. 1	$ 500 00		Feb. 1	16	$ 20 80		$	16	$ 20 80	
3	1,010 00		2	32	44 80			32	44 80	
5	551 20		3	52	72 80			52	72 80	
			4	52	72 80			52	72 80	
			5	52	72 80			52	72 80	
			W/E 13	126	178 00	1,340	1,742 00	1,466	1,920 00	
	$2,061 20			330	$ 462 00	1,340	$1,742 00	1,670	$2,204 00	

Date cost sheet completed (actual basis)

SUMMARY	Actual	Summarized By	Date
Materials.........................	$2,061 20		
Labor.............................	2,204 00	George North	Feb. 28, 19__
Factory expense:		Finished Goods Ledger	Date
1,670 hours @ $.8196+..............	1,368 73		
Total cost........................	$5,633 93	Finished Goods Journal	Date
Cost per unit.....................	$ 4 27		

12 | Applying actual expense rate to hours which have been posted to cost sheets during month

Figure 9-8

Note that this particular order was completed on February 12 and held until the end of the month for the application of factory expense. Where costs are used for the measurement of performance, holding the cost sheets until the end of the month is a disadvantage of actual basis. Where the performance by a cost sheet is unsatisfactory, the management wants to follow up as soon as possible. A delay from the twelfth of the month until the end of the month might be serious. The application of actual factory expense rates to cost sheets may give important information as to product costs as such, but the information is usually too late to be of value for control purposes.

The illustration (page 190) shows the entry on one cost sheet. The factory expense rate for February would be applied to *all* the cost sheets which received labor postings during the month. If such an order is not actually finished, the charge is recorded in small figures, so that the charge for next month can be added at the end of next month. Any order receives an application of factory expense each month that it is worked upon.

13. *Make General Journal to Record Total Factory Expense Applied.* At the end of the month, a general journal entry is made to record the total of factory expense applied to the cost sheets. The entry is a debit to Factory Expense in Process and a credit to Factory Expense, as shown. The amount is:

$$\begin{array}{ccc} \text{Actual hours} & \times & \dfrac{\text{Actual expense rate}}{} = \dfrac{\text{Total expense applied}}{} \\ 7{,}930 & & \$.8196+ \qquad\qquad \$6{,}500 \end{array}$$

Under the actual basis, total expense applied to the cost sheets agrees with the total of actual debits to the Factory Expense account, since the *rate* applied to the cost sheets ($.8196+) is computed on the basis of the debit balance of the Factory Expense account at the end of the month. The journal entry to record expense applied accordingly closes the Factory Expense account.

Actual factory expense rates in a seasonal business. The chart "Illustrative Actual Factory Expense Rates in a Seasonal Business" (Figure 9-9) shows graphically how factory expense rates might vary over the months of the year in a seasonal business. The fluctuation in the actual rate suggests what might be expected in any seasonal business. (The fluctuation would be greater in some businesses than in others.)

Direct labor hours are plotted as line (A). Note that the factory operates at the lowest level (6,000 hours) in January. Production rises to a peak (10,000 hours) in April and May and then goes down to 6,000 in November and December.

Rates per hour are plotted as line (B). The rate per hour is highest in the months of lowest production measured in hours, and lowest in months of highest production. The rates range from a high of $.84 per hour at the 6,000 hour level in January to a low of $.695 per hour at the 10,000 hour level in April and May.

The rates per hour which were plotted by months in Figure 9-9 were calculated on the basis of the data assembled in Figure 9-10, "Factory Expense and Factory Expense Rates by Level of Production."

Figure 9-10 is a graph used to project factory expense rates for all levels from zero to 100 per cent of capacity. The graph is based upon the factory expense budget for the 8,000 hour level ($2,200 of fixed expense and $3,800 of variable expense), set up by the cost accountant as shown in Figure 9-3. Use of the graph makes it possible to determine the rate for any other level

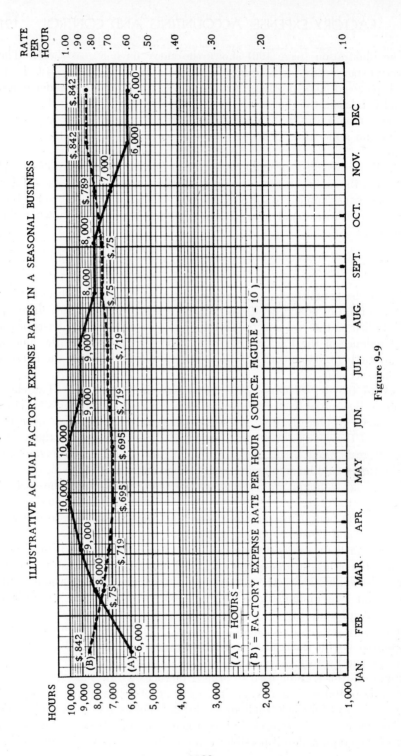

ILLUSTRATIVE ACTUAL FACTORY EXPENSE RATES IN A SEASONAL BUSINESS

(A) = HOURS

(B) = FACTORY EXPENSE RATE PER HOUR (SOURCE: FIGURE 9 – 10)

Figure 9-9

**Factory Expense and Factory Expense Rates
by Level of Production**

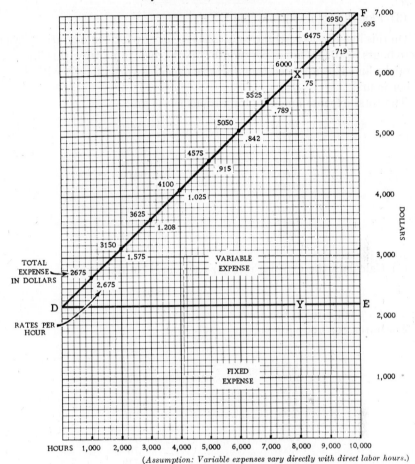

(*Assumption: Variable expenses vary directly with direct labor hours.*)

Figure 9-10

from the factors used in calculating the rate at 8,000 hours.   The assumption is made that variable expenses vary directly with direct labor hours.

This assumption may not be strictly valid, but it does suffice to support the illustration that actual factory expense rates do vary with level of production, due to the existence of fixed expenses.

To prepare the projection in Figure 9-10 from the budget data in Figure 9-3, the steps are:

(1) Plot the fixed expense ($2,200) as the same amount for all levels by setting out the horizontal line D-E.

(2) Plot X. the total factory expense ($6,000) at the 8,000 hour level.

Note that the vertical distance XY is *variable* expense at the 8,000 hour level.

(3) Plot the total expense line DXF.

On this line can be read the total expense for any level of operations from zero hours to 10,000 hours per month.   Note that, in plotting this line as a straight line, it is assumed that variable expenses vary directly with direct labor hours.

The total expense amounts for various levels are:

Hours	*Amounts*
1,000	$2,675.00
2,000	3,150.00
3,000	3,625.00
4,000	4,100.00
5,000	4,575.00
6,000	5,050.00
7,000	5,525.00
8,000	6,000.00
9,000	6,475.00
10,000	6,950.00

(4) Calculate the expense rate for each level by the formula

$$\text{Expense} \div \text{Hours} = \text{Rate}$$

and enter each rate on the chart.

The rates per hour for various levels are:

Hours	*Rate*
1,000	$2.675
2,000	1.575
3,000	1.208
4,000	1.025
5,000	.915
6,000	.842
7,000	.789
8,000	.75
9,000	.719
10,000	.695

V. EXPENSE APPLIED: NORMAL BASIS

Significance of the normal rate as a predetermined rate.   It was stated above that the normal rate is computed at the beginning of a year, that it is not ordinarily changed during the year, and that it is applied to the cost sheet of a production order as soon as the order is finished.   There are a number of implications in the fact that the normal rate is predetermined and, therefore, used in this manner.   In the first place, use of normal rates makes it unnecessary to hold the cost sheets until the end of the month; they can be completed as soon as the job is finished and action can be taken on them immediately.

In the second place, since they are computed for a full year in advance, they can be used as the basis for catalog prices. In fact, normal rates *have* to be used for predetermined costs where price lists have to be sent out before the goods are produced. Furthermore, normal rates are not high in periods of low production and the reverse, as actual rates would be. They are, therefore, more suitable from the standpoint of price list requirements. It is not likely to be possible to cancel a price list and issue a new one—with higher prices—when the volume falls. The price list has to reflect an average rate for the slack season and the busy season.

Procedure for normal basis. The procedure for (a) compiling actual expense and (b) applying expense to cost sheets by means of normal rates involves the following steps:

(1)-(10)—Compile actual expense during each month and charge totals to Factory Expense at the end of each month. This is the same as for actual basis.

(11) At the *beginning of the year*, compute the normal expense rate on the basis of expected expense and hours for the year.

(12) During each month, when an order is finished, apply the normal expense rate to the cost sheet and complete the costing of the production order.

(13) At the end of each month, make a general journal entry to record the expense applied to cost sheets during the month.

11. *At the Beginning of the Year, Calculate Normal Expense Rate.* The normal expense rate is calculated at the beginning of the year on the basis of the best estimate that can be made of expense and hours for the coming period. The formula is:

$$\text{Normal expense rate per hour} = \frac{\text{Expense for normal month}}{\text{Hours for normal month}}$$

The rate is calculated:

$$\frac{\$6,000}{8,000 \text{ hours}} = \$.75 \text{ per hour}$$

12. *When a Production Order is Finished, Apply Normal Expense Rate.* Under normal basis, expense is applied to a cost sheet *as soon as the order is finished in the factory.* Expense applied to a cost sheet = actual hours worked and posted to the cost sheet multiplied by the normal expense rate. In the illustration, the amount of factory expense applied to the cost sheet for Production Order No. 104 is:

$$1,670 \text{ hours} \times \$.75 \text{ per hour} = \$1,252.50$$

This is the same order that was illustrated previously in this chapter. It was completed in the factory on February 12. Under the normal basis, the rate would be applied the next day and the cost sheet completed. Note

APPLYING FACTORY EXPENSE TO COST SHEETS

(Normal Basis)

Cost Sheet

Pro~~~~ *rder No.*   104

Date Re.

Quantity and Description   1,320 Units Product A

Date Started

Made For

Date Completed   Feb. 12, 19__

MATERIALS				Cutting		Assembly		Total	
Date 19__	Amount	Date 19__		Hours	Amount	Hours	Amount	Hours	Amount
Feb. 1	$ 500 00	Feb.	1	16	$ 20 80		$	16	$ 20 80
3	1,010 00		2	32	44 80			32	44 80
5	551 20		3	52	72 80			52	72 80
			4	52	72 80			52	72 80
			5	52	72 80			52	72 80
		W/E	13	126	178 00	1,340	1,742 00	1,466	1,920 00
	$2,061 20			330	$ 462 00	1,340	1,742 00	1,670	$2,204 00

LABOR

Date cost sheet completed (normal basis)

SUMMARY	Actual		Summarized	Date
Materials..................................	$2,061 20			
Labor.....................................	2,204 00		George North	Feb. 13, 19__
Factory expense:			*Finished Goods Ledger*	Date
1,670 hours @ $.75.....................	1,252 50			
Total cost............................	$5,517 70		*Finished Goods Journal*	Date
Cost per unit........	$ 4 18			

> **12** When an order is finished, apply normal factory expense rate to cost sheet

Figure 9-11

that if no orders were actually finished during the month, no entries would be made on the cost sheets. When an order *is* finished, the normal rate for a given year is applied to the total of hours worked during the year as shown by that cost sheet.

13. *At End of Month Make Journal Entry for Expense Applied; Underabsorbed Expense.* Under normal basis, expense applied for the month is recorded by a general journal entry debiting Factory Expense in Process and crediting Factory Expense Applied. The amount is:

$$\underset{7,930}{\text{Actual hours}} \times \underset{75¢}{\text{Normal expense rate}} = \underset{\$5,947.50}{\text{Total expense applied}}$$

13

Make general journal entry to record expense applied

General Journal

Month of February   }   19___

Date 19___		Particulars	Miscellaneous Accounts		
			A/c	Debits	Credits
Feb.	27	Factory expense in process........	143	$5,947 50	$
		Factory expense applied......	500A		5,947 50
		To record factory expense applied:			
		7,930 hours @ 75¢ = $5,947.50			

Factory Expense Control   No. 500

19___			F	Amount	19___			F	Amount
Feb.	27	Disbursement vouchers.....	VR6	$3,260 93					
	27	Requisitions....	RJ2	41 00					
	27	General journal items........	GJ3	3,198 07					
				$6,500 00					

Factory Expense Applied   No. 500A

19___		F	Amount	19___			F	Amount
				Feb.	27	Applied expense		$5,947 50

Unabsorbed expense = $6,500.00 − $5,947.50 = $552.50

Factory Expense in Process Control   No. 143

19___			F	Amount	19___			F	Amount
Feb.	1	Inventory......		$1,012 50					
		Expense applied	GJ	5,947 50					

Figure 9-12

Under the normal basis, expense applied will not agree with the actual expense for the month except by coincidence.   In the illustration, the debit balance of Factory Expense account ($6,500) exceeds the credit balance of Factory Expense Applied account ($5,947.50).   The excess of the debit balance over the credit balance ($552.50) is called "Underapplied (or Underabsorbed) Factory Expense."   If the credit balance of the Factory Expense Applied account exceeds the debit balance of the Factory Expense account, the difference is known as "Overapplied (or Overabsorbed) Factory Expense."

Statement of factory expense and factory expense applied.   A statement of factory expense and factory expense applied is illustrated on page 199.   It is similar to the factory expense statement shown on page 179, except for the applied expense and underabsorbed section at the bottom.

The bottom of the statement (below "Actual Factory Expense, Total") is an analysis of underabsorbed expense by causes.   This section is useful in answering the manager's question, when the underabsorbed expense is large, as to what caused it.

Note: In Column (1), the net underabsorbed expense is $552.50.   This is the difference between actual expense, $6,500, and applied expense, $5,947.50.

In Column (3), the excess of actual spending over the budget, ($500) (one of the causes of underabsorbed expense) is actual expense, $6,500 minus budget expense, $6,000.

In Column (2), the underabsorbed expense due to volume is budget expense, $6,000, less applied expense, $5,947.50.   Note that if volume were 8,000 hours, as expected, instead of 7,930 hours, the full $6,000 of the budget would have been charged to cost sheets and eventually to cost of sales, to be recovered through shipments billed to customers.

Behavior of the underabsorbed expense balance over the year. In the operation of the Factory Expense account and the Factory Expense Applied account over the year, the following facts are pertinent:

In a slack month, it would be expected that the credit to Factory Expense Applied (being based upon a relatively small number of hours) will tend to be less than the debit to Factory Expense.   In other words, less expense will be charged to the cost sheets than was actually incurred.

In a busy month, it would be expected that the credit to Factory Expense Applied account (being based upon a relatively large number of hours) will be greater than the debit to Factory Expense.   In other words, more expense will be charged to the cost sheets than was actually incurred.

Over the course of a full year (a full normal cycle), it is expected that the accumulated credits to the Factory Expense Applied account will just about balance the accumulated debits to the Factory Expense account. They *will* balance if the expense for the year agrees with the estimated or

BENSON MANUFACTURING COMPANY
Statement of Factory Expense and Factory Expense Applied

Month of February, 19—

	(1) Actual Expense	(2) Budget Expense	(3) Excess (Saving*) over Budget
Object Accounts			
Hours..............................	7,930	8,000	
VARIABLE EXPENSE:			
Indirect labor......................	$1,951.60	$1,710.00	$241.60
Overtime premium...................	8.40		8.40
F.I.C.A. tax.......................	250.74	264.60	13.86*
Unemployment insurance.............	242.46	235.00	7.46
Indirect materials, supplies and			
repair parts......................	750.00	600.00	150.00
Heat, light, and power..............	99.43	190.00	90.57*
Freight on materials................	800.00	600.00	200.00
Unclassified.......................	160.00	163.03	3.03*
Total variable expense...........	$4,262.63	$3,762.63	$500.00
FIXED EXPENSE:			
Depreciation—Machinery and equipment	$ 266.66	$ 266.66	$
Insurance—Machinery and equipment..	200.88	200.88	
Taxes—Machinery and equipment......	277.33	277.33	
Rent on building....................	1,492.50	1,492.50	
Total fixed expense..............	$2,237.37	$2,237.37	$
ACTUAL FACTORY EXPENSE, TOTAL........	$6,500.00	$	$
BUDGET FACTORY EXPENSE, TOTAL........		6,000.00	
Excess spending over budget..........			500.00
APPLIED FACTORY EXPENSE..............	5,947.50	5,947.50	
Unabsorbed expense—volume..........		$ 52.50	
NET UNDERABSORBED EXPENSE...........	$ 552.50		

Figure 9-13

normal expense and the actual hours for the year agree with the estimated or normal hours on which the expense rate was based.

Figure 9-14 is a chart of the expected cumulative under- and overapplied factory expense balance over the months of a full year (that is, the balances as estimated when the normal rate was computed at the beginning of the year). The balance of the account is zero at the end of the year, showing that overapplied expense is expected to balance underapplied expense over the year. Figure 9-15 shows the detail calculations.

It is possible that, under the actual operation of the business during the year, there may be some net underabsorbed expense in the accounts at the end of the year. This would be caused by, say, the actual expense for the

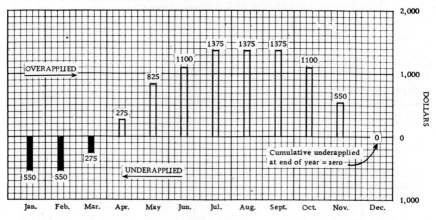

**Expected Cumulative Under- and Overapplied
Factory Expense, by Months
Year 19___**

Figure 9-14

year being greater than the normal ("excess spending"), or the actual
hours being less than the normal ("too little volume"), or both.

Disposition of the underabsorbed expense balance. In the above
illustration (Figure 9-15) the Factory Expense account and the Factory
Expense Applied account are allowed to remain open during the months

Expected Cumulative Under- and Overapplied Factory Expense by Months, Year 19___

	(1) Expected Actual Factory Expense‡	(2) Expected Actual Hours (Figure 9-9)	(3) Applied Factory Expense (Col. 2 × $.75)	(4) Cumulative Actual	(5) Cumulative Applied	Cumula- tive Under- (Over-*) Applied
Month						
January......	$ 5,050.00	6,000	$ 4,500.00	$ 5,050.00	$ 4,500.00	$ 550.00
February.....	6,000.00	8,000	6,000.00	11,050.00	10,500.00	550.00
March.......	6,475.00	9,000	6,750.00	17,525.00	17,250.00	275.00
April........	6,950.00	10,000	7,500.00	24,475.00	24,750.00	275.00*
May........	6,950.00	10,000	7,500.00	31,425.00	32,250.00	825.00*
June........	6,475.00	9,000	6,750.00	37,900.00	39,000.00	1,100.00*
July........	6,475.00	9,000	6,750.00	44,375.00	45,750.00	1,375.00*
August.......	6,000.00	8,000	6,000.00	50,375.00	51,750.00	1,375.00*
September....	6,000.00	8,000	6,000.00	56,375.00	57,750.00	1,375.00*
October......	5,525.00	7,000	5,250.00	61,900.00	63,000.00	1,100.00*
November....	5,050.00	6,000	4,500.00	66,950.00	67,500.00	550.00*
December....	5,050.00	6,000	4,500.00	72,000.00	72,000.00	0.00
	$72,000.00	96,000	$72,000.00			

‡ The expected actual expense for each level is obtained from page 194.

Figure 9-15

of the year, and they are closed to Profit and Loss at the end of the year. The theory on which this illustration is based is that a net debit balance for the year is in the nature of a loss for the year, and a net credit balance is in the nature of a gain. It is expected or hoped that the overabsorbed expense of busy months will balance the underabsorbed expense of slack months.

On the financial statements prepared during interim months, underabsorbed expense is shown on the Balance Sheet as a prepaid expense. Overabsorbed expense is shown as a deferred credit. There are other theories for disposing of the underabsorbed expense balance. Further discussion appears in Chapter 11.

QUESTIONS

9-1. What is an object classification of expense accounts? Give examples of accounts in an object classification.

9-2. What is the distinction between (a) factory expense and (b) selling and shipping expense?

9-3. (a) In general, what distinction is drawn between direct costs and indirect costs in Chapter 9?

(b) Distinguish indirect materials proper, factory operating supplies, maintenance supplies, and repair parts.

(c) Distinguish indirect labor from the other categories of labor chargeable to factory expense, naming those categories.

(d) Distinguish the two categories of indirect expense indicated in Chapter 9.

(e) From the standpoint of control of factory expense against excessive spending, why is it desirable to distinguish as far as possible the categories indicated in parts (a)-(c)?

9-4. (a) In regard to factory expense, what is meant by variable expense? Fixed expense?

(b) Give a number of examples of factory expense object accounts which you think are variable.

(c) Give a number of examples of factory expense object accounts which you think are fixed.

(d) Give a number of examples of factory expense object accounts which you think are a combination of variable and fixed expense.

(e) Why is it useful for the cost accountant and the management to keep in mind the fact that some expenses are variable and some are fixed?

9-5. (a) What means of control of expense against excess spending are likely to be used in small manufacturing concerns?

(b) It is said that some expenses are controlled by *executive decision* as to what constitutes a reasonable amount for a period. Discuss.

9-6. Name the journals from which charges to Factory Expense Control account come, and give examples of charges which come from each journal.

9-7. (a) What is meant by actual basis for applying factory expense to production orders? Normal basis?

(b) Under what conditions might it be necessary or desirable to use normal basis? Actual basis?

9-8. (a) Name the steps of procedure for the application of factory expense to production orders (including the end-of-the-month journal entry) on the actual basis.

(b) Name the steps of procedure for normal basis.

9-9. (a) What is meant by "underabsorbed expense"? What causes it?

(b) How does underabsorbed expense appear in the accounts?

(c) How is an underabsorbed expense balance disposed of?

EXERCISES

9-1. The following "fill-in" forms are presented in the Workbook:

Voucher register

Requisition journal

General journal

Cost sheets

Control accounts for (a) factory expense and factory expense applied and (b) work in process.

Required:

(1) Foot and cross-foot the journals; post the pertinent totals to Factory Expense account.

(2) Make the entry in the general journal to charge expense applied into work in process; post this entry to the accounts provided. Use the normal rate given. Note that the normal rate given is applied to the hours worked during the current year. It is not applicable to the opening inventory of work in process.

(3) Prepare an analysis of underabsorbed factory expense. (All information required for this analysis is given on the charts.)

PROBLEMS

9-1. Draft entries in simple journal entry form (that is, assuming that only a simple general journal is used) to record the following transactions. After each entry indicate (a) which basic accounting paper is used for the original writing of the transaction, (b) what factory expense ledger account is debited, and (c) what special journal would be used for summarizing the particular type of transaction.

(1) Salary of factory foreman accrued, $400.

(2) Company's share of F.I.C.A. tax on direct and indirect labor, $84.

(3) Provision for vacation pay for week, $42.

(4) Workmens' insurance expense for week, $66.

(5) Factory supplies drawn from materials storeroom for current use, $23.

(6) Repair bill (for repairing machinery) received from outside repair company, $65.

(7) Received bill for technical society dues (engineering and manufacturing), $30.

(8) Depreciation on factory machinery for period, $100.

(9) Insurance expense on factory machinery for period, $50.

(10) Taxes expense on factory machinery for period, $100.

The basic accounting paper for transactions 2-4 and 8-10 is a journal voucher.

9-2. The following transactions of the Phillips Manufacturing Co. relate to factory expense:

Jan. 2—Vouchered and paid factory rent for month, McLeod Realty Co., $400.

Jan. 4—Received from Folts & Co., machine repair parts, $60. (Charge to expense immediately upon receipt.)

Jan. 5—Purchased printed forms from Wilson Printing Co., for use in factory, $20.

Jan. 6—Factory and shipping payroll for week vouchered and paid:

Class	Hours	Amount
Direct labor	360	$570.00
Indirect labor	80	100.00
Shipping labor	60	80.00
Total	500	$750.00

Jan. 13—Factory and shipping payroll for week vouchered and paid:

Class	Hours	Amount
Direct labor	420	$615.00
Indirect labor	90	125.00
Shipping labor	60	80.00
Total	570	$820.00

(Payroll entries for remaining weeks of month eliminated from problem.)

Jan. 31—Vouchered and paid electric power bill, Commonwealth Electric Co., $60.

Jan. 31—Inventory of machine repair parts, $20.

Jan. 31—Estimated depreciation for month on factory machinery, $40.

Jan. 31—Estimated taxes for month on factory machinery, $50.

Jan. 31—Insurance expired for month on factory machinery, $30.

Jan. 31—Record the entry for factory expense applied for month:

$$\text{Normal direct labor hour rate} = \frac{\text{Normal factory expense}}{\text{Normal direct labor hours}} = \frac{\$800}{800} = \$1 \text{ per hour}$$

Actual direct labor hours = 780.

Required:

(1) Using columnar analysis paper, set up the following forms:
    (a) Voucher register,
    (b) Check register, and
    (c) General journal
(2) Enter the above transactions in the proper journals.
(3) Set up "T" accounts and post the journals to the accounts.

9-3. The ABC Company uses a job order cost system. Factory expense is applied on a normal basis using direct labor hours. The budgeted expense for the month is $1,200 and the budgeted hours are 800. The following costs appear on the cost sheets at the end of the first month of operations:

	Material	Labor Hours	Labor Cost
Job 101	$500.00	200	$300.00
102	400.00	100	400.00
103	700.00	200	300.00
104	200.00	50	200.00

The materials ledger shows the following:

	Received	Issued
Material A	100 units @ $15.00............	90 units @ $15.00
Material B	200 units @ $ 5.00............	{ 90 units @ $ 5.00 { 10 units @ $ 5.00**

The factory expense ledger accounts show the following:

Indirect labor................	$260.00
Indirect material.............	50.00**
Heat, light, and power........	500.00
Depreciation.................	300.00

Required:

(a) Compute the amount of factory expense applicable to each job.

(b) Using T accounts, enter the above data in the following accounts and show the source of all postings:

Materials control	Factory expense in process
Materials in process	Factory Expense
Labor in process	Factory expense applied

(c) Prepare a statement of over- or underapplied factory expense. (Analyze the amount of over- or underapplied.)

(d) If this company had applied actual rather than normal factory expense, what amount of factory expense would be applicable to each job?

9-4. The Factory Expense Control account and Factory Expense Ledger accounts for Brunswick Manufacturing Company appear as follows after posting journal entries for the month of February:

(In General Ledger)

Factory Expense Control

19__		F	Amount	19__		F	Amount
Feb.	Journal entries	GJ	$195 64				
	Materials	RJ	100 00				
	Disbursement						
	vouchers	VR	27 76				

FACTORY EXPENSE LEDGER

Indirect Labor

19__		F	Amount	19__		F	Amount
Feb.	Payroll	GJ	$128 80				

Overtime Premium

19__		F	Amount	19__		F	Amount
Feb.	Payroll	GJ	$ 3|10				

F.I.C.A. Tax

19__		F	Amount	19__		F	Amount
Feb.	Journal charge	GJ	$ 8|74				

Indirect Materials, Supplies, and Repair Parts

19__		F	Amount	19__		F	Amount
Feb.	Indirect materials	RJ	$100|00				

Power

19__		F	Amount	19__		F	Amount
Feb.	Disbursement voucher	VR	$ 27|76				

Depreciation

19__		F	Amount	19__		F	Amount
Feb.	Journal charge	GJ	$ 30 00				

Insurance

19__		F	Amount	19__		F	Amount
Feb.	Journal charge	GJ	$ 10 00				

Taxes

19__		F	Amount	19__		F	Amount
Feb.	Journal charge	GJ	$ 15 00				

Cost sheets (summarized) show the following information for the month:

PRODUCTION ORDER COST SHEETS

Production Order Cost Sheet   *No.* 41

MATERIALS			LABOR		
19__ Date	Req. No.	Amount	19__ Date	Hours	Amount
2/11	104	$600 00	W/E 2/20	71	$111 30

Production Order Cost Sheet   No. 42

MATERIALS			LABOR		
19__ Date	Req. No.	Amount	19__ Date	Hours	Amount
2/ 3 /12	101 105	$150 00 185 00	W/E 2/20	61	$ 93 90

Production Order Cost Sheet   No. 43

MATERIALS			LABOR		
19__ Date	Req. No.	Amount	19__ Date	Hours	Amount
2/7	103	$140 00	W/E 2/20	64	$ 99 40

Required:

(1) Set up an expense statement for the month.

(2) Give formula for direct labor hour (factory expense) rate, and compute the rate on the actual basis.

(3) Draft a statement showing the amount of factory expense applicable to each production order for the month of February.

(4) Draft the general journal entry required to charge expense into work in process for the month.

9-5. Referring to the data in Problem 9-4, assume that factory expense is applied to production orders on the normal basis instead of the actual basis. Normal expense per month is $320 and normal hours, 200.

Required:

(1) Give the formula for direct labor hour (factory expense) rate, and compute the rate on the normal basis.

(2) Draft a statement showing the amount of factory expense applicable to each production order for the month of February under normal basis.

(3) Draft the general journal entry required to charge factory expense into Work in Process for the month under normal basis.

(4) Prepare an analysis of underabsorbed expense.

Chapter 10 ~~~~~~

FACTORY EXPENSE: ALLOCATION TO PRODUCTS

Meaning of the term "allocation." Allocation of factory expense to products is the application of factory expense totals or factory expense segments to products. It is accomplished by the use of rates based upon some factor common to all products, such as direct labor hours expended on the products. Chapter 9 illustrates the use of direct labor hour rates for the allocation of factory expense to products. In what is called the actual basis (page 189), a factory expense rate per hour is computed by the formula:

$$\text{Factory expense rate per direct labor hour} = \frac{\text{Factory expense for month}}{\text{Direct labor hours for month}}$$

and the resulting rate is applied to the cost sheets by the formula:

Factory expense applied to cost sheet = Direct labor hours × Direct labor hour rate

In the illustration in Chapter 9, the entire factory expense for the Benson Manufacturing Company is charged to cost sheets by means of a single rate. A single rate was used for illustrative purposes merely for convenience in opening the subject. In practice, the rate structure by which factory expense is applied to cost sheets may comprise a number of rates, each intended to give effect to a separate factor in the aggregate factory expense picture. For instance, the expense incurred to get the materials into the factory and care for them until they are used may be applied to cost sheets by means of a rate based upon materials as a factor. The remainder of factory expense may then be applied to cost sheets by means of a rate based upon labor. This handling of materials overhead is suggested in Chapter 6, dealing with the classification of materials and expense.

Equitable costing; Importance to the management. The purposes of cost accounting might be defeated if expense is not applied equitably to the cost sheets. Equitable costing would mean that no production order should be penalized by expense application to the undue advantage of some other production order, and similarly that no product would be penalized to the undue advantage of some other product.

Consider, first, the use of cost accounting in the measurement of performance and, second, the use of product costs as a factor in setting selling

208

prices. A production order charged with too small a factory expense application might appear to represent a satisfactory performance in the factory, whereas the performance was unsatisfactory, and ought to be investigated.

Similarly, a product overcosted by the cost man may become a product overpriced by the sales department influenced by such reported cost. Although it is true that the sales manager does not necessarily set his selling prices with direct reference to the costs in his factory, he may be influenced by them and inadvertently price one of his products out of the market because of a "high cost."

Classification of factory expense for allocation to products. Chapter 9 sets out a classification of factory expense for control purposes (page 176) in a small manufacturing business. In this business, one man (the manager) is responsible for the control of expense. For the purposes of his monthly expense statement, expenses are classified according to the nature of the expense item itself and according to the nature and degree of remedial action possible. This classification of accounts is carried in the factory expense ledger. For a complete control plan, it is necessary to decide what each expense varies with (if it does vary), and to set up allowances which are related to activity.

A different classification might be useful for deciding how expense should be allocated to product. This classification (actually a *re*classification) would not be carried in the books and most likely it would not be formal or complete. It constitutes the vehicle for decision by the cost accountant who must decide upon the rate structure.

A theoretical classification of factory expense accounts for allocation purposes is shown on page 210. In considering this classification, the cost accountant would recognize that in general:

(1) The manufacture of products consists in bringing together materials, labor, and manufacturing facilities.

(2) Certain objects of factory expense have a more or less definite relationship to the materials or labor which go into the product or the facilities used to make the product.

Note that the classification illustrated provides, in addition to the classification of accounts at the left, a column for overhead related to materials, one for overhead related to labor and two for overhead related to plant (one for machinery, and one for building). The cost accountant considers each object account to decide whether it relates to materials, labor, or plant and places the object account number in the proper column to the right of the classification. Some of the object accounts fall clearly into one class. The classification of others is debatable. The cost accountant places the latter items according to his best opinion. When the spread is completed, it is possible to form an opinion as to whether the factory expense falls predominantly into one class.

An alternative procedure would be to use a trial balance and to spread the balances of the accounts in the distribution columns. Often it is possible to form an opinion without spreading the trial balance, by using the method shown in Figure 10-1.

Factory Expense

Theoretical Classification of Object Accounts for Allocation Purposes

Object Classification (Accounts grouped for control)	Materials Overhead	Labor Overhead	Plant Overhead		
			Machinery	Building	General
510 Indirect labor:					
511 Supervision	—	511	—	—	—
512 Production control clerks and dispatchers	512	—	—	—	—
513 Timekeepers and payroll clerks	—	513	—	—	—
514 Cost clerks	—	—	—	—	514
515 Shop porters	515	—	—	—	—
516 Machinists	—	—	516	—	—
517 Janitors, firemen, and watchmen	—	—	—	517	—
519 Overtime premium	—	519	—	—	—
520 Payroll taxes, insurance, and reserves:					
521 F.I.C.A. taxes	—	521	—	—	—
522 Workmen's insurance	—	522	—	—	—
523 Provision for vacation pay	—	523	—	—	—
530 Indirect materials and operating supplies:					
531 Pattern paper; chalk	531	—	—	—	—
532 Needles	—	—	532	—	—
540 Maintenance and repairs; repair parts:					
541 Machinery	—	—	541	—	—
542 Building	—	—	—	542	—
550 Purchased services:					
551 Heat	—	—	—	551	—
552 Light	—	—	—	552	—
553 Power	—	—	553	—	—
554 Water	—	—	—	554	—
555 Freight-in	555	—	—	—	—
556 Engineers fee (time study)	—	556	—	—	—
560 Travel	—	560	—	—	—
570 Unclassified	—	—	—	—	570
580 Fixed charges:					
581 Depreciation on machinery	—	—	581	—	—
582 Insurance on machinery	—	—	582	—	—
583 Taxes on machinery	—	—	583	—	—
584 Rent on building	—	—	—	584	—

Figure 10-1

Types of factory expense rates. Particular objects of factory expense have a recognizable relationship to particular factors of the manufacturing function, and it is desirable to consider some of the types of rate available for the application of factory expense to products.

The following types of rate will be explained:

(1) Product unit rate
(2) Rates based upon the direct labor factor in products:
   (a) Direct labor hour
   (b) Direct labor cost
(3) Rates which recognize direct materials as a factor in products:
   (a) Prime cost rate
   (b) Materials overhead rate

(4) Rates which recognize facilities overhead expense separately (machine rates).

I. PRODUCT UNIT RATE

Formula and use. The formula for amount per product unit is:

$$\text{Factory expense per product unit} = \frac{\text{Factory expense for month}}{\text{Product units for month}}$$

The amount per unit for the Benson Manufacturing Company, computed on the actual basis is:

$$\frac{\$6,500}{5,000} = \$1.30 \text{ per product unit}$$

This type of rate is used logically where a single product is produced. If the Benson Manufacturing Company produced only Product X, for instance, the cost accountant might consider applying expenses by this type of rate.

The unit product rate would probably be adequate for such a simple costing situation. It does put the factory expense on the product unit. Note, however, that it may not be sufficiently refined to serve all the purposes of cost accounting. For instance, it would show the same unit factory expense cost for all production orders produced during the month, even though some of the orders were produced at more labor *time* per unit than others. It might be argued that the product units which required more time to produce received the benefit of more factory expense than did the others and that the product unit rate failed to show that fact. The unit product costs might therefore not be considered suitable for the measurement of performance.

II. RATES BASED UPON THE DIRECT LABOR FACTOR IN PRODUCT

Direct labor hour rate. The direct labor hour rate was explained in Chapter 9. The formula for direct labor hour rate is:

$$\text{Direct labor hour rate} = \frac{\text{Factory expense for month}}{\text{Direct labor hours for month}}$$

The rate for the Benson Manufacturing Company, computed on the actual basis, is:

$$\frac{\$6,500}{7,930} = \$.8196+ \text{ per direct labor hour}$$

If direct labor hour rates were used, the application to Production Order No. 104 would be:

$$\begin{array}{cc} \text{Direct labor hours} \\ \text{for Order No. 104} \\ 1{,}670 \end{array} \times \begin{array}{c} \text{Direct labor} \\ \text{hour rate} \\ \$.8196+ \end{array} = \begin{array}{c} \text{Applied factory expense} \\ \$1{,}368.73 \end{array}$$

The direct labor hour rate applies factory expense to products in production to the amount of time required to produce them, measured in direct labor hours. It operates on the assumption that the production orders which require more time to produce receive the benefit of more factory expense. This assumption may have some justification if, in fact, a significant part of the factory expense items do accrue on a time basis.

Direct labor cost rate. The formula for direct labor cost rate is:

$$\text{Direct labor cost rate} = \frac{\text{Factory expense for month}}{\text{Direct labor cost for month}}$$

The rate for the Benson Manufacturing Company, computed on the actual basis, is:

$$\frac{\$6{,}500}{\$10{,}577} = 61.45\% \text{ of direct labor cost}$$

If direct labor cost rates were used, the application to Production Order No. 104 would be:

$$\begin{array}{cc} \text{Direct labor cost} \\ \text{for Order No. 104} \\ \$2{,}204 \end{array} \times \begin{array}{c} \text{Direct labor} \\ \text{cost rate} \\ 61.45\% \end{array} = \begin{array}{c} \text{Applied factory expense} \\ \\ \$1{,}354.36 \end{array}$$

Note that the expense applied to Order No. 104 by actual direct labor cost rate above is almost the same as expense applied to that order by actual direct labor hour rate. Expense applied by direct labor cost rate is $1,354.36 and expense applied by direct labor hour rate is $1,368.73, because the average rate of wages paid the workmen on Order No. 104 (direct labor cost, $2,204 ÷ labor hours, 1,670 = $1.32) is approximately the same as the average rate of wages paid all workmen (total direct labor cost, $10,577 ÷ total direct labor hours, 7,930 = $1.34). If there had been a *single* rate of wages for all workmen in the factory (say $1.30 an hour), expense applied by direct labor cost rate would be exactly the same as expense applied by direct labor hour rate.

Where the average rate of wages on each job is likely to be approximately the same as the average for the factory, the cost man will probably select the direct labor cost rate rather than the direct labor hour rate for applying expense. There is a clerical saving in the use of the direct labor cost rate, since labor hours do not have to be posted to the cost sheets. (Labor *dollars*, which would have to be posted in any case, is the base for applying expense.)

Where the average rate of wages varies significantly from employee to employee, the effect of using direct labor cost rate is to apply proportionately more expense to the labor of employees who are paid high rates per hour.   One hour of work of an employee who is paid $1.30 per hour will be charged 30 per cent more factory expense than one hour of work of an employee who is paid $1 per hour.

The effect of *rate of wages* upon the expense application would raise a question as to the validity of the direct labor cost rate compared with the direct labor hour method.   The employees who worked on Order No. 101 (Product A) were paid an average of $1.23 per hour, whereas the employees who worked on Order No. 104 (Product B) were paid an average of $1.32 an hour.   The extra factory expense application to Order No. 104 (Product B) under the direct labor cost method can be justified only on the theory that (a) the higher priced employees do require more factory expense per hour or receive more benefit per hour than the lower priced ones or (b) a significant part of factory expense is labor overhead which does accrue proportionately to labor cost.

It is sometimes said that direct labor cost rate should be used for applying expense when a piece-rate wage payment plan is in effect.   The arguments are:

(1)   It is not desirable to keep track of hours worked on each order, especially since clock hours on each order may not be required for any wage payment calculation.

(2) Under a piece-rate wage payment plan, employees tend to average out approximately the same earned rate per hour as they become experienced in their operations.   Therefore, a direct labor cost rate would apply to each job approximately the same amount of expense as a direct labor hour rate.

The first argument is valid for the use of direct labor cost rates in connection with piece-rate wage payment plans.   The second argument is open to examination in the light of specific conditions in the factory in question.   It is not a foregone conclusion that in a specific factory using a piece-rate wage payment plan, there will not be a considerable disparity in average earned rates per hour among employees.

III.   RATES BASED UPON THE MATERIALS FACTOR IN PRODUCT COST

Prime cost rate.   The prime cost rate, unlike the rate described in the following section, is intended to apply *total* expense to product.   The formula for prime cost rate is:

$$\text{Prime cost rate} = \frac{\text{Factory expense for month}}{\text{Direct materials} + \text{Direct labor for month}}$$

The rate for Benson Manufacturing Company, computed on the actual basis, is:

$$\frac{\$6,500}{\$7,389 + \$10,577} = 36.18\% \text{ of prime cost}$$

If prime cost rates were used, the application to Production Order No. 104 would be:

Prime cost for Order No. 104 × Prime cost rate = Factory expense applied
$4,265.20   ×   36.18%   = $1,543.16

When the prime cost rate is used, the expense application to a particular order varies with two factors: the cost of the labor and the cost of the materials. Use of the prime cost rate is an attempt to recognize the fact that some of the factory expense (freight on materials, for instance) is really *materials* overhead. The theory is that orders with a large materials content should be charged with more factory expense than should orders with small materials content, other factors remaining constant.

This line of thinking is illustrated in the costing of Order No. 104. The expense application by prime cost method, as above, is $1,543.16. The expense application by direct labor cost method is $1,354.36. In this connection, note that Order No. 104 does have a relatively high material cost and would therefore be expected to have a relatively high expense application under prime cost method. The average of materials cost to prime cost for Order No. 104 is 48.33 per cent (materials, $2,061.20 ÷ prime cost, $4,265.20), whereas the average materials cost to prime cost for all orders is 41.90 per cent (materials, $7,429.20 ÷ prime cost, $17,730.20).

Note, however, that *any* order with a prime cost of $4,265.20 (prime cost of Order No. 104) would receive a factory expense application of $1,543.16 under the use of prime cost rates, regardless of how much or how little material the order comprised.

Procedure: Separate rate for storage and handling expense.   The procedure for using a separate rate for materials storage and handling expense is:

(1) At the beginning of the period, compute a rate for materials storage and handling expense by the formula:

$$\frac{\text{Rate for materials storage}}{\text{and handling expense}} = \frac{\text{Estimated materials storage and handling expense}}{\text{Estimated direct materials cost}}$$

The rate computed:

$$\frac{\$800}{\$7,200} = 11.1\% \text{ of direct materials cost}$$

(2) When each production order is completed, post a charge for materials storage and handling expense to the cost sheets. For Order No. 104, the charge is:

Materials cost × Rate = Total charge
$2,061.20   × 11.1% = $228.79

(A special section would be provided on the cost sheet form in which to post charges of this kind.)

(3) During the month, as expense bills are received, record them by debits to Material Storage and Handling Expense and appropriate credits.

(4) At the end of the month, make a general journal entry to charge Factory Expense in Process and credit Materials Storage and Handling Expense for materials cost for the month multiplied by the materials storage and handling expense rate.

The storage and handling rate is a *partial* rate, in that it is intended to apply to only one segment of overhead (storage and handling expense). Some other type of rate, such as a direct labor hour rate or machine rates, must be used with the materials storage and handling rate to apply those items of factory expense not covered by the latter rate.

IV. RATES THAT RECOGNIZE FACILITIES OVERHEAD EXPENSE SEPARATELY

Meaning and purpose. In Chapter 9 it was assumed that factory expense is (a) *controlled* and (b) *applied* to production for the factory as a whole. The statement of factory expense (page 199), used as the instrument of control, represented the entire factory. Whatever expense rate was selected for the application of expense would likewise be based upon the expense of the entire factory.

In some cases, it might be desirable to apply expense to production by the use of several rates, each of which is related to some organizational and physical segment of the whole factory. Thus, if there were two assembly departments in the Benson Manufacturing Company factory, each of which produced a separate product, each of them might be regarded as a separate small factory, as far as expense application is concerned, and a separate rate computed and applied for each department. It would seem reasonable that each product should bear the factory expense of the department in which it was made.

The organizational and plant units for the application of expense are known as *factory expense centers*, and the rate for such a center is known as a *machine rate*.

The process of dividing the factory into small units for the computation and application of factory expense rates might extend down below the departmental level. In the pressroom of a job printing plant, for instance, each press or each group of identical presses might become a plant unit for a separate factory expense rate. A separate rate might be computed for each press to make it possible to charge each product with the capacity cost and the operating cost of the equipment used to make the product.

To illustrate, consider the case of the printing plant in which there are three presses (see Figure 10-2). Press #1 is a small one-color press which is used for letterheads, business and calling cards, and small fliers. Press #2 is two-color, used for small catalogs and brochures. Press #3 is a four-color press, used for seed catalogs and similar work. A separate factory expense rate for Press #1 would be $3 an hour; for Press #2, $6 an hour, and for Press #3, $10 an hour. An average rate for the whole press department would be $7.50 per hour.

However, if all jobs were quoted to include factory expense at the average rate of $7.50 an hour, the company would not be likely to get any work for Press #1. Competing companies, equipped only with presses of the same

FACTORY EXPENSE RATES FOR PRINTING PLANT

PRESS DEPARTMENT

PRESS NO. 1	PRESS NO. 2	PRESS NO. 3	Average rate for Department, $7.50 per hour
$ 3.00 per hour	$ 6.00 per hour	$10.00 per hour	

Figure 10-2

type as Press #1, cannot be expected to include factory expense at $7.50 per hour in their bids.

Likewise, if four-color work on Press #3 was quoted at $7.50 an hour, the company would probably be able to sell out the capacity of the press. It would, however, spend more than that amount for every hour of work done on the press.

Consequently, where the factory expense cost of equipment is significant, and where different products require the use of different units of equipment, it is necessary to consider using separate factory expense rates for various units of equipment.

Factory expense centers are the segments into which a factory is divided for the effective application of expense to products. From what has been said above, it would appear that a factory expense center is an area of plant, including its machinery and equipment and the indirect labor personnel assigned to it whose factory expense is applied to product by means of separate rate.

Factory expense centers illustrated; Calculation of expense rates. Figures 10-3a to 10-3d are an illustrative set of worksheets for dividing the Benson Manufacturing Company into factory expense centers. Figures 10-3b through 10-3d provide an allocation of the expenses to factory expense centers.   The worksheets in the series are:

Figure 10-3a—Factory Expense Budget and Rates.

This master schedule is supported by:

Figure 10-3b—Budget of Indirect Labor and Related Accounts.
Figure 10-3c—Budget of Factory Expense: Supplies and Services.
Figure 10-3d—Budget of Fixed Charges (except labor).

Note the arrangement of factory expense centers set up by the cost man, as shown by figure 10-3a.   There are three expenses centers altogether: one for the cutting department as a whole and two for the assembly department —one for the benches in which several of the products are assembled by hand and one for the large machine which assembles the one product automatically.   There are thirty people in the bench assembly center and two people in the automatic machine center.   (The latter two people feed cut materials into the machine, which positions them, fastens them together, and paints them.)

There is a considerable difference in factory expense rate per hour for the three centers.   Although the rate per hour for the whole factory is $.75, the rates for the separate centers are:

Cutting department.................... $1.70 per hour
Assembly department:
    Benches............................   .38 per hour
    Automatic machine.................   2.50 per hour

These rates are normal expense rates, since the data used are all normal data.

Figures 10-3b to 10-3d, which support Figure 10-3a, illustrate how the total budget expense for each object account is allocated to the three factory expense centers.   The basic data required for allocation are different for (1) indirect labor and related accounts, (2) supplies and services, and (3) fixed charges.   This is the reason for organizing the budget in three schedules.

In Figure 10-3b, Indirect labor and Related Accounts—F.I.C.A. Tax and Workmen's Insurance—the basic data are labor hours and dollars.   Note that although the foreman of the assembly department and the shop porter are allocated on the basis of estimates of their own activity, other indirect labor is allocated on the basis of *direct* labor hours.

In Figure 10-3c, Supplies and Services, supplies and indirect materials are allocated on the basis of the foreman's estimate.   Heat, light, and power is allocated on the basis of estimated kilowatt hour consumption in each factory expense center.

In Figure 10-3d, Fixed Charges, depreciation, insurance, and taxes on machinery and equipment are allocated on the basis of value of machinery and equipment.   Rent is allocated on the basis of floor space.

BENSON MANUFACTURING COMPANY
Factory Expense Budget and Rates

(One-Month Period)

Accounts	Supporting Schedule (Figure No.)	Total Plant	Cutting Department	Assembly Department		
				Total	Benches	Automatic Machine
510 Indirect labor....................	10-3b	$1,710.00	$ 817.00	$ 893.00	$ 707.50	$ 185.50
530 Payroll taxes and Workmens' insurance.....	10-3b	499.60	124.34	375.26	340.55	34.71
540 Supplies and indirect materials.........	10-3c	600.00	80.00	520.00	330.00	190.00
560 Purchased services...............	10-3c	790.00	640.00	150.00	30.00	120.00
580 Unclassified..................	10-3c	163.03	17.44	145.59	115.80	29.79
590 Fixed charges (Except Labor).........	10-3d	2,237.37	1,041.22	1,196.15	756.15	440.00
500 Total factory expense...............		$6,000.00	$2,720.00	$3,280.00	$2,280.00	$1,000.00
Direct labor hours, by department.........		8,000	1,600	6,400	6,000	400
Direct labor hour rates, by department......		$ .75	$ 1.70	$ .5125	$ .38	$ 2.50
Machine rate per hour (200 machine hours) ...						$ 5.00

Figure 10-3a

BENSON MANUFACTURING COMPANY
Budget of Indirect Labor and Related Accounts
(with Allocation to Expense Centers)
(One-Month Period)

Accounts	Total Plant	Cutting Department	Assembly Department — Total	Benches	Automatic Machine
LABOR STATISTICS:					
Normal machine hours	200		200		200
Normal direct labor hours	8,000	1,600	6,400	6,000	400
(a) Normal direct labor dollars	$11,520.00	$2,400.00	$9,120.00	$8,320.00	$800.00
INDIRECT LABOR:					
510 Indirect labor—					
511 Foreman—assembly:			500.00	$375.00	$125.00
512 Assistant foreman—Cutting	500.00	300.00			
513 Shop porter—Moving materials:	300.00	75.00	75.00	50.00	25.00
514 Factory storekeeper and clerical (estimate)	150.00		150.00	125.00	25.00
515 Other indirect labor:	550.00	400.00			
	150.00		168.00	157.50	10.50
(b) Total indirect labor	$ 1,710.00	$ 817.00	$ 893.00	$ 707.50	$185.50
(c) Total labor—direct (line [a]) plus indirect (line [b])	$13,230.00	$3,217.00	$10,013.00	$9,027.50	$985.50
530 Payroll taxes and unemployment insurance:					
531 F.I.C.A. tax (2% of total labor—line [c])	$ 264.60	$ 64.34	$ 200.26	$180.55	$ 19.71
532 Workmens' insurance (various rates)	235.00	60.00	175.00	160.00	15.00
	$ 499.60	$ 124.34	$ 375.26	$340.55	$ 34.71

511 Foreman—assembly:

Center	Foreman's Time Estimate	Salary Allocated
Benches	75%	$375.00
Machine	25%	125.00
Total	100%	$500.00

513 Shop porter—Moving materials:

Center	Porter's Hours	% to Total	Porter Allocated
Cutting	75	50%	$ 75.00
Assembly:			
Benches	50	33⅓%	50.00
Machine	25	16⅔%	25.00
Total	150	100%	$150.00

515 Other indirect labor:

Center	Direct Labor Hours	% to Total	Indirect Labor Allocated
Cutting	1,600	20%	$ 42.00
Assembly:			
Benches	6,000	75%	157.50
Machine	400	5%	10.50
Total	8,000	100%	$210.00

Figure 10-3b

219

BENSON MANUFACTURING COMPANY
Budget of Factory Expense—Supplies and Services
(with Allocation to Expense Centers)
(One-Month Period)

Accounts	Total Plant	Cutting Department	Assembly Department		
			Total	Benches	Automatic Machine
Kilowatt hour statistics (light and power)	4,750	1,000	3,750	750	3,000
Supplies and services accounts:					
540 Supplies and indirect materials—					
541 Factory operating supplies (estimate)	$100.00	$ 50.00	$ 50.00	$ 20.00	$ 30.00
542 Indirect materials (estimate)	400.00		400.00	300.00	100.00
543 Repairs and repair parts (estimate)	100.00	30.00	70.00	10.00	60.00
Totals	$600.00	$ 80.00	$520.00	$330.00	$190.00
560 Purchased services:					
561 Heat, light, and power	$190.00	$ 40.00	$ 150.00	$ 30.00	120.00
562 Freight on materials, (all to cutting)	600.00	600.00			
Totals	$790.00	$640.00	$150.00	$ 30.00	$120.00
580 Unclassified (average per month—past year)	$163.03	$ 17.44	$145.59	$115.80	$ 29.79

561 Heat, light, and power:

Center	K.W. Hours	Rate per K.W. Hr.	Amount
Cutting	1,000	$.04	$ 40.00
Assembly:			
Benches	750	.04	30.00
Machine	3,000	.04	120.00
Total	4,750	.04	$190.00

Figure 10-3c

BENSON MANUFACTURING COMPANY
Budget of Fixed Charges—Manufacturing (except Labor)

(with Allocation to Expense Centers)
(One-Month Period)

Accounts	Total Plant	Cutting Department	Assembly Department		
			Total	Benches	Automatic Machine
Plant statistics:					
(a) Floor space—square feet.................		14,925	7,190	6,290	900
(b) Value of machinery and equipment..........	$30,000.00	$10,000.00	$20,000.00	$5,000.00	$15,000.00
Fixed charges (except labor) accounts:					
590 Fixed charges (except labor)—					
591 Depreciation—machinery & equipment:					
Rate per year (per cent of value)...........		12%		10%	10%
Amount per month...........	$ 266.66	$ 100.00	$ 166.66	$ 41.66	$ 125.00
592 Insurance—machinery & equipment:					
Rate per year (per cent of value)...........		8%		7.5%	8%
Amount per month...........	200.88	69.72	131.16	31.16	100.00
593 Taxes—machinery and equipment:					
Rate per year (per cent of value)...........		11%		13%	10%
Amount per month...........	277.33	98.00	179.33	54.33	125.00
599 Rent on building:					
(@ $.10 per square foot per month)......	1,492.50	773.50	719.00	629.00	90.00
Total fixed charges (except labor)........	$ 2,237.37	$ 1,041.22	$ 1,196.15	$ 756.15	$ 440.00

Rates shown are approximate.

Figure 10-3d

QUESTIONS

10-1. (a) What is meant by "equitable expense application" to products?

(b) Of what importance is it to management that expense application be equitable?

10-2. What is meant by materials overhead, labor overhead, machine overhead?

10-3. (a) Set up an object classification of factory expense accounts from memory, using a grouping that would be logical for control purposes.

(b) Name the accounts that you think are materials overhead, labor overhead, building overhead, and machine overhead.

10-4. Name the types of factory expense rates which are based upon:

(1) the direct labor factor in products
(2) the direct materials factor in products
(3) facilities overhead as a factor.

10-5. Give the formula for each rate that you have listed in your answer to Question 10-4. Indicate clearly whether each rate is a percentage of something or a rate per hour.

10-6. (a) Which rate(s) in your answer to Question 10-4 are obviously intended to be used in combination with other rates to make up the complete allocation structure? (In other words, which rate(s) are not intended to be the sole rate used for the application of factory expense to products?)

(b) In general, what is the advantage of using a multiple rate structure for the allocation of factory expense to products? What is the disadvantage?

10-7. (a) What is a factory expense center?

(b) What is the reason for setting up factory expense centers for the allocation of expense to products?

(c) If a factory is divided into factory expense centers for the allocation of factory expense to products, is it necessary to use a machine hour rate in each center, or can some other type of rate be used in each center?

10-8. Discuss the conditions under which you would use the product unit rate for applying factory expense.

10-9. Discuss the conditions under which you would use the direct labor hour rate.

10-10. Discuss the conditions under which you would use the percentage of direct labor cost rate.

10-11. Discuss the conditions under which you would use a materials overhead rate.

10-12. Discuss the conditions under which you would use the prime cost rate.

10-13. Discuss the conditions under which you would use machine rates.

10-14. If a factory is divided into factory expense centers for the application of expense to products, does it follow that factory expense accounts must be operated to compile actual factory expense according to the same classification?

EXERCISES

10-1. The Illinois Manufacturing Company uses a machine rate plan for applying factory expense to products. The following worksheet forms are presented in the Workbook:

Factory expense rates—by expense center
Indirect labor and related accounts
Supplies and purchased services
Fixed charges (except supervisory labor)

Required:

Complete the worksheets and compute for each expense center:
  (a) Rate per operating hour
  (b) Rate per direct labor hour

10-2 through **10-6.** Using the blanks provided in the Workbook, solve Exercises 10-2 through 10-6.

PROBLEMS

10-1. The cost accountant for the Thompson Manufacturing Company is attempting to decide which of two factory expense rates is more equitable. He accordingly computes (a) direct labor cost rate, and (b) direct labor hour rate, and then determines the cost of four orders, first using one rate and then using the other. He finds differences between results, and asks your opinion as to which rate should be used as a matter of consistent practice.

The rates were computed on the basis of the following information:

Particulars	Total Month	*Job No.* 101	102	103	104
Product no..............		14	12	14	16
Quantity (units).........		100	200	100	300
Materials................	$1,120.00	$200.00	$300.00	$220.00	$400.00
Labor hours.............	600	100	190	110	200
Labor cost..............	$ 900.00	$180.00	$246.00	$154.00	$320.00
Factory expense (actual)..	$1,800.00				

Required:

  (1) Compute actual direct labor cost rate and actual direct labor hour rate.
  (2) Compute total cost of each of the four orders, using each of the two rates.
  (3) Write a paragraph in good English explaining (a) what is meant by equitable costing (with reference to this problem), and (b) which rate results in the more equitable costing.
  (4) One executive in the company says that it does not make any difference which type of rate is used, since either rate will result in applying the full $1,800 of actual factory expense. What is your answer?

10-2. Following are (a) accounts relating to factory expense and (b) cost sheets (summarized) for the Tech Manufacturing Company for the month of March.

Factory Expense

19—			
March 31	Actual		$1,845

Factory Expense in Process

Cost Sheets

*Product*____100 units A____   *P.O. No.*____101____

| Materials | LABOR | |
	Hours	Amount
$ 500	200	$320 00

*Product*____200 units A____   *P.O. No.*____102____

| Materials | LABOR | |
	Hours	Amount
$1,200	440	$616 00

*Product*____200 units B____   *P.O. No.*____103____

| Materials | LABOR | |
	Hours	Amount
$ 514	360	$540 00

Required:

(1) Compute (a) direct labor hour rate, (b) direct labor cost rate, and (c) prime cost rate.
(2) Set up a statement showing cost of each production order under each of the three types of rate. Show materials, labor, expense, and total cost of each order; also total cost of each order; also total cost per unit of each order.
(3) Draft the general journal entry for total expense applied for the month.
(4) Discuss reasons for the difference in expense applied to orders as among the three methods.

10-3. The ABC Company manufactures widgets. Factory expense is applied on the basis of normal direct labor hours. Given below are the factory expense accounts as they appeared at the end of June. The budget for June is $2,400, and the normal factory expense rate is $2 per hour.

Factory Expense in Process

$2,000	

Factory Expense

$3,000	

Factory Expense—Applied

	$2,000

1. How many direct labor hours appear on the cost sheets?
2. Prepare an analysis of over- or underapplied factory expense.
3. If an actual rate based upon direct labor hours rather than a normal rate based upon direct labor hours had been used, what amount of factory expense would have been applied?
4. If the budgeted and actual wage rate is $3 per hour,
   (a) compute an actual rate based upon direct labor cost.
   (b) compute a normal rate based upon direct labor cost.
   (c) what amounts of factory expense would have been applied, using each of the above rates?

10-4. Using the following information, set up factory expense budget and machine rates for a one-month period for the Rochester Company:

	Total Plant	Drill Presses	Lathes	Planer
Labor statistics:				
Normal machine hours....................	3,000	1,000	1,500	500
Normal direct labor hours.................	3,000	1,000	1,500	500
Normal direct labor dollars...............	$ 6,250.00	$ 2,000.00	$ 3,000.00	$ 1,250.00
Kilowatt hours of power used..............	4,000	1,000	2,000	1,000
Plant statistics:				
Floor space—square feet..................	4,200	2,000	2,000	200
Value of machinery and equipment.........	$75,000.00	$20,000.00	$40,000.00	$15,000.00

A/C No.	Account	Notes	Total Monthly Amount	Bases of Allocation		
511	Foreman..........................	(1)	$ 600.00	25%	50%	25%
513	Shop porter—moving materials........	(2)	300.00	100 hrs.	50 hrs.	50 hrs.
515	Other indirect labor..................		600.00	Direct labor hours, as above		
531	F.I.C.A. tax.......................		155.00	2% of total labor		
532	Workmen's insurance................		77.50	1% of total labor		
541	Factory operating supplies............		190.00	$50.00	$60.00	$80.00
542	Indirect materials...................		120.00	30.00	40.00	50.00
543	Repairs and repair parts.............		190.00	60.00	70.00	60.00
561	Heat, light, and power..............		160.00	Kilowatt hours used, as above		
562	Unclassified (average per month—past year)......		380.00	$80.00	$264.75	$35.25
591	Depreciation—machinery and equipment		750.00	12% (per year) of value, as above		
592	Insurance—machinery and equipment...		375.00	6% (per year) of value, as above		
593	Taxes—machinery and equipment......		187.50	3% (per year) of value, as above		
599	Rent on building....................		2,100.00	Square feet, as above		
	Total............................		$6,185.00			

(1) Foreman's estimate
(2) Porter's hours

10-5.

NORMAN MANUFACTURING COMPANY
Factory Expense Budget
(One-Month Period)

Account	Totals Per Month	Basis of Distribution
Indirect labor:		
Supervision....................	$ 516.00	Labor hours
Factory clerical................	258.00	Labor hours
Machine repairmen............	336.00	Machine hours
Supplies and repair parts:		
Operating supplies..............	50.00	Estimate based upon experience
Maintenance supplies..........	55.00	Estimate based upon experience
Repair parts...................	70.50	Estimate based upon experience
Power.........................	114.00	Horsepower hours
Fixed charges:		
Depreciation...................	350.00	Valuation of equipment
Insurance.....................	175.00	Valuation of equipment
Taxes.........................	87.50	Valuation of equipment
Rent—building................	500.00	Square feet of floor space
	$2,512.00	

NORMAN MANUFACTURING COMPANY
Statistics for Allocation of Expense to Machine Centers

	Total	Center No. 1	Center No. 2	Center No. 3
Labor hours.....................	1,720	800	600	320
Machine hours....................	560	200	200	160
Estimate—Operating supplies.......	$ 50.00	$ 30.00	$ 15.00	$ 5.00
Estimate—Maintenance supplies....	55.00	20.00	25.00	10.00
Estimate—Repair parts............	70.50	30.00	20.00	20.50
Horsepower hours.................	2,280	800	1,000	480
Valuation of equipment............	$35,000.00	$20,000.00	$10,000.00	$5,000.00
Depreciation rate per year..........	12%			
Insurance rate per year............	6%			
Taxes rate per year...............	3%			
Square feet of floor space..........	5,000	2,500	1,250	1,250

The Norman Manufacturing Company applies factory expense to jobs by machine hour rates. The factory expense budget and statistics for allocation of expense to factors are presented herewith.

Required:

(1) Calculate factory expense rate per machine hour for each center.
(2) Draft the entry to charge expense into work in process for the month of January, assuming that hours of machine time are being compiled on cost sheets. Machine time for the month is:

No. 1..................	180
No. 2..................	180
No. 3..................	140
	500

10-6. The Norman Manufacturing Company (Problem 10-5) uses machine hour rates for application of expense to jobs. In this company, the relationship of direct labor hours to machine hours is constant, because a standard crew of operators is used when each factor operates. Machine hours, labor hours, and standard crew for each center are:

Center No.	Machine Hours	Labor Hours	Men in Crew
1..................	200	800	4
2..................	200	600	3
3..................	160	320	2
Totals...........	560	1,720	

Assume that labor dollars and hours are being compiled on job order cost sheets. How would you adjust the rates per machine hour computed in Problem 10-5 to make them applicable to labor hours posted to cost sheets?

Chapter 11 ~~~~~~

COSTS OF FACTORY OPERATION— MANUFACTURING AND CAPACITY COSTS

Control of job order costs. Previous chapters have explained the managerial information provided by the job order cost system in regard to materials, labor, and factory expense, together with cost accounting procedures designed to get the information. It was pointed out that a good cost system, in addition to providing managerial information, operates to protect the manufacturer against losses of materials and labor. Accounting for cost of goods manufactured and sold similarly produces reports useful to the management and affords an element of protection against loss of finished goods.

Actually, the basic principle of a job order cost system is that production is controlled through the medium of production orders (in certain factories) and that costs are likewise determined for those production orders. The management studies the costs of successive production orders, or jobs, to determine whether the manufacturing operation is proceeding profitably and whether the selling prices are high enough to leave a gross profit. The statement of profits sets out the final summary of sales, cost of sales, and gross profits, of course, and it is the accounting for cost of goods manufactured and cost of goods sold which assembles the segments for that statement.

The accounting function described in this chapter includes operating a perpetual inventory of finished goods in the warehouse. This record shows running balances of goods on hand, as to quantity, value, or both, as desired by the management. Running balances in quantities would be used (with other information) by the planning and production control people to keep production and finished goods on hand in line with sales. Running balances in dollars would be used by the financial managers of the business to determine how much working capital is tied up in various classes of finished goods.

A perpetual inventory can also be used as a tool for the protection of goods against theft or the other improper release from the warehouse. Checking the quantity of goods actually on hand against the quantity shown by the perpetual inventory sometimes signals shortages that ought to be investigated.

Organization for physical control.   Proper physical control over finished goods is necessary in its own right for the protection of the goods. It is also a necessary foundation for the integrity, or "truthfulness" of the accounting records.   The unit cost computed on the cost sheet is not correct if the number of good units shown by the cost sheet is more than the quantity of goods actually put into the warehouse.   If there is not proper physical control over the goods checked into the warehouse, the cost sheets may be wrong because of incorrect quantities.   It is also true that the balances in the finished goods ledger may be incorrect if there is no one in the warehouse to check goods in and out.

In the Benson Manufacturing Company, attention has been paid to maintaining a suitable organization for the physical control of finished goods.   A well-arranged and protected warehouse is provided for finished goods.   There is adequate shelf and bin space, and the stock is kept in good order in the proper place.   The storekeeper is responsible for the warehouse. He accepts completed goods from the inspector in the factory, rechecking the inspector's count as he does so.   The goods on each production order are moved intact through the factory operations and into the warehouse. The inspection bench is therefore a check point against loss of product in the factory as well as a control point of quantities put into the warehouse.

The storekeeper is permitted to release goods from the warehouse only upon receipt of a proper shipping order from the office.   Order pickers pull goods from stock on the basis of the shipping orders.   A shipping clerk in the shipping room checks the quantities pulled against the shipping order to locate possible discrepancies.

Organization for accounting.   In the Benson Manufacturing Company, the cost man posts the cost sheets and computes total costs and unit costs when production orders are completed.   He also acts as finished goods ledger clerk, posting completed cost sheets to finished goods ledger accounts and posting the office copies of sales invoices likewise to those accounts.

The general ledger bookkeeper operates a finished goods journal and a sales journal, described later in this chapter.

Managerial information: Statement of cost of goods sold; Statement of cost of goods completed.   The monthly Statement of Cost of Goods Sold (Figure 11-1) is prepared from the abstract of the Finished Goods account (Figure 11-13).   It is constructed by the formula:

Opening inventory + Goods completed − Closing inventory = Cost of goods sold

Note that, in addition to showing the mathematical makeup of cost of goods sold, this statement provides a comparison of the totals of finished goods inventories at the beginning and end of the month.   In the statement illustrated, the closing inventory was $24,217.09 and the opening inventory was $23,300, indicating a slight increase during the month.   The statement also provides the information for computing finished goods inventory turnover.   The company attempts to maintain an inventory equal to about one month's sales, and the statement indicates that during the last month, the plan has been substantially adhered to.   Average inventory is slightly greater than cost of sales for the month.

The cost of goods sold balance on the Statement of Cost of Goods Sold is carried to the Statement of Profits.

The Statement of Cost of Goods Completed (Figure 11-2) is prepared from the abstract of the in-process inventory accounts (page 243).   It comprises a separate section for each element.   Each section is derived from the in-process account to which it is related, by the formula:

Opening inventory + Input of the element − Closing inventory =
Amount of the element in goods completed

Compare the "cost accounting" form of the Statement of Cost of Goods Completed, shown on page 231, with the "financial accounting" form of statement shown on page 29.   The cost accounting form, which is prepared from the in-process accounts, shows materials, labor, and expense in *goods completed*.   The financial accounting form, prepared from a single Work in Process account, shows materials, labor, and expense put *into* process.

The former type of statement is a more dependable measure of cost performance than the latter.   In the latter type, the percentage of materials, labor, and expense total can change from month to month simply because the amount of materials started in process has changed from month to month.   This can happen even though percentages of materials, labor, and expense in goods completed has remained fairly constant from month to month.   In months when production lines are being started and work in process inventories built up, considerably more materials may be put into

Exhibit III

BENSON MANUFACTURING COMPANY
Statement of Cost of Goods Sold

for the Month of February, 19__

Particulars	Amount
Finished goods inventory, February 1, 19__........	$23,300.00
Add—Goods completed (Exhibit IV).............	23,662.70
Goods available for sale.......................	$46,962.70
Less—Finished goods inventory, February 28, 19__	24,217.09
Cost of goods sold (Exhibit II).................	$22,745.61

Figure 11-1

production than are taken out. (Note, however, that in the illustrated statement, input and output are approximately equal for the month of February. The lines were started in January and production is leveling off during February.)

The Statement of Cost of Goods Completed illustrated in Figure 11-2 is useful for the control of investment in work in process, as well as for the measurement of cost performance. The foreman of the Benson Manufacturing Company believes that an inventory of about one week's production should be maintained in the work in process banks and on the benches to avoid having any operators run out of work. Note that the illustration shows that an average inventory of approximately one week's production has been maintained during the month and that (as stated above) the input during the month has been about the same as the output.

The manager agrees with the foreman that a certain amount of in-process inventory is necessary to avoid having bottlenecks, with operators at later points running out of work. He is just as anxious, however, to avoid

Exhibit IV

BENSON MANUFACTURING COMPANY
Statement of Cost of Goods Completed

for the Month of February, 19__

MATERIALS:

Materials in process inventory, February 1, 19__	$ 2,268.00	
Add—Materials used	7,389.00	
Total	$ 9,657.00	
Less—Materials in process inventory, February 28, 19__	2,227.80	
Materials in goods completed		$ 7,429.20

LABOR:

Labor in process inventory, February 1, 19__	$ 1,597.50	
Add—Labor used	10,577.00	
Total	$12,174.50	
Less—Labor in process inventory, February 28, 19__	1,873.50	
Labor in goods completed		10,301.00

FACTORY EXPENSE:

Factory expense in process inventory, February 1, 19__	$ 1,012.50	
Add—Expense applied	5,947.50	
Total	$ 6,960.00	
Less—Factory expense in process inventory, February 28, 19__	1,027.50	
Factory expense in goods completed		5,932.50

TOTAL COST OF GOODS COMPLETED (Exhibit III) | | $23,662.70

Figure 11-2

carrying too much work in process inventory as too little. He points out that excess inventories tie up working capital and increase the hazard of inventory losses. He contends further that too large an inventory would actually impede production by obstructing easy movement of goods out of the work in process banks.

Managerial information: Production orders; Products. In the Benson Manufacturing Company, the manager and the foreman want to know the cost of each production order as soon as possible after it is completed. Through the use of normal factory expense rates, it is possible for the cost man to complete a cost sheet the day after the order is finished in the factory. The inspector notifies the cost man when an order is finished.

For the control of direct materials and direct labor on regular stock items, the cost man uses the predetermined costs set up at the beginning of the year. These predetermined costs were drawn up by the cost man, working with the manager and the foreman, and they were approved by the latter before the price lists were issued. The manager naturally wants to know whether the factory is getting out the goods at the cost which was projected at the time. If the factory is running over the predetermined cost, the manager wants to find out the cause and correct it if poor performance is indicated.

Control of direct costs is implemented by a tabular report and a chart. One report and one chart are kept in the manager's office. For the foreman's use, an identical report and an identical chart are kept in his office. New reports and charts are started at the beginning of each month.

The tabulated report in Figure 11-3 is a record of the performance on particular orders. It provides two columns for materials ("actual" and "estimated"), two for labor, two for expense, and two for total. On the form, there is a line for each production order. The illustration shows the report as it would appear at the end of the month although, as stated above, each production order is actually entered as soon as the cost sheet is completed.

The chart in Figure 11-4, "Cumulative Direct Material and Direct Labor Cost," is in three sections: materials, labor, and total. The horizontal reading in each chart is days and the vertical reading is dollars. The solid line on each section represents cumulative estimated cost and the dotted line, cumulative actual cost.

The illustration shows how the chart appeared after entry for Order No. 106, completed on February 25. Two orders were completed on February 12, and actual and estimated costs of those orders were plotted *on that date*. Two more orders were completed on February 13; cumulative actual and cumulative estimated costs (for four orders) were plotted on that date. One order was finished on February 18, and one was finished February 25. Actual costs ran slightly ahead of estimated costs throughout the month.

Comparison of Unit Costs on Production Orders, by Element
Month of February, 19___

Date	P.O. No.	Quantity	Product	Materials Actual	Materials Estimated	Labor Actual	Labor Estimated	Factory Expense Actual	Factory Expense Estimated	Total Actual	Total Estimated
12	104	1,320	A	$1.56	$1.50	$1.67	$1.63	$ .95	$ .84	$4.18	$3.97
12	101	300	B	1.16	1.20	2.22	2.26	1.35	1.16	4.73	4.62
13	102	600	A	1.56	1.50	1.59	1.63	.97	.84	4.12	3.97
13	103	600	C	1.64	1.60	2.17	2.26	1.35	1.16	5.16	5.02
18	105	1,190	C	1.64	1.60	2.37	2.26	1.33	1.16	5.34	5.02
25	106	990	B	1.16	1.20	2.38	2.26	1.33	1.16	4.87	4.62

Figure 11-3

In presenting the chart, a table showing the dollar values from which the chart was prepared would be shown as a supplement.

The manager and the foreman look at the chart frequently during the month to get a measure of performance to date, for all orders completed. Since the amounts shown are cumulative, the chart begins to indicate toward the middle of the month whether operations have been profitable, as far as the factory has been concerned. For the month of February, actual materials and labor costs exceed estimated costs by $348. If the goods had been *sold* during February, actual gross profit would have been less than estimated profit by that amount. Since the goods were not sold during the month of February, however, the impact of the higher manufacturing cost upon cost of sales will not be felt until the goods are sold.

The Benson Manufacturing Company occasionally manufactures goods

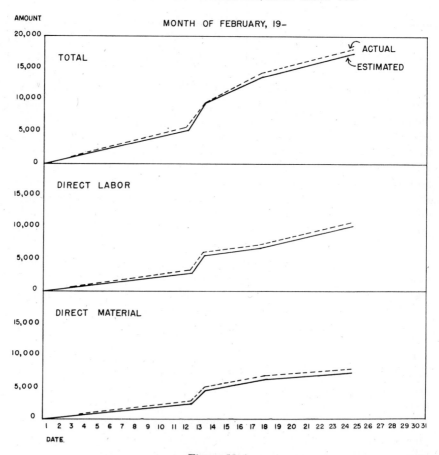

Figure 11-4

to customers' order. The goods are shipped and billed as soon as they are completed. Goods thus manufactured are similar to goods manufactured for stock, except for certain features which the customer specifies. These orders are usually obtained on a bid basis, and the sales manager makes the bid with knowledge of the estimated cost of the job. In most cases, the bid is higher than the estimated cost.

For the control of direct materials and labor on custom production, the cost man uses the estimated cost which was furnished the sales manager before he made his bid. As these orders are shipped out the cost man completes the cost sheets, determines the total cost and unit cost on the order, and also computes the actual gross profit on the order.

For management information the cost and profit on custom orders is recorded on a report of that name, as illustrated in Figure 11-5. This report provides columns for a comparison of actual cost with estimated cost for each element of cost, and also for a comparison of actual gross profit with estimates. This report is kept in the manager's office. The cost man makes the appropriate entries as each cost sheet is completed. At the end of the month, he enters the totals for the month. Actual gross profit per this report should agree with gross profit shown by the Statement of Profits for the month.

The Cost and Profit on Custom Orders report will show for each order on which there was a loss whether the order was (a) "sold at a loss" or (b) "made at a loss" or (c) both. An order is sold at a loss if the selling price is less than the estimated cost. It is made at a loss if the actual cost is greater than the estimated cost. The manager wants to know whether an order was made at a loss or sold at a loss since the responsibility is different in each situation. In Figure 11-5, note that no job was sold at a loss, since the actual selling price for each job was greater than the estimated cost. On the other hand, the actual cost of each job was greater than the estimated cost. The total estimated gross profit was $8,915 and the actual profit, $7,720.30.

A Schedule of Gross Profit by Product Class (Figure 11-6) is prepared monthly for the manager and the sales manager. This report shows sales, cost of sales, and gross profit for each product, with totals for all products. Both month and year to date figures are shown. All the custom jobs would be carried as Product Class X on this report.

The Schedule of Gross Profit shows which product class is most profitable. In the Benson Manufacturing Company, the sales manager tells the salesmen to push the most profitable products, and the sales manager accordingly watches the Schedule of Gross Profit to see to what extent this is being done. The salesmen agree to try to push the most profitable products but, since they are paid straight commission on sales dollars, they are naturally more interested in sales dollar volume than they are in selective selling. Most customers (being retailers of complete lines) like to

Cost and Gross Profit on Custom Orders
(Illustrative)
Month of February, 19___

Date	P.O. No.	Made For	Product	Materials Actual	Materials Estimated	Labor Actual	Labor Estimated	Factory Expense Actual	Factory Expense Estimated	Total Cost Actual	Total Cost Estimated	Actual Sales Amount	Gross Profit Estimated	Gross Profit Actual
Feb. 12	104	Brown	X—31	$2,061.20	$1,980.00	$ 2,204.00	$ 2,151.60	$1,252.50	$1,108.80	$ 5,517.70	$ 5,240.40	$ 7,128.00	$1,887.60	$1,610.30
12	101	Carter	X—15	348.00	360.00	664.50	678.00	405.00	348.00	1,417.50	1,386.00	1,890.00	504.00	472.50
13	102	Lincoln	X—16	936.00	900.00	956.00	978.00	577.50	504.00	2,469.50	2,382.00	3,240.00	858.00	770.50
13	103	Jones	X—01	984.00	960.00	1,303.00	1,356.00	795.00	696.00	3,082.00	3,012.00	4,320.00	1,308.00	1,238.00
18	105	Myers	X—03	1,951.60	1,904.00	2,820.50	2,689.40	1,582.50	1,380.40	6,354.60	5,973.80	8,568.00	2,594.20	2,213.40
26	106	March	X—21	1,148.40	1,188.00	2,353.00	2,237.40	1,320.00	1,048.40	4,821.40	4,473.80	6,237.00	1,763.20	1,415.60
				$7,429.20	$7,292.00	$10,301.00	$10,090.40	$5,932.50	$5,085.60	$23,662.70	$22,468.00	$31,383.00	$8,915.00	$7,720.30

Figure 11-5

Note: This statement is prepared for illustrative purposes on the assumption that all goods manufactured this month were custom production. Actually, the Benson Manufacturing Company produced only for stock in February.

Schedule of Gross Profit by Product Class

Month of February, 19___

| | Sales | | Cost of Sales | | Gross Profit | | | |
| | | | | | Month | | Year to Date | |
Product	Month	Year to Date	Month	Year to Date	Amount	% to Sales	Amount	% to Sales
A	$ 9,288.00	$15,768.00	$ 6,901.61	$11,701.61	$2,386.39	25.69	$ 4,066.39	25.79
B	8,857.00	15,157.00	6,394.00	10,994.00	2,463.00	27.81	4,163.00	27.46
C	13,230.00	21,870.00	9,450.00	15,450.00	3,780.00	28.57	6,420.00	29.35
X								
Total	$31,375.00	$52,795.00	$22,745.61	$38,145.61	$8,629.39	27.51	$14,649.39	27.74

Figure 11-6

Sales and Inventory Position Report
(In Product Units)

February 28, 19___

| | Sales This Month | Sales Year to Date | Unfilled Sales Orders | | | Inventories February 28, 19___ | |
			March	April	May	Work in Process	Finished Goods
Product							
A	1,720	2,920	2,000	1,600	1,200	280	1,800
B	1,390	2,390	1,600	1,200	1,000	410	1,400
C	1,890	3,090	2,100	1,500	1,300	710	1,900
Total	5,000	8,400	5,700	4,300	3,500	1,400	5,100

Figure 11-7

be supplied entire lines by the manufacturer. This fact, too, induces the salesman to try to sell the complete line rather than to concentrate on the most profitable items. (The sales manager is considering paying different commission rates for the various products, but as yet has reached no decision.)

In addition to the above cost and profit information, the management of the Benson Manufacturing Company uses finished goods inventory reports, illustrated in Figure 11-7. This report shows inventory at the end of the month for each product, together with sales for the old month, and unfilled sales orders for each of the following three months. The sales figure shows in general how well a product is selling. The inventory balances, when compared with sales, may give some indication of whether the inventory is out of line with sales. For certain products, orders are taken for future delivery. For these products, the production clerk is guided by the volume of unfilled orders as well as by the inventory (and other factors) in planning production of the coming periods.

Cost analysis. In some cases, the actual manufacturing cost of a production order is significantly higher than the estimated cost. When this is the case, the cost man makes an analysis of the actual cost as shown by the cost sheet. He does this to discover, if possible, any bookkeeping error that may have caused the apparent high cost and to anticipate the manager's inevitable question as to why the cost is high. Sometimes, the apparent high cost is caused by such bookkeeping errors as charging a requisition or a job ticket to the wrong cost sheet (which fact is not brought to light in proving the cost sheets against the in-process control accounts). More often, the cost man's analysis shows that:

(a) Actual performance was unsatisfactory as compared with the estimates, which are still regarded as sound by the management, or
(b) The estimates were "too tight," as the management now agrees.

Analysis is sometimes a tedious process, since it may involve comparing actual costs with estimated costs in the most minute detail. Sometimes, the cost man can detect the high costs as he posts job tickets and, more particularly, requisitions to the cost sheets. If a material price is high, the cost man is likely to observe the fact when he posts the requisition to the cost sheet.

When a detailed analysis is necessary to determine why total actual cost is greater than total estimated cost, the cost man proceeds from totals to details. First, he compares total actual materials cost with total estimated materials cost, and total actual labor cost with total estimated labor cost to determine which element is high. If materials are high, he compares actual cost with estimated cost for each type of material. If the actual cost of a specific type of material is high, he determines whether the price paid was high, or if the quantity used was greater than the quantity estimated.

Analysis of Differences Between Actual and Estimated Cost

Order No. 104   1,320 Units Product A   Completed February 12, 19—

Particulars	Actual Costs Per Cost Sheet			Estimates			Excess (Saving*) Actual Over Estimate
	Quantity or Hours	Average Price or Rate	Amount	Quantity or Hours	Price or Rate	Amount	Amount
Materials:							
Material "a".........	4,060 yds.	$ .5076/yd.	$2,061.20	3,960 yds.	$ .50/yd.	$1,980.00	$ 81.20
Labor:							
Cutting...........	330 hrs.	1.40/hr.	$ 462.00	330 hrs.	1.40/hr.	$ 462.00	
Assembly........	1,340 hrs.	1.30/hr.	1,742.00	1,320 hrs.	1.28/hr.	1,689.60	52.40
	1,670 hrs.		$2,204.00	1,650 hrs.		$2,151.60	$ 52.40
Factory expense......	1,670 hrs.	.75/hr.	$1,252.50	1,650 hrs.	.672/hr.	$1,108.80	$143.70
Total cost.........			$5,517.70			$5,240.40	$277.30
Cost per unit........			$ 4.18			$ 3.97	$ .21

Figure 11-8

If total actual labor cost is greater than total estimated labor cost, the cost man compares actual with estimate by department and then (if desired and feasible) by operation. In the Benson Manufacturing Company estimated costs by operation are not available, and it is therefore not possible to make a comparison of actual with estimate by operation. The comparison is made, however, by department.

An analysis of difference between actual and estimated cost for Order No. 104 appears in Figure 11-8. Note:

(1) Total actual cost of the order exceeded the estimated cost by $277.30. Of this total;

(2) Actual cost of materials exceeded estimated cost by $81.20. This excess was caused by using 100 yards more of materials than allowed for in the estimate and spending slightly more per yard than the estimated price per yard. In the Benson Manufacturing Company, excess yardage used is considered the responsibility of the cutting room supervisor. Excess prices are considered to be the result of faulty forecasting.

(3) Actual cost of labor exceeded the estimate by $52.40. Analysis of labor costs by department shows that the entire amount occurred in the assembly department. Twenty extra hours of labor were used (which was the responsibility of the assembly department supervisor), and the average actual rate per hour was higher than the estimated rate (which would be the responsibility of the same supervisor if he used higher rated labor than he should have used for the work done).

(4) Factory expense included in the actual cost is greater than that included in the estimate by $143.70. This is caused by excess hours used on the order and by the fact that the rate applied to the cost sheets ($.75 per hour) is greater than the rate used by the estimator.

Forms. Forms used in accounting for cost of goods manufactured and cost of goods sold (excepting the report forms discussed above) include cost sheets (Figure 11-9), finished goods journal (Figure 11-11), finished goods ledger accounts (Figure 11-16), and sales journal (Figure 11-13).

They also include the *shipping order* (not illustrated), which is written instruction to the warehouse people to pick goods of specified quantities and descriptions and to the shipping clerk to ship them to the customer named, and the *sales invoice* (not illustrated). The original sales invoice is mailed to the customer as notice of amount due for goods shipped. A copy is used by the accounting department as the source document for (a) sales value of the shipment and (b) cost of the goods shipped. (Cost is picked up after the invoice has been typed and the office copy separated from the original.)

I. PROCEDURE

Procedure for cost of goods completed. The steps for recording cost of goods completed are:

(1) Complete the cost sheet when the production order is finished, and

(2) Post completed cost sheet to the finished goods ledger.

(3) Enter the cost sheet in the finished goods journal.

(4) At the end of the month, post column totals of finished goods journal to inventory control accounts in the general ledger.

These steps are explained and illustrated in the following sections.

1. *Complete the Cost Sheet.* The cost sheet of a finished production order is completed by totaling the materials charges and the labor hours and amounts, applying the expense rate (in the illustration, 1,670 hours @

COMPLETED JOB ORDER COST SHEET

1 | Complete the cost sheet

*Production Order No.*____104____

Cost Sheet

*Date Promised*_____

*Quantity and Description*___1,320 Units Product A___   *Date Started*_____

*Made For*_____   *Date Completed*___Feb. 12, 19__

MATERIALS			LABOR						
				Cutting		Assembly		Total	
Date 19__	Amount	Date 19__	Hours	Amount	Hours	Amount	Hours	Amount
Feb. 1	$ 500 00	Feb. 1	16	$ 20 80		$	16	$ 20 80
	$2,061 20		330	$ 462 00	1,340	$1,742 00	1,670	$2,204 00

SUMMARY	Actual		Summarized By George North	Date Feb. 13, 19__
Materials........................	$2,061	20	*Finished Goods Ledger*	Date
Labor...........................	2,204	00		
Factory expense: 1,670 hours @ $.75..............	1,252	50		
Total cost.....................	$5,517	70	*Finished Goods Journal*	Date
Cost per unit.................	$ 4	18		

Totals, by element; cost per unit

Figure 11-9

$.75 = \$1,252.50$), and finally determining the total cost of the job and the cost per unit in the summary section.

The total cost of Order No. 104 in the illustration is \$5,517.70, and the cost per unit is \$4.18 (\$5,517.70 ÷ 1,320).

2. *Post Completed Cost Sheet to Finished Goods Ledger.* The cost sheet for Order No. 104 is entered in the Finished Goods account for Product A as shown. Details are date (February 12), P.O. No. (104), quantity (1,320), cost each (\$4.18), and amount (\$5,517.70).

Note also that new balances for quantity and amount are entered in the two right-hand columns. The formula is previous new balance plus goods completed on this order equals new balance.

FINISHED GOODS ACCOUNT
Illustrating Entry For Completed Cost Sheet

2

> Post completed cost sheet

> New balances: quantity and amount

Finished Goods Account

Description _____ Product A

		COMPLETED					SHIPPED				BALANCE	
Date 19__	P.O. No.	Quan-tity	Cost Each	Amount		Date 19__	Invoice No.	Quan-tity	Cost Each	Amount	Quan-tity	Amount
Feb. 1	Inven	tory	$4 00	$					$	$	1,600	$ 6,400 00
12	104	1,320	4 18+	5,517 70							2,920	11,917 70

Figure 11-10

3. *Enter Cost Sheet in Finished Goods journal.* The cost sheet for Order No. 104 is entered on the first line of the finished goods journal illustrated. Note that separate columns are provided for materials (\$2,061.20), labor (\$2,204), expense (\$1,252.50), and total for the order (\$5,517.70).

4. *Post Totals of Finished Goods Journal to Control Accounts at End of Month.* At the end of the month, the finished goods journal is footed and cross-footed to determine that the debit totals equal credit totals. The totals are posted directly to control accounts in the general ledger. Credit Materials in Process, Labor in Process, and Factory Expense in Process, respectively, with the totals of the elements for the month, and debit Finished Goods for the grand total.

3 [Enter cost sheet]

FINISHED GOODS JOURNAL

Finished Goods Journal

Month of __February__ 19__

Date 19__		P.O. No.	Quan-tity	Product	151 Finished Goods, Debit		Work In Process, Credit		
							141 Materials	142 Labor	143 Factory Expense
Feb.	12	104	1,320	A	$ 5,517 70		$2,061 20	$ 2,204 00	$1,252 50
	12	101	300	B	1,417 50		348 00	664 50	405 00
	13	102	600	A	2,469 50		936 00	956 00	577 50
	13	103	600	C	3,082 00		984 00	1,303 00	795 00
	18	105	1,190	C	6,354 60		1,951 60	2,820 50	1,582 50
	25	106	990	B	4,821 40		1,148 40	2,353 00	1,320 00
					$23,662 70		$7,429 20	$10,301 00	$5,932 50
					(151)		(141)	(142)	(143)

4 [Post totals to control accounts]

Finished Goods Inventory Control — No. 151

19__			F	Amount		19__		F	Amount
Feb.	1	Inventory		$23,300 00		19__			
	28	Goods completed	FG4	23,662 70					

Materials in Process Inventory Control — No. 141

19__			F	Amount		19__			F	Amount
Feb.	1	Inventory		$ 2,268 00		Feb.	28	Goods completed	FG4	$ 7,429 20
	28	Materials used	RJ2	7,389 00				Balance		2,227 80
				$ 9,657 00						$ 9,657 00
Mar.	1	Inventory		$ 2,227 80						

Labor in Process Inventory Control — No. 142

19__			F	Amount		19__			F	Amount
Feb.	1	Inventory		$ 1,597 50		Feb.	28	Goods completed	FG4	$10,301 00
	28	Labor used	GJ3	10,577 00				Balance		1,873 50
				$12,174 50						$12,174 50
Mar.	1	Inventory		$ 1,873 50						

Factory Expense in Process Inventory Control — No. 143

19__			F	Amount		19__			F	Amount
Feb.	1	Inventory		$ 1,012 50		Feb.	28	Goods completed	FG4	$ 5,932 50
	27	Expense applied	GJ3	5,947 50				Balance		1,027 50
				$ 6,960 00						$ 6,960 00
Mar.	1	Inventory		$ 1,027 50						

Figure 11-11

Procedure for cost of goods sold. The steps for recording cost of goods sold are:

(1) Post sales invoice to the finished goods ledger and enter cost of the goods shipped on the invoice.
(2) Enter the invoice in the sales journal.
(3) At the end of the month, post totals of sales journal to control accounts in the general ledger.

These steps are explained and illustrated in the following sections.

1. *Post Invoice to Finished Goods Ledger; Enter Cost on Invoice.* This is actually a two-phase operation, although only the first phase is illustrated below. The phase illustrated can be described:

(a) From the invoice (office copy), enter date (February 3), invoice number (51), and quantity (1,390) in the shipped section of the Finished Goods account.

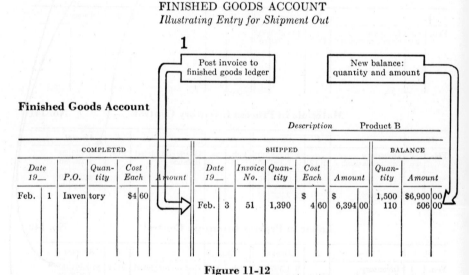

FINISHED GOODS ACCOUNT
Illustrating Entry for Shipment Out

Figure 11-12

(b) Compute the cost of the goods shipped by use of the unit cost appearing in the Completed section (1,390 units × $4.60 = $6,394). Enter cost each and total cost of the shipment in the Shipped section, as illustrated.

The second phase (not illustrated) is to write the unit cost ($4.60) and the total cost ($6,394) on the invoice.

(c) Enter the new balance (quantity 110 and value $506) in the two right-hand columns of the account. The formula for the calculation is previous new balance minus this shipment equals new balance.

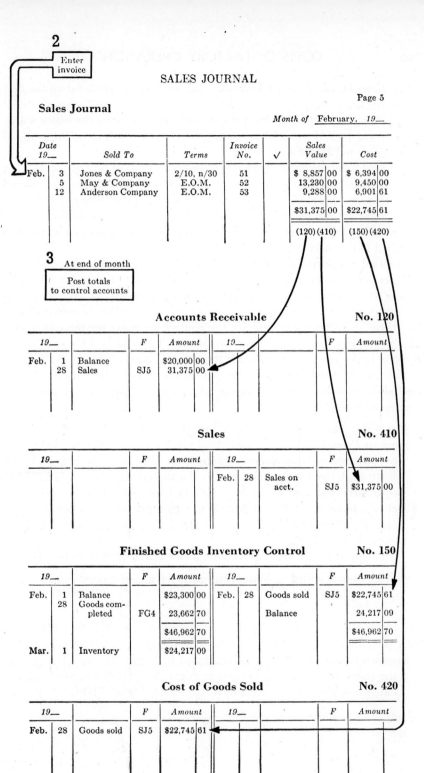

2

Enter invoice

SALES JOURNAL

Sales Journal

Page 5

Month of February, 19___

Date 19___		Sold To	Terms	Invoice No.	✓	Sales Value		Cost	
Feb.	3	Jones & Company	2/10, n/30	51		$ 8,857	00	$ 6,394	00
	5	May & Company	E.O.M.	52		13,230	00	9,450	00
	12	Anderson Company	E.O.M.	53		9,288	00	6,901	61
						$31,375	00	$22,745	61
						(120) (410)		(150) (420)	

3 At end of month

Post totals to control accounts

Accounts Receivable — No. 120

19___			F	Amount		19___			F	Amount
Feb.	1	Balance		$20,000	00					
	28	Sales	SJ5	31,375	00					

Sales — No. 410

19___		F	Amount		19___			F	Amount	
					Feb.	28	Sales on acct.	SJ5	$31,375	00

Finished Goods Inventory Control — No. 150

19___			F	Amount		19___			F	Amount	
Feb.	1	Balance		$23,300	00	Feb.	28	Goods sold	SJ5	$22,745	61
	28	Goods completed	FG4	23,662	70			Balance		24,217	09
				$46,962	70					$46,962	70
Mar.	1	Inventory		$24,217	09						

Cost of Goods Sold — No. 420

19___			F	Amount		19___		F	Amount
Feb.	28	Goods sold	SJ5	$22,745	61				

Figure 11-13

245

2. *Enter Invoice in Sales Journal.* Invoice No. 51 is entered on the first line of the sales journal. Sales value ($8,857) and cost ($6,394) are entered in adjoining columns. During the month, the items in the Sales Value column are posted as debits to the customers accounts. (These detail postings are not illustrated.)

3. *Post Totals of Sales Journal to Control Accounts at End of Month.* At the end of the month, the two columns in the sales journal are totaled and the totals are posted to control accounts in the general ledger. The posting of total sales is a debit to Accounts Receivable and a credit to Sales. The posting of total cost is a debit to Cost of Sales account and a credit to Finished Goods account.

Control accounts and proofs of subsidiary ledgers. The relationship between the subsidiary ledgers of the job order cost system and their respective control accounts is illustrated on page 247. The Materials Inventory Control account is the control account for the materials ledger. The three in-process accounts are the control accounts for the cost sheets which comprise the work in process ledger. The Finished Goods Control account is the control account for the finished goods ledger. At the end of the month, the balances in the subsidiary ledgers are proved against the balances of the control accounts, as a proof posting. These proofs are illustrated as follows:

Materials: This proof is illustrated on page 249.

Work in Process: The open cost sheets in the work in process ledger are proved against the control accounts as illustrated in Figure 11-15. Note that the total of charges to the materials columns ($2,227.80) equals the balance of the Materials in Process account shown in the chart, page 247. The total of the charges to the labor columns ($1,873.50) equals the balance of the Labor in Process Control account in the chart.

The proof of factory expense chargeable to the open cost sheet is:

$$\begin{array}{ccccc} \text{Labor hours posted} & & \text{Normal expense} & & \text{Expense applicable, per} \\ \text{to cost sheets} & \times & \text{rate} & = & \text{balance of control account} \\ \text{1,370 hours} & \times & \$.75 & = & \$1,027.50 \end{array}$$

Note that the expense applicable as computed by this formula agrees with the balance of the control account in the chart (Figure 11-14).

Finished Goods: This proof is illustrated in Figure 11-16. The sum of the balances in the finished goods ledger ($24,217.09) agrees with the balance of the control account in the chart, Figure 11-14.

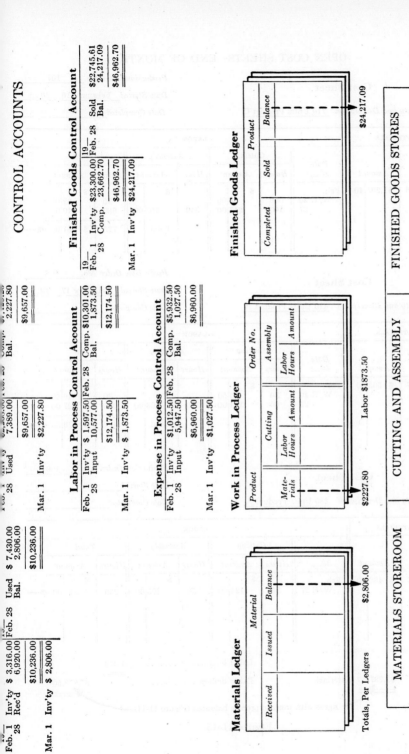

CONTROL ACCOUNTS

Finished Goods Control Account

19— Feb. 1	Inv'ty	$23,300.00	19— Feb. 28	Sold	$22,745.61
28	Comp.	23,662.70		Bal.	24,217.09
		$46,962.70			$46,962.70
Mar. 1	Inv'ty	$24,217.09			

Labor in Process Control Account

Feb. 1	Inv'ty	$1,597.50	Feb. 28	Comp.	$10,301.00
28	Input	10,577.00		Bal.	1,873.50
		$12,174.50			$12,174.50
Mar. 1	Inv'ty	$1,873.50			

Expense in Process Control Account

Feb. 1	Inv'ty	$1,012.50	Feb. 28	Comp.	$5,932.50
28	Input	5,947.50		Bal.	1,027.50
		$6,960.00			$6,960.00
Mar. 1	Inv'ty	$1,027.50			

(partial, left edge)

Feb. 1	Inv'ty	$3,316.00	Feb. 28	Used	$7,430.00
	Rec'd	6,920.00		Bal.	2,806.00
		$10,236.00			$10,236.00
Mar. 1	Inv'ty	$2,806.00			

Finished Goods Ledger

Product			
Completed	Sold	Balance	

$24,217.09

Work in Process Ledger

Product   Order No.

Materials	Cutting		Assembly	
	Labor Hours	Amount	Labor Hours	Amount

$2227.80   Labor $1873.50

Materials Ledger

Material		
Received	Issued	Balance

Totals, Per Ledgers $2,806.00

MATERIALS STOREROOM	CUTTING AND ASSEMBLY	FINISHED GOODS STORES
Materials Received	Materials Issued → Goods Completed →	Goods Sold

Figure 11-14

OPEN COST SHEETS—END OF MONTH

Cost Sheet

Production Order No. _____ 107
Date Started February 16, 19__
Date Completed _____

Quantity and Description 710 Units Product C

MATERIALS		LABOR							
			Cutting		Assembly		Total		
Date 19__	Amount	Date 19__	Hours	Amount	Hours	Amount	Hours	Amount	
Feb. 16	$1,205 40	Feb. W/E 20	40	$ 62 00		$	40	$ 62 00	
		27	140	217 00	540	702 00	680	919 00	
						Total	720	$ 981 00	←

Cost Sheet

Production Order No. _____ 108
Date Started February 17, 19__
Date Completed _____

Quantity and Description 410 Units Product B

MATERIALS		LABOR							
			Cutting		Assembly		Total		
Date 19__	Amount	Date 19__	Hours	Amount	Hours	Amount	Hours	Amount	
Feb. 17	$ 533 60	Feb. W/E 20	30	$ 46 50		$	30	$ 46 50	
		27	80	124 00	310	403 00	390	527 00	
						Total	420	$ 573 50	←

Cost Sheet

Production Order No. _____ 109
Date Started _____
Date Completed _____

Quantity and Description 280 Units Product A

MATERIALS		LABOR							
			Cutting		Assembly		Total		
Date 19__	Amount	Date 19__	Hours	Amount	Hours	Amount	Hours	Amount	
Feb. 23	$ 488 80	Feb. W/E 27	80	$ 124 00	150	$ 195 00	230	$ 319 00	←

$2,227.80 Materials ←

Labor hours............ 1,370

Labor dollars........... $1,873.50

Agree with work in process balances (Figure 11-14)

Figure 11-15

248

PROOF OF FINISHED GOODS LEDGER

Finished Goods Account — Description: Product A

COMPLETED

Date 19—	P.O. No.	Quantity	Cost Each	Amount
Feb. 1	Inventory			$
12	104	1,320	$ 4 18+	5,517 70
13	102	600	4 12−	2,469 50

SHIPPED

Date 19—	Invoice No.	Quantity	Cost Each	Amount
Feb. 12	{ 53	1,600	$ 4 00	$ 6,400 00
	53	120	4 18	501 61

BALANCE

Quantity	Amount
1,600	$ 6,400 00
1,200	5,016 09
1,800	7,485 59

Finished Goods Account — Description: Product B

COMPLETED

Date 19—	P.O. No.	Quantity	Cost Each	Amount
Feb. 1	Inventory		$4 60	$
12	101	300	4 72½	1,417 50
25	106	990	4 87+	4,821 40

SHIPPED

Date 19—	Invoice No.	Quantity	Cost Each	Amount
Feb. 3	51	1,390	$ 4 60	$ 6,394 00

BALANCE

Quantity	Amount
1,500	$ 6,900 00
110	506 00
410	1,923 50
1,400	6,774 90

Finished Goods Account — Description: Product C

COMPLETED

Date 19—	P.O. No.	Quantity	Cost Each	Amount
Feb. 1	Inventory		$5 00	$
13	103	600	5 14−	3,082 00
18	105	1,190	5 34	6,354 60

SHIPPED

Date 19—	Invoice No.	Quantity	Cost Each	Amount
Feb. 5	52	1,890	$5 00	$9,450 00

BALANCE

Quantity	Amount
2,000	$10,000 00
110	550 00
710	3,632 00
1,900	9,986 60

Proof: Sum of balances, $24,217.09, agrees with balance of Finished Goods account (Figure 11-14).

Figure 11-16

II. BASES FOR THE CALCULATION OF ESTIMATED FACTORY EXPENSE RATES

Bases named: Capacity. Two bases for the calculation of factory expense rates were explained and illustrated in Chapter 9: actual basis and estimated basis. Under the *actual* basis, factory expense rates are calculated at the end of each month, reflecting the actual expense and actual hours (or other rate factor) for the month. Under the estimated basis, factory expense rates are calculated at the beginning of some selected period, reflecting a specified volume of production decided upon by the management.

Estimated rates may reflect any one of three volumes as indicated in the table "Calculation of Estimated Factory Expense Rates" below.

Calculation of Estimated Factory Expense Rates:
Three Bases*

	(1)	(2)	(3)	(4)	(5)
			Variable		*Total Rate*
		Fixed	*Expense*	*Total*	*Per Hour*
Bases	*Hours*	*Expense*	*(1) × $.475*	*Expense*	*(4) − (1)*
Practical capacity	10,000	$2,200.00	$4,750.00	$6,950.00	.695
Average capacity	9,000	2,200.00	4,275.00	6,475.00	.719
Expected actual	8,000	2,200.00	3,800.00	6,000.00	.75
	7,000	2,200.00	3,325.00	5,525.00	.789
	6,000	2,200.00	2,850.00	5,050.00	.842
	5,000	2,200.00	2,375.00	4,575.00	.915
	4,000	2,200.00	1,900.00	4,100.00	1.025
	3,000	2,200.00	1,425.00	3,625.00	1.208
	2,000	2,200.00	950.00	3,150.00	1.575
	1,000	2,200.00	475.00	2,675.00	2.675

* This table is based upon the chart "Factory Expense Rates by Level of Production," page 193.

Figure 11-17

(1) The expected average actual volume for the coming year ($.75 per hour). The so-called "normal" rate illustrated in Chapter 9 was assumed to be based upon the volume for the coming year.* When such a rate is used, it is expected that cumulative applied expense will balance cumulative actual expense over the year (and that there will be no underabsorbed expense at the end of the year). In fact, there *will be* no underabsorbed expense at the end of the year if actual expense and actual hours for the year agree with normal expense and normal hours.

In some businesses, there are a busy season and a slack season each year, and an estimated rate of the kind described would average out the *seasonal*

* The term "normal" was introduced for convenience in Chapter 9. Some cost accountants describe other estimated rates as "normal" rates.

fluctuations due to volume. Such rates would not iron out the *cyclical* fluctuations which occur over a period of several years ("good" years and "poor" years).

There would be a new estimated rate at the beginning of each year. The estimated rate for any year would tend to be low for expected "good" years and high for expected "poor" years.

(2) The expected average sales volume for a period of years ($.719), which is assumed here to be "capacity to make and sell." The average sales capacity rate is expected to iron out the fluctuations due to cyclical factors as well as seasonal factors.

(3) Practical capacity for the plant ($.695 per hour). This is the number of hours that the plant, as set up by the engineers, is expected to operate, on a single-shift, two-shift, or three-shift plan as specified. (The supervisory organization and certain other factors vary as among single-shift and multiple-shift operation, and consequently, practical capacity is calculated with specific reference to the number of shifts to be worked.)

Practical capacity is distinguished from theoretical capacity, the latter of which is the number of hours the plant can operate in, say, a single-shift plan *with no down time*. Practical capacity is theoretical capacity minus a reasonable allowance for unavoidable down time for repairs. Note that in some assembly line production, the amount of production that can come off the end of the line is limited by one particular machine on the line—the bottleneck operation. Under practical capacity, normal hours would be the number of labor hours the plant would operate up to the limit imposed on the plant by the bottleneck operation.

In the dye house of a fabric mill, for instance, the drier (a large oven-like structure with a conveyor to carry the fabric through) may be the bottleneck operation. Each fabric goes through the drier regardless of the combination of operations which precede and follow the drier.

It might be pointed out that the expected actual volume, or the average capacity volume, might be considerably *lower* in an actual case than the levels indicated in this illustration. This would mean that the rates per hour would be higher. The selection of capacity level for factory expense rates would be of great importance to the management. It is obvious, of course, that in an actual case, "expected actual" level could be higher than "average capacity."

Cumulative underabsorbed expense under the several bases. The cumulative underabsorbed and overabsorbed expense at the end of a year would be different as among the several possible bases:

(1) If the estimated rate is based upon expense and hours expected for one year, it is expected that factory expense of the year will all be absorbed by the end of the year. This situation is illustrated in the cumulative expense table in Chapter 9 (page 200).

(2) If the estimated rate is based upon sales capacity, it is expected that there will be underabsorbed expense or overabsorbed expense at the end of any year.   It is expected that over a period of years representing the cycle, overabsorbed expense would balance underabsorbed expense.   (In practice, when an average sales capacity basis is used, any under- or overabsorbed expense existing at the end of a year is likely to be closed to Profit and Loss even though it is theorized that such balances would cancel each other out over a period of years.)   The cumulative underabsorbed expense statement, illustrated in Figure 11-18, shows that where the average sales capacity rate ($.71944+ per hour) is used, the underabsorbed expense balance at the end of the year is expected to be $2,933.34.

Expected Cumulative Under- and Overabsorbed Factory Expense
by Months, Year 19—

Estimated Rate Based Upon Average Sales Capacity

	(1)	(2)	(3)	(4)	(5)	(6)
	Expected Actual Factory Expense	Expected Actual Hours	Absorbed Factory Expense (Col. 2 × $.71944 +)	Cumulative		Cumulative Underabsorbed*
				Actual	Absorbed	
January........	$ 5,050.00	6,000	$ 4,316.67	$ 5,050.00	$ 4,316.67	$ 733.33
February......	6,000.00	8,000	5,755.56	11,050.00	10,072.23	977.77
March.........	6,475.00	9,000	6,475.00	17,525.00	16,547.23	977.77
April..........	6,950.00	10,000	7,194.44	24,475.00	23,741.67	733.33
May..........	6,950.00	10,000	7,194.44	31,425.00	30,936.11	488.89
June..........	6,475.00	9,000	6,475.00	37,900.00	37,411.11	488.89
July..........	6,475.00	9,000	6,475.00	44,375.00	43,886.11	488.89
August........	6,000.00	8,000	5,755.56	50,375.00	49,641.67	733.33
September.....	6,000.00	8,000	5,755.56	56,375.00	55,397.23	977.77
October.......	5,525.00	7,000	5,036.11	61,900.00	60,433.34	1,466.66
November.....	5,050.00	6,000	4,316.66	66,950.00	64,750.00	2,200.00
December.....	5,050.00	6,000	4,316.66	72,000.00	69,066.66	2,933.34
	$72,000.00	96,000	$69,066.66			

*Underabsorbed expense is idle capacity loss: 12,000 hrs. × $.244 = $2,933.34

Figure 11-18

(3) If the estimated rate is based upon practical capacity, there will be underabsorbed expense at the end of *any* year when actual hours worked is less than the practical capacity of the plant.   There will likewise be overabsorbed expense at the end of any year when the actual hours worked exceed practical capacity as calculated.   The cumulative underabsorbed expense statement in Figure 11-19 shows that where the practical capacity rate ($.695 per hour) is used to apply expense, the underabsorbed expense is expected to be $5,280 at the end of the year.

Expected Cumulative Under- and Overabsorbed Factory Expense

by Months, Year 19—

Estimated Rate Based Upon Practical Capacity

	(1) Expected Actual Factory Expense (Fig. 9-15)	(2) Expected Actual Hours (Fig. 9-15)	(3) Absorbed Factory Expense (Col. 2 × $.695)	(4) Cumulative Actual	(5) Cumulative Absorbed	(6) Cumulative Underabsorbed*
January.......	$ 5,050.00	6,000	$ 4,170.00	$ 5,050.00	$ 4,170.00	$ 880.00
February......	6,000.00	8,000	5,560.00	11,050.00	9,730.00	1,320.00
March........	6,475.00	9,000	6,255.00	17,525.00	15,985.00	1,540.00
April.........	6,950.00	10,000	6,950.00	24,475.00	22,935.00	1,540.00
May..........	6,950.00	10,000	6,950.00	31,425.00	29,885.00	1,540.00
June..........	6,475.00	9,000	6,255.00	37,900.00	36,140.00	1,760.00
July..........	6,475.00	9,000	6,255.00	44,375.00	42,395.00	1,980.00
August........	6,000.00	8,000	5,560.00	50,375.00	47,955.00	2,420.00
September,....	6,000.00	8,000	5,560.00	56,375.00	53,515.00	2,860.00
October.......	5,525.00	7,000	4,865.00	61,900.00	58,380.00	3,520.00
November.....	5,050.00	6,000	4,170.00	66,950.00	62,550.00	4,400.00
December.....	5,050.00	6,000	4,170.00	72,000.00	66,720.00	5,280.00
	$72,000.00	96,000	$66,720.00			

*Underabsorbed expense is idle capacity loss: 24,000 hrs. × $.22 = $5,280.00

Figure 11-19

Effect of estimated rate basis upon expense rates and product costs.

The estimated rates calculated under each of the several volumes are:

(1) Expected actual for the coming year: $.75 per hour.
(2) Average sales capacity: $.71944 + per hour.
(3) Practical capacity: $.695 per hour.

The rates differ according to the volume upon which they are based. Unit product costs would likewise be different as among the various bases that might be used. Thus, in selecting the particular volume on which to base estimated rates, the management must consider (1) the effect upon unit costs which are presumably considered when the price lists are made up and (2) the probable behavior of the underabsorbed factory expense balance.

Idle capacity loss. The underabsorbed factory expense amounts shown on Figures 11-18 and 11-19 are *idle capacity losses*—the result of acquiring factory capacity and supervisory organization, and failing to operate the factory to capacity level.

Capacity loss (or in this case, *anticipated* capacity loss) can be calculated by a method other than setting up an underabsorbed expense table to show how factory expense and factory expense applied amounts will accumulate in the accounts (which was done in Figures 11-18 and 11-19). This method involves computing directly the loss in fixed expenses due to operating the plant a lesser number of hours than the capacity selected for expense rate purposes.

(1) Assuming that the estimated rate selected is based upon average sales capacity (9,000 hours per month or 108,000 hours per year):

  (a) Fixed expense per capacity hour = Fixed expense per month ($2,200) ÷ Capacity hours per month (9,000) = $.244+ per hour.
  (b) Lost hours for year = Capacity hours (108,000) − Expected actual hours (96,000) = 12,000.
  (c) Idle capacity loss = Lost hours (12,000) × Fixed expense per capacity hour ($.244+) = $2,933.34. This amount agrees with the cumulative underabsorbed expense amount in Figure 11-18.

(2) Assuming that the normal rate selected is based upon practical capacity (10,000 hours per month or 120,000 hours per year):

  (a) Fixed expense per capacity hour = Fixed expense per month ($2,200) ÷ Capacity hours per month (10,000) = $.22 per hour.
  (b) Lost hours for year = Capacity (120,000) − Expected actual hours (96,000) = 24,000.
  (c) Idle capacity loss = Lost hours (24,000) × Fixed expenses per capacity hour ($.22) = $5,280. This amount agrees with the cumulative underabsorbed expense amount in Figure 11-19.

QUESTIONS

11-1. State concisely what is included in the function of accounting for cost of goods manufactured and cost of goods sold.

11-2. What is meant by the term "organization for physical control" in connection with finished goods?

11-3. Name and describe briefly various managerial reports concerned with cost of goods manufactured and cost of goods sold. Indicate the use that the management might make of each report.

11-4. Compare the "cost accounting" form of Statement of Cost of Goods Completed shown on page 231 with the "financial accounting" form of the statement shown on page 29.

11-5. What is meant by cost analysis? How might cost analysis be involved in following up the reports on cost of goods manufactured?

11-6. Name the principal forms used in accounting for cost of goods manufactured and cost of goods sold, and state briefly the purpose of each form.

11-7. (a) Name the steps of procedure in accounting for cost of goods manufactured in a job order cost system.

(b) Name the steps of procedure in accounting for cost of goods sold.

11-8. What proofs of posting are operated in connection with (a) cost sheets and (b) finished goods ledger accounts?

11-9. (a) Name several bases for calculating estimated factory expense rates.

(b) Why is the selection of basis important when costs are to be used as a factor in selling prices? Explain fully.

11-10. Describe the expected behavior of the underabsorbed expense balance under each of the three bases.

11-11. The cost of idle capacity is determined in Figures 11-18 and 11-19 as budget expense minus (actual hours worked × estimated expense rate). State a different formula for determining the cost of idle capacity.

11-12. Where does underabsorbed factory expense appear on the Balance Sheet? Overabsorbed expense?

DISCUSSION QUESTIONS

11-13. (a) State the arguments in favor of using practical capacity as a basis for estimated burden rates. State the arguments against using practical capacity.

(b) State the arguments in favor of using average sales capacity as a basis for estimated burden rates. State the arguments against using average sales capacity.

11-14. The sales manager states that the industry in which his company is doing business is "operating at 60 per cent of capacity" and that the factory expense rates of his company should likewise be set at 60 per cent of capacity to provide costs on which to base selling prices. What is your opinion?

11-15. Assume that estimated factory expense rates were set at the beginning of a calendar year and that the rates have been in use for several months, being charged to cost sheets and likewise used to absorb expense into Work in Process account.

If the volume of sales and production suddenly drops significantly below budget volume, should the factory expense rates be changed to reflect the change in volume?

11-16. Is idle capacity cost, determined as in your answer to Question 11-11, strictly speaking a cost or a loss? How should it be disposed of in the accounts?

11-17. The Farwell Manufacturing Company, which has a large factory in Chicago, is planning to build a factory with a finished goods warehouse in a town several hundred miles from Chicago. The warehouse in the new factory will be used to store only goods produced in that factory.

The assistant controller is setting up a classification of accounts for the factory and warehouse. The question arises as to whether the cost of operating the warehouse should be charged to factory expense or to selling expense.

Discuss the arguments for charging to one account or the other from the standpoint of (a) the chief manufacturing executive and (b) the chief marketing executive.

11-18. Should the cost of boxes, bottles, or other containers in which the product is sold be charged to factory expense or to selling expense?

11-19. The Taylor Manufacturing Company operates shops in which specialty products are made on a contract basis. When the sales department turns up a prospective customer, the industrial engineers and the cost estimators examine the proposed job to determine how it would be done in the factory and how much it would cost. Certain "premanufacturing" is the same whether or not the sales department succeeds in selling the job. If the sales department sells the job, the industrial engineers complete the premanufacturing work and put the job into production.

The vice president in charge of marketing says that all premanufacturing cost should be charged to factory expense, since it must be incurred before any manufacturing can be done. The vice president in charge of production says that it should be charged to selling expense since premanufacturing must be done to make any sales.

What is your opinion?

11-1. The blanks in the Workbook are in three parts:
Part I   —Journals of the Rogers Manufacturing Company
Part II —Ledgers
Part III—Trial Balance

Required:

  (1) Complete all entries in the journals
  (2) Complete all postings from journals to ledgers
  (3) Prepare the trial balance
  (4) Prepare a balance sheet, statement of profits, statement of cost of goods sold, and statement of cost of goods completed.
Detach and submit all parts together with the statements.

11-2. Hear-Avision Incorporated produces Products X and Y from Materials A and B. A job order cost system is used. Factory expense is applied at a normal rate of $1 per direct labor hour. The FIFO method of costing is used with both materials and finished goods.

During February, no collections on account were made. All suppliers' invoices were paid 5 days after receipt. The monthly payroll was paid February 28.

During February, Job Nos. 101 and 102 were completed. Job No. 101 was completed February 6 and Job No. 102 was completed February 20.

The documents, journals, and ledgers for February are in the Workbook. Journalize and make all the postings for February and prepare a statement of cost of goods manufactured during February.

11-3. The following "fill-in" forms are presented in the Workbook:

  Finished goods journal
  Sales journal
  Cost sheets
  Finished goods ledger accounts
  Control accounts for work in process and finished goods, and certain other accounts.

Required:

  (1) Make all entries and postings necessary to record the following transactions:

      Jan. 8—Production Order No. 101 completed. Apply factory expense rate of $1.00 per hour to Jan. 1 balance; $1.50 per hour to hours worked in January.
      Jan. 12—Sold to Lincoln Company, 25 units Item X @ $200 per unit; Invoice No. 31.
      Jan. 22—Production Order No. 102 completed.
      Jan. 24—Sold to Miller & Co., 15 units Item Y @ $40 per unit; Invoice No. 32.

  (2) Assuming that there are no further transactions, foot and cross-foot the journals and post to the accounts.

11-4. The following completed journals for the month of January, 19__ are presented in the Workbook:

  Voucher register
  Requisition journal
  General journal

Finished goods journal
Sales journal

Uncompleted ("fill-in") account forms are also presented.

Required:

Post the journals to the account forms provided. Bring down closing balances in the accounts.

PROBLEMS

11-1. Draft entries in simple journal entry form to record the following transactions. After each entry, indicate (a) what basic accounting paper is used for the original writing of the transaction, (b) what subsidiary ledger account (if any) would be debited and what subsidiary ledger account (if any) would be credited, and (c) what special journal would be used for summarizing the particular type of transaction.

(1) Production Order No. 128, covering 100 units of Product T made for stock, is completed. The cost sheet shows the following totals:

Materials...................	$200.00
Labor......................	340.00
Factory expense.............	225.00
Total......................	$765.00

(2) Production Order No. 136 was spoiled in process, with no scrap value. The cost sheet shows the following totals to point of spoilage:

Materials...................	$ 50.00
Labor......................	25.00
Factory expense.............	20.00
Total.....................	$ 95.00

(Charge Factory Expense account = Spoiled work)

(3) Production Order No. 138, made for Clayton Brown, is completed and shipped. Mr. Brown was billed for $1,000. The cost sheet shows the following totals:

Materials...................	$225.00
Labor......................	360.00
Factory expense.............	230.00
Total.....................	$815.00

(Charge Cost of Sales.)

(4) Shipped 50 units of Product T from stock to William Ordway, billing @ $9 per unit.

(5) Received freight bill from N.Y.C. Railroad for $50 covering the shipment of Product T to William Ordway. The goods were shipped freight prepaid to Ordway, who is to be billed for the freight.

(6) Ordway returned 10 units of Product T for credit. He states that we did not meet our delivery date promise, and that he cannot handle the full

original order. He shipped the goods freight collect, and we voucher the freight bill ($10) for payment.

(7) Shipped 25 units of Product T to Fred Park, billing him @ $9 per unit. We agree to stand the freight, which is $30. State the entry for freight.

(8) We pay for repair of one unit of Product L returned by the customer, under the 30-day warranty. No charge to customer. The repair charge, which we pay to an outside repairman, is $10.

11-2. Following is a summary of charges to production order cost sheets of the Phillips Manufacturing Company for the month of January, 19___.

	Completed		Uncompleted	
Production Order No.	101	102	103	Totals
Product.....................	A	B	C	
Quantity....................	10 units	20 units	10 units	
Materials...................	$130.00	$ 77.50	$120.00	$ 327.50
Labor hours.................	300	170	310	780
Labor cost..................	$450.00	$270.00	$465.00	$1,185.00

Sales for the month:

				Sales Value	
Customer	Invoice No.	Product	Quantity	Each	Total
W. C. Brown................	81	A	5	$120.00	$ 600.00
P. C. Smith.................	82	B	5	40.00	200.00
Fred Barish.................	83	B	10	40.00	400.00
			20		$1,200.00

Required:

(1) Draft entries in simple journal entry form for:

    (a) Production orders completed (Factory expense rate: $1 per hour)
    (b) Cost of goods sold.
    (c) Sales value of goods sold.

(2) Set up "T" accounts and post entries in (1).

11-3. The cost sheets for the Blaine Manufacturing Company are shown below. In addition, the following data are available to you:

Materials inventory January 1..........		$1,300.00
Materials purchased during January......		9,500.00
Finished goods inventory January 1......		—
Factory expense incurred during January		
Department 1......................	$175.00	
Department 2......................	320.00	
Department 3......................	210.00	$ 705.00
Total		
Budget for January		
Department 1 (150 hrs.)..............	$150.00	
Department 2 (200 hrs.)..............	300.00	
Department 3 (250 hrs.)..............	225.00	

Job Nos. 101, 102 and 103 are completed in January. Job Nos. 101 and 102 are sold in January.

The company uses normal departmental factory expense rates.   The same normal rates were used in December.

Required:

Using T accounts, reconstruct all general ledger inventory accounts, factory expense, factory expense applied, and cost of goods sold, showing all entries for January.   Indicate the source of each entry in the accounts.

Job No. __101__   *Manufactured for:*   ___Jones Equipment Co.___

*Completed*___Jan. 18___   *Delivered*___Jan. 25___

*Sales Price*___$6,200.00___

	Material	Labor	\multicolumn{4}{c}{Labor Hours by Departments}
			1	*2*	*3*	*Total*
Jan. 1 Bal.	$1,200.00	$ 600.00	110	10	60	180
Jan. Charges	600.00	700.00	—	70	70	140
Total	$1,800.00	$1,300.00	110	80	130	320

Summary of Costs:		*Factory Expense*		
Material...............	$1,800.00	Department 1	110 @ $1.00	$110.00
Labor................	1,300.00	Department 2	80 @ $1.50	$120.00
Factory Exp.	347.00	Department 3	130 @ $ .90	$117.00
Total Cost............	$3,447.00	Total		$347.00

Job No. __102__   *Manufactured for:*   ___King & Co.___

*Completed*___Jan. 25___   *Delivered*___Jan. 29___

*Sales Price*___$5,800.00___

	Material	Labor	\multicolumn{4}{c}{Labor Hours by Departments}
			1	*2*	*3*	*Total*
Jan. 1 Bal.	$1,000.00	$ 450.00	100	—	—	100
Jan. Charges	900.00	725.00	10	76	100	186
Total	$1,900.00	$1,175.00	110	76	100	286

Summary of Costs:		*Factory Expense:*		
Material...............	$1,900.00	Department 1	110 @ $1.00	$110.00
Labor................	1,175.00	Department 2	76 @ $1.50	$114.00
Factory Exp.	314.00	Department 3	100 @ $ .90	$ 90.00
Total Cost............	$3,389.00	Total		$314.00

Job No.   103   Manufactured for: Adams Inc.

Completed   Jan. 31   Delivered

Sales Price

	Material	Labor	Labor Hours by Departments			
			1	2	3	Total
Jan. Charges	$1,900.00	$1,200.00	100	60	100	260
Total	$1,900.00	$1,200.00	100	60	100	260

Summary of Costs:

Material............... $1,900.00

Labor................. 1,200.00

Factory Exp........... 280.00

Total Cost............ $3,380.00

Factory Expense:

Department 1   100 @ $1.00 $100.00

Department 2   60 @ $1.50 $ 90.00

Department 3   100 @ $ .90 $ 90.00

Total $280.00

Job No.   104   Manufactured for: Queen's Courts

Completed   Delivered

Sales Price

	Material	Labor	Labor Hours by Departments			
			1	2	3	Total
Jan. Charges	$900.00	$300.00	30	—	—	30
Total						

Summary of Costs:

Material...............

Labor.................

Factory Exp...........

Total Cost............

Factory Expense:

Department 1   @ $1.00

Department 2   @ $1.50

Department 3   @ $ .90

Total

Data for Problems **11-4** *through* **11-6**:

	Normal Month	Totals	Actual Month Job No. 101	Job No. 102	Job No. 103
Materials...........	$15,000.00	$11,000.00	$6,000.00	$3,000.00	$2,000.00
Labor					
Hours............	12,000	9,000	4,000	3,000	2,000
Amount...........	$15,000.00	$12,000.00	$5,000.00	$4,500.00	$2,500.00
Factory expense.....	$15,000.00	$12,000.00	—	—	—

11-4. The Tech Company operates a job order cost system controlled by the following inventory accounts in the general ledger:

    Materials control
    Materials in process control
    Labor in process control
    Factory expense in process
    Finished goods control

The data above cover the first month of the business. Job No. 101 was still in process at the end of the month. Job No. 102 and Job No. 103 were completed during the month. Job No. 103 was sold (and shipped) during the month. Factory expense is applied to jobs by a normal direct labor hour rate.

Required:

Draft all entries required to operate the inventory accounts, so far as data are given. Use simple journal entry form. In the explanation of each entry, include the name of the journal in the cost system from which the postings to general ledger accounts would actually come.

11-5. Prepare a Statement of Cost of Goods Manufactured of the "cost" type that would be identified with this system.

11-6. Draft a statement of underabsorbed expense.

11-7. The following information is presented herewith:
    Trial balance as of January 31, 19—, after recording transfer entries.
    Analysis of all general ledger accounts for January, 19—.

Required:

(1) Prepare Statement of Cost of Goods Sold and Statement of Cost of Goods Manufactured from the appropriate inventory accounts.
(2) Prepare Statement of Profits and Balance Sheet from the trial balance.

Trial Balance—January 31, 19__

Accounts	Debits	Credits
Cash	$ 4,970.80	$
Accounts receivable	3,580.00	
Raw materials inventory	2,625.00	
Materials in process inventory	300.00	
Labor in process inventory	220.00	
Factory expense in process inventory	90.00	
Finished goods inventory	1,865.60	
Prepaid insurance	165.00	
Office furniture and fixtures	2,400.00	
Reserve for depreciation—Office furniture and fixtures		140.00
Machinery and equipment	9,600.00	
Reserve for depreciation—Machinery and equipment		560.00
Vouchers payable		1,745.00
Accrued taxes		150.00
Capital stock		15,000.00
Surplus		6,713.00
Sales		5,600.00
Cost of goods sold	3,405.40	
Factory expense	925.20	
Factory expense applied		594.00
Selling expense	280.00	
Administrative expense	75.00	
	$30,502.00	$30,502.00

Cash

19__				19__			
Jan. 1	Balance		$3,618.00	Jan. 31	Payments		$4,847.20
31	Receipts		6,200.00	31	Balance		4,970.80
			$9,818.00				$9,818.00
Jan. 31	Balance		$4,970.80				

Accounts Receivable

19__				19__			
Jan. 1	Balance		$4,180.00	Jan. 31	Received on account		$6,200.00
31	Sales	SJ5	5,600.00	31	Balance		3,580.00
			$9,780.00				$9,780.00
Jan. 31	Balance		$3,580.00				

Raw Materials Inventory

19—				19—				
Jan. 1	Inventory		$ 250.00	Jan. 31	Materials used	RJ2	$ 925.00	
31	Purchases	VR1	3,300.00	31	Balance		2,625.00	
			$3,550.00				$3,550.00	
Jan. 31	Inventory		$2,625.00					

Materials in Process Inventory

19—				19—				
Jan. 1	Inventory		$ 100.00	Jan. 31	Materials in goods			
31	Materials used	RJ2	825.00		completed	FGJ4	$ 625.00	
				31	Balance		300.00	
			$ 925.00				$ 925.00	
Jan. 31	Inventory		$ 300.00					

Labor in Process Inventory

19—				19—				
Jan. 1	Inventory		$ 200.00	Jan. 31	Labor in goods			
31	Labor used	VR1	912.00		completed	FGJ4	$ 892.00	
				31	Balance		220.00	
			$1,112.00				$1,112.00	
Jan. 31	Inventory		$ 220.00					

Factory Expense in Process Inventory

19—				19—				
Jan. 1	Inventory		$ 100.00	Jan. 31	Factory expense in			
31	Expense applied GJ3		594.00		goods completed			
						FGJ4	$ 604.00	
				31	Balance		90.00	
			$ 694.00				$ 694.00	
Jan. 31	Inventory		$ 90.00					

Finished Goods Inventory

19—				19—				
Jan. 1	Inventory		$3,150.00	Jan. 31	Goods sold	SJ5	$3,405.40	
31	Goods completed FGJ4		2,121.00	31	Balance		1,865.60	
			$5,271.00				$5,271.00	
Jan. 31	Inventory		$1,865.60					

Prepaid Insurance

19—				19—				
Jan. 1	Prepaid	$ 180.00		Jan. 31	Insurance expense	GJ3	$	15.00
					Balance			165.00
		$ 180.00					$	180.00
Jan. 31	Prepaid	$ 165.00						

Office Furniture and Fixtures

19—		
Jan. 1	Balance	$2,400.00

Reserve for Depreciation—Office Furniture and Fixtures

	19—				
	Jan. 1	Balance		$	120.00
	31	Provision for month	GJ3		20.00

Machinery and Equipment

19—		
Jan. 1	Balance	$9,600.00

Reserve for Depreciation—Machinery and Equipment

	19—				
	Jan. 1	Balance		$	480.00
	31	Provision for month	GJ3		80.00

Vouchers Payable

19—			19—			
Jan. 31	Vouchers paid	$4,847.20	Jan. 1	Balance		$1,465.00
31	Balance	1,745.00	31	Vouchers issued	VR1	5,127.20
		$6,592.20				$6,592.20
			Jan. 31	Vouchers unpaid		$1,745.00

Accrued Taxes

			19—			
			Jan. 31	Accrued	GJ3	$ 150.00

Capital Stock

			19—		
			Jan. 1	Balance	$15,000.00

Surplus

			19—		
			Jan. 1	Balance	$6,713.00

Sales

			19—			
			Jan. 31	Sales for month	SJ5	$5,600.00

Cost of Goods Sold

19—			
Jan. 31	Cost of goods sold for month	SJ5	$3,405.40

Factory Expense

19—			
Jan. 31	Voucher items	VR1	$ 635.20
31	Indirect materials	RJ2	100.00
31	Journal charges	GJ3	190.00

Factory Expense Applied

	19—			
	Jan. 31	Applied for month's production	GJ3	$ 594.00

Selling Expense

19—			
Jan. 31	Voucher items	VR1	$ 280.00

Administrative Expense

19—			
Jan. 31	Journal charges	GJ3	$ 75.00

11-8. The management of the Steel Container Company makes a survey of all conditions relating to volume:

(1) The productive capacity of its machinery
(2) The estimated average annual sales for the following six years
   (The business is seasonal, and it is believed that six years constitute a normal cycle of years.)
(3) The expected sales volume for next year

All goods are made to order, there is no finished goods inventory, and the work in process inventory is not generally a significant factor. Fixed charges are a significant part of expense.

The cost accountant, in considering the computation of factory expense rates, assembles the following information:

	Covering Year	Average Sales	Manufacturing Capacity
Per cent of practical capacity.........	60%	80%	100%
Direct labor hours...................	10,800	14,400	18,000
Factory expense:			
Fixed...........................	$18,000.00	$18,000.00	$18,000.00
Variable.......................	10,800.00	14,400.00	18,000.00
Totals.......................	$28,800.00	$32,400.00	$36,000.00

The sales manager argues that factory expense rates should be based upon manufacturing capacity, and the factory superintendent argues in favor of setting the rate on the basis of sales for the coming year.

Required:

(1) Compute the factory expense rate for each basis:
   (a) Expected volume, coming year
   (b) Average sales
   (c) Practical capacity
(2) Assume that the actual sales volume for the coming year turns out to be exactly as estimated (10,800 hours) and that actual expenses incurred were as forecast ($28,800). Compute the amount of underabsorbed expense which would result during the coming year if the rate had been set on the basis of:
   (a) Expected volume, coming year
   (b) Average sales
   (c) Practical capacity

Discuss the validity of the sales manager's argument.

11-9. The following statements by months (six months) for the Stevens Manufacturing Company are presented herewith:

Exhibit I —Statement of Profits
Exhibit II —Statement of Cost of Goods Completed
Exhibit III—Statement of Factory Expense Applied

The president of the company asks you to explain why the profits decrease successively for the months of May and June although the sales were 1,100 units each month for April, May, and June. You note that the profits for those months were:

April.................	$4,640.00
May..................	3,706.67
June.................	2,706.67

11-9 Continued:

Exhibit I

STEVENS MANUFACTURING COMPANY
Statement of Profits, by Months
Six Months Ending June 30, 19__

Particulars	January Units	January Amount	February Units	February Amount	March Units	March Amount	April Units	April Amount	May Units	May Amount	June Units	June Amount	Six Months Units	Six Months Amount
Sales	200	$2,400.00	600	$7,200.00	800	$9,600.00	1,100	$13,200.00	1,100	$13,200.00	1,100	$13,200.00	4,900	$58,800.00
Less—Cost of goods sold:														
Finished goods, opening inventory		$	400	$2,800.00	600	$4,200.00	800	$5,600.00	900	$6,300.00	600	$4,200.00		$
Add—Goods completed (Exhibit II)	600	4,200.00	800	5,600.00	1,000	7,000.00	1,200	8,400.00	800	5,600.00	500	3,500.00	4,900	34,300.00
Totals	600	$4,200.00	1,200	$8,400.00	1,600	$11,200.00	2,000	$14,000.00	1,700	$11,900.00	1,100	$7,700.00	4,900	$34,300.00
Deduct—Finished goods, closing inventory	400	2,800.00	600	4,200.00	800	5,600.00	900	6,300.00	600	4,200.00				
Cost of goods sold	200	$1,400.00	600	$4,200.00	800	$5,600.00	1,100	$7,700.00	1,100	$7,700.00	1,100	$7,700.00	4,900	$34,300.00
Gross profit		$1,000.00		$3,000.00		$4,000.00		$5,500.00		$5,500.00		$5,500.00		$24,500.00
Deduct—Selling and general expense:														
Commission and other variable expense		$ 120.00		$ 360.00		$ 480.00		$ 660.00		$ 660.00		$ 660.00		$ 2,940.00
Fixed expense		1,000.00		1,000.00		1,000.00		1,000.00		1,000.00		1,000.00		6,000.00
Total expense		$1,120.00		$1,360.00		$1,480.00		$1,660.00		$1,660.00		$1,660.00		$ 8,940.00
Net profit (Loss*)		$ 120.00*		$1,640.00		$2,520.00		$3,840.00		$3,840.00		$3,840.00		$15,560.00
Underabsorbed (Overabsorbed*) expense (Exhibit III)		133.34		133.33		333.33*		800.00*		133.33		1,133.33		400.00
Net income		$ 253.34*		$1,506.67		$2,853.33		$4,640.00		$3,706.67		$2,706.67		$15,160.00

* Red.

Exhibit II

STEVENS MANUFACTURING COMPANY
Statement of Cost of Goods Completed, by Months
Six Months Ending June 30, 19__

Particulars	January Units	January Amount	February Units	February Amount	March Units	March Amount	April Units	April Amount	May Units	May Amount	June Units	June Amount
Opening inventory, work in process		$	200	$1,400.00	200	$1,400.00	200	$1,400.00	200	$1,400.00	200	$1,400.00
Add—												
Materials		800.00		800.00		1,000.00		1,200.00		800.00		300.00
Labor		1,600.00		1,600.00		2,000.00		2,400.00		1,600.00		600.00
Factory expense by normal rate		3,200.00		3,200.00		4,000.00		4,800.00		3,200.00		1,200.00
Totals	800	$5,600.00	1,000	$7,000.00	1,200	$8,400.00	1,400	$9,800.00	1,000	$7,000.00	500	$3,500.00
Less—Closing inventory, work in process	200	1,400.00	200	1,400.00	200	1,400.00	200	1,400.00	200	1,400.00		
Goods completed (Exhibit I)	600	$4,200.00	800	$5,600.00	1,000	$7,000.00	1,200	$8,400.00	800	$5,600.00	500	$3,500.00

Exhibit III

STEVENS MANUFACTURING COMPANY
Statement of Factory Expense Applied, by Months
Six Months Ending June 30, 19___

Particulars	January	February	March	April	May	June	Six Months
Actual expense for month:							
Variable expense................	$1,333.34	$1,333.33	$1,666.67	$2,000.00	$1,333.33	$ 333.33	$ 8,000.00
Fixed expense...................	2,000.00	2,000.00	2,000.00	2,000.00	2,000.00	2,000.00	12,000.00
Totals..................	$3,333.34	$3,333.33	$3,666.67	$4,000.00	$3,333.33	$2,333.33	$20,000.00
Applied expense for month (Exhibit II)......	3,200.00	3,200.00	4,000.00	4,800.00	3,200.00	1,200.00	19,600.00
Underabsorbed expense—Month (Exhibit I)..	$ 133.34	$ 133.33	$ 333.33*	$ 800.00*	$ 133.33	$1,133.33	$ 400.00
Underabsorbed expense—Cumulative........	133.34	266.67	66.66*	866.66*	733.33*	400.00	400.00

* Red.

Required:

Write a short letter to the president, answering his question.   If any alternative method of accounting would result in a different profit showing for the six successive months, describe the method and set up a schedule to show what the profits by month would be under that method.   State the reasons why the alternate method should, or should not, be used.

Chapter 12

DEPARTMENTAL FACTORY EXPENSE ACCOUNTS

Organization of the Benson & West Manufacturing Company.
Chapters 5 to 11 have explained and illustrated the cost accounting used by
two small manufacturing concerns: John Benson, Manufacturer, and
Benson Manufacturing Company. The present chapter explains the
factory expense reports used by the management of a larger manufacturing
company and also the journals and ledgers used to compile the information
for those reports. The Benson & West Manufacturing Company is the
basis for all illustrations in this chapter. This new business was organized
by John Benson, majority stockholder of the Benson Manufacturing Company and Fred West, a salesman for that company.

The new business obtained capital by sale of common stock to John
Benson, Fred West, and certain other people. It acquired the assets of the
Benson Manufacturing Company and bought the building which had been
occupied by that company. It added a new product to the line, which the
management expected to sell in considerable volume, and built an extension
on the factory and office.

The organization chart of the new company, the Benson & West Manufacturing Company, appears in Figure 12-1, and the floor plan of the new
factory in Figure 12-2. The new company is organized in four divisions:
general administration—headed by the president; sales—headed by a vice-
president; manufacturing—headed by a vice-president; and accounting
and cost accounting—headed by the controller. The managerial organization of the factory now comprises:

(1) The general factory administration, consisting of the factory superintendent, with:
    (a) Industrial engineer, who makes recommendations on the product
        design (from the standpoint of production economy) and the
        methods of manufacture.
    (b) Head clerk, planning and production control, who schedules
        production of the various products through the various depart-
        ments to keep production and inventories in line with sales.
    (c) Master mechanic, who with his mechanics, keeps the factory
        machinery in running order.

ORGANIZATION CHART

BENSON AND WEST MANUFACTURING COMPANY

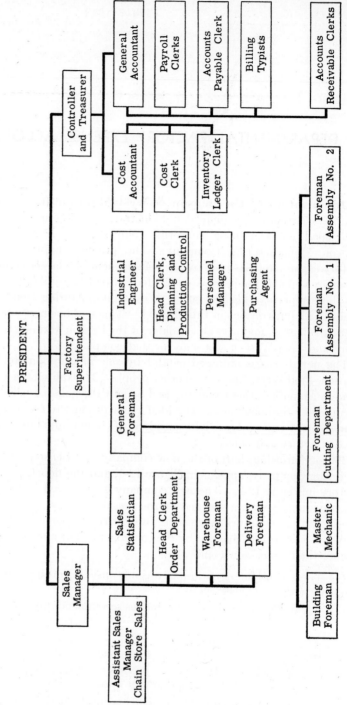

Figure 12-1

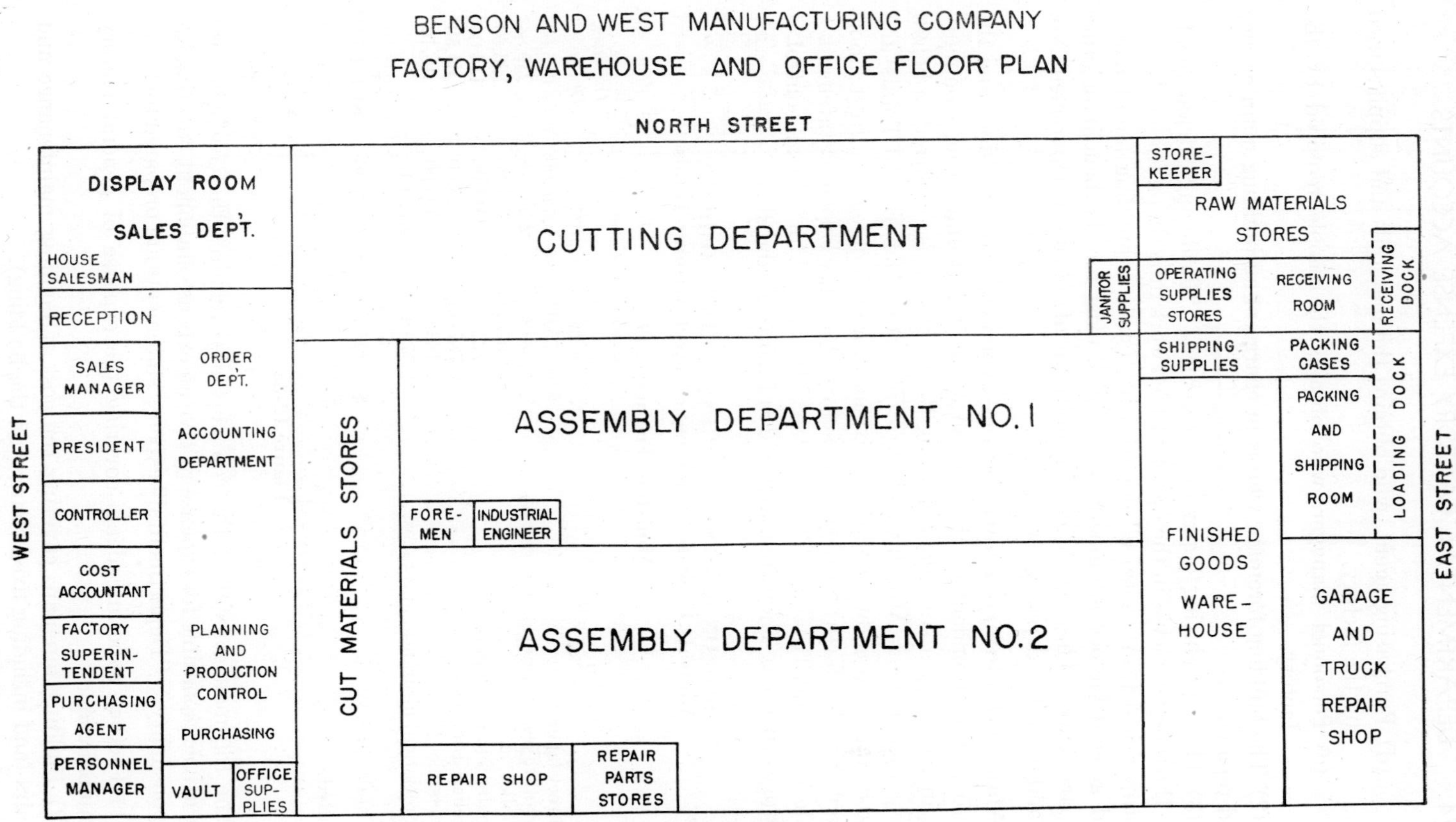

BENSON AND WEST MANUFACTURING COMPANY

FACTORY, WAREHOUSE AND OFFICE FLOOR PLAN

NORTH STREET

EAST STREET

WEST STREET

STORE-KEEPER

RAW MATERIALS STORES

RECEIVING ROOM

OPERATING SUPPLIES STORES

JANITOR SUPPLIES

RECEIVING DOCK

PACKING CASES

SHIPPING SUPPLIES

PACKING AND SHIPPING ROOM

LOADING DOCK

GARAGE AND TRUCK REPAIR SHOP

FINISHED GOODS WAREHOUSE

CUTTING DEPARTMENT

ASSEMBLY DEPARTMENT NO. 1

FORE-MEN

INDUSTRIAL ENGINEER

ASSEMBLY DEPARTMENT NO. 2

REPAIR PARTS STORES

REPAIR SHOP

CUT MATERIALS STORES

DISPLAY ROOM

SALES DEPT.

HOUSE SALESMAN

RECEPTION

ORDER DEPT.

ACCOUNTING DEPARTMENT

PLANNING AND PRODUCTION CONTROL

PURCHASING

OFFICE SUPPLIES

VAULT

SALES MANAGER

PRESIDENT

CONTROLLER

COST ACCOUNTANT

FACTORY SUPERINTENDENT

PURCHASING AGENT

PERSONNEL MANAGER

Figure 12-2

273

(d) Purchasing agent, who obtains the materials and supplies used by the factory.

(e) Personnel manager, who obtains the people required by the factory.

(2) The building foreman, who is in charge of all building maintenance and repairs.

(3) Three producing department foremen. "Producing" departments are those departments in the factory which work directly on the product as distinguished from "service" departments (such as building maintenance and general factory administration) which exist for the benefit of other departments. They are the cutting department, assembly department No. 1, and assembly department No. 2.

Managerial information: Factory expense. The president and the factory superintendent of the Benson & West Manufacturing Company require monthly a statement showing the total expense incurred in behalf of each department (Monthly Expense Statement—Department Totals) and also a statement showing the total expense for each object (indirect labor, supplies, and so forth) for the entire factory (Monthly Expense Statement—Object Account Totals). These statements are used for over-all control of factory expense. They are illustrated in Figures 3a and 3b.

BENSON & WEST MANUFACTURING COMPANY
Monthly Expense Statement—Object Account Totals
Month of February, 19__

Account	Budget	Actual	Increase, Decrease*
Indirect labor	$10,075.00	$ 9,440.00	$ 635.00*
Payroll taxes, insurance, and reserves	2,534.62	2,294.78	239.84*
Supplies	907.50	781.00	126.50*
Repairs and repair parts	725.00	611.00	114.00*
Purchased services	787.50	723.00	64.50*
Unclassified	486.90	505.00	18.10
Depreciation, insurance, and taxes	2,779.18	2,779.18	
Totals	$18,295.70	$17,133.96	$1,161.74*

* Red.

Figure 12-3a

The top management of the company also requires that each factory executive responsible for expense receive an expense statement covering his responsibility. "Departmental" expense statements are prepared for:

(1) Factory superintendent, covering the expense of general factory administration.

(2) Building foreman, covering the cost of building maintenance and repairs (and including fixed charges on the building).

(3) Each of the three producing department foremen, covering the expenses of their respective departments.

BENSON & WEST MANUFACTURING COMPANY
Monthly Expense Statement—Departmental Totals

Month of February, 19__

Department	Budget	Actual	Increase, Decrease*
Building maintenance and fixed charges....	$ 4,021.07	$ 4,156.25	$ 135.18
General factory........................	5,473.20	5,159.16	314.04*
Cutting department.....................	3,203.09	2,612.20	590.89*
Assembly department No. 1..............	2,706.32	2,430.45	275.87*
Assembly department No. 2..............	2,892.02	2,775.90	116.12*
Totals...........................	$18,295.70	$17,133.96	$1,161.74*

* Red.

Figure 12-3b

Three of the departmental statements are illustrated on pages 276 to 278. Note that on the producing department statement (page 278), the producing department is charged with (a) all expenses which originate within the department (called "direct departmental expenses") and (b) a share of general factory administrative expense and a charge for "rent" to cover building maintenance and repairs and fixed charges. General factory administration and building maintenance and fixed charges are charged to the producing departments on the theory that the producing departments receive benefit. The bases for charging these expenses to using departments are explained on page 293. (The statements for assembly department No. 1 and assembly department No. 2—not illustrated —are the same in form as the statement for cutting department.)

Classification of accounts. The classification of expense accounts used to produce the statements illustrated in the previous section appears on page 279. The classification comprises a set of object accounts for each of the five departments. There are 13 accounts for Building Maintenance and Fixed Charges, 17 accounts for the General Factory, and 15 accounts for each of the three producing departments.

The classification illustrated is a part of a complete general ledger classification which comprises the following groups:

    100   Assets
    200   Liabilities and Net Worth
    300   Sales and Cost of Sales
    400   Factory Expense
    500   Selling Expense
    600   Administrative Expense
    900   Financial Income and Expense

BENSON & WEST MANUFACTURING COMPANY
Departmental Expense Statement

		Building Maintenance
	Department	and Fixed Charges

Month of ___ February, ___ 19__

Object	*Budget Expense*	*Actual Expense*	*Excess or Savings* over Budget*
Indirect labor:			
Supervisory............................	$ 500.00	$ 500.00	
Janitors, firemen, and watchmen...........	1,100.00	1,150.00	$ 50.00
Totals............................	$1,600.00	$1,650.00	$ 50.00
Payroll taxes, reserves, and insurance:			
F.I.C.A. tax..........................	$ 32.00	$ 33.00	$ 1.00
Workmen's insurance....................	8.00	8.25	.25
Provision for vacation pay...............	32.00	33.00	1.00
Totals............................	$ 72.00	$ 74.25	$ 2.25
Supplies:			
Janitors' supplies.......................	$ 40.00	$ 42.00	$ 2.00
Coal.................................	190.00	195.00	5.00
Totals............................	$ 230.00	$ 237.00	$ 7.00
Repairs to building.......................	$ 300.00	$ 280.00	$ 20.00*
Electric light and power...................	$ 200.00	$ 210.00	$ 10.00
Unclassified.............................	$ 119.07	$ 205.00	$ 85.93
Depreciation, insurance, and taxes:			
Depreciation on building.................	$ 800.00	$ 800.00	
Insurance on building....................	400.00	400.00	
Taxes on building.......................	300.00	300.00	
Totals............................	$1,500.00	$1,500.00	
Total departmental expense.................	$4,021.07	$4,156.25	$135.18
Expense charged to other departments:			
Administrative and selling................	$ 820.00	$ 847.57	
General factory........................	400.00	413.46	
Cutting department.....................	895.51	925.61	
Assembly department No. 1...............	993.81	1,027.21	
Assembly department No. 2...............	911.75	942.40	
Total, as above........................	$4,021.07	$4,156.25	

Figure 12-4a

BENSON & WEST MANUFACTURING COMPANY
Departmental Expense Statement

Department   General Factory Administration

Month of   February,   19__

Object	Budget Expense	Actual Expense	Excess or Saving* over Budget
Indirect labor:			
Supervisory...........................	$3,200.00	$3,200.00	
Clerical and production control...........	950.00	850.00	$100.00*
Machinists............................	500.00	350.00	150.00*
Totals............................	$4,650.00	$4,400.00	$250.00*
Payroll taxes, reserves, and insurance:			
F.I.C.A. tax...........................	$ 93.00	$ 88.00	$ 5.00*
Workmen's insurance....................	23.25	22.00	1.25*
Provision for vacation pay...............	93.00	88.00	5.00*
Totals............................	$ 209.25	$ 198.00	$ 11.25*
Printed forms and office supplies...........	$ 177.50	$ 156.00	$ 21.50*
Purchased services:			
Electric light and power..................	$ 106.50	$ 95.00	$ 11.50*
Telephone and telegraph.................	71.00	63.00	8.00*
Professional engineers fees...............	100.00	100.00	
Totals............................	$ 277.50	$ 258.00	$ 19.50*
Unclassified............................	$ 101.79	$ 90.00	$ 11.79*
Depreciation, insurance, and taxes:			
Depreciation on office furniture and fixtures	$ 9.16	$ 9.16	
Depreciation on machinery and equipment	25.00	25.00	
Insurance on office furniture and fixtures...	2.00	2.00	
Insurance on machinery and equipment....	6.00	6.00	
Taxes on office furniture and fixtures.......	3.00	3.00	
Taxes on machinery and equipment........	12.00	12.00	
Totals............................	$ 57.16	$ 57.16	
Total direct departmental expense...........	$5,473.20	$5,159.16	$314.04*
Rent..................................	400.00	413.46	
Total department........................	$5,873.20	$5,572.67	
Expense charged to other departments:			
Cutting department.....................	$1,240.82	$ 950.67	
Assembly department No. 1...............	1,323.54	1,182.96	
Assembly department No. 2...............	3,308.84	3,438.99	
Totals, as above....................	$5,873.20	$5,572.62	

Figure 12-4b

BENSON & WEST MANUFACTURING COMPANY
Departmental Expense Statement

Department _____ Cutting _____

Month of _____ February, _____ 19__

Object	Budget Expense	Actual Expense	Excess or Saving* over Budget
Indirect labor:			
Supervision.............................	$ 800.00	$ 700.00	$100.00*
Shop porters...........................	700.00	600.00	100.00*
Other indirect labor.....................	75.00	60.00	15.00*
Totals.............................	$1,575.00	$1,360.00	$215.00*
Payroll taxes, insurance, and reserves:			
F.I.C.A. tax...........................	$ 256.50	$ 190.88	$ 65.62*
Workmen's insurance...................	64.12	47.72	16.40*
Provision for vacation pay...............	256.50	190.88	65.62*
Totals.............................	$ 577.12	$ 429.48	$147.64*
Factory operating supplies.................	$ 300.00	$ 210.00	$ 90.00*
Repairs and repair parts...................	$ 225.00	$ 160.00	$ 65.00*
Electric light and power...................	$ 150.00	$ 110.00	$ 40.00*
Unclassified.............................	$ 108.25	$ 75.00	$ 33.25*
Depreciation, insurance and taxes:			
Depreciation on machinery and equipment	$ 100.00	$ 100.00	
Insurance on inventory...................	44.72	44.72	
Insurance on machinery and equipment....	25.00	25.00	
Taxes on inventory......................	48.00	48.00	
Taxes on machinery and equipment........	50.00	50.00	
Totals.............................	$ 267.72	$ 267.72	
Total direct departmental expense...........	$3,203.09	$2,612.20	$590.89*
Service department charges:			
Rent..................................	895.51	925.61	
General factory administration............	1,240.82	950.67	
Total department........................	$5,339.42	$4,488.48	

Figure 12-4c

BENSON & WEST MANUFACTURING COMPANY
Classification of Expense Accounts—by Department

Object A/c	Object	1 Building Maintenance & Fixed Charges	2 General Factory	3 Cutting	4 Assembly No. 1	5 Assembly No. 2
411	Supervisory labor	4111	4112	4113	4114	4115
412	Clerical and production control		4122			
413	Shop porters			4133	4134	4135
414	Machinists		4142			
415	Janitors, firemen, and watchmen	4151				
416	Other indirect labor			4163	4164	4165
421	F.I.C.A. tax	4211	4212	4213	4214	4215
422	Workmen's insurance	4221	4222	4223	4224	4225
423	Provision for vacation pay	4231	4232	4233	4234	4235
431	Printed forms and office supplies		4312			
432	Janitors' supplies	4321				
433	Coal	4331				
434	Factory operating supplies			4343	4344	4345
435	Repairs and repair parts	4351		4353	4354	4355
441	Electric light and power	4411	4412	4413	4414	4415
442	Telephone and telegraph		4422			
443	Professional engineers fees		4432			
460	Unclassified	4601	4602	4603	4604	4605
471	Depreciation on building	4711				
472	Depreciation on office furniture and fixtures		4722			
473	Depreciation on machinery and equipment		4732	4733	4734	4735
474	Insurance on building	4741				
475	Insurance on inventory			4753	4754	4755
476	Insurance on office furniture and fixtures		4762			
477	Insurance on machinery and equipment		4772	4773	4774	4775
481	Taxes on buildings	4811				
482	Taxes on inventory			4823	4824	4825
483	Taxes on office furniture and fixtures		4832			
484	Taxes on machinery and equipment		4842	4843	4844	4845

Figure 12-5

Note that the *general ledger* classification proper comprises three-digit numbers. The 400 series is the Factory Expense accounts. These accounts are grouped into object groups as follows:

400   Indirect labor   (6 accounts, in all)
420   Payroll taxes, insurance, and reserves (3 accounts)
430   Supplies   (5 accounts)
440   Purchased services   (3 accounts)
460   Unclassified   (1 account)
480 ⎫
490 ⎭ Depreciation, insurance, and taxes   (11 accounts)

The *departmental expense* account classification illustrated on page 279 has been formed by adding a digit to the right of the object digits, to identify the department. The department digits are:

1 Building maintenance and fixed charges
2 General factory
3 Cutting
4 Assembly No. 1
5 Assembly No. 2

Thus, a complete four-digit number is built up as follows:

4113 Factory expense
  1   Indirect labor
    1   Supervision
      3 Cutting department

Expense account forms; Journal forms.   The Benson & West Manufacturing Company uses a factory expense ledger which comprises a double-page columnar account for each of the five departments. (See the illustration on page 286.)   The five columnar accounts take the place of 75 conventional "T" account forms which might otherwise have been used. The columnar account for Building Maintenance and Fixed Charges comprises 13 columns, one for each of 13 object accounts.   The columnar account for General Factory comprises 17 columns for that number of object accounts.   Each of the columnar accounts for the three producing departments provides 15 columns for 15 objects.

The voucher register used in conjunction with the columnar expense ledger is illustrated on page 281. It provides among others a Factory Expense, Debit column, for each of the five departments. The general journal (page 284), likewise, includes a Factory Expense, Debit column, for each department.

PROCEDURE

Voucher register

1. *Enter Disbursement Vouchers in Voucher Register.*   The voucher register on page 281 illustrates entries for various purchases of supplies and

Voucher Register

During the month, enter disbursement vouchers for supplies and purchased services in voucher register

(Miscellaneous columns omitted)

Month of _____ February, 19___

Date	Issued To	Vo. No.	Paid Check No.	Paid Date	Vouchers Payable Credit	Building Maintenance and Fixed Charges A/c	Amount	General Factory A/c	Amount	Cutting Department A/c	Amount	Assembly Department No. 1 A/c	Amount	Assembly Department No. 2 A/c	Amount	Selling Expense, Debit A/c	Amount	Administrative Expense, Debit A/c	Amount
19—																	$		$
Feb. 3	Peacock Coal Co.	111			$ 195 00	433	$195 00												
8	Building Supply Co.	112			42 00	432	42 00												
15	Engineering Associates	113			100 00			443	$100 00										
19	Mill Supply Co.	114			388 00					434	$210 00	434	$100 00	434	$ 78 00				
21	Mason & Wilson	115			280 00	435	280 00												
22	Mechanics Repair Co.	116			331 00			431	156 00	435	160 00	435	132 00	435	39 00				
25	Horders Printing Co.	117			156 00			460	90 00										
Various	Factory Petty Cash	118			505 00	460	205 00			460	75 00	460	110 00	460	25 00				
28	Commonwealth Power Co.	119			560 00	441	210 00	441	95 00	441	110 00	441	67 00	441	78 00				
28	Bell Telephone Co.	120			63 00			442	63 00										
					$2,620 00		$932 00		$504 00		$555 00		$409 00		$220 00				

Credit Vouchers Payable, $2,620.00

Total debit to Factory Expense Control, $2,620.00

At end of month, post column totals to control accounts in general ledger (See Figure 12-7)

Figure 12-6

281

services.   The vouchers represent purchases of coal, various operating supplies, repairs by an outside service, power, telephone, and so forth.   For each voucher, enter the numbers of the expense accounts to be charged in the folio column of the proper department.

2. *At End of Month, Post Column Totals to Control Accounts in General Ledger.*   The voucher register (page 281) illustrates the posting of column totals at the end of the month.   Debit Factory Expense Control account in the general ledger for the grand total of the five Factory Expense, Debit columns, and credit Vouchers Payable account for the total of Vouchers Payable Credit column.   From the voucher register illustrated, there would be no other posting of factory expense items to the general ledger: just one debit and one credit.   This posting, of course, leaves the general ledger in balance.

POSTING COLUMN TOTALS TO CONTROL ACCOUNTS
IN THE GENERAL LEDGER

Vouchers Payable

19__		F	Amount	19__		F	Amount
				Feb. 28	Vouchers for month	VR8	$2,620

Factory Expense Control

19__		F	Amount	19__		F	Amount
Feb. 28	Disbursement vouchers	VR8	$2,620				

(The debit to Factory Expense Control account is the total of Factory Expense Debit columns.)

Figure 12-7a

General journal

3. *During the Month, Enter Payrolls in the General Journal.*   The first entry in the general journal (page 284) is a payroll entry involving debits to the various indirect labor accounts of the five departments.   To save space, only one entry has been shown.   In practice, there would be one entry for each of the weekly payrolls, and one entry for the monthly salaries.

4. *At the End of the Month, Record Accruals and Deferrals in the General Journal.*   The general journal illustrates entries for:

(a) Labor costs other than direct payroll:
   Company's share of F.I.C.A. tax
   Workmen's insurance expense
   Provision for vacation pay
(b) Depreciation, insurance, and taxes on plant and inventories.

Note that the expense debits in each entry are recorded in the Factory Expense, Debit column, of the department affected. The number of the account to be charged is entered in the A/c column beside the amount. The credits of all entries illustrated appear in the Miscellaneous Credits column, since these amounts are to be posted to general ledger accounts (and not to expense accounts). The credits are posted individually to the general ledger accounts. This may be done day by day if desired instead of at the end of the month.

5. *Post Column Totals to Control Accounts in General Ledger.* Post the grand total of the five expense columns to Factory Expense Control account in the general ledger and credit various liability, reserve, and other accounts. This posting to Factory Expense Control account is illustrated below.

FACTORY EXPENSE CONTROL ACCOUNT
(Postings Completed)

Factory Expense Ledger Control Account

19__		F	Amount	19__		F	Amount
Feb. 28	Disbursement						
	vouchers	VS	$ 2,620.00				
28	Journal entries	G6	14,513.96				
			$17,133.96				

Figure 12-7b

There is no other posting of factory expense items to the general ledger (in this chapter). This posting leaves the general ledger in balance.

Factory expense ledger

6. *Post the Items in Each Factory Expense Debit Column in the Voucher Register to Related Columnar Expense Account.* The illustration on page 285 shows the posting of details *and* the total of the building Maintenance and Fixed Charges column of the voucher register to the account of the same name in the factory expense ledger. Each of the four other expense columns of the voucher register is posted in the same manner to the proper departmental expense account in the factory expense ledger. Thus, the total of all charges to the accounts in the factory expense ledger would agree with the debit of $2,620 in the Factory Expense Control account in the general ledger.

During the month, enter payrolls in the general journal

General Journal

Month of __February__, 19__

Date	Particulars	J.V. No.	Misc. A/c	Misc. Debits	Misc. Credits	Building Maintenance and Fixed Charges A/c	Amount	General Factory A/c	Amount	Cutting Department A/c	Amount	Assembly Department No. 1 A/c	Amount	Assembly Department No. 2 A/c	Amount
19__ Various	Supervisory labor					411	$500 00	411	$3,200 00	411	$700 00	411	$650 00	411	$500 00
	Clerical and production labor							412	850 00	413	600 00	413	325 00	413	300 00
	Shop porters														
	Machinists														
	Janitors, firemen, and watchmen					415	1,150 00	414	350 00	416	60 00	416	135 00	416	120 00
	Other indirect labor														
	Accrued payroll		221		$9,440 00										
Feb. 28	F.I.C.A. tax					421	33 00	421	88 00	421	190 88	421	193 02	421	515 00
	Accrued F.I.C.A. tax		222		1,019 90										
	Company's share of F.I.C.A. tax for month.														
28	Unemployment insurance expense					422	8 25	422	22 00	422	47 72	422	48 76	422	128 75
	Prepaid insurance		140		254 98										
	Insurance expense for month														
28	Provision for vacation pay					423	33 00	423	88 00	423	190 88	423	193 02	423	515 00
	Reserve for vacation pay		229		1,019 90										
	Provision for vacation pay based upon wages paid for month														
28	Depreciation—Building					471	800 00								
	Depreciation—Office furniture and fixtures							472	9 16						
	Depreciation—Machinery and equipment							473	25 00	473	100 00	473	170 00	473	170 00
	Reserve for depreciation— Building		170R		800 00										
	Office furniture and fixtures		181R		9 16										
	Machinery and equipment		185R		465 00										
	Estimated depreciation for month														
28	Insurance—Building					474	400 00								
	Insurance—Inventory							476	2 00						
	Insurance—Furniture and fixtures							477	6 00	475	44 72	475	89 50	475	89 50
	Insurance—Machinery and equipment		140		736 72					477	25 00	477	40 00	477	40 00
	Prepaid insurance														
	Insurance expired for month														
28	Taxes—Building					481	300 00								
	Taxes—Inventory							483	3 00						
	Taxes—Office furniture and fixtures							484	12 00	482	48 00	482	96 00	482	96 00
	Taxes—Machinery and equipment		231		768 30					484	50 00	484	81 65	484	81 65
	Accrued property taxes														
	Taxes for month														
			$		$14,513 96		$3,224 25		$4,655 16		$2,057 20		$2,021 45		$2,555 90

Post credits from Miscellaneous column on daily basis, in detail

At end of month, post column totals to control accounts in general ledger

Total Factory Expense, $14,513.96

At end of month, record entries for accruals and deferrals

Figure 12-8

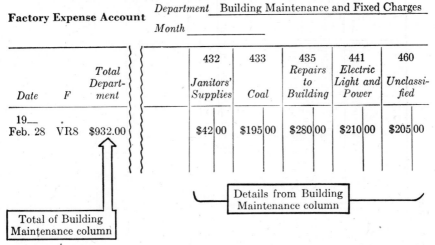

Figure 12-9

7. *Post the Items in the Factory Expense Debit Columns in the General Journal to Columnar Expense Accounts.* The postings from the Building Maintenance and Fixed Charges column of the general journal to the expense account of that name are illustrated in Figure 12-10a.

Complete set of columnar expense accounts illustrated. The complete set of columnar expense accounts appears on pages 286-290. Postings from the voucher register and the general journal, respectively, are shown on the first two lines. The illustration also shows postings from the expense worksheet, as explained in the following sections.

Thus, the entry to distribute building maintenance and fixed charges ("rent") in the departmental ledger would be:

General factory administration.........	$ 413.46	
Cutting department.................	925.61	
Assembly department No. 1...........	1,027.21	
Assembly department No. 2...........	942.40	
Selling and administrative expense......	847.57	
Building maintenance and fixed charges		$4,156.25

Selling and Administrative Expense is charged for building maintenance and fixed charges on the space occupied by the sales department and the administrative department. An account form (not illustrated) would have to be put in the departmental factory expense ledger to receive the charge of $847.57, to keep the ledger in balance. This amount is transferred from the departmental factory expense ledger and charged to Selling and Administrative Expense account in the general ledger, as explained in the following section.

Departmental Expense Account

Date	F	Total Department	411 Supervisory Labor	415 Janitors, Firemen, and Watchmen	421 F.I.C.A. Tax	422 Workmens' Insurance	423 Provision for Vacation Pay	432 Janitors' Supplies	433 Coal	435 Repairs to Building	441 Electric Light and Power
19_ Feb. 28	VR8	$ 932 00	$	$ 1,150 00	$	$	$	$42 00	$195 00	$280 00	$210 00
28	GJ6	3,224 25	500 00		33 00	8 25	33 00				
Totals		$4,156 25	$500 00	$1,150 00	$33 00	$8 25	$33 00	$42 00	$195 00	$280 00	$210 00

Department Building Maintenance and Fixed Charges
Month of February 19_

460 Unclassified	471 Depreciation—Building	474 Insurance—Building	481 Taxes—Building		Distributed to Other Departments
$205 00	$ 800 00	$ 400 00	$ 300 00		
$205 00	$800 00	$400 00	$300 00		$4,156 25*

7 Post the items in the Factory Expense, Debit columns of the general journal to columnar expense accounts

Figure 12-10a

*Credit

Departmental Expense Account

Date	F	Total Department	411 Supervisory Labor	412 Clerical and Production Control Labor	414 Machinists	421 F.I.C.A. Tax	422 Workmen's Insurance	423 Provision for Vacation Pay	431 Printed Forms and Office Supplies	441 Electric Light and Power	442 Telephone and Telegraph	443 Professional Engineers Fees
19__ Feb. 28	VR8	$ 504 00										
28	GJ6	4,655 16	$3,200 00	$ 850 00	$ 350 00	$ 88 00	$ 22 00	$ 88 00	$156 00	$95 00	$63 00	$100 00
Service distribution		413 46										
		$5,572 62	$3,200 00	$850 00	$350 00	$88 00	$22 00	$88 00	$156 00	$95 00	$63 00	$100 00

Department ___ General Factory

Month of ___ February, 19___

460 Unclassified	472 Depreciation—Office Furniture & Fixtures	473 Depreciation—Machinery & Equipment	476 Insurance—Office Furniture & Fixtures	477 Insurance—Machinery & Equipment	483 Taxes—Office Furniture & Fixtures	484 Taxes—Machinery & Equipment	— Service Charge Received: Rent	Distributed to Other Departments
								$
							$	
$90 00	$ 9 16	$ 25 00	$ 2 00	$ 6 00	$ 3 00	$ 12 00		
							413 46	$5,572 62*
$90 00	$9 16	$25 00	$2 00	$6 00	$3 00	$12 00	$413 46	$5,572 62*

*Credit

Figure 12-10b

Departmental Expense Account

Date	F	Total Department	411 Supervisory Labor	413 Shop Porters	416 Other Indirect Labor	421 F.I.C.A. Tax	422 Workmen's Insurance	423 Provision for Vacation Pay	434 Factory Operating Supplies	435 Repairs and Repair Parts	441 Electric Light and Power
19__ Feb. 28	VR8	$ 555.00							$210.00	$160.00	$110.00
28	GJ6	2,057.20	$ 700.00	$ 600.00	$ 60.00	$ 190.88	$ 47.72	$ 190.88			
Service distribution		1,876.28									
		$4,488.48	$700.00	$600.00	$60.00	$190.88	$47.72	$190.88	$210.00	$160.00	$110.00

Department __Cutting__
Month of __February__ 19__

460 Unclassified	473 Depreciation—Machinery and Equipment	475 Insurance—Inventory	477 Insurance—Machinery and Equipment	482 Taxes—Inventory	484 Taxes—Machinery and Equipment	Service Charges Received	
						Rent	General Factory Administration
$75.00	$ 100.00	$ 44.72	$ 25.00	$ 48.00	$ 50.00	$ 925.61	$ 950.67
$75.00	$100.00	$44.72	$25.00	$48.00	$50.00	$925.61	$950.67

Figure 12-10c

Departmental Expense Account

Date	F	Total Depart- ment	411 Super- visory Labor	413 Shop Porters	416 Other Indirect Labor	421 F.I.C.A. Tax	422 Work- men's Insurance	423 Provision for Vacation Pay	434 Factory Operating Supplies	435 Repairs and Repair Parts	441 Electric Light and Power
19__ Feb. 28	VR8	$ 409 00							$100 00	$132 00	$67 00
28	GJ6	2,021 45	$ 650 00	$ 325 00	$ 135 00	$ 193 02	$ 48 26	$ 193 02			
Service distri- bution		2,210 17									
		$4,640 62	$650 00	$325 00	$135 00	$193 02	$48 26	$193 02	$100 00	$132 00	$67 00

Department   Assembly No. 1
Month of   February,   19__

460 Unclas- sified	473 Depre- ciation Machinery and Equipment	475 Insur- ance Inventory	477 Insur- ance— Machinery and Equipment	482 Taxes— Inventory	484 Taxes— Machinery and Equipment	Service Charges Received	
						Rent	General Factory Adminis- tration
$110 00	$ 170 00	$ 89 50	$ 40 00	$ 96 00	$ 81 65	$	$
						1,027 21	1,182 96
$110 00	$170 00	$89 50	$40 00	$96 00	$81 65	$1,027 21	$1,182 96

Figure 12-10d

Departmental Expense Account

Date	F	Total Department	411 Supervisory Labor	413 Shop Porters	416 Other Indirect Labor	421 F.I.C.A. Tax	422 Workmen's Insurance	423 Provision for Vacation Pay	434 Factory Operating Supplies	435 Repairs and Repair Parts	441 Electric Light and Power
19__ Feb. 28	VR8	$ 220 00									
28	GJ6	2,555 90	$ 500 00	$ 300 00	$ 120 00	$ 515 00	$ 128 75	$ 515 00	$ 78 00	$ 39 00	$ 78 00
Service distribution		4,381 39									
		$7,157 29	$500 00	$300 00	$120 00	$515 00	$128 75	$515 00	$78 00	$39 00	$78 00

Department _____ Assembly No. 2

Month of _____ February _____ 19 ___

	460 Unclassified	473 Depreciation—Machinery and Equipment	475 Insurance—Inventory	477 Insurance—Machinery and Equipment	482 Taxes—Inventory	484 Taxes—Machinery and Equipment	Service Charges Received Rent	Service Charges Received General Factory Administration
	$25 00	$ 170 00	$ 89 50	$ 40 00	$ 96 00	$ 81 65	$	$
							942 40	3,438 99
	$25 00	$170 00	$89 50	$40 00	$96 00	$81 65	$942 40	$3,438 99

Figure 12-10e

The entry to distribute general factory administration expense would be:

Cutting department..................	$ 950.67	
Assembly department No. 1...........	1,182.96	
Assembly department No. 2..........	3,438.99	
General factory administration expense		$5,572.62

Trial balance of factory expense ledger. The charge to Selling and Administrative Expense for building maintenance and fixed charges would be recorded in the general ledger by the entry:

Selling and administrative expense.........	$847.57	
Factory expense....................		$847.57
To record rent charge to sales and administrative departments.		

After this entry is recorded the Factory Expense account has a debit balance of $16,286.39.

The trial balance of the factory expense ledger would show the following balances:

Cutting department...........................	$ 4,488.48
Assembly department No. 1....................	4,640.62
Assembly department No. 2................... .	7,157.29
Total, agreeing with the control account........	$16,286.39

EXPENSE WORKSHEET

Worksheet procedure. An expense worksheet (page 292) is used to assemble dollar information relating to (a) the cost of operating each service department and (b) charges to each using department for service received from the service departments.   The worksheet provides a column for each department and a line for each group of object accounts (lines 1-8). At the bottom of the worksheet is a line for recording the charge to each department for building maintenance and fixed charges ("Rent")(line 9) and a line for recording the charge to each department for general factory expense (line 11).

The worksheet is set up as follows:

(1) Enter on lines 1-8 the total of each object class for each department, obtaining the amounts from the accounts in the factory expense ledger.   Note that to save space on the worksheet, object group totals have been taken from the expense ledger instead of individual object totals.

(2) Enter total direct expense for each department on line 8.

(3) Charge each of the using departments for its share of building maintenance and fixed charges and credit Building Maintenance and Fixed Charges for the total cost of the department for the month, as shown on line 9.   (The charge is described as rent.)   The total of the Maintenance Department account per the worksheet is $4,156.25. This amount is allocated to the other departments on the basis of the square feet of floor space (as shown on page 293).

BENSON & WEST MANUFACTURING COMPANY
Expense Worksheet

Showing Distribution of Actual Service Department Expense Per Factory Expense Accounts to Using Departments

	Object Classes	Service Departments		Producing Departments			Selling and Administrative Expense	Totals
		Building Maintenance and Fixed Charges	General Factory	Cutting	Assembly Department No. 1	Assembly Department No. 2		
1	Indirect labor........ (410 group)	$1,650.00	$4,400.00	$1,360.00	$1,110.00	$ 920.00		$ 9,440.00
2	Payroll taxes, reserves, and insurance..... (420 group)	74.25	198.00	429.48	434.30	1,158.75		2,294.78
3	Supplies............ (431–434)	237.00	156.00	210.00	100.00	78.00		781.00
4	Repairs and repair parts (435)	280.00	258.00	160.00	132.00	39.00		611.00
5	Purchased services.... (440 group)	210.00	−90.00	110.00	67.00	78.00		723.00
6	Unclassified.......... (460)	205.00		75.00	110.00	25.00		505.00
7	Depreciation, insurance and taxes..... (470–480)	1,500.00	57.16	267.72	477.15	477.15		2,779.18
8	Total direct departmental expense	$4,156.25	$5,159.16	$2,612.20	$2,430.45	$2,775.90		$17,133.96
9	Rent distributed (Figure 12-12)	4,156.25*	413.46	925.61	1,027.21	942.40	$847.57	
10			$5,572.62					
11	General factory distributed (Figure 12-13).............		5,572.62*	950.67	1,182.96	3,438.99		
12	Total department.....			$4,488.48	$4,640.62	$7,157.29	$847.57	

Figure 12-11

(4) Determine the total of general factory administration expense, including the rent charge to that department. The total is $5,572.62; enter it on line 10.

(5) Charge each of the producing departments for its share of factory administrative service received and credit General Factory Administration account, as shown on line 11. The total of General Factory Administration account on the worksheet is $5,572.62. This amount is allocated to the using departments on the basis of the number of labor hours worked in the respective departments (as shown on page 294).

(6) Determine the total expense for each producing department and enter the totals on line 12 on the worksheet.

Preparing the departmental expense statements. The departmental expense statements are illustrated on pages 276-278. Those statements are prepared by obtaining the object account totals from the departmental expense accounts (pages 286-288), and the service charges to using departments from the expense worksheet (page 292).

Entering service charges to using departments in the expense ledger accounts. The service charges to using departments shown on the worksheet and the departmental expense statements may also be posted to the departmental expense accounts, if desired. (This is done as illustrated in the expense accounts on pages 286-290.) Note that the service department accounts show the credits and the producing using departments show the debits.

ALLOCATION OF ACTUAL BUILDING MAINTENANCE AND FIXED CHARGES TO USING DEPARTMENTS

Building maintenance and fixed charges:

$$\text{Rate per square foot} = \frac{\text{Total building maintenance and fixed charges}}{\text{Square feet of floor space}}$$

$$= \frac{\$4,156.25}{40,210.5} = \$.10336 +$$

Allocation of building maintenance and fixed charges to departments (@ $.10336 per square foot):

Department	Square Feet	Amount
Selling and administrative.........	8,200	$ 847.57
Factory administration............	4,000	413.46
Cutting.........................	8,955	925.61
Assembly No. 1..................	9,938	1,027.21
Assembly No. 2..................	9,117.5	942.40
	40,210.5	$4,156.25

Figure 12-12

Normal departmental factory expense rates. *Normal* departmental factory expense rates are calculated at the beginning of the year

ALLOCATION OF ACTUAL GENERAL FACTORY EXPENSE TO
USING DEPARTMENTS

General factory expense:

$$\text{Rate per hour} = \frac{\text{Total general factory expense (including ``rent'')}}{\text{Total actual labor hours}}$$

$$= \frac{\$5,572.62}{30,950} = \$.180052$$

Allocation of general factory expense to departments ($.180052 per labor hour):

Department	Labor Hours	Amount
Cutting...................	5,280	$ 950.67
Assembly No. 1............	6,570	1,182.96
Assembly No. 2............	19,100	3,438.99
	30,950	$5,572.62

Figure 12-13

on the basis of (a) the expense budget for each department as shown in the departmental expense statements, and (b) the expected hours (or other volume measure) for each department.   The rates are calculated as shown in Figure 12-14.   Note that in this calculation, the expense budgets of service departments are allocated to producing departments.

The normal expense rates for producing departments are:

	Rate per Hour
Cutting department.....................	$.71
Assembly department No. 1..............	$.63
Assembly department No. 2..............	$.36

These rates are applied to cost sheets as jobs are finished, in the same manner as normal rates in general.   At the end of the month, total expense applied is recorded by the general journal entry:

Factory expense in process.............. $14,763.90
    Factory expense applied............ $14,763.90
To record factory expense applicable to
production for the month, as follows:

Department	Actual Hours	Normal Rate	Total Applied
Cutting....................	5,280	$.71	$ 3,748.80
Assembly No. 1............	6,570	.63	4,139.10
Assembly No. 2............	19,100	.36	6,876.00
	30,950		$14,763.90

The net underabsorbed expense for the factory would be:

BENSON & WEST MANUFACTURING COMPANY

Normal Departmental Expense Rates

Particulars	Building Maintenance and Fixed Charges	Administrative and Selling	General Factory Administration	Cutting Department	Assembly Department No. 1	Assembly Department No. 2	Totals
1 Normal hours........			35,500	7,500	8,000	20,000	
2 Direct departmental expenses......	$4,021.07	$	$5,473.20	$3,203.09	$2,706.32	$2,892.02	$18,295.70
3 Building maintenance and fixed charges: ("rent") @ $.10+ per square foot:		820.00	400.00	895.51	993.81	911.75	
4 Total general factory administration......			$5,873.20				
5 General factory administration distributed @ $.16544 per normal hour:	4,021.07*		5,873.20*	1,240.82	1,323.54	3,308.84	
6 Total producing department (and administrative and selling)......		$820.00		$5,339.42	$5,023.67	$7,112.61	$18,295.70
7 Rates per hour......				$ .71192	$ .62796	$ .35563	
Use......				$ .71	$ .63	$ .36	

Building maintenance and fixed charges:

Department	Square Feet	Amount
Administrative and selling............	8,200	$ 820.00
General factory.....................	4,000	400.00
Cutting department..................	8,955	895.51
Assembly department No. 1...........	9,938	993.81
Assembly department No. 2...........	9,117.5	911.75
Totals.........................	40,210.5	$4,021.07

General factory administration distributed:

Department	Normal Hours	Amount
Cutting department..................	7,500	$1,240.82
Assembly department No. 1...........	8,000	1,323.54
Assembly department No. 2...........	20,000	3,308.84
Totals.........................	35,500	$5,873.20

Figure 12-14

295

NORTHCOTT MANUFACTURING COMPANY
Normal Departmental Expense and Normal Expense Rates
(One-Month Period)

| | | Service Departments | | | | Producing Departments | | | |
		(1) Building Maintenance and Fixed Charges	(2) General Factory Administration	(3) Electric Power Plant	(4) Repair Shop	(10) Shearing	(11) Parts	(12) Assembly	Totals
Line	Particulars								
	Statistics:								
1	Square feet of floor space		400	600	600	1,000	1,400	2,000	6,000
2	Indirect labor hours	500	1,000	400	400	400	400	400	3,500
3	Direct labor hours					4,000	6,000	8,000	18,000
4	Total labor hours	500	1,000	400	400	4,400	6,400	8,400	21,500
5	Kilowatt hours of power used				1,000	15,000	10,000	3,000	29,000
6	Repair hours used					400	300	200	900
	Expense dollars:								
7	Indirect labor	$1,200.00	$2,500.00	$800.00	$800.00	$1,600.00	$1,500.00	$1,200.00	$9,600.00
8	Maintenance supplies	100.00		30.00		80.00	200.00	80.00	490.00
9	Operating supplies		200.00	100.00	30.00	50.00	200.00	150.00	730.00
10	Purchased service	600.00	500.00	50.00	50.00	50.00	100.00	150.00	1,500.00
11	Unclassified	100.00					30.00	50.00	180.00
12	Fixed charges	1,000.00	100.00	100.00	50.00	100.00	200.00	250.00	1,800.00
13	Totals	$3,000.00	$3,300.00	$1,080.00	$930.00	$1,880.00	$2,230.00	$1,880.00	
	Service department allocations:*								
14	Building maintenance and fixed charges (@ 50¢ per sq. ft. × line 1)	3,000.00*	200.00	300.00	300.00	500.00	700.00	1,000.00	
15			$3,500.00						
16	General factory administration (@ $.175 per hour × line 4)		3,500.00*	70.00	70.00	770.00	1,120.00	1,470.00	
17				$1,450.00					
18	Electric power (@ 5¢ per K.W. hour × line 5)			1,450.00*	50.00	750.00	500.00	150.00	
19					$1,350.00				
20	Repair shop expense (@ $1.50 per repair hour × line 6)				1,350.00*	600.00	450.00	300.00	
21	Total expenses (producing departments)					$4,500.00	$5,000.00	$4,800.00	$14,300.00
22	Expense rates per hour for producing departments (line 21 ÷ line 3)					$1.125	$.83⅓	$.60	

* Rates for allocation of service are computed in Figure 12-16.

Figure 12-15

Actual factory expense, per debit balance of Factory Expense account..............................	$16,286.39
Applied factory expense, per credit balance of Factory Expense Applied account........................	14,763.90
Net underabsorbed expense........................	$ 1,522.49

The underabsorbed expense for any department may be calculated by applying the same formula to department balances.

Other service departments: Expense worksheet illustrated.   In addition to the general factory administration department and the building maintenance department, a number of other service departments might be found in large companies; for example:

(a) Power plants of various types—electric, steam, compressed air, and hydraulic.   In very large companies, all these plants might be operated. A separate expense account would be maintained for each plant.   At the end of each month, the departments which use a particular kind of power would be charged on the basis of metered or estimated consumption, and the service department which produced the power would be credited.

(b) Repair shops of various kinds, such as machine shops, carpenter shops, tin shops, electric shops, and boiler shops.   Each of the shops might have its own building and equipment and each of them might be supervised by a foreman.   An expense account would be kept for each shop.   Departments using a particular repair service would be charged with the appropriate repair shop overhead on the basis of the number of hours of repair service.

A worksheet illustrating the allocation of the expenses of four service departments appears on page 298:

(1)   Building maintenance and fixed charges
(2)   General factory administration
(3)   Electric power
(4)   Repair shop

On the worksheet, the statistics used for the allocation of service expense appear on lines 1-6:

Line 1—Square feet of floor space, used to allocate building maintenance and fixed charges.
Line 4—Total labor hours, used to allocate general factory administration.
Line 5—Kilowatt hours of power used, to allocate electric power plant expense.
Line 6—Repair hours used, to allocate repair shop expense.

Expense incurred by departments is shown on lines 7-13.   Allocations of service department expenses to using departments are shown on lines 14-20.

Note that building maintenance and fixed charges is allocated to all departments—service departments as well as producing departments. (Factory office, the electric power plant, and the repair shop are charged for "rent" on the basis of floor space occupied.)   Likewise, general factory administration is charged to power plant and repair shop as well as to the producing departments.

The *rates* used for allocation of service department expense are computed below:

RATES FOR ALLOCATION OF SERVICE DEPARTMENT EXPENSE

Building maintenance and fixed charges:

$$\text{Rate per square feet of floor space} = \frac{\text{Total expense (col. 1, line 13)}}{\text{Total square feet (line 1)}}$$

$$= \frac{\$3,000}{6,000} = \$.50 \text{ per sq. ft.}$$

General factory administration:

$$\text{Rate per labor hour} = \frac{\text{Total expense (col. 2, line 15)}}{\text{Total labor hours (line 4)}}$$

$$= \frac{\$3,500}{20,000} = \$.175 \text{ per labor hour}$$

(Labor hours for building maintenance and general factory administration are excluded.)

Electric power:

$$\text{Rate per kilowatt hour} = \frac{\text{Total expense (col. 3, line 17)}}{\text{Total kilowatt hours (line 5)}}$$

$$= \frac{\$1,450}{29,000} = \$.05 \text{ per kilowatt hour}$$

Repair shop expense:

$$\text{Rate per repair hour} = \frac{\text{Total expense (col. 4, line 19)}}{\text{Total repair hours (line 6)}}$$

$$= \frac{\$1,350}{900} = \$1.50 \text{ per repair hour}$$

Figure 12-16

Expense rates per hour for producing departments are entered on line 22. The formula is:

$$\text{Expense rate for producing department} = \frac{\text{Expense for department}}{\text{Direct labor hours for department}}$$

The resulting normal rates are:

	Rate per Hour
Shearing department..................	$1.125
Parts department....................	.83⅓
Assembly department.................	.60

Normal rates for producing departments would be used to apply expense to production order cost sheets and to charge the Factory Expense in Process account at the end of the month.

Summary: Operating departmental factory expense accounts.
The steps for operating departmental factory expense accounts and preparing expense statements for management are:

Voucher Register

(1) During the month, enter disbursement vouchers for supplies and purchased services in the voucher register.

(2) At the end of the month, foot and cross-foot the voucher register. Post column totals to control accounts in the general ledger.

General Journal

(3) During the month, enter payrolls in the general journal.

(4) At the end of the month, record the entries for accruals and deferrals affecting factory expense in the general journal. Post the credits to general ledger accounts from Miscellaneous Credits column on a day-to-day basis.

(5) Foot and cross-foot the general journal. Post column totals to control accounts in general ledger.

Factory Expense Ledger

(6) Post the items in each Factory Expense, Debit column of the voucher register to the related columnar expense account in the factory expense ledger.

(7) Post the items in the Factory Expense, Debit columns, of the general journal to the columnar accounts in the factory expense ledger.

Expense Worksheet and Expense Statement

(8) Prepare a worksheet for distributing service department expense to using departments. Prepare departmental expense statements from the worksheet.

(9) If desired, post entries for service used from the expense worksheet to credit service departments for service provided by them and charge using departments for service received. (This is an optional step.)

REVIEW QUESTIONS

12-1. (a) What are producing departments? Service departments?
(b) Name typical producing departments; service departments.

12-2. With reference to factory expense accounts, what is an object classification? Describe the arrangement of an object classification suitable for a large business. Explain the purposes of arranging the accounts in groups.

12-3. What factory expense reports would usually be prepared for the management of a manufacturing concern operating producing departments and service departments? For what purpose(s) would each report be used?

12-4. Describe a plan of departmental expense account numbers for a manufacturing concern operating producing departments and service departments.

12-5. What journals are the sources of postings to the departmental expense accounts? What types of charges originate in each journal?

12-6. (a) On what basis is building maintenance and fixed charges allocated to using departments?   Give formula for rate.

(b) On what basis is general factory administration allocated?   Give formula for rate.

DISCUSSION QUESTIONS

12-7. Are the bases for allocation of the services mentioned in Question 12-6 reasonable?

12-8. Name a number of service departments other than those mentioned in Question 12-6, indicating a basis for the allocation of each service to the using departments.   Discuss the reasonableness of each basis.

12-9. The foreman of the assembly department complains to the cost accountant that even though he uses the same quantity of power each month for several months, he is sometimes charged different dollar amounts.   He points out that he might be charged $.04 per kw. hr. one month and $.05 the next month.

(a) What would cause the difference in rate per kw. hr. from one month to the next?

(b) Is the foreman justified in complaining about the increase in rate per kw. hr.?

(c) If the foreman is justified in complaining, what is your recommendation?

12-10. Referring to Question 12-9, is it desirable to charge using departments for power used at the rate(s) quoted by the local independent power company? Is it feasible from a cost accounting standpoint?

12-11. Suppose that in the text illustrations of service department accounts in Chapter 12, there had been an electric power plant and a repair shop, among other departments.   How would you proceed to charge (a) the repair shop for electric power received and (b) the power plant for repair work done by the repair shop?

EXERCISES

12-1. The L. Jarson Manufacturing Company has three departments: two producing departments and one service department.   Compute normal factory expense rates based upon direct labor hours using the form in the Workbook.

12-2. The L. Jarson Manufacturing Company referred to in Exercise 12-1 uses departmental factory expense accounts.   All transactions for the month of January except those given below have been journalized, and the daily postings have been made.

Using the journals and accounts in the Workbook, enter the transactions given below and complete all posting for the month of January.

(1) January 31—Received the power bill for January from Public Electric Co. It is to be charged as follows:

Producing department 1..............	$100.00
Producing department 2..............	30.00
Repair department..................	70.00
Total...........................	$200.00

(2) January 31—Insurance expired on equipment during January:

Producing department 1..............	$ 25.00
Producing department 2.............	38.00
Repair department	12.00
Total credit to Unexpired Insurance..	$ 75.00

NORTH MANUFACTURING COMPANY
Departmental Expense Data
Month of January, 19__

Particulars	Building Maintenance & Fixed Charges	Service Departments			Producing Departments			Totals
		General Factory Administration	Electric Power Plant	Repair Shop	Shearing	Punch Press	Assembly	
Statistics:								
Sq. ft. of floor space....		500	500	400	500	600	1,000	3,500
Direct labor hours.....					2,000	2,000	6,000	10,000
Indirect labor hours.....	600	1,200	1,600	400	1,200	1,600	1,200	7,800
Total labor hours......	600	1,200	1,600	400	3,200	3,600	7,200	17,800
Kilowatt hours (power)....				2,000	15,000	14,000	5,000	36,000
Repair hours..........					200	400	600	1,200
Expense dollars:								
Indirect labor.........	$1,200.00	$3,000.00	$1,800.00	$ 400.00	$1,600.00	$2,400.00	$2,400.00	$12,800.00
Operating supplies......		100.00	500.00	50.00	100.00	50.00	100.00	900.00
Maintenance supplies.....	100.00		100.00		50.00	100.00	100.00	450.00
Purchased services......	300.00	150.00	50.00	200.00	200.00	100.00	50.00	1,050.00
Unclassified.........	200.00	50.00	50.00	50.00	100.00	50.00	100.00	600.00
Fixed charges........	1,700.00	200.00	200.00	100.00	300.00	200.00	400.00	3,100.00
Totals........	$3,500.00	$3,500.00	$2,700.00	$ 800.00	$2,350.00	$2,900.00	$3,150.00	$18,900.00

(3) January 31—On the basis of service rendered, $275 of the repair department expense is to be allocated to producing department 1: the balance of the repair department expense is to be charged to producing department 2.
Detach the forms from the Workbook and submit them.

12-3. From your Solutions to Exercise 12-1 and Exercise 12-2, prepare the following reports:
(1) For the president:
    (a) Monthly Expense Statement showing object totals (see Figure 12-3a)
    (b) Monthly Expense Statement showing departmental totals (see Figure 12-3b)
(2) For the foreman of producing department 1:
    (a) Monthly Expense Statement for producing department 1 (see Figure 12-4c)
(Note that the budget prepared in Exercise 12-1 was a budget for a year and not one month.)

12-4. The cost sheets for January show 900 direct labor hours in producing department 1 and 400 direct labor hours in producing department 2.
    (a) On the basis of normal rates computed in Exercise 12-1, how much factory expense is applied in January?
    (b) Prepare a statement showing the amount of over- or underapplied factory expense by department.

12-5. A "fill-in" form departmental expense worksheet for the Lang Manufacturing Company appears in the Workbook. You are asked to (a) distribute service department expenses and (b) compute factory expense rates for producing departments.

PROBLEMS

12-1. Departmental expense statistics and dollars for the North Manufacturing Company for January, 19— appear in the tabulation presented herewith.

Required:

Prepare a departmental expense worksheet, allocating service department expense to using departments. Charge building maintenance and fixed charges to all other departments, including service departments. Charge general factory administration to all departments except building maintenance and fixed charges. Charge electric power and repair shop to all using departments.

12-2. The Crull Company uses normal departmental rates based upon direct labor hours to apply factory expense. The budget and computation of these rates for 19— are shown on page 303.

During 19— factory expense was not recorded in departmental expense accounts, but the information on page 304 was collected to facilitate departmentalizing the expenses on a worksheet.

Using the information given on page 304, prepare:

(a) A worksheet to departmentalize factory expense.
(b) A statement of factory expense by object totals.
(c) A statement of factory expense by departmental totals
(d) A statement of under- or overapplied factory expense by departments.

Statistics	Total	Cutting Department	Assembly Department	Repair Department	General Works Department
Number of employees	20	7	6	3	4
Labor hours	39,200	14,000	12,000	6,000	7,200
Floor space (sq. ft.)	10,000	3,500	4,500	1,000	1,000
Valuation of equipment	$75,000.00	$40,000.00	$30,000.00	$3,000.00	$ 2,000.00

Costs	Basis of Allocation	Total	Cutting Department	Assembly Department	Repair Department	General Works Department
Salaries—supervision	Number of employees	$18,000.00	$ 6,300.00	$ 5,400.00	$2,700.00	$ 3,600.00
Salaries—clerical	Services used	13,200.00	2,400.00	2,400.00		8,400.00
Rent	Floor space	15,000.00	5,250.00	6,750.00	1,500.00	1,500.00
Heat, light, and power	Service used	2,400.00	1,500.00	580.00	200.00	120.00
Depreciation	Valuation of equipment	7,500.00	4,000.00	3,000.00	300.00	200.00
Supplies	Supplies used	2,000.00	700.00	497.00	499.00	304.00
Insurance	Valuation of equipment	750.00	400.00	300.00	30.00	20.00
Miscellaneous	Number of employees	1,200.00	420.00	360.00	180.00	240.00
Total direct departmental expense		$60,050.00	$20,970.00	$19,287.00	$5,409.00	$14,384.00
Allocation of service departments:						
General works—labor hours			6,293.00	5,394.00	2,697.00	14,384.00*
					$8,106.00	
Repair department—service rendered			2,702.00	5,404.00	8,106.00*	
Totals		$60,050.00	$29,965.00	$30,085.00		
Normal rates based upon direct labor hours			$ 2.14	$ 2.51		

* Red.

Statistics	Total	Cutting Department	Assembly Department	Repair Department	General Works Department
Number of employees....	15	5	6	2	2
Labor hours............	29,000	10,000	11,000	4,000	4,000
Floor space (sq. ft.).....	10,000	3,500	4,500	1,000	1,000
Valuation of equipment..	$75,000.00	$40,000.00	$30,000.00	$3,000.00	$2,000.00
Clerical services used....	$12,000.00	$ 3,000.00	$ 3,000.00		$6,000.00
Heat, light, and power...	$ 2,500.00	$ 1,500.00	$ 600.00	$ 250.00	$ 150.00
Supplies used...........	$ 2,000.00	$ 600.00	$ 400.00	$ 800.00	$ 200.00
Salaries—Supervision....	$15,000.00				
Rent.................	$15,000.00				
Depreciation...........	$ 7,500.00				
Insurance.............	$ 750.00				
Misc. expense..........	$ 690.00				

Repair department charge: All but $1,598.00 charged to cutting department.

12-3. The following data relative to the Jones Equipment Company are submitted for your consideration:

Trial Balance, January 31, 19__

Cash.................................	$ 7,300.00	
Accounts receivable....................	18,430.00	
Reserve for bad debts..................		$ 785.00
Raw materials inventory, January 1, 19__	5,200.00	
Work in process inventory, January 1, 19__	7,100.00	
Finished goods inventory, January 1, 19__	9,700.00	
Land................................	10,000.00	
Building.............................	75,000.00	
Machinery and equipment..............	100,000.00	
Reserve for depreciation...............		12,950.00
Prepaid insurance.....................	3,700.00	
Accounts payable.....................		7,430.00
Bank loan...........................		5,000.00
Mortgage payable (due in 10 yrs.).......		25,000.00
Capital stock........................		100,000.00
Surplus.............................		77,350.00
Sales...............................		52,040.00
Purchase of materials..................	14,300.00	
Direct labor.........................	9,740.00	
Indirect labor........................	680.00	
Factory supplies......................	740.00	
Heat, light, & power..................	420.00	
Miscellaneous factory expense...........	120.00	
Selling expense.......................	9,800.00	
General expense......................	8,200.00	
Interest expense......................	125.00	
	$280,555.00	$280,555.00

The following additional information has not been recorded:

Materials requisitioned
Direct materials.................................... $15,000.00
Indirect materials.................................. 750.00

Unpaid wages
Direct labor.....................................	1,620.00
Indirect labor...................................	130.00
Salesmen's commissions...........................	320.00
Insurance expired................................	1,500.00
Depreciation on building.........................	625.00
Depreciation on machinery and equipment..............	1,000.00
Unused factory supplies at January 31, 19___............	60.00
Cost of goods manufactured.........................	29,630.00
Cost of goods sold :................................	28,300.00

Departmental factory expense rates based upon direct labor hours are used. The factory expense applied in January is based upon the following:

	Labor Hours	Normal Rate
Department 1.............	1,800	$1.25
Department 2.............	2,200	1.20
Department 3.............	600	1.40

The schedule below shows the distribution of factory expense to the various departments.

You are asked to prepare:

(a) Statement of Cost of Goods Manufactured.
(b) Statement of Cost of Goods Sold.
(c) Income Statement.
(d) Balance Sheet.
(e) Statement of Over- or Underapplied Factory Expense by Departments.
(f) Statement of Factory Expense by Objects for Department 1.

JONES EQUIPMENT COMPANY
Distribution of Factory Expense
for the Month of January 19___

Accounts to Be Credited

Account to Be Debited.	Total	Indirect Materials	Indirect Labor	Factory Supplies	Heat, Light, & Power
General works dept.	$ 305.00	$	$ 40.00	$ 80.00	$ 40.00
Repair dept.............	625.00	50.00	70.00	130.00	80.00
Department 1............	1,885.00	300.00	100.00	40.00	95.00
Department 2............	2,100.00	200.00	300.00	300.00	85.00
Department 3............	1,920.00	200.00	300.00	130.00	120.00
Totals................	$6,835.00	$750.00	$810.00	$680.00	$420.00

Accounts to Be Credited (Continued)

	Prepaid Insurance	Depreciation— Machine & Equipment	Depreciation— Building	Miscellaneous Factory Exp.	Repair Department	Gen. Works Department
	$ 80.00	$ 20.00	$ 25.00	$ 20.00		
	70.00	135.00	25.00	20.00		45.00
	550.00	365.00	225.00	40.00	75.00	95.00
	350.00	280.00	175.00	30.00	300.00	80.00
	450.00	200.00	175.00	10.00	250.00	85.00
Totals.....	$1,500.00	$1,000.00	$625.00	$120.00	$625.00	$305.00

12-4. The Waverly Manufacturing Company has decided to change its method of distributing factory burden to its products, all of which are manufactured on special order. You are asked (a) to develop appropriate departmental rates, based on the company's operations for the first half of 19__, and (b) to illustrate their use by determining the cost of Job Order No. 987 by applying the rates you develop.

The trial balance of the company's factory ledger (cents omitted), for the six months ended June 30, 19__ is as follows:

	Debit	Credit
Materials and manufacturing supplies.....	$ 85,321.00	
Work in process—material................	86,105.00	
Work in process—labor................	82,872.00	
Work in process—manufacturing expenses	161,480.00	
Indirect labor........................	41,740.00	
Factory rent.........................	2,400.00	
Insurance—machinery and equipment.....	4,216.00	
Compensation insurance................	2,486.00	
Superintendence......................	6,000.00	
Factory clerical salaries................	4,950.00	
Machinery maintenance and repairs......	31,010.00	
Depreciation of machinery and equipment	42,800.00	
Fuel................................	3,172.00	
Electricity...........................	2,178.00	
Manufacturing supplies used............	3,617.00	
Social security taxes...................	9,210.00	
Factory office supplies.................	879.00	
Miscellaneous factory expense...........	1,212.00	
Manufacturing expense applied..........		$158,200.00
General ledger control.................		413,448.00
	$571,648.00	$571,648.00

Additional data:

The manufacturing operations are carried on in three production departments, A, B, and C, with the aid of two service departments, numbered 1 and 2, respectively. Other data are as follows:

			Departments			
	Total	A	B	C	1	2
Plant floor space (sq. ft.)...	30,000	10,000	5,000	2,000	7,500	5,500
Number of employees......	109	50	20	4	25	10
Number of labor hours.....	113,360	52,000	20,800	4,160	26,000	10,400
Number of machine hours...	47,952	31,912	9,640	560	5,840	
Salaries and wages.........	$161,317.00	$76,180.00	$28,472.00	$9,975.00	$37,230.00	$9,460.00
Cost of machinery and equipment..................	$1,019,047.00	$623,225.00	$250,960.00	$20,210.00	$112,862.00	$11,790.00
Annual depreciation rates...		8%	8%	10%	10%	20%

In developing burden rates, expenses not distributed in the above table shall be distributed to departments as follows:

On the basis of floor space:
  Factory rent; fuel; ¼ of electricity
On the basis of salaries and wages:
  Compensation insurance
  Superintendence
  Manufacturing supplies used
  Social security taxes

Factory office supplies

Miscellaneous factory expense

On the basis of investment in machinery and equipment:

Insurance, machinery and equipment

Machinery maintenance and repairs

¾ of electricity

Factory clerical salaries and $4,510 of indirect labor are charged to department No. 2.   The balance of indirect labor is charged to department No. 1.

Expenses of department No. 1 are to be distributed, 1/10 to department No. 2, the balance to all other departments on the basis of machine hours.

Expenses of department No. 2 are to be distributed to departments A, B, and C, on the basis of labor hours.

The departmental burden rates are to be based on machine hours for departments A and B, and on labor hours for department C.

Data applicable to Job Order No. 987 are as follows:

Material, $487.92; direct labor, $465.

Machine hours: Department A, 50 hours.

Department B, 12 hours.

Labor hours: Department C, 20 hours.

(*American Institute of Certified Public Accountants*—Adapted)

Chapter 13

PROCESS COSTS

Definition and general discussion. A process cost system is one in which unit product costs are determined *for a period* with reference to (a) production costs and (b) units produced for the period. The unit cost is accordingly an average cost for a period. The period is often one month, but it may be of any length, for instance, a day or a week. Having a regular cutoff based upon a period of time, it is to be distinguished from job order costing in which a unit product cost is computed for each *production order*. In a job order cost system, it will be recalled, the unit cost is based upon the cost of a particular production order and the units produced on the order.

Process cost systems are used in industries in which the product moves through the factory as a flow, rather than as a succession of separate orders. They are used, for instance, in cement mills. Here lime and clay are ground and burned into clinkers, which in turn are ground with gypsum to make cement. Records are kept of cost of production and barrels produced month by month, and an average cost per barrel of cement is computed each month. Other examples are found in milling industries where grains are ground to make flour, in breweries where beer is produced, and in power plants where electricity is produced. Note that in some cases, the product is liquid and it literally flows through the plant. In other cases, the product is solid but to all intents and purposes it flows through the plant, since separate lots are not identified.

In addition to the situation where process costing *must* be used, as indicated in the previous paragraph; there are cases where process costing is used as a matter of choice. In a washing machine factory which produces a single model of product in large quantities, it might be considered not worth the effort to post requisitions and job tickets to a large number of production orders. The management may decide to use process costing. This would involve simply keeping track of production cost and units produced according to the desired periods, which could be one week. Process costing would probably be cheaper to operate than job order costing.

In this chapter, two examples of process costing are illustrated and explained:

(1) Single-stage process costing, used where the raw material passes through a single stage or department in the conversion to finished product.

(2) Multiple-stage process costing, used where the material passes through several departments in succession in the conversion to finished goods. Unit cost of production is determined for each department in succession.

I. SINGLE-STAGE PROCESS COSTING

Description of product and process. This illustration is concerned with the manufacture of pig iron using iron ore, limestone, and coke. Large quantities of these "materials" are bought and stored in piles unit used. (Actually, only the iron ore is, strictly speaking, a material, since it is the substance which is converted into product. Coke is a fuel and limestone is a flux. All these items are accounted for as materials.) Measured quantities of materials are charged into a huge furnace, known as a blast furnace. They are hoisted to the top of the furnace and dumped in at regular intervals. Molten pig iron is likewise tapped from the base of the furnace at intervals. It is poured into moulds in which it cools and hardens into the blocks of iron known as "pigs." The pig iron is sold to other companies which process it further.

Careful weight records are kept of materials put into the piles, materials used, pig iron tapped, and pig iron sold. The record of materials charged into the furnace, for instance, is kept by the stock house foreman, who reports it to the accounting department at the end of each month. The record of the tons of pig iron tapped is kept by the cast house foreman, who likewise reports it to the accounting department at the end of each month. And finally, the tally of tons shipped is kept by the shipping clerk.

Managerial information: Statement of cost of pig iron produced.

Figure 13-1 is a statement of cost of pig iron produced, which is typical of process cost statements prepared in single-stage process cost systems. This statement covers a one-month period. Note that it shows:

(a) *Tons produced* (5,000). This tonnage figure is the basis for the unit costs shown on the statement.

(b) *Materials.* This section shows the quantities and amounts of each material used during the month and the unit cost per ton of pig iron produced ($20).

(c) *Conversion cost.* This is the sum of labor and expense incurred in converting materials to finished product. In this statement, conversion cost is set out by object class (supplies and repair parts, purchased service, and so on). Total conversion cost is $90,000 and conversion cost per ton of pig iron is $18.

(d) *Total cost ($190,000) and total cost per ton ($38).*

(e) *Material yield.* This is output in tons divided by input in tons.

The theoretical yield is determined by the technicians in the company laboratory who test samples of the iron ore to determine how much iron a ton of ore should yield.   In this case, they have determined that one ton of ore should yield .52 ton of iron; in other words, that the yield should be 52 per cent.   The actual yield, computed by the accounting department, is 5,000 tons output divided by 10,000 tons input equals 50 per cent.   The actual yield was therefore less than the expected yield.   The blast furnace superintendent did not get as much iron out of the iron ore as he was expected to get.

WESTERN IRON COMPANY
Statement of Cost of Pig Iron Produced

Month of January, 19__

(Process Cost System)

Particulars	Tons	Price Per Ton	Amount	Per Ton of Iron Produced
Tons produced:...............			5,000	
Materials:				
Iron ore....................	10,000	$ 8.00	$ 80,000.00	
Limestone.................	2,000	5.00	10,000.00	
Coke.....................	1,000	10.00	10,000.00	
Totals....................	13,000		$100,000.00	$20.00
Conversion cost:				
Labor......................		$60,000.00		
Supplies and repair parts......		5,000.00		
Purchased service...........		8,000.00		
Depreciation................		5,000.00		
Relining expense............		1,250.00		
Insurance...................		3,750.00		
Taxes......................		7,000.00		
Totals....................			$ 90,000.00	18.00
Total cost..................			$190,000.00	$38.00
Material yield:				
Theoretical yield.....................			52%	
Actual yield (5,000 tons output ÷ 10,000 tons input)......			50%	

Figure 13-1

Note that the unit conversion cost and the material yield percentage are considered to be measures of the performance of the blast furnace superintendent. The superintendent is not considered responsible for the prices per ton paid for the various materials, and consequently conversion cost is separated as the part of cost for which he *is* responsible. The superintendent is considered responsible for obtaining a satisfactory yield. Note that the theoretical yield with which actual yield is compared is a standard based upon good production performance.

Accounts. A list of inventory and cost accounts required to produce the process cost statement illustrated in the previous section appears in Figure 13-2. Note that it includes among others, an account for each of the three materials and for finished pig iron, an account for cost of production (in process—pig iron) and accounts for labor and factory expense.

WESTERN IRON COMPANY
Inventory and Cost Accounts

Inventories:

Iron Ore Inventory
Limestone Inventory
Coke Inventory
In Process—Pig Iron
Finished Pig Iron Inventory
Supplies and Repair Parts Inventory

Factory Expense Accounts:

Supplies and Repair Parts
Purchased Service
Depreciation
Relining expense
Insurance
Taxes

Sales, Cost of Sales, and Production Cost:

Sales of Pig Iron
Cost of Pig Iron Sales
Labor
Factory Expense Control

Figure 13-2

Quantity control. A tabulation of quantities reported to the accounting department is prepared as illustrated in Figure 13-3. Note that for each material it shows opening inventory, tons purchased, tons used, and closing inventory. For pig iron, it shows opening inventory, tons produced, tons sold, and closing inventory. The basic purpose of this quantity control record is to determine the accuracy of the usage information and other quantity information reported to the accounting department. During the year, the accountant can judge the reasonableness of the quantities of materials used and quantities of iron produced by noting whether the relationship between cumulative input and cumulative output has changed significantly.

Any change could be caused by either a poor-yield showing or incorrect quantity figures. When there is a significant change, the accountant attempts to find out whether there have been any operating difficulties which would account for a poor-yield showing.

The final determination of the accuracy of the reporting is made at physical inventory time. At that time the balances on hand per the

WESTERN IRON COMPANY
Materials Used: Pig Iron Production and Sales (in Tons)

Month of January, 19___

	Opening Inventory	Debits	Credits	Closing Inventory
Iron ore.............	8,000	12,000	10,000	10,000
Limestone............	2,000	3,000	2,000	3,000
Coke................	2,000	1,000	1,000	2,000
Total materials.....	12,000	16,000	13,000	15,000
Pig iron.............	5,000	5,000	4,000	6,000

Figure 13-3

quantity control record are proved against the quantities determined by physical inventory.

The need for quantity control in a process cost system is clear. In the first place, quantity control safeguards the accuracy of the quantity figures used in computing unit costs. Obviously, the unit costs are not correct if the quantities upon which they are based are wrong. In the second place, quantity control is an over-all check on cash payments for materials. If the materials quantities per the control record tie to physical inventory, it is reasonably certain that the quantities of materials paid for on incoming invoices were the correct quantities. And finally, quantity control is an over-all check on billing to customers. If the pig iron quantities tie to physical inventory, there is assurance that the quantities of pig iron billed to the customers on outgoing invoices were correct.

Procedure outlined. The procedure for operating the accounts and preparing the process cost statement in a single-stage process cost system is outlined:

During the month:

Compile tons of materials received and tons used; also tons of iron produced and tons sold, as illustrated in Figure 13-3.

(1) Compile cost of materials and supplies purchased, and labor and expense incurred.

At the end of the month: Draft entries to—

(2) Record cost of materials used, charging In Process—Pig Iron account.

(3) Close labor and factory expense accounts to In Process—Pig Iron account.

(4) Record cost of pig iron produced.

(5) Record cost of pig iron sold.

All these entries are based upon the quantities in Figure 13-3 and costs compiled as indicated in (1).

These steps are illustrated in the following sections.

1. *Materials and Supplies Purchased; Labor and Expense Incurred.*
Entries in general journal form for cost of materials and supplies purchased
and labor and expense incurred follow:

(a) Purchase of materials:

Iron ore inventory..............................	$88,000.00	
Limestone inventory...........................	17,000.00	
Coke inventory................................	12,000.00	
Vouchers payable.........................		$117,000.00
Materials purchased during the month, and freight-in, as follows:		

Invoices

	Tons	Per Ton	Amount	Freight	Total
Iron ore.........	12,000	$ 7.00	$ 84,000.00	$4,000.00	$ 88,000.00
Limestone.......	3,000	5.00	15,000.00	2,000.00	17,000.00
Coke...........	1,000	11.00	11,000.00	1,000.00	12,000.00
	16,000		$110,000.00	$7,000.00	$117,000.00

(b) Labor accrued:

Labor...	$60,000.00	
Accrued labor.............................		$60,000.00
Labor used in production of pig iron during month		

(c) Purchase of supplies, repair parts, and purchased services:

Supplies and repair parts inventory...............	$ 4,000.00	
Factory expense—Purchased service...............	8,000.00	
Vouchers payable...........................		$12,000.00
Purchases during month		

(d) Supplies and repair parts used:

Factory expense—Supplies and repair parts........	$ 5,000.00	
Supplies and repair parts inventory...........		$ 5,000.00
Supplies and repair parts used during month		

(e) Depreciation on buildings, furnace, and equipment:

Factory expense—Depreciation....................	$ 5,000.00	
Reserve for depreciation......................		$ 5,000.00
Estimated depreciation on buildings, furnace, and equipment for month		

(f) Depreciation on brick lining of furnace:

Factory expense—Relining.......................	$ 1,250.00	
Reserve for relining.........................		$ 1,250.00
Estimated depreciation on furnace lining:		
5,000 tons @ 25¢ per ton........... $1,250.00		

(g) Insurance:

Factory expense—Insurance......................	$ 3,750.00	
Prepaid insurance.............................		$ 3,750.00
Insurance expired during month		

(h) Taxes:

Factory expense—Taxes.........................	$ 7,000.00	
Accrued taxes.............................		$ 7,000.00
Estimated taxes for month		

2. *Cost of Materials Used.* After the first entry above has been posted, the materials inventory accounts appear as shown in Figure 13-4.

Materials Inventory Accounts

Postings from Voucher Register

Particulars		Tons	Per Ton	Amounts	
Iron ore inventory (debits):					
Opening inventory........		8,000	$ 9.00	$ 72,000.00	
Purchases—invoices.......	(1a)	12,000	7.00	84,000.00	
Freight.................	(1a)			4,000.00	
		20,000		$160,000.00	Average $8
Limestone inventory (debits):					
Opening inventory........		2,000	$ 4.00	$ 8,000.00	
Purchases—invoices.......	(1a)	3,000	5.00	15,000.00	
Freight.................	(1a)			2,000.00	
		5,000		$ 25,000.00	Average $5
Coke inventory (debits):					
Opening inventory........		2,000	$ 9.00	$ 18,000.00	
Purchases—invoices.......	(1a)	1,000	11.00	11,000.00	
Freight.................	(1a)			1,000.00	
		3,000		$ 30,000.00	Average $10

Figure 13-4

The average price per ton of materials in opening inventory and purchases, including freight-in, is:

	Per Ton
Iron ore..............	$ 8.00
Limestone.............	5.00
Coke.................	10.00

These average prices are used at the end of the month for determining the cost of materials used. The journal entry for recording cost of materials used is:

(2) In process—Pig iron............................	$100,000.00	
Iron ore inventory...........................		$80,000.00
Limestone inventory.........................		10,000.00
Coke inventory..............................		10,000.00

Materials used during month, as follows:

	Tons	Per Ton*	Amount
Iron ore..............	10,000	$ 8.00	$ 80,000.00
Limestone.............	2,000	5.00	10,000.00
Coke................	1,000	10.00	10,000.00
	13,000		$100,000.00

* As determined in inventory accounts, Figure 13-4.

3. *Close Labor and Factory Expense Accounts.* The entry to close labor and factory expense accounts is:

In process—Pig iron..........................	$ 90,000.00	
Labor.....................................		$ 60,000.00
Factory expense..........................		30,000.00

To charge In Process—Pig Iron with balances of labor and factory expense accounts for the month

4. *Record Cost of Pig Iron Produced:* The entry to record Cost of Pig Iron Produced is:

Pig iron inventory............................	$190,000.00	
In process—Pig iron.......................		$190,000.00

To close balance of In Process—Pig Iron account to Pig Iron Inventory account. (The unit cost per ton of pig iron produced is: $190,000 ÷ 5,000 = $38)

5. *Record Cost of Pig Iron Sold.* After Entry (4) has been posted, the debit side of the Pig Iron Inventory account appears:

Pig Iron inventory (debits):

Particulars		Tons	Per Ton	Amount	
Opening inventory.....		5,000	$40.00	$200,000.00	
Pig iron produced.....	(4)	5,000	38.00	190,000.00	
		10,000		$390,000.00	Average $39

Figure 13-5

The average cost per ton of opening inventory and pig iron produced during the month is $390,000 ÷ 10,000 tons or $39 per ton. This average is used for determining cost of pig iron sold as shown in the following entry:

(5) Cost of pig iron sold:

Cost of pig iron sales..........................	$156,000.00	
Pig iron inventory.........................		$156,000.00

Cost of pig iron sold during month:
4,000 tons @ $39*............. $156,000.00

* As determined in Pig Iron Inventory account, Figure 13-5.

Accounts posted: Preparing the statement. The complete set of posted accounts appears on pages 316-317. The statement of Cost of Pig

Iron Produced illustrated on page 310 is prepared from In Process—Pig Iron, with supporting details from the Factory Expense account and the Journal Entry for materials used (Entry (2)).

COMPLETE SET OF INVENTORY AND COST ACCOUNTS, POSTED

Iron Ore Inventory

Particulars		Tons	Per Ton	Amount	Particulars		Tons	Per Ton	Amount
Opening inventory		8,000	$ 9	$ 72,000	Used	(2)	10,000	$ 8	$ 80,000
Purchases—Invoices	(1a)	12,000	7	84,000					
Freight	(1a)			4,000	Balance		10,000	8	80,000
		20,000	8	$160,000			20,000	8	$160,000
Closing inventory		10,000	$ 8	$ 80,000					

Limestone Inventory

Particulars		Tons	Per Ton	Amount	Particulars		Tons	Per Ton	Amount
Opening inventory		2,000	$ 4	$ 8,000	Used	(2)	2,000	$ 5	$ 10,000
Purchases—Invoices	(1a)	3,000	5	15,000					
Freight	(1a)			2,000	Balance		3,000	5	15,000
		5,000	5	$ 25,000			3,000	5	$ 25,000
Closing inventory		3,000	$ 5	$ 15,000					

Coke Inventory

Particulars		Tons	Per Ton	Amount	Particulars		Tons	Per Ton	Amount
Opening inventory		2,000	$ 9	$ 18,000	Used	(2)	1,000	$10	$ 10,000
Purchases—Invoices	(1a)	1,000	11	11,000					
Freight	(1a)			1,000	Balance		2,000	10	20,000
		3,000	10	$ 30,000			3,000	10	$ 30,000
Closing inventory		2,000	$10	$ 20,000					

Pig Iron Inventory

Particulars		Tons	Per Ton	Amount	Particulars		Tons	Per Ton	Amount
Opening inventory		5,000	$40	$200,000	Pig iron sold	(5)	4,000	$39	$156,000
Pig iron produced	(4)	5,000	38	190,000	Balance		6,000	39	234,000
		10,000	39	$390,000			10,000	39	$390,000
Closing inventory		6,000	$39	$234,000					

Figure 13-6a

II. MULTIPLE-STAGE PROCESS COSTING

Description of product and processes. As was stated in the first section of this chapter, multiple-stage process costing is used where the material passes through several departments in succession in the conversion to finished goods. The manufacture of steel wire from steel ingots bought outside will be used to illustrate this type of process costing. Ingots are

In Process—Pig Iron

Materials	(2)	$100,000	Close to Pig Iron Inventory	(4)	$190,000
Labor	(3)	60,000			
Factory Expense	(3)	30,000			
		$190,000			$190,000

Supplies and Repair Parts Inventory

Opening inventory		$ 8,000	Used	(1d)	$ 5,000
Purchases	(1c)	4,000	Balance		7,000
		$12,000			$12,000
Closing inventory		$ 7,000			

Cost of Pig Iron Sales

Cost of sales for month	(5)	$156,000

Labor

Labor accrued	(1b)	$60,000	Close to In Process—Pig Iron	(3)	$60,000

Factory Expense

Purchased services	(1c)	$ 8,000	Close to In Process—Pig Iron	(3)	$30,000
Supplies and repair parts	(1d)	5,000			
Depreciation—Buildings, Furnace and equipment	(1e)	5,000			
Depreciation—Lining	(1f)	1,250			
Insurance	(1g)	3,750			
Taxes	(1h)	7,000			
		$30,000			$30,000

Figure 13-6b

large blocks of steel. In the manufacture of wire, the material would be processed successively in three departments:

(1) The blooming mill, in which the ingots are heated and rolled into blooms. In this operation, the hot ingot is passed between rolls. The effect is to increase the length of the ingot and reduce the other dimensions to form the bloom.

(2) The rod mill, in which the blooms are heated and rolled into rod.

(3) The wire mill, in which the rods are drawn through dies to produce wire.

In the illustration which follows, it is assumed for the sake of simplicity that only one size of wire is produced. It is also assumed that none of the blooms or rod are sold as such. All the good output of the blooming mill passes to the rod mill and all the good output of the rod mill passes to the wire mill.

In addition to the three producing departments, there are four service departments: general factory, electric power, repair shop, and shop transportation.

Managerial information: Statement of cost of wire produced. The following statements are prepared monthly for the management:

(1) A cost of production statement for each of the three producing departments: one for the cost of blooms produced, one for the cost of rod produced, and one for the cost of wire produced.

The Statement of Cost of Wire Produced is illustrated in Figure 13-7. It

EASTERN STEEL AND WIRE COMPANY
Statement of Cost of Wire Produced
for the Month of January, 19—

Particulars		Amount	Cost Per Ton
Tons of wire produced....................		940	
Labor....................................		$ 2,000.00	$ 2.13
Direct departmental expense:			
Indirect labor...........................	$600.00		
Supplies and repair parts.................	110.00		
Purchased service.......................	100.00		
Depreciation............................	175.00		
Insurance..............................	225.00		
Taxes..................................	200.00		
Total direct departmental expense......		1,410.00	1.50
Service department expense distributed:			
General factory expense..................	$400.00		
Electric power..........................	80.00		
Machine repair shop.....................	120.00		
Shop transportation.....................	190.00		
Total service department expense.......		790.00	.84
Total conversion cost......................		$ 4,200.00	$ 4.47
Materials: 950 tons Rod @ $50.00...........		47,500.00	50.53
Total cost of production...................		$51,700.00	$55.00

Shrinkage: 10 tons (loss) ÷ 940 tons (output) = 1.00%

Figure 13-7

is similar in outline to the Statement of Cost of Pig Iron Produced shown in Figure 13-1. It shows labor and expense for the wire mill, including charges to the wire mill for services received from the four service departments, and total conversion cost for the wire mill ($4,200). Unit costs per ton of wire produced are shown, as well as total costs.

Under the heading of materials, the statement show "950 tons rod @ $50.53 per ton = $47,500." This item is the total cost of rod produced by the rod mill. (Similarly, the Statement of Cost of Rod Produced would show, under material, the cost of the blooms delivered to the rod mill by the blooming mill.)

(2) A departmental expense statement for each of the seven departments. These statements are similar to the ones illustrated in Chapter 12 (Figure 12-3).

Accounts: Flow of cost diagrammed. A list of the inventory and cost accounts used to produce the statements described in the previous section appears below. Note that there are (a) inventory accounts for ingots and finished wire, (b) departmental expense accounts for the four service departments and three producing departments, (c) a cost of production account for each of the three producing departments.

EASTERN STEEL AND WIRE COMPANY
Inventory and Cost Accounts

Inventories:

Ingots Inventory
Supplies and Repair Parts Inventory
Finished Wire Inventory

In Process Accounts:

In Process—Blooming Mill
In Process—Rod Mill
In Process—Wire Mill

Departmental Expense Accounts:

Service Departments:

General Factory Expense
Electric Power Plant Expense
Repair Shop Expense
Shop Transportation Expense

Producing Departments:

Blooming Mill Expense
Rod Mill Expense
Wire Mill Expense

Sales and Cost of Sales:

Sales of Wire
Cost of Wire Sold

Figure 13-8

EASTERN STEEL AND WIRE COMPANY

Diagram: Inventory and Production Accounts

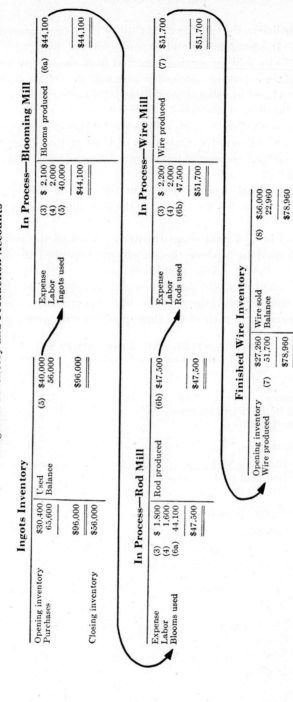

Ingots Inventory

Opening inventory	$30,400	Used	(5)	$40,000
Purchases	65,600	Balance		56,000
	$96,000			$96,000
Closing inventory	$56,000			

In Process—Blooming Mill

Expense	(3)	$ 2,100	Blooms produced	(6a)	$44,100
Labor	(4)	2,000			
Ingots used	(5)	40,000			
		$44,100			$44,100

In Process—Rod Mill

Expense	(3)	$ 1,800	Rod produced	(6b)	$47,500
Labor	(4)	1,600			
Blooms used	(6a)	44,100			
		$47,500			$47,500

In Process—Wire Mill

Expense	(3)	$ 2,200	Wire produced	(7)	$51,700
Labor	(4)	2,000			
Rods used	(6b)	47,500			
		$51,700			$51,700

Finished Wire Inventory

Opening inventory	$27,260	Wire sold	(8)	$56,000
Wire produced	(7) 51,700	Balance		22,960
	$78,960			$78,960
Closing inventory	$22,960			

Figure 13-9

A diagram of the inventory and production accounts appears on page 320. It shows how cost flows from the ingots account, through the Blooming Mill, Rod Mill, and Wire Mill production accounts, to the Finished Wire account.

Quantity control. The quantity control summary for the Eastern Steel and Wire Company appears below. It is similar to the one shown on page 312, except that it also shows tonnage in and out for each of the three producing departments. In this illustration it is assumed that there is no inventory in process at the end of any month, and there is no inventory between departments.

Note that shrinkage is shown as loss occurs in each of the producing departments. Since there are no in process inventories, shrinkage in a department is the difference between the input and the output.

EASTERN STEEL AND WIRE COMPANY
Quantity Control Summary (in tons)
for the Month of January 19__

Inventory or Department	Opening Inventory	Trans- ferred In	Trans- ferred Out	Shrinkage or Loss	Closing Inventory
Ingots inventory...........	800	1,600	1,000	0	1,400
Blooming mill department...	0	1,000	980	20	0
Rod mill department.......	0	980	950	30	0
Wire mill department......	0	950	940	10	0
Finished wire.............	470	940	1,000		410

Figure 13-10

Procedure outlined. The steps of procedure for operating the accounts and producing the statements are:

Compile tons of ingots received and tons used, also tons of processed materials transferred from the Blooming Mill to the Rod Mill account and from the Rod Mill to the Wire Mill account.

Draft entries to record:

(1) Expense incurred by departments
(2) Charge to using departments for service received from service departments
(3) Transfer producing departments expense to in process accounts
(4) Charge to the in process accounts for operating labor
(5) Charge to the In Process—Blooming Mill account for ingots used
(6) Processed materials transferred from one in process account to another
(7) Finished wire produced
(8) Cost of wire sold

These steps are illustrated and explained in the following sections.

Compile tonnage received, used, transferred and sold. Tonnage received, used, transferred, and sold are compiled currently. The totals are set up in a reconciliation similar to Figure 13-10 at the end of the month. Tonnage totals are used in preparing the process cost worksheet and journal entries for materials used, wire produced, and wire sold, as explained later.

1. *Expense Incurred by Departments.* Entries for expense incurred by departments follow. Note that in each entry, each department is charged with the total of an expense object used.

(a) Indirect labor distribution:

General factory expense	$800.00	
Electric power plant expense	200.00	
Repair shop expense	200.00	
Shop transportation expense	300.00	
Blooming mill expense	600.00	
Rod mill expense	500.00	
Wire mill expense	600.00	
Accrued labor		$3,200.00
To record indirect labor by departments for month		

(b) Supplies and repair parts issued from stores:

General factory expense	$200.00	
Electric power plant expense	30.00	
Repair shop expense	20.00	
Shop transportation expense	28.00	
Blooming mill expense	130.00	
Rod mill expense	34.00	
Wire mill expense	110.00	
Supplies and repair parts inventory		$ 552.00
To record supplies and repair parts distribution for month		

(c) Purchased services vouchered:

General factory expense	$430.00	
Electric power plant expense	40.00	
Repair shop expense	48.00	
Shop transportation expense	30.00	
Blooming mill expense	50.00	
Rod mill expense	70.00	
Wire mill expense	100.00	
Vouchers payable		$ 768.00
To record distribution of disbursement vouchers for purchased service for month		

(d) Estimated depreciation:

General factory expense	$ 50.00	
Electric power plant expense	40.00	
Repair shop expense	40.00	
Shop transportation expense	20.00	
Blooming mill expense	75.00	
Rod mill expense	50.00	
Wire mill expense	175.00	
Reserve for depreciation		$ 450.00
To record distribution of depreciation for month		

(e) Insurance expired:

General factory expense	$100.00	
Electric power plant expense	30.00	
Repair shop expense	20.00	
Shop transportation expense	25.00	
Blooming mill expense	90.00	
Rod mill expense	90.00	
Wire mill expense	225.00	
Prepaid insurance		$ 580.00

To record distribution of insurance expense for month

(f) Estimated property taxes:

General factory expense	$100.00	
Electric power plant expense	20.00	
Repair shop expense	20.00	
Shop transportation expense	25.00	
Blooming mill expense	125.00	
Rod mill expense	60.00	
Wire mill expense	200.00	
Accrued taxes		$ 550.00

To record distribution of property taxes expense for month

2. *Charge Using Departments for Service Received.* Entries to charge using departments for service received follow. These entries are based upon the expense distribution worksheet on page 324.

(a) General factory administration:

Electric power plant expense	$ 40.00	
Repair shop expense	40.00	
Shop transportation expense	60.00	
Blooming mill expense	520.00	
Rod mill expense	620.00	
Wire mill expense	400.00	
General factory expense		$1,680.00

To distribute general factory expense to using departments (line 2a of the worksheet, Figure 13-11).

(b) Electric power:

Repair shop expense	$ 32.00	
Shop transportation expense	8.00	
Blooming mill expense	160.00	
Rod mill expense	120.00	
Wire mill expense	80.00	
Electric power plant expense		$ 400.00

To distribute electric power expense to using departments (line 2b of the worksheet).

EASTERN STEEL AND WIRE COMPANY
Expense Distribution, by Departments
for Month of January, 19___

Particulars	Service Departments				Producing Departments			Totals
	General Factory	Electric Power Plant	Repair Shop	Shop Transportation	Blooming Mill	Rod Mill	Wire Mill	
Statistics:								
(a) Labor hours worked		200	200	300	2,600	3,100	2,000	8,400
(b) Kw. Hours of power used			800	200	4,000	3,000	2,000	10,000
(c) Hours of repair service received				150	250	100	200	700
(d) Tons of materials transferred in					1,000	980	950	2,930
Labor and expense:								
(1a) Labor	$ 800.00	$200.00	$200.00	$300.00	$ 600.00	$ 500.00	$ 600.00	$3,200.00
(1b) Supplies and repair parts	200.00	30.00	20.00	28.00	130.00	34.00	110.00	552.00
(1c) Purchased service	430.00	40.00	48.00	30.00	50.00	70.00	100.00	768.00
(1d) Depreciation	50.00	40.00	40.00	20.00	75.00	50.00	175.00	450.00
(1e) Insurance	100.00	30.00	20.00	25.00	90.00	90.00	225.00	580.00
(1f) Taxes	100.00	20.00	20.00	25.00	125.00	60.00	200.00	550.00
Total direct departmental expense	$1,680.00	$360.00	$348.00	$428.00	$1,070.00	$ 804.00	$1,410.00	$6,100.00
General factory administration expense:								
Rate per labor hour (8,400 Hours) = 20¢								
(2a) Expense allocated (line a × 20¢)	1,680.00*	40.00	40.00	60.00	520.00	620.00	400.00	
Total		$400.00						
Electric power:								
Rate per Kw. hours (10,000 Kw. Hours) = 4¢								
(2b) Expense allocated (line b × 4¢)		400.00*	32.00	8.00	160.00	120.00	80.00	
Total			$420.00					
Repair shop expense:								
Rate per repair hour (700 hours) = 60¢								
(2c) Expense allocated (line c × 60¢)			420.00*	90.00	150.00	60.00	120.00	
Total				$586.00				
Shop transportation expense:								
Rate per ton (2,930 tons) = 20¢								
(2d) Expense allocated (line d × 20¢)				586.00*	200.00	196.00	190.00	
Total service department allocations to producing departments					$1,030.00	$ 996.00	$ 790.00	
(3) Total expense—Producing departments					$2,100.00	$1,800.00	$2,200.00	$6,100.00

* Credit.

Figure 13-11

(c) Repair shop:

Shop transportation expense..............	$ 90.00	
Blooming mill expense..................	150.00	
Rod mill expense......................	60.00	
Wire mill expense.....................	120.00	
Repair shop expense................		$ 420.00
To distribute repair shop expense to using departments (line 2c of the worksheet).		

(d) Shop transportation expense:

Blooming mill expense..................	$200.00	
Rod mill expense......................	196.00	
Wire mill expense.....................	190.00	
Shop transportation expense.........		$ 586.00
To distribute shop transportation expense to using departments (line 2d of the worksheet).		

3. *Transfer Producing Department Expense to In Process Accounts.* After the using departments have been charged for service received (Entries 2a-2d), the service department accounts are closed, and the producing department expense accounts show the following balances:

Blooming mill..............	$2,100.00
Rod mill..................	1,800.00
Wire mill..................	2,200.00
Total..................	$6,100.00

The producing department expense balances are closed to the in process accounts by the following entry:

(3) In process—Blooming mill.............	$2,100.00	
In process—Rod mill................	1,800.00	
In process—Wire mill................	2,200.00	
Blooming mill expense............		$2,100.00
Rod mill expense.................		1,800.00
Wire mill expense...............		2,200.00
To transfer balances of producing department expense accounts to the in process accounts		

4. *Charge In-Process Accounts for Operating Labor.* The entry to record operating labor in producing department is:

(4) In process—Blooming mill.............	$2,000.00	
In process—Rod mill................	1,600.00	
In process—Wire mill................	2,000.00	
Accrued wages..................		$5,600.00
To record operating labor for month		

5. *Charge In Process—Blooming Mill for Ingots Used.* Assume that the Ingots Inventory account shows the following debits for the month:

Ingots Inventory Account

(*Debits*)

Particulars	Tons	Per Ton	Amount
Opening inventory..........	800	$38.00	$30,400.00
Purchases..................	1,600	41.00	65,600.00
Total debits............	2,400		$96,000.00
Average cost per ton.........		$40.00	

The entry to record ingots used during the month, based upon the average cost per ton shown by the account, is:

(5) In process—Blooming mill..........	$40,000.00	
Ingots inventory...............		$40,000.00

To record cost of ingots used during the month:
1,000 tons @ $40.... $40,000.00

6. *Processed Materials Transferred from One In Process Account to Another:* Entries to record transfers of processed materials from one department to the next (assuming no inventories in producing departments) follow:

(a) In process—Rod mill..............	$44,100.00	
In process—Blooming mill.......		$44,100.00

To transfer the cost of blooms produced (980 tons) to In Process—Rod Mill account, as follows:

Particulars	Entry No.	Amount
Expense—Blooming mill...............	3	$ 2,100.00
Labor—Blooming mill.................	4	2,000.00
Ingots charged to blooming mill........	5	40,000.00
Total cost of blooms..............		$44,100.00

(b) In process—Wire mill..............	$47,500.00	
In process—Rod mill..........		$47,500.00

To transfer the cost of rod produced (950 tons) to In Process—Wire Mill account, as follows:

Particulars	Entry No.	Amount
Expense—Rod mill..................	3	$ 1,800.00
Labor—Rod mill....................	4	1,600.00
Blooms charged to rod mill...........	6a	44,100.00
Total cost of rod................		$47,500.00

7. *Finished Wire Produced.* The entry for finished wire produced (assuming no closing inventory in the Wire Mill account) is:

Finished wire inventory.............	$51,700.00	
In process—Wire mill..........		$51,700.00

To transfer the cost of wire produced (940 tons) to Finished Wire Inventory account, as follows:

Particulars	Entry No.	Amount
Expense—Wire mill...................	3	$ 2,200.00
Labor—Wire mill.....................	4	2,000.00
Rod charged to wire mill.............	6b	47,500.00
Total cost of finished wire.........		$51,700.00

8. *Cost of Wire Sold.* After Entry (7) is posted, the Finished Wire Inventory account shows the following debits:

Finished Wire Inventory Account

(Debits)

Particulars	Entry No.	Tons	Per Ton	Amount
Opening inventory..............		470	$58.00	$27,260.00
Produced.....................	7	940	55.00	51,700.00
Total debits..............		1,410		$78,960.00
Average cost per ton........			$56.00	

The entry to record cost of wire sold, based upon the average cost per ton shown in the account, is:

(8) Cost of wire sold...................	$56,000.00	
Finished wire inventory........		$56,000.00

To record cost of wire sold during the month:
1,000 tons @ $56.... $56,000.00

Inventory accounts completed. After all entries have been posted, the inventory accounts appear as shown on page 328. The balances of the accounts represent closing inventories at average prices.

Process cost worksheet. A process cost worksheet which may be used to facilitate preparation of (a) transfer entries and (b) producing department statements appears on page 329. The worksheet provides three columns (tons, per ton, and amount) for each producing department. It is used for assembling dollar and tonnage information and computing total and per ton cost of blooms (line 6a), rod (line 6b) and wire (line 7).

The tonnage information [lines (a)-(c)] is obtained from the quantity control record (page 321) and total expense (line 3) for each producing department from the expense distribution worksheet (page 324). The cost of materials used is determined by multiplying the quantity of materials received by the blooming mill (1,000 tons of ingots) by the average price per ton for the month computed on the debit side of the Ingots Inventory account (below), which is $40. Operating labor is posted to the worksheet from the direct labor distribution prepared by the payroll department.

Ingots Inventory

	Tons	Per Ton	Amount			Tons	Per Ton	Amount
Opening inventory	800	$38	$30,400	Used	(5)	1,000	$40	$40,000
Purchases	1,600	41	65,600	Balance		1,400	40	56,000
	2,400	40	$96,000			2,400	$40	$96,000
Closing inventory	1,400	$40	$56,000					

Finished Wire Inventory

	Tons	Per Ton	Amount			Tons	Per Ton	Amount
Opening inventory	470	$58	$27,260	Sold	(8)	1,000	$56	$56,000
Produced (7)	940	55	51,700	Balance		410	56	22,960
	1,410	56	$78,960			1,410	$56	$78,960
Closing inventory	410	$56	$22,960					

Cost of Wire Sales

Cost of sales for month	(8)	$56,000

Figure 13-12

The steps in preparing the process cost worksheet are:

(a) Enter the quantity information on lines (a-c).
(b) Enter the total expense for each producing department on line 3 from the Expense Distribution Worksheet (Figure 13-11).
(c) Enter the operating (direct) labor of each producing department on line 4. This information would be obtained from a distribution prepared by the payroll department (not illustrated).
(d) Enter the total of labor and expense for each department on line 4a. This is total conversion cost. For each department, divide total conversion cost by good units produced (units transferred to the next department) to determine unit conversion cost:

EASTERN STEEL AND WIRE COMPANY

Process Cost Worksheet—Month of January, 19___

Particulars	Blooming Mill Tons	Per Ton	Amount	Rod Mill Tons	Per Ton	Amount	Wire Mill Tons	Per Ton	Amount	Totals
Tonnage:										
(a) Received	1,000			980			950			
(b) Lost	20			30			10			
(c) Transferred to next department	980			950			940			
Cost:										
3 Expense (Line 3, Figure 13-11)		$ 2.14	$ 2,100.00		$ 1.90	$ 1,800.00		$ 2.34	$ 2,200.00	$ 6,100.00
4 Labor		2.04	2,000.00		1.68	1,600.00		2.13	2,000.00	5,600.00
4a Total conversion cost	980	$ 4.18	$ 4,100.00	950	$ 3.58	$ 3,400.00	940	$ 4.47	$ 4,200.00	$11,700.00
5 Materials (ingots)		40.82	40,000.00							40,000.00
6a Total cost of blooms produced		$45.00	$44,100.00		46.42	44,100.00				
Blooms transferred to rod mill	980*	45.00	44,100.00*							
6b Total cost of rod produced					$50.00	$47,500.00		50.53	$47,500.00	
Rod transferred to wire mill				950*	50.00	47,500.00*				
7a Total cost of wire produced								$55.00	$51,700.00	$51,700.00
Wire transferred to finished goods warehouse.							940*	55.00	51,700.00*	51,700.00*

* Credit.

Figure 13-13

329

Per Ton

Blooming mill	$4.18
Rod mill	3.58
Wire mill	4.47

(e) Compute the cost of materials (10,000 tons × $40 = $40,000), and enter in the Blooming Mill amount column. Compute the material cost per ton of good blooms produced ($40,000 ÷ 980 tons = $40.82). Enter in the per ton column for Blooming Mill.

(f) Enter total and per ton cost of blooms on line 6a.

(g) Enter the cost of blooms transferred from the Blooming Mill to the Rod Mill on the line below 6a. Credit Blooming Mill columns for the entire cost of blooms produced ($44,100) and debit Rod Mill. (Recall that there is no closing inventory in process in any producing department.)

(h) In the same manner as for the Blooming Mill, enter the total cost of rod produced (line 6b) and transferred; also the total cost of wire produced (line 7) and transferred.

QUESTIONS

13-1. (a) Define job order costing, process costing.

(b) What is meant by single-stage process costing? multiple-stage?

13-2. In process costing, what cost reports are prepared for the management?

13-3. Give the formulas for:

(a) Unit conversion cost

(b) Unit product cost

(c) Materials yield percentage

What is the significance of each unit cost or percentage to the management?

13-4. (a) What is meant by quantity control in a process cost system?

(b) What are the purposes of quantity control?

13-5. From the standpoint of (a) the account classification and (b) bookkeeping entries, what is the basic difference between single-stage process costing and multiple-stage process costing?

13-6. The superintendent of the Compton Iron Company has received the Statement of Cost of Pig Iron Produced prepared from the data in Problem 13-1. He tells you, the cost accountant, that the statement is not a fair measure of his operating performance because he has no control over the source of the ore which is bought for his use. He points out that the price of the ore changes from time to time, and that the freight varies according to distance, and so on.

What is your answer? Does the statement provide a good measure of performance?

EXERCISES

13-1. The Jolton Block Company manufactures cement blocks that are used in landscaping. Cement, crushed rock, and sand are mixed together with water. The mixture is poured into forms and removed after it has become hard.

The data relating to January production are given on page 331.

	Quantity	Amount
Cement inventory, January 1...........	1,960 lbs.	$ 27.00
Crushed rock inventory, January 1......	10 cu. yds.	25.00
Sand inventory, January 1.............	8 cu. yds.	16.00
Purchases:		
Cement.........................	77,420 lbs.	1,066.50
Crushed rock.....................	100 cu. yds.	250.00
Sand..........................	95 cu. yds.	180.00
Requisitioned:		
Cement.........................	78,400 lbs.	1,080.00
Crushed rock....................	90 cu. yds.	225.00
Sand...........................	85 cu. yds.	170.00
Direct labor......................		3,000.00
Depreciation.....................		200.00
Rent............................		200.00
Insurance.......................		75.00
Water and electricity................		50.00
Miscellaneous supplies..............		75.00

During the month 20,000 blocks were completed. Of these 19,000 were sold. There were no blocks on hand at the beginning of January. There were no unfinished blocks on hand at either the beginning or end of January.

Required:

1. Journalize all transactions for January.
2. Post to the T accounts provided in the Workbook.
3. Prepare a statement of cost of blocks produced.

13-2. The Thackery Company manufactures table tops of a standard size. The tops are made by applying a special paint-like mixture called "Glassid" to a plywood base. The plywood is cut in the cutting department and sent to the surfacing department where Glassid is sprayed on the plywood.

During the month of September the following costs were incurred in producing 10,000 tops:

Material:	
Plywood..................	$6,000.00
Glassid..................	2,000.00
Labor:	
Cutting..................	5,000.00
Surfacing...............	3,000.00
Factory expense:	
Cutting..................	2,800.00
Surfacing...............	1,200.00

There were no inventories in process at the beginning or end of the period.

Required:

1. Prepare general journal entries to record the above information.
2. Post the journal entries to the T accounts provided in the Workbook.

13-3. Complete the process cost worksheet for the Walton Company in the Workbook.

PROBLEMS

13-1. The Compton Iron Company manufactures pig iron, using iron ore, limestone, and coke. The company operates a process cost system. You are asked to prepare a Statement of Cost of Pig Iron Produced, for the month of January,

19__, using appropriate information from the following list.   Show the appropriate "Per Ton of Iron Produced" amounts on the statement.

	Tons	Amount
Inventories, Jan. 1:		
Iron ore	3,000	$24,000.00
Limestone	2,000	8,000.00
Coke	1,000	6,000.00
Pig iron	0	0
Purchases:		
Iron ore	10,000	70,000.00
Limestone	8,000	40,000.00
Coke	6,000	42,000.00
Freight:		
Iron ore		3,500.00
Limestone		3,000.00
Coke		1,000.00
Depreciation		9,000.00
Insurance		6,000.00
Labor		22,000.00
Power		8,000.00
Supplies and repair parts		5,000.00
Taxes		2,200.00
Materials used:		
Iron ore	9,000	
Limestone	8,000	
Coke	6,000	
Iron yielded by the ore used:		
Theoretical		52%
Actual		50%

13-2. The Bowman Cement Co. produces cement, using clay, lime, and gypsum. The accounting department operates the following inventory and cost accounts:

Inventory accounts:
Clay Inventory
Lime Inventory
Gypsum Inventory
Finished Cement Inventory
Sales, Cost of Sales, and Production Cost
Sales of Cement
Cost of Cement Sales
In Process—Cement
Labor
Factory Expense (one account)

The summary of materials used, cement production and sales (in tons) for the month of March, 19__, follows:

Particulars	Opening Inventory	Received	Used	Closing Inventory
Clay	2,000	8,000	7,000	3,000
Lime	1,000	4,000	3,000	2,000
Gypsum	500	600	800	300
Total materials	3,500	12,600	10,800	5,300
		Produced	Sold	
Finished cement	2,000	10,800	9,800	3,000

The opening inventories are valued as follows:

Particulars	Tons	Per Ton	Amount
Clay..........................	2,000	$4.00	$8,000.00
Lime...........................	1,000	3.00	3,000.00
Gypsum........................	500	5.00	2,500.00
Finished cement.................	2,000	4.77	9,540.00

Transactions for the month of March, 19__:

(1) Charges to inventory accounts for materials received (post invoice amounts and freight amounts separately)

Invoices

	Tons	Per Ton	Amount	Freight	Total
Clay..........	8,000	$4.50	$36,000.00	$1,000.00	$37,000.00
Lime.........	4,000	3.50	14,000.00	500.00	14,500.00
Gypsum......	600	4.75	2,850.00	150.00	3,000.00
	12,600		$52,850.00	$1,650.00	$54,500.00

(2) Charges to Labor account,* $8,000.
(3) Charges to Factory Expense account:

    (a) Gas bill received*........ $2,000.00
    (b) Depreciation............ 1,000.00
    (c) Insurance............... 500.00 (credit Prepaid Insurance)
    (d) Taxes.................. 800.00 (credit Accrued Taxes)
    * Credit Vouchers Payable.

At the end of the month:

(4) Materials used. (Charge In Process—Cement account.) For each material, calculate the average cost per ton (example, Clay):

Particulars	Tons	Per Ton	Amount
Opening inventory.....	2,000	$4.00	$ 8,000.00
Purchases for month....	8,000	4.50	36,000.00
Freight..............			1,000.00
Totals for the month...	10,000		$45,000.00 Average $4.50

Materials used charge = Tons used × Average cost per ton.

(5) Close Labor and Factory Expense accounts to In Process—Cement account.
(6) Close In Process—Cement account to Finished Cement account. (10,800 tons of cement were produced.)
(7) Credit Finished Cement account for cost of cement sold. Calculate the average cost per ton for opening inventory of cement plus cement produced. Cost of cement sold = Tons sold × Average cost per ton.
(8) Make entry for sales value of cement sold @ $8 per ton.

Required:

(1) Set up T accounts for the classification shown above. In the inventory accounts, provide columns for tons, per ton, and amount on each side of the account, as illustrated on page 316. Enter opening inventories.
(2) Draft entries in simple journal form for the eight transactions.

(3) Post the journal entries to the accounts.

(4) Prepare Statement of Cost of Cement Produced.

13-3. The Lew Barson Company manufactures a single product—a standard-size wooden storm window. The lumber is cut in a cutting department, and the frame is assembled in the assembly department. The frame is sent to a third department for the installation of the glass. In addition to these producing departments, there is a repair department which services the various machines used in production. Any costs not directly assignable to these four departments are collected in a General Factory Burden account and distributed to the other departments at the end of each month.

The following costs were incurred during the month of October while completing 10,000 storm windows:

	Cutting Department	Frame Assembly Department	Glass Assembly Department	Repair Department	General Factory Burden
Materials:					
Lumber.........	$2,000.00				
Glass..........			$2,500.00		
Labor............	2,000.00	$3,100.00	2,800.00	$ 300.00	$1,200.00
Rent.............	100.00	100.00	100.00	50.00	50.00
Heat, light, & power	50.00	25.00	25.00	25.00	25.00
Supplies used......	20.00	300.00	500.00	100.00	30.00
Depreciation......	100.00	10.00			
Other burden......	30.00	10.00	20.00	5.00	45.00

General factory burden was allocated as follows: 1/3 to the cutting department; 1/3 to the frame assembly department; 2/9 to glass assembly department; and 1/9 to the repair department.

There were $20 of the repair department charges assigned to the frame assembly department, and the remainder assigned to the cutting department.

Required:

1. Prepare the journal entries required to record all the above information.
2. Post the journal entries to T accounts.

13-4. Using the data given in Problem 13-3, prepare a process cost work sheet.

PROCESS COSTS: DEPARTMENTAL INVENTORIES
IN PROCESS

The problem of departmental inventories in process. This chapter is a continuation of Chapter 13 in which the subject of process costs was introduced. Like Chapter 13, it is concerned with costing for a product which passes through several departments in succession in the conversion from raw materials to finished goods. In Chapter 13, it was assumed that there were no inventories in process (either opening or closing) to be accounted for when computing monthly product costs. The entire cost of production incurred in one department was transferred to the next department.

In the present chapter it is assumed that there *are* inventories in process in the various producing departments. It is necessary to determine the cost of the inventory remaining in a department as well as the cost of the goods transferred to the next department. The first part of this chapter explains methods of determining the cost of inventory in process in each stage or department, *completed and ready to be transferred* to the next department. The second part explains methods of determining the cost of inventory in process in each stage, *partly finished as regards labor* in the stage.

It will be noted that the accounts and the entries are similar to those explained in Chapter 13. Valuation and recording of the departmental closing inventories constitute the new subject matter. Two bases of valuation are illustrated: (a) average costs per ton and (b) first-in, first-out.

I. DEPARTMENTAL INVENTORIES, COMPLETED AND
READY FOR TRANSFER

Quantity control. This illustration is concerned with the manufacture of steel wire from ingots as outlined on pages 316-318. In this illustration, it is assumed that:

(1) Ingots are rolled into blooms in the blooming mill. Part of the blooms are transferred to the rod mill and part remain as inventory in the blooming mill.

(2) Blooms are rolled into rod in the rod mill. Part of the rod is transferred to the Wire Mill and part remains as inventory in the rod mill.

(3) Rod is drawn into wire in the wire mill. Part of the wire is transferred to the warehouse and part remains as inventory in the Wire Mill.

The quantity control record for this production operation appears in Figure 14-1. Note that the control sheet provides a column for each department. The formula for each department is:

Opening inventory + Tonnage received = Shrinkage loss in the department + Transfers to the next department + Closing inventory in the department.

Note also that tons *produced* is computed for each department, for use in calculating unit conversion cost (illustrated in the next section). Tons produced for the blooming mill (for example) is:

Tons of blooms finished and transferred to rod mill............................ 900
Add—Tons of blooms in closing inventory ready for transfer................. 100

Gross production.. 1,000
Less—Tons of blooms in opening inventory ready for transfer............... 200

Tons produced.. 800

A similar calculation for the rod mill and wire mill also appears in the quantity control sheet.

WESTERN STEEL AND WIRE COMPANY
Quantity Control Sheet

Month of January, 19—

		Blooming Mill	Rod Mill	Wire Mill
Tonnage:				
Opening inventories.........................	(a)	200	100	200
Received.................................	(b)	820	900	900
Totals..............................		1,020	1,000	1,100
Lost in process (shrinkage).................		20	30	10
Transferred to next department.............	(c)	900	900	990
Closing inventories (ready for transfer)........	(d)	100	70	100
Totals..............................		1,020	1,000	1,100
Tons produced (c+d−a)		800	870	890

Figure 14-1

Process cost worksheet: Inventories @ average per ton costs.
A process cost worksheet, showing inventories @ average cost per ton of
opening inventory plus goods produced during the month, appears in
Figure 14-2a. It provides three columns for each department (Tons, Per
Ton, and Amount), and a pair of summary columns at the right for assem-
bling totals for Cost of Production.

The tonnage information in the top section of the worksheet comes
directly from the quantity control sheet, Figure 14-1. The labor and
expense dollars on lines 1 and 2 come from the departmental labor and
expense accounts. The materials used amount on line 4, which is ingots
used by the blooming mill ($32,800), is tons used multiplied by the average
cost per ton per the Ingots Inventory account.

The opening inventories for this period (lines 6, 10, and 14) come from
the ledger accounts, being the closing inventories recorded at the end of the
previous period. These are the basic data. The remaining entries on the
worksheet are all computed from data on the worksheet.

The worksheet is set up by the following steps:

Line 3—Conversion cost. Total conversion cost for each department is Labor
+ Factory expense. Unit conversion cost is Total conversion cost ÷
Tons produced. (For blooming mill, $4,100 ÷ 800 = $5.125.)

Line 4—Materials cost per ton of blooms produced is $32,800 ÷ 800 = $41.

Line 5—Total cost of blooms produced during the month ($46.125 per ton;
$36,900 total). This is line 3 + line 4.

Line 6—Opening inventory of blooms. From the inventory accounts, as recorded at the end of the previous month.

Line 7—Total production available—blooms (1,000 tons, $45,900). This is
line 5 + line 6. $45.90 is the *average cost per ton* of blooms: Opening
inventory + Blooms produced during the month.

Line 8—Blooms to rod mill (900 tons @ $45.90 = $41,310). This is Tons
transferred × Average cost per ton (Opening inventory + Blooms
produced).

Line 17—Closing inventory (of blooms, 100 tons @ $45.90 = $4,590). This is
Total production available, line 7 − Blooms to rod mill, line 8.

Lines 9-12 and 13-16—Computed in the same manner as lines 5-8.

Line 17—Closing inventories. For each department, this is Total production
available − Tonnage transfer to the next department.

Note that the closing process inventories (line 17) are all valued at
average costs per ton:

Blooming mill @ $45.90, average cost per ton of production available, per
line 7.

Rod mill @ $51.50, average cost per ton of production available, per line 11.

Wire mill @ $56.70, average cost per ton of production available, per line 15.

**Process cost worksheet: Inventories valued on first-in, first-out
basis.** Figure 14-2b is a process cost worksheet for the Western Steel
and Wire Company, which is the same as Figure 14-2a except that the

WESTERN STEEL AND WIRE COMPANY
Process Cost Worksheet—Month of January, 19__

(Inventories @ Average Per Ton Costs)

Particulars		Blooming Mill Tons	Per Ton	Amount	Rod Mill Tons	Per Ton	Amount	Wire Mill Tons	Per Ton	Amount	SUMMARY Cost of Production Debits	Credits
Tonnage:												
Opening inventories	(a)	200			100			200				
Received	(b)	820			900			900				
Totals		1,020			1,000			1,100				
Lost in process (shrinkage)		20			30			10				
Transferred to next department	(c)	900			900			990				
Closing inventories	(d)	100			70			100				
Totals		1,020			1,000			1,100				
Tons produced (c+d −a)		800			870			890				
Cost:												
1 Labor				$ 2,000.00			$ 1,600.00			$ 2,000.00	$ 5,600.00	
2 Factory expense				2,160.00			1,800.00			2,200.00	6,100.00	
3 Total conversion cost		800	$ 5.125	$ 4,100.00	870	$ 3.91	$ 3,400.00	890	$ 4.72	$ 4,200.00		
4 Materials			41.00	32,800.00							32,800.00	
Blooming mill:												
5 Cost of goods produced during month			$46.125	$36,900.00								
6 Opening inventory of blooms		200	45.00	9,000.00							9,000.00	
7 Total production available		1,000	$45.90	$45,900.00								
8 Blooms to rod mill		900*	45.90	41,310.00*		47.48	41,310.00					
Rod mill:												
9 Cost of goods produced during month					870	$51.39	$44,710.00					
10 Opening inventory rod					100	52.45	5,245.00				5,245.00	
11 Total production available					970	51.50	$49,955.00					
12 Rod to wire mill					900*	51.50	46,350.00*		52.08	46,350.00		
Wire mill:												
13 Cost of goods produced during month								890	$56.80	$50,550.00		
14 Opening inventory of wire								200	56.26+	11,253.00	11,253.00	
15 Total production available								1,090	56.70	$61,803.00		
16 Wire to warehouse								990*	56.70	56,133.00*		$56,133.00
17 Closing inventories		100	45.90	$ 4,590.00	70	51.50	$ 3,605.00	100	56.70	$ 5,670.00		13,865.00
											$69,998.00	$69,998.00

* Red

Figure 14-2a

WESTERN STEEL AND WIRE COMPANY
Process Cost Worksheet—Month of January, 19___

(Inventories @ First-In, First-Out)

Particulars	Blooming Mill Tons	Per Ton	Amount	Rod Mill Tons	Per Ton	Amount	Wire Mill Tons	Per Ton	Amount	SUMMARY Cost of Production Debits	Credits
Cost:											
1 Labor...................			$ 2,000.00			$ 1,600.00			$ 2,000.00	$ 5,600.00	$
2 Factory expense........			2,100.00			1,800.00			2,200.00	6,100.00	
3 Total conversion cost...	800	$ 5.125	$ 4,100.00	870	$ 3.900	$ 3,400.00	890	$ 4.72	$ 4,200.00		
4 Materials...............		41.000	32,800.00							32,800.00	
Blooming mill:											
5 Cost of goods produced during month		46.125	36,900.00								
6 Opening inventory of blooms........	200	45.000	9,000.00							9,000.00	
7 Total production available........	1,000	45.900	$45,900.00								
8 Blooms to rod mill—											
Opening inventory (line 6).........	200	45.000	$ 9,000.00								
Balance of the transfer............	700	46.125	32,287.50								
Total transfer............	900*	45.875	$41,287.50*			41,287.50					
Rod mill:											
9 Cost of goods produced during month.......				870	51.364+	$44,687.50					
10 Opening inventory of rod........				100	52.450	5,245.00				5,245.00	
11 Total production available.......				970		$49,932.50					
12 Rod to wire mill—											
Opening inventory (line 10)........				100	52.450	$ 5,245.00					
Balance of the transfer........				800	51.364+	41,091.92					
Total transfer........				900*	51.364	$46,336.92*			46,336.92		
Wire mill:											
13 Cost of goods produced during month........							890	56.783	$50,536.92		
14 Opening inventory of wire.........							200	56.265	11,253.00	11,253.00	
15 Total production available.......							1,090		$61,789.92		
16 Wire to warehouse—											
Opening inventory (line 14)........							200	56.265	$11,253.00		
Balance of the transfer........							790	56.783	44,858.61		
Total transfer........							990*		$56,111.61		56,111.61
17 Closing inventories........	100	46.125	$ 4,612.50	70	51.364	$ 3,595.58	100	56.783	$ 5,678.31		13,886.39
										$69,998.00	$69,998.00

* Red

Figure 14-2b

inventories are valued on first-in, first-out basis. The two worksheets are identical from lines 1 to 7, total production available—blooming mill.

Using the first-in, first-out basis of valuing inventories, the *transfer* of blooms to rod mill would be computed as shown on line 8. Here it is indicated that the opening inventory was the first goods transferred out. Of the 900 tons transferred out, 200 was the opening inventory (@ $45 per ton per line 6 = $9,000). The balance of the transfer, 700 tons, was valued at the cost per ton of blooms produced *during the month* (@ $46.125 per ton per line 5 = $32,287.50).

The closing inventory of blooms (line 17) is also valued at the average cost per ton of blooms produced during the month ($46.125).

The transfer of rod to wire mill (900 tons in all) on line 12 includes the entire opening inventory of rod (100 tons @ $52.45 = $5,245) plus 800 tons of the rod produced during the month (@ $51.364 = $41,091.92). The closing inventory of rod in the rod mill (line 17) is valued at the cost per ton of rod produced during the month ($51.364).

The transfer of wire to the finished goods warehouse (990 tons) on line 16 includes the entire opening inventory (200 tons @ $56.265 = $11,253) plus 790 tons of the wire produced during the month (@ $56.783 = $44,858.61). The closing inventory of wire in the wire mill is valued at the cost per ton of wire produced during the month ($56.783).

Entry to record closing inventories and cost of goods produced. The following summary entry to record closing inventories and cost of wire produced may be prepared from the summary columns on the worksheet, Figure 14-2a. Where a summary entry is used, it takes the place of individual transfer entries from department to department, as illustrated in Chapter 13.

Wire inventory (wire produced).........................	$56,133.00	
In process inventories (closing inventories).................	13,865.00	
Labor (labor used)....................................		$ 5,600.00
Factory expense (expense used)......................		6,100.00
Ingots inventory (ingots used).......................		32,800.00
In process inventories (opening inventories)............		25,498.00

To close the opening in process inventories, labor and factory expense accounts; to credit Ingots Inventories for ingots used, and record cost of wire produced and closing in process inventories.

II. DEPARTMENTAL INVENTORIES, PARTLY FINISHED

Product and processes described. The factory that is the basis of this illustration produces a single style of work garment from denim. The denim is bought in bales, each comprised of a number of bolts, which are stored in a storeroom until used. The producing departments are:

Cutting room. In this department, the denim is spread in plies on a cutting table, marked from patterns, and cut with electric shears. Twenty to fifty plies of denim may be spread in one lay. The top ply is marked, and all plies in the lay are cut at one time.

After the lay is cut, the cut pieces of denim are gathered from the cutting table in bundles of a predetermined number of pieces. Serial number tags are fastened to the bundles, and the bundles in each lay are put on hand trucks for movement to the sewing room when that department is ready for them.

Note that there are never any partly finished lays on the cutting table at an inventory date. Any lay on the table on an inventory date is finished and bundled for inventorying. There are usually a number of sets of bundles of cut piece goods in the cutting room (on an inventory date) ready to be transferred to the sewing room. These bundles are of course 100 per cent completed as far as regards cutting room labor and expense.

Sewing room. In this department, the various pieces of cut denim move in bundles from operator to operator. Each operator performs a particular operation on all the pieces in the bundle. (There may be as many as 50 standard sewing operations in a work garment.) Bundle boys move the bundles from operator to operator.

Note that at the end of any month (except at the end of a style season when the room is "sewed out"), there is an inventory in process in the sewing room. There will be one or more bundles at each operator's work place, and other bundles of partly processed garments at in process banks located between one set of operators and another set. An operator performs a single operation or group of operations on all the garments in a bundle. The bundle then goes to another operator, who performs one or several operations, or to an in-process bank. When the bundle has passed the last operator, the garments are finished. In the middle of the manufacturing season, an inventory can be said to be "on the average 50 per cent completed" because the total bundles are spread fairly evenly through the room. At the beginning of the season, however, an inventory is likely to be, say "on the average 25 per cent completed." There are likely to be more bundles in the early operations than in the later operations since the sewing room inventory is building up. At the end of the manufacturing season, the inventory is likely to be on the average 75 per cent completed." There are likely to be more bundles in the later operations than in the early operations.

As will be noted in the following sections, it is necessary for the accountant to know not only the number of dozens of garments in the sewing room but also the average stage of completion. He may obtain an estimate of stage of completion from the sewing room foreman.

Quantity control. The quantity control summary of the garment factory appears in Figure 14-3. The controls for cutting room, sewing

TULANE GARMENT COMPANY
Quantity Control Summary

Month of January, 19—

	Yards	Bundles*		Dozens of Garments
Cutting room:				
Opening inventory of cut materials ready for transfer............................	2,400	10	(a)	100
Materials received in bolts.................	24,000			1,000
Totals............................	26,400			1,100
Cut materials transferred to sewing room.....	21,600	90	(b)	900
Closing inventory of cut materials ready for transfer (balance)........................	4,800	20	(c)	200
Totals............................	26,400			1,100
Dozens cut (b + c − a)....................		100		1,000
Actual yards per dozen (24,000 yards ÷ 1,000 dozens)...............................				24
Sewing room:				
Opening inventory of garments in process.....		30		300†
Cut materials received in bundles...........		90		900
Total.............................				1,200
Completed garments to warehouse...........				1,000
Closing inventory of garments in process (balance).............................		20		200‡
Total.............................				1,200
Warehouse—finished garments:				
Opening inventory.........................				150
Garments received........................				1,000
Total.............................				1,150
Garments sold............................				1,025
Closing inventory (balance).................				125
Total.............................				1,150

* A bundle is assumed to be 10 dozen garments for the purpose of this illustration.
† On the average 50% completed as to sewing labor and expense.
‡ On the average 60% completed as to sewing labor and expenses.

Figure 14-3

room, and warehouse—finished garments—are illustrated. In practice, controls for materials yardage (not illustrated) would also be kept. Sources of quantity information are as follows:

(1) Yards of materials used and dozens cut are reported to the accounting department by the cutting room foreman.
(2) Dozens moved from cutting room to the sewing room are reported by the cutting room foreman. (An entire production order—called a cutting order—is moved at one time.)
(3) Dozens moved from the sewing room to the warehouse—finished garments—are reported to the accounting department by the inspectors.
(4) Dozens sold are tallied from the invoices by the accounting department.

In Figure 14-3, note that the cutting room summary shows that cut materials for 900 dozen garments was transferred to the sewing room during the month, and that cut materials for 200 dozens remained in the Cutting Room at the end of the month. This inventory is 100 per cent completed as regards materials and cutting room labor and expense. It is ready to be transferred to the sewing room.

The sewing room summary shows that 1,000 dozen completed garments were transferred to finished garments warehouse. Two hundred dozen garments were still in the sewing room. These garments were 100 per cent complete as regards body materials, since all the body materials for a production order come from the cutting room at the same time. They are estimated to be 60 per cent complete as regards sewing room labor and expense.

Process cost worksheets (*Example 1, Closing Inventories @ Average Price*). Process cost worksheets for the garment factory are illustrated in Figures 14-4a and 14-4b. A separate sheet or a separate horizontal section of a sheet is prepared for each department: Figure 14-4a for the cutting room and Figure 14-4b for the sewing room. On each sheet, the quantity control data appear at the top of the worksheet. Costs, transfers, and inventories are computed in the bottom section of each worksheet, using *average* unit costs. Also on each sheet three columns (Dozens of garments, Cost per dozen garments, and Total amount) are provided for materials and three for conversion cost. In the sewing room worksheet, this separation of conversion cost from materials facilitates calculation of unit conversion costs and closing inventories where the inventory in a department is only partly completed.

In Figure 14-4a, Process Cost Worksheet—Cutting Room, the in process inventory at the end of the month is fully completed and ready for transfer to the sewing room. The following points are illustrated:

TULANE GARMENT COMPANY (Example I)
Process Cost Worksheet—Cutting Department
Month of January, 19__

Particulars	Materials: Dozens of Garments	Effective Dozens	Cost per Dozen Garments	Total Amount	Conversion Cost: Dozens of Garments	Effective Dozens	Cost per Dozen Garments	Total Amount	Total Cost: Effective Dozens	Cost per Dozen Garments	Total Amount
Dozens:											
Opening inventory cut materials (ready for transfer)......	(a) 100				(a) 100						
Materials received (24,000 yards)......	1,000				1,000						
Totals......	1,100				1,100						
Cut materials transferred to sewing......	(b) 900				(b) 900						
Closing inventory of cut materials (ready for transfer)......	(c) 200				(c) 200						
Totals......	1,100				1,100						
Dozens cut (b+c−a)......	1,000				1,000						
Cost:											
1 Materials......		1,000	$12.00	$12,000.00		1,000			1,000	$12.00	$12,000.00
2 Labor......							$.75	$ 750.00		.75	750.00
3 Expense......							.25	250.00		.25	250.00
4 Totals......			$12.00	$12,000.00			$1.00	$1,000.00		$13.00	$13,000.00
5 Opening inventory—cut materials......		100	14.75	1,475.00		100	1.22	122.00	100	15.97	1,597.00
6 Production available......		1,100	12.25	$13,475.00		1,100	1.02	$1,122.00	1,100	13.27	$14,597.00
7 Less Closing inventory—cut materials......		200	12.25	2,450.00		200	1.02	204.00	200	13.27	2,654.00
8 Cut materials transferred to sewing......		900	12.25	$11,025.00		900	1.02	$ 918.00	900	13.27	$11,943.00

Figure 14-4a

Note: This worksheet covers one department only—the cutting department.

TULANE GARMENT COMPANY (Example I)
Process Cost Worksheet—Sewing Department
Month of January, 19___

Particulars	Materials			Conversion Cost			Totals
	Dozens of Garments	Stage of Completion	Effective Dozens	Dozens of Garments	Stage of Completion	Effective Dozens	
Dozens:							
Opening inventory of garments in process	300	100%	(a) 300	300	50%	(a) 150	
Cut materials received	900			900			
Totals	1,200			1,200			
Completed garments to warehouse	1,000	100%	(b) 1,000	1,000	100%	(b) 1,000	
Closing inventory of in process garments	200	100%	(c) 200	200	60%	(c) 120	
Totals	1,200			1,200			
(d) Dozens produced (b+c−a)			900			970	

Cost:	Materials			Conversion Cost			Totals	
	Effective Dozens	Cost per Dozen Garments	Total Amount	Effective Dozens	Cost per Dozen Garments	Total Amount	Per Dozen	Amount
1 Cut materials from cutting room	900	$13.27	$11,943.00		$	$	$	$11,943.00
2 Labor					4.00	3,880.00		3,880.00
3 Expense					2.00	1,940.00		1,940.00
4 Totals		$13.27	$11,943.00	970	$6.00	$5,820.00		$17,763.00
5 Opening inventory of garments in process	300	13.39	4,017.00	150	6.74+	1,012.00		5,029.00
6 Production available	1,200	13.30	$15,960.00	1,120	6.10	$6,832.00		$22,792.00
7 Less—Closing inventory of garments in process	200	13.30	2,660.00	120	6.10	732.00		3,392.00
8 Garments transferred to warehouse	1,000	13.30	$13,300.00	1,000	6.10	$6,100.00	19.40	$19,400.00

Figure 14-4b

Note: This worksheet covers one department only—the sewing department.

Line 1—Compute materials cost per dozen garments cut: $12,000 ÷ 1,000 = $12 per dozen.

Line 4—Compute conversion cost per dozen garments cut: $1,000 ÷ 1,000 = $1 per dozen.

Line 5—Add opening inventory to cut materials to arrive at production available (line 6).

Line 6—Compute available materials cost per dozen in production available: $13,475 ÷ 1,100 = $12.25. Compute average conversion cost per dozen ($1.02).

Line 7—Subtract closing inventory of cut materials. For materials it is 200 dozens × $12.25 (from line 6) = $2,450. For conversion cost, it is 200 dozens × $1.02 = $204.

Line 8—Cut materials transferred to sewing ($11,943) is production available (line 6)—Closing inventory (line 7).

In Figure 14-4b, Process Cost Worksheet—Sewing Room, the in process inventory at the end of the month is 100 per cent complete as regards materials, but 60 per cent complete as regards sewing labor and expense. No new features are illustrated in the Materials columns, except that line 1, Cut materials from cutting room, is brought to this sheet from line 8 (total column) of the cutting room sheet.

The following new points (all relating to the Conversion Cost columns) are illustrated in Figure 14-4b:

Line (d) Effective dozens produced (970). This is the number of dozens of garments the sewing room foreman gets credit for producing this month. As indicated, the formula is:

(b) Completed garments to warehouse..................... 1,000
(c) Closing inventory of garments in process. The foreman gets only 60% credit for these garments since they are only 60% completed............................... 120

1,120

(a) Less—The number of effective dozens in the opening inventory in process (which the foreman was given credit for last month): 50% of 300....................... 150

Effective dozens for which the foreman is given credit this month.. 970

Line 4—Unit conversion cost is $5,820 ÷ 970 (effective dozens produced) = $6 per dozen.

Line 5—Opening inventory of garments in process is 150 (the *effective* units in process) × $6.74+ (the average unit conversion cost of product available for the previous period, used in costing the inventory) = $1,012.

Line 6—Production available ($6,832). This is conversion cost ($5,820) + Opening inventory ($1,012). Unit labor and expense cost of production available is Production available ($6,832) ÷ Effective production available (1,120) = $6.10 per dozen.

Line 7—Closing inventory of garments in process ($732). This is 120 (*effective* units in process) × $6.10 (the full unit labor and expense cost).

Line 8—Garments transferred to warehouse ($6,100). This is 1,000 (dozens transferred to warehouse) × $6.10.

Process Cost Worksheet—Sewing Department
Month of January, 19___

(Closing inventory calculated on first-in, first-out basis)

Dozens section

Particulars	Cut Materials — Dozens of Garments	Stage of Completion	Effective Dozens	Conversion Cost — Dozens of Garments	Stage of Completion	Effective Dozens	Totals
Dozens:							
Opening inventory of garments in process	300	100%	(a) 300	300	50%	(a) 150	
Cut materials received	900			900			
Totals	1,200			1,200			
Completed garments to warehouse	1,000	100%	(b) 1,000	1,000	100%	(b) 1,000	
Closing inventory of in process garments	200	100%	(c) 200	200	60%	(c) 120	
Totals	1,200			1,200			
(d) Dozens produced (b+c−a)			900			970	

Cost section

Particulars	Cut Materials — Effective Dozens	Cost per Dozen Garments	Total Amount	Conversion Cost — Effective Dozens	Cost per Dozen Garments	Total Amount	Per Dozen	Amount
Cost:								
1. Cut materials from cutting room	900	$13.27	$11,943.00					$11,943.00
2. Labor				970	$4.00	$3,880.00		3,880.00
3. Expense				970	2.00	1,940.00		1,940.00
4. Totals, this month's production	900	$13.27	$11,943.00	970	$6.00	$5,820.00		$17,763.00
5. Opening inventory of garments in process	300	13.39	4,017.00	150	6.74+	1,012.00		5,029.00
6. Production available	1,200	13.30	$15,960.00	1,120	6.10	$6,832.00		$22,792.00
7. Less—Closing inventory of garments in process	200	13.27	2,654.00	120	6.00	720.00		3,374.00
8. Garments transferred to warehouse	1,000	13.30+	$13,306.00	1,000	6.11+	$6,112.00	19.42	$19,418.00
Alternate calculation of cost of garments transferred:								
4a. Totals	900	$13.27	$11,943.00	970	$6.00	$5,820.00		$17,763.00
5a. Opening inventory of garments in process	300	13.39	4,017.00	150	6.74+	1,012.00		5,029.00
6a. Production available	1,200	13.30	$15,960.00	1,120	6.10	$6,832.00		$22,792.00
7a. Less—Garments transferred to warehouse								
Opening inventory	300	13.39	$4,017.00	300	(½) 6.74+	$1,012.00		
Amount to complete opening inventory					(½) 6.00	900.00		
Balance of transfer	700	13.27	9,289.00	700	6.00	4,200.00		
Total transfer	1,000	13.30+	$13,306.00	1,000	6.11+	$6,112.00	19.42	19,418.00
8a. Closing inventory	200	13.27	$2,654.00	120	6.00	$720.00		$3,374.00

Figure 14-5

Note: This worksheet covers one department only—the sewing department.

The total cost of garments transferred to warehouse is $19,400 (Totals column).

Process cost worksheets (*Example II, Closing Inventory @ First-in, First-out*).   Figure 14-5 illustrates how the sewing room inventory of the Tulane Garment Company would be calculated on a first-in, first-out basis. This worksheet is the same as Example I (Figure 14-4b) except for the calculation of the closing inventory.

Two methods of calculating the closing inventory and the transfer-out are illustrated.   In the first illustration (lines 4-8), the formula is Total production available (line 6) − Computed closing inventory (line 7) = Garments transferred to warehouse (line 8).   The closing inventory is calculated as effective dozens multiplied by the cost per dozen for the month's production (line 7):

Materials, 200 effective dozens × $13.27................	$2,654.00
Conversion cost, 120 effective dozens × $6.00..........	720.00
Total closing inventory.............................	$3,374.00

In the second illustration (lines 4a-8a), the formula is Total production available (line 6a) − Computed garments transferred to warehouse (line 7a) = Closing inventory (line 8a).   The garments transferred consists of the opening inventory (which under first-in, first-out is assumed to be the first goods to be transferred out) plus, in this case, a quantity out of the current month's production. · The calculation for materials in goods transferred out (line 7a) is:

Opening inventory,	300 effective dozens @ $13.39....	$ 4,017.00
Balance of transfer,	700 effective dozens @ $13.27....	9,289.00
Total transfer	1,000...........................	$13,306.00

Note that in the case of materials the opening inventory was 100 per cent complete and ready for transfer.   No additional materials had to be supplied for these garments.

The calculation for conversion cost transferred out (line 7a) is:

Opening inventory, 300 dozen ½ complete @ $6.74+....	$1,012.00
Conversion cost to complete the opening inventory, 300 dozen @ (½ of $6)* (The $6 is this month's unit conversion cost)..	900.00
Balance of transfer, 700 dozens @ $6..................	4,200.00
Total transfer, 1,000 dozens.........................	$6,112.00

* Note that if the opening inventory in process had been 40 per cent completed, the "conversion cost to complete" would have been based upon 60 per cent of this month's unit conversion cost.

The results are the same under both methods—Closing inventory in process is $3,324 and Cost of garments transferred is $19,418.

In process inventories partially completed as to materials, labor, and expense.   It is possible for a closing inventory in process within a department to be partially completed as regards certain *materials* as well as partially completed as regards labor and expense.   Thus, in the manufacture of work garments, *trim* (pocket facings, loops, labels, zippers, and buttons) may be drawn directly from stores by the sewing room and applied during various sewing operations to the body material which came from the cutting room.   In this case, a closing inventory in the sewing room which is 100 per cent completed as regards body material, and 60 per cent completed as regards sewing labor and expense may be only 50 per cent completed as regards the trim applied.   (More of the trim is applied in the later operations than in the earlier operations.)

Figure 14-6 is a process cost worksheet which illustrates, among other things, the determination of (a) trim cost per dozen garments, (b) closing inventory of trim in process, and (c) trim cost in garments completed.   The worksheet provides three columns (effective dozens, cost per dozen garments, and total amount) for body materials, three for trim and three for sewing labor and expense.   All entries in the body materials columns and the sewing labor and expense columns are the same as in the previous illustration (Figure 14-4b).

In Figure 14-6, effective dozens are computed for trim in the top section of the worksheet.   This quantity (980) is used in the lower section to compute the trim cost per dozen for the month.   Closing inventory of trim in process and trim cost in garments completed are determined in the same manner as for labor and expense.

QUESTIONS

14-1. Give the formula for effective production, assuming that both the opening inventory and the closing inventory are partially completed.

14-2. Give the formula for valuation of closing inventory in process using average costs, assuming that the inventory is fully complete as regards materials and partially complete as regards labor and expense.

14-3. Give the formula for valuation of closing inventory in process using first-in, first-out costs, assuming that the inventory is fully complete as regards materials and partially complete as regards labor and expense.

14-4. How does shrinkage in process affect effective production?

EXERCISES

14-1. Complete the process cost worksheet for the Lang Manufacturing Company given in the Workbook.

14-2. Complete the process cost worksheet for the Lawrence Manufacturing Company given in the Workbook.

14-3. Complete the process cost worksheets for the Harrison Manufacturing Company given in the Workbook.

14-4. Complete the process cost worksheet for the Alton Axle Co. given in the Workbook.

TULANE GARMENT COMPANY (Example II)
Process Cost Worksheet—Month of January, 19__

Particulars	Body Materials (from Cutting Room) Dozens of Garments	Trim (from Storeroom) Dozens of Garments	Stage of Completion	Effective Dozens	Sewing Labor and Expense Dozens of Garments	Stage of Completion	Effective Dozens
Dozens:							
Opening inventory of garments in process (a)	300	300	40%	(a) 120	300	50%	(a) 150
Materials received	900	900			900		
Totals	1,200	1,200			1,200		
Completed garments to warehouse (b)	1,000	1,000	100%	(b) 1,000	1,000	100%	(b) 1,000
Closing inventory of garments in process (c)	200	200	50%	(e) 100	200	60%	(c) 120
Totals	1,200	1,200			1,200		
Dozens produced (b+c−a)	900			980			970

	Body Material Effective Dozens	Cost per Dozen Garments	Total Amount	Trim Effective Dozens	Cost per Dozen Garments	Total Amount	Sewing Labor and Expense Effective Dozens	Cost per Dozen Garments	Total Amount	Totals Per Dozen	Amount
Cost:										$	$
Cut body materials from cutting room	900	$13.27	$11,943.00		$	$		$	$		$11,943.00
Trim added in sewing room				980	.54	529.20					529.20
Labor								4.00	3,880.00		3,880.00
Expense								2.00	1,940.00		1,940.00
Totals		$13.27	$11,943.00		$ .54	$529.20	970	$6.00	$5,820.00		$18,292.20
Opening inventory of garments in process	300	13.39	4,017.00	120	1.09	130.80	150	6.74+	1,012.00		5,159.80
Totals	1,200	13.30	$15,960.00	1,100	.60	$660.00	1,120	6.10	$6,832.00		$23,452.00
Less—Closing inventory of garments in process	200	13.30	2,660.00	100	.60	60.00	120	6.10	732.00		3,452.00
Garments completed	1,000	13.30	$13,300.00	1,000	.60	$600.00	1,000	6.10	$6,100.00	20.00	$20,000.00

Figure 14-6

Note: This worksheet covers one department only—the sewing department.

PROBLEMS

14-1. Using the process cost data for the Middleton Manufacturing Company presented herewith, prepare a process cost worksheet for the month of January.

MIDDLETON MANUFACTURING COMPANY
Process Cost Data

Month of January, 19__

Particulars	Dept. A	Dept. B
Product units:		
Opening inventory.....................	200*	300*
Materials (equivalent units).............	1,000	
Received from previous department......		1,080
Totals...........................	1,200	1,380
Lost in process (shrinkage).............	20	30
Transferred to next department.........	1,080	1,150
Closing inventory.....................	100*	200*
Totals...........................	1,200	1,380
Cost:		
Labor...............................	$ 980.00	$ 525.00
Expense.............................	980.00	525.00
Materials...........................	1,940.00	
Opening inventories...................	820.00	$1,515.00

* Fully completed.

14-2. The LST Company manufactures a single product. Department 1 produces a semifinished product, X, and department 2 produces another semifinished product, Y. X and Y are combined in department 3 to obtain finished product Z. The production and cost figures for September are given below:

	Dept. 1	Dept. 2	Dept. 3
Production:			
Opening inventories..........	40	20	40
Received....................	510	600	500
Transferred to Dept. 3........	500	500	
Transferred to finished goods...			405
Closing inventories...........	40	100	10
Costs:			
Material....................	$7,500.00	$2,900.00	
Labor......................	6,000.00	2,000.00	$10,000.00
Factory expense..............	2,750.00	900.00	6,200.00
Opening inventories..........	1,250.00	300.00	3,000.00

All opening and closing inventories are valued on a first-in, first-out basis, and all inventories in process are complete and awaiting transfer to department 3. Prepare a process cost worksheet.

14-3. The KTP Company manufactures a single product. Department 1 produces product A which is transferred to department 2 where it is converted into product B. Product B is transferred to department 3, where additional conversion costs are incurred to produce the final product C.

Production and cost figures for July are given below:

	Dept. 1	Dept. 2	Dept. 3
Production:			
Opening inventories........	200	400	200
Received..................	500	600	800
Transferred to next dept.....	600	800	750
Closing inventories.........	100	100	250
Costs:			
Material..................	$9,000.00		
Labor....................	5,000.00	$18,000.00	$60,000.00
Factory expense............	5,000.00	10,000.00	12,000.00
Opening inventories........	9,000.00	38,000.00	48,000.00

Inventories are valued on an average cost basis. All inventories remaining in process are complete and awaiting transfer to the next department.

Prepare a process cost worksheet.

14-4. The Morton Screen Company manufactures a standard-size screen. There are three stages to the manufacture:

1. Cutting out the frames
2. Assembling the frames
3. Assembling the wire screen.

In the first stage, lumber is cut to proper length and the joints are made. The frame is put together and glued in the second stage. In the last department, the screen is put on the frames.

The principal materials are the lumber and screen. The lumber is issued in the first stage and the screen in the last stage.

The screens are manufactured in lots of 100. A first-in, first-out method of pricing is used. The results of the first three months of operation are given below.

Required:

Prepare a process cost worksheet for each month of operations.

The results of the first month of operation are given below:

	Cutting Dept.	Frame Assembly Dept.	Screen Assembly Dept.
Production:			
Completed & transferred...	400 lots	400 lots	400 lots
No inventories............			
Costs:			
Lumber.................	$20,000.00		
Screen.................			$40,000.00
Conversion costs.........	$40,000.00	$30,000.00	10,000.00

The results of the second month of operation are given below:

	Cutting Dept.	Frame Assembly Dept.	Screen Assembly Dept.
Production:			
Completed & transferred..............	550 lots	500 lots	400 lots
Closing inventories			
Complete & ready for transfer........	100 lots		
Complete except for conversion;			
Conversion ½ complete.............		50 lots	100 lots
Costs:			
Lumber..........................	$78,000.00		
Screen..........................			$25,000.00
Conversion costs...................	$65,000.00	$39,375.00	$11,250.00

The results of the third month are given below:

	Cutting Dept.	Frame Assembly Dept.	Screen Assembly Dept.
Production:			
Completed and Transferred............	550 lots	500 lots	400 lots
Beginning inventory (closing inventory of second month):			
Complete and ready for transfer........	100 lots		
Complete except for conversion; conversion ½ complete....................		50 lots	100 lots
Closing inventory:			
Complete as to material; ½ complete as to conversion.........................	50 lots		
½ complete as to conversion............		100 lots	
½ complete as to screen and conversion costs...............................			100 lots

One hundred of the assembled frames received in the screen assembly department were cut too small and had to be discarded.

Costs:			
Beginning inventory (should agree with your worksheet for the second month)	$22,000.00	$12,875.00	$35,750.00
Lumber........................	60,000.00		
Screen.........................			$10,500.00
Conversion costs.................	$47,500.00	$41,475.00	$24,000.00

14-5. The Johnson Company manufactures a standard product. In the process of manufacture the product passes from department 1 to department 2 to department 3. An average cost method of pricing is used.

The production and cost statistics for June are given below:

	Dept. 1	Dept. 2	Dept. 3
Production:			
Opening inventory			
Fully complete and awaiting transfer...	50	200	
Complete as to material and transfer charges; ½ complete as to conversion costs...........................			50
Received...........................	1,000	1,000	1,000
Transferred to the next dept...........	1,000	1,000	800
Closing inventory			
Fully complete and awaiting transfer...		200	
Complete as to materials and transfer charges; ½ complete as to conversion costs........................	40		100
Costs:			
Conversion costs.....................	$38,897.00	$10,000.00	$15,840.00
Materials............................	9,999.00	25,000.00	8,500.00
Opening inventory			
Materials and transfer costs..........	401.00	16,200.00	6,400.00
Conversion costs..................	1,903.00	800.00	310.00

Prepare a process cost worksheet. Use a separate page for each department, showing separate columns for materials and conversion cost.

14-6. The X and P Company uses a process cost system. Department 1 transfers its final product to department 2. Departments 2 and 3 both transfer their final products to department 4. The costs incurred by departments were:

	Dept. 1	Dept. 2	Dept. 3	Dept. 4
Materials..........	$3,600.00		$15,000.00	
Conversion costs....	4,200.00	$3,850.00	4,500.00	$11,250.00

Departments 3 and 4 had beginning inventories of $4,000 and $18,000 respectively. Department 3 beginning inventory was fully complete and department 4 beginning inventory was complete as to transfer costs but only ½ complete as to conversion costs.

The units produced this month were:.

	Dept. 1	Dept. 2	Dept. 3	Dept. 4
Beginning Inventory....			100	200
Received...............	600	600	700	400
Transferred out........	600	500	500	500
Ending inventory.......		100	100	100

All ending inventories were fully complete except for conversion costs; they were ½ complete as to conversion costs.

A Fifo method of costing was used.

Prepare a process cost worksheet. Show proof of all inventory values. Deduct closing inventories from production available to determine transfers.

14-7. The Superior Hammer Company produces an expensive line of hammers. It operates its own handle department and a foundry department to produce the hammer heads. Assembly and finishing is a separate department.

In the foundry department, equal parts, by weight, of pig iron and coke, together with special alloy materials, are introduced into a furnace where the materials are reduced to molten metal which is poured into molds. The day's work in the foundry is as follows:

(1) Remove and clean the heads cast on the previous day.
(2) Set the molds for the current day's melt.
(3) Load and "burn" the melt for the day.
(4) Pour the metal into the molds.

One-fourth of the labor cost is estimated to be applicable to step number 1.

In the assembly and finishing department, the hammer heads are finished and the handles inserted. Handles are frequently spoiled in the process. Finished hammers are transferred to the stock room immediately.

On October 1, 19__, there was no inventory of any kind in the foundry department. During October, 20,000 heads were completed and transferred to the assembly and finishing department. At the end of the month 1,500 good cleaned heads were on hand in the foundry and 1,000 heads had been poured on the last day. A total of 22 tons of pig iron, coke, and alloy materials costing $1,248 were placed in production. Direct labor costs for the month amounted to $4,380. Indirect costs were applied at 30 per cent of direct labor cost. A hammer head weighs one pound. An average of 10 per cent of the heads poured are not perfect and are remelted.

On October 1 there were 400 hammer heads in the assembly and finishing department on which no work had been done. Their cost was $128.24. There were no handles on hand. During October 20,000 handles costing $9,876 were received in this department. All the handles were used in completing 19,800 finished hammers. Labor cost amounted to $1,834 and indirect costs to $1,252.

(*AICPA*)

DEPARTMENTAL INVENTORIES IN PROCESS 355

Required:

Prepare departmental cost and production reports showing unit production costs and the assignment of these costs to interdepartmental transfers or inventories for the month of October, 19__, for the foundry department and the assembly and finishing department. The company uses weighted average cost in its accounts. Unit cost computations should be carried to five decimal places.

14-8. The P.A.R. Company, which is engaged in manufacturing a single product, uses a process cost system to cost its product and to determine inventory values.

You are to prepare a summary of costs and production for October, 19__, and a summary schedule of inventory values by processes at October 31, 19__. In costing units out of each process, use the first-in, first-out, basis.

Material is used at various stages of production as follows: Material L is placed in process at the beginning of work in department 1 (that is, at the beginning of process A); material T is put into the process at the beginning of the second process (process B) in department 1. When the production of process A reaches process B, it is mixed with material T.

Costing of production is on a pound basis. There is a weight loss in the department, all of which takes place in the second (B) process.

The following data cover the operations for the month of October 19__:

	Work in Process 10/1/__ (pounds)	Work in Process 10/31/__ (pounds)	Transferred to Department 2 Month (pounds)
Process A	2,000	3,000	
Process B	4,000	2,000	36,000

During October, 25,000 pounds of material L costing $4,250 were issued to process A, and 12,000 pounds of material T costing $2,720 were issued to process B.

Labor cost during October for process A was $13,832 and for process B $14,878. Overhead is 100 per cent of labor cost. Work on the inventory in process A as of October 1, 19__ had been 40 per cent completed. The cost of material, labor, and overhead had amounted to $1,284. The inventory in process B has been 60 per cent completed in that process and had an accumulated total cost of $5,384. The inventories on October 31, 19__, were 50 per cent complete in both processes.

(AICPA—Adapted)

Chapter 15

PROCESS COSTS: BY-PRODUCT METHOD
AND JOINT-PRODUCT METHOD

Subdivision of materials: Secondary processing. In some lines of manufacture, a single material passes through a primary process in which it is broken down physically or chemically into other materials. These materials in turn pass through secondary processing from which a variety of salable products emerges. Basic characteristics of the material and the products are: (1) The buyer of the material often has no choice as to the composition of the specific materials. He takes it as it is, or rejects it; (2) There is a determinable numerical relationship among the products which will be yielded by the lot of materials; (3) The buyer often has some latitude as to the nature and extent of secondary processing to be done. In some cases, he may elect not to do certain secondary processing and even to abandon some of the materials that come out of the primary process. Or he may elect to do extended secondary processing of certain of the materials in order to make a greater final profit on the products that are offered for sale.

Examples of the type of manufacture described above are:

(1) Mining and smelting, in which copper, silver, and gold may be produced from a single ore.
(2) Meat packing, in which a number of grades of meat may be produced from a single animal.
(3) The distillation of petroleum, which yields lubricants, burning oils, and automotive and aviation fuels of various kinds.
(4) The production of lumber in which various grades of lumber are secured from the same logs.
(5) The production of coke, gas, and various other products from coal.

Cost accounting of a form that is basically process costing may be used for any of the types of manufacture described above. An account may be set up for each product or process and transfers may be made from one account to another, finally to arrive at product cost (s). Within the process costing classification, there are two basic methods of accounting for groups of products of the type described above:

356

(1) By-product method
(2) Joint-product method

These methods are explained and illustrated in the following sections.   It will be noted that in some cases, either method of accounting can be used for a given set of products from a common material, depending upon the nature of the information desired by the management.

I. BY-PRODUCT METHOD OF ACCOUNTING

Description of by-product method.   Under the by-product method of accounting, one of the products of the group is designated as the major product and a process or product account is set up for it.   The major product is charged for the cost of the primary processing and credited with the net returns of the by-products.

Statement of gross profits illustrated.   To provide a basis for illustration, assume that the Chicago Gas and Coke Company manufactures gas and coke from coal.   The primary process consists in heating coal in an oven for a number of hours, during which time gas is collected from the top of the oven.   At the end of the production period, the coke is discharged from the oven.   A separate secondary process is operated for each of the two products.   The secondary process for coke involves cooking the hot coke that comes out of the oven, screening it, and loading it in cars for shipment.   The secondary process for gas consists in filtering it and washing it.   The gas is pumped into a main which is connected to the distribution system.

A table of data showing the cost of operating the primary process for the month and also the cost of secondary processing of coke and gas appears below.   In this example, it is assumed that coke is the major product and gas the incidental product.

		Secondary Processing		
Particulars	Primary Process	Coke	Gas	Totals
Sales......................		$15,000.00	$5,000.00	$20,000.00
Coal......................	$ 6,000.00	$	$	$ 6,000.00
Labor.....................	2,000.00	2,000.00	500.00	4,500.00
Expense..................	2,000.00	1,000.00	500.00	3,500.00
Total cost................	$10,000.00	$ 3,000.00	$1,000.00	$14,000.00

Figure 15-1

The Statement of Gross Profits appears on page 358.   It consists of two parts:

(a) Sales of the major product (which is coke, in this case).

(b) Cost of sales of the major product. The application of the rule stated above is illustrated. The gross cost of coke (consisting of the entire cost of the primary processing, $10,000, plus the secondary processing cost for coke, $3,000) is credited with the net returns of gas (sales, $5,000 less secondary processing of gas, $1,000 equals net returns, $4,000). The cost of coke sold is $9,000. In this case, there are no inventories of finished coke—either opening or closing—and cost of coke sold is the same as cost of coke produced.

CHICAGO GAS AND COKE COMPANY
Statement of Gross Profits: By-Product Method

for the Month of February, 19___

Sales of coke............................			$15,000.00
Cost of coke sales:			
Gross cost of coke—			
Cost of primary process...............		$10,000.00	
Secondary processing—coke...........		3,000.00	
Gross cost........................		$13,000.00	
Less—Net returns from sales of gas—			
Sales of gas.........................	$5,000.00		
Less—Secondary processing............	1,000.00		
Net returns......................		4,000.00	
Cost of coke sales......................			9,000.00
Gross profit—coke......................			$ 6,000.00

Figure 15-2

Accounts. Following are the sales and cost accounts used to produce the statement illustrated in the previous section:

Inventory and Cost Accounts	*Sales and Cost of Sales*
Coal Inventory	Sales of Coke
Coke Inventory	Cost of Coke Sales
Primary Processing—Coke	Sales of Gas
Secondary Processing—Coke	
Secondary Processing—Gas	

During the month, the cost of coal and the labor and expense of operating the oven are charged to the Primary Processing account. The cost of cooling, screening, and loading the coke is charged to the Secondary Processing—Coke account, and the cost of filtering and washing the gas and pumping it into the main are compiled in the Secondary Processing—Gas account.

Note that the operation of these accounts provides an illustration of multiple-stage process costing. The oven process is the first stage. The two secondary processes (operating simultaneously) represent the second stage. In practice, a unit conversion cost is computed for the primary processing (Labor + Expense ÷ Tons of coke = Unit conversion cost) and for each of the secondary stages. Unit conversion cost of secondary processing of coke is Secondary cost ÷ Tons of coke. Unit conversion cost of secondary processing of gas is Cost ÷ Cubic feet of gas delivered.

Transfer entries. At the end of the month the following transfer entries are made formally to set up the cost of coke produced, crediting it with the net returns from gas:

(1)

Coke inventory............................	$10,000.00	
Primary processing.....................		$10,000.00
To close Primary Processing account		

(2)

Coke inventory............................	$ 3,000.00	
Secondary processing—coke.............		$ 3,000.00
To close Secondary Processing—Coke account		

(3)

Sales of gas..............................	$ 5,000.00	
Secondary processing—gas...............		$ 1,000.00
Coke inventory.......................		4,000.00
To credit cost of coke with net returns on sales of coke		

(4)

Cost of coke sales.........................	$ 9,000.00	
Coke inventory.......................		$ 9,000.00
To charge Cost of Coke Sales account with cost of coke sold		

In this case, it is assumed that all the coke produced during the month was sold: there is no closing inventory. If, on the other hand, 900 tons had been produced and 800 tons sold, Cost of Coke Sales would have been charged for $8,000. (The cost per ton would have been $9,000 ÷ 900 = $10, and the cost of 800 tons would have been 800 × $10 = $800.) There would have been a balance of $1,000 in the Coke Inventory account, representing the closing inventory.

Accounts illustrated. After the entries in the previous section are posted, the accounts appear as illustrated on page 360.

Inventory of by-products. In the illustration of by-product method above, it is assumed that there were no inventories of gas—either opening or closing. There is no gas storage or holder and all gas is delivered to the customer as produced. If the inventory of gas in the holder is of significant cost (and not of constant amount from period to period), the inventory would be recorded. The entry for a closing inventory is debit Inventory of Gas in Holder and credit Secondary Processing—Gas. The amount is based upon the cost debits in the latter account. A cost per thousand cubic feet (MCF) for the month is calculated and the entry determined by multiplying MCF by cost per MCF.

PROCESS COST ACCOUNTS—BY-PRODUCT METHOD

Sales of Coke

		Sales for month	$15,000

Cost of Coke Sales

Coke sold	(4) $9,000		

Sales of Gas

To close	(3) $ 5,000	Sales for month	$ 5,000

Coke Inventory

Primary processing—coke	(1)	$10,000	Net returns from sales of gas		
Secondary processing—coke	(2)	3,000	(Sales, $5,000—secondary		
			processing, $1,000)	(3)	$ 4,000
			Coke sold (balance)	(4)	9,000
		$13,000			$13,000

Primary Processing—Coke

Coal	$ 6,000	To close	(1)	$10,000
Labor	2,000			
Expense	2,000			
	$10,000			$10,000

Secondary Processing—Coke

Labor	$ 2,000	To close	(2)	$ 3,000
Expense	1,000			
	$ 3,000			$ 3,000

Secondary Processing—Gas

Labor	$ 500	To close	(3)	$ 1,000
Expense	500			
	$ 1,000			$ 1,000

Figure 15-3

II. JOINT-PRODUCT METHOD OF ACCOUNTING

Description of joint-product method. Under the joint-product method of accounting, all products are assumed to have market importance and a separate cost account is set up for primary processing and for each of the products or product groups. A theoretically complete cost is compiled for *each* product or product group. Each product is charged with (a) a share of primary processing cost and (b) its own secondary processing cost.

Statement of gross profits illustrated (no inventories). A table of sales and cost data for the Chicago Coal Products Company which produces coke, tar, sulphate, and benzol from coal appears below. The basic process is the same as that by which coke and gas are produced, as assumed in the previous illustration. In the present case, however, the gas is further processed to obtain tar, sulphate, and benzol, instead of being sold as gas. Each of the three products named requires secondary processing in a separate plant built for the purpose. It is assumed that there are no opening or closing inventories.

The Statement of Gross Profits prepared for the Chicago Coal Products Company appears on page 362. Note that it provides, in addition to a Primary Process column, a column for each of the products and a column for totals of all products. Each of the product columns shows sales, direct costs, share of primary cost allocated, and gross profit for the product.

CHICAGO COAL PRODUCTS COMPANY
Sales and Cost Data

for the Month of April, 19__

Particulars	Primary Process	Coke	Tar	Sulphate	Benzol	Totals
Sales.........		$6,000.00	$6,000.00	$5,000.00	$3,000.00	$20,000.00
Coal.........	$ 6,000.00	$	$	$	$	$ 6,000.00
Labor........	2,000.00	1,000.00	700.00	500.00	300.00	4,500.00
Expense......	2,000.00	1,000.00	200.00	200.00	100.00	3,500.00
Total cost...	$10,000.00	$2,000.00	$ 900.00	$ 700.00	$ 400.00	$14,000.00

Figure 15-4

Note that the total of primary process cost ($10,000) is allocated to products on the basis of sales. The percentage of sales of each product to total sales appears on the second line of the statement. These percentages are used to allocate the total of primary process cost on line 8. The total product cost for each product is shown on line 9 and the gross profit for each product on line 10.

Accounts. To produce the statement illustrated on page 362, the following accounts are kept:

Inventory and Cost Accounts

Coke Inventory
Tar Inventory
Sulphate Inventory
Benzol Inventory
Primary Processing
Secondary Processing—Coke
Secondary Processing—Tar
Secondary Processing—Sulphate
Secondary Processing—Benzol

Sales and Cost of Sales Accounts

A sales account and a cost of sales account for each product.

CHICAGO COAL PRODUCTS COMPANY
Statement of Gross Profits—Joint-Product Method
for the Month of April, 19__

	Particulars	*Primary Process*	*Coke*	*Tar*	*Sulphate*	*Benzol*	*Totals*
1	Sales.....................		$6,000.00	$6,000.00	$5,000.00	$3,000.00	$20,000.00
2	% to total sales...........		30%	30%	25%	15%	100%
3	Less—Cost of sales:						
4	Coal..................	$ 6,000.00	$	$	$	$	$ 6,000.00
5	Labor.................	2,000.00	1,000.00	700.00	500.00	300.00	4,500.00
6	Expense...............	2,000.00	1,000.00	200.00	200.00	100.00	3,500.00
7	Total direct costs..........	$10,000.00	$2,000.00	$ 900.00	$ 700.00	$ 400.00	$14,000.00
8	Primary process allocated ...	10,000.00*	3,000.00	3,000.00	2,500.00	1,500.00	
9	Total product cost........		$5,000.00	$3,900.00	$3,200.00	$1,900.00	
10	Gross profits.............		$1,000.00	$2,100.00	$1,800.00	$1,100.00	$ 6,000.00

* Credit.

Figure 15-5

At the end of the month, the balance of the Primary Processing account is allocated to the inventory accounts, and the secondary processing accounts are closed to their respective inventory accounts. And finally, the inventories are credited for cost of goods sold, with corresponding debits to the cost of goods sold accounts.

Journal entries and accounts illustrated. The journal entries to record cost of production and cost of sales are:

(1)

Coke inventory............................	$3,000.00	
Tar inventory.............................	3,000.00	
Sulphate inventory........................	2,500.00	
Benzol inventory..........................	1,500.00	
Primary processing......................		$10,000.00

    To record allocation of cost of primary processing to products produced

(2)

Coke inventory............................	$2,000.00	
Tar inventory.............................	900.00	
Sulphate inventory........................	700.00	
Benzol inventory..........................	400.00	
Secondary Processing—Coke..............		$ 2,000.00
Secondary Processing—Tar..............		900.00
Secondary Processing—Sulphate..........		700.00
Secondary Processing—Benzol...........		400.00

    To close the secondary processing accounts

(3)

Cost of coke sales...........................	$5,000.00	
Cost of tar sales............................	3,900.00	
Cost of sulphate sales.......................	3,200.00	
Cost of benzol sales.........................	1,900.00	
Coke inventory.........................		$ 5,000.00
Tar inventory..........................		3,900.00
Sulphate inventory.....................		3,200.00
Benzol inventory.......................		1,900.00
To record cost of sales for month		

T accounts for inventories, primary processing, and secondary processing showing the postings of the above entries appear on pages 364 and 365. Sales and cost of sales accounts were omitted to save space.

Bases for allocating cost of primary processing.   Bases for allocating the cost of primary processing in the joint-product method of accounting are:

(1) *Weight or other physical measure* (such as tons, gallons, or cubic feet). This basis is considered where the various products are all measured by a common unit of measure and where there is no great difference in market value per unit among the various products.

(2) *Sales value or net value (sales less secondary costs) of products yielded.* An allocation based upon sales value is illustrated in Figure 15-5. Value bases provide a common denominator for all products. They are also useful where there is significant difference in unit value among products.

Statement of profits (inventories).   The Statement of Gross Profits on page 367 and the supporting Statement of Cost of Goods Sold on page 368 illustrate a method of valuing closing inventories under the joint-product method of accounting. As will be seen, the cost of primary processing is allocated to the various products on the basis of value of products yielded. Cost of production of each product is then allocated to inventories and cost of goods sold on the basis of physical units of each product.

The two statements are based upon the Inventory and Cost Statistics on page 366. The latter schedule shows sales @ average selling prices (these figures are simply the credits to sales accounts for the month), closing inventories at selling prices on inventory date, and production cost— primary processing and secondary processing.

All the allocating is done on the Statement of Cost of Goods Sold (page 368). Lines 1-4 show the production by product class. Line 9 shows the allocation of primary processing cost to products on the basis of value of product yielded and line 11, the average cost per unit (tons, gallons, or barrels, as appropriate). On lines 12-14, cost of production for each product is allocated to inventories and cost of goods sold on the basis of physical units. The allocation of the Statement of Cost of Goods Sold is carried to the Statement of Gross Profits.

PROCESS COST ACCOUNTS—JOINT-PRODUCT METHOD

Coke Inventory

Share of primary processing	(1)	$ 3,000	Sold	(3)	$ 5,000
Secondary processing	(2)	2,000			
		$ 5,000			$ 5,000

Tar Inventory

Share of primary processing	(1)	$ 3,000	Sold	(3)	$ 3,900
Secondary processing	(2)	900			
		$ 3,900			$ 3,900

Sulphate Inventory

Share of primary processing	(1)	$ 2,500	Sold	(3)	$ 3,200
Secondary processing	(2)	700			
		$ 3,200			$ 3,200

Benzol Inventory

Share of primary processing	(1)	$ 1,500	Sold	(3)	$ 1,900
Secondary processing	(2)	400			
		$ 1,900			$ 1,900

Primary Processing

Coal	$ 6,000	Allocation to products	(1)	$10,000
Labor	2,000			
Expense	2,000			
	$10,000			$10,000

Figure 15-6a

364

Secondary Processing—Coke

Labor	$ 1,000	To close	(2) $ 2,000
Expense	1,000		
	$ 2,000		$ 2,000

Secondary Processing—Tar

Labor	$ 700	To close	(2) $ 900
Expense	200		
	$ 900		$ 900

Secondary Processing—Sulphate

Labor	$ 500	To close	(2) $ 700
Expense	200		
	$ 700		$ 700

Secondary Processing—Benzol

Labor	$ 300	To close	(2) $ 400
Expense	100		
	$ 400		$ 400

Figure 15-6b

Journal entries and accounts illustrated (inventories). The accounts are the same as for the previous illustration. The journal entries are:

(1)

Coke inventory............................	$3,200.00	
Tar inventory.............................	3,000.00	
Sulphate inventory.......................	2,400.00	
Benzol inventory.........................	1,400.00	
Primary Processing..................		$10,000.00

To record allocation of cost of primary processing to products produced (Figure 15-9, line 9)

CHICAGO COAL PRODUCTS COMPANY
Inventory and Cost Statistics
for the Month of April, 19___

Particulars	Primary Process	Coke		Tar		Sulphate		Benzol		Total Amounts
	Amount	Tons	Amount	Barrels	Amount	Tons	Amount	Gallons	Amount	
Sales @ average selling prices		600	$6,000.00	1,200	$6,000.00	4,000	$5,000.00	12,000	$3,000.00	$20,000.00
Closing inventories @ selling prices		180	2,000.00	300	1,500.00	1,000	1,000.00	3,000	500.00	5,000.00
Total production @ selling prices		780	$8,000.00	1,500	$7,500.00	5,000	$6,000.00	15,000	$3,500.00	$25,000.00
Production cost:										
Coal	$ 6,000.00									$ 6,000.00
Labor	2,000.00		$1,000.00		$ 700.00		$ 500.00		$ 300.00	4,500.00
Expense	2,000.00		1,000.00		200.00		200.00		100.00	3,500.00
Total production cost	$10,000.00		$2,000.00		$ 900.00		$ 700.00		$ 400.00	$14,000.00

Figure 15-7

CHICAGO COAL PRODUCTS COMPANY
Statement of Gross Profits—Joint-Product Method

for the Month of April, 19—

	Particulars	Coke	Tar	Sulphate	Benzol	Totals
1	Sales................	$6,000.00	$6,000.00	$5,000.00	$3,000.00	$20,000.00
2	Less—Cost of sales					
	(Fig. 15-9, line 13)...	4,000.00	3,120.00	2,480.00	$1,440.00	11,040.00
3	Gross profit..........	$2,000.00	$2,880.00	$2,520.00	$1,560.00	$ 8,960.00

Figure 15-8

(2)

Coke inventory.........................	$2,000.00	
Tar inventory..........................	900.00	
Sulphate inventory.....................	700.00	
Benzol inventory.......................	400.00	
Secondary processing—Coke...........		$2,000.00
Secondary processing—Tar............		900.00
Secondary processing—Sulphate........		700.00
Secondary processing—Benzol........		400.00

To close secondary processing cost accounts to the inventory accounts (Figure 15-9, line 8)

(3)

Cost of coke sales.......................	$4,000.00	
Cost of tar sales........................	3,120.00	
Cost of sulphate sales...................	2,480.00	
Cost of benzol sales.....................	1,440.00	
Coke inventory......................		$4,000.00
Tar inventory......................		3,120.00
Sulphate inventory..................		2,480.00
Benzol inventory....................		1,440.00

To record cost of sales (Figure 15-9, line 13)

Scrap credits. Scrap is defined in Chapter 6 as the incidental residue from certain types of manufacture, recoverable without further processing. Chapter 6 presents a number of examples of manufacturing operations in which scrap is recovered. The worksheet on page 371 illustrates how credits from scrap recovery are handled in process costs.

The illustration is the process cost worksheet for a wire mill in which a certain part of the rod production and a certain part of the wire production are both sold as scrap without further processing. The quantity control is recapped at the top of the worksheet. Note that the Cost of Good Rods Produced is credited for the sales of scrap rod (20 tons @ $20 = $400) and the Cost of Good Wire Produced is credited for the sales of scrap wire (20 tons @ $20 = $400).

CHICAGO COAL PRODUCTS COMPANY
Statement of Cost of Goods Sold—Joint-Product Method
for the Month of April, 19—

	Particulars	Primary Process	Coke Units (Tons)	Coke Amount	Tar Units (Barrels)	Tar Amount	Sulphate Units (Tons)	Sulphate Amount	Benzol Units (Gallons)	Benzol Amount	Total Amounts
1	Goods sold @ average selling prices		600	$6,000.00	1,200	$6,000.00	4,000	$5,000.00	12,000	$3,000.00	$20,000.00
2	Closing inventories @ selling prices		180	2,000.00	300	1,500.00	1,000	1,000.00	3,000	500.00	5,000.00
3	Total production @ selling prices...		780	$8,000.00	1,500	$7,500.00	5,000	$6,000.00	15,000	$3,500.00	$25,000.00
4	% to Total...			32%		30%		24%		14%	
5	Coal...	$ 6,000.00									$ 6,000.00
6	Labor...	2,000.00		$1,000.00		$ 700.00		$ 500.00		$ 300.00	4,500.00
7	Expense...	2,000.00		1,000.00		200.00		200.00		100.00	3,500.00
8	Total direct cost...	$10,000.00		$2,000.00		$ 900.00		$ 700.00		$ 400.00	$
9	Primary cost allocated to production; basis line 4...	10,000.00*		3,200.00		3,000.00		2,400.00		1,400.00	
10	Total product cost...			$5,200.00		$3,900.00		$3,100.00		$1,800.00	$14,000.00
11	Average cost per unit...			$6.67		$2.60		$ .62		$ .12	
12	Closing inventory @ average cost per unit...		180	$1,200.00	300	$ 780.00	1,000	$ 620.00	3,000	$ 360.00	$ 2,960.00
13	Cost of goods sold @ average cost per unit...		600	4,000.00	1,200	3,120.00	4,000	2,480.00	12,000	1,440.00	11,040.00
14	Total product cost, as above...		780	$5,200.00	1,500	$3,900.00	5,000	$3,100.00	15,000	$1,800.00	$14,000.00

Figure 15-9

* Credit.

PROCESS COST ACCOUNTS—JOINT-PRODUCT METHOD

Coke Inventory

Share of primary processing	(1)	$ 3,200	Sold	(3)	$ 4,000	
Secondary processing	(2)	2,000	Balance down		1,200	
		$ 5,200			$ 5,200	
Inventory		$ 1,200				

Tar Inventory

Share of primary processing	(1)	$ 3,000	Sold	(3)	$ 3,120	
Secondary processing	(2)	900	Balance down		780	
		$ 3,900			$ 3,900	
Inventory		$ 780				

Sulphate Inventory

Share of primary processing	(1)	$ 2,400	Sold	(3)	$ 2,480	
Secondary processing	(2)	700	Balance down		620	
		$ 3,100			$ 3,100	
Inventory		$ 620				

Benzol Inventory

Share of primary processing	(1)	$ 1,400	Sold	(3)	$ 1,440	
Secondary processing	(2)	400	Balance down		360	
		$ 1,800			$ 1,800	
Inventory		$ 360				

Primary Processing

Coal	$ 6,000	Allocation to products	(1)	$10,000
Labor	2,000			
Expense	2,000			
	$10,000			$10,000

Secondary Processing—Coke

Labor	$ 1,000	Close to inventory account	(2)	$ 2,000
Expense	1,000			
	$ 2,000			$ 2,000

Figure 15-10

Secondary Processing—Tar

Labor	$	700	Close to inventory account	(2) $	900
Expense		200			
	$	900		$	900

Secondary Processing—Sulphate

Labor	$	500	Close to inventory account	(2) $	700
Expense		200			
	$	700		$	700

Secondary Processing—Benzol

Labor	$	300	Close to inventory account	(2) $	400
Expense		100			
	$	400		$	400

Cost of Coke Sales

Shipments for month	(3) $ 4,000

Cost of Tar Sales

Shipments for month	(3) $ 3,120

Cost of Sulphate Sales

Shipments for month	(3) $ 2,480

Cost of Benzol Sales

Shipments for month	(3) $ 1,440

Figure 15-10 (*continued*)

Process Cost Worksheet—Scrap Credits

Particulars	Blooming Mill			Rod Mill			Wire Mill			Totals
	Tons	Per Ton	Amount	Tons	Per Ton	Amount	Tons	Per Ton	Amount	
Tonnage:										
1 Received	1,000			980			930			
2 Lost	20			30			10			
3 Scrap				20			20			
4 Transferred to next department	980			930			900			
Cost:		Per Ton	Amount		Per Ton	Amount		Per Ton	Amount	
5 Labor		$ 2.04	$ 2,000.00			$ 1,600.00			$ 2,000.00	$ 5,600.00
6 Expense		2.14	2,100.00			1,800.00			2,200.00	6,100.00
7 Total conversion cost	980	$ 4.18	$ 4,100.00	930	$ 3.66	$ 3,400.00	900	$ 4.67	$ 4,200.00	$11,700.00
8 Materials received	1,000									
9 Lost in process	20									
10 Net materials cost	980	40.82	$40,000.00	980	45.00	44,100.00				40,000.00
11 Total cost of blooms produced		$45.00	$44,100.00							
12 Blooms transferred to rod mill	980*	45.00	44,100.00*							
13 Lost in process—Rod mill				30*						
14 Scrap rod sold				20*	20.00	400.00*				400.00*
15 Net materials cost				930	46.99	$43,700.00				
16 Total cost of rod produced						$47,100.00				
17 Rod transferred to wire mill				930*	50.65	47,100.00*	930	50.65	47,100.00	
18 Lost in process—Wire mill							10*			
19 Scrap sold							20*	20.00	400.00*	400.00*
20 Net materials cost							900	51.88	$46,700.00	
21 Total cost of wire produced									$50,900.00	
22 Wire transferred to finished goods warehouse							900*	56.55	50,900.00*	$50,900.00

* Credit.

Figure 15-11 (*continued*)

371

QUESTIONS

15-1. (a) What is meant by subdivision of materials?
(b) Give examples.

15-2. (a) What is meant by by-product method of accounting?
(b) What is meant by joint-product method of accounting?

15-3. How would you value an inventory of by-products under the by-product method of accounting?

15-4. Name and discuss the bases for allocating cost of primary processing under the joint-product method of accounting.

15-5. How are returns from sales of scrap recorded in a process cost system?

EXERCISES

15-1. The Lerchin Company manufactures one major product called "Chup." In processing "Chup" a by-product called "Bluch" is produced. The sales and cost statistics for the first month of operations are given below:

Costs	Materials	Labor	Factory Expense
Primary processing—Chup..............	$10,000.00	$7,500.00	$3,000.00
Secondary processing—Chup............		4,000.00	1,000.00
Secondary processing—Bluch............		700.00	300.00

Sales	
Sales of Chup........................	$40,000.00
Sales of Bluch.......................	1,500.00

Required:

1. Using the information above and the T accounts provided in the Workbook, make all entries required during the first month.
2. Prepare a Statement of Gross Profits for the month.

15-2. The Altoona Corporation uses a joint-product method of costing. Costs of the primary process are allocated to the products on the basis of sales value. The costs and sales statistics for the first month of operations are given below:

	Primary Process	Product 1	Product 2	Product 3	Total
Sales................		$20,000.00	$30,000.00	$25,000.00	$75,000.00
Production costs:					
Material...........	$15,000.00				15,000.00
Labor.............	5,000.00	2,000.00	3,000.00	2,000.00	12,000.00
Factory expense.....	10,000.00	3,000.00	3,000.00	2,000.00	18,000.00

There are no inventories at the end of the period.

Required:

1. Using the information above and the T accounts provided in the Workbook, make all the entries required for the month.
2. Prepare a Statement of Gross Profits for the month.

PROBLEMS

15-1. The McBaken Corporation produces a major product called "Ket." A by-product called "Mos" is also produced. The sales and cost statistics for the first month of operations are given below:

Costs	Material	Labor	Factory Expense
Primary processing—Ket................	$8,000.00	$3,500.00	$2,500.00
Secondary processing—Ket..............		2,400.00	1,600.00
Secondary processing—Mos.............		1,200.00	300.00

Sales	
Sales of Ket...........................	$35,000.00
Sales of Mos..........................	2,500.00

Required:

Prepare a worksheet for the month.

15-2. The Jonesten Corporation produces one major product and two by-products. The sales and cost statistics for the first month of operations are given below:

Costs	Material	Labor	Factory Expense]
Primary process.......................	$6,000.00	$2,000.00	$1,000.00
Secondary processing—Major product......		2,500.00	1,300.00
Secondary processing—By-product 1.......		300.00	200.00
Secondary processing—By-product 2......		750.00	150.00

Sales	
Sales of major product.................	$23,000.00
Sales of by-product 1..................	600.00
Sales of by-product 2..................	1,500.00

Required:

Prepare a Statement of Gross Profit for the month.

15-3. Jergens Alton Company uses a joint-product method of costing. Costs of the primary process are allocated to the products on the basis of sales value. The cost and sales statistics for the first month of operations are given below:

	Primary Process	Product 1	Product 2	Product 3	Total
Sales................		$60,000.00	$15,000.00	$25,000.00	$100,000.00
Production costs:					
Material............	$35,000.00				35,000.00
Labor..............	2,000.00	2,500.00	1,500.00	4,000.00	10,000.00
Factory expense.....	1,000.00	1,000.00	1,500.00	1,500.00	5,000.00

There are no inventories at the end of the period.

Required:

Prepare a Statement of Gross Profits for the month.

15-4. The XYZ Company uses a joint-product method of costing for Products A, B, and C. Costs of the primary process are allocated to the products on the basis of sales value. The cost and sales statistics for the first month of operations are given below:

	Primary Process		Product A		Product B		Product C		Total
	Gal.	Amount	Gal.	Amount	Gal.	Amount	Gal.	Amount	
Sales.............			400	$40,000.00	5,000	$25,000.00	900	$18,000.00	$ 83,000.00
Closing inventories @ sales value....			100	10,000.00	1,000	5,000.00	100	2,000.00	17,000.00
			500	$50,000.00	6,000	$30,000.00	1,000	$20,000.00	$100,000.00
Production cost									
Materials........	7,500	$ 6,000.00							$ 6,000.00
Labor..........		12,000.00		$ 7,000.00		$ 6,000.00		$ 3,000.00	28,000.00
Factory expense..		2,000.00		2,000.00		4,000.00		2,000.00	10,000.00
		$20,000.00		$ 9,000.00		$10,000.00		$ 5,000.00	$ 44,000.00

Heading for Product A, B, C columns: Secondary Process

Required:

1. Set up T accounts and make all entries required by the above data.
2. Prepare a Statement of Gross Profits.
3. Prepare a Statement of Cost of Goods Sold.

15-5. The Kraxton Awning Company builds metal awnings of a standard size. The awnings are cut from metal sheets in department 1, and each part of the awnings is given an enameled coating in department 2. The metal scraps are sold to a novelty company.

The costs and production figures for the first month of operation are given below:

	Department 1	Department 2
Materials purchased		
Metal....................	2 tons @ $40 per ton	
Paint....................		10 gallons @ $4.50 per gal.
Labor....................	$600.00	$300.00
Factory expense..........	900.00	450.00

Sale of scrap: 250 lbs. of metal at a total sales price of $5.

Production: 150 awnings are completed, and there are no inventories in process at the end of the period.

Required:

Prepare a worksheet showing unit material and unit conversion costs in each department.

15-6. The Alnod Chemical Company produces two major products, Whatzip and Whozip. The process of manufacture is described below:

Raw products Wen and Wear are mixed together in the ratio of 2 parts Wen to 1 part Wear. From the mixing, two products emerge, Notik and Gluk. Notik is sold as a by-product. Gluk is cooked, strained, and allowed to settle in wooden casks. Whatzip is skimmed from the top of the casks, and the remainder represents the other major product Whozip. Cooking, straining, and settling costs are allocated to the major products on the basis of gallons produced. Residue from the straining is sold to a fertilizer company, and the proceeds of the sale are credited to cooking, straining, and settling costs.

During the first month of operations 800 gallons of Wen and 400 gallons of Wear were used. The average costs per gallon of the products were $5 and $10, respectively. The labor and burden charges incurred in mixing totaled $3,000. There were 250 gallons of Notik produced and sold for $2,500. Bottling costs of Notik were $1,500. There were 800 gallons of Gluk sent to the cooking department. There were no inventories of Notik or Gluk at the end of the month.

The total conversion costs incurred in cooking, straining, and settling were $8,000. There were 50 gallons of residue from straining sold for $750. Bottling costs were $.30 a gallon, for Whatzip and $1 a gallon for Whozip. There were 250 gallons of Whatzip produced, bottled, and sold and 450 gallons of Whozip produced, bottled, and sold. The only inventory at the end of the month was 50 gallons of Whozip which had not been bottled.

Required:

Prepare a worksheet showing:
  (a) Cost per gallon for Whatzip.
  (b) Cost per gallon for Whozip.
  (c) Cost of Whatzip sold.
  (d) Cost of Whozip sold.

Part Two

COST CONTROL

ESTIMATE COSTS

Historical costs and predetermined costs. Historical costs are costs compiled as or after production takes place. The job order cost system explained in Chapters 4 to 12 and the process cost system explained in Chapters 13 and 14 illustrate historical costs. Predetermined costs are costs compiled before production takes place. Chapters 16 and 17 discuss the uses of predetermined costs and explain the operation of cost accounting procedures based upon predetermined costs.

There are two types of predetermined costs:

(1) Estimate costs
(2) Standard costs

There is no rigid distinction between the two types of predetermined costs. In general, it may be said that standard costs are scientifically determined costs, often representing a considered judgment of what the cost should be under good performance. A great deal of time of engineers and cost accountants may be required to set standard costs. Estimate costs are costs set by methods immediately expedient. They may or may not represent satisfactory operating performance.

Managerial information: Estimate costs. As a basis for illustration of estimate costs and estimate cost procedure, assume that John Benson, whose factory is diagrammed on page 26, desires:

(1) Predetermined costs (estimate costs) of his product line for the coming manufacturing season, which he can review before setting selling prices for his line. Note that in some cases, where the estimated cost of a product is greater than the price he thinks the customers will pay, he may withdraw the product from the line or modify it somewhat.

(2) A cost accounting procedure for comparing actual costs incurred with estimated cost of production, at frequent intervals. If the factory superintendent is not producing the goods at the estimate which was set up before the price lists were released, the manager wants to know it as soon as possible. In some cases, it may be possible to correct the situation, and the manager wants to do so with a minimum of delay.

(3) Simple records that will be economical to operate. He does not desire actual job costs.

The Estimate Cost Card and the Variance Statement (Figures 16-1 and 16-2) illustrate the information provided by the estimate cost procedure.

Estimate Cost Card. One of these cards is prepared for each product when the product is set up for manufacture and sale. Each card shows the estimated cost of one unit of a product for the period to which the cost applies—a style season, say, or a year. The form provides a section for each element of cost and columns for (a) original estimate and (b) revision. The *materials* section would comprise a list of materials required to produce a unit of product, together with the estimated quantity of materials, the expected price, and the extension of quantity and price. The *labor* section may show a list of labor operations with the estimated time and wage rate for each, or it may show total labor and average wage rate for each department, or simply total labor for all departments. In many cases, labor data by operation may not be available because no studies by operation have been made. The *factory expense* rate illustrated is a normal direct labor hour rate, computed as explained in Chapter 9. The rate illustrated ($.75) is based upon estimated expense of $6,000 and estimated total hours of 8,000.

Estimate Cost Card

Cost Per Product Unit   *Product*   X

Spring, 19__   *Computed*   Dec. 28, 19__

                                 Revised _____

                                               Revision
                                    _____

                                               Date _____

Particulars	Original Estimate	Price or Rate	Amount
Materials:			
1 piece material "a" @ $1.00..	$1.00		
Labor			
0.5 hour @ $1.50.............	$ .75		
Factory expense:			
0.5 hour @ $.75.............	.375		
Labor and expense...........	$1.125		
Total cost..................	$2.125		

Figure 16-1

The *revision* columns may be used for periodic revision of the original estimates. Use of these columns may save the work of setting up complete new cards, when only a few of the factors in the original estimate have been changed. This would be the case where the product specifications and the materials quantities and labor hour allowances have not changed, but the materials prices and labor and expense rates have changed. As a matter of company policy, the estimates may be revised at the beginning of a specified calendar period, such as one month, six months, or a year. The need for current information for (a) new price lists and (b) inventory valuation for balance sheet purposes is a factor in deciding upon the frequency of revision.

Note that in "pricing the line" (setting selling prices for the price list), the management is likely to give some consideration to (a) the estimated cost of the product, as nearly as the cost man can estimate it with the information available, and (b) the gross profit requirements of the business. The management may have in mind a certain dollar volume of sales, a certain turnover of inventories, and a certain percentage of gross profit necessary to cover selling and general expenses and leave a net profit. These latter factors may be worked out informally by studying recent profits statements.

Variance Statement. The statement of variances from estimate for a one-month period provides a comparison of actual cost with cost of the month's production stated at estimate. This statement is of vital interest to the management since it shows the extent to which the management is failing to meet the costs estimated before the price lists were released to customers. The statement illustrated analyses the difference, called the *variance*, by element. For purposes of this comparison, it is necessary to include not only goods completed but also the work done on goods still in process. (It is assumed in this illustration that there was no opening inventory in process. If there had been one, it would be subtracted from goods completed plus closing work in process to determine production.) Note that during the month of February, the company exceeded the estimate on materials by $1,420), and the estimate on labor and expense applied by $1,699. The management would investigate these variances to determine whether it is possible to correct them.

Accounts. The following accounts among others are required to produce the statement illustrated in the previous section and the Statement of Profits on page 391.

Materials Inventory	Sales
In Process—Materials	Cost of Sales—Materials
In Process—Labor and Expense	Cost of Sales—Labor and Expense
In Process Clearing Account	Variance from Estimated Cost
Finished Goods—Materials	Factory Expense
Finished Goods—Labor and Expense	Factory Expense Applied
	Selling and General Expense

Variance Statement

for the Month of February, 19__

Particulars	Actual Cost	Estimated Cost of Production			Variance from Estimate	Variance Percentage
		Goods Completed	Inventory in Process	Total Production		
Materials....................	$13,420.00	$10,000.00	$2,000.00	$12,000.00	$1,420.00	11.83%
Labor......................	$ 9,424.00					
Factory expense*..........	4,650.00					
Total labor and expense...	$14,074.00	11,250.00	1,125.00	12,375.00	1,699.00	13.73%
Total—all elements.......	$27,494.00	$21,250.00	$3,125.00	$24,375.00	$3,119.00	12.79%

* Normal factory expense applied.

Figure 16-2

ESTIMATE COST PROCEDURE

Materials Inventory

Purchases @ actual (1) $14,300	Used @ actual (2) $13,420
	Balance (inventory) 880

In Process—Materials Inventory

Materials used @ actual (2) $13,420	Materials in goods completed @ estimate (6) $10,000
	Inventory @ estimate (7) 2,000

Finished Goods—Materials Inventory

Materials in goods completed @ estimate (6) $10,000	Materials in goods sold @ estimate (8) $8,000

Cost of Sales—Materials

Materials in goods sold @ estimate (8) $3,000	

In Process—Labor and Expense Inventory

Labor used @ actual (3) $ 9,424	Labor and expense in goods completed @ estimate (6) $11,250
Expense (5) 4,650	Inventory @ estimate (7) 1,125

Finished Goods—Labor and Expense Inventory

Labor and expense in goods completed @ estimate (6) $11,250	Labor and expense in goods sold @ estimate (8) $9,000

Cost of Sales—Labor and Expense

Labor and expense in goods sold @ estimate (8) $9,000	

Figure 16-3

Operation of the inventory and cost of sales accounts is diagrammed on page 381. Note that separate materials accounts are kept for in process, finished goods, and cost of sales. Separate materials accounts are carried because the management desires to know the investment in materials—raw, in process, and finished. This arrangement also facilitates the adjustment of inventories for materials price variances. Labor and expense accounts are likewise provided for in process, finished goods, and cost of sales.

Materials inventory is charged and credited at actual cost. In process materials is charged at actual and credited at estimate:

In Process Materials

Materials used @ actual	Materials in goods completed @ estimate
	In process inventory @ estimate

The balance of the account represents materials *variance*, the excess of actual materials used over the estimated amount required for (a) goods completed and (b) the in process inventory to the present stage of completion (or the reverse, saving). This figure is important to the management because it shows how nearly the company is meeting the estimate on which selling prices are based. The In Process Labor account operates in a manner similar to the In Process Material account.

The finished goods accounts and the cost of goods sold accounts are carried at estimated values.

Job order cost sheets are not kept in the procedure illustrated. The elimination of job order cost sheets, with the posting of requisitions and job tickets, in some cases provides very considerable clerical economies.

PROCEDURE

Journal entries: Materials, labor, and factory expense into production. Journal entries to record actual materials, actual labor, and actual expense incurred and normal expense applied follow:

(1)

Materials.................................		$14,300.00
Accounts payable.......................		$14,300.00
To record purchase of Material "a" @ actual:		
13,000 pieces @ $1.10...................	$14,300.00	

(2)

In process—Materials......................		$13,420.00
Materials..............................		$13,420.00
To record actual quantity of Material "a"		
used @ actual price:		
12,200 pieces @ $1.10..................	$13,420.00	

(3)

In process—Labor and expense................	$ 9,424.00	
Accrued wages.........................		$ 9,424.00
To record actual cost of direct labor used:		
6,200 hours @ $1.52.....................	$ 9,424.00	

(4)

Factory expense.............................	$ 4,000.00	
Accrued factory expense.................		$ 4,000.00
To record actual factory expense for month		

(5)

In process—Labor and expense................	$ 4,650.00	
Factory expense applied..................		$ 4,650.00
To record normal factory expense applied:		
6,200 hours @ $.75.....................	$ 4,650.00	

Cost of goods completed; Closing work in process; Cost of goods sold. Entries to record cost of goods completed, closing work in process inventories (based upon physical inventory), and cost of goods sold—all at estimate are:

(6)

Finished goods—Materials............................	$10,000.00	
Finished goods—Labor and expense.....................	11,250.00	
In process—Materials...............................		$10,000.00
In process—Labor and expense......................		11,250.00
To record cost of goods completed @ estimate (10,000 units):		

	Estimated Cost	
Element	Per Unit	Total
Materials........................	$1.000	$10,000.00
Labor and expense................	1.125	11,250.00
Totals.........................	$2.125	$21,250.00

(7)

Work in process clearing account........................	$ 3,125.00	
In process—Materials...............................		$ 2,000.00
In process—Labor and expense......................		1,125.00
To record closing work in process inventory @ estimate		
(2,000 units, 50% completed as regards labor and expense)		
per inventory worksheet, page 387, item (a):		

		Estimated Cost	
Element	Stage	Per Unit	Total
Materials..............	100%	$1.000	$ 2,000.00
Labor and expense......	50%	1.125	1,125.00
Totals..............		$2.125	$ 3,125.00

(8)

Cost of sales—Materials................................	$ 8,000.00	
Cost of sales—Labor and expense.......................	9,000.00	
Finished goods—Materials...........................		$ 8,000.00
Finished goods—Labor and expense..................		9,000.00
To record cost of goods sold @ estimate (8,000 units):		

	Estimated Cost	
Element	*Per Unit*	*Total*
Materials........................	$1.000	$ 8,000.00
Labor and expense...............	1.125	9,000.00
Totals........................	$2.125	$17,000.00

Sales; Selling and general expense.   Entries to record sales value at actual and selling and general expense at actual are:

(9)

Accounts receivable.........................		$20,000.00
Sales....................................		$20,000.00
To record sales value of goods sold:		
8,000 units @ $2.50....................	$20,000.00	

(10)

Selling and general expense...................		$ 3,420.00
Accrued selling and general expense........		$ 3,420.00
To record actual selling and general expense for month		

Variances.   After the above entries are posted, the in process inventory accounts will appear as shown below:

IN PROCESS INVENTORY ACCOUNTS POSTED

In Process Materials Inventory

Materials used @ actual	(2) $13,420	Materials in goods completed @ estimate	(6)	$10,000
		Closing inventory @ estimate	(7)	$ 2,000
Balance (variance from estimate)	$ 1,420			

In Process Labor and Expense Inventory

Labor used @ actual	(3) $ 9,424	Labor and expense in goods		
Factory expense applied	(5) 4,650	completed @ estimate	(6)	$11,250
		Closing inventory @ estimate	(7)	1,125
Balance (variance from estimate)	$ 1,699			

Figure 16-4

The In Process Materials account shows a balance of $1,420, representing variance from estimate.   The sum of $13,420 was spent for production which at estimated costs would total $12,000 (completed plus in process). Similarly, the In Process Labor and Expense account shows a balance of $1,699, representing variance from estimate.   The variances are reported to management on the variance report, page 380.

Revising the estimate cost cards. At the end of each month before the Balance Sheet and Statement of Profits are prepared, the estimate cost cards are revised to reflect any significant changes in *prices* (that is, differences between actual *prices* being paid and the estimated prices shown on the estimate cost cards). They may also be revised to reflect changes in *quantities* of materials and labor per product unit (that is, differences between actual quantities of material and labor being used per unit of product and the estimated quantities shown on the estimate cost card). Revisions of quantities are likely to be made when the management believes that the original quantity estimates are not sound measures of quantity performance.

Figure 16-5 is the Estimate Cost Card for Product X (as shown in Figure 16-1) revised for changes in materials prices and wage rates. The new materials price is $1.10 per yard and the new wage rate is $1.52 per hour. Note that the quantity factors (1 piece of material and 0.5 hour of labor per unit of product) have not been changed because the management believes they are satisfactory measures of performance. Likewise, no revision of normal expense rates has been made.

ESTIMATE COST CARD

Cost per Product Unit Product .   X

Spring, 19—   Computed December 28, 19—

Revised   January 28, 19—

Revision

Date

Particulars	Original Estimate	Price or Rate	Amount
Materials:			
1 piece material "a" @ $1.00 .	$1.00	$1.10	$1.10
Labor:			
0.5 hour @ $1.50............	$ .75	1.52	.76
Factory expense:			
0.5 hour @ $.75............	.375		.375
Labor and expense............	$1.125		$1.135
Total cost.................	$2.125		$2.235

Figure 16-5

Adjusting in process, finished goods, and cost of sales accounts. The entry to close variances out of the in process accounts (the balances of those accounts at this point) is:

(11)

Variance from estimated cost...........................	$3,119.00	
In process—Materials................................		$1,420.00
In process—Labor and expense......................		1,699.00
To close variances from the in process accounts to the variance account		

(12)

In process—Materials....................................	$2,000.00	
In process—Labor and expense..........................	1,125.00	
Work in process clearing account......................		$3,125.00
To reverse Entry (7). (This entry is posted after Entry (11) has been posted and the in process accounts balanced and double ruled.) Use of the clearing account facilitates (a) getting the in-process inventory on the books and (b) producing the variance balance		

The Inventory and Cost of Sales Worksheet (page 387) is used for assembling the adjustments to inventories and cost of sales to convert them from estimate to actual. In addition to columns for Original Estimate, it provides columns for Restated and Adjustment. The prices per unit in the Restated columns are obtained from the Estimate Cost Card (Figure 16-5), which now shows the latest actual prices for materials and the latest rates for wages.

Journal Entry (13) records the adjustment of in process materials, finished goods materials, and cost of sales materials as shown in the adjustment column of the worksheet (Figure 16-6). Journal Entry (14) records the adjustment of in process labor and expense, finished goods labor and expense, and cost of sales labor and expense shown on the worksheet.

In some cases, only one element (say materials) will need to be adjusted. Only the control accounts affecting materials would be involved. In process materials, finished goods materials, and cost of sales materials would be adjusted "across the board." Journal Entry (14) for labor and expense would be omitted.

(13)

In process—Materials....................................	$ 200.00	
Finished goods—Materials..............................	200.00	
Cost of sales—Materials................................	800.00	
Variance from estimate...............................		$1,200.00
To adjust inventory and cost of sales accounts to reflect increase in actual materials prices over estimated prices, per Inventory and Cost of Sales Worksheet (page 387):		

Classification	Balances @ Original Estimate	Balances Restated	Adjustment for Price
In process..............	$ 2,000.00	$ 2,200.00	$ 200.00
Finished...............	2,000.00	2,200.00	200.00
Sold..................	8,000.00	8,800.00	800.00
Totals...............	$12,000.00	$13,200.00	$1,200.00

Inventory and Cost of Sales Worksheet

Product and Element	Units	Stage of Completion (In Process)	Inventories and Cost of Sales @ Original Estimate		Restated for Changes in Prices (c)		Adjustment for Changes in Price
			Per Unit	Total	Per Unit	Total	
Work in process							
Product A—	2,000						
Materials..........		100%	$1.000	$ 2,000.00	$1.100	$ 2,200.00	$ 200.00
Labor and expense....		50%	1.125	1,125.00	1.135	1,135.00	10.00
				(a) $ 3,125.00		$ 3,335.00	
Finished goods							
Product A—	2,000						
Materials...........			$1.000	$ 2,000.00	$1.100	$ 2,200.00	200.00
Labor and expense....			1.125	2,250.00	1.135	2,270.00	20.00
				(b) $ 4,250.00		$ 4,470.00	
Cost of sales							
Product A—	8,000						
Materials..........			$1.000	$ 8,000.00	$1.100	$ 8,800.00	800.00
Labor and expense....			1.125	9,000.00	1.135	9,080.00	80.00
				$17,000.00		$17,880.00	
Totals...........				$24,375.00		$25,685.00	$1,310.00

Figure 16-6

Notes:

(a) Work in process amount per Inventory Worksheet is *physical* inventory priced at original estimate. It is *recorded* in Work in Process Clearing account by J/E (7).

(b) Finished goods amount per Inventory Worksheet is likewise physical inventory priced at original estimate. It is used to *prove the bal-* ance of Finished Goods after cost of goods completed (Entry 6) and cost of sales (Entry 8) have been recorded.

(c) Inventories Restated amounts show inventory values at *current* prices.

387

(14)

In process—Labor and expense................................	$ 10.00	
Finished goods—Labor and expense.........................	20.00	
Cost of sales—Labor and expense............................	80.00	
Variance from estimate....................................		$ 110.00

To adjust inventory and cost of sales accounts to reflect increase in actual wage rates over estimated rates, per Inventory Worksheet:

Classification	Balances @ Original Estimate	Balances Restated	Adjustment for Price
In process................	$ 1,125.00	$ 1,135.00	$ 10.00
Finished.................	2,250.00	2,270.00	20.00
Sold.....................	9,000.00	9,080.00	80.00
Totals................	$12,375.00	$12,485.00	$ 110.00

Accounts posted. After the above entries have been posted, the accounts appear as follows. Note that the inventories and cost of sales are based upon the original estimated quantities with adjustments (Entries 13 and 14) to reflect current replacement prices of materials and current rates of wages.

Accounts Receivable

Sales for month	(9) $20,000	

Materials Inventory

Purchases @ actual	(1) $14,300	Used @ actual	(2)	$13,420
		Balance		880
	$14,300			$14,300
Closing inventory @ actual	$ 880			

In Process—Materials

Materials used @ actual	(2) $13,420	Materials in goods completed @ estimate	(6)	$10,000
		Closing inventory @ estimate	(7)	2,000
		Variance from estimate	(11)	1,420
	$13,420			$13,420
Closing inventory @ estimate (12)	2,000			
Adjustment—price (13)	200			

In Process—Labor and Expense

Labor used @ actual	(3)	$ 9,424	Labor and expense in goods		
Factory expense applied	(5)	4,650	completed @ estimate	(6)	$11,250
			Closing inventory @ estimate	(7)	1,125
			Variance from estimate	(11)	1,699
		$14,074			$14,074
Closing inventory @ estimate	(12)	$ 1,125			
Adjustment—labor rate	(14)	10			

Work in Process Clearing Account

Closing inventory @ estimate	(7)	$ 3,125	To reverse	(12)	$ 3,125

Finished Goods—Materials

Materials in goods completed @ estimate	(6)	$10,000	Materials in goods sold @ estimate	(8)	$ 8,000
Adjustment—Materials price	(13)	200	Balance		2,200
		$10,200			$10,200
Closing inventory, adjusted for price		$ 2,200			

Finished Goods—Labor and Expense

Labor and expense in goods completed @ estimate	(6)	$11,250	Labor and expense in goods sold @ estimate	(8)	$ 9,000
Adjustment for wage rates	(14)	20	Balance		2,270
		$11,270			$11,270
Closing inventory, adjusted for wage rates		$ 2,270			

Accounts Payable and Accruals

		Accounts payable	(1)	$14,300
		Accrued wages	(3)	9,424
		Accrued factory expense	(4)	4,000
		Accrued selling and general expense	(10)	3,420

Sales

	Goods sold for month	(9) $20,000

Cost of Sales—Materials

Goods sold for month	(8) $ 8,000		
Adjustment—materials price (13)	800		

Cost of Sales—Labor and Expense

Goods sold for month	(8) $ 9,000		
Adjustment—labor rates (14)	80		

Variance from Estimate Cost

Variance for month	(11) $ 3,119	Adjustment of inventories and cost of sales:		
		Materials price	(13) $ 1,200
		Labor rate	(14) 110
Balance = $1,809 debit			

Factory Expense

Actual expense for month	(4) $ 4,000	

Factory Expense Applied

	Applied for month	(5) $ 4,650

Selling and General Expense

Actual expense for month	(10) $ 3,420	

Note that overabsorbed expense (the difference between the debit balance of Factory Expense account, $4,000, and the credit balance of Factory Expense Applied, $4,650) is not allocated. The two accounts are allowed to remain open until the end of the year, in the expectation that they will nearly balance out over the period. Any balance remaining at the end of the year is closed to Profit and Loss.

The balance of the Variance from Estimate account ($1,809 debit) appears on the Statement of Profits as an addition to Cost of Sales. It represents the cost of using larger quantities of materials and more labor (and expense) hours than were called for in the estimate cost cards. (Materials and labor *price* variances were removed from the variance account by Entries 13 and 14.)

Statement of profits. The Statement of Profits prepared from the above accounts appears below. Note that the balance of the variance account is added to Cost of Sales.

JOHN BENSON
Statement of Profits

for the Month of February, 19__

Sales...		$20,000.00
Less—Cost of sales:		
Estimated cost adjusted for price changes...............	$17,880.00	
Variance from estimate: due to quantity factors..........	1,809.00	
Total...		19,689.00
Gross margin...		311.00
Less—Selling and general expense.......................		3,420.00
Net loss...		$ 3,109.00

Figure 16-7

Summary: Operating the accounts. The operating procedure explained in the previous sections may be outlined:

(1) Record actual materials used, actual labor and expense incurred, and normal expense applied.

(2) Record cost of goods completed, closing work in process inventories (based upon physical inventory), and cost of goods sold—all at estimate.

(3) Record sales value at actual and selling and general expense at actual.

(4) At the end of each month (if required) set up revised estimate costs in special columns provided on the estimate cost cards.

(5) At the end of the month (if required), adjust the in process, finished goods, and cost of sales accounts.

(6) Prepare monthly statements for the management.

OTHER METHODS OF HANDLING VARIANCES

Adjusting inventories only and closing the balance of variance account to cost of sales. In some cases, the clerical work in the adjustment procedure is shortened by

(1) restating the inventories only (using a worksheet similar to the Inventories sections of Figure 16-6), and

(2) making an entry to adjust inventories, at the same time crediting (in this case) the variance account, and

(3) closing the balance of the variance account to Cost of Sales.

This should give the same result as the method shown and it does save the restating of cost of sales. It does not provide the mathematical balancing that a complete restatement of inventories and cost of sales provides.

Adjustment of inventories by use of percentages. The adjustment of inventories illustrated above was accomplished by revising the estimate cost cards to reflect (a) replacement prices of materials and (b) replacement rates for wages. This method involves repricing each material item separately, which may be desirable where different products use different materials. It should also be considered where the cost of materials is a significant part of the cost of the product and where changes in prices are significant.

In some cases, it may be desirable to adjust the estimate cost cards and the inventory balances by use of the variance percentages shown on the Variance Statement (page 380). Note that the variance percentage for materials (11.83%) could be used for restating the original materials figure on the estimate cost cards and likewise for restating the in process materials balance and the finished goods materials balance. It is particularly desirable to carry materials accounts "across the board" (materials, in process materials, and finished goods materials) when adjustments are to be made by percentages. The variance percentages are thus calculated by element and applied by element to inventory accounts.

The labor and expense variance percentage could be similarly used for adjustment purposes. Note that the percentage for materials would represent not only the increase of actual prices over estimated prices, but also the excess of actual quantities used over quantities estimated on the Estimate Cost Card. A similar combination of price and quantity exists in the labor and expense variance percentage.

Sometimes it may be desirable to make adjustments of materials by *repricing items* and to make adjustments of labor and expense by *use of percentages*. Adjustment of labor by percentages should be considered where there has been a blanket increase or decrease in wage rates.

Variances by Department. In some cases, it may be desired to analyze labor and expense variances by department. This might be the case where it is believed that the quality of performance varies considerably among departments. Such an analysis would make it possible to localize responsibility for variances.

QUESTIONS

16-1. (a) Define historical costs; predetermined costs.
(b) Name and distinguish two types of predetermined costs.

16-2. (a) What is meant by "pricing the line"?
(b) Explain how the management might use estimate cost cards in pricing the line. What accounting information in addition to that shown on the estimate cost card might the management require in pricing the line?

16-3. Assume that the manager has asked for a "cost accounting procedure for comparing actual costs incurred with estimated cost of production, at frequent intervals." In general, how does an estimate cost procedure operate in the matter of comparing actual costs with estimated cost of production? Express the comparison in terms of a formula.

16-4. (a) Make a list of typical inventory, variance, and cost of goods sold accounts that might be operated in an estimate cost procedure.
(b) Why may it be desirable to carry the materials control accounts "across the board" (raw materials, materials in process and finished goods, and materials in cost of goods sold) in an estimate cost procedure?

16-5. (a) Why is good quantity control necessary to the successful operation of an estimate cost procedure?
(b) Why is a reasonably accurate evaluation of stage of completion of work in process inventory necessary in an estimate cost procedure?

16-6. How do you dispose of variances in estimate cost procedure?

16-7. In revising the estimate cost cards to bring them up to date, under what conditions would you use variance percentages generated in the in process accounts? If you do not use the variance percentages, how would you revise the cards?

16-8. Why might an estimate cost procedure be cheaper to operate than a job order cost system for the same factory?

16-9. What generalizations can you draw regarding the minuteness of analysis of variances in an estimate cost procedure?

EXERCISE

16-1. The Bell Manufacturing Company operates an estimate cost system. Following is the Estimate Cost Card for Product X:

PRODUCT X

Estimate Cost per Unit

Materials...................	$10.00
Labor......................	10.00
Factory expense.............	5.00
Total cost per unit..........	$25.00

Entries for actual and estimated cost of goods produced and sold appear in the "fill-in" T accounts presented in the Workbook.

Required:

Make the entries (directly in the T accounts) to:

(a) record net variance from estimated cost of manufacture and

(b) distribute the entire variance to inventories and cost of goods sold, assuming that the estimates were faulty.

Calculate and use a separate variance percentage for each element.

PROBLEMS

16-1. The Stockman Manufacturing Company operates an estimate cost system. The Estimate Cost Card for Product A appears:

PRODUCT A

Estimate Cost per Unit of Product

(Based upon budget of 100 units: 500 hours: $500 factory expense)

Materials:	
10 pieces "a" @ $2..................	$20.00
Labor:	
5 hours @ $2......................	10.00
Factory expense:	
5 hours @ $1 (normal rate)..........	5.00
Total cost per unit...................	$35.00
Selling price per unit................	$50.00

Inventories and cost of sales accounts appear below.

Required:

(1) Revise the Estimate Cost Card to reflect the current material price. Assume that the quantity estimates per unit of product for all elements are considered satisfactory by the management.
(2) Set up an Inventory and Cost of Sales Worksheet like Figure 16-6.
(3) Draft the entry (or entries) necessary to adjust inventories and cost of sales for price changes.
(4) Set up a Statement of Profits as completely as possible with the information given. Add net variance after price adjustment to cost of sales.

In Process—Material Inventory

Actual materials used—		Materials in goods completed		
950 pieces @ $2.10	$1,995	@ estimate—80 units @ $20	(2)	$1,600
		Materials in process @ estimate—10 units @ $20	(4)	200
		Variance from estimate (balance)	(7)	195
	$1,995			$1,995

In Process—Labor and Expense Inventory

Actual labor used:			Labor and expense in goods		
450 hours @ $2		$ 900	completed @ estimate:		
Expense applied @ normal rate:			80 units @ $15	(3)	$1,200
450 hours @ $1	(1)	450	Labor and expense in process		
			@ estimate:		
			10 units @ ½ ($15)	(4)	75
			Variance from estimate		
			(balance)	(8)	75
		$1,350			$1,350

Work in Process Clearing Account

Inventory in process		
@ estimate:	(4)	$ 275
Materials—		
10 units @ $20	$200	
Labor and expense—		
10 units @ ½ ($15)	75	

Finished Goods—Materials Inventory

Materials in finished goods			Materials in finished goods		
completed @ estimate:			sold @ estimate:		
80 units @ $20	(2)	$1,600	60 units @ $20	(5)	$1,200
			Inventory @ estimate		
			(balance down)		400
		$1,600			$1,600
Closing inventory @ estimate:					
20 units @ $20		$ 400			

Finished Goods—Labor and Expense Inventory

Labor and expense in finished			Labor and expense in finished		
goods completed @ esti-			goods sold @ estimate		
mate			60 units @ $15	(6)	$ 900
80 units @ $15	(3)	$1,200	Inventory @ estimate		
			(balance down)		300
		$1,200			$1,200
Closing inventory @ estimate					
20 units @ $15		$ 300			

Cost of Goods Sold—Materials

Materials in finished goods sold @ estimate 60 units @ $20	(5) $1,200

Cost of Goods Sold—Labor and Expense

Labor and expense in goods sold @ estimate 60 units @ $15	(6) $ 900

Variance from Estimate

Materials	(7) $ 195
Labor and expense	(8) 75

Factory Expense

Actual expense	$ 550

Factory Expense Applied

Expense applied: 450 hours @ $1	(1) $ 450

16-2. The Universal Corporation, which produces Product L, operates an estimate cost system. The Estimate Cost Card follows:

PRODUCT L

Estimate Cost per Unit* of Product

Particulars	Original Estimate Price or Rate	Total	Revised (date) Price or Rate	Total
Materials 8 pieces "T"	$ .40/pc.	$ 3.20		
Labor 6 hours	$1.50/hr.	9.00		
Factory expense 6 hours	$1.25/hr.	7.50		
Total		$19.70		

* Based upon production of 800 units per month.

Transactions for May, 19—

(1) Purchased 7,000 pcs. "T" @ $.42 = $2,940
(2) Used 6,200 pcs. "T"

(3) Direct labor used: 4,400 hrs. @ $1.55 per hour
(4) Actual factory expense incurred for month $6,100
(5) Factory expense applied: 4,400 hrs. @ $1.25 per hour
(6) Goods completed: 700 units Product L
(7) In process inventory at close: 50 units Product L, 50% complete as to labor and expense
(8) and (9) Goods sold, 690 units L @ $25
(10) Actual selling and general expense incurred for month, $1,500

The following accounts pertinent to this problem are operated in the general ledger:

Accounts Receivable	Sales
Materials Inventory	Cost of Sales—Materials
In Process—Materials	Cost of Sales—Labor and Expense
In Process—Labor and Expense	Variance from Estimated Cost
Work in Process Clearing Account	Factory Expense
Finished Goods—Materials	Factory Expense Applied
Finished Goods—Labor and Expense	Selling and General Expense
Accounts Payable and Accruals	

Required:

(1) Draft journal entries to record the transactions and also to adjust inventories and cost of sales to the $.42 actual price for materials and the $1.55 rate for labor.
(2) Post the entries to T accounts.
(3) Prepare an Estimate Cost Card for Product L, showing both the original estimate and the revised estimate. In making the revised estimate, assume that the original quantity estimates are satisfactory measures of performance.
(4) Prepare an Inventory and Cost of Sales Worksheet, for allocating the price variance to inventories and cost of sales.
(5) Prepare a Statement of Profits. Charge the balance of the variance account to Cost of sales.
(6) Prepare a Variance Statement for month.

16-3. The Donnell Company produces a single product, "Y," from a single material, "S." The company operates an estimate cost system with separate in process, finished goods, and cost accounts for (1) materials and (2) direct labor and expense. The Estimate Cost Card for Product Y is based upon a complete budget. Budget data for one month and actual results for January, 19__ follow:

Particulars	Budget Month	Actual Month: January, 19__
Product units of Y:		
Sold during month.................		400 units*
Completed during month............	1,000 units	500 units
In process at end of month (50% completed as regards labor and expense)		100 units
Charges to materials account		
Pieces of S.........................	6,000	3,500
Total amount.......................	$12,000.00	$7,350.00

* Selling price, $30.00 per unit.

Particulars	Budget Month	Actual Month: January, 19__
Charges to work in process account		
Materials		
Pieces...........................	5,000	3,030
Total amount....................	$10,000.00	$6,363.00
Labor		
Hours...........................	6,000	3,630
Total amount....................	$ 9,600.00	$5,989.50
Factory expense applied		
Hours...........................	6,000	3,630
Total amount....................	$ 6,600.00	$3,993.00
Factory expense incurred..............	$ 6,600.00	$4,200.00
Selling and general expense incurred.....		2,000.00

Required: Set up T accounts for an estimate cost system. Draft journal entries to operate the accounts for the month of January, and post entries to accounts. Set up an Estimate Cost Card with revision columns which reflect current actual prices for materials and wage rates for labor. Adjust inventories and cost of sales for price variances. Assume no opening inventories.

Prepare a Statement of Profits and a Variance Statement for month.

16-4. The National Uniform Company manufactures one style of uniform. Estimated cost per uniform is:

Estimate Cost per Unit

	Materials	Labor	Expense	Total
Cloth....................	$36.00	$	$	$36.00
Cutting:				
Labor.................		3.60		
Expense..............			2.40	
Total...............				6.00
Sewing:				
Labor.................		8.00		
Expense..............			4.00	
Total...............				12.00
Pressing:				
Labor.................		.40		
Expense..............			.20	
Total...............				.60
Total per unit...........	$36.00	$12.00	$6.60	$54.60
Expected selling price......				$80.00

The following inventory accounts are operated to localize variances between estimated and actual cost:

> Materials in Process
> Cutting Labor in Process
> Sewing Labor in Process
> Pressing Labor in Process
> Factory Expense in Process

Actual costs and production statistics for January, 19__ follows:

Actual Costs for January, 19__

Particulars	Materials	Labor	Expense	Totals
Cloth......................	$10,000.00	$	$	$10,000.00
Cutting labor...............		1,000.00		1,000.00
Sewing labor................		1,900.00		1,900.00
Pressing labor..............		100.00		100.00
Factory expense.............			1,600.00	1,600.00
	$10,000.00	$3,000.00	$1,600.00	$14,600.00
Materials purchased..........	$12,000.00			

Production and Closing Inventories in Process

Units completed and transferred to finished goods....... 200
Units in cutting room, ready for sewing room........... 20
Units in sewing room, average ½ through sewing........ 30
Units in pressing room, ready for pressing............. 10
Units sold... 100

Required:

(1) Draft journal entries to record the above data. Charge *actual* factory expense to Factory Expense in Process account.

(2) Set up T accounts for inventories and post the journal entries.

16-5. The Morris Manufacturing Company operates an estimate cost system. Accounts are kept for Materials in Process, Labor in Process, Factory Expense in Process, Finished Goods, and Cost of Goods Sold. The Estimate Cost Card and transactions for January, 19__ are presented herewith:

PRODUCT A

Estimate Cost per Unit

(Based upon budget of 1,250 units per month)

Materials:
    5 pieces Aa @ $1.12................. $ 5.60
Labor:
    4 hours @ $2.00.................... 8.00
Factory expense:
    4 hours @ 60¢..................... 2.40

    Total factory cost per unit......... $16.00

Transactions for January, 19__

(1) Purchases of materials, $8,050.00
(2) Materials used, $6,210.00
(3) Direct labor used, $9,030.00
(4) Actual factory expense incurred, $3,225.00
(5) Units of Product A completed, 1,000

(6) Units of Product A in process, one-half completed as to labor and expense, 100

(7) & (8) Units of Product A sold @ $25.00 per unit, 800

(9) Actual expense accrued:
Selling expenses, $1,800.00
Administrative expense, $1,400.00
Total $3,200.00

Required:

(1) Draft entries in simple journal form to record the transactions. Charge total *actual* factory expense to work in process. Calculate a single variance percentage for each element (netting price and quantity factors). Assume that variances are caused by faulty estimates and distribute all variances over inventories and cost of sales.

(2) Set up T accounts and post the entries.

16-6. The LOS Company uses an estimate cost system. Separate In Process, Finished Goods, and Cost of Goods Sold accounts for materials are operated. The actual and estimated costs for the year are shown below:

	Actual	*Estimate*
Production:		
Completed......................	1,000	1,000
Inventory in process, which is complete as to materials and ½ complete as to labor and expense...............	200	
Sold................................	900	900
Costs:		
Material........................	$62,400.00	$50,000.00
Labor...........................	36,300.00	30,000.00
Factory expense..................	19,800.00*	20,000.00

* Charge actual expense to Work in Process.

Required:

Using T accounts, show all entries to the in process inventories, finished goods, and cost of sales including the distribution of all variances from estimate cost.

16-7. The predetermined cost of a unit of Whip, based upon a production of 1,000 units, is shown below:

Materials:	
5 pieces @ $1.......................	$ 5.00
Labor:	
2 hours @ $2.......................	4.00
Factory expense:	
2 hours @ 50¢......................	1.00
	$10.00

The actual costs incurred the first month were:

Materials purchased:	
4,800 pieces @ $1.50..............	$7,200.00
Material requisitioned:	
4,400 pieces @ $1.50..............	6,600.00
Labor incurred:	
3,000 hours @ $1.................	3,000.00
Factory expenses incurred..........	3,000.00*

* Charge actual expense to Work in Process.

During the month 900 units were completed. Of these 800 were sold. In addition there were 200 units still in process that were complete as to materials but only ½ complete as to labor and factory expense.

Assuming that an estimate cost system were used, show how the above data would appear in the accounts. (Distribute all variances.)

STANDARD COSTS: OPERATION
OF THE ACCOUNTS

Measurement of performance. Chapter 16 explained how estimate costs are set up and how actual costs for a period are compared with estimated cost of production to determine whether factory performance is coming within the estimates. This follow-up, or measurement of performance, is important because selling prices are set with knowledge of estimate costs. If the factory is not operating within these costs, it is necessary to take whatever remedial action is possible.

It was also stated that an estimate cost is intended to anticipate actual performance and it may reflect a certain amount of inefficiency. It is not set by such industrial engineering methods as time study and materials utilization study, and it is not intended to be a primary measure of performance. Often, the variances between actual cost and estimate cost are not analyzed very minutely.

Inevitably, however, questions arise as to whether the predetermined cost *is* a satisfactory yardstick, whether the factory is doing as well as it should, and if not, who is responsible. Standard cost systems of the types described in this text are intended to help answer these questions. The answers proceed from setting the predetermined costs on the basis of acceptable performance in the first place and then analyzing variances in such manner as to establish responsibility.

To present the over-all picture of a standard cost system first, this chapter describes some of the information which is provided for management purposes and the methods of getting it (that is, the methods of operating the accounts). As will be seen, the method of operating the accounts to be used depends upon the frequency and minuteness of the desired analysis of variances. One type of system is intended to provide an end-of-the-month analysis, not too detailed in character. The other type is intended to provide an analysis as frequently as daily and in sufficient detail to identify the supervisor or even the operator responsible for an off-standard performance. This chapter explains the operation of the accounts under both systems.

"Standard" and "standard cost." The term "standard" implies that an attempt has been made to find the best way to make the product, that proper productive machines and methods have been set up, and that materials handling has been carefully worked out and controlled. It does not necessarily imply that perfection has been attained; the term refers rather to the best means and methods that have been evolved and put into effect at the present time. Quantity standards, as set by qualified people, represent good performance attainable by the average employee.

Quantity standards for labor and material are standards of performance stated in physical units. Examples are: (a) *Standard hours* allowed to perform a specified labor operation on one unit of product, and (b) *standard pieces* of each material allowed to produce one unit of product of a specific design. Quantity standards are based upon definite specifications for the product and carefully established methods of manufacture, since obviously a quantity standard would be meaningless if product and methods of manufacture were changed at will.

A standard product cost is a predetermined product cost based upon quantity standards and predetermined prices and rates, called standard prices and rates. The Estimate Cost Card illustrated on page 385 might serve as a standard cost card if the word "estimate" were changed to "standard." It will be used as the basis for the mathematical illustration of standard costs which follows.

PRODUCT X

Standard Cost per Unit

Particulars	Amount
Materials:	
1 piece material "a" @ $1.00	$1.00
Labor:	
0.5 hour @ $1.50	$ .75
Factory Expense:	
0.5 hour @ $0.75	.375
Labor and expense	$1.125
Total cost	$2.125

Figure 17-1

The standard price for material is the average price expected during the coming year. The standard rate for labor is the average rate expected for the coming year under the labor contract in force. The standard rate for factory expense is the normal rate for the coming year, determined as explained in Chapter 9.

Uses of standard costs. As stated above, since standard costs represent what the costs should be under good performance, they are specifically intended to be used for the *measurement of performance*. Further, since standard costs are predetermined costs, they are useful in businesses where it is necessary to get out *catalog prices* and *price lists* at the beginning of a manufacturing season, that is, before the goods are actually manufactured. It is necessary in this case for the manufacturer to use predetermined costs because actual costs come too late.

Standard costs may be carried in the inventory accounts (as explained and illustrated in this chapter), in which case they are used for the *valuation of inventories* in the cost accounting records. (Note, however, that for financial accounting purposes, it is sometimes necessary to adjust such values by setting up inventory reserves.)

JOHN BENSON
Statement of Profits
for the Month of __, 19__

Sales............................		$20,000.00
Less—Cost of goods sold (@ standard).....		17,000.00
Expected gross margin.................		$ 3,000.00
Less—Variances from Standard Cost:		
Materials quantity variance...........	$ 100.00	
Materials price variance..............	1,210.00	
Labor time variance..................	900.00	
Labor rate variance..................	122.00	
Factory expense time variance.........	450.00	
Factory expense overabsorbed..........	575.00*	
Net variance.....................		2,207.00
Actual gross margin....................		$ 793.00

* Credit.

Figure 17-2

In some cases, standard costs are installed for *clerical economy* reasons. Where a standardized product is being manufactured repetitively by standardized methods, it is often most economical from a clerical standpoint simply to compare certain actual costs by period with total standard costs of the goods produced or operations performed during those periods. In a full-fledged standard cost system, the job order cost sheets may be eliminated, with the postings of materials requisitions and job tickets that they require. It may be cheaper simply to compare actual cost totals for periods with standard cost totals for the same periods than to operate job order cost sheets.

Managerial information: Statement of profits. One of the best examples of managerial information provided by a standard cost system is the statement of profits itself. A Statement of Profits prepared in a standard cost system appears below. It is set up to show in what respects performance was or was not satisfactory as compared to standard, and to show the effect upon profits of any off-standard performance.   On this statement variances from the predetermined cost are analyzed more minutely than they are in an estimate cost procedure.   Each element is analyzed into *quantity* and *price* factors.

The statement illustrated shows the following information:

Sales, $20,000.   This is the conventional sales figure: Quantity sold × Actual selling price.

Cost of Goods Sold, $17,000.   This is Actual quantity sold (8,000 units) × Standard cost per unit ($2.125).

Expected Gross Margin, $3,000.   Sales less cost of sales @ standard.   As this caption indicates, this is the gross profit that would have been realized on the units sold if the standards had been met and if there had been no underabsorbed expense due to volume.

Less, Variance (netting $2,207).   The variances show losses of expected profit (or additions to expected profit) due to off-standard performance in regard to materials, labor, and factory expense.   Both price and quantity factors are shown.   In this illustration, all variances are closed to Profit and Loss.

Actual Gross Margin, $793.   This is the gross margin which remains after subtracting the variances, the cost of off-standard performance.

Meaning of the variances.   The variances shown in the Statement of Profits (page 404) are separated by *price* and *quantity* factors and by *element*.   This division is significant because the people who are responsible for price performance are likely to be different from the people who are responsible for quantity performance.   In a garment manufacturing plant, for instance, the merchandise manager or purchasing agent may be responsible for piece goods prices.   The cutting room foreman, on the other hand, would be responsible for piece goods quantity performance, that is, for using no more yardage than the standard yards allowed for the garments cut.   In some cases, it may be considered that relatively little control over prices is possible, but that a satisfactory control over quantity performance can be achieved.

Referring to the Statement of Profits (page 404), materials quantity variance can be described as the cost of using more pieces of materials than the standard quantity allowed for the product produced.   (Formulas which describe the variances in mathematical terms appear later in this chapter.)   Materials price variance is the cost of paying higher prices for materials than the standard prices which appear on the standard cost cards.

Labor time variance is the labor cost of using more hours than the standard hours allowed for the product produced.   The foreman would likely be responsible for this variance.   Labor rate variance is the cost of paying higher rates than the standard rates which appear on the standard cost cards.   If the rate increase is the result of a new union contract, the foreman would not be responsible.

Factory expense time variance is the factory expense cost of using more hours than the standard hours allowed for the product produced. Factory expense underabsorbed is the difference between the actual factory expense incurred and the expense chargeable to the actual hours worked (assuming a direct labor rate for applying expense.)

In a particular situation, any of the variances can be *excess costs* over standard or *savings* over standard.

PROCEDURE

Methods of operating in process accounts in a standard cost system. Two methods of operating the in process accounts, using the type of standard costs described in the previous pages are:

(1) Charge Work in Process for the actual cost incurred and credit it for standard cost of goods completed (and standard value of closing work in process inventory.) The balance of the in process account is *net variance* for the month, and it is analyzed into its factors (if desired) at the end of the month. This method is explained on pages 406-412.

(2) Charge Work in Process for standard value of operations completed and credit it for standard value of finished goods completed. The balance of the Work in Process account is standard value of work in process at the end of the period. Variances are isolated and analyzed from the original media (invoices, requisitions, job tickets, and so forth) used for building up the debit to Work in Process. They can accordingly be analyzed in any desired frequency and in any desired detail. This method is explained on pages 413-421.

Charging in process at actual and crediting at standard: Entries. Under this method of recording standard costs, work in process accounts are operated according to the same principle as for estimate costs described in the previous chapter. The accounts are charged at actual cost (or normal for factory expense) and credited for goods produced at standard. In this system only one finished goods account and one cost of sales account are operated. They are carried at standard values.

Journal entries to record actual materials, actual labor, and actual expense incurred and normal expense applied follow:

(1)

Materials....................................		$14,300.00
Accounts payable.....................		$14,300.00
To record purchase of Materials "a" @ actual:		
13,000 pieces @ $1.10...................	$14,300.00	

(2)

Materials in process.......................		$13,310.00
Materials..............................		$13,310.00
To record actual quantity of Materials "a" used @ actual price:		
12,100 pieces @ $1.10...................	$13,310.00	

(3)

Labor in process............................	$ 9,272.00	
Accrued wages.........................		$ 9,272.00

To record actual cost of direct labor used:
6,100 hours @ $1.52..................... $ 9,272.00

(4)

Factory expense............................	$ 4,000.00	
Accrued factory expense...............		$ 4,000.00

To record actual factory expense for month.

(5)

Factory expense in process..................	$ 4,575.00	
Factory expense applied...............		$ 4,575.00

To record normal factory expense applied:
6,100 hours @ $.75..................... $ 4,575.00

Entries to record cost of goods completed, closing work in process inventories (based upon physical inventory), and cost of goods sold—all at standard—are:

(6)

Finished goods..	$21,250.00	
Materials in process.............................		$10,000.00
Labor in process................................		7,500.00
Factory expense in process........................		3,750.00

To record cost of goods completed @ standard:
(10,000 units):

	Standard Cost	
Element	Per Unit	Total
Materials.................	$1.000	$10,000.00
Labor....................	.75	7,500.00
Factory expense...........	.375	3,750.00
Totals...............	$2.125	$21,250.00

(7)

Work in process clearing account........................	$ 3,125.00	
Materials in process.............................		$ 2,000.00
Labor in process................................		750.00
Factory expense in process........................		375.00

To record closing work in process inventory @ standard
(2,000 units, 50% completed as regards labor and expense):

		Standard Cost	
Element	Stage	Per Unit	Total
Materials...........	100%	$1.000	$2,000.00
Labor...............	50%	.75	750.00
Factory expense.....	50%	.375	375.00
Totals..........		$2.125	$3,125.00

(8)

Cost of Sales..	$17,000.00	
Finished Goods................................		$17,000.00

To record cost of goods sold @ standard (8,000 units):

	Standard Cost	
Element	Per Unit	Total
Materials.................	$1.000	$ 8,000.00
Labor and expense...........	1.125	9,000.00
Totals.................	$2.125	$17,000.00

Entries for variances.   It was stated above that the balances of the in process inventory accounts represent net variances.   If it is desired to record a formal analysis of variances, the entries are:

(9)

Materials quantity variance.................		$ 100.00	
Materials in process.................			$ 100.00

To record materials quantity variance for month:

Actual pieces used.........................	12,100 pcs.

Standard pieces allowed for goods produced:

Goods completed................	10,000	
In process......................	2,000	12,000
Excess pieces............................		100 pcs.
Standard price per piece..................		$ 1.00
Materials quantity variance...............		$ 100.00

(10)

Materials price variance.....................		$ 1,210.00	
Materials in process....................			$ 1,210.00

To record materials price variance for month:

Actual price per piece....................	$ 1.10
Standard price per piece..................	1.00
Excess price paid.......................	$ .10
Actual pieces used......................	12,100 pcs.
Materials price variance..................	$1,210.00

(11)

Labor time variance.........................		$ 900.00	
Labor in process.....................			$ 900.00

To record labor time variance for month:

Actual hours used.......................	6,100 hrs.

Standard hours allowed for goods produced:

Goods completed...............	5,000	
In process.....................	500	5,500
Excess hours.............................		600 hrs.
Standard rate per hour...................		$ 1.50
Labor time variance.....................		$ 900.00

(12)

Labor rate variance..........................		$ 122.00
Labor in process......................		$ 122.00

To record labor rate variance for month:

Actual rate per hour.....................	$ 1.52
Standard rate...........................	1.50

Excess rate paid.......................	$ .02
Actual hours used......................	6,100 hrs.

Labor rate variance......................	$ 122.00

(13)

Factory expense time variance................		$ 450.00
Factory expense in process.............		$ 450.00

To record factory expense time variance for month:

Actual hours used.......................		6,100 hrs.
Standard hours allowed for goods produced:		
Goods completed...........	5,000	
In process................	500	5,500

Excess hours...........................		600 hrs.
Standard expense rate..................		$ .75

Factory expense time variance............	$ 450.00

In process accounts posted.   Three in process accounts are shown on pages 410-412. Note that these accounts are charged at actual and credited at standard, and that the balance of each account is net variance from standard.

The accounts illustrated also show the analysis of net variance into quantity and price factors.   In practice, the details of this analysis would not be shown in the account but would be shown in schedules supporting the journal entries.   The details of analysis were included in the same illustration as the operation of the accounts to show how the analysis ties to the In Process account.

Summary: Formulas for variances.   Formulas for variances used in the previous pages of this chapter may be described as follows:

Materials Quantity Variance = Cost of the excess quantity* of materials used. Computed as (Actual quantity of materials used − Standard quantity allowed for the product produced) × Standard price per unit of materials.

Materials Price Variance = Total excess price paid for the actual materials used. Computed as (Actual price − Standard price) × Actual pieces of materials used.

* All the descriptions apply to *debit* variances.   In practice, it is possible also for any variance to be a credit.

ANALYSIS OF VARIANCES IN A STANDARD COST SYSTEM: MATERIALS

Materials in Process Account

Materials used @ actual (Entry 2)..................$13,310.00

Actual Pieces	Actual Price	Actual Amount
12,100	$1.10	$13,310.00

$13,310.00

Materials in goods completed @ standard (Entry 6) $10,000.00

Product Units	Standard Pieces Per Unit	Total	Standard Price/Piece	Total Materials @ Standard
10,000	1 piece "a"	10,000	$1.00	$10,000.00

Materials in closing process inventory @ standard (Entry 7)........ 2,000.00

Product Units	% Completed	Per Unit	Total	Standard Price/Piece	Total Materials @ Standard
2,000	100%	1	2,000	$1.00	$ 2,000.00

Net variance (balance)................. 1,310.00

$13,310.00

Actual Pieces	Actual Price	Actual Amount
12,100	$1.10	$13,310.00

Standard Pieces	Standard Price	Standard Amount
12,000	$1.00	$12,000.00

Total standard materials allowed........

Materials quantity variance—
Excess pieces (12,100 − 12,000) × Standard price per piece ($1.00)......... $ 100.00
Materials price variance—
Actual pieces used (12,100) × Excess price (actual $1.10 − standard $1.00)........... 1,210.00

Net variance, as above................. $1,310.00

Figure 17-3

ANALYSIS OF VARIANCES IN A STANDARD COST SYSTEM: LABOR

Labor in Process Account

Labor used @ actual (Entry 3) $9,272.00

Actual Hours	Actual Rate	Actual Amount
6,100	$1.52	$9,272.00

Labor in goods completed @ standard (Entry 6, labor) $7,500.00

Product Units		Standard Hours		Standard Price/Hour	Total Labor @ Standard
	Per Unit		Total		
10,000	0.5 hour		5,000	$1.50	$7,500.00

Labor in closing process inventory @ standard (Entry 7, labor) .. 750.00

Product Units	% Completed	Standard Hours		Standard Price/Hour	Total Labor @ Standard
		Per Unit	Total		
2,000	50%	0.5	500	$1.50	$ 750.00

Net variance (balance) 1,022.00

       $9,272.00 $9,272.00

	Standard Hours	Standard Rate	Standard Amount
	5,500	$1.50	$8,250.00

Total standard labor allowed.........

Labor time variance—
  Excess hours (actual 6,100 − standard allowed 5,500) × Standard price per hour ($1.50)............ $ 900.00

Labor rate variance—
  Actual hours used (6,100) × Excess price (actual $1.52 − standard $1.50)........................ 122.00

                                 $1,022.00

Net variance, as above.................

Figure 17-4

ANALYSIS OF VARIANCES IN A STANDARD COST SYSTEM: FACTORY EXPENSE

Factory Expense in Process Account

Expense applied @ normal (Entry 5) $4,575.00

Actual Hours	Standard Rate	Amount Applied
6,100	$ .75	$4,575.00

6,100		

$4,575.00

Expense in goods completed @ standard (Entry 6) $3,750.00

Product Units	Standard Hours Per Unit	Total	Standard Rate/Hour	Total Expense @ Standard
10,000	0.5 hour	5,000	$ .75	$3,750.00

Expense in closing inventories @ standard (Entry 7) 375.00

Product Units	% Completed	Standard Hours Per Unit	Total	Standard Rate/Hour	Total Expense @ Standard
2,000	50%	0.5	500	$ .75	$ 375.00

Time variance (balance) 450.00

5,500 hours		$4,575.00

Factory expense time variance = Excess hours (6,100 − 5,500) × Standard expense rate ($ .75) = $450 as above.
Net overabsorbed expense = Factory expense ($4,000) − Expense applied ($4,575) = $575.

* Red.

Figure 17-5

Labor Time Variance = Cost of the excess hours of labor used.
Computed as (Actual labor hours used − Standard hours allowed for the quantity of product produced) × Standard price per hour for labor.

Labor Price Variance = Total excess price paid for the actual labor used.
Computed as (Actual rate per hour − Standard rate per hour) × Actual hours of labor used.

Factory Expense Time Variance = Cost of the excess hours of factory expense used.
Computed as (Actual labor hours used − Standard hours allowed for the quantity of product produced) × Standard rate per hour for factory expense.

Factory Expense Underabsorbed
Computed as Actual factory expense − (Actual labor hours × Standard factory expense rate).

Charging in process at standard and crediting at standard. The operation of the Work in Process account (and the other inventory accounts) under this method is diagrammed on page 414 and explained in the following paragraphs.

Materials Inventory account is charged for the standard value of materials purchased and credited for (a) standard value of the standard quantity of materials allowed for production and (b) standard value of the excess pieces of materials drawn from stores. The balance of the Materials Inventory account is the inventory of materials on hand, valued at standard prices.

Work in Process Inventory account is charged for the standard value of materials, labor, and expense allowed for operations performed and credited for standard value of units of product completed. The balance of Work in Process Inventory account is the inventory of work in process, valued at standard.

Finished Goods Inventory account is charged for standard value of units of product completed and credited for standard value of units of product sold. The balance of Finished Goods Inventory account is the inventory of finished goods, valued at standard.

A separate variance account is operated for each variance in the statement of profits. The diagram shows variance accounts for materials price, materials quantity, labor, and factory expense. (To reduce the size of the illustration, price and quantity variances for labor have been combined into one account; likewise, variances for factory expense have been combined into one variance account.) The journal entries necessary to operate the inventory and variance accounts are presented later in this chapter.

Transactions. The following transactions are the bases for the illustrative entries in the next section.

(1) Materials "a" purchased:

Actual pieces @ actual price
13,000 $1.10   = $14,300

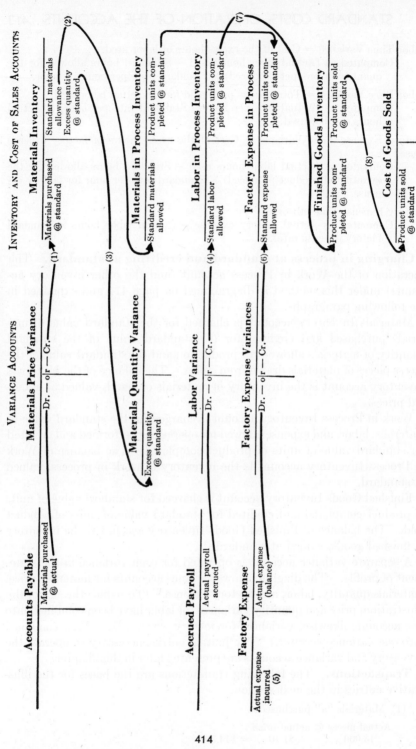

INVENTORY, COST OF SALES, AND VARIANCE ACCOUNTS
STANDARD COST SYSTEM

Figure 17-6

(2) Standard materials allowed for month production per standard bills of materials issued by production control:

	Product Units	Standard Pieces per Unit	Total Standard Pieces
Goods completed this month.........	10,000	1	10,000
In process end of month............	2,000	1	2,000
Totals......................	12,000	1	12,000

(3) Excess pieces of materials used over standard, 100.

(4a) Standard labor hours allowed for month production per job tickets issued by production control:

	Product Units	Standard Hours per Unit	Total Standard Hours
Goods completed this month.........	10,000	0.5	5,000
In process end of month............	2,000 (½)	0.5	500
Totals......................	12,000	0.5	5,500

(4b) Actual labor used:

Actual hours @ actual rate
6,100 $1.52   = $9,272

(5) Actual factory expense, $4,000.
Actual selling and shipping expense, $2,000.
Actual administrative expense, $1,420.

(6) Standard hours of factory expense in month production (same as 4a), 5500 hours.

(7) Goods completed, 10,000 units.

(8) Goods sold, 8,000 units.

Charging work in process @ standard and crediting @ standard.
The entries to record charges to work in process and variances from standard cost follow:

(1)

Materials inventory.........................	$13,000.00	
Materials price variance.....................	1,300.00	
Accounts payable.....................		$14,300.00

Purchases of materials "a" for month, as follows:
Actual pieces @ Actual price
13,000   @ $1.10............... $14,300.00
Actual pieces @ Standard price
13,000   @ $1.00.............. 13,000.00

Price variance......................... $ 1,300.00

(2)

Materials in process........................	$12,000.00	
Materials inventory...................		$12,000.00

Standard materials "a" allowed for month's production, per standard bills of material extended @ standard:
12,000 pieces @ $1.00 per yard............ $12,000.00

(3)

Materials quantity variance.................	$ 100.00	
Materials inventory...................		$ 100.00

Excess pieces of materials used over standard
during month, priced @ standard:

100 pieces @ $1.00.....................	$ 100.00	

(4)

Labor in process inventory (a)................	$ 8,250.00	
Labor time variance (c) − (a)..........	900.00	
Labor rate variance (b) − (c)..........	122.00	
Accrued payroll (b)................		$ 9,272.00

To record standard labor value of operations
completed, actual labor accrued and variances
for month:

Standard hours @ Standard rate (a)		
5,500 @ $1.50..............	$ 8,250.00	
Actual hours @ Standard rate (c)		
6,100 @ $1.50..............	9,150.00	
Actual hours @ Actual rate (b)		
6,100 @ $1.52..............	9,272.00	

(5)

Factory expense............................	$ 4,000.00	
Selling and shipping expense.................	2,000.00	
Administrative expense......................	1,420.00	
Accrued expense.....................		$ 7,420.00

To record actual factory expense for month

(6)

Factory expense in process inventory..........	$ 4,125.00	
Factory expense variance...............		$ 125.00
Factory expense......................		4,000.00

To record standard factory expense value of
operations completed and net variance for
month:

Standard value of operations completed:

Standard hours @ Standard rate		
5,500 @ $.75.............	$ 4,125.00	
Actual factory expense................	4,000.00	
Variance (credit).....................	$ 125.00	

(7)

Finished goods inventory.....................	$21,250.00	
Materials in process inventory..........		$10,000.00
Labor in process inventory.............		7,500.00
Factory expense in process inventory....		3,750.00

Goods completed during the month
(10,000 units) @ standard:

	Per Unit	Amount
Materials.................	$1.000	$10,000.00
Labor.....................	.75	7,500.00
Factory expense...........	.375	3,750.00
Totals................	$2.125	$21,250.00

(8)

Cost of goods sold...........................	$17,000.00	
Finished goods inventory...............		$17,000.00
Goods sold during the month @ standard cost:		
8,000 units @ $2.125....................	$17,000.00	

(9)

Accounts receivable.........................	$20,000.00	
Sales......................................		$20,000.00
Goods sold during the month @ actual selling		
price		

Inventory and variance accounts posted.   After the journal entries in the previous section are posted, the accounts appear as follows.   Note that the closing balances of the inventory accounts (including Work in Process accounts) represent closing inventories @ standard value.

Accounts Receivable

Sales for month @ actual selling prices	(9) $20,000	

Materials Inventory

Purchases @ standard	(1) $13,000	Standard allowances for operations completed, per bills of materials	(2)	$12,000
		Excess pieces used, per waste piece requisitions	(3)	100
		Balance		900
	$13,000			$13,000
Closing inventory @ standard	$ 900			

Materials in Process Inventory

Standard allowances for operations completed @ standard	(2) $12,000	Goods completed @ standard (7)	$10,000
		Balance	2,000
	$12,000		$12,000
Closing inventory @ standard	$ 2,000		

Labor in Process Inventory

Standard labor in operations completed	(4) $ 8,250	Goods completed @ standard (7)	$ 7,500
		Balance	750
	$ 8,250		$ 8,250
Closing inventory @ standard	$ 750		

Factory Expense in Process Inventory

Standard expense in operations completed	(6) $ 4,125	Goods completed @ standard	(7)	$ 3,750
		Balance		375
	$ 4,125			$ 4,125
Closing inventory @ standard	$ 375			

Finished Goods

Goods completed @ standard	(7) $21,250	Goods sold @ standard	(8)	$17,000
		Balance		4,250
	$21,250			$21,250
Closing inventory @ standard	$ 4,250			

Accounts Payable and Accrued Expense

	Materials purchases	(1)	$14,300
	Labor accrued	(4)	9,272
	Expense accrued	(5)	7,420

Sales

	Goods sold @ actual selling prices	(9) $20,000

Cost of Goods Sold

Goods sold @ standard cost   (8) $17,000

Materials Quantity Variance

Variance for month   (3) $ 100

Materials Price Variance

Variance for month   (1) $ 1,300

Labor Time Variance

Variance for month	(4) $ 900	

Labor Rate Variance

Variance for month	(4) $ 122	

Factory Expense Variance

	Variance for month	(6) $ 125

Factory Expense

Actual expense for month	(5) $ 4,000	To close	(6) $ 4,000

Selling and Shipping Expense

Actual expense for month	(5) $ 2,000	

Administrative Expense

Actual expense for month	(5) $ 1,420	

Statement of profits.   The statement of profits prepared under the method described in the last half of this chapter appears on page 420.

Note that the material price variance ($1,300) under the system of standard costs explained in the latter part of this chapter is recorded at the time the material is *received*, whereas the material price variance under the system explained in the first part of the chapter is recorded when the material is *used*.

The Statement of Profits suggests one of the cardinal principles exemplified in the reports produced in a standard cost system: the *principle of exceptions*.   In its application, this principle means that the exceptions to standard performance are reported.   They are the cost performances which should be brought to the attention of the manager.   The manager

Statement of Profits

(Standard Cost System)

Sales (8,000 units @ $2.50).....................		$20,000.00
Cost of sales @ standard (8,000 units @ $2.125)		17,000.00
Expected gross margin.....................		$ 3,000.00
Less, Variances from standard		
Material quantity variance................	$ 100.00	
Material price variance...................	1,300.00	
Labor time variance......................	900.00	
Labor rate variance......................	122.00	
Factory expense variance.................	125.00*	
Total variances.......................		2,297.00
Actual gross margin.......................		$ 703.00
Less, selling, shipping, and administrative expense		
Selling and shipping expense..............	$2,000.00	
Administrative expense...................	1,420.00	3,420.00
Net loss............................		$ 2,717.00

* Red.

Figure 17-7

can then decide, by noting the amount of a variance, whether he wants to investigate further. If he does want to investigate it, he can call for detailed variance reports which support the variances on the statement of profits. In a full-fledged standard cost system these supporting reports are sufficiently detailed to encompass every phase of the manufacturing operations of the business.

Source papers: Controlling material and labor variances at the source. In a standard cost system of the second type described in this chapter, the design and use of basic forms is particularly important because variances are determined and analyzed from those forms, as and when the variances occur. The following forms are related to the accounting procedures presented in this chapter:

Purchase invoices, showing actual quantities and actual prices, as they come in from the suppliers. In the accounting department, standard prices are entered (usually in spaces provided by applying a rubber stamp), and the extensions of Actual quantities × Standard prices are computed and entered. The invoices thus extended are summarized for Journal Entry (1) shown on page 415.

Standard bill of material, which is a list of materials required to produce a specified quantity of product, stating the standard allowance of each material for that quantity of product. The standard bill of materials for a production order is issued by the production control clerk at the time he issues the production order. Where the nature of the materials and the quantities involved make it feasible, the materials storekeeper may release all the materials (standard allowance) at one time.

Excess piece requisition, issued by the foreman when a workman fails to complete his operation with the original allowance of materials, because of defective materials or defective work. Note that the issue of an excess piece requisition gives the foreman notice to investigate the need for excess materials. Use of excess piece requisitions is an example of controlling variances at the source.

Job tickets, issued for each operation performed by each employee each day. A job ticket shows not only actual time and actual rate of wages but also *standard time* and (after the operation is finished) standard rate and the dollar extension at standard. The standard time is put on the job ticket before it is issued to indicate to the workman what time performance is expected on the operation. From the completed job tickets, Journal Entry (4) illustrated on page 416 is prepared. Ordinarily, a frequent analysis (sometimes daily) is made for the foremen to see what operations are not being performed at standard.

In the accounting procedures, separate entries are made for:

(a) the total standard value of materials released on standard bills of materials. The entry is (2) on page 415: debiting Materials in Process Inventory and crediting Materials Inventory.

(b) the total standard value of materials released on excess piece requisitions. The entry is (3) on page 416: debiting Materials Quantity Variance and crediting Materials Inventory.

Note that the excess piece requisitions can be analyzed as frequently as desired to provide reports to management.

QUESTIONS

17-1. What does the term "standard" mean in connection with standard costs?

17-2. Discuss briefly the uses of standard costs.

17-3. Describe the statement of profits prepared in a standard cost system, explaining the significant balances.

17-4. Name the variances from standard and state the formula for each variance.

17-5. (a) What is meant by the "principle of exceptions"?

(b) What is meant by analysis of variances at the source?

17-6. Describe two methods of operating work in process accounts in standard cost systems.

17-7. Name the papers used in the operation of a standard cost system of the second type explained in this chapter. Explain the use of each paper. What journal entry is obtained from the summary of each paper?

17-8. (a) What does the balance of each inventory account in the second type of system represent at the end of a period?

(b) How do you prove the balance of the work in process accounts at the end of a period?

EXERCISES

17-1. The Bell Manufacturing Company operates a standard cost system, charging Work in Process with actual costs and crediting it with standard costs. Following is the standard cost card for Product X.

PRODUCT X

Standard Cost per Unit

(Factory expense budget = $1,000: 1,000 hours: 200 units)

Materials:
10 pieces @ $1.00 per piece.................... $10.00
Labor:
5 hours @ $2.00 per hour..................... 10.00
Factory Expense:
5 hours @ $1.00 per hour..................... 5.00

Total factory cost per unit................ $25.00

Entries for actual and standard cost of goods produced appear in the "fill-in" T accounts presented in the Workbook.

Required:

Make the entries (directly in the T accounts) to record all variances from standard cost. You may enter the calculations supporting the variances in the particulars spaces of the accounts.

17-2. The Acme Company operates a standard cost system charging actual costs to the work in process accounts and crediting these accounts for the standard cost of goods completed and in process. Variances are analyzed at the end of each month and transferred to separate accounts. The following information is presented:

Standard cost of one lamp:
Raw materials—10 pieces at $.50.......... $ 5.00
Direct labor   — 5 hours at $1.00.......... 5.00
Factory expense —5 hours at $2.00........ 10.00

Total............................. $ 20.00

Budget for one month:
Factory expense........................ $10,000.00
Direct labor hours....................... 5,000.00
Factory expense rate per hour.............. $ 2.00
Actual cost for the month of August:
Raw materials used—10,000 pieces at $.40... $ 4,000.00
Direct labor   — 4,500 hours at $.90... 4,050.00
Factory expense........................ 11,000.00

Actual production for the month of August:
700 lamps completed
200 lamps in process at the end of August,
50% completed as to *all* elements of cost.

There were no inventories of work in process at August 1.

Required:

Complete the T accounts using the form in the Workbook.

17-3. Calculate variances, using the data shown in the Workbook and enter in the spaces provided.

PROBLEMS

17-1. The Astra Manufacturing Company produces metal ash trays of a simple design on a continuous process basis. The engineers have determined that one ash tray should use one pound of metal and should require one hour of direct labor after making allowances for waste, some spoilage, and employee fatigue. The standard price for metal is set at $1 per pound, and the standard rate for direct labor at $2 per hour. The budget for factory expense per month is $3,000, and the expected average volume of production per month is 1,000 ash trays to be made in 1,000 direct labor hours.

Compute the standard cost of one ash tray.

17-2. During the month of *January*, the Astra Manufacturing Company (Problem 17-1) completed 900 ash trays. There were no inventories of work in process at the beginning or end of the month. The following costs were incurred during January:

> Materials used: 950 pounds of metal at $1.10 per pound.
> Direct labor: 940 hours at $2.15 per hour.
> Factory expense: $3,150.

Set up the following three T accounts:

> Materials in Process
> Direct Labor in Process
> Factory Expense in Process

For the month of January, enter the historical costs incurred as debits to the above accounts. (Charge Factory Expense in Process account for actual hours × standard rate.) Credit these accounts for the standard cost of goods completed and for the variances from standard cost. Analyze materials and direct labor variances as to the price and quantity factors. Analyze factory expense variance as to factory expense time variance and factory expense underabsorbed. Show your computations.

17-3. During the month of *February*, the Astra Manufacturing Company (Problem 17-1) completed 1,060 ash trays and had started an additional 40 ash trays which were still in process at February 28. All the metal had been issued for the 40 ash trays in process, and they were on the average one-half completed. The following costs were incurred during February:

> Materials used: 1,090 pounds of metal at $1.10 per pound.
> Direct labor: 1,200 hours at $1.80 per hour.
> Factory expense: $2,800.

Draft journal entries to record:

(a) Historical costs incurred. (Charge Factory Expense in Process account for actual hours × Standard rate.)
(b) Standard cost of goods completed.
(c) Transfer of goods in process at standard to a work in process clearing account.
(d) Transfer of six variances from standard costs to separate variance accounts.

Post these entries to T accounts.

17-4. The Morris Manufacturing Company operates a standard cost system charging Work in Process with materials @ actual, labor @ actual, and expense @ standard rate and crediting it with standard costs. The standard cost card and transactions for January, 19— are presented below.

PRODUCT A

Standard Cost per Unit

(Based upon budget of 1,250 units per month)

Materials:		
5 pieces Aa @ $1.12..................................	$	5.60
Labor:		
4 hours @ $2.00......................................		8.00
Factory expense:		
4 hours @ $.60.......................................		2.40
Total factory cost per unit........................	$	16.00

Transactions for January, 19—

(1) Purchases of materials:	
7,000 pieces Aa @ $1.15...........................	$8,050.00
(2) Materials used:	
5,400 pieces Aa @ $1.15...........................	6,210.00
(3) Direct labor used:	
4,300 hours @ $2.10..............................	9,030.00
(4) Actual factory expense incurred......................	3,225.00
(5) Units of Product A completed........................	1,000
(6) Units of Product A in process, one half completed as to all	
elements..	100
(7 & 8) Units of Product A sold @ $25.00 per unit.........	800
(9) Actual expense accrued:	
Selling expense........................ $1,800.00	
Administrative expense.................. 1,400.00	
Total..............................	$3,200.00

Required:

(1) Draft entries in simple journal form to record the transactions and also a complete analysis of variances from standard cost for the month.
(2) Set up T accounts and post the entries.
(3) Prepare a Statement of Profits.

17-5. The Lawson Company operates a standard cost system, charging Work in Process with materials @ actual, labor @ actual, and expense @ standard rate and crediting it at standard. The standard cost card follows:

PRODUCT R

Standard Cost per Unit

(Based upon budget of 1,200 units per month)

Materials:		
8 pieces B @ $2.00.....	$	16.00
Labor:		
6 hours @ $1.30.....		7.80
Factory Expense:		
6 hours @ $1.25.....		7.50
Total Factory Cost per Unit.....	$	31.30

Transactions for June 19__

(1) Purchases of materials:	
10,000 pieces B @ $2.10.....	$21,000.00
(2) Materials used:	
9,300 pieces B @ $2.10.....	19,530.00
(3) Direct labor used:	
7,000 hours @ $1.35.....	9,450.00
(4) Actual factory expense incurred.....	9,200.00
(5) Product R completed.....	1,100 units
(6) Product R in process, one-half completed as to labor	
and expense.....	100 units
(7 & 8) Units of Product A sold @ $40.00 per unit.....	1,000 units
(9) Actual expense accrued	
Selling expense..... $2,000.00	
Administrative expense..... 1,000.00	
Total.....	$ 3,000.00

Required:

(1) Draft entries to record the above transactions and a complete analysis of variances for the month.

(2) Set up T accounts and post the entries.

(3) Prepare a Statement of Profits.

Chapter 18

MATERIALS AND LABOR CONTROL

Organization for cost control. Cost control is the function of measuring cost performance to determine whether expenditures have been excessive. It involves setting up measures of what the cost should be, comparing actual costs with the measures to determine whether actual costs were excessive, and initiating action to reduce the expenditures to proper levels. In the field of materials and labor, the control function is partly the work of industrial engineers and partly the work of cost accountants. The task of setting up quantitative measures of materials and labor (called "physical standards") usually falls to the industrial engineer, and the task of translating the quantitative measures into dollars and collecting dollar information for report purposes usually falls to the accountant.

In the organization chart of the Benson & West Manufacturing Company (page 272), note that there is an industrial engineer reporting to the vice-president in charge of manufacturing and a cost accountant reporting to the controller. These two men perform the work of cost control for materials and labor.

Phases of a cost control program. A cost control program which is typical of many used by small well-run companies is explained under the following major headings:

(1) Setting standards for cost control: direct materials and direct labor (this chapter).
(2) Budgeting indirect labor (this chapter).
(3) Recording variances from standard cost (Chapter 17 and Chapter 19).

I. SETTING STANDARDS FOR COST CONTROL: DIRECT MATERIALS AND DIRECT LABOR

This section explains all the steps in setting standards by means of an actual case—the manufacture of the cardboard box illustrated on page 427. This example was selected because the product is familiar to everyone and because the steps can be described completely in part of a chapter. The boxes are not the main product of the Benson & West Manufacturing Company, but they provide an excellent example of how standards and standard costs are set.   (The brand name is fictitious.)

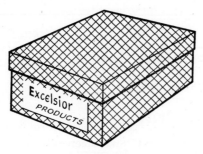

Figure 18-1

It should be mentioned that most of the work of setting standards is done by the industrial engineers.   The cost accountant sets up the standard cost cards from those standards.   It is desirable for the cost accountant to have a good understanding of how standards are set.

Specification sheet for each product.   A specification sheet for a product is a written or coded description of the main features of a product, such as will relate it to other products in the company line and at the same time distinguish it from the others.   It is based upon the general classification plan which the company uses for setting up catalogs, price lists, perpetual inventory accounts, and planning and production control records. The specification sheet may not cover all features of each product, but it does cover all features which identify the product and distinguish it from other products in the line.   It is often supplemented by drawings, photographs, or models of the product.

The specification sheet for the cardboard box appears on page 428.   It shows the capacity of the box, the size of the box and the size of the cover, description of the cardboard and the paper, and description of the label.

Product specification sheets for major products are used first by top management in making decisions as to what products shall be put in the line.   In the Benson & West Manufacturing Company it is usually the sales department which makes the request that a new product be put in the line, on the basis of a demand they think exists.   There are conferences with the industrial engineer and the factory superintendent as to manufacturing facilities and methods, and with the cost accountant as to the probable cost of the new product.   Finally, the president, the sales manager, and the production superintendent decide whether the product will be put in the line.   The controller is consulted about any problems of financing that might be involved.

How a cardboard box is made: Process chart used by the engineer.

SPECIFICATION SHEET

**BOX CAPACITY
AND DESCRIPTION**   Small Utility Box - 6" deep   **DATE 9/15/-**

DIMENSIONS   Width   Length   Depth
  Box   :   10 x   12   x   6
  Cover: 10 1/4 x 12 1/4 x 1 1/2

MATERIALS SPECIFICATIONS
  CARDBOARD

	Supplier	Kind	Size Sheet	Ply
Box :	Jones	Warrior	24 x 42	41
Ends :	Jones	Warrior	32 x 42	50
Cover:	Jones	Warrior	28 x 32	32

  PAPER (Box and Cover)

	Supplier	Description (Imprint)	Width	Length
	Nolton	Coated paper - B - W	30"	2500'

  LABEL

	Supplier	Description (Imprint)
	Carroll	Excelsior Products

Figure 18-2

A pictorial chart showing how a box is made appears on page 429. This chart names the operations from the time the cardboard sheets and rolls of paper are taken out of the storeroom until the box is lidded and labeled. It shows what the materials look like after each operation, and it is presented to help the reader visualize the operations.

The industrial engineer who is going to lay out the production line would use a more technical type of chart known as a *process* chart. This chart would show in proper sequence the direct labor operations required to produce each part and to assemble the parts into the final product. It is a means of setting out graphically the sequence of operations and the flow of production through the productive facilities of the plant. Using this type of chart, the industrial engineer can show not only the sequence of operations but also, where there is a choice, the particular machine to be used for each operation. Often the industrial engineer will prepare several such charts in succession while he is making decisions on how the product should be put together. Each chart represents a more advanced stage of thinking than the previous one. When the engineer is satisfied that he has devised the best method possible at the present time, he uses the process

Setting Standards: How a Cardboard Box Is Made

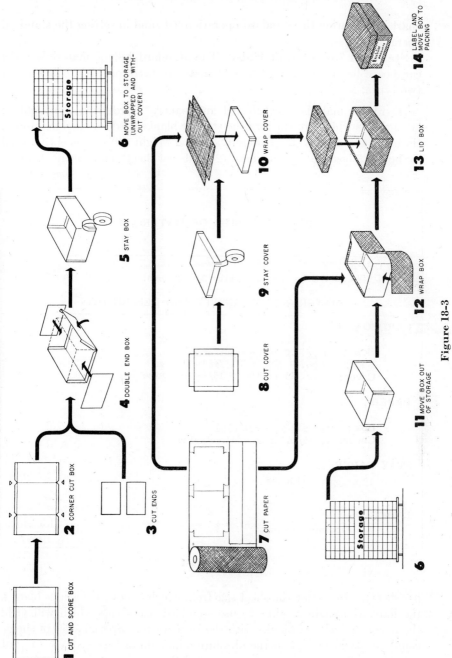

1 CUT AND SCORE BOX

2 CORNER CUT BOX

3 CUT ENDS

4 DOUBLE END BOX

5 STAY BOX

Storage

6 MOVE BOX TO STORAGE (UNWRAPPED AND WITHOUT COVER)

7 CUT PAPER

8 CUT COVER

9 STAY COVER

10 WRAP COVER

Storage

6

11 MOVE BOX OUT OF STORAGE

12 WRAP BOX

13 LID BOX

14 LABEL AND MOVE BOX TO PACKING

Figure 18-3

429

chart in preparing the standard operation lists and in setting the standard operation times.

Standard bill of materials. The standard bill of materials for a cardboard box is shown below. The materials used for this product are of two types:

(1) Major materials: cardboard and paper. Cardboard is bought in large sheets which are cut into the smaller blanks used for the box proper, the ends, and the cover. Different size and weight ("ply") sheets are used for boxes (3 boxes per sheet), ends (20 ends per sheet), and covers (4 covers

---

STANDARD BILL OF MATERIALS

BOX CAPACITY
AND DESCRIPTION   Small Utility Box 6" deep   DATE 9/15/-

MATERIALS : QUANTITY AND DESCRIPTION

CARDBOARD

    Box :   1 pc. 22" x 13½" cut size
    Ends: 2 pc. 9 7/8" x 5 15/16" cut size
    Cover: 1 pc. 15 1/4" x 13 15/16" cut size

PAPER

    Box :   46" x 7 5/8" cut size
    Cover: 16 15/16" x 14 3/8" cut size

STAY PAPER

    13 oz. per 100 boxes

LABEL

    1 - Excelsior Products

Figure 18-4

per sheet). In setting the sheet size from which to cut the various blanks, the industrial engineer aims to use standard size sheets which will yield the particular sizes of blanks with the least waste. Special sizes of sheets could be specified to yield the absolute minimum of waste, of course, but special sizes of sheet cost more per pound than standard sizes.

Note that the ends are made out of heavier cardboard than are the box and top. This point suggests that, in setting the standards, it is necessary first to decide how sturdy a box is required for the intended use.

STANDARD OPERATION LIST		
Product Small Utility Box – 6" Deep		Date 9/15/–
Operation No.	Operation Name and Description	Machine
1	Cut and score box (square cut)	Scoring machine
2	Corner cut box (mitre cut)	Corner cutter
3	Cut ends	Scoring machine
4	Double end box The machine automatically folds the box piece into the shape of a box and glues the two ends on.	Double ender
5	Stay box. Glues a strip of stay paper on the vertical edges of the box.	Large stayer
6	Move box to storage	Hand truck
7	Cut paper Machine slits rolls 30" wide into three strips – two for boxes and one for covers	Slitter
8	Cut cover	Corner cutter
9	Stay cover	Small stayer
10	Wrap cover	Automatic wrapper
11	Move boxes out of storage	Hand truck
12	Wrap boxes	Stripper
13	Lid boxes Lids are put on by hand	Table
14	Label boxes	Table
15	Move lidded boxes to packing	Hand trucks

Standard times not shown.

Figure 18-5

Paper, coated and imprinted with the company name, is bought in rolls, in this case 30" wide and 2,500' long. In Operation #7, Cut Paper, the roll of paper is put into a slitter which unrolls it and splits it lengthwise into three strips, each 2,500' long. Two of these strips are the same width: they are in turn sliced into box papers. The other strip (wider) is sliced into cover papers. As in the case of cardboard, the engineer aims to specify the roll size which will yield the box papers and cover papers with the least waste practicable.

(2) Minor materials, such as stay paper for fastening the edges of

the box and the edges of the top together, and labels. The stay paper (gummed paper) is a standard width. To determine the standard allowance, the actual usage was measured by running a test lot of 100 boxes through the stayer. The roll of stay paper was weighed before and after the test run, and it was found to take 13 ounces of paper per 100 boxes. (This paper is quoted by the pound.)

Standard operation list; standard times. The operation list for the cardboard box appears on page 431. This list is prepared directly from the process chart. The *standard* times which would be shown on the list were set by the industrial engineer. To set standard times, he observed an average operator perform each operation, determined the best way to do the operation, taught the operator to do the operation by the correct method, and then time-studied the operator after he had built up the requisite experience in performing the operation. The standard time for each operation represents the performance that an average operator should achieve with reasonable, consistent effort. The standard time includes an allowance for "PFD" (personal factors, delay, and fatigue). (Standard times are omitted from Figure 18-5 because the box manufacturer considers them restricted information.)

Standard operating instructions. Standard operating instructions are written for each direct labor operation. The instructions describe (a) the equipment to be used, (b) the handling of materials into the operation and out of the operation (pickup and disposal), and (c) the method of performing the operation. They also show the standard time allowed. Formal instructions are useful as a record of the conditions upon which the standard times are based. The standard time for an operation as shown by the operations list may not be applicable if any of the particulars named above have been changed. It may therefore be useful to check the actual prevailing particulars against the standard particulars occasionally. Sometimes it is found that the operation is no longer being performed the standard way and that a labor variance results from that fact.

Standard operating instructions may also be useful in training new operators. Sometimes the instructions are intended to be read by the operator. Often they are intended to be read by the foreman or other instructor, who shows the operator how to perform the operation.

Incentive wage plan. After the time studies have been completed and the standard times set for labor operations, an incentive wage plan is formulated by the industrial engineer. There are numerous types of incentive wage payment plans, but one typical plan includes the following features (illustrated in Chapter 8):

(1) Each employee is paid on the basis of his own production. The plan is an individual incentive plan rather than a group incentive plan in which each member of a group is paid on the basis of the production of the group.

(2) Each employee is given credit for his production in terms of standard

hours produced.   Thus, if the employee performs Operation #101 on 100 units of Product A, and the standard time allowance per unit is .02 hours, the employee is given credit for 2 standard hours produced.   The credit is given regardless of the actual time taken: if the employee performed the operation in 1.8 clock hours, he gets credit for 2 standard hours.

(3) The employee receives certain allowances for clock time spent "Off-standard" during the work period, through no fault of his own.   "Off-standard" time is either nonproductive time or time spent on an operation for which the operator was not trained and on which he is not likely to achieve the standard time performance.   Examples of off-standard allowances are payments for:

(a) Waiting time, which is idleness due to the fact that there is no work on hand for the operator.

(b) Machine delay, which is idleness due to machine breakdown.

(c) Transfer time, which is time spent on an operation other than the one for which the operator was trained.   To keep production moving it is sometimes necessary to transfer an operator from one operation to another to fill the place of an absentee.

(4) In addition to the "off-standard" allowances described in paragraph (3), employees may be paid:

(a) Make-up to guarantee, where the incentive pay plan includes a provision that the employee is guaranteed earnings at a specified rate, say, $1.25 per hour.   If, in a week of 40 hours, the operator fails to earn as much as $40 \times \$1.25$ in incentive pay and allowances, the employee will nevertheless be paid a total of $50 under the guarantee.   The difference between the amount that the employee earned in incentives and allowances and the guaranteed payment is known as make-up to guarantee.

(b) Overtime premium, which is an amount paid to the employee for hours worked over eight in one day or hours worked over 40 in one week, depending upon the agreement in effect.   (The calculation of overtime premium under an incentive wage payment plan is illustrated in Chapter 8.)

Standard cost card.   Figure 18-6 is the standard cost card for a cardboard box.   It shows:

(a) A complete description of all the materials used, together with the standard quantities allowed as described on page 430.   It is possible to list all the materials, since the number is small.   If the numbers were large, only *total* costs could be shown on the standard cost card.   The details would be shown on a supporting form.

(b) The list of operations and the standard time per unit of product for each operation.

Standard prices and wage rates.   The standard *prices* of *materials* are set by the purchasing agent.   They are average or mean prices expected to be paid during the coming period for the quantities which he expects

STANDARD COST CARD		
		Date 9/15/-

BOX CAPACITY AND DESCRIPTION Small Utility Box – 6" deep		Amount Per Box
MATERIALS		
CARDBOARD		
Box: :1 pc. __" x __" cut size		
Ends : 2 pc. __" x __" cut size		
Cover: 1 pc. __" x __" cut size		
COATED PAPER IMPRINTED		
Box : __" x __" cut size		
Cover: __" x __" cut size		
STAY PAPER		
13 oz. for 100 boxes		
LABEL		
Total materials		$

LABOR	Standard Minutes	
1 Cut and score box		
2 Corner cut box		
3 Cut ends		
4 Double end box		
5 Stay box		
6 Move box to storage		
7 Cut paper		
8 Cut cover		
9 Stay cover		
10 Wrap cover		
11 Move boxes out of storage		
12 Wrap boxes		
13 Lid boxes		
14 Label boxes		
15 Move lidded boxes to packing		
Total standard minutes		
Standard rate per hour		
Total standard labor amount		$
		$
FACTORY EXPENSE (@ per standard labor hour)		
TOTAL COST PER BOX		

Pro-forma illustration: times and amounts omitted.

Figure 18-6

to buy. The prices are entered on the standard cost cards by the cost accountant, who extends standard prices and standard quantities to determine standard materials costs per unit of product.

Under the incentive wage payment plan outlined above, there are two types of wage rate:

(a) Standard base rate. This rate is applicable (in this particular plan) to all operations and all operators. It is the multiplier applied to standard

434

hours for an operation to determine standard labor cost. The industrial engineer sets the rate at such level that an operator who performs at the standard hour allowance (that is, meets standard time) will receive a payment about 20 per cent higher than the going rate in the community for the same class of work paid on a straight hourly rate. (In other words, the industrial engineer sets the standard times *and* the standard base rate in such manner as to provide the employee with an extra 20 per cent for the effort which he would be expected to put forth under the incentive plan.)

(b) Guaranteed rates. This is the rate per actual hour which the employer guarantees to pay the employee, as explained above. The guaranteed rate becomes effective for an employee if his total incentive earnings and allowances for the pay period do not exceed actual hours × the guaranteed rate for the employee.

In extending labor on standard cost cards, the cost accountant multiplies standard hours shown on the card by the standard base rate. The extension is *standard labor cost* for the product. Some cost accountants also apply to standard labor cost a percentage to cover probable allowances, make-up, and overtime premium, on the theory that it is not possible for a foreman to operate the factory without *some* payments for those factors. The percentage added is based upon the amount of such payments which the industrial engineer would consider reasonable under efficient management.

Summary: Setting standards for cost control. The steps involved in setting standards for cost control of direct materials and direct labor have been described in the previous sections of this chapter. They are:

(1) Set up specification sheet for each product.

(2) Make a process chart for each product, showing the direct labor operations required to produce each part and to assemble the parts into final assemblies.

(3) Set up a bill of materials for each product, listing all the materials required to produce the product, and showing the quantity of each material allowed per unit of finished product.

(4) Prepare an operations list for each product, listing the labor operations in sequence.

(5) Set standard time per unit of product (or for some other specified quantity of product) for each operation shown on the operations list.

(6) Formulate an incentive wage payment plan based upon the standard times set up in (5). Such a plan usually comprises payment for (a) operations performed on the product by an employee while on his regular operation and (b) special allowances.

(7) Write standard practice instructions (for the employees) covering the performance of each operation for which standard time has been set.

Formal instructions can be used (a) as a guide in teaching the employees how they are expected to perform the operation and (b) for reference in case of question as to what the standard practice is and whether standard practice is being followed.

(8) Write a formal description of the incentive wage payment plan for the guidance of (a) the employees, who should be fully informed on the amounts and conditions of payment under the incentive plan, and (b) the payroll clerks, who have to compute the pay due each employee under the plan.

(9) Set up a standard cost card for each product, using the specification sheet (1, above), the bill of materials, the operations list, and the standard times by operation.

The above steps represent the physical aspects of cost control. To translate physical standards into cost standards, it is necessary to:

(10) Set a standard price for each material and apply standard prices to the standard cost cards to determine standard materials cost for each product.

(11) Set standard wage rates for labor operations and apply standard rates to the standard cost cards.

Planning custom work and setting standard costs. The manufacture of boxes described in the previous pages is a *mass production* operation, and the standards for materials and labor comprise the basis for day-to-day control of operations.   In the same plant, certain custom work is done, and the predetermined costs of that work are used for planning and control.

The custom work is the art work for labels and coated cover paper and the printing of labels.   In this segment of the manufacture of boxes, there was no real control of costs before predetermined costs were instituted. If a certain design of paper or label was desired, the art department and the printing department proceeded to manufacture it without any formal planning.   Often, the cost of a completed job was excessive simply because it had not been decided how the work was to be done before it was started.

There are, of course, a number of methods and processes by which a particular end result in such printing can be achieved.   In the past, it always seemed after the job was done that the most expensive methods had been used.   Now, the art department and the printing department are required to submit formal plans and cost estimates for all proposed jobs. Once a proposal is accepted, these departments are not permitted to change methods without authorization from the department that placed the order.

II. BUDGETING INDIRECT LABOR

Importance of controlling indirect labor: Job classifications. *Direct* labor has been defined as labor identified with a work unit or cost unit and which can be measured and charged to the cost unit.   The identification of labor with some cost unit is the means of setting up a control. Once the relationship of labor time or dollars to cost units has been established, it can be determined whether actual labor expenditure during a particular period is excessive.

Indirect labor is not identified with a particular cost unit such as a product unit and therefore cannot be measured and charged to the cost unit.   If it is assumed that the product unit is the cost unit, indirect labor may sometimes include such groups as supervisory, accounting, and production control; machine repairmen; materials and scrap handlers; supply room attendants; inspection, product repairs, and seconds people; learners; experimental work; nonstandard productive labor; and building maintenance people.

Although the layman might have the idea that indirect labor is "incidental" labor, actually it is likely to be anything but incidental in its effect upon profits.   In some factories, there is a surprisingly large number of jobs which the management classifies as indirect labor.   Unless some control is put on these jobs, the number of people is likely to go up as the production curve goes up, and fail to come down as the curve descends.

Reclassifying indirect labor: Making it direct. Sometimes it is possible to put certain labor jobs under control by changing them from indirect labor to direct labor.   To illustrate, assume that the cost unit in a certain department is a product unit and that the labor of handling semifinished products in the department is considered as indirect labor.   Materials handlers, so called, are charged to factory expense.   In some cases, it might be possible to set standard times for materials handling per product unit and to treat the materials handling operation as a direct labor operation, putting the standard cost of the operation on the standard cost card for the product.   This would be an example of reclassifying an indirect labor operation to make it direct labor, by deciding to measure it in terms of the product unit.

It is also possible to put labor under control by finding a cost unit or work unit other than the product unit.   To illustrate, assume that all janitors, watchmen, painters, and other job classifications under building maintenance are charged to a Building Maintenance and Fixed Charges account, which is a departmental account in the factory expense ledger. In a large plant, it might be possible to set standards for (a) sweeping and (b) painting *per square yard*.   In fact, the maintenance superintendent would very likely know approximately how many square yards of floor a sweeper ought to sweep in a certain department in an hour, and how many square yards of floor a painter ought to paint under certain conditions.

Note that in these cases, although sweeping and painting would be indirect labor if the product unit is considered the cost unit, it would be direct if the square yard of floor is considered the cost unit.

The amount of reclassifying of indirect labor that can be done is, of course, limited because of the problem of finding suitable cost units or work units. Most alert managements examine the indirect labor job classifications from time to time, however, to see whether suitable work units can be found for measuring the productivity of each of them. Most fruitful are job classifications in which the employee performs the same operation or a limited set of closely integrated operations repetitively.

Indirect labor allowances. In some cases, indirect labor is controlled by setting allowances based upon the capacity of a department or cost center. Thus, it may be considered that a department will require one foreman, one clerk, two machine repairmen and one sweeper-watchman when operating at the capacity for which it was set up. (Capacity may be measured in machine hours or labor hours, depending upon whether machines or labor is the controlling factor in production.) It may further be decided that, if the volume of production drops below capacity, one foreman and one sweeper-watchman would still be required, but that less than the full time of a clerk and the full time of two machinists would be required. It is considered that the foremen complement and the sweeper-watchman complement are *fixed* and the others are *variable*.

The complement might be set up by the industrial engineer who designed the production line and determined its capacity, and the quantitative relationship of each of the jobs to capacity might likewise be set by him. He may have the opinion that a certain job classification is *directly variable* with the volume of production. This would mean that, if the volume is 50 per cent of capacity, the allowance for that job classification would be 50 per cent of the allowance at capacity. Or he may be of the opinion that the allowance for a certain job classification cannot be varied directly with volume of production, but that it may be moved up and down in steps. Thus, if a factory has a bank of three freight elevators, the successive allowance steps would be one operator, two operators, and finally three operators as volume approaches capacity. Such allowances are *semivariable*.

Setting up indirect labor allowances in this manner may not provide as tight control as is possible when indirect labor can be converted to direct labor through the selection of suitable work units. It does, however, provide the means and advantage of a close examination of each job classification in relationship to the amount of direct labor time or machine time in a department or cost center.

Indirect labor control report. An indirect labor control report (not the Benson & West Manufacturing Company) is shown on page 439. In this company, the budget is set at capacity, and it is assumed that variable job classifications vary directly with standard direct labor hours produced (that is, the standard labor hours in operations performed.) Fixed job classifications are recognized, but not semivariable job classifications. In

INDIRECT LABOR CONTROL REPORT BY JOB CLASSIFICATION			
Department	Week ending		19
JOB CLASSIFICATION	Allowance	Actual	Excess or Saving
Supervisory, Accounting and Production Control			
111 Foremen and assistant foremen			
112 Teachers			
113 Timekeepers and payroll clerks			
114 Factory accounting			
115 Planning and production clerks			
Machine Repairmen			
Materials and Scrap Handlers			
131 Receiving clerks (storeroom)			
132 Assembling materials			
133 Truck rollers			
134 Scrap and waste handlers			
Supply Room			
141 Supply room clerks			
142 Small supply production			
Inspectors, Repairs, Seconds			
151 Inspectors			
152 Product repair girls			
153 Seconds handling			
Learners			
Experimental Work			
Building Maintenance			
191 Janitors and watchmen			
192 Firemen			
193 Building repair			
Total Department			

Figure 13-7

this case, the foremen were given allowances of the fixed items unadjusted plus the variable items adjusted directly to level of production. Labor control reports on which semivariable as well as variable and fixed allowances appear are illustrated in Chapter 19.

III. LABOR STANDARDS FOR PROCESS MANUFACTURE

Job order manufacture and process manufacture compared. The setting of labor standards differs between job order manufacturing situations and process manufacturing situations. Under job order manufacture, each job or order is identified by a production order. The job may pass from work place to work place in a tote box or on a pallet or in a bundle. At each work place, one or more operations are performed on the job, often by a single workman. There are time standards for individual direct labor operations. The standard labor cost of any product is the sum of the standard operation costs for the product. The efficiency of the individual operator is determined by comparing the standard time allowed for the quantity of work which the operator has produced with the actual time which he spent.

FLOW CHART SHOWING METHODS OF MANUFACTURE
Batch vs. Continous

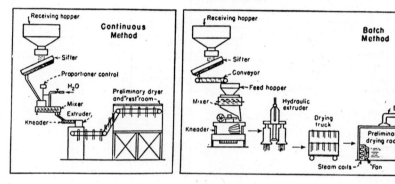

Figure 18-8

In process manufacturing situations, the product or products may pass through a number of work centers, each of which is staffed with one or more operators, depending upon the work load scheduled for the day and the particular kinds of products making up the work load. Thus, the dye house in a knitting mill may comprise the following work centers: dye tubs (normally say two men operating three tubs), extractors which squeeze the moisture from dyed cloth (one man on each extractor), drier (an oven manned by two men), napper, which brushes up the nap of the cloth (one man operating two machines), and turner and folder (two men operating two machines).

Controlling labor in the dye house consists in setting up the production schedule for each day and determining the standard labor allowance for each job classification for the particular load and the particular assortment of cloth styles. Note that labor is not directly variable with pounds of cloth processed. The number of workmen allowed for each work center is likely to vary in steps.

Labor variance in this case is the difference between standard labor allowed for the load and the mix, and actual labor used. This is the foreman's operating variance. Note that there is also a *practice* variance, for which the foreman is not responsible. It is the difference between the

---

WORK SCHEDULES AT DIFFERENT OPERATING LEVELS

Manufacturing Dept. - Long Cut Section - Vertical Presses

Standards Of Accomplishment

Production Group	Lbs. Per Hour	Hours Per Lb.
Group No. 1	300	.0033
" No. 2	400	.0025
" No. 3	200	.0050
" No. 4	350	.0029

MAN-HOUR RATIOS

Job Classification	No. 1 Men	Hrs.	No. 2 Men	Hrs.	No. 3 Men	Hrs.	No. 4 Men	Hrs.	No. 5 Men	Hrs.	No. 6 Men	Hrs.	No. 7 Men	Hrs.	No. 8 Men	Hrs.
Mixer Men	1	9.0	1	9.0	1	9.0	1	9.0	1	10.0	1	10.0	1	10.0	1	10.0
Mixer Helpers		-		-	1	8.0	1	8.0		-		-	1	9.0	1	9.0
Kneader Men	3	24.0	4	32.0	5	40.0	6	48.0	3	27.0	4	36.0	5	45.0	6	54.0
Kneader Helpers	3	11.0	3	11.0	4	18.0	5	19.0	3	12.0	3	12.0	4	20.0	5	21.0
Spreaders	6	48.0	8	64.0	10	80.0	12	96.0	6	54.0	8	72.0	10	90.0	12	108.0
Macaroni Hangers	1	8.0	2	16.0	2	16.0	2	16.0	1	9.0	2	18.0	2	18.0	2	18.0
Scrap Men	1	8.0		-	1	8.0	1	8.0	1	9.0		-	1	9.0	1	9.0
Elevator Men	2	6.0	2	8.0	2	10.0	2	12.0	2	8.0	2	10.0	2	12.0	2	14.0
TOTALS	17	114.0	20	140.0	26	189.0	30	216.0	17	129.0	20	158.0	26	213.0	30	243.0
Vertical Press Hrs.		48.0		64.0		80.0		96.0		54.0		72.0		90.0		108.0
Ratio		2.38		2.18		2.36		2.25		2.39		2.19		2.37		2.25

Operating Schedules

Schedule No. 1 - 6 Presses - 8 Hours
Schedule No. 2 - 8 Presses - 8 Hours
Schedule No. 3 - 10 Presses - 8 Hours
Schedule No. 4 - 12 Presses - 8 Hours
Schedule No. 5 - 6 Presses - 9 Hours
Schedule No. 6 - 8 Presses - 9 Hours
Schedule No. 7 - 10 Presses - 9 Hours
Schedule No. 8 - 12 Presses - 9 Hours

Figure 18-9

---

standard labor allowed the foreman for the load and the mix, and the standard value of the day's production if priced at the standard amounts shown on the standard cost cards. The latter (which are used as a factor in setting selling prices) are based upon an estimated load and mix for a period of time. The practice variance can be described as a volume and mix variance.

Labor standards for process manufacture. An interesting example of labor standards for process manufacture appears in "Labor Cost Controls for a Macaroni Plant" by John W. Sheets.*

For thirty years or more macaroni making confined itself to the intermittent or batch operation. This method makes use initially of power driven mixers in which a projecting arm revolves around an horizontal axis in a metal tub, agitating the seminola or flour, so that each particle comes in contact with water to form dough. Kneading and extrusion operations follow. The continuous method of making macaroni has been in operation in this country so few years that most of the larger macaroni plants are using both the intermittent and the continuous methods in getting out their production. In the continuous method, the mixing, kneading and forming of the product is done in a contained unit. The two methods are compared (and contrasted) in the depictographs [in Figure 18-8]. . . .

A review of plant operations over a period of time will indicate the activity levels for which labor requirements must be determined. Different operating schedules necessitate different labor requirements. If these operating schedules are definitely established beforehand and incorporated into manpower requirements, the supervisor will know what action to take as conditions change. A co-operative approach on the part of those directly concerned with this problem will lead to a better understanding and a satisfactory solution. In a small company, the foreman may contribute his knowledge of the job to the thinking of the factory superintendent, the cost accountant, and the individual assigned to cost reduction. . . .

The planning of the operation schedules cannot be accomplished with maximum efficiency without the use of standards of accomplishment, for standards provide supervision with the means of utilizing labor effectively. In the development of labor standards, two factors, standard hourly rates and standard time units are primarily involved. . . .

The labor standards at various operating levels are shown in Figure 18-9. Note that the schedule shows the number of men in each job classification for each of eight work schedules. A daily labor variance report (not illustrated here) shows actual hours by job classification and total standard hours allowed for the day's production, bonus hours, and bonus per cent.

QUESTIONS

18-1. (a) What is meant by "cost control"?

(b) Discuss organization for cost control as it might exist in a small manufacturing concern.

18-2. What are "physical standards"?

18-3. What is each of the following forms:

(a) a specification sheet
(b) a process chart
(c) an operation list
(d) a bill of materials
(e) standard practice instructions
(f) standard cost card?

* *Bulletin of the National Association of Cost Accountants*, October, 1950, pp. 185–194. Excerpts are presented here by permission.

18-4. In general, what are the steps in setting standards for direct materials and direct labor? Discuss each step briefly.

18-5. Discuss the use of standards in planning custom work. Give a specific example.

18-6. (a) Explain the importance of formal job classifications in the control of indirect labor.

(b) What is meant by "making indirect labor direct" to get it under control?

18-7. (a) Explain a general plan for budgeting indirect labor.

(b) Describe an indirect labor control report.

18-8. In what basic respect is the structure of labor standards for process manufacture different from the structure of standards for job order manufacture?

EXERCISES

18-1. Assume that the Acme Company (Exercise 17-2) operates a standard cost system wherein variances are determined *before* charges to Work in Process are made. Variances are therefore entered directly into variance accounts and Work in Process is charged for the *standard* costs of production. The materials price variance is computed at the time goods are purchased.

In addition to the data presented in Exercise 17-2, only the following information is necessary:

Purchases for August, 12,000 pieces of material at $.40.

Using the T accounts form provided in the Workbook, make all entries required under this method of operating standard costs in the accounts.

PROBLEMS

18-1. Assume that the Stockman Manufacturing Company operates a standard cost system of the type in which Work in Process is charged and credited at standard. The standard cost for Product A appears:

PRODUCT A

Standard Cost per Unit of Product

(Based upon budget of 100 units: 500 hours: $500 factory expense)

Materials:
10 pieces "a" @ $2............................. $20.00
Labor:
5 hours @ $2.................................... 10.00
Factory expense:
5 hours @ $1 (normal rate)...................... 5.00

Total cost per unit............................. $35.00

Selling price per unit.......................... $50.00

Transactions for the month of January, 19—:

(1) Materials purchased @ actual:
1,000 pieces "a" @ $2.10, $2,100

(2) Standard quantity of materials allowed per B/M at standard prices:

Classification	Product Units	Standard Amount Per Unit	Standard Amount Total
Completed and transferred to finished goods.....	80	$10.00	$800.00
In process at end of month...................	10	10.00	100.00
Totals................................	90	10.00	$900.00

(3) Excess pieces of materials used, 50

(4) Standard hours of labor allowed at standard rates:

Classification	Product Units	Stage of Completion	Standard Amount Per Unit	Standard Amount Total
Completed and transferred to finished goods	80	100%	$5.00	$400.00
In process at end of month.............	10	50%	5.00	25.00
Totals...........................	90			$425.00

(5) Actual hours of direct labor @ actual rate:
   450 hours @ $2.10, $945.00

(6) Actual factory expense, $550.00

(7) Goods completed, 80 units.

(8) Goods sold (@ standard selling price), 60 units.

Required:

(1) Draft journal entries to record the above information.

(2) Post the entries to T accounts.

(3) Prepare a proof of work in process balances.

18-2. The Bolting Manufacturing Company produces metal ash trays of a simple design on a continuous process basis. The engineers have determined that one ash tray should use one pound of metal and should require one hour of direct labor after making allowances for waste, some spoilage, and employee fatigue. The standard price for metal is set at $1 per pound, and the standard rate for direct labor at $2 per hour. The budget for manufacturing overhead per month is $3,000 and the expected average volume of production per month is 1,000 ash trays to be made in 1,000 direct labor hours.

Compute the standard cost of one ash tray.

Note: This problem, which comprises data identical to Problem 17-1, is used in this chapter as the basis for Problems 18-3 and 18-4.

18-3. During the month of January, the Bolting Manufacturing Company (Problem 18-2) completed 900 ash trays. There were no inventories of work in process at the beginning or end of the month. The following costs were incurred during January:

Materials purchased: 1,100 pounds of metal at $1.10 per pound.

Materials used: 950 pounds of metal. Materials price variance is entered in the Variance account at the time materials are purchased. Materials used are therefore priced at the standard cost.

Direct labor: 940 hours at $2.15 per hour.

Manufacturing overhead: $3,150.

Set up the following T accounts. Make these accounts large enough for two months' transactions.

Raw Materials
Materials Price Variance
Accounts Payable and Other Credits
Materials in Process
Direct Labor in Process
Manufacturing Overhead in Process
Materials Quantity Variance
Direct Labor Rate Variance
Direct Labor Time Variance
Factory Expense Variance
Finished Goods Inventory.

For the month of January, enter the costs incurred and production. The Bolting Manufacturing Company computes variances at their source. Variances are therefore charged directly to the variance accounts, and Work in Process is both debited and credited at standard costs. Show your computations.

18-4. During the month of February, the Bolting Manufacturing Company (Problem 18-2) completed 960 ash trays and had started an additional 100 ash trays which were still in process at February 28. All the metal had been issued for the 100 ash trays in process, and they were on the average one-half completed. The following costs were incurred during February:

Materials purchased: 1,000 pounds of metal at $.90 per pound.
Materials used: 1,050 pounds of metal.
Direct labor: 1,020 hours at $1.90 per hour.
Manufacturing overhead: $3,100.

For the month of February, enter the foregoing transactions in the T accounts set up in Problem 18-3.

18-5. Assume that the Lawson Company (Problem 17-5) operates a standard cost system charging and crediting Work in Process @ standard. Using the information given in Problem 17-5, draft entries to operate the system and post to T accounts. Prepare a Statement of Profits.

18-6. The Lee Roberts Manufacturing Company uses a standard cost system in accounting for the cost of its single product. Their standard was set as follows:

Standard output per month: 10,000 units.
Standard direct labor per unit: 8 hours @ $1.30 per hour.
Standard direct material per unit:
  Material P—10 pounds @ $.275 per pound.
  Material Q—5 units @ $.64 per unit.
Total standard cost per unit, including overhead on a direct labor hour basis: $23.55.

The following operating data were taken from the records for the month of March, 19—:

In process first of month: None.
Completed during month: 8,000 units.
In process end of month: 1,000 units, which are one-half complete as to labor and have had all of material P issued for them and sufficient material Q for one-half of them.

Direct labor: $88,440 (at a rate of $1.32 per hour).
Material issued to production:
  94,000 pounds of P @ $.26 per pound.
  42,600 units of Q @ $.65 per unit.
Overhead for the month: $61,640.

You are to prepare a schedule showing the variance of actual cost from standard cost and an analysis of variance for labor and material, separating each into the factors which caused them. Show all computations supporting your schedule.

(*AICPA*)

18-7. There are ten men working as a group on a particular project. When the weekly production of the group exceeds a standard number of pieces per hour, each man in the group is paid a bonus for the excess production in addition to his wages at hourly rates. The amount of the bonus is computed by first determining the percentage by which the group's production exceeds the standard. One-half of this percentage is then applied to a wage rate of $1.25 to determine an hourly bonus rate. Each man in the group is paid, as a bonus, this bonus rate applied to his total hours worked during the week. The standard rate of production before a bonus can be earned is two hundred pieces per hour.

On the basis of the production record stated below, compute:

(a) The rate and amount of bonus for the week.
(b) The total wages of Allen, who worked forty hours at a base rate of $1.00 per hour, and of Knoll, who worked thirty-nine and one-half hours at a base rate of $1.50 per hour.

Production Record

	Hours Worked	Production
Monday................	72	17,680
Tuesday................	72	17,348
Wednesday.............	72	18,000
Thursday..............	72	18,560
Friday.................	71.5	17,888
Saturday..............	40	9,600
	399.5	99,076

(*AICPA*)

18-8. From the information following, prepare an income statement showing therein appropriate manufacturing cost variances of Bunsom Co., for January, 19–6, supported by journal entries of transactions for the month.

The Bunsom Co. makes unit M. The manufacturing of unit M is based on three successive and continuous operations, namely, operations M-10 to M-12, inclusive, in which the manufacturing cost of such unit is developed as shown by the following tabulation of percentages of cost of manufacture:

Percentages of Cost of Manufacture of Unit M

Operation	Material	Labor	Overhead
M-10..............	20%	20%	40%
M-11..............		35	40
M-12..............	80%	45	20
Total.........	100%	100%	100%

(The company does not record the actual labor charges applicable to each operation.)

The Bunsom Co. operates a cost accounting system based on standard costs which are incorporated in the manufacturing cost accounts. The differences between standard costs and actual costs are reflected in appropriate variance accounts, namely, material price, material usage, direct labor rate, direct labor time, and over-all manufacturing overhead. The material price variance is assumed to be realized at the time of purchase, irrespective of time of usage.

The standard manufacturing costs used for unit M (based on a planned monthly production ranging between 8,000 and 12,000 units M) are as follows:

	Per Unit M	
	Quantity or Hrs.	Amount
Material:		
Item M-a (issued in operation M-10)...................	1	$ .50
Item M-b (issued in operation M-12)..................	1	2.00
Direct labor (total for all operations at uniform rate of $5 per hour)..	¼ hr.	1.25
Overhead (applicable to operations as a whole):		
Variable expenses.....................................		.60
Fixed expenses..		.90
Manufacturing cost per unit.......................		$5.25

The inventories applicable to unit M as at December 31, 19–5, stated in accordance with the foregoing schedule of standard costs, are as follows:

> Material: Item M-a, 100 units; item M-b, 100 units.
> Work in progress: 50 units complete through operation M-10.
> Finished goods: None.

Transactions during January, 19–6, are submitted as follows:
The voucher register reflects applicable transactions paid and incurred as follows:

	Amount
Material purchases:	
Item M-a—12,000 units @ $.45 per unit...............	$ 5,400
Item M-b—12,000 units @ $2.10 per unit..............	25,200
Payroll for all operations:	
Direct labor—3,100 hours @ $1.2625 per ¼ hr...........	15,655
Indirect labor.......................................	1,500
Manufacturing overhead, other than indirect labor.......	15,000
Selling, administrative, and general expenses.............	25,000

Other facts are:

During January, 19–6, 11,000 units M were transferred to the finished goods warehouse and 10,500 units were sold at $9 per unit M.

As at January 31, 19–6, 100 units of work in progress are complete through operation M-11.

Stores requisitions indicate issuances of material items M-a and M-b in the quantities required for the production carried through the respective operations. A supplementary stores requisition, however, indicates that item M-a actually used was 2% in excess of standard quantity required.

(*AICPA*)

FACTORY EXPENSE CONTROL: FLEXIBLE BUDGETS

Factory expense control in general. Control of factory expense requires determining whether expense incurred was excessive and, if so, who was responsible for the excess spending. It involves maintaining expense accounts for the various supervisors who have authority to incur expense to determine how much expense each of them did incur during the period. These accounts may be set up by department or function (as in Chapter 12) where one supervisor has undivided authority for the expense of a particular department. Control of factory expense also involves determining how much expense each supervisor or department is *allowed* during a period for the activities performed. The amount of excess spending is calculated by comparing actual expenses for a period with allowed expenses for the period.

In some factories, factory expense is a major element of cost, and the opportunity for saving expense through the operation of proper controls is important. Although there are expenses over which the foreman has no control (for example, depreciation and taxes), there are likely to be other expenses over which the foreman does have authority. Examples of the latter expenses are certain indirect labor job classifications, supplies and repair parts of various kinds, and certain services. If there is no control plan, that is, if supervisors can add indirect labor job classifications and can requisition supplies and services more or less at will, there is almost certain to be waste. If there *is* a control plan, supervisors will realize that excess spending will be questioned, and they will give more careful consideration to adding indirect labor jobs and requisitioning supplies and services.

The expense allowances may be displayed for reporting purposes according to either of two plans. One plan is the fixed budget (described in Chapter 12) in which the original budget is formulated in relationship to expected volume, with no adjustment of the budget in case actual volume is different from the expected volume. Certain differences between actual expense and budget expense have to be interpreted in the light of actual volume compared with expected volume. The other plan is the flexible budget in which, for measurement of spending performance, the original budget is adjusted downward or upward to conform with current volume of operations. This plan is described in the present chapter. It will be noted that the so-called "control plan" comprises the mechanics of allocation (the calculation of expense rates for allocation of expense to standard cost cards) as well as true control (measurement of spending performance).

There are several methods of setting standards for factory expense, that is, of deciding how much the supervisor should be allowed per standard direct labor hour or other factor for measuring volume. They vary in simplicity and scientific accuracy. The allowances may be based upon intelligent guesses, or analysis of past actual expenses in relationship to volume, or industrial engineering studies of the same kind as the time and material standards described in the previous chapter.

The factory expense control plan of the Benson & West Manufacturing Company. This chapter describes the factory expense control plan of the Benson & West Manufacturing Company whose organization and plant were described in Chapter 12.

The plan comprises three parts:

(1) The calculation of a set of standard departmental expense rates at the beginning of each year, based upon expected volume, and the application of those rates to standard cost cards for products. As was indicated in Chapter 12, there are five departments, each of which would have its own standard expense rate:

> Service departments:
> General factory administration
> Building maintenance and fixed charges
>
> Producing departments:
> Cutting
> Assembly Department No. 1
> Assembly Department No. 2

(2) A set of departmental expense statements, similar to those in Chapter 12, but with special provision for *adjusting the budget of each department to current volume*, so that spending performance can be measured accurately.

(3) A "flexible budget," which is a budget set up for various volumes of operation. The flexible budget is intended to facilitate the operation of Part (1) and Part (2) of the control plan.

I. DEPARTMENTAL EXPENSE RATES AND STANDARD PRODUCT COSTS

Calculating standard expense rates. Standard departmental expense rates are a type of normal departmental expense rates, explained in Chapter 12. They are predetermined rates based upon some selected volume of operations for a specified period (often expressed in standard labor hours) and based upon a budget of factory expenses for that volume. Where there are both service departments and producing departments, as in this case, it is necessary to calculate standard expense rates for the service departments first and then to assess the producing departments for service expected to be used by them.

The calculation of standard factory expense rates for the Benson & West Manufacturing Company is illustrated in the table on page 451 (Figure 19-1a). It is exactly the same as the calculation of normal departmental expense rates in Chapter 12 (page 295), except that in the present case expected volume of operations is assumed to be measured in *standard* direct labor hours. It is expected that the departments will produce the following standard direct labor hours per month:

Cutting department....................	7,500
Assembly department No. 1............	8,000
Assembly department No. 2...........	20,000
Total.............................	35,500

The labor operations to be performed in the three departments, measured in the standard time set by the engineers, would total 7,500 for cutting department, 8,000 for assembly department No. 1, and 20,000 for assembly department No. 2.

The budget of factory expenses for the various departments at the volumes indicated appears on page 452 (Figure 19-1b). It is expected that the foremen can operate their departments on the following direct departmental expense budgets (totals) for the volumes shown:

Building maintenance and fixed charges.......	$4,021.07
General factory administration..............	5,473.20
Cutting department	3,203.09
Assembly department No. 1.................	2,706.32
Assembly department No. 2................	2,892.02

The standard departmental expense rates are calculated in the table on page 451 by the following steps:

(1) Compute a *standard rate per square foot* for building maintenance and fixed charges. $4,021.07 ÷ 40,210.5 square feet = $.10 per square foot. Distribute to the using departments on line 3.

(2) Enter the total of general factory administration expense, including its share of building maintenance and fixed charges ("rent") on Line 4. The total is $5,873.20.

(3) Compute a *rate per standard hour* for general factory administration. $5,873.20 ÷ 35,500 standard hours = $.165+ per standard hour. Distribute the total of general factory administration expense to the producing departments on the basis of budgeted standard hours (Line 5).

(4) Determine the total expense including service for each producing department. Enter on Line 6.

(5) Determine the total expense rate per standard hour for each producing

BENSON & WEST MANUFACTURING COMPANY
Standard Departmental Expense Rates

	Particulars	Building Maintenance and Fixed Charges	Administrative and Selling	General Factory Administration	Cutting Department	Assembly Department No. 1	Assembly Department No. 2	Totals
1	Expected hours to be produced..........			35,500	7,500	8,000	20,000	
2	Direct departmental expenses (from Figure 19-1b).....	$4,021.07	$	$5,473.20	$3,203.09	$2,706.32	$2,892.02	$18,295.70
3	Building maintenance and fixed charges: ("rent") @ $.10+ per square foot:		820.00	400.00	895.51	993.81	911.75	
	(distributed)	4,021.07*						
4	Total general factory administration.....			$5,873.20				
5	General factory administration distributed at $.16544 per standard hour:			5,873.20*	1,240.82	1,323.54	3,308.84	
6	Total producing department (and Administrative and Selling)..		$820.00		$5,339.42	$5,023.67	$7,112.61	
7	Rates per standard hour.....				$ .71192	$ .62796	$ .35563	
	Use.....				$ .71	$ .63	$ .36	

Building maintenance and fixed charges:

Department	Square Feet	Amount
Administrative and selling.........	8,200	$ 820.00
General factory.........	4,000	400.00
Cutting department.........	8,955	895.51
Assembly department No. 1.........	9,938	993.81
Assembly department No. 2.........	9,117.5	911.75
Totals.........	40,210.5	$4,021.07

General factory administration:

Department	Standard Hours	Amount
Cutting department........	7,500	$1,240.82
Assembly department No. 1........	8,000	1,323.54
Assembly department No. 2........	20,000	3,308.84
Totals........	35,500	$5,873.20

*Credit

Figure 19-1a

department and enter on Line 7.   The formula is Total Expense (Line 7) ÷ Total standard hours (Line 1) = Expense rate per standard hour.   The rates are as follows:

Cutting department	$.71
Assembly department No. 1	.63
Assembly department No. 2	.36

BENSON & WEST MANUFACTURING COMPANY
Budget Factory Expense, by Departments: One Month

(Expected volume = 80% of practical capacity)

	Building Maintenance and Fixed Charges	General Factory Administration	Cutting Department	Assembly Department No. 1	Assembly Department No. 2
Standard Hours		35,500	7,500	8,000	20,000
Supervisory labor	$ 500.00	$3,200.00	$ 800.00	$ 700.00	$ 600.00
Clerical and production control labor		950.00	700.00	370.00	300.00
Machinists		500.00			
Janitors, watchmen, and firemen	1,100.00				
Other indirect labor			75.00	160.00	120.00
F.I.C.A. tax	32.00	93.00	256.50	224.60	520.40
Workmen's insurance	8.00	23.25	64.12	56.15	130.10
Provision for vacation pay	32.00	93.00	256.50	224.60	520.40
Printed forms and office supplies		177.50			
Factory operating supplies			300.00	120.00	80.00
Janitor supplies	40.00				
Coal	190.00				
Repairs to building	300.00				
Repairs and repair parts			225.00	160.00	40.00
Electric light and power	200.00	106.50	150.00	80.00	80.00
Telephone and telegraph		71.00			
Professional engineers' fees		100.00			
Unclassified	119.07	101.79	108.25	133.82	23.97
Depreciation on building	800.00				
Depreciation on office furniture and fixtures		9.16			
Depreciation on machinery and equipment		25.00	100.00	170.00	170.00
Insurance on building	400.00				
Insurance on office furniture and fixtures		2.00			
Insurance on machinery and equipment		6.00	25.00	40.00	40.00
Insurance on inventory			44.72	89.50	89.50
Taxes on building	300.00				
Taxes on furniture and fixtures		3.00			
Taxes on machinery and equipment		12.00	50.00	81.65	81.65
Taxes on inventory			48.00	96.00	96.00
	$4,021.07	$5,473.20	$3,203.09	$2,706.32	$2,892.02

Figure 19-1b

Standard product costs per unit.   The standard expense rates per hour are applied to the standard hours on standard cost cards for products. They are then extended to obtain the expense application to products. This step is illustrated on page 453.

II. DEPARTMENTAL EXPENSE STATEMENTS

Budget adjusted to current volume.   As was indicated at the beginning of this chapter, it is often useful to measure a supervisor's spending

BENSON & WEST MANUFACTURING COMPANY
Standard Product Costs per Unit and Standard Selling Prices per Unit

Based upon volume of 80% of practical capacity

Element and Department	Product A			Product B			Product C			Product D		
	Yards or Hours per Unit	Price or Rate	Total Amount per Product Unit	Yards or Hours per Unit	Price or Rate	Total Amount per Product Unit	Yards or Hours per Unit	Price or Rate	Total Amount per Product Unit	Yards or Hours per Unit	Price or Rate	Total Amount per Product Unit
Materials..........	3 yards	$ .50	$1.50	2 yards	$ .60	$1.20	2 yards	$ .80	$1.60	2 yards	$1.50	$ 3.00
Labor:												
Cutting department........	.25 hour	1.50	.375	.25 hour	1.50	.375	.25 hour	1.50	.375	.5 hour	1.50	.75
Assembly department No. 1....	1.0 hour	1.25	1.25	1.5 hour	1.25	1.875	1.5 hour	1.25	1.875	2.0 hours	1.25	2.50
Assembly department No. 2....												
Factory expense:												
Cutting department.........	.25 hour	.71	.178	.25 hour	.71	.178	.25 hour	.71	.178	.5 hour	.71	.355
Assembly department No. 1....	1.0 hour	.63	.63	1.5 hour	.63	.945	1.5 hour	.63	.945	2.0 hours	.36	.72
Assembly department No. 2....												
Totals per product unit..........			$3.933			$4.573			$4.973			$ 7.325
Standard (desired average) selling prices per unit..........			$7.10			$7.90			$8.40			$10.50

Figure 19-2

performance by comparing his actual expense with budget expense which has been adjusted to current volume of operations.   Essentially, this plan requires separating the expense accounts of a department into three groups: *fixed expenses*, which in the short run do not vary with changes in volume, *variable expenses*, which vary directly with changes in volume measured in standard hours produced, and *semivariable expenses*, which vary with changes in volume but not directly with those changes.

Under this plan, a supervisor's budget for variable expenses is increased currently as volume goes up.   His budget for fixed expenses is not changed, except in special circumstances.   His budget for semivariable expenses is increased in steps as volume of production goes up, as will be illustrated in this chapter.

The departmental expense statements for the Benson & West Manufacturing Company shown on the following pages illustrate how the statements are set up.   They also provide numerous examples of expense accounts which may be considered fixed, variable, and semivariable, respectively.

Statements illustrated.   Three departmental expense statements are illustrated herewith:

> Building Maintenance and Fixed Charges, page 455.
> General Factory Administration, page 457.
> Cutting Department, page 459.

These statements are the same as those for the same departments in Chapter 12 (pages 276 to 278), except for the adjustment of budget to current level and the method of showing expense charged out of the departments.

The Building Maintenance and Direct Charges statement is based upon a fixed budget.   The budget is set up at the beginning of the year by estimating each of the accounts and arriving at the total for one month ($4,021.07), which amount is not adjusted during the year.   As shown on page 455, the spending variance is simply the difference between actual expense (column 2) and the original budget (column 1).

The General Factory Administration statement (page 457) and the Cutting Department statement (page 459) are both based upon flexible budgets.   In the former case, the original budget totaling $5,473.20 (total departmental expense) is based upon a volume of 35,500 hours.   During March, the factory worked only 30,950 hours, and the total budget was reduced to $5,101.15 (total departmental expense).   *How* the adjustment is made is explained later.   Spending variance for General Factory Administration (column 5) is accordingly Actual Expense (column 4) minus Budget Adjusted to Current Volume (column 3).   The excess spending is $58.01.

Use of the Budget Adjusted to Current Volume column is a formal attempt to recognize the fact that, if the level of operations falls, certain expenses (called the "variable" expenses) should be expected to fall also, whereas other expenses (the "fixed" expenses) cannot be expected to fall. The theory is that the original budget is not a satisfactory measure of spending performance when the level of operation is significantly below the level on which the original budget was based. The adjusted budget is used in an attempt to make the spending variance a more satisfactory measure of spending performance than one computed on the basis of the original budget.

The Cutting Department statement shows a similar adjustment. Note that current volume for March is 5,150 standard hours against the original budget of 7,500 standard hours, and the total direct departmental expense is accordingly adjusted downward from $3,203.09 to $2,565.49.

BENSON & WEST MANUFACTURING COMPANY
Expense Variance Report

Illustrating statement based upon fixed budget

Department   Building Maintenance and Fixed Charges

Month   March   19__

Particulars	(1) Original Budget	(2) Actual Expense	(3) Spending Variance
Direct department expense:			
Supervision......................	$ 500.00	$ 500.00	$
Janitors, firemen, and watchmen........	1,100.00	1,150.00	50.00
F.I.C.A. tax (2% of labor).............	32.00	33.00	1.00
Workmen's insurance (½% of labor).....	8.00	8.25	.25
Provision for vacation pay (2% of labor)	32.00	33.00	1.00
Janitors' supplies....................	40.00	42.00	2.00
Coal.................................	190.00	195.00	5.00
Repairs to building...................	300.00	280.00	20.00*
Electric light and power..............	200.00	210.00	10.00
Unclassified.........................	119.07	205.00	85.93
Depreciation on building..............	800.00	800.00	
Insurance on building.................	400.00	400.00	
Taxes on building....................	300.00	300.00	
Total direct departmental expense.....	$4,021.07	$4,156.25	$135.18
($4,021.07 + 40,210.5 square feet = $.10+ per square foot)			
Expense charged to other departments.....	$4,021.07*	4,021.07*	
Spending variance.....................		$ 135.18	

* Red.

Column (1) is the *original budget* set at the beginning of the year. Standard rate per square foot for rent = $4,021.07 ÷ 40,210.5 square feet = $.10+ per square foot (same as Figure 19-1a).

Figure 19-3

PROCEDURE

Preparing the expense report: Building maintenance and fixed charges. The Building Maintenance and Fixed Charges report (page 455) is based upon a *fixed budget*. Column (1) is the original budget as set up at the beginning of the year when the standard expense rates were calculated. Note that the total original budget is $4,021.07, which was the amount used in calculating the standard rate for rent (page 451). Column (2) is actual expenses by object classification per the expense account for the department. (The departmental expense account is in Chapter 12, page 286.) Column (3) is the spending variance for the month (column [2] − column [1]). This column shows what object accounts were overspent and what ones showed a saving over the budget for the month. The total (or net) spending variance is shown at the bottom of the report.

Note the method of calculating F.I.C.A. tax, workmen's insurance, and provision for vacation pay on expense reports on this statement (and on Figures 19-4 and 19-5).

Preparing the expense reports: Budget adjusted to current volume. The second and third expense reports are based upon flexible budgets. In the General Factory Administration report (page 457), note that column (2) is the original budget adopted at the beginning of the year when the expense rates were computed. It includes (a) the estimated direct departmental expense for 35,500 standard hours (broken down by expense account), totaling $5,473.20 and (b) the charge for building maintenance and fixed charges ("rent") *calculated at the beginning of the year* (4,000 square feet @ $.10 per square foot = $400, page 451).

Note the standard rate per hour for general factory administration expense calculated at the foot of the Original Budget column: $5,873.20 ÷ 35,500 = $.16544 per hour. This calculation is of course the same as in the standard rate calculations at the beginning of the year (page 451). In fact, once the original budget and the standard rate have been determined at the beginning of the year (worksheet for standard rates, page 451), they are the same each month for the full year.

Column (3)—Budget adjusted to current volume—is based upon total actual hours worked by all the producing departments during March (30,950 hours).

> Fixed expense items (F) are the same as in column (2).
>
> Variable expense items (V) are 30,950 (actual hours) × the appropriate budget rate/hour, column (1). Thus for printed forms and office supplies: 30,950 hours × $.005 per hour = $154.75. Variable expense rates are taken from the flexible budget explained on page 466.
>
> Semivariable expenses (S-V) are obtained from the flexible budget (explained on pages 462-474), which shows at what points an expense allowance changes.

BENSON & WEST MANUFACTURING COMPANY
Expense Variance Report

Department __General Factory Administration__

Month _____   March, 19___

Illustrating adjustment of budget to current volume

Particulars	Variability	(1) Budget Rate/Hour: Variable	(2) Original Budget for Normal Volume 35,500	(3) Budget Adjusted to Current Volume 30,950	(4) Actual Expense	(5) Spending Variance (4) − (3)
Budget hours................				30,950		
Actual hours................						
Direct departmental expense:						
Supervisory labor...........	F		$3,200.00	$3,200.00	$3,200.00	$
Clerical and production control labor......	S-V		950.00	825.00	850.00	25.00
Machinists........	S-V		500.00	325.00	350.00	25.00
F.I.C.A. tax (2% of labor).......	S-V		93.00	87.00	88.00	1.00
Workmen's insurance (½% of labor)......	S-V		23.25	21.75	22.00	.25
Provision for vacation pay (2% of labor).....	S-V		93.00	87.00	88.00	1.00
Printed forms and office supplies........	V	.005	177.50	154.75	156.00	1.25
Electric light and power.........	V	.003	106.50	92.85	95.00	2.15
Telephone and telegraph.......	V	.002	71.00	61.90	63.00	1.10
Professional engineers' fees......	F		100.00	100.00	100.00	
Unclassified.............	V	.002+	101.79	88.74	90.00	1.26
Depreciation on office furniture and fixtures......	F		9.16	9.16	9.16	
Depreciation on machinery and equipment.......	F		25.00	25.00	25.00	
Insurance on office furniture and fixtures.......	F		2.00	2.00	2.00	
Insurance on machinery and equipment........	F		6.00	6.00	6.00	
Taxes on office furniture and fixtures.......	F		3.00	3.00	3.00	
Taxes on machinery and equipment......	F		12.00	12.00	12.00	
Total direct departmental expense........			$5,473.20	$5,101.15	$5,159.16	$58.01
Rent: 4,000 square feet @ $.10 per square foot......	F		400.00	400.00	400.00	
Total department (Standard expense rate calculated)........		$.16544	$5,873.20	$5,501.15	$5,559.16	$58.01
		.16544				
	35,500 hours	30,950 hours				
General factory administration expense charged to other departments......				5,120.37*	5,120.37*	
Volume variance (Budget adjusted to current volume − Charges to other departments).......				$ 380.78		
Net variance (Actual expense − Charges to other departments)......					$ 438.79	

Budget adjusted to current volume (March)

Column (2) is the *original budget* set at the beginning of the year. Standard rate per hour for general factory administration is: $5,873.20 ÷ 35,500 = $.165+ (same as Figure 19-1a)

* Red.

Figure 19-4

On the flexible budget (page 466), use the expense allowance shown in the column for 26,625 hours, which is the tabulated level next below 30,950 hours (30,950 is not a tabulated level).   Total clerical and production control labor (actually one F occupation and three S-V occupations) is $825.00.

Column (4) is actual expenses by object classification per the expense account for the department.   (The actual direct departmental expenses shown on this report are obtained from the General Factory Administration Expense account in Chapter 12, page 287.)   Note that the charge for rent is 4,000 square feet @ *the standard rate of $.10 per square foot* = $400.

Column (5) is Spending Variance: Column (4) Actual Expense minus Column (3) Budget Adjusted to Current Volume.

General Factory Administration Charged to Other Departments (at the bottom of the statement) is Actual hours (30,950) × *Standard rate* per hour ($.16544) = $5,120.37.

Note that an analysis of underabsorbed expense appears at the bottom of the statement:

Spending variance:		
Actual expense..........................	$5,559.16	
Budget adjusted to current volume.........	5,501.15	
Excess over budget......................		$ 58.01
Volume variance:		
Budget adjusted to current volume.........	$5,501.15	
Expense charged to other departments......	5,120.37	
Volume variance....................		380.78
Total variance...........................		$438.79

Preparing the expense report for the cutting department.   In the Cutting Department Expense Report (page 459):

Column (2) is the original budget for one month at the expected volume of 7,500 hours.   It includes direct departmental expense for the expected volume, a charge for rent, and a charge for general factory administration (7,500 hours @ the standard rate of $.165+ per hour).

Note the standard rate per hour for cutting expense calculated at the foot of the Original Budget column: $5,339.42 ÷ 7,500 hours = $.71 per hour.   This calculation is the same as in the standard rate calculation at the beginning of the year (worksheet for standard rates, page 451.)

Column (3) is the budget adjusted to current volume.   This adjusted budget is based upon *standard hours produced* by the department during March (5,150 standard hours).

Column (4) is the actual expense for March per the expense account for the cutting department.   The actual direct departmental expenses shown on this report are obtained from the Cutting Department expense account in Chapter 12, page 288.)   Service charges include rent (8,955 square feet @ *standard rate* of $.10+ per square foot = $895.51) and general factory

Department .... Cutting

Month .... March .... 19..

Particulars	Variability	(1) Budget Rate/Hour: Variable	(2) Original Budget for Normal Volume 7,500	(3) Budget Adjusted to Current Volume 5,150	(4) Actual Expense 5,280	(5) Variance (4) − (3)
Budget hours..........			7,500			
Standard hours produced..........				5,150		
Actual hours..........					5,280	
Direct labor cost (Standard rate. $1.50)..........			$11,250.00	$7,725.00	$8,184.00	$459.00
Total indirect labor (as below)..........			1,575.00	1,351.50	1,360.00	8.50
						Spending Variance
Direct departmental expense:						
Supervision..........	S-V		$ 800.00	$ 700.00	$ 700.00	$
Clerical..........	S-V		700.00	600.00	600.00	
Other indirect labor..........	V	.01	75.00	51.50	60.00	8.50
F.I.C.A. tax (2% of total labor at top of column)..........	S-V		256.50	181.53	190.88	9.35
Workmen's insurance (½% of total labor)..........	S-V		64.12	45.38	47.72	2.34
Provision for vacation pay (2% of total labor)..........	S-V		256.50	181.53	190.88	9.35
Factory operating supplies..........	V	.04	300.00	206.00	210.00	4.00
Repairs and repair parts..........	V	.03	225.00	154.50	160.00	5.50
Electric light and power..........	V	.02	150.00	103.00	110.00	7.00
Unclassified..........	V	.01+	108.25	74.33	75.00	.67
Depreciation on machinery and equipment..........	F		100.00	100.00	100.00	
Insurance on inventory..........	F		44.72	44.72	44.72	
Insurance on machinery and equipment..........	F		25.00	25.00	25.00	
Taxes on inventory..........	F		48.00	48.00	48.00	
Taxes on machinery and equipment..........	F		50.00	50.00	50.00	
Total direct departmental expense..........			$ 3,203.09	$2,565.49	$2,612.20	$ 46.71
Service charges:						
Rent: 8,955 square feet @ $.10+ per square foot..........	F		895.51	895.51	895.51	
General factory administration:	V					
Original budget..........			1,240.82			
Adjusted budget..........				852.02		
Actual..........					873.52	21.50
Total department expense (Standard expense rate calculated)..........		.71	$ 5,339.42	$4,313.02	$4,351.23	$ 68.21
Cutting department expense charged to Work in Process (Standard hours produced)..........		.71		3,656.50	3,656.50	
Volume variance (Budget adjusted to current volume − charge to Work in Process)..........				$ 656.52		
Net variance (Actual expense − charge to Work in Process)..........						$ 724.73

7,500 hours   .16544
5,150 hours   .16544
5,280 hours   .16544
7,500 hours   .71

5,150 hours   .71

Budget adjusted to current volume (March)

Column (2) is the *original budget* set at the beginning of the year. Standard rate per hour for cutting department is:
$5,339.42 ÷ 7,500 = $.71 (Same as Figure 19-1a)

Figure 19-5

administration (5,280 actual hours @ *standard rate* of $.165+ per hour = $873.52).

Column (5) is spending variance (total, $68.21).

Volume variance ($656.52) and net variance ($724.73) are shown at the bottom of the report.

The expense reports for assembly department No. 1 and assembly department No. 2 are similar to the expense report for the cutting department. They are illustrated in Appendix I.

Operating the departmental expense accounts. The *actual direct* departmental expenses shown on the reports above are obtained from departmental expense accounts illustrated in Chapter 12 (departmental expense accounts). Charges to using departments for service received *may* or *may not* be recorded in the expense accounts depending upon whether it is desired to show variances *by department* in the accounts. (They would in any case be shown on the statements, as illustrated above.) If they *are* recorded, the using departments are charged at standard rates, as was done on the statements above.

Illustrative entries for service department charges to using departments. This illustration assumes that service charges are recorded in the accounts, as well as on the statements. Each department is charged for actual service used × the *standard rate*.

(1)

Administrative and selling expense	$ 820.00	
General factory administration	400.00	
Cutting department	895.51	
Assembly department No. 1	993.81	
Assembly department No. 2	911.75	
Building maintenance and fixed charges		$4,021.07

To charge using departments for rent at standard rate of $.10 per square foot:

Department	Square Feet	Standard Charges
Administrative and selling	8,200	$ 820.00
Factory administration	4,000	400.00
Cutting department	8,955	895.51
Assembly department No. 1	9,938	993.81
Assembly department No. 2	9,117.5	911.75
Totals	40,210.5	$4,021.07

(2)

Cutting department	$ 873.52	
Assembly department No. 1	1,086.94	
Assembly department No. 2	3,159.91	
General factory administration		$5,120.37

To charge using departments for general factory administration at standard rate of $.16544 per actual hour:

Department	Actual Hours	Amount
Cutting department...............	5,280	$ 873.52
Assembly department No. 1........	6,570	1,086.94
Assembly department No. 2........	19,100	3,159.91
Totals......................	30,950	$5,120.37

Charge expense into work in process. The expense charge to Work in Process is computed by the formula: Standard hours produced × Standard factory expense rate. Assuming the following production:

	Standard Hours
Cutting department............	5,150
Assembly department No. 1....	6,545
Assembly department No. 2....	19,000
Total....................	30,695

The entry to charge expense into work in process is:

(3)

Work in Process..	$14,619.85	
Cutting department....................................		$3,656.50
Assembly department No. 1............................		4,123.35
Assembly department No. 2............................		6,840.00

To charge Work in Process for factory expense applicable to production:

Department	Standard Hours Produced	Standard Expense Rate	Standard Expense Applied
Cutting department..........	5,150	$.71	$ 3,656.50
Assembly department No. 1...	6,545	.63	4,123.35
Assembly department No. 2...	19,000	.36	6,840.00
Totals..................	30,695		$14,619.85

Expense accounts posted. After the entries in the previous sections have been posted, the expense accounts appear as follows:

Building Maintenance and Fixed Charges

Total direct departmental expense (VR & GJ) $ 4,156.25 Net variance $135.18	Rent charged to other departments	(1) $4,021.07

General Factory Administration

Total direct departmental expense (VR & GJ) $ 5,159.16 Rent (1) 400.00 Net variance $438.79	Charged to other departments	(2) $5,120.37

Cutting Department

Total direct departmental expense	(VR & GJ)	$ 2,612.20	Charged to Work in Process	(3)	$3,656.50
Rent	(1)	895.51			
General factory administration	(2)	873.52			
Net variance $724.73					

Assembly Department No. 1

Total direct departmental expense	(VR & GJ)	$ 2,430.45	Charged to Work in Process	(3)	$4,123.35
Rent	(1)	993.81			
General factory administration	(2)	1,086.94			
Net variance $387.85					

Assembly Department No. 2

Total direct departmental expense	(VR & GJ)	$ 2,775.90	Charged to Work in Process	(3)	$6,840.00
Rent	(1)	911.75			
General factory administration	(2)	3,159.91			
Net variance $7.56					

Work in Process

Standard expense applied	(3)	$14,619.85

Administrative and Selling Expense

Rent	(1) $	820.00

The net variances per the departmental expense accounts agree with the net variances per the reports.

III. FLEXIBLE EXPENSE BUDGETS

What flexible expense budgets are: Uses.   Flexible expense budgets are multiple level budgets. They are intended to show what the expense should be at each of several selected levels of operation. They are based upon recognition of the fact that some expenses can be expected to rise and fall with level of operations, and certain other expenses cannot be expected to so rise and fall.

Flexible expense budgets are set up at the beginning of the year. They are the basis for (1) calculating the standard expense rates (after standard volume of operating for the coming period has been set) as explained on page 450, and (2) setting up expense reports at the end of each month, with budget-adjusted-to-current-volume allowances for measuring spending performance.

Budgets illustrated. Expense budgets for the various departments of the Benson & West Manufacturing Company appear on pages 464-469:

The Building Maintenance and Fixed Charges Budget is shown on page 464. It is assumed in this illustration that this budget is set from year to year and that, for any particular year, it is a fixed budget. Note that in practice, such an item as repairs to building might be changed from year to year. The management may change the repairs budget from year to year on the basis of what projects have to be undertaken, according to the opinion of qualified maintenance engineers. It may also change the allowance for financial reasons.

The General Factory Administration Budget is shown on page 466. This is a flexible budget, providing expense allowances for three levels: 100 per cent, 80 per cent, and 60 per cent of practical capacity. At capacity, the producing departments of the factory can produce goods equivalent to 44,375 standard labor hours. At 80 per cent of capacity, the factory can produce 35,500 standard hours and at 60 per cent, the factory can produce 26,625 standard hours.

The flexible budgets for the cutting room, assembly department No. 1 and assembly department No. 2 appear on pages 467-469. They are constructed in the same manner as the flexible budget for general factory administration.

A Schedule of Non-Cash Fixed Charges on Assets appears on page 470. This worksheet was used by the accountant to collect the fixed charges information needed to prepare the budgets.

The superintendent and the accountant set up the budgets. Note that in this connection, the degree of variability of the accounts is significant. The fixed expenses (designated "F") are the ones which the management believes cannot be expected to change in amount through any of the three levels of operation tabulated in the budget. The supervisory salaries and accounts in the depreciation, insurance, and taxes group are in this category. Each of the fixed expense account allowances is inserted in the same amount for each of the three levels.

The variable expenses (designated "V") are assumed in this illustration to vary with volume of production measured in standard hours produced.

For the purpose of this illustration, printed forms and office supplies, and certain accounts in the purchased services group are assumed to be in this category.

BENSON & WEST MANUFACTURING COMPANY

Factory Expense Budget
Building Maintenance and Fixed Charges

(*Period: One Month*)

Indirect labor:	
Supervisory—	
Building foreman...........................	$ 500.00
Janitors, fireman, and watchman—	
Janitors..................................	500.00
Fireman..................................	300.00
Watchman................................	300.00
Total indirect labor......................	$1,600.00
Payroll taxes, reserves, and insurance:	
F.I.C.A. tax...............................	$ 32.00
Workmen's insurance........................	8.00
Provision for vacation pay..................	32.00
Total.................................	$ 72.00
Supplies:	
Janitors' supplies...........................	$ 40.00
Coal..	190.00
Total.....................................	$ 230.00
Repairs to building...........................	$ 300.00
Electric light and power.......................	$ 200.00
Unclassified...................................	$ 119.07
Depreciation, insurance, and taxes:	
Depreciation on building.....................	$ 800.00
Insurance on building........................	400.00
Taxes on building............................	300.00
Total depreciation, insurance, and taxes.....	$1,500.00
Total department.............................	$4,021.07

Figure 19-6

The variable expenses are set on the basis of a study of actual spending for some periods in the past, made by the accountants, to determine the relationship which has existed between volume and expense. For each account, the amount allowed for capacity is entered in the 100 per cent column, 80 per cent of that amount in the next column, and 60 per cent of the capacity figure in the 60 per cent column.

Note that a *rate per hour* for each variable expense has been calculated and entered in the flexible budget, Figure 19-7:

	Rate per Hour
Printed forms and office supplies.........	$.005
Electric light and power................	.003
Telephone and telegraph................	.002
Unclassified.........................	.002+

The rate per hour for a variable expense is the total budgeted amount at practical capacity ÷ 44,375 hours. Since the flexible budgets are set up for only three levels (60 per cent, 80 per cent, and 100 per cent), the rates for variable expense are useful for interpolating at some level other than one of the three tabulated levels.

The semivariable expenses (designated "S-V") are those which are neither fixed nor variable directly with level of production. In some cases, they move up in steps as production increases. Thus, one inventory records clerk, one payroll clerk, and one machinist can handle all the work involved in their respective functions at the 60 per cent level. At the 80 per cent level a part-time person must be added in each of the three categories to help take care of the load, and at capacity, still more help will be required. The superintendent and the accountant decide *how much* help it is reasonable to add at each level.

The items in the payroll taxes, reserves, and insurance group, which are based upon total labor, are computed after total indirect labor has been set up in the budget for each of the three levels.

Note that in the above illustration, various object accounts have been arbitrarily included in variable or semivariable categories. The purpose has been to illustrate the mechanics of setting up the flexible budget. In a particular actual case, the grouping might be different from the one illustrated.

AN ALTERNATIVE METHOD OF HANDLING SEMIVARIABLE ALLOWANCES

Substituting fixed and variable allowances for semivariable allowances. In the previous sections of this chapter, expenses are classified for control purposes as variable, semivariable, and fixed. For each variable expense, a rate per standard hour was set. For each semivariable expense, a dollar amount was set for each volume of operations: the dollar amounts increased in irregular steps as volume increased. For each fixed expense a dollar allowance, constant for all levels of production normally expected, was set.

BENSON & WEST MANUFACTURING COMPANY
Flexible Budget—Factory Expense—General Factory Administration

(Period: One Month)

Object Classification	Variability	Variable: Rate per Hour	60% 26,625 Fixed	60% Variable and Semi-variable	80% 35,500 Fixed	80% Variable and Semi-variable	100% 44,375 Fixed	100% Variable and Semi-variable
Per cent of capacity								
Expected actual hours								
Indirect labor:								
Supervisory—	F							
Factory superintendent			$1,000.00	$	$1,000.00	$	$1,000.00	$
Purchasing agent			500.00		500.00		500.00	
Personnel manager			400.00		400.00		400.00	
Industrial engineer			500.00		500.00		500.00	
Master mechanic			450.00		450.00		450.00	
Head clerk, planning and production control			350.00		350.00		350.00	
Clerical and Production control—								
Planning and production clerks	F		300.00		300.00		300.00	
Inventory record clerk	S-V			250.00		300.00		350.00
Payroll clerks	S-V			275.00		350.00		425.00
Machinists	S-V			325.00		500.00		650.00
Payroll taxes, reserves, and insurance:								
F.I.C.A. tax	S-V			87.00		93.00		98.50
Workmen's insurance	S-V			21.75		23.25		24.63
Provision for vacation pay	S-V			87.00		93.00		98.50
Printed forms and office supplies	V	.005		133.13		177.50		221.88
Purchased services:								
Electric light and power	V	.003		79.88		106.50		133.13
Telephone and telegraph	V	.002		53.25		71.00		88.75
Professional engineers' fees	F		100.00		100.00		100.00	
Unclassified	V	.0028673		76.34		101.79		127.24
Depreciation, insurance, and taxes:	F							
Depreciation on office furniture and equipment			9.16		9.16		9.16	
Depreciation on machinery and equipment			25.00		25.00		25.00	
Insurance on office furniture and equipment			2.00		2.00		2.00	
Insurance on machinery and equipment			6.00		6.00		6.00	
Taxes on office furniture and equipment			3.00		3.00		3.00	
Taxes on machinery and equipment			12.00		12.00		12.00	
Total department: fixed and variable			$3,657.16	$1,388.35	$3,657.16	$1,816.04	$3,657.16	$2,217.63
Grand total				$5,045.51		$5,473.20		$5,874.79

Figure 19-7

466

BENSON & WEST MANUFACTURING COMPANY
Flexible Budget—Factory Expense—Cutting Department

(Period: One Month)

Object Classification	Varia-bility	Variable Expense: Rate/ Standard Hour	60% 5,625 Fixed	60% 5,625 Variable and Semi-variable	80% 7,500 Fixed	80% 7,500 Variable and Semi-variable	100% 9,375 Fixed	100% 9,375 Variable and Semi-variable
Per cent of capacity								
Standard hours								
Direct labor cost @ standard rate ($1.50 per hour)				$8,437.50		$11,250.00		$14,062.50
Total indirect labor				1,356.25		1,575.00		1,593.75
Total direct and indirect labor				$9,793.75		$12,825.00		$15,656.25
Indirect labor:								
Supervision—								
Cutting room foreman	F		$400.00		$400.00		$400.00	
Storekeepers	S-V•			$ 300.00		$ 400.00		$ 400.00
Clerical—								
Stores clerk	F		300.00		300.00		300.00	
Receiving clerks	S-V			300.00		400.00		400.00
Other indirect labor	V	.01		56.25		75.00		93.75
Payroll taxes, reserves, and insurance:								
F.I.C.A. tax	S-V			195.88		256.50		313.13
Workmen's insurance	S-V			48.97		64.12		78.28
Provision for vacation pay	S-V			195.88		256.50		313.13
Factory operating supplies; indirect materials	V	.04		225.00		300.00		375.00
Repairs and repair parts	V	.03		168.75		225.00		281.25
Electric light and power	V	.02		112.50		150.00		187.50
Unclassified	F	.0144338		81.19		108.25		135.32
Depreciation, insurance, and taxes:								
Depreciation on machinery and equipment—								
Materials storage			16.66		16.66		16.66	
Cutting			83.34		83.34		83.34	
Insurance on inventory			44.72		44.72		44.72	
Insurance on machinery and equipment—								
Materials storage			4.16		4.16		4.16	
Cutting			20.84		20.84		20.84	
Taxes on inventory			48.00		48.00		48.00	
Taxes on machinery and equipment—								
Materials storage			8.33		8.33		8.33	
Cutting			41.67		41.67		41.67	
Total department: fixed and variable			$967.72	$1,684.42	$967.72	$ 2,235.37	$967.72	$ 2,577.36
Grand total				$2,652.14		$ 3,203.09		$ 3,545.08

Per cent of capacity: 60%, 80%, 100%
Standard hours: 5,625 — 7,500 — 9,375

Figure 19-8

BENSON & WEST MANUFACTURING COMPANY
Flexible Budget—Factory Expense—Assembly Department No. 1

(Period: One Month)

Object Classification	Varia-bility	Variable Expense: Rate/ Standard Hour	60% 6,000 Fixed	60% 6,000 Variable and Semi-variable	80% 8,000 Fixed	80% 8,000 Variable and Semi-variable	100% 10,000 Fixed	100% 10,000 Variable and Semi-variable
Per cent of capacity								
Standard hours								
Direct labor cost @ standard rate (@ $1.25 per hour)				$7,500.00		$10,000.00		$12,500.00
Total indirect labor (as shown below)				1,020.00		1,230.00		1,400.00
Total direct and indirect labor				$8,520.00		$11,230.00		$13,900.00
Indirect labor:								
Supervision	S-V			$ 600.00		$ 700.00		$ 800.00
Clerical labor	S-V			300.00		370.00		400.00
Other indirect labor	V	.02		120.00		160.00		200.00
Payroll taxes, reserves, and insurance:								
F.I.C.A. tax	S-V			170.40		224.60		278.00
Workmen's insurance	S-V			42.60		56.15		69.50
Provision for vacation pay	S-V			170.40		224.60		278.00
Factory operating supplies	V	.015		90.00		120.00		150.00
Repairs and repair parts	V	.020		120.00		160.00		200.00
Electric light and power	V	.010		60.00		80.00		100.00
Unclassified	F	.016728		100.37		133.82		167.28
Depreciation, insurance, and taxes:								
Depreciation on machinery and equipment			170.00		170.00		170.00	
Insurance on inventory			89.50		89.50		89.50	
Insurance on machinery and equipment			40.00		40.00		40.00	
Taxes on inventory			96.00		96.00		96.00	
Taxes on machinery and equipment			81.65		81.65		81.65	
Total department: fixed and variable			$477.15	$1,773.77	$477.15	$2,229.17	$477.15	$ 2,642.78
Grand total				$2,250.92		$ 2,706.32		$ 3,119.93

Figure 19-9

468

BENSON & WEST MANUFACTURING COMPANY
Flexible Budget—Factory Expense—Assembly Department No. 2

(Period: One Month)

Object Classification	Variability	Variable Expense: Rate/Standard Hour	60% 15,000 Fixed	60% 15,000 Variable and Semi-variable	80% 20,000 Fixed	80% 20,000 Variable and Semi-variable	100% 25,000 Fixed	100% 25,000 Variable and Semi-variable
Per cent of capacity								
Standard hours								
Direct labor cost @ standard rate ($1.25 per hour)				$18,750.00		$25,000.00		$31,250.00
Total indirect labor (as shown below)				890.00		1,020.00		1,250.00
Total direct and indirect labor				$19,640.00		$26,020.00		$32,500.00
Indirect labor:								
Supervision	S-V		$	$ 500.00	$	$ 600.00	$	$ 700.00
Clerical labor	S-V			300.00		300.00		400.00
Other indirect labor	V	.006		90.00		120.00		150.00
Payroll taxes, reserves, and insurance:								
F.I.C.A. tax	S-V	.004		392.80		520.40		650.00
Workmen's insurance	S-V	.002		98.20		130.10		137.50
Provision for vacation pay	S-V	.004		392.80		520.40		650.00
Factory operating supplies	V	.004		60.00		80.00		100.00
Repairs and repair parts	V	.002		30.00		40.00		50.00
Electric light and power	V	.004		60.00		80.00		100.00
Unclassified	V	.0011985		17.98		23.97		29.96
Depreciation, insurance and taxes:	F							
Depreciation on machinery and equipment			170.00		170.00		170.00	
Insurance on inventory			89.50		89.50		89.50	
Insurance on machinery and equipment			40.00		40.00		40.00	
Taxes on inventory			96.00		96.00		96.00	
Taxes on machinery and equipment			81.65		81.65		81.65	
Total department: fixed and variable			$477.15	$ 1,941.78	$477.15	$ 2,414.87	$477.15	$ 2,967.46
Grand total				$ 2,418.93		$ 2,892.02		$ 3,444.61

Figure 19-10

469

BENSON & WEST MANUFACTURING COMPANY
Schedule of Noncash Fixed Charges on Assets
(Period: One Month)

Noncash Charges	Totals	General Administration	Sales Department	Order Department and Cash Collecting	Finished Goods Warehouse	Garage and Delivery Department	Building and Building Maintenance	General Factory	Repair Shop	Raw Materials Storage	Cutting Department	Assembly Department No. 1	Assembly Department No. 2
Depreciation:													
Building	$ 800.00	$	$	$	$	$	$ 800.00	$	$	$	$	$	$
Office furniture and equipment	175.82	33.33	33.33	100.00				9.16					
Display fixtures	33.33		33.33										
Autos	275.00		275.00										
Delivery trucks	125.00					125.00							
Machinery and equipment	673.34				166.67	41.67			25.00	16.66	83.34	170.00	170.00
Total depreciation	$2,082.49												
Insurance:													
Inventory (estimated)	$ 358.72				135.00					44.72		89.50	89.50
Building	400.00						400.00						
Office furniture and equipment	43.66	8.33	8.33	25.00				2.00					
Display fixtures	8.33		8.33										
Autos	91.67		91.67										
Delivery trucks	33.34					33.34							
Machinery and equipment	152.66				33.33	8.33			6.00	4.16	20.84	40.00	40.00
Total insurance	$1,088.38												
Taxes:													
Inventory (estimated)	$ 390.00				150.00					48.00		96.00	96.00
Building	300.00						300.00						
Office furniture and equipment	52.00	10.00		35.00				3.00					
Display fixtures	4.00		4.00										
Autos	45.83		45.83										
Delivery trucks	40.00					40.00							
Machinery and equipment	287.30				50.00	12.00			12.00	8.33	41.67	81.65	81.65
Automobile and truck licenses	25.83		20.00			5.83							
Total taxes	$1,144.96												
Total noncash charges	$4,315.83	$51.66	$523.82	$160.00	$535.00	$266.17	$1,500.00	$14.16	$43.00	$121.87	$145.85	$477.15	$477.15

Figure 19-11

In some flexible budget plans, the semivariable expense classification is in effect eliminated by resolving each semivariable expense into fixed and variable components.   Thus, instead of setting up a dollar allowance for each specified level for indirect labor, the budget man would make a two-way allowance: a fixed allowance of say $760 and a variable allowance of say $.046 per standard direct labor hour.

When this is done, the preparation of budgets for any level of operations is simplified.   To prepare a budget for *any* level, it is necessary to know the rates per standard hour and the fixed allowances applicable to each expense account.

One of the advantages claimed for this plan is that it can be easily taught to foremen and used by foremen.   Instead of working with budgets tabulated in a series of levels, the foreman works with a set of rates per standard hour and a set of fixed allowances.   From these factors, he can compute his budget for any level.   It is often important to give the foreman the means of figuring his budget at the beginning of the month, when he is planning his operations.   This may be better than to give him nothing but a variance report after the end of the month when the operations have been completed.

Figure 19-12 illustrates one method of setting fixed and variable expense allowances for a semivariable expense (in this case, indirect labor for assembly department No. 1).   Assume that standard hours produced and actual indirect labor for a six-month period are:

Month	Hours	Amount
January..................	8,500	$1,220.00
February...............	5,000	1,000.00
March.................	6,050	1,021.00
April...................	7,950	1,059.00
May...................	9,900	1,249.00
June.................	5,750	1,015.00

The procedure for setting a fixed and a variable allowance for indirect labor is:

(1) Plot indirect labor dollars and standard direct labor hours by month on a graph illustrated in Figure 19-12.   The vertical scale is dollars and the horizontal scale is standard hours.   Note that the numbers in circles identify the months (1 = January, 2 = February, and so on).

(2) Draw a trend line (*AB*) by sight through the plotted positions so that there are roughly as many plotted positions below the line as there are above the line. This is the variable expense line.

(3) Draw the horizontal fixed charge line (*AC*).   This line is drawn horizontally from the point where the variable expense line (*AB*) intersects the zero standard hours line (that is, from point *A*).

(4) Read the fixed expense allowance.   It is $760 for any volume.

(5) Read the variable expense total for practical capacity (10,000 hours).   It is $480.

(6) Compute the variable expense rate *per standard hour*.   It is $480 ÷ 10,000 = $.048 per standard hour.

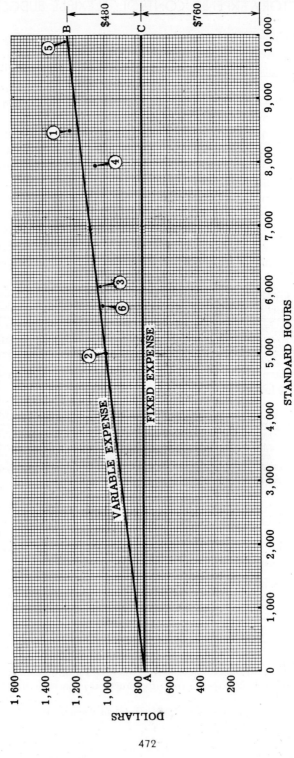

Indirect Labor—Assembly Department No. 1
Analysis of Totals for Six Months Into Fixed and Variable Components

STANDARD HOURS

Figure 19-12

BENSON & WEST MANUFACTURING COMPANY

Budget Factory Expense: Assembly Department No. 1
By Months—Six Months Ending June 30, 19___

Particulars	Variability	Variable Expense Rate/Standard Hour	January 8,500 Fixed	Variable	February 5,000 Fixed	Variable	March 6,050 Fixed	Variable	April 7,950 Fixed	Variable	May 9,960 Fixed	Variable	June 5,760 Fixed	Variable
Direct labor cost @ standard rate ($1.25/hour)			$	$10,625.00	$	$6,250.00	$	$7,562.50	$	$ 9,937.50	$	$12,437.50	$	$7,187.50
Total indirect labor (as shown below)			760.00	408.00	760.00	240.00	760.00	290.40	760.00	381.60	760.00	477.60	760.00	276.00
Total labor			$ 760.00	$11,033.00	$ 760.00	$6,490.00	$ 760.00	$7,852.90	$ 760.00	$10,319.10	$ 760.00	$12,915.10	$ 760.00	$7,463.50
Indirect labor		.048	$ 760.00	$ 408.00	$ 760.00	$ 240.00	$ 760.00	$ 290.40	$ 760.00	$ 381.60	$ 760.00	$ 477.60	$ 760.00	$ 276.00
Payroll taxes, reserves, and insurance (4½% of labor)		.015	34.20	496.13	34.20	292.11	34.20	353.38	34.20	464.35	34.20	581.18	34.20	335.86
Factory operating supplies		.020		127.50		75.00		90.75		119.25		149.25		86.25
Repairs and repair parts		.010		170.00		100.00		121.00		159.00		199.00		115.00
Electric light and power		.016728		85.00		50.00		60.50		79.50		99.50		57.50
Unclassified				142.19		83.64		101.20		132.99		166.44		96.18
Depreciation on machinery and equipment	F		170.00		170.00		170.00		170.00		170.00		170.00	
Insurance on inventory	F		89.50		89.50		89.50		89.50		89.50		89.50	
Insurance on machinery and equipment	F		40.00		40.00		40.00		40.00		40.00		40.00	
Taxes on inventory	F		96.00		96.00		96.00		96.00		96.00		96.00	
Taxes on machinery and equipment	F		81.65		81.65		81.65		81.65		81.65		81.65	
Total factory expense: Fixed and variable			$1,271.35	$ 1,428.82	$1,271.35	$ 840.75	$1,271.35	$1,017.23	$1,271.35	$ 1,336.70	$1,271.35	$ 1,672.97	$1,271.35	$ 966.79
Total factory expense: together				$ 2,700.17		$2,112.10		$2,288.58		$ 2,608.05		$ 2,944.32		$2,238.14

Figure 19-13

Using fixed allowances and variable rates to set the factory expense budget.   Figure 19-13 is a six-month budget for assembly department No. 1, set by the use of fixed allowances and variable expense rates:

Account	Fixed Allowance per Month	Expense Rate per Standard Hour
Indirect labor...........................	$760.00	$.048
Payroll taxes, reserves, and insurance....	4½% of labor	
Factory operating supplies..............		.015
Repairs and repair parts...............		.020
Electric light and power...............		.010
Unclassified...........................		.016728
Depreciation on machinery and equipment	$170.00	
Insurance on inventory.................	89.50	
Insurance on machinery and equipment..	40.00	
Taxes on inventory.....................	96.00	
Taxes on machinery and equipment......	81.65	

Note the allowances for indirect labor: January, $760 fixed + (8,500 × $.048 = $408); February, $760 fixed + (5,000 × $.048 = $240), and so forth.   All the other accounts are assumed to be either purely variable or purely fixed.   In practice, some of the items shown as variable might actually be semivariable and therefore be resolved to fixed and variable allowances as illustrated for indirect labor.

IV. SUMMARY

The steps in a complete plan.   The various parts of a complete plan of expense control have been explained in this chapter.   The author began with the part with which the reader was already familiar: the calculation of expense rates.   This was done to provide an easy introduction.   It is now useful to indicate the chronological order in which the steps would be performed in actual operation.

At the beginning of the year:

(1) Set up flexible expense budgets, one for each department, to show the expected expense for each of several levels of operation (say 60 per cent, 80 per cent, and 100 per cent of capacity).

(2) Compute standard expense rate for each department on the basis of some particular volume of operation.

(3) Apply the producing department expense rates to the standard cost cards.

At the end of each month:

(4) Draft entries to:

    (a) Charge actual direct departmental expenses to the departmental expense accounts.

(b) Charge service department expense to the using departments in the accounts (if desired).

(c) Charge expense of producing departments to Work in Process.

(5) Prepare departmental expense reports. On these reports, compare actual expense with budget adjusted to the volume of operations attained. To adjust the budget, use appropriate factors (with reference to variable and fixed expense) previously set up in the flexible expense budgets (paragraph 1).

QUESTIONS

19-1. (a) What is a flexible budget for the control of factory expense?

(b) Define variable expense, semivariable expense, and fixed expense.

(c) Discuss briefly the uses of a flexible expense budget.

19-2. Compare the worksheet for calculating standard departmental expense rates (Figure 19-1a) with the worksheet for calculating normal departmental expense rates (Figure 12-14). Discuss any differences.

19-3. Name the uses of standard factory expense rates for (a) producing departments and (b) service departments.

19-4. What are the fundamental differences between the departmental expense reports illustrated in Chapter 19 and those illustrated in Chapter 12?

19-5. (a) "The foreman of a department is charged (in the actual column of his departmental expense statement) with actual floor space × standard rate per square foot for rent, actual hours worked in his department × standard rate for general factory administration, and actual kw. hrs. × standard rate per kw. hr. for power supplied by the company power plant." Is this statement correct?

(b) If you were the foreman, would you prefer being charged with *actual* rates for service as in Chapter 12, or with standard rates for service, as in Chapter 19?

19-6. (a) "In the Budget Adjusted to Current Volume column, variable expenses are entered at standard hours produced × the standard rate per hour for the particular expense, semivariable expense is entered at the amount shown for the particular expense in the flexible budget, and fixed expenses are entered at the amount shown in the original budget set up at the beginning of the year." Is this statement correct with reference to a producing department?

(b) Assume that in setting up the budget adjusted to current volume on a department report, you find that standard hours produced by the department was 6,500. For a certain semivariable expense, the allowance at the 6,000 hour level is $800 and the allowance at the 8,000 hour level is $900. What allowance for that expense would you enter on the report?

19-7. (a) "It is optional whether entries to charge using departments for service received from service departments are recorded in the departmental accounts in the factory expense ledger." Discuss this statement.

(b) How does net expense variance appear in the departmental expense accounts? In the control accounts in the general ledger?

19-8. (a) What is meant by converting a semivariable expense into its fixed expense and variable expense elements? Describe a method for doing it.

(b) What is gained by so converting semivariable expenses?

19-9. Discuss this statement: "The foreman should be provided with the means of planning his expenses."

EXERCISE

19-1. (*Part 1*). The S&J Foundry computes standard factory expense rates at the beginning of each year on the basis of anticipated expense dollars and anticipated volume expressed as standard direct labor hours. This company has five departments as follows:

	Basis for Allocation to Other Departments
Service departments:	
Building maintenance and fixed charges	Square feet of space occupied
General factory administration	Standard direct labor hours worked in producing departments
Producing departments:	
Moulding	Charged to Work in Process on the basis of
Casting	standard direct labor hours in operations
Finishing	completed at standard rates.

Required:

Compute standard factory expense rates and standard product costs, using the form in the Workbook.

(*Part 2*). The S&J Foundry compiles flexible budgets to measure performance. The flexible budget for the moulding department for a one-month period follows:

Per cent of capacity........		70% 7,000		80% 8,000	
Standard direct labor hours					
	Variable Expense Rate per Standard Hour	*Fixed*	*Variable and Semi-variable*	*Fixed*	*Variable and Semi-variable*
Direct labor cost...........	$2.50		$17,500.00		$20,000.00
Total indirect labor........			1,500.00		1,500.00
Total labor cost........			$19,000.00		$21,500.00
Direct departmental expense:					
Supervision.............		$ 900.00		$ 900.00	
Other indirect labor......			$ 600.00		$ 600.00
Employee benefits........	(a)		1,900.00		2,150.00
Supplies................	.05		350.00		400.00
Repairs and repair parts..	.10		700.00		800.00
Depreciation, insurance, and taxes............		1,800.00		1,800.00	
Totals...............		$2,700.00	$ 3,550.00	$2,700.00	$ 3,950.00
Grand totals.........			$6,250.00		$6,650.00

(a) 10 per cent of total labor cost.

Required:

Complete the Expense Variance Report—Moulding Department, using the form in the Workbook.

PROBLEMS

19-1. The Jergens Company operates a standard cost system, using a flexible budget for factory expense. There are no service departments, and the company uses a single factory expense rate.

The factory expense budget for one month follows:

Particulars	Variable Expense Rate per Hour	Volume of Operations			
		70%	80%	90%	100%
Standard hours............		700	800	900	1,000
Variable expense............	$.50	$ 350.00	$ 400.00	$ 450.00	$ 500.00
Semivariable expense........		400.00	400.00	500.00	500.00
Fixed expense.............		1,000.00	1,000.00	1,000.00	1,000.00

The standard cost card for the single product which the company makes provides the following information:

Standard Cost Per Product Unit

Materials
  10 pcs. X @ $.20.................... $2.00
Labor
  2 hrs. @ $1.50...................... 3.00
Factory expense
  2 hrs. @ ?.........................

Actual operations for the month of July, 19__ were:

Product units produced............. 410
Materials used (actual)
  4200 pcs. @ $.22................. $ 924.00
Labor used (actual)
  830 hrs. @ $1.60................. $1,328.00
Variable factory expense............ $ 430.00
Semivariable factory expense......... $ 420.00
Fixed factory expense.............. $1,000.00

Required:

(1) The manager wants to know the cost of product per unit of product at 70 per cent, 80 per cent, 90 per cent, and 100 per cent of capacity of the factory. Compute standard factory expense rates at those volumes and set up standard product costs per unit at those volumes.

(2) Assume that the budget for factory expense and standard product costs are set at 80 per cent of factory capacity. Draft a factory expense variance statement for the month of July.

To determine the budget adjusted to current volume for semivariable expenses, refer to the tabular flexible budget and determine whether the standard hours produced happens to be a tabulated level. If it is not, locate the tabulated level next below the standard hours produced for the month. Use the semivariable expense allowance for *that* tabulated level.

(3) Assuming that actual factory expenses for July have been recorded in a Factory Expense account, draft a journal entry to charge expense into Work in Process and to record the factory expense variances.

19-2. The Norton Company operates a standard cost system using a flexible budget for factory expense.   The flexible budgets for a one-month period are as follows:

	Per Cent of Capacity		
	80%	*90%*	*100%*
General factory administration			
Standard hours....................	4,800	5,400	6,000
Variable expense....................	$ 96.00	$ 108.00	$ 120.00
Semivariable expense................	84.00	100.00	150.00
Fixed expense.....................	300.00	300.00	300.00
Producing department A			
Standard hours....................	3,200	3,600	4,000
Variable expense....................	$ 352.00	$ 396.00	$ 440.00
Semivariable expense................	1,528.00	1,800.00	1,800.00
Fixed expense.....................	1,000.00	1,000.00	1,000.00
Producing department B			
Standard hours....................	1,600	1,800	2,000
Variable expense....................	$ 160.00	$ 180.00	$ 200.00
Semivariable expense................	880.00	950.00	1,000.00
Fixed expense.....................	1,200.00	1,200.00	1,200.00

Actual results for April, 19— are:

Particulars	*General Factory Administration*	*Producing Department A*	*Producing Department B*
Standard hours produced..............	5,000	3,000	2,000
Actual hours........................	5,300	3,200	2,100
Variable expense......................	$ 110.00	$ 350.00	$ 210.00
Semivariable expense..................	90.00	1,530.00	1,020.00
Fixed expense........................	300.00	1,000.00	1,200.00

Required:

Assuming that the budget and standard factory expense rates for the period have been set at 80 per cent for all departments, draft expense variance statements for:

(1) General Factory Administration
(2) Producing Department A
(3) Producing Department B

19-3. The Lincoln Manufacturing Company operates a standard cost system. Factory expense budgets (by department) follow:

BUILDING MAINTENANCE AND FIXED CHARGES:
All levels............... $4,000.00

GENERAL FACTORY ADMINISTRATION DEPARTMENT (500 square feet):

		80%		90%		100%	
Per cent of capacity.....							
Expected actual hours....		12,000		13,500		15,000	
	Variable Rate/ Standard Hour	Variable	Fixed; Semi- variable	Variable	Fixed; Semi- variable	Variable	Fixed; Semi- variable
Variable...............	.01	$120.00		$135.00		$150.00	
Semivariable...........			$ 400.00		$ 565.00		$ 565.00
Fixed.................			1,500.00		1,500.00		1,500.00
Totals................		$120.00	$1,900.00	$135.00	$2,065.00	$150.00	$2,065.00

CUTTING DEPARTMENT (1,500 square feet):

		80%		90%		100%	
Per cent of capacity.....							
Standard hours.........		4,000		4,500		5,000	
	Variable Rate/ Standard Hour	Variable	Fixed; Semi- variable	Variable	Fixed; Semi- variable	Variable	Fixed; Semi- variable
Variable...............	.02	$ 80.00		$ 90.00		$100.00	
Semivariable...........			$ 500.00		$ 610.00		$ 610.00
Fixed.................			1,400.00		1,400.00		1,400.00
Totals................		$ 80.00	$1,900.00	$ 90.00	$2,010.00	$100.00	$2,010.00

ASSEMBLY DEPARTMENT (2,000 square feet):

		80%		90%		100%	
Per cent of capacity.....							
Standard hours.........		8,000		9,000		10,000	
	Variable Rate/ Standard Hour	Variable	Fixed; Semi- variable	Variable	Fixed; Semi- variable	Variable	Fixed; Semi- variable
Variable...............	.03	$240.00		$270.00		$300.00	
Semivariable...........			$4,000.00		$4,430.00		$4,430.00
Fixed.................			5,000.00		5,000.00		5,000.00
Totals................		$240.00	$9,000.00	$270.00	$9,430.00	$300.00	$9,430.00

ACTUAL OPERATING DATE (one month):

Particulars	Building Mainte- nance and Fixed Charges	General Factory Adminis- tration	Cutting	Assembly
Standard hours produced.......................			4,000	9,500
Actual hours.................................			4,100	9,600
Variable expense.............................	$	$ 140.00	$ 86.00	$ 295.00
Semivariable expense.........................		570.00	520.00	4,500.00
Fixed expense................................	4,000.00	1,550.00	1,400.00	5,000.00
	$4,000.00	$2,260.00	$2,006.00	$9,795.00

Required:

Assume that standard expense rates for all departments are set at the 90 per cent level.   Draft expense variance statements for:

(a) General Factory Administration,
(b) Cutting Department, and
(c) Assembly Department.

19-4 (*Part 1*). The L-T Company breaks down all factory expense between that portion which is fixed and that which is variable, by segregating the fixed and variable elements of each semivariable cost.   A recent six-month history of indirect labor in the assembly department is as follows:

	Standard Direct Labor Hours	Factory Expense
January	10,000	$1,500.00
February	9,000	1,440.00
March	8,000	1,400.00
April	4,000	1,190.00
May	5,000	1,250.00
June	6,000	1,310.00

Required:

Determine the fixed charge per month and the variable rate per standard direct labor hour.

(*Part 2*). The following additional data is presented for the assembly department:

	Budget for Normal Volume	Fixed Allowance per Month	Rate per Standard Hour	Actual for July
Direct labor hours	8,000			7,000
Direct labor dollars	$12,000.00			$11,000.00
Indirect labor	$ 1,400.00	See above	See above	$ 1,375.00
Supplies	640.00	$	$.08	545.00
Depreciation, insurance and taxes	620.00	620.00		620.00
Employee benefits	1,340.00	10% of total labor dollars		1,238.00
Totals	$ 4,000.00			$ 3,778.00
Standard hours in operations completed for July				6,000

Required:

Prepare the expense variance report for the assembly department for the month of July.

19-5. The Winton Company operates a standard cost system with flexible budgets for expense control. Four departments are recognized for control purposes:

> Building maintenance and fixed charges
> General factory administration
> Assembly A
> Assembly B

Building maintenance operates on a fixed budget. The other departments operate on flexible budgets. Budgets for all departments are presented herewith.

Required:

(1) Compute expense rates for all departments, assuming that the producing departments operate at 80 per cent level. Allocate rent on the basis of square feet:

	Square Feet
General factory	500
Assembly A	4,500
Assembly B	5,000

(2) Draft expense variance reports for (a) building maintenance and fixed charges, (b) general factory administration, and (c) Assembly A department for July, 19___. Use, in addition to the budget information, the Actual Hours, Standard Hours Produced, and Actual Expenses, by Department presented herewith. In calculating budget adjusted to current volume for F.I.C.A., workmen's insurance, and provision for vacation pay, apply the appropriate percentages to the total indirect labor as adjusted to current volume. Drop the cents in these calculations.

Problem **19-6** (*continuation of Problem* **19-5**). Draft the expense variance report for Assembly B department of the Winton Company for July, 19___.

Factory Expense Budget
Building Maintenance and Fixed Charges
Object Groups and Accounts

Indirect labor:	
Supervisory.............................	$ 500.00
Janitors, firemen, and watchmen...........	1,200.00
Payroll taxes, reserves, and insurance:	
F.I.C.A. tax............................	34.00
Workmen's insurance....................	17.00
Provision for vacation pay................	34.00
Supplies:	
Janitor's supplies.......................	80.00
Coal....................................	120.00
Repairs.................................	75.00
Purchased services:	
Electric light and power..................	60.00
Unclassified..............................	80.00
Depreciation, insurance, and taxes:	
Depreciation on building.................	500.00
Insurance on building....................	200.00
Taxes on building.......................	300.00
Total department......................	$3,200.00

General Factory
Factory Expense Budget, by Level of Operations

			One Four-Week Period		
Object Groups and Accounts	Variable Rate/ Standard Hour		60% 3-day Week 11,250 Std. Hrs.	80% 4-day Week 15,000 Std. Hrs.	100% 5-day Week 18,750 Std. Hrs.
Indirect labor:					
Supervisory		S-V	$ 800.00	$1,200.00	$1,200.00
Clerical and production control		S-V	400.00	400.00	700.00
Machinists		S-V	400.00	400.00	600.00
Overtime premium		S-V			100.00
Payroll taxes, reserves, and insurance:					
F.I.C.A. tax		S-V	32.00	40.00	52.00
Workmen's insurance		S-V	16.00	20.00	26.00
Provision for vacation pay		S-V	32.00	40.00	52.00
Printed forms and office supplies	.005	V	56.25	75.00	93.75
Repairs and repair parts	.011	V	123.75	165.00	206.25
Purchased services:					
Electric light and power	.008	V	90.00	120.00	150.00
Telephone and telegraph		S-V	50.00	70.00	80.00
Professional engineers' fees		S-V	400.00	600.00	600.00
Unclassified	.008	V	90.00	120.00	150.00
Depreciation, insurance, and taxes:					
Depreciation on equipment		F	80.00	80.00	80.00
Insurance on equipment		F	50.00	50.00	50.00
Taxes on equipment		F	60.00	60.00	60.00
Total department			$2,680.00	$3,440.00	$4,200.00

Assembly A Department
Factory Expense Budget, by Level of Operations

			One Four-Week Period		
Object Groups and Accounts	Variable Rate/ Standard Hour		60% 3-day Week 3,750 Std. Hrs.	80% 4-day Week 5,000 Std. Hrs.	100% 5-day Week 6,250 Std. Hrs.
Indirect labor:					
Supervision		S-V	$ 700.00	$ 700.00	$1,000.00
Shop porters	.112	V	420.00	560.00	700.00
Other indirect labor	.08	V	300.00	400.00	500.00
Overtime premium		S-V			100.00
Totals			$1,420.00	$1,660.00	$2,300.00
Payroll taxes, insurance, and reserves:					
F.I.C.A. tax		S-V	$ 28.00	$ 33.00	$ 46.00
Workmen's insurance		S-V	14.00	16.00	23.00
Provision for vacation pay		S-V	28.00	33.00	46.00
Totals			$ 70.00	$ 82.00	$ 115.00
Factory operating supplies	.016	V	$ 60.00	$ 80.00	$ 100.00
Repairs and repair parts		S-V	80.00	100.00	120.00
Electric light and power	.032	V	120.00	160.00	200.00
Unclassified	.04	V	150.00	200.00	250.00
Depreciation, insurance, and taxes:					
Depreciation on machinery and equipment		F	$ 338.00	$ 338.00	$ 338.00
Insurance on inventory		F	80.00	80.00	80.00
Insurance on machinery and equipment		F	100.00	100.00	100.00
Taxes on inventory		F	160.00	160.00	160.00
Taxes on machinery and equipment		F	200.00	200.00	200.00
Totals			$ 878.00	$ 878.00	$ 878.00
Total department			$2,778.00	$3,160.00	$3,963.00

Assembly B Department
Factory Expense Budget, by Level of Operations

			One Four-Week Period		
Object Groups and Accounts	Variable Rate/ Standard Hour		60% 3-day Week 7,500 Std. Hrs.	80% 4-day Week 10,000 Std. Hrs.	100% 5-day Week 12,500 Std. Hrs.
Indirect labor:					
Supervision........................		F	$ 900.00	$ 900.00	$ 900.00
Shop porters......................	.08	V	600.00	800.00	1,000.00
Other indirect labor................	.04	V	300.00	400.00	500.00
Overtime premium.................		S-V			150.00
Totals...........................			$1,800.00	$2,100.00	$2,550.00
Payroll taxes, insurance, and reserves:					
F.I.C.A. tax......................		S-V	$ 36.00	$ 42.00	$ 51.00
Workmen's insurance...............		S-V	18.00	21.00	25.00
Provision for vacation pay..........		S-V	36.00	42.00	51.00
Totals...........................			$ 90.00	$ 105.00	$ 127.00
Factory operating supplies............	.016	V	$ 120.00	$ 160.00	$ 200.00
Repairs and repair parts..............		S-V	100.00	120.00	150.00
Electric light and power..............	.02	V	150.00	200.00	250.00
Unclassified.......................	.016	V	120.00	160.00	200.00
Depreciation, insurance, and taxes:					
Depreciation on machinery and equipment.....................		F	$ 505.00	$ 505.00	$ 505.00
Insurance on inventory.............		F	100.00	100.00	100.00
Insurance on machinery and equipment		F	120.00	120.00	120.00
Taxes on inventory.................		F	180.00	180.00	180.00
Taxes on machinery and equipment...		F	250.00	250.00	250.00
Totals...........................			$1,155.00	$1,155.00	$1,155.00
Total department....................			$3,535.00	$4,000.00	$4,632.00

Actual Hours, Standard Hours Produced, and Actual Expense, by Department

Month of July, 19__

	Building Maintenance and Fixed Charges	General Factory	Assembly		Total
			A	B	
Actual hours....................		13,800	4,600	9,200	
Standard hours produced........			4,500	9,000	
Indirect labor:					
Supervisory.....................	$ 550.00	$1,230.00	$ 750.00	$ 920.00	$ 3,450.00
Clerical and production control....		420.00			420.00
Machinists.....................		430.00			430.00
Shop porters...................			520.00	750.00	1,270.00
Janitors, firemen, and watchmen..	1,180.00				1,180.00
Other indirect labor.............			370.00	380.00	750.00
Totals......................	$1,730.00	$2,080.00	$1,640.00	$2,050.00	$ 7,500.00
Payroll taxes, reserves, and insurance:					
F.I.C.A. tax....................	$ 35.00	$ 41.00	$ 33.00	$ 41.00	$ 150.00
Workmen's insurance...........	18.00	20.00	16.00	21.00	75.00
Provision for vacation pay........	35.00	41.00	33.00	41.00	150.00
Totals......................	$ 88.00	$ 102.00	$ 82.00	$ 103.00	$ 375.00
Supplies and repairs:					
Janitors supplies................	$ 90.00	$	$	$	$ 90.00
Coal...........................	105.00				105.00
Printed forms and office supplies..		70.00			70.00
Factory operating supplies........			75.00	148.00	223.00
Repairs to building.............	185.00				185.00
Repairs and repair parts..........		135.00	110.00	125.00	370.00
Totals......................	$ 380.00	$ 205.00	$ 185.00	$ 273.00	$ 1,043.00
Purchased services:					
Electric light and power..........	$ 85.00	$ 100.00	$ 150.00	$ 195.00	$ 530.00
Telephone and telegraph.........		60.00			60.00
Professional engineers' fees.......		650.00			650.00
Totals......................	$ 85.00	$ 810.00	$ 150.00	$ 195.00	$ 1,240.00
Unclassified.....................	$ 90.00	$ 90.00	$ 130.00	$ 155.00	$ 465.00
Depreciation, insurance, and travel:					
Depreciation on building........	$ 500.00	$	$	$	$ 500.00
Depreciation on machinery and equipment....................		100.00	400.00	500.00	1,000.00
Insurance on building...........	200.00				200.00
Insurance on inventory..........			80.00	100.00	180.00
Insurance on machinery and equipment....................		50.00	100.00	120.00	270.00
Taxes on building..............	350.00				350.00
Taxes on inventory.............			160.00	180.00	340.00
Taxes on machinery and equipment		65.00	200.00	250.00	515.00
Totals......................	$1,050.00	$ 215.00	$ 940.00	$1,150.00	$ 3,355.00
Total direct departmental expense...	$3,423.00	$3,502.00	$3,127.00	$3,926.00	$13,978.00

Chapter 20

COST REDUCTION THROUGH ANALYSIS
OF VARIANCES

Cost reduction through the use of a standard cost system. Possibilities for reducing manufacturing cost arise at a number of points in the operation and use of a standard cost system. Cost reduction is accomplished, for instance, by setting the standards carefully in the first place, so that they do represent good performance. When a new or proposed standard is set, it is compared with the current actual cost to determine what cost savings are likely. The act of setting a new standard is thus often a step in the direction of cost reduction.

The aims of cost reduction are likewise supported by telling the employees what the labor standards are, so that they will know what they have to do to meet the standards. In many factories, standard times are put on the job tickets before they are issued to the workmen for that purpose. The aims may be even further supported by teaching the supervisor how the standards for factory expense are put together and used to make it possible for them to plan their expenditures. Thus, if it appears early in the month that the volume of production will be low, the supervisor can scale his expenditures down accordingly while there is still time.

Providing for quick and frequent reporting of variances will also assist in the accomplishment of cost reduction aims. In this connection, it should be noted that the first system of standard costs explained in Chapter 17 provides for analysis of variances monthly, which is after all not very frequent. The second system provides for analysis of materials and labor daily, if desired, from the requisitions and job tickets. Variance reports can accordingly be issued daily. As a matter of fact, requiring supervisors to sign excess piece requisitions and labor allowance tickets as and when they are issued puts cost control information in their hands with the ultimate frequency.

Providing for analysis of variances to determine the cause and who is responsible is the cap-stone of the cost reduction program. Some of this analysis is *accounting analysis;* it involves setting up classifications of accounts for variances; sorting invoices, job tickets, and requisitions down to the classifications; and taking off dollar amounts of variances. All standard cost systems comprise a regular series of variance reports which come under the heading of accounting analyses. They are prepared for supervisors of all levels, and they highlight off-standard conditions for the attention of the supervisors.

Another form of variance analysis is *engineering* or *operations* analysis; it involves going back of variances to the actual working situation to determine the underlying causes of the variances and finding out what can be done to correct them. Analysis of this kind is likely to be pursued on a project basis. The accounting variances may point up a situation that needs to be investigated and an engineering analysis may be started to determine causes and remedies.

In large companies, the analysis and control of variances may be assigned to one or more specialized departments. As an example, one company has a personnel efficiency department that devotes its entire time to the study of labor costs and analysis of labor variances. In other companies, the work is often done by cost analysts attached to the cost accounting department but who, at the same time, are acquainted with and work as a team with production management. Where company size does not justify specialization, the function is performed by members of the regular cost accounting staff in cooperation with factory personnel.*

This chapter explains accounting analysis (for specific order situations and for process manufacture) and presents a case description of engineering analysis.

ACCOUNTING ANALYSIS

Change of standards; Change of standards variance. It was stated before that a standard for materials or labor or factory expense is a performance measure based upon methods considered feasible during the period to which the standard applies. A standard does not necessarily represent the best possible performance. As a matter of fact, in well-managed companies, efforts are constantly made to find better ways of doing things—and to reduce standard costs.

The comparison of a new standard with an old standard provides an element in the measurement of cost reduction. If the industrial engineer has devised a new method of performing a labor operation at a cost of $.18 per unit, whereas the old method cost $.20, the labor saving is $.02 per unit. Obviously, such factors as the number of units to be produced and the cost of training and equipment in changing the operation has to be considered, but the comparison of the new standard with the old standard is the key point. When a change is under consideration, the industrial engineer will make a formal proposal to the management. If the proposal is accepted, the change will be made.

---

* "The Analysis of Manufacturing Cost Variances," *N.A.C.A. Bulletin* (August, 1952) Research Series No. 22, p. 1556.

The question of *when* the change becomes effective is important for cost accounting purposes. In some cases, the changes are intended to become effective when the next product models go into production. In this case, the new standards are used when the new set of standard cost cards is drawn up at the beginning of the style season. It is necessary, of course, for the cost accountant to be certain that the new standard cost cards do reflect all the new standards.

In other cases, the management desires to change a method and a standard during a cost period, after the standard cost cards have been set up and the selling price lists issued. When the number of standard cost cards is very large, it may be particularly desirable to continue the old standard costs in the Inventory and Cost of Sales accounts until the end of the style season, thus:

Work in Process	Finished Goods		Cost of Goods Sold	
Old standard $.20	Old standard $.20	Old standard $.20	Old standard $.20	

After the new standard for the operation is put into effect, Work in Process will be charged for the new standard. Continuing the above illustration relating to one labor operation on one unit of product, Work in Process would stand charged at the new standard and credited at the old standard:

Cash		Work in Process	
	$.18	New standard $.18	Old standard $.20

At the end of the period, the change of standard variance would be taken out of Work in Process by a debit to Work in Process for $.02 and a credit to Change of Standards Variance for the same amount. Of course, the actual amount of the entry would be determined by multiplying the number of units processed through the operation by the $.02 saving. The credit balance in the Change of Standards Variance account represents cost reduction through devising new methods and installing new standards.

In some cases, no attempt is made to isolate the change of standards variance for labor and it accordingly gets buried in the Labor Variance account, along with price and quantity factors. The balance of that account may actually be a balance of debits and credits. It may be necessary to analyze the account to determine the true variance situation.

Materials price variance reports. The Materials Price Variance

Report below analyzes price variance by *class of materials* into four major classes. The formula for price variance is:

Price variance = Actual quantities @ actual prices − Actual quantities @ standard prices.

The report shows whether the major classes of material are being purchased at the prices which have been put on the standard cost cards and presumably provided for in the selling prices of the product. The dollar variance shows the amount of loss (or gain) due to the difference between actual and standard prices.

Standard prices are set by the purchasing agent at the beginning of the year. They represent his forecast of prices that will be paid during the coming year. The variances are accordingly a measure of the success of the forecasting. They are not necessarily a measure of performance in the sense of securing the lowest possible prices during the period. Note, however, that some companies state that price variances have a limited usefulness in evaluating purchasing activities. A price variance may be caused by an emergency small quantity purchase at a price higher than the contract prices reflected in the standards.

Materials Price Variance Report

for the Month of March, 19__

Class of Materials	Actual Quantities @ Standard Prices	@ Actual Prices	Price Variance
a....................	$ 2,500.00	$ 2,600.00	$100.00
b....................	1,500.00	1,450.00	50.00*
c....................	2,800.00	2,870.00	70.00
d....................	22,500.00	22,800.00	300.00
Totals.........	$29,300.00	$29,720.00	$420.00

*Credit

Figure 20-1

The Materials Price Variance Report is prepared by recapping the purchase invoices. When the invoices are received, each invoice is rubber stamped to provide space for entering standard prices and extensions of actual quantities and standard prices. This information is entered on the invoice. The invoices are sorted by product class, the standard and actual values for each product class are recapped, and Price Variance Report is prepared.

Materials quantity variance reports. The Materials Quantity Variance Report below analyzes quantity variances by *class of materials* into four major classes. The formula for quantity variance is:

(1) Quantity variance = Actual quantities @ standard prices − Standard quantities allowed (for the production of the period) @ standard prices, or

(2) Quantity variance = (Actual quantity used − Standard quantity allowed) × Standard prices

Materials Quantity Variances by Class of Materials

for the Month of March, 19__

(@ Standard Prices)

Class of Materials	Actual Quantities	Standard Quantities	Quantity Variance
a...............	$ 3,400.00	$ 3,200.00	$ 200.00
b...............	1,300.00	1,200.00	100.00
c...............	3,000.00	2,600.00	400.00
d...............	21,500.00	21,000.00	500.00
Totals........	$29,200.00	$28,000.00	$1,200.00

Figure 20-2

Standard allowed quantity of each material per unit of product is set by the industrial engineer who works out the specifications for the materials that go into each product. The specifications are set with direct reference to the desired quality of the end-product and the quantity standards are then set to reflect satisfactory utilization of the materials in the manufacturing process. In some cases, setting the quantity standard for a particular material is a matter of simple mathematics. Each unit of a certain product may require six units of one material and one unit of another material. In other cases, as where the material is cut or sheared in the production operations, it may be necessary for the industrial engineer to determine how the material is to be laid out for cutting and what sizes of particular materials are available. The problem is to cut out the parts with the least waste of materials.

A materials quantity variance means that more (or less) material was used per unit of product than the standard called for. Ordinarily, a debit variance indicates an unsatisfactory performance in the utilization of materials. It is possible, however, that an engineering or operation analysis of the variance may show that nonstandard or defective materials are being used, or that the cutting or shearing operations are not being performed as set up when the materials quantity standards were formulated, or possibly that the materials quantity standards were set incorrectly in the first place.

In some cases, it is possible to determine the cause of a material quantity variance at the time excess pieces of material are used. A coding scheme for the various causes may be worked out, for instance: 01 nonstandard material, 02 defective material, 03 nonstandard operation, 04 nonstandard equipment, 05 trainee operator, etc. The supervisor who signs an excess piece requisition will indicate on it the code number of the cause of the variance. From these coded requisitions, a Quantity Variance by Cause report may be prepared as follows:

Materials Quantity Variances by Cause

for the Month of March, 19__

01	Nonstandard material............	$ 200.00
02	Defective material...............	300.00
03	Nonstandard operation...........	300.00
04	Nonstandard equipment..........	100.00
05	Trainee operator................	300.00
	Total.....................	$1,200.00

Figure 20-3

On the matter of cost control at the source of the variances, the *N.A.C.A. Bulletin* cited previously in this chapter states:

Control over current costs must obviously be exercised before the fact rather than after the fact. Preventive cost control depends upon actions taken at the point where losses and waste can occur, or where savings can be made. This type of control uses basic operating standards expressed in terms of material specifications, operation methods and times, preferred equipment and facilities. Such standards need to be current at all times—i.e., they must represent the methods which should be followed when the work is done.*

Daily materials yardage report. The Daily Materials Yardage Report below is an example of a materials quantity variance report in physical units (yards) used as a primary measure of performance. This report is used in the cutting room of a work garment factory, but numerous other examples of quantity variance reports in physical units can be found. The yardage report is an extremely valuable report because of the large losses in piece goods that can pile up if cutting is not controlled.

The formula for yardage variance is:

Yardage variance = Actual yards used − Standard yards allowed
for the product units cut.

The daily report is prepared from the production orders completed by the cutting room each day. When the production order is issued by the production control clerk, it shows among other things, the standard yards allowed for the quantity of product indicated on the order. The cutting room foreman is thus made aware of the quantity standard he is supposed to meet, *before the material is cut.* After the material for the order is cut, actual yards used is entered on the cutting order. The Daily Materials

* *Op. cit.,* p. 1548.

Yardage Report is a summary of the production orders. The monthly report is a summary of all the daily reports for the month.

Daily Materials Yardage Report

March 3, 19__

Product Class	Product Units Produced	Standard Yards	Actual Yards	Variance (in Yards)
A.................	800	1,600	1,800	200
B.................	1,000	2,500	2,600	100
C.................	900	1,800	1,850	50
D.................	15,000	30,000	30,100	100
	17,700	35,900	36,350	450

Figure 20-4

Any large variance is investigated promptly, for it may mean that the mark-up man has done a poor job of laying out the patterns for maximum utilization of the piece goods.   Note, however, that the standard yards per dozen garments might be based upon an *average* size and that the day's production orders of a certain product may show a preponderance of large sizes rather than a normal curve of sizes.   The variance shown on the report would have to be interpreted in the light of the preponderance of large sizes.

Substitution of materials variance.   When the standard item called for in the bill of materials is not available, a substitute material is sometimes used instead.   A Substitution of Materials Report (not illustrated) is drawn to show the gain or loss on substitution.   Thus, if the standard bill of materials calls for 10 pieces of Material A @ $2 = $20, and the substitution slip shows 10 pieces Material X @ $2.50, the substitution variance would be a debit of $5.   This debit is a cost of failing to have the proper materials on hand.

Note that if a journal entry is made to separate substitutions from regular issues, the entry is:

Dr. Work in process (for standard value of standard materials)
    Substitution of materials variance (for difference)
        Cr. Materials (for standard value of actual materials drawn from stores)

If no separate entry is made, any substitution variance is buried in the Materials Quantity Variance account.   (This would be the case where the accountant debits Work in Process for the standard value of the standard items allowed for production, credits Materials for the standard value of the actual items drawn from stores, and debits or credits the balancing figure to Materials Quantity Variance.)   In some cases, substitution of materials is a real cost factor, and formal analysis of the materials quantity variance balance is a necessary part of the cost reduction program.

Labor variance reports; Incentive plans. A Weekly Report of Labor Allowances, Makeup, and Overtime Premium: Piece Work (Figure 8-3) is described on page 165. This report is typical for factories operating (a) piece work with certain allowances or (b) standard hours @ base rate with certain allowances. (The latter plan is described on page 432.) Basically, the report is a control on allowances made by the foreman. Since the allowances are made because of conditions beyond the control of the employee (conditions over which the management has some control), the report is often a valuable cost reduction tool.

The Daily Labor Performance Report below is prepared for the foreman. It shows *for each employee:* standard hours produced, actual hours worked, and performance per cent (Standard hours produced ÷ Actual hours worked). It is expected that the performance percentages will hover around 100. Above average performers will show percentages above 100 and below average performers, percentages below 100. New, inexperienced employees will show percentages less than 100, but the percentage for such employees is expected to rise during the training period (which is from three weeks to two months, depending upon the operation in a particular case).   In reading the report, therefore, the foreman must take into consideration the length of time a trainee has been on the job.

Daily Labor Performance Report—Assembly Department No. 1

by Operator

March 3, 19__

Employee Name	No.	Standard Hours Produced	Actual Hours Worked	Performance Per Cent
George Smith..........	101	10	8	125
Fred Wilson...........	102	8	8	100
Milton Simon..........	103	6	8	75
Total department.......		260	240	108.33

Figure 20-5

Labor variances; Hourly rated wages.   In hourly rated wage payment plans, it is possible to analyze labor variance into *rate* and *time* factors.   The formula for rate variance is:

Rate variance = (Actual hours × Actual rate) − (Actual hours × Standard rate)

The formula for time or efficiency variance is:

Time variance = (Actual hours × Standard rate) − (Standard hours in operations completed × Standard rate)

To illustrate the calculation of variances, assume that (Actual hours $\times$ Actual rate) = 1,100 $\times$ \$1.10 = \$1,210 and that (Standard hours in operations completed $\times$ Standard rate) = 1,000 $\times$ \$1 = \$1,000.

Rate variance =

Actual hours	$\times$ Actual rate		
1,100	$\times$ \$1.10	= \$1,210.00	
Actual hours	$\times$ Standard rate		\$110.00
1,100	$\times$ \$1.00	= 1,100.00	

Time variance =

Actual hours	$\times$ Standard rate		
1,100	$\times$ \$1.00	= \$1,100.00	
Standard hours	$\times$ Standard rate		\$100.00
1,000	$\times$ \$1.00	= 1,000.00	

Net variance =

Actual hours	$\times$ Actual rate		
1,100	$\times$ \$1.10	= \$1,210.00	
Standard hours	$\times$ Standard rate		\$210.00
1,000	$\times$ \$1.00	= 1,000.00	

If it is desired to analyze labor variances currently at the source, job tickets can be designed to provide for entry of standard time allowed for the operation covered by the ticket (to be shown when the ticket is issued), standard rate, actual time taken, and actual rate. If a job ticket is issued for each operation on which each man works during the day, variances can be analyzed down to the individual man and the individual operation. Daily reports can be issued showing the efficiency of each man and the net efficiency of the department.

Reports can also be issued covering *rate* variances. Such variances can exist where it is possible for a foreman to assign a man who has a relatively high wage rate to an operation with a relatively low standard rate. Rate variances can also arise when actual wage rates are changed (say by reason of a new union contract) during the period for which standard cost cards have already been set. Assume that standard wage rates reflected on the standard cost cards are the same as actual wage rates in effect at the beginning of the standard cost period, but that actual wage rates will be increased at the middle of the period. If the standard wage rates are not changed at that time, there will be a debit rate variance during the remainder of the period. Actual hours $\times$ Actual rate for the remainder of the period will be different from Actual hours $\times$ Standard rate.

Spoiled work. In some businesses, the costs of spoiled work are significant. Reports on such costs may be obtained in a standard cost system by costing the inspector's spoiled work tickets and summarizing them with the desired frequency. It is necessary for the inspector who rejects the job to write the number of the last operation completed on the ticket. The cost man then costs the ticket at the cumulative standard cost through the last operation completed. The costs are reported to the management. Where the jobs are large, it may be desired to list them separately and to have the foreman or the industrial engineer indicate the cause of spoilage in each case (defective material, faulty machine tools, operator error, and so forth).

The monthly entry to remove the cost of spoiled work from the Work in Process Inventory account is:

> Dr. Spoiled work inventory
> Cr. Work in process inventory
> To record the cost of spoiled work per the
> summary of spoiled work tickets.

Factory expense variances. There are two plans for analysis of factory expense variances: the two-variance plan and the three-variance plan. The two-variance plan (explained originally in Chapter 19) and the three-variance plan are illustrated below on the basis of a single set of data.

The flexible expense budget shows:

Per cent of capacity	80%	90%	100%
Standard hours	8,000	9,000	10,000
Variable expense	$4,000.00	$4,500.00	$5,000.00
Fixed expense	4,000.00	4,000.00	4,000.00

Assume further that the volume for the coming period was estimated at 8,000 standard hours and the standard expense rate therefore ($4,000 + $4,000) ÷ 8,000 = $1 per hour.

Actual performance was:

Per cent of capacity	90%
Standard hours produced	9,000
Actual hours	9,200
Variable expense	$4,700.00
Fixed expense	$4,000.00
Total actual expense	$8,700.00

The variances calculated under the two-variance plan are:

Controllable variance
Actual expense.......................... $8,700.00
Budget adjusted to current volume
(9,000 standard hours)................... 8,500.00

Variance................................. $200.00
Volume variance
Budget adjusted to current volume
(as above)............................... $8,500.00
Standard expense charged to process
(9,000 standard hours @ $1) 9,000.00

Variance................................. 500.00*

Net variance............................. $300.00*

*Credit

Under the three-variance plan, the following variances would be calculated:

Spending variance
   Actual expense.......................... $8,700.00
   Budget adjusted to 9,200 actual hours
      Variable expense: 9,200 × $.50... $4,600.00
      Fixed expense................ 4,000.00   8,600.00

   Variance.................................. $100.00
Capacity variance
   Budget adjusted to 9,200 actual hours........ $8,600.00
   Actual hours × Standard rate ($1)........... 9,200.00

   Variance..................................   600.00*
Time variance
   Actual hours × Standard expense rate........ $9,200.00
   Standard hours in operations completed
      @ standard expense rate
      9,000 standard hours × $1 per hour........ 9,000.00

   Variance..................................   200.00

  Net variance.................................. $300.00*

* Credit

Note that the time variance for factory expense (above) is comparable to the time variance for labor (page 493). The latter represents the labor cost of taking more than the standard allowed hours for the month's output and the former represents the factory expense cost of the same excess usage of hours.

Typical set of variance reports (list). On page 496 is the list of variance reports prepared for Franklin Manufacturing Company (fictitious name) which manufactures a toy from sheet steel. The list will be of interest to the reader because it illustrates what particular variances are set out in a typical situation and how the variances are built into an integrated report structure.

VARIANCE REPORTS FOR PROCESS INDUSTRIES

Materials price, mixture, and yield variances. Figure 20-8 (page 497) is a materials price, mixture, and yield variance report for a process industry in which Materials A, B, and C are put into process at the same time according to formula to produce a single product "X."
The materials formula for one dozen units of Product X is:

Material	*Pounds*
Material A.............................	6.18
Material B.............................	3.09
Material C.............................	3.09
Gross input.........................	12.36
Standard shrinkage (3% of good output)..	.36
Net weight per dozen..................	12.00

FRANKLIN MANUFACTURING COMPANY
Variance Reports

Change of Standard Variance Report
Materials Price Variance Report, showing separate variances for
    Sheet steel
    Steel rod
    Steel wire
    Steel tubing
    Paint
    Miscellaneous (washers, cotter pins, nuts)
Materials Quantity Variance and Scrap Reports
    Sheet Steel Tonnage Variance—Shearing Department
    Sheet Steel Tonnage Variance—Punch Press Department
    Scrap Report—Spot Weld Department
    Paint Quantity Variance—Painting Department
Substitution of Materials—Assembly Department
Labor Variances
    Direct Labor Variances (Hourly rated wage)—Shearing Department
    Direct Labor Variances (Piece work, with allowances)
       —Punch Press Department
       —Spot Weld Department
    Direct Labor Variances (Group bonus)—Assembly Department
    Direct Labor Variances (Hourly rated wage)—Painting Department
Factory Expense Variances (Controllable and Volume variances)
    Separate variance report for each department:
    General Factory Administration
    Building Maintenance and Fixed Charges
    Shearing Department
    Punch Press Department
    Spot Weld Department
    Assembly Department
    Painting Department

Figure 20-6

The standard cost card (materials only) for Product X appears below:

Standard Cost Card

Materials Cost Per Dozen—Product X

Particulars	Pounds	Per Pound	Amount
Material A..........................	6.18	$.20	$1.236
Material B........................	3.09	.20	.618
Material C.........................	3.09	.40	1.236
	12.36	.25	3.090
Standard shrinkage (3% of good output)	.36		
Net material cost per dozen............	12.00		3.090

Figure 20-7

Although there is a standard formula, it is possible for the foreman to vary the proportions.   (The foreman is responsible for weighing the charges

Materials Price, Mixture, and Yield Variances

Particulars (Materials Classification) Formula	(1) Actual Input (Pounds)	(2) Actual Price per Pound	(3) Actual Input @ Actual Price (1 × 2)	(4) Standard Price per Pound	(5) Actual Input @ Standard Price (1 × 4)	Price Variance on Input (3–5)	(6) Total Actual Input @ Average Standard Cost/Pound ($.25/#)	(7) Production for Period @ Standard Yield ($.25/#)	(8) Mix Variance (5–6)	(9) Yield Variance (6–7)
Dozens output.........								1,000		
Standard pounds input......								12,360		
Actual input............	12,480		12,480		12,480		12,480			
Material A........	6,600	$.22	$1,452.00	$.20	$1,320.00					
Material B........	3,000	.23	690.00	.20	600.00					
Material C........	2,880	.42	1,209.60	.40	1,152.00					
	12,480		$3,351.60		$3,072.00	$279.60	$3,120.00	$3,090.00	$48.00*	$30.00

* Credit.

Figure 20-8

497

into process.) In fact, if operations are not performed properly in all respects, it is necessary to use extra quantities of some of the materials to produce a product which will pass inspection. For this reason, it is possible for the foreman to have a yield variance, due to using a greater aggregate quantity of materials than was called for in the formula, and a mixture variance, due to using a greater proportion of the more expensive material than was called for in the formula. These variances, which together make up a quantity variance, are found in addition to the usual price variance.

To illustrate the calculation of these variances, assume that input and production for a certain day were as follows:

Production and Input: Product X

Particulars	Actual Quantity	Actual Price	Amount
Product X produced...........	1,000 dozens		
Actual input			
Material A................	6,600 pounds	$.22 per pound	$1,452.00
Material B................	3,000 pounds	.23 per pound	690.00
Material C................	2,880 pounds	.42 per pound	1,209.60
	12,480 pounds		$3,351.60

Figure 20-9

The materials price, mixture, and yield variances in the report (page 497) are computed according to the formulas on the first line of the report:

The *price variance* is (Actual quantities @ actual prices) − (Actual quantities @ standard prices).

The *mixture variance* is (Actual quantities used @ standard prices, extended at the standard prices for the separate materials) − (Total actual quantity used × Average standard price per pound).

The *yield variance* is (Total actual pounds used × Average standard price per pound) − (Total standard input quantity allowed × Average standard price per pound).

The variances shown in Figure 20-8 are:

Price variance............................	$279.60
Mixture variance.........................	48.00*
Yield variance...........................	30.00
Net variance.........................	$261.60

* Credit

The net variance obtained by adding the individual variances agrees with the net variance computed as follows:

Actual input @ actual prices.............. $3,351.60
Production for period @ standard yield.... 3,090.00

Net variance, as above.............. $ 261.60

Labor crew, volume, and yield variances.   Figure 20-10 (page 500) is a Labor Crew, Volume, and Yield Variance Report for a process plant (assumed to be the one on which the materials report, Figure 20-8, is based) in which a standard crew is allowed to process a particular volume of input.   There may accordingly be *crew* variances, when the actual crew exceeds the standard; volume variances, when the actual input is less than the capacity for which the crew was set; and yield variance, when the output of good product is less than the input minus the standard shrinkage.

In the variance report (page 500), the standard crew for the actual input is listed by job classification in Columns 4, 5, and 6.   Note that direct labor is not perfectly variable with input.   One particular complement of crew will take care of production up to a certain point, another larger crew will take care of production from that point up to a certain higher point, and so on.   The crew shown will take care of 1,200 dozens a day output, or 14,832 pounds input.   This crew capacity is larger than the actual 12,480 pounds that were processed, and the difference represents a labor loss on volume.

The formulas on the first line indicate how the variance calculations are made:

The *Crew Variance from Standard* is (Actual hours worked × Actual wage rates) − (Standard hours allowed for the expected volume × Standard wage rates).

The *Volume Variance* is (Standard hours allowed for the expected volume × Standard wage rates) − (Total actual input in pounds × Average standard labor cost per pound).

The *Yield Variance* is (Total actual input in pounds × Average standard labor cost per pound) − (Standard pounds allowed for the goods produced × Average standard labor cost per pound).

The variances shown in Figure 20-10 are:

Crew variance................. $12.00
Volume variance.............. 27.91
Yield variance................ 1.43

Total variance............ $41.34

The net variance obtained by adding the individual variances agrees with the net variance computed as follows:

Actual crew @ actual rates........................ $188.00
Production for period @ standard yield (subtract).... 146.66

Total variance, as above........................ $ 41.34

Labor Crew, Volume, and Yield Variance

Particulars (Job Classification) Formula	(1) Actual Crew (Hours)	(2) Actual Rate per Hour	(3) Actual Crew @ Actual Rate (1 × 2)	(4) Standard Hours	(5) Standard Rate per Hour	(6) Standard Amount (4 × 5)	Crew Variance from Standard (3–6)	(7) Total Actual Input @ Average Standard Cost/Pound	(8) Production for Period @ Standard Yield	(9) Volume Variance (6–7)	(10) Yield Variance (7–8)
Crew capacity.........						14,832#					
Dozens output........									1,000		
Standard pounds input.....									12,360		
Actual pounds input......	12,480							12,480			
Foreman..........	8	$2.00	$ 16.00	8	$2.00	$ 16.00					
Material loader.........	16	1.25	20.00	16	1.25	20.00					
Dye tub tenders.........	32	1.50	48.00	24	1.50	36.00					
Extractor tenders........	16	1.25	20.00	16	1.25	20.00					
Drier tenders.........	16	1.50	24.00	16	1.50	24.00					
Napper tenders.........	24	1.25	30.00	24	1.25	30.00					
Turner and folder tenders..	16	1.25	20.00	16	1.25	20.00					
Folder unloader.........	8	1.25	10.00	8	1.25	10.00					
	136		$188.00	128		$176.00	12.00	$148.09	$146.66	$27.91	$1.43

(5) Standard crew for volume up to 1,200 dozen × 12.36 pounds = 14,832 pounds
    Standard labor cost per pound = $176.00 ÷ 14,832 pounds = $.011866
(7) 12,480 pounds × $.011866 = $148.09
(8) 12,360 pounds × $.011866 = $146.66

Figure 20-10

ENGINEERING ANALYSIS TO DETERMINE CAUSE
OF VARIANCES

Description of an engineering analysis (excerpt). Although a study of the mathematics of variances might indicate to the reader that the variances "automatically" show the supervisor what is wrong, the fact is that variances often show what *needs to be investigated further*. In some companies that operate standard cost systems, full-time analysts make surveys of operations to determine the cause of variances and make recommendations on the correction of operating practices.

An explanation of the technical details of engineering analysis of variances is outside the scope of this book, but a case description of such an analysis is interesting and useful at this point. An example of a survey made in a steel plant follows:

In the steel industry—as in many other industries dealing with large volumes of material and many stages of processing—we find that practice changes, even though involving relatively small percentage yield effects, have a disconcertingly frequent habit of showing up in the variance (and, therefore, in the profit and loss) statements as very real and significant items. The problem of isolating and identifying the cause of out-of-line materials costs occasionally results in a study reaching back into a prior operation, since, in these cases, the responsibility where the loss occurs may well have been forced into a nonstandard practice due to something which a prior operation may have done or not done. This was the case [in Figure 20-11] in which a study was made to determine the cause of an overstandard metal loss in a small rolling mill producing billets directly from ingots.

We find that the first clue to the nature of the problem in the statement of variances, which indicates that in terms of finished product (in the case, billets), the materials input cost was excessive for the period involved by $33,000 offset to some extent by overnormal recovery of scrap. In this operation, by way of explanation, the unusable portion of the steel ingot is sheared off at the top and bottom as "crop ends." It follows, rather naturally, that where the input is excessive, the scrap will generally be also, particularly where there is no latitude allowed in the dimensions of the product being produced from the ingot. . . . A review of the scheduling practice for the furnace department indicated that the ingots were ordered poured to the correct height to provide for the proper number of billets per ingot and, further, that the tonnage scheduled to be produced in the furnaces was correctly computed as to the total desired billet weight, plus the standard allowance for scrap occuring in the furnace department in the pouring of the ingots through splashing, loss in weight, and other causes. Thus, no blame could be laid at the door of the scheduling department, although as a matter of fact, it was frequently accused of insufficient providing for the mill using the billets.

The analysis proceeded further to observation of actual practices and it soon became evident that the length of the clearing, or final, crop end was considerably in excess of the amount allowed in the standard practice. . . . Although the steel pourers could hardly be expected to admit readily that they were not following standard practice in pouring the ordered height, it was possible to take physical measurements of an adequate sampling of ingots after they were stripped from the mold but before rolling in the mill. This indicated that certain of the steel pourers

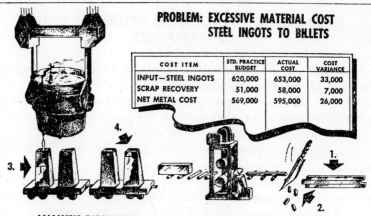

PROBLEM: EXCESSIVE MATERIAL COST STEEL INGOTS TO BILLETS

COST ITEM	STD. PRACTICE BUDGET	ACTUAL COST	COST VARIANCE
INPUT—STEEL INGOTS	620,000	653,000	33,000
SCRAP RECOVERY	51,000	58,000	7,000
NET METAL COST	569,000	595,000	26,000

ANALYSIS DISCLOSES:

1. NO. OF BILLETS PRODUCED FROM EACH INGOT AS SCHEDULED, BUT ORDERS FREQUENTLY SHORT ON INGOTS.
2. SHEARMAN STATES THAT CLEARING CROPS ARE EXCESSIVE.
3. BUTT (UNUSABLE SHORT) INGOT OCCURRENCE OVER STANDARD.
4. INGOT LENGTH FOUND TO BE CONSISTENTLY OVER ORDERED LENGTH.

CONCLUSION:

1. REVIEW SCHEDULING, MOLD MARKING & POURING PRACTICES FOR ALL GRADES.
2. INSTRUCT STEEL POURERS TO FOLLOW STANDARD PRACTICES.
3. METALLURGISTS TO FOLLOW UP ON RESULTS OVERALL AND AS BETWEEN GRADES.

RESULTS:

1. INCREASED GOOD PRODUCT YIELD BOTH AT FURNACES (DUE TO FEWER SHORT INGOTS) AND AT ROLLING MILL (DUE TO LESS GOOD STEEL LOST AT SCRAP SHEAR).
2. REDUCED RE-SCHEDULING TO MAKE UP DEFICIENCIES, IMPROVED PERFORMANCE ON SHIPPING PROMISES.

Figure 20-11

consistently poured their ingots over the scheduled height and the loss on "butt" ingots (the last one poured and too short for that use) was over standard consistently on the same heats.*

QUESTIONS

20-1. The P Company operates a job order standard cost system under specific order production control. Excess piece requisitions are issued for materials used in addition to those on the standard bills of materials. Direct labor time tickets are issued for specific tasks. The materials quantity variance for the week just ended was unfavorable in the amount of $10,691. The direct labor quantity variance for the week just ended was unfavorable in the amount of $8,921. You are asked to make an investigation and prepare a report. Prepare such a report, assuming whatever additional facts are necessary as to the causes of these variances.

20-2. The Q Company operates a process standard cost system under repetitive order production control. Quantities of inputs and production are summarized daily. Direct labor is recorded on time cards by each employee, each day by operations performed. Each man generally performs the same operations repetitively. The materials quantity variance for the week just ended was unfavorable in the amount of $12,934. The direct labor quantity variance for the week just ended was unfavorable in the amount of $8,645. You are asked to make an investigation and prepare a report. Prepare such a report, assuming whatever additional facts are necessary as to the causes of these variances.

20-3. The R Furniture Manufacturing Company purchases five basic types of wood, and three basic types of upholstery materials. The only other important raw material, dollar-wise, is steel wire for coil springs. The unfavorable materials price variance for the month just ended was $64,359. Prepare an informative analysis for management, assuming whatever details are necessary.

20-4. The S Company operates an incentive pay system wherein the production employees are guaranteed a basic minimum hourly wage, but paid approximately 120 per cent of that minimum for standard performance. Idle time due to lack of orders, machine breakdown, changeover, etc., is identified by special operation numbers. Time and one-half is paid for time worked over 40 hours per week. Unfavorable direct labor quantity variance for the week just ended was $3,221. Unfavorable direct labor rate variance for the week just ended was $2,233. Prepare the analyses for management, assuming whatever details are necessary.

EXERCISE

20-1. A department of the North Baking Company produces one type of biscuit on a continuous process basis. The standard materials, crew, and production are as follows:

Production *per day*, 13,140 biscuits using 1,314 pounds of raw materials and a standard crew of 48 labor hours.

Raw Materials:

Standard input per day—

* Lewis W. Roe, "How Standard Costs Help in Managing a Steel Company," *N.A.C.A. Bulletin* (February, 1955), pp. 775–77.

	Quantity	Price	Amount
Flour (in lbs.).............................	1,000	$.20	$200.00
Milk (in gals.).............................	8	.60	4.80
Shortening (in lbs.).....................	250	.232	58.00
Total (in lbs.).....................	1,314		$262.80

Average standard price per pound ($262.80 ÷ 1,314 lbs.)...............		.20	
Yield, at ten biscuits per pound..........	13,140 biscuits		

Direct labor:
Standard crew per day:

	Hours	Rate	Amount
Material handler..........................	8	$1.50	$12.00
Mixers....................................	8	2.00	16.00
Cutters...................................	16	2.00	32.00
Oven-men.................................	16	2.00	32.00
Total...............................	48		$92.00

Average standard labor cost per pound of starting materials ($92.00 ÷ 1,314 lbs.).........		.07

Required:

Complete the following analyses presented as Form 1 and 2 in the Workbook.

Analysis of Materials Price, Mixture, and Yield Variances—Form 1.
Analysis of Labor Crew, Volume, and Yield Variances—Form 2.

PROBLEMS

20-1. The Miller Company operates a standard cost system. Physical standards for materials and labor are set by the industrial engineering department and standard cost cards are set up by the cost accounting department. Yearly models are produced, and a new set of standard cost cards is drawn at the beginning of each year.

In some cases, new standards which would bring about cost reduction are put into effect during the year, although the standard cost cards are not changed until the end of the year.

Assume that a standard cost card shows the following information:

Standard Cost per Unit

Materials	
10 pcs. @ $2.00.............	$20.00
Labor	
5 hrs. @ $1.50...............	7.50
Factory expense	
5 hrs. @ $1.00...............	5.00
Total cost per unit.............	$32.50

Labor transactions for February, 19__ are:

(1) Product units completed................ 100
(2) New labor standard used in the factory
    4½ hours per product unit
(3) Labor used: 460 hours @ $1.55......... $713.00

There were no work in process inventories, beginning or ending.

Required:

(1) Draft entries to record (a) cost of goods completed and (b) labor rate, labor time, and change of standards variances.
(2) Set up T accounts for labor in process, the three variances, and accrued wages, and post the entries.

20-2. The Miller Company (Problem 20-1) used nonstandard Material Y during part of the month of February. Fifty units of product were produced using 510 pieces of standard Material X @ $2.10 per piece, and 50 units were produced using 520 pieces of nonstandard Material Y @ $2.50 per piece.

Required:

(1) Draft entries to record (a) cost of goods completed and (b) materials price, materials quantity, and substitution of materials variance. Assume that materials accounts are carried at actual prices.
(2) Set up T accounts for materials in process, the three variances, and materials inventory, and post the variances.

20-3. Assume that in the month of March, the Miller Company (Problem 20-1) produces 90 units of good product and 20 units of spoiled product. All materials required for the latter are in the product, but they are only half completed as regards labor and expense.

Draft the entry for spoiled work.

20-4. The flexible expense budget of the Comet Company for a one-month period follows:

Per cent of capacity......	80%	90%	100%
Standard hours..........	640	720	800
Variable expense........	$ 384.00	$ 432.00	$ 480.00
Fixed expense...........	$1,008.00	$1,008.00	$1,008.00

It is expected that the factory will operate at 90 per cent of capacity and the standard factory expense rate is set on that basis.

Actual performance for the month of August, 19__ was:

Per cent of capacity.............	80%
Standard hours produced.........	640
Actual hours...................	660
Variable expense...............	$ 390.00
Fixed expense..................	$1,020.00
Total actual expense...........	$1,410.00

Required:

(1) Calculate expense variances for August under the two-variance plan.
(2) Calculate expense variances for August under the three-variance plan.

20-5. The Copperhead Company operates a process standard cost system for its separating department using a standard crew. Summaries for the week just ended show:

For raw materials:

Actual cost of inputs...	$10,692.00
Actual inputs used at standard prices.............................	10,213.00
Total weight of inputs at the average standard price for all inputs......	10,355.00
Standard inputs for the production attained at standard prices........	9,886.00

For direct labor:

Actual labor cost of the crew......................................	$ 957.00
Normal hours of standard crew at standard rates. (Capacity of crew equals 20,000 pounds per week)..................................	900.00
Actual weight of materials handled at standard labor cost per pound....	845.00
Standard weight of materials for the production attained at standard labor cost per pound..	814.00

Required:

(1) Prepare a simple analysis of the variances for raw materials in summary form.

(2) Prepare a simple analysis of the variances for direct labor in summary form.

20-6. The North Carolina Knitting Mills produces Product T, using the following formula for materials:

	Pounds
Material X..............................	5.10
Material Y..............................	3.10
Material Z..............................	2.00
Gross input............................	10.20
Standard shrinkage (2% of good output)......	.20
Net weight per dozen.....................	10.00

The standard cost card shows the following costs per dozen for materials:

Standard Cost Card
Materials Cost per Dozen

Particulars	*Pounds*	*Per Pound*	*Amount*
Material X...............................	5.10	$.30	$1.53
Material Y...............................	3.10	.40	1.24
Material Z...............................	2.00	.50	1.00
	10.20	.3696*	$3.77
Standard shrinkage (2% of good output).......	.20		
Net material cost per dozen.................	10.00	$.377	$3.77

* Use $.37

Production and input for October 1, 19__ are:

Production and Input: Product T

Particulars	*Actual Quantity*	*Actual Price*	*Amount*
Product T produced................	800 dozens		
Actual input			
Material X........................	4,150 pounds	$.32	$1,328.00
Material Y........................	2,520 pounds	.43	1,083.60
Material Z........................	1,630 pounds	.55	896.50
	8,300 pounds		$3,308.10

Required:

Calculate materials price, mixture, and yield variances.

20-7. The Dye House of the North Carolina Knitting Mill (Problem 20-6) has a capacity of 1,000 dozens of Product T (10.2 pounds gross input weight per dozen), using the standard crew shown below:

October 1, 19___

	Standard Crew (Hours)	Standard Rate per Hour	Actual Crew (Hours)	Actual Rate
Foreman....................	8	$2.00	8	$2.00
Material loaders................	16	1.50	20	1.50
Dye tub tenders...............	16	1.60	20	1.60
Extractor tenders..............	24	1.50	24	1.50
Drier tenders.................	16	1.70	16	1.70
Napper tenders................	16	1.50	16	1.50
Turner and folder tenders........	16	1.60	18	1.60
Folder unloader...............	8	1.40	8	1.40

Prepare an analysis of labor crew, volume, and yield variance, using the above information and pertinent information from Problem 20-6.

GENERAL ADMINISTRATIVE EXPENSE CONTROL; OFFICE AND CLERICAL LABOR CONTROL

I. GENERAL ADMINISTRATIVE EXPENSE CONTROL

General administrative function; Expense control. General administrative expense control is concerned with the expense of top management, which is responsible for planning, coordinating, and supervising the major activities of the business, such as manufacturing and marketing. Organization-wise, it includes the president and the immediate staff which assists him in performing those functions. The work of these people is related jointly to manufacturing and marketing, rather than to one or the other directly and exclusively.

True general administrative activities do not lend themselves to work measurement by means of statistical units. Staff work of a creative or exploratory nature is not likely to be directly related to such units as product units produced, or orders received, or invoices typed. For this reason, general administrative expense control consists in careful consideration of what staff is required to do the current job of planning, coordinating, and top supervising, and what will be the cost in salaries and expenses of maintaining that staff. Accounts in the general administrative expense budget are likely to be controlled by executive decision as to what is needed.

A formal control plan for general administrative expense is useful because it provides for periodic re-examination of personnel complements, salaries, and expenses. The object would be, not to eliminate necessary activities, but to provide adequately for them, and at the same time to prevent administrative expense from rising by osmosis.

General administrative expense accounts should not include expenses which can be readily identified with the marketing function (such as order and billing expense) or the manufacturing function (such as factory payroll clerks). Better control is likely to be achieved by identifying such activities as order and billing and factory payroll with the functions to which they are directly related than by carrying them in the general administrative expense accounts.

Function, organization, and plant: Benson & West Manufacturing Company. The Administrative Department of the Benson & West Manufacturing Company exercises general supervision over the manufacturing departments and the distribution departments. Personnel of the department consists of the president, controller and treasurer, cost accountant, head bookkeeper, and receptionist. The plant used by the Administrative Department consists of the office space occupied by general administrative personnel, together with the furniture and fixtures in the offices.

Expense control: Budget. Administrative expense is controlled by means of a budget of the fixed type. It is not adjusted for ordinary changes in level of operations during the period to which it applies. The budget is shown on page 510. At the beginning of each period, executive salaries for the coming period are set up on the basis of positions to be maintained and salaries to be paid. The other object accounts (except Noncash Charges) are set up through review of the actual accounts for the previous period, modified for expected price changes and to some extent by administrative decision. Such accounts as dues and subscriptions and donations are controlled almost entirely by administrative decision, and travel is partly so controlled. The Noncash Charges section comprises depreciation, insurance, and taxes on office furniture and fixtures, and rent for the office. These charges are same as last period, except where changes in equipment and space cost are expected.

Actual expense is compared with the budget each period to determine how well the management has stayed within the budget. A comparative statement appears in Appendix I.

II. OFFICE AND CLERICAL LABOR CONTROL

Office and clerical labor in large organizations. The following sections of this chapter describe and illustrate the types of information which the management needs to control the cost of clerical operations, together with several methods of setting standards for clerical operations. "Order Department and Cash Collecting," comprising all the steps of paper work involved in recording the customer's order (on open charge account), filling the order, and finally collecting the cash, is used to illustrate standards. This example has been chosen because it fits numerous medium-sized and large businesses. The methods of control described can be used for all mass production clerical operations.

When studying standards for clerical operations, it is interesting to compare paper work procedures found in large offices with production procedures used in the factory. In large organizations, the processing of accounting papers follows standardized procedures from the point where they are written to the point where they are finally filed. Particular types of accounting papers may move in batches from desk to desk in somewhat

Administrative Expense Budget

(Excluding Order Department and Cash Collecting)

Account	Amount
Salaries:	
Executive salaries—	
President	$1,800.00
Controller and treasurer	1,000.00
Cost accountant	700.00
Head bookkeeper	500.00
Total	$4,000.00
Office salaries—	
Receptionist	300.00
Total salaries	$4,300.00
Supplies:	
Printed forms	$ 40.00
Office supplies	30.00
Total supplies	$ 70.00
Purchased services:	
Electric light and power	$ 20.00
Telephone and telegraph	60.00
Legal and accounting fees	200.00
Dues and subscriptions	50.00
Donations	60.00
Total purchased service	$ 390.00
Travel	$ 200.00
Unclassified	$ 40.00
Noncash charges:	
Depreciation—Furniture and equipment	$ 33.33
Insurance—Furniture and equipment	8.33
Taxes—Furniture and equipment	10.00
Rent	164.00
Total noncash charges	$ 215.66
Total department	$5,215.66

Figure 21-1

the same way as materials in the factory move from work center to work center, and each clerk may perform a single integrated set of operations upon each batch of papers. Certain sets of operations, such as order writing and invoice typing, are likely to be mass production operations. In a large company there may be a dozen or so billing machine operators producing invoices.

In large organizations it may also be possible to apply some of the principles of work measurement to clerical operations that are used for factory production operations. Where one office employee performs a single operation or a set of integrated operations, it is usually not difficult to find a *work unit* which is a good measure of the employee's clerical output. In some cases, the number of each form (orders, invoices, and so on) handled may be satisfactory, and a basic work measure might be orders (or invoices, or some other form) processed per hour.

Often in setting up a program of clerical standards, it is found that satisfactory work units are already being collected and recorded. Customers' orders are numbered serially as they come in, for instance, and the number of orders received each day is being recorded. Likewise, sales invoices may be serially numbered and each day's count recorded. In other cases, it is necessary for the standards man to devise and install work units to make it possible to control clerical costs properly. He may find, for instance, that the number of lines in the body of invoices varies considerably from season to season and that the number of invoices typed is not a satisfactory measure of billing typist output. He may decide that it will be necessary to collect *line items* as well as number of *invoices*.

One further point may be made by way of introduction to the study of clerical standards. After the work units have been selected and installed, the computed standards may be either *cost* standards or *time* standards, depending upon the basic plan the standards man follows. Both types of standards are explained and illustrated in the following sections.

Managerial information: Benson & West Manufacturing Co. (cost standards). Office and clerical labor is an important cost in the Benson & West Manufacturing Company. In the organization chart, page 272, the following positions appear:

Sales Statistician
Head Clerk—Order Department
Head Clerk—Planning and Production Control
Purchasing Agent
Cost Clerk
Inventory Ledger Clerk
Payroll Clerks
Accounts Payable Clerk
Billing Typists
Accounts Receivable Clerks

In this company the supervisors desire the following analyses of Order Department and Cash Collecting Costs:

(1) Cost by object, monthly.
(2) Cost of performing certain operations or subfunctions; total and per unit (in terms of work performed).

These analyses are explained and illustrated in the following sections.
Order department and cash collecting costs by object. The

Statement of Expenses by Object for Order Department and Cash Collecting appears on page 513. As was indicated previously, the object accounts analyze expenses according to the nature of the goods or services used. On each statement, the object accounts are grouped in general according to the nature and degree of control which is possible.

The object groups are:

> Labor
> Supplies
> Repairs and Repair Parts
> Purchased Services
> Unclassified
> Bad Debts
> Fixed Charges

This grouping is a rough separation according to variability, since the expenses that are susceptible to short-run action are placed at the top, and those susceptible to long-run action (for example, the fixed charges) at the bottom.

This statement is used to provide an over-all control of expenses. This control involves studying gross profit percentages and object expense account percentages to determine whether the latter exceed allowable limits. The managers have determined through experience what the percentages should be for a given volume of sales—leaving a balance of profit—and they investigate unsatisfactory percentages immediately to see if corrective action is possible.

Analysis of order department and cash collecting costs by function: Work units. A classification of costs by function is a classification according to the nature of the work done. The table on page 514 is an analysis of order department and cash collecting costs by function.

The functions indicated in this analysis are:

> Credit investigations—prospective customers
> Passing orders for credit
> Editing orders
> Typing shipping orders
> Entering orders in order register and following up orders
> Invoicing
> Charging customers' accounts
> Preparing customers' monthly statements
> Recording cash sales
> Receiving cash on account and crediting customers' accounts

Note that this analysis is likely to be more useful than analysis by *object* for the measurement of performance according to local work areas and responsibilities. Thus it is likely to be more useful to know the cost of passing orders for credit, editing orders, and so on, than it is to know the total cost of labor, the total cost of supplies, and so on.

Statement of Expenses by Object
for Month of December, 19__

Order Department and Cash Collecting Department

	Month		Year to Date	
Object	Amount	% to Sales	Amount	% to Sales
Labor........................	$2,390.00		$	
Supplies:				
Printed forms...............	$ 231.00		$	
Office supplies..............	149.00			
Totals...................	$ 380.00		$	
Repairs and repair parts........	$ 15.00		$	
Purchased services:				
Electric light and power.......	$ 3.00		$	
Credit association dues........	867.00			
Postage....................	48.00			
Totals...................	$ 918.00		$	
Bad debts....................	$ 700.00		$	
Fixed charges:				
Depreciation................	$ 100.00		$	
Insurance..................	33.33			
Taxes.....................	50.00			
Rent......................	54.50			
Totals...................	$ 237.83		$	
Total order department and				
cash collecting...........	$4,640.83		$	

Figure 21-2

A *work unit*, as the name indicates, is a unit for the measurement of work done. Work units which may be used in connection with Order Department and Cash Collecting functions are:

Function	Work Unit
Credit investigations	Investigations
Passing orders for credit	Charge orders
Editing orders	Orders shipped
Typing shipping orders	Orders shipped
Order register and follow-up	Orders shipped
Invoicing:	
Typing headings	Invoices
Typing line items	Line items
Charging customers accounts	Invoices
Preparing customers monthly statements	Statements mailed
Recording cash sales	Cash orders
Crediting customers accounts	Receipts

Analysis of Actual Order Department and Cash Collecting Costs—by Object and Function for the Month of December, 19___

	By Object					By Function		
Functional Account	Labor	Supplies	Repairs and Repair Parts	Purchased Services (1); Noncash Charges (2)	Total Amount	Description of Unit	Number of Units	Cost per Unit
Credit investigations—prospective customers...	$ 70.00			(1) $ 650.00	$ 720.00	Investigations	160	$4.50
Passing orders for credit...	93.00			(1) 217.00	310.00	Charge orders	3,100	.10
Editing orders...	870.00				900.00	Orders shipped	3,000	.30
Typing shipping orders...	330.00	$ 30.00	$ 5.00		450.00	Orders shipped	3,000	.15
Order register and follow up...	153.00	115.00			180.00	Orders shipped	3,000	.06
Invoicing—headings...	315.00	27.00	5.00		480.00	Invoices	3,200	.15
Invoicing—line items...	42.00	160.00			42.00	Line items	4,200	.01
Charging customers accounts...	47.00	25.00	5.00	(1) 3.00	80.00	Invoices	3,200	.025
Customers monthly statements...	48.00			(1) 48.00	96.00	Statements mailed	1,600	.06
Recording cash sales...	4.00	2.00			6.00	Cash orders	200	.03
Crediting customers accounts...	43.00	21.00			64.00	Receipts	1,600	.04
Total charges to functional accounts...	$2,015.00	$380.00	$15.00	$ 918.00	$3,328.00			
Bad debts...				(2) $ 700.00	$ 700.00			
Capacity costs								
Supervision...	$ 375.00				$ 375.00			
Depreciation...				(2) $ 100.00	100.00			
Insurance...				(2) 33.33	33.33			
Taxes...				(2) 50.00	50.00			
Rent...				(2) 54.50	54.50			
Total capacity cost...	$ 375.00			$ 237.83	$ 612.83			
Totals by object group...	$2,390.00	$380.00	$15.00	$1,855.83	$4,640.83			

Figure 21-3

514

Budget of Order Department and Cash Collecting Costs and Standard Functional Unit Costs
One Month Period: Effective January 1, 19___

Budget

Functional Account	Labor	Supplies	Repairs and Repair Parts	Purchased Services (1); Noncash Charges (2)	Total Amount
Credit investigations—prospective customers	$ 40.00			(1) $ 520.00	$ 560.00
Passing orders for credit	90.00	$ 14.00		(1) 130.00	234.00
Editing orders	736.00	20.00			756.00
Typing shipping orders	276.00	125.00	$ 4.00		405.00
Orders register and follow-up	109.00	26.00			135.00
Invoicing—headings	281.00	135.00	4.00		420.00
Invoicing—line items	40.00				40.00
Charging customers accounts	29.50	20.00	4.00	(1) 2.50	56.00
Customers monthly statements	14.00	28.00		(1) 42.00	84.00
Recording cash sales	5.00	2.50			7.50
Crediting customers accounts	24.00	12.00			36.00
Total charges to functional accounts	$1,644.50	$382.50	$12.00	$ 694.50	$2,733.50
Bad debts				(2) 690.00	$ 690.00
Capacity cost					
Supervision	$ 400.00				$ 400.00
Depreciation				(2) $ 100.00	100.00
Insurance				(2) 33.33	33.33
Taxes				(2) 50.00	50.00
Rent				(2) 54.50	54.50
Total capacity cost	$ 400.00			$ 237.83	$ 637.83
Totals by object group	$2,044.50	$382.50	$12.00	$1,622.33	$4,061.33

Standard Functional Unit Costs

Description of Unit	Number of Units	Cost per Unit
Investigations	140	$4.00
Charge order	2,600	.09
Orders shipped	2,700	.28
Orders shipped	2,700	.15
Orders shipped	2,700	.05
Invoices	2,800	.15
Line items	4,000	.01
Invoices	2,800	.02
Statements mailed	1,400	.06
Cash orders	250	.03
Receipts	1,200	.03

Figure 21-4

A *functional unit cost* is the cost of a function per work unit performed. The formula is Cost of the function ÷ Work units produced. In Figure 21-3, the unit cost of typing shipping orders is $.15 per shipping order. The cost of the bookkeeping operation of charging customers accounts is $.025 per invoice charged. (Figure 21-3 also shows functional unit costs for all the other functions named above.)

The functional unit costs shown in Figure 21-3 are *actual* unit costs. They are determined by dividing actual cost of a function by actual work units produced. To measure the performance of the various functions, the management may compare the current actual functional unit costs with past actual unit costs. If a functional unit cost is rising, the supervisor may investigate it to determine whether the increase was caused by higher salaries or by reduction in number of work units produced for a given period of time. Or the management may compare current actual unit costs with *standard* unit costs which have been set on the basis of good performance.

Setting standard functional unit costs by analysis of actual functional unit costs. In some cases, standard functional unit costs may be set by analysis of actual functional unit costs. The procedure would be:

(1) Compile actual expenses in functional expense accounts for one month and at the same time collect work units produced for each of the functions. At the end of the month, determine actual functional unit costs as shown in Figure 21-3.

(2) Review the actual functional unit costs to eliminate the wild costs. These are the costs which are obviously out of line when compared with past actual costs or which appear to the supervisors to be too high on the basis of experience.

(3) Determine the number of work units required for the coming period. Set up a budget of costs by function and standard functional unit costs as shown in Figure 21-4. This budget is based upon the actual costs of the previous period, with appropriate adjustments to correct the out-of-line unit costs of that period and also for any anticipated changes in salaries and other prices.

III. OPERATION TIME ALLOWANCES AND CLERICAL WORK LOADING

Control of clerical labor through clerical work loading. Clerical work loading consists in (a) determining allowed time per work unit for each clerical operation and (b) setting up the total labor allowance for a coming period, by persons or occupations on the basis of expected work load. In this case, the control covers labor only (unlike the control described above, which covers all elements of cost), and it is set up in hours (instead of dollars). The total loading for a coming period becomes the labor budget for the period.

Several features of clerical work loading as a management tool are noteworthy. In the first place, loading itself is a method of distributing the work load equitably among the clerks. In some cases, the work load assigned to the employees of a department may have become very inequitable over a period of time. This could be because there was no measurement of work and because clerical employees tend to adapt their speed to whatever

Operation Chart—Order and Billing Procedure

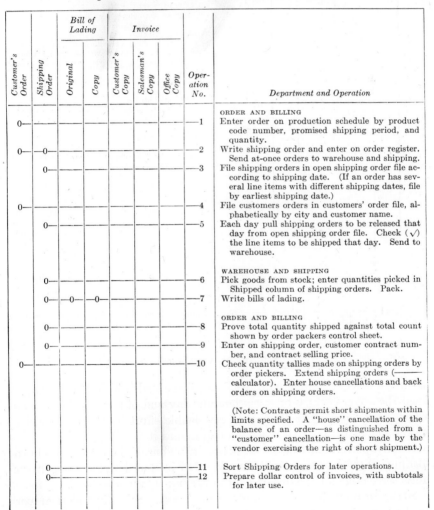

| Customer's Order | Shipping Order | Bill of Lading | | Invoice | | | | Oper-ation No. | Department and Operation |
		Original	Copy	Customer's Copy	Salesman's Copy	Office Copy			
									ORDER AND BILLING
0—								—1	Enter order on production schedule by product code number, promised shipping period, and quantity.
0—	0—							—2	Write shipping order and enter on order register. Send at-once orders to warehouse and shipping.
	0—							—3	File shipping orders in open shipping order file according to shipping date. (If an order has several line items with different shipping dates, file by earliest shipping date.)
0—								—4	File customers orders in customers' order file, alphabetically by city and customer name.
	0—							—5	Each day pull shipping orders to be released that day from open shipping order file. Check (✓) the line items to be shipped that day. Send to warehouse.
									WAREHOUSE AND SHIPPING
	0—							—6	Pick goods from stock; enter quantities picked in Shipped column of shipping orders. Pack.
	0—	0—	0—					—7	Write bills of lading.
									ORDER AND BILLING
	0—							—8	Prove total quantity shipped against total count shown by order packers control sheet.
	0—							—9	Enter on shipping order, customer contract number, and contract selling price.
0—								—10	Check quantity tallies made on shipping orders by order pickers. Extend shipping orders (———— calculator). Enter house cancellations and back orders on shipping orders.
									(Note: Contracts permit short shipments within limits specified. A "house" cancellation of the balance of an order—as distinguished from a "customer" cancellation—is one made by the vendor exercising the right of short shipment.)
	0—							—11	Sort Shipping Orders for later operations.
	0—							—12	Prepare dollar control of invoices, with subtotals for later use.

Figure 21-5

Operation Chart—Order and Billing Procedure

Customer's Order	Shipping Order	Bill of Lading		Invoice			Operation No.	Department and Operation
		Original	Copy	Customer's Copy	Salesman's Copy	Office Copy		
	0						13	Put (invoice) serial number and date on shipping orders. (Numbering stamp.)
	0			0	0	0	14	Type and extend invoice (——— computing billing machine.)
						0	15	Take office copies of invoices to sales department.
						0	16	SALES DEPARTMENT Check prices on office copies of invoices.
		0	0	0			17	ORDER AND BILLING Separate original bills of lading from copies. Match original bills of lading with original invoices. Staple original bills to original invoices. Mail invoices.
			0				18	File copies of bills of lading.
						0	19	ACCOUNTS RECEIVABLE Post invoices to customers' accounts (——— bookkeeping machine).
						0	20	OFFICE MANAGER Prove dollars posted to customers' accounts (per bookkeeping machine proof sheet) against billing dollar control (Operation 12)
						0	21	SALES DISTRIBUTION Post sales totals (from Operation 12) to sales distribution.
						0	22	Make distribution of shipments by product number.
					0		23	Enter invoices in commission record. Send salesmen's copies to salesmen.
						0	24	File invoices by invoice serial number.
	0						25	ORDER AND BILLING Enter shipment dates (or completions) on order register.
	0						26	File completed shipping orders in completed shipping order file.
	0						27	File uncompleted shipping orders in open shipping order file.

Figure 21-5 (*Continued*)

volume is in sight. Some employees may have loads which would normally keep them consistently busy six hours a day and others may have loads which could actually be done with reasonable effort in four hours a day.

Another feature is that work loading makes it possible to measure the actual net performance of the department. Thus, if the total hours in the loading is 1,000 and the actual hours of labor paid for is 1,200, the performance percentage for the department is $1,000 \div 1,200 = 83\frac{1}{3}\%$.

Steps in a clerical work loading program. Steps in a clerical work loading program are:

(1) Trace the path of each of the major office forms through the various

operations, and prepare an operation list or flow chart of each sequence or "process," as it is sometimes called.

(2) Determine actual time required to do each of the operations, by observing actual batches in work.

(3) On the basis of expected clerical volumes, set up labor time allowed for each operation and total for the department.

These steps are explained and illustrated in the following sections. The illustrations are based upon actual cases (not the Benson & West Manufacturing Company), but the number of operations has been reduced and the actual times have been changed to simplify the presentation.

Operation list or flow chart. An operation list setting out the operations (27 in all) in an order and billing procedure is shown on pages 517-518. The list was prepared by a methods analyst who went from desk to desk observing the operations. The operations are listed in the order in which they are performed. Department names (order and billing, warehouse and shipping, sales, etc.) are inserted as appropriate to indicate where each operation is performed on the batch of papers as it moves.

Note that several columns have been added to the left of the operation list—one column for each form or copy of a form:

Customer's order
Shipping order
Bill of lading—
    Original
    Copy
Invoice—
    Customer's copy
    Salesman's copy
    Office copy.

The purpose of these columns is to show which forms are involved in each operation. The horizontal line opposite an operation indicates what forms are in use in that operation.

Operation times. A table of "Operation Times—Selected Batches in Actual Production" appears on pages 520-521. The times were taken after the flow chart, described above, was completed. To obtain these actual times, certain batches of documents were observed in work. Start and finish times were obtained for each operation. Minutes elapsed and minutes per form were calculated. (In actual situations, the batches were smaller than the ones indicated in Figure 21-6, and the analyst was able to observe many of the operations through complete batches. Any significant interruptions were noted.)

Work loading. A work loading table based upon 1,000 orders and 500 invoices per week is shown on pages 522-523 and one based upon 500 orders and 1,000 invoices per week on pages 524-525. In preparing both loading tables, the operation times appearing in Figure 21-6 were used.

Operation Times—Selected Batches in Actual Production

Operation No.	Operation Description	Form Handled (Operator)	Quantity in Sample (Date)	Start: Finish	Minutes Elapsed	Minutes per Form
1	Enter order on production schedule by product code number, promised shipping period, and quantity	Customer Orders (B. Smith)	200 7/2/—	8:00 A 5:00 P	480	2.40
2	Write shipping order and enter on order register	Shipping Orders (J. Thomas)	200 7/3/—	8:00 A 3:00 P	360	1.80
3	File shipping orders in open shipping file according to shipping date	Shipping Order	200 7/3/— 7/4/—	3:00 P 5:00 P 8:00 A 9:00 A	180	.90
4	File customers orders in customers' order file alphabetically by city and customer's name	Customers Orders (A. Morgan)	200 7/4/—	9:00 A 10:30 A	90	.45
5	Each day, pull shipping orders to be released that day from the open shipping order file	Shipping Orders (A. Morgan)	Not timed	Fixed daily allowance 10 min.		
6	Pick goods from stock; enter quantities picked in Shipped column of Shipping Orders. Pack	Shipping Department	Not timed			
7	Write bills of lading	Shipping Department	Not timed			
8	Prove total quantity shipped against total count shown by order packers' control sheet	Shipping Orders (F. Lord)	320 7/2/—	4:22 P 5:00 P	38	.12
9	Enter customer contract number and contract price on shipping order	Shipping Orders (T. Lombard)	320 7/3/—	2:00 P 4:40 P	160	.50
10	Check quantity tallies made on shipping orders by order pickers. Extend shipping orders (—— calculator). Enter house cancellations and back orders on shipping orders	Shipping Orders (E. North)	320 7/3/—	8:00 A 5:00 P	480	1.50
11	Sort shipping orders for later operations	Shipping Orders (F. Lord)	320 7/4/—	8:00 A 8:57 A	57	.18
12	Prepare dollar control of invoices, with subtotals for later use	Invoices (E. North)	320 7/5/—	9:20 A 10:30 A	70	.22
13	Put (invoice) serial number and date on shipping orders. (Numbering stamp)	Shipping Orders (F. Lord)	320 7/4/—	8:57 A 9:19 A	22	.07
14	Type and extend invoices (—— Computing billing machine)	Invoices (E. North)	129 7/4/—	9:19 A 1:45 P	206	1.60
15	Take office copies of invoices to sales department	Invoices (E. North)	Not timed	Fixed daily allowance 10 min.		
16	Check prices on office copies of invoices	Sales Department	Not timed			
17	Separate original bills of lading from copies. Match original bills of lading with original invoices. Staple original bills to original invoices. Mail invoices.	B/L Use Invoices (E. North)	320 7/4/—	2:00 P 4:40 P	160	.5
18	File copies of bills of lading	B/L Use Invoices (E. North)	320 7/5/—	8:00 A 9:20 A	80	.25
19	Post invoices to customers accounts (—— bookkeeping machine)	Invoices (P. Schultz)	320 7/5/—	10:30 A 1:51 P	141	.44
20	Prove dollars posted to customers account (per bookkeeping machine proof sheet) against billing dollar control (Operation 12).	Not timed				
21	Post sales totals (from Operation 12) to sales distribution	Tape (J. Ward)			10/day	
22	Make distribution of shipments by product number	Invoices (J. Ward)	320 7/5/—	3:00 P 4:20 P	80	.25
23	Enter invoices in commission record. Send salesmens copies to salesmen.	Invoices (A. Morgan)	320 7/5/—	4:20 P 4:52 P	32	.10
24	File invoices by invoice serial number.	Invoices (A. Morgan)	320 7/5/—	4:52 P 5:00 P	8	—

Figure 21-6

Operation Times—Selected Batches in Actual Production

Opera-tion No.	Operation Description	Form Handled (Operator)	Quantity in Sample (Date)	Start: Finish	Minutes Elapsed	Minutes per Form
25	Enter shipment dates (or completions) on order register	Shipping Orders (B. Smith)	320 7/5/— 7/6/—	2:00 P 5:00 P 8:00 A 9:00 A	240	.75
26	File completed shipping orders in completed shipping order file	Shipping Orders (A. Morgan)	200 7/6/—	9:00 A 10:30 A	90	.45
27	File uncompleted shipping orders in open shipping order file	Shipping Orders (A. Morgan)	120 7/6/—	10:30 A 1:18 P	108	.90

Figure 21-6 (*Continued*)

In the situation illustrated, orders are taken for future delivery. In certain months, the office must process 1,000 incoming orders per week and half that many invoices representing shipments. In other months, the office must process 1,000 invoices, but half as many incoming orders. The load for particular operations changes from season to season, and the work force must be trained so that to some extent employees can be shifted from one operation to another.

The charts show that for a work load of 1,000 orders and 500 invoices, 154.0 clerk hours must be provided. In a work load of 500 orders and 1,000 invoices, 172.6 clerk hours must be provided. These standards do not include allowances for personal factors, fatigue, and delay. In the actual situation these standard time totals were multiplied by $1\frac{1}{3}$ to take care of those factors.

Note that the loading tables are headed "measured work." It should be pointed out that there is certain "unmeasured work" in the function, such as (in this case) supervision, taking dictation, look ups to answer customer complaints, and other tasks. A reasonable addition is made to the clerical work budget to take care of unmeasured work. A task is moved from the unmeasured to the measured class when it is feasible to set up a unit measurement for the task and where the work load for the task justifies measurement.

QUESTIONS

21-1. Discuss the methods of controlling administrative expense in a medium-size concern.

21-2. What is an object classification of expense accounts? a functional classification?

21-3. (a) What is a "work unit"?

(b) Give examples of work units for manufacturing concerns, trading concerns, and institutions.

(c) Discuss the importance of the selection of proper work units where unit costs are to be used in the control of expense.

21-4. In many businesses, large volume clerical operations are found in (a) order and billing and (b) payroll.

(a) Name work units which might be used in order and billing in a large business.

Loading—Measured Work—Based upon Actual Operation Times

(Period—One Week)

Work load per week:
1,000 orders
500 invoices

Opera-tion No.	Operation Description	Production Schedule Clerk — Orders; Minutes per Order	Total Minutes Week	Order Clerk — Orders; Minutes per Order	Total Minutes Week	Biller — Invoices; Minutes per Invoice	Total Minutes Week	Accounts Receivable Operator — Invoices; Minutes per Invoice	Total Minutes Week	Distribution Clerk — Invoices; Minutes per Invoice	Total Minutes Week	File Clerk — Minutes per Paper	Total Minutes Week
1	Enter order on production schedule	1,000 2.40	2,400										
2	Write shipping order and enter on order register			1,000 1.80	1,800								
3	File shipping orders in open shipping order file											1,000 .9	900
4	File customers order in customers' order file											1,000 .45	450
5	Pull shipping orders from file for release											500 10/day	50
6	Pick goods from stock; pack (warehouse)	Not timed											
7	Write bills of lading (warehouse)	Not timed											
8	Prove total quantity shipped			500 .12	60								
9	Enter customer contract number and contract price on shipping order			500 .5	250								
10	Check quantity tallies on shipping orders. Enter house cancellations and back orders			500 1.5	750								
11	Sort shipping orders for later operation			500 .18	90								
12	Prepare dollar control of invoices			200 .22	44								
13	Put serial numbers and date on shipping orders					500 .07	35						

Figure 21-7 — continuation of operations list (operations 14–27)

No.	Operation	Quantity	Rate	Minutes
14	Type and extend invoices (_____ computing billing machine)	500	1.6	800
15	Take office copies of invoices to sales department	500	10/day	50
16	Check prices on office copies of invoices		Not timed	
17	Separate bills of lading. Match with invoices and staple. Mail	500	.5	250
18	File copies of bills of lading	500	.25	125
19	Post invoices to customers' accounts (_____ bookkeeping machine)	500	.44	220
20	Prove dollars posted to customer accounts		Not timed	
21	Post sales totals to sales distribution sheet		10/day	50
22	Make distribution of shipments by product number	500	.25	125
23	Enter invoices in commission record. Send salesmen's copies to salesmen	500	.10	50
24	File invoices by serial number	500	10/day	50
25	Enter shipment dates (or completions) on order register	500	.75	375
26	File completed shipping orders in completed shipping order file	300	.45	135
27	File uncompleted shipping orders in open shipping order file	200	.9	180

Column totals:

	I	II	III	IV	V	VI
Total minutes (All operations, 9,239 minutes)	2,400	3,369	1,135	220	225	1,890
Total hours (All operations, 154.0 hours)	40	56.2	18.9	3.7	3.7	31.5

Figure 21-7

523

Loading—Measured Work—Based upon Actual Operation Times

(Period—One Week)

Work load per week:
500 orders
1,000 invoices

Operation No.	Operation Description	Production Schedule Clerk Orders; Minutes per Order	Total Minutes Week	Order Clerk Orders; Minutes per Order	Total Minutes Week	Biller Invoices; Minutes per Invoice	Total Minutes Week	Accounts Receivable Operator Invoices; Minutes per Invoice	Total Minutes Week	Distribution Clerk Invoices; Minutes per Invoice	Total Minutes Week	File Clerk Minutes per Paper	Total Minutes Week
1	Enter order on production schedule	500 2.40	1,200										
2	Write shipping order and enter on order register			500 1.80	900								
3	File shipping orders in open shipping order file											500 .9	450
4	File customers order in customers' order file											1,000 .45	450
5	Pull shipping orders from file for release											1,000 20/day	100
6	Pick goods from stock; pack (warehouse)	Not timed											
7	Write bills of lading (warehouse)	Not timed											
8	Prove total quantity shipped			1,000 .12	120								
9	Enter customer contract number and contract price on shipping order			1,000 .5	500								
10	Check quantity tallies on shipping orders. Extend. Enter house cancellations and back orders			1,000 1.5	1,500								
11	Sort shipping orders for later operations			1,000 .18	180								
12	Prepare dollar control of invoices			1,000 .22	220								
13	Put serial numbers and date on shipping orders					1,000 .07	70						

No.	Operation	Volume	Rate	Minutes
14	Type and extend invoices (——— computing billing machine)	1,000	1.6	1,600
15	Take office copies of invoices to sales department		10/day	50
16	Check prices on office copies of invoices. Not timed			
17	Separate bills of lading. Match with invoices and staple. Mail.	1,000	.5	500
18	File copies of bills of lading	1,000	.25	250
19	Post invoices to customers' accounts (——— bookkeeping machine)	1,000	.44	440
20	Prove dollars posted to customers accounts. Not timed			
21	Post sales totals to sales distribution sheet		10/day	50
22	Make distribution of shipments by product number	1,000	.25	250
23	Enter invoices in commission record. Send salesmen's copies to salesmen	1,000	.10	100
24	File invoices by serial number	1,000	10/day	50
25	Enter shipment dates (or completions) on order register	1,000	.75	750
26	File completed shipping orders in completed shipping order file	600	.45	270
27	File uncompleted shipping orders in open shipping order file	400	.9	360

	Column totals					
Total minutes (all operations, 10,360 minutes)	1,200	4,170	2,220	440	400	1,930
Total hours (all operations, 172.6 hours)	20	69.5	37	7.3	6.7	32.1

Figure 21-8

Do this by listing the functional accounts in the sequence in which an order and invoice would go through the department, with the unit (the functional unit) which would be used for each function work account.

(b) Name work units which might be used in a large timekeeping and payroll activity. You may refer to the chapter on accounting for labor (Chapter 7), list the major clerical steps described there, and indicate what work unit you think would be appropriate for each step. Assume that the company is a large one, and that the documents flow in large batches from person to person in the accounting department.

21-5. In general, what is the difference between a program of controlling clerical costs by the use of functional unit costs and controlling them by clerical work loading?

21-6. Name and discuss briefly the steps in a program of controlling clerical costs by the use of functional unit costs.

21-7. Name and discuss briefly the steps in a program of controlling clerical costs by clerical work loading.

EXERCISES

21-1. The following exhibits for the Van Norden Company are presented herewith:

(a) Budget of Order Department and Cash Collecting Costs and Standard Functional Unit Costs for a one-month period (page 527).
(b) Analysis of Actual Order Department and Cash Collecting Costs—by Object and Function for January, 19__ (page 528).

Required:

(1) Prepare an Expense Variance Statement, using the form in the Workbook.
(2) The Order Department and Cash Collecting Function spent $24.50 less than budget for the month. Using your solution to Required Part (1) as a basis, write an analysis of the favorable factors and the unfavorable factors contributing to the $24.50 net saving.

21-2. From the additional information which follows, complete Form 1 and Form 2 of this exercise in the Workbook.

Labor and supplies have been analyzed, and the distribution by functional accounts is as follows:

Functional Account	Budget Labor	Budget Supplies	Actual for January, 19__ Labor	Actual for January, 19__ Supplies
Credit investigations................	$ 60.00	$	$ 60.00	$
Passing orders for credit...........	100.00	20.00	94.00	16.00
Editing orders....................	725.00	25.00	730.00	20.00
Typing shipping orders.............	240.00	114.00	272.00	98.00
Order register and follow up........	100.00	20.00	100.00	25.00
Invoicing—headings...............	335.00	139.00	320.00	117.00
Invoicing—line items..............	64.00		48.00	
Charging customers' accounts.......	33.00	20.00	50.00	18.00
Customers' monthly statements.....	20.00	12.00	12.00	6.00
Recording cash sales..............	6.00	3.00	6.00	4.00
Crediting customers' accounts......	32.00	16.00	20.00	12.00
Totals.....................	$1,715.00	$369.00	$1,712.00	$316.00

THE VAN NORDEN COMPANY

Budget of Order Department and Cash Collecting Costs and Standard Functional Unit Costs

One Month Period: Effective January 1, 19___

	Budget					Standard Functional Unit Costs		
Functional Account	Labor	Supplies	Repairs and Repair Parts	Purchased Services (1); Noncash Charges (2)	Total Amount	Description of Units	Number of Units	Cost per Unit
Credit investigations—prospective customers..	$ 110.00			(1) $ 35.00	$ 145.00	Investigations	50	$2.90
Passing orders for credit..........	203.00				203.00	Charge orders	2,900	.07
Editing orders.............	728.00	$ 40.00			768.00	Orders shipped	3,200	.24
Typing shipping orders.........	350.00	120.00	$10.00		480.00	Orders shipped	3,200	.15
Order register and follow-up.....	110.00	18.00			128.00	Orders shipped	3,200	.04
Invoicing—headings...........	250.00	98.00		(1) 87.00	435.00	Invoices	2,900	.15
Invoicing—line items.........	43.50				43.50	Line items	4,350	.01
Charging customers' accounts......	40.00	10.00	8.00		58.00	Invoices	2,900	.02
Customers' monthly statements.....	50.00	10.00		(1) 90.00	150.00	Statements mailed	3,000	.05
Recording cash sales...........	7.00	2.00			9.00	Cash orders	300	.03
Crediting customers' accounts......	80.00	10.00			90.00	Receipts	3,000	.03
Total charges to functional accounts......	$1,971.50	$308.00	$18.00	(1) $ 212.00	$2,509.50			
Bad debts......				(2) $ 580.00	$ 580.00			
Capacity cost								
Supervision.............	$ 375.00				$ 375.00			
Depreciation............				(2) $ 100.00	100.00			
Insurance.............				(2) 25.00	25.00			
Taxes.............				(2) 50.00	50.00			
Rent.............				(2) 60.00	60.00			
Total capacity cost......	$ 375.00	$	$	(2) $ 235.00	$ 610.00			
Totals by object group......	$2,346.50	$308.00	$18.00	$1,027.00	$3,699.50			

527

THE VAN NORDEN COMPANY

Analysis of Actual Order Department and Cash Collecting Costs—by Object and Function
for the Month of January, 19___

	By Object					By Function		
Functional Account	Labor	Supplies	Repairs and Repair Parts	Purchased Services (1); Noncash Charges (2)	Total Amount	Description of Units	Number of Units	Cost per Unit
Credit investigations—prospective customers...	$ 120.00			(1) $ 60.00	$ 180.00	Investigations	60	$3.00
Passing orders for credit...	192.00				192.00	Charge orders	2,400	.08
Editing orders...	700.00	$ 50.00			750.00	Orders shipped	3,000	.25
Typing shipping orders...	340.00	100.00	$10.00		450.00	Orders shipped	3,000	.15
Order register and follow-up...	120.00	30.00			150.00	Orders shipped	3,000	.05
Invoicing—headings...	208.00	80.00		(1) 72.00	360.00	Invoices	2,400	.15
Invoicing—line items...	48.00				48.00	Line items	4,800	.01
Charging customers' accounts...	40.00	5.00	3.00		48.00	Invoices	2,400	.02
Customers' monthly statements...	66.00	15.00		(1) 81.00	162.00	Statements mailed	2,700	.06
Recording cash sales...	16.00	2.00			18.00	Cash orders	600	.03
Crediting customers' accounts...	100.00	32.00			132.00	Receipts	3,300	.04
Total charges to functional accounts...	$1,950.00	$314.00	$13.00	(1) $ 213.00	$2,490.00			
Bad debts...				(2) $ 600.00	$ 600.00			
Capacity cost								
Supervision...	$ 350.00				$ 350.00			
Depreciation...				(2) $ 100.00	100.00			
Insurance...				(2) 25.00	25.00			
Taxes...				(2) 50.00	50.00			
Rent...				(2) 60.00	60.00			
Total capacity cost...	$ 350.00	$	$	(2) 235.00	$ 585.00			
Totals by object group...	$2,300.00	$314.00	$13.00	$1,048.00	$3,675.00			

Other items should be distributed as follows:

	Amounts	
	Budget	Actual for January, 19__
Repairs and repair parts............................	$ 18.00	$ 15.00
Distribute one-third to each of the following:		
Typing shipping orders.......................		
Invoicing—headings..........................		
Charging customers' accounts.................		
Credit association dues and fees......................	700.00	790.00
Distribute $130.00 each month to "Passing orders for credit." Balance to "Credit investigations"........		
Electricity..	3.00	5.00
Distribute total each month to "Charging customers' accounts"		
Postage..	48.00	54.00
Distribute total each month to "Customers' monthly statements"		

Charges not allocable to functional accounts are:

	Amounts	
	Budget	Actual for January, 19__
Bad debts.......................................	$700.00	$550.00
Supervision......................................	400.00	425.00
Depreciation, insurance, and taxes..................	200.00	200.00

After the two schedules on Form 1 and 2 have been completed, write a memo to the controller commenting upon the performance of the order and cash collection department for the month of January, 19__.

PROBLEMS

21-1. The following exhibits for the L.&A. Company are presented herewith:

(a) Budget of Order Department and Cash Collecting Cost for period of one month (page 530)

(b) Actual Order Department and Cash Collecting Costs for month of November, 19__ (page 531).

Required:

Draft a variance report, analyzing variances between actual expenses and budget expenses for the functional accounts into (1) variances due to quantity of work units and (2) variances due to price of work units. For capacity costs, show net variance for each account. Devise your own form of report.

The following formulas are suggested:

Units		Price	
Actual	@	Actual	} Price
Actual	@	Standard	}
Budget	@	Standard	} Quantity

THE L.&A. COMPANY

Budget of Order Department and Cash Collecting Costs

One-Month Period: Effective January 1, 19___

Functional Account	Labor	Supplies	Repairs and Repair Parts	Purchased Service (1); Noncash Charges (2)	Total Amount	Description of Unit	Number of Units
		Budget					
Credit investigations—prospective customers	$ 150.00			(1) $ 50.00	$ 200.00	Investigations	100
Passing orders for credit	288.00				288.00	Charge orders	3,600
Editing orders	400.00				400.00	Orders shipped	4,000
Typing shipping orders	465.00	$120.00	$15.00		600.00	Orders shipped	4,000
Order register and follow-up	300.00	20.00			320.00	Orders shipped	4,000
Invoicing—headings	358.00	110.00		(1) 108.00	576.00	Invoices	3,600
Invoicing—line items	162.00				162.00	Line items	5,400
Charging customers' accounts	121.00	18.00	5.00		144.00	Invoices	3,600
Customers' monthly statements	94.00	20.00		(1) 114.00	228.00	Statements mailed	3,800
Recording cash sales	16.00				16.00	Cash orders	400
Crediting customers' accounts	114.00				114.00	Receipts	3,800
Total charges to functional accounts	$2,468.00	$288.00	$20.00	$ 272.00	$3,048.00		
Bad debts				(2) $ 600.00	$ 600.00		
Capacity cost:							
Supervision				(2) $ 600.00	$ 600.00		
Depreciation				(2) 400.00	400.00		
Insurance				(2) 200.00	200.00		
Taxes				(2) 700.00	700.00		
Rent				(2) 800.00	800.00		
Total capacity cost				(2) $2,700.00	$2,700.00		
Totals by object group	$2,468.00	$288.00	$20.00	$3,572.00	$6,348.00		

THE L.&A. COMPANY

Actual Order Department and Cash Collecting Costs—by Object

for the Month of November, 19__

	By Object					By Function	
Functional Accounts	Labor	Supplies	Repairs and Repair Parts	Purchased Service (1); Nomcash Charges (2)	Total Amount	Description of Unit	Number of Units
Credit investigations—prospective customers....	$ 128.00			(1) $ 40.00	$ 168.00	Investigations	80
Passing orders for credit............	259.00				259.00	Charge orders	3,700
Editing orders...........	451.00				451.00	Orders shipped	4,100
Typing shipping orders............	$387.00	$130.00	$16.00		533.00	Orders shipped	4,100
Order register and follow-up..........	390.00	20.00			410.00	Orders shipped	3,700
Invoicing—headings............	329.00	115.00		(1) 111.00	555.00	Invoices	3,700
Invoicing—line items............	180.00				180.00	Line items	6,000
Charging customers' accounts..........	123.00	20.00	5.00		148.00	Invoices	3,700
Customers' monthly statements.........	94.00	20.00		(1) * 114.00	228.00	Statements mailed	3,800
Recording cash sales..........	12.00				12.00	Cash orders	400
Crediting customers' accounts..........	114.00				114.00	Receipts	3,800
Total charges to functional accounts........	$2,467.00	$305.00	$21.00	$ 265.00	$3,058.00		
Bad debts...........				(2) $ 630.00	$ 630.00		
Capacity cost:							
Supervision...........				(2) $ 650.00	$ 650.00		
Depreciation...........				(2) 400.00	400.00		
Insurance..........				(2) 220.00	220.00		
Taxes...........				(2) 800.00	800.00		
Rent...........				(2) 800.00	800.00		
Total capacity cost..........				(2) $2,870.00	$2,870.00		
Totals by object group.........	$2,467.00	$305.00	$21.00	$3,765.00	$6,558.00		

21-2. As methods analyst for the Searco Company, you have made a thorough study of the labor operations in the order and billing departments. A simplified version of your report of standard operation times is as follows:

Operation	Form	Busy Season		Slack Season	
		Quantity per Employee per Eight-Hour Day	Minutes per Form	Quantity per Employee per Eight-Hour Day	Minutes per Form
(1) Editing customer's order	Customer's order	240	2	240	2
(2) Prepare shipping order and send to shipping department	Shipping order	240	2	240	2
(3) Receive shipping order after shipment is completed. Price and extend	Shipping order	120	4	240	2
(4) Prepare invoice in triplicate	Invoice	120	4	240	2
(5) Mail invoice	Invoice	480	1	480	1
(6) Enter duplicate invoice on accounts receivable and file	Invoice	480	1	480	1
(7) Prepare daily sales analyses from triplicate invoice and file	Invoice	120	4	240	2
(8) Receive cash and prepare cash receipt ticket	Cash receipt ticket	480	1	480	1
(9) Credit Accounts receivable	Cash receipt ticket	480	1	480	1

The additional time required to process certain forms during the busy season is due to the greatly increased number of items per order.

It is estimated that personal and fatigue time will add about 20 per cent to the foregoing standard times. You are asked to estimate the personnel requirements for the order and billing department for the coming six months during which severe fluctuations in selling volume is normal. These months and the number of orders, etc., anticipated are as follows:

	Anticipated Quantity per Day			
	Customers' Orders	Shipping Orders	Invoices	Cash Receipt Tickets
Busy season:				
October..............	600	600	600	300
November............	720	720	720	360
December............	840	840	840	420
Slack season:				
January..............	240	240	240	120
February.............	300	300	300	150
March...............	360	360	360	180

Required (Part 1):

Prepare an estimate of the personnel requirements (daily basis) of the order and billing department for the six months shown above.

During the month of September, just ended, which is a busy season month, the following quantities of forms were actually processed:

	Customers' Orders	Shipping Orders	Invoices	Cash Receipt Tickets
Average per day........	630	600	660	420

Actual labor times during September were analyzed by operations. These times, expressed as averages per working day, are as follows:

Operation	Actual Hours per Working Day
(1) Editing customer's order	24
(2) Prepare shipping order and send to shipping department	24
(3) Receive shipping order after shipment is complete—price and extend	48
(4) Prepare invoice in triplicate	56
(5) Mail invoice	16
(6) Enter duplicate invoice on account receivable and file	16
(7) Prepare daily sales analyses from triplicate invoices and file	56
(8) Receive cash and prepare cash receipt ticket	8
(9) Credit accounts receivable	16
Total hours	264
Number of employees	33

Required (Part 2):

Prepare an analysis comparing the actual versus the standard time allowed by operations for the month of September.

Required (Part 3):

Write a memo to the controller of the Searco Company commenting upon the performance of the order and billing department personnel for the month of September.

DISTRIBUTION COST CONTROL

The need for distribution cost control. The function of distribution involves such activities as:

(1) Getting the customer's order. This function includes *direct selling* by salesmen and *sales promotion* through catalogs, direct mail pieces, and newspaper advertising.

(2) Filling the order and collecting the cash. This function includes order department and cash collecting activities and warehouse activities.

(3) Delivering the order.

In some companies a large part of the sales dollar is spent for distribution; in fact, the cost of distributing the product may be larger than the cost of manufacturing it. The sales force and the sales offices, the warehouse employees and the warehouses, the order department personnel with their offices and equipment, and finally the delivery department people with their garages and trucks may together make up an imposing organization and plant structure. Some large manufacturing companies have numerous sales offices, order department offices, and warehouses located in various states. The distribution activities of large oil companies, for instance, involve the maintenance and operation of bulk storage facilities for gasoline over vast areas, served by great transportation organizations.

Distribution activities require careful planning which in turn suggests the need for cost control. When a set of plans is being drawn up, it is necessary to consider the cost of implementing those plans. When those plans are carried out, it is useful to determine how the actual costs compare with the expected costs.

The tools of cost control of distribution activities are budgets and standards, in general the same as those used in the factory. As will be seen in this chapter, however, the use of those tools varies from function to function in the field of distribution. In some functions such as delivery by truck, it is possible to make a great deal of use of standard costs based upon work units for the measurement of spending performance. In other functions, such as direct selling and promotion, it may be possible to make only limited use of such standards. Complete budgets may be used, however, to set up the expected cost to carry out certain plans or to achieve certain goals. The budgets would be used not so much as a basis for measuring spending performance but rather as a means of indicating whether people responsible for spending money had actually made cost commitments to carry out the plans on which the budget was based.

This chapter (like the related Chapters 28 and 29) is concerned with the distribution cost problems of manufacturers who maintain their own warehouses and other distribution facilities, rather than with the distribution problems of wholesalers. It should be noted, however, that many of the same techniques of cost control used by the manufacturer-distributor are also used by the wholesaler.*

Function and organization: Benson & West Manufacturing Company. The organization chart on page 536 and the factory floor plan on page 537 show, respectively, the supervisory personnel and the plant used by the Benson & West Manufacturing Company to perform the distribution function.

The *selling organization* of the Benson & West Manufacturing Company consists of the sales manager who supervises the activity, the assistant sales manager who sells to chain stores, a number of outside salesmen, a house salesman, and sales clerical employees. The salesmen sell to retail stores, wholesalers, and industrial customers. All the sales department employees, except the outside salesmen, are paid straight salaries. The latter salesmen are paid commission plus certain allowances for automobile and subsistence.

Plant used by the selling organization consists of the sales manager's office and the sales department display room, both equipped with furniture and fixtures. It also includes the automobiles used by the salesmen, which are owned by the company.

The selling function includes sales promotion through catalogs and other direct mail pieces, and newspaper advertising. The actual planning of advertising is done by an advertising agency, which is paid a discount by publishers and others with whom it places advertising. The sales manager reviews proposed programs submitted by the agency and accepts or rejects them for the company.

The *order department and cash collecting* organization consists of the credit manager and the head of the order department, together with typists (shipping orders and invoices), order record clerks, accounts receivable bookkeeper, and part-time receiving cashier. Plant used by the organization consists of the office space of the order department, equipped with office furniture and fixtures.

* Because of the rapid and relatively recent development of distribution cost accounting, and the widespread interest in the subject, the author has supplemented these chapters with an annotated bibliography on distribution costs (Appendix III). This bibliography covers over a thousand pages of the most significant bulletins on the subject.

ORGANIZATION CHART

BENSON AND WEST MANUFACTURING COMPANY

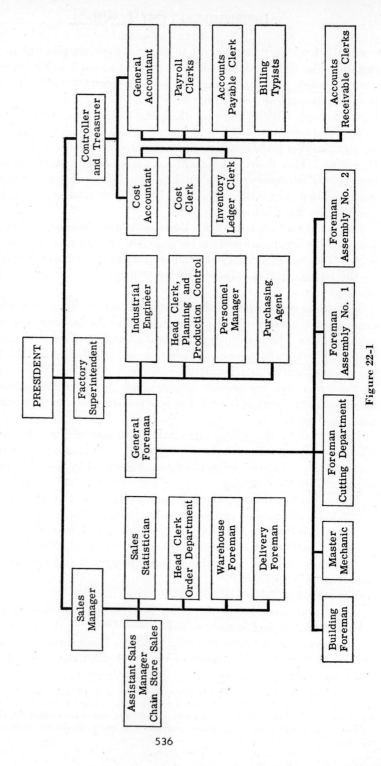

Figure 22-1

BENSON AND WEST MANUFACTURING COMPANY
FACTORY, WAREHOUSE AND OFFICE FLOOR PLAN

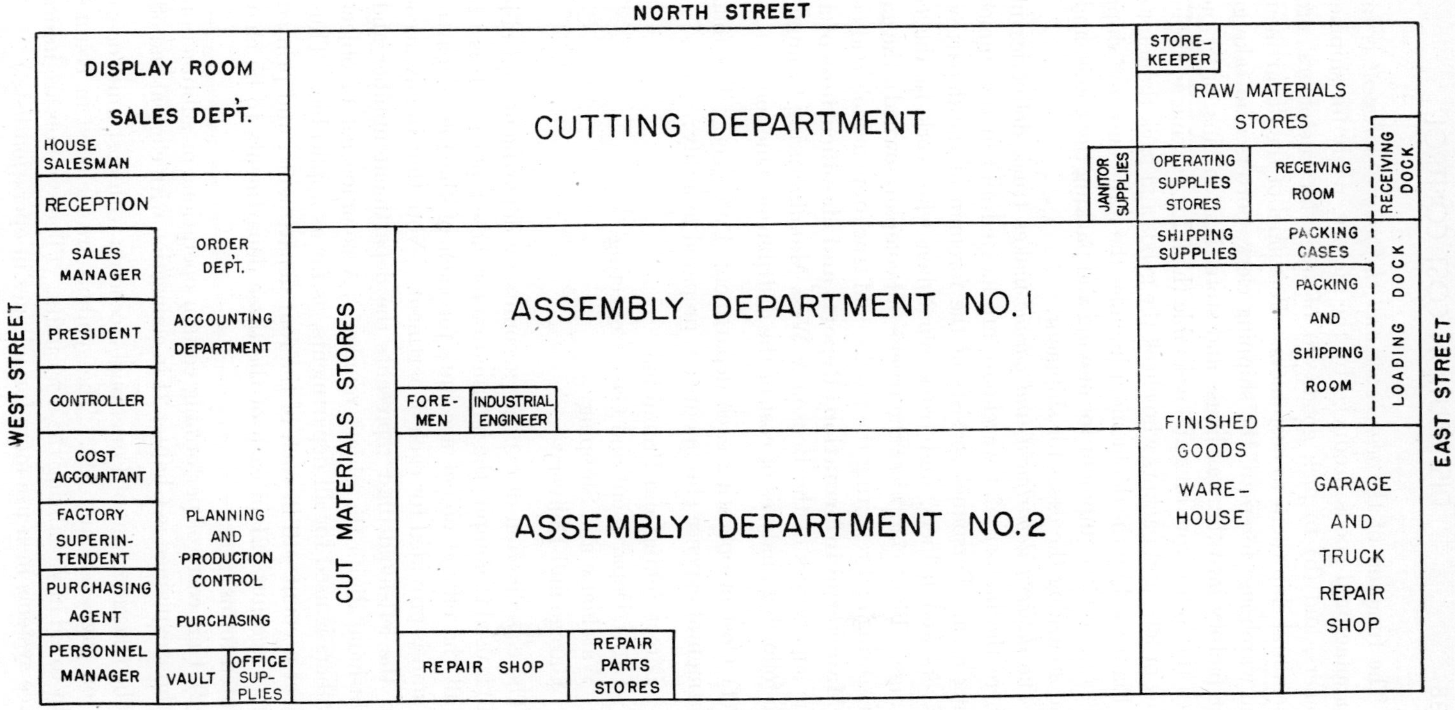

Figure 22-2

537

The function of the *warehouse and shipping department* is (a) to store manufactured goods produced by the factory, ready for shipment to customers, and (b) to pick goods out of stock for customers' orders, pack them and ship them to customers. Personnel of the department includes the warehouse foreman, the shipping clerk, porters who take goods from the factory into the warehouse and store them in bins, order pickers who pick the items from bins and assemble them for packing according to shipping orders, and packers who check the goods and pack them for shipment.

Plant used by the department includes the warehouse and shipping room space; also the equipment for moving and packing the goods, and weighing and stenciling the cases for shipment.

The *delivery department and garage* makes truck deliveries in the city where the factory and warehouse are located and in the immediate outlying area. Personnel consists of the foreman of the department, truck drivers and helpers, and truck repairmen who work in the company's garage. Plant comprises the trucks (all company-owned), the garage used for storing and repairing the trucks, and truck repair tools and equipment.

Managerial information: Reports and classifications of accounts. The supervisors of the Benson & West Manufacturing Company require the following analyses of cost of the distribution function:

(1) Cost of operating each department, by object. The following departmental expense statements are prepared monthly:

> Direct Selling and Promotion
> Order Department and Cash Collecting
> Warehouse and Shipping
> Garage and Delivery

The classification of expense accounts by department and object (page 539) is used to compile the information for these reports. It is a tabulation of all the official object accounts for each of the four departments. A column is provided for each department. Note that in any account number, the left-hand digit represents the department number and the two right-hand digits the object number. A common set of object account numbers is used for all departments, as far as applicable. Thus, labor is object account #10 in each of the four departments, and printed forms is object account #21 in each of the three departments to be charged with printed forms used.

(2) Unit costs of performing certain operations or subfunctions similar to those explained in Chapter 21 in connection with clerical and office costs.

The Classification of Functional Accounts with cost units or work units are on pages 540 and 541. The symbols are included in columns at the right to aid in visualizing the work units. (The symbols are informal ones. Office systems men use more formal ones in operation lists.)

BENSON & WEST MANUFACTURING COMPANY

Classification of Distribution Cost Accounts
by Department and Object

Department → Object	600 Direct Selling & Promotion	700 Order Dept. and Cash Collecting	800 Warehouse and Shipping	900 Garage and Delivery
10 Labor	610	710	810	910
20 Supplies:				
21 Printed forms	621	721	821	
22 Office supplies		722		
23 Shipping supplies			823	
24 Packing cases			824	
25 Gas				925
26 Oil				926
27 Garage supplies				927
30 Repairs and repair parts	630	730	830	930
40 Purchased services:				
41 Telephone and telegraph	641			
42 Electric light and power		742	842	942
43 Credit association dues		743		
44 Postage		744		
50 Advertising:				
51 Catalogs	651			
52 Direct mail prices	652			
53 Newspaper advertising	653			
54 Sales training manuals	654			
60 Travel and entertainment:				
61 Automobile variable	661			
62 Travel—public transport	662			
63 Subsistence	663			
64 Entertainment	664			
70 Unclassified	670			
80 Bad debts		780		
90 Fixed charges:				
91 Depreciation	691	791	891	991
92 Insurance	692	792	892	992
93 Taxes	693	793	893	993
94 Licenses	694			994
95 Rent	695	795	895	995

Figure 22-3

BENSON & WEST MANUFACTURING COMPANY

Functional Accounts, Work Units

Functional Accounts	Work Units
Direct selling and promotion department:	
01 Direct selling (salaries and commission)	
02 Subsistence	Days subsisted
03 Travel: Automobile variable	Miles traveled
04 Travel: Public transport	
05 Sales promotion	
06 Sales office clerical activities	Orders
Order department and cash collecting department:	
01 Credit investigations—Prospective customers	Investigations
02 Passing orders for credit	Charge orders
03 Editing orders	Orders shipped
04 Typing shipping orders	Orders shipped
05 Order register and follow-up	Orders shipped
06 Invoicing: Headings	Invoices
07 Invoicing: Lines	Line items
08 Charging customers' accounts	Invoices
09 Customers' monthly statements	Statements mailed
10 Recording cash sales	Cash orders
11 Crediting customers' accounts	Receipts
Warehouse and shipping room:	
01 Putting goods into stock	Product units received
02 Order picking	Product units picked
03 Packing	Product units packed
04 Packing cases	Orders packed
05 Warehouse equipment maintenance, repairs, and operation	Product units picked
06 Shipping department clerical	Orders packed
Garage and delivery department:	
01 Loading and unloading	Loading and unloading hours
02 Truck operation: Wages	Operating hours
03 Truck operation: Gas and oil	Miles
04 Truck repairs	Miles

Figure 22-4

Discussion of the work units shown in the chart follows. Consideration of alternate work units appears later.

The cost units for direct selling relate to the salesmen. They are *days subsisted* (for subsistence) and *miles traveled* (for automobile variable expense). No work unit has been found for sales promotion. The company controls advertising on a project basis.

The cost units for order department and cash collecting are related to the documents handled. They are *orders* (for passing orders for credit, editing orders, typing orders, and so on), *invoices* (for typing headings of invoices, for posting invoices to customers, accounts, and so on), *statements* (for

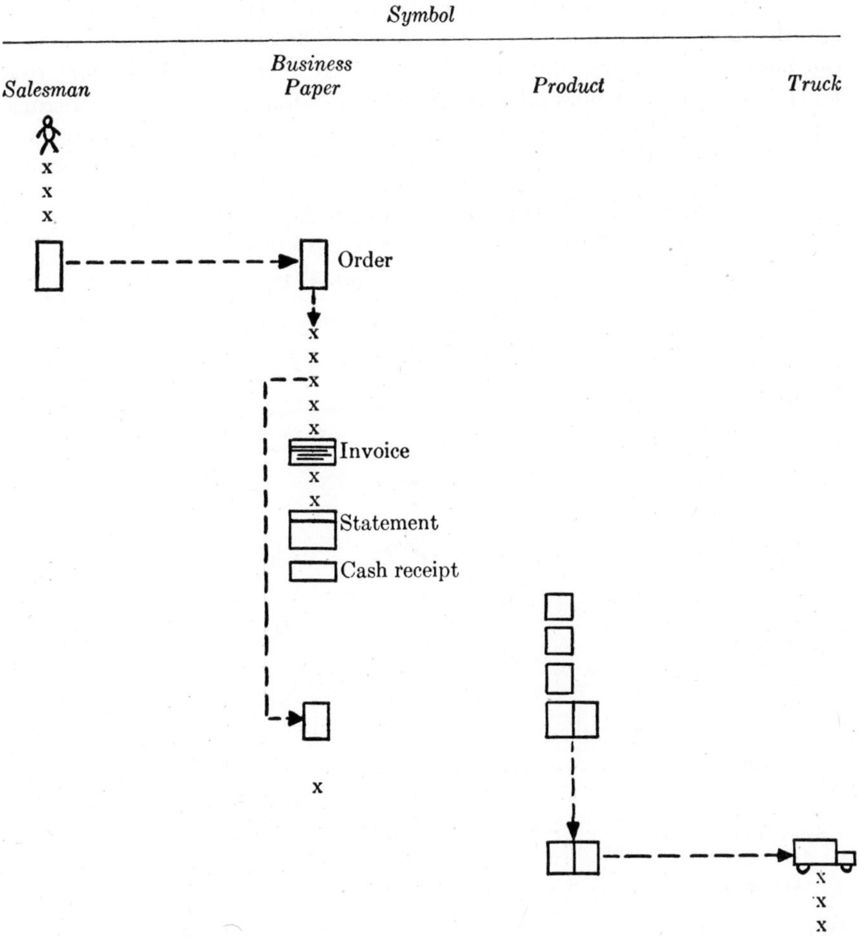
Symbol
Salesman
Business Paper
Product
Truck
Order
Invoice
Statement
Cash receipt

Figure 22-4 (*Continued*)

typing and postage of the monthly statements), and *cash receipts* (for receiving cash and crediting customers' accounts). The labor, supplies, and expense in each of the functional accounts are supposed to vary with the output of the function stated in terms of the work unit indicated.

The work units for warehouse and shipping room relate to product units and orders packed. *Product units received* is used for measuring putting goods into stock, *product units picked* for order picking, and *product units packed* for packing labor and expense. *Orders packed* is used for packing cases and shipping department clerical. Note that product units have been used in this case because all products are approximately the same size, shape, and weight. In many cases, it is not feasible to use product units because of the disparity of size and weight among products. It may be necessary to use other work units as indicated on page 548.

The work units for garage and delivery department relate to the trucks and the men (drivers and helpers) on them. They are *loading and unloading* hours (for loading and unloading trucks), *truck operating hours* (for truck operation: wages), and *miles* (truck operation: gas and oil) and truck repairs. Note that a set of functional unit costs would be computed for each size of truck. Also, separate sets of functional unit costs would be

BENSON & WEST MANUFACTURING COMPANY
Statement of Expenses, by Object

for the Month of December, 19__

Direct Selling and Promotion Department

Object	Month (Sales, $)		Year to Date (Sales, $)	
	Amount	% to Sales	Amount	% to Sales
Payroll:				
Salaries......................	$ 1,750.00		$	
Commissions.................	1,800.00			
Totals.....................	$ 3,550.00		$	
Printed forms...................	$ 200.00		$	
Repairs and repair parts.........	100.00			
Telephone and telegraph.........	600.00			
Advertising:				
Catalogs.....................	2,600.00			
Direct mail pieces.............	2,500.00			
Newspaper advertising.........	3,800.00			
Sales training manuals.........	350.00			
Totals.....................	$ 9,250.00		$	
Travel:				
Automobile variable...........	$ 720.00		$	
Travel—public transport........	550.00			
Subsistence...................	1,700.00			
Totals.....................	$ 2,970.00		$	
Fixed charges:				
Depreciation..................	$ 341.66		$	
Insurance.....................	108.33			
Taxes........................	53.83			
Rent—Sales office.............	164.00			
Totals.....................	$ 667.82		$	
Total direct selling and promotion	$17,337.82		$	

Figure 22-5

computed for city delivery trucks (having a great deal of stop and go) and for line haul trucks (on long distance hauls with a minimum of stop and go).

One final point should be stated with reference to cost units and work units used in distribution cost analysis and control. The validity of the functional unit costs depends upon the reasonableness of the cost unit or work unit. Obviously, if the cost unit is not reasonable to begin with, the resulting functional unit costs will not be valid.

Statements of expenses by object illustrated. A Statement of Expenses by Object for a department is illustrated on page 542. One of these statements is prepared for each of the four departments. (The four statements are identical in format.) The president of the company receives all four statements, and each department head receives the statement relating to his department. As indicated previously, the object accounts analyze expenses according to the nature of the goods or services used. On each statement, the object accounts are grouped in general according to the nature and degree of control which is possible. These statements are used for determining the trend of expenses in relationship to sales. Note that cumulative figures would be shown.

Analysis of expense by object and function illustrated. An Analysis of Expenses by Object and Function for a department is illustrated on page 544. One of these statements is prepared for each of the four departments. The advantage of these statements is that they relate expense dollars to volume of work done through the use of (a) functional expense accounts and (b) work units appropriate to the functional expense account.

Each statement shows the object classification (at the left) which is the same as on the Object Statement and the reclassification into function accounts at the right. The functional unit costs shown in the extreme right-hand column are a valuable tool to determine whether costs are getting out of line in comparison with volume of work done. Besides providing a current measure of spending performance, they are used in planning future spending, as illustrated on pages 545-551.

Analysis procedure. The analysis procedure for producing a set of department expenses by object statements is:

(1) Enter payrolls (labor) in the general journal which provides a column for each department. Each department column is ruled with a folio column for object account numbers to identify the dollar amounts entered in the columns.

(2) Enter purchase invoices and salesmen's expense accounts (original media for supplies, repairs and repair parts, purchased services, travel and entertainment, and unclassified) in the voucher register. The voucher register is provided with a column for each department, as is the general journal.

(3) Enter journal vouchers for bad debts and fixed charges in the general journal.

BENSON & WEST MANUFACTURING COMPANY

Analysis of Actual Direct Selling and Promotion Costs—by Object and Function
for the Month of December, 19—

Object Classification

Accounts	Amount
Payroll	
Supervisory	$ 800.00
Salesmen's salaries	650.00
Commissions	1,800.00
Clerical salaries	300.00
Total	$ 3,550.00
Travel	
Subsistence	$ 1,700.00
Automobile—Variable	720.00
Travel—Public transport	550.00
Total	$ 2,970.00
Advertising	
Catalogs	$ 2,600.00
Direct mail pieces	2,500.00
Newspaper advertising	3,800.00
Sales training manuals	350.00
Total	$ 9,250.00
Printed forms	$ 200.00
Repairs and repair parts	100.00
Telephone and telegraph	600.00
Direct charges	
Depreciation	341.66
Insurance	108.33
Taxes	53.83
Rent—Sales office	164.00
Total	$ 667.82
Total direct selling and promotion	$17,337.82

Functional Classification

Accounts	Amount	Description of Unit	Number of Units	Actual Cost per Unit
Direct selling by salesmen				
Salesmen's salaries	$ 650.00			
Commissions	1,800.00			
Total	$ 2,450.00	None		
Subsistence	$ 1,700.00	Days subsisted	200	$8.50
Travel				
Automobile—Variable	720.00	Miles traveled	12,000	.06
Public transport	550.00	None		
Sales promotion				
Catalogs	2,600.00			
Direct mail pieces	2,500.00			
Newspaper advertising	3,800.00			
Sales training manuals	350.00			
Total	$ 9,250.00	None (project basis)		
Sales office clerical				
Salaries	$ 300.00			
Printed forms	200.00			
Repairs and repair parts	100.00			
Telephone and telegraph	600.00			
Total	$ 1,200.00	Orders	3,000	.40
Capacity cost				
Supervisory salaries	$ 800.00			
Depreciation	341.66			
Insurance	108.33			
Taxes	53.83			
Rent—Sales office	164.00			
Total	$ 1,467.82	None		
Total direct selling and promotion	$17,337.82			

Figure 22-6

(4) Post the general journal and the voucher register to the departmental expense accounts for distribution. These accounts comprise a set of object accounts for each of the four departments, as listed in the Classification of Distribution Cost Accounts, by Department and Object (Figure 22-3).

(5) Prepare the set of expense reports, department expenses by object (Figure 22-5) from the posted accounts. This set of statements supports the Statement of Profits prepared in the usual manner from the general ledger.

Where, in addition, it is desired to make a regular analysis of costs by functional account, such analysis is done from the original media (job tickets or time sheets, showing the function on which the clerk spends time, and so on). These media have to be coded by functional account as well as by department and object, at the time they are written. Cost units or work units (orders, invoices, statements, cash receipts, and so forth) would also be collected currently. Expenses are then analyzed by function as illustrated.

Expense control: Direct selling and promotion expense. Selling expenses are controlled by a budget (page 546) which is set up by the following methods:

Direct selling by salesmen:

Salaries, by reviewing the payroll and deciding upon additions and reductions in staff and raises in salaries, necessary to carry out the plans of the sales department for the coming year. It is generally expected that sales department salaries should not exceed a certain per cent of sales, but it is recognized that sales salaries are not perfectly variable. Sometimes additions are made to the staff in one period to implement the plans of future periods.

Commissions. This is the regular commission rate applied to the estimated sales volume on which commissions are paid.

Subsistence:

Expected days subsisted × Standard cost per day
200 × $9.50 = $1,900

The number of days is estimated on the basis of the number of men who will be traveling. The new standard cost per day is last year's actual cost per day, raised $1 to provide for increased food and room costs.

Travel:

Automobile—variable.

Expected miles traveled × Standard rate per mile
12,000 × $.06 = $720

BENSON & WEST MANUFACTURING COMPANY

Budget of Direct Selling and Promotion Costs and Standard Functional Unit Costs

(Period: One Month)

Accounts	Description Functional Unit	Actual, December, 19__			Budget, January, 19__		
		Total Amounts, by Account	Number of Units	Actual Cost per Unit	Total Amounts, by Account	Number of Units	Standard Cost per Unit
Direct selling by salesmen							
Salesmen's salaries		$ 650.00			$ 700.00		
Commissions		1,800.00			1,729.50		
Total	None	$ 2,450.00			$ 2,429.50		
Subsistence	Days subsisted	$ 1,700.00	200	$8.50	$ 1,900.00	200	$9.50
Travel	Miles traveled						
Automobile—variable		720.00	12,000	.06	910.00	13,000	.07
Public transport		550.00			500.00		
Sales promotion							
Catalogs		2,600.00			2,400.00		
Direct mail pieces		2,500.00			2,300.00		
Newspaper advertising		3,800.00			4,000.00		
Sales training manuals		350.00			300.00		
Total	None (project basis)	$ 9,250.00			$ 9,000.00		
Sales office clerical							
Salaries		300.00			280.00		
Printed forms		200.00			140.00		
Repairs and repair parts		100.00			110.00		
Telephone and telegraph		600.00			496.00		
Total	Orders	$ 1,200.00	3,000	.40	$ 1,026.00	2,850	.36
Capacity costs							
Supervisory salaries		800.00			900.00		
Depreciation		341.66			341.66		
Insurance		108.33			108.33		
Taxes		53.83			73.83		
Rent—sales office		164.00			164.00		
Total	None	$ 1,467.82			$ 1,587.82		
Total direct selling and promotion		$17,337.82			$17,353.32		

Figure 22-7

The automobiles are company owned. The automobile variable standard covers only the expenses that the salesmen pay (gas, oil, and authorized garage work), for which they are reimbursed on their expense accounts.

The number of miles is estimated on the basis of the number of men who will be traveling and the geographical coverage expected (in present territories and new territories). The new standard cost per day is last year's actual cost per mile, raised $1 to provide for increased fuel and repair costs.

Public transport. There is no standard. The budget total is based upon last year's figure, with such change as would be justified by plans for the coming year's staff. In general, any control is, by administrative decision, on an "Is this trip necessary?" basis.

Sales promotion:

Project basis. The sales manager approves or rejects projects proposed by the advertising agency on the basis of estimated cost of project and estimated, or hoped for, results.

Sales office clerical activities:

Orders × Standard cost per order
2,850 × $.36 = $1,026

The number of orders is estimated on the basis of change in volume of business compared with last year, with consideration of any change in the nature of the coverage. The standard cost per order is likewise based upon last year's salaries, printed forms, office supplies, and telephone and telegraph with consideration of changes in prices.

Note that, although the calculation of standard functional unit costs on the basis of last year's actual functional unit may not appear to be scientific, it does subject past results and future plans to close scrutiny. Each expense function is considered carefully with reference to volume of business, prices to be paid, and whether last year's unit cost apparently contained waste. Sometimes, a supervisor will agree that last year's unit cost (for a certain function) is so high as to be completely unreasonable, and that it should be reduced.

Capacity costs:

Supervision, Fixed charges (except rent), *Rent.* These are personnel and organization costs required to maintain a readiness-to-operate. In setting up the budget for next year, price and salary changes would be recognized. Changes in desired capacity would also be considered. Thus, if it were planned to open an additional sales office, or to close one, there might be significant changes in this section of the budget. Minor changes in the operating plan, on the other hand, might have very little effect upon this section of the budget.

The complete budget of direct selling and promotion costs and standard functional unit costs for a one-month period are presented on page 546.

Expense control: Warehousing and shipping expense. For the control of variable labor and expense, the Benson & West Manufacturing Company uses the following standard functional unit costs:

Function	Work Unit
Putting goods into stock	Product units received
Order picking	Product units picked
Packing	Product units packed
Warehouse equipment—Maintenance, repairs, and operation	Product units picked
Shipping department clerical	Orders packed

Product units is used as the work unit (instead of weight of product or standard allowed hours per unit for each product) because the various products are similar in size and weight. The standard costs for the coming period are shown on page 549, Budget of Warehouse Costs and Standard Functional Unit Costs. This budget was set up from the analysis of actual warehouse costs for the previous period shown on the same sheet. In setting the new budget, changes in prices and volume of operations were considered and obvious inefficiencies in actual performance were eliminated.

Other work units which may be used for warehouse operations are:

Weighted product units. A company which manufactures radio and television sets has worked out a table of unit equivalents for its products, intended to show the relative effort required to move and handle each of the various products. Thus the smallest item is assigned the value of 1 unit, the next larger product 1 1/8 units, the next 1 1/4, and so forth. To determine, for budget purposes or other control purposes, the number of units put into stock, multiply actual product units by the proper unit equivalent. When this method is used, the larger radios and television sets count for a larger number of budget work units than do the smaller ones.

Pounds, yards, gallons, or other common units of measure for bulk goods.

Standard *time* per product unit for each warehouse operation for each product. Standards in time units are sometimes set where there are significant differences in size, weight, and amount of movement required for various products. Note that, in order to set standard times which will be meaningful, it is necessary to have standardized plant and operating conditions in the warehouse.

In setting up the budget, packing cases were included at an estimated average cost per order packed. It was recognized that the cost of the packing case varied with the number of units of product in the order, but it was believed that for the purpose of budgeting, it would not be necessary to set separate standards for orders of different sizes.

Budget of Warehouse Costs and Standard Functional Unit Costs

(Period: One Month)

Accounts	Description of Functional Unit	Actual, December, 19___			Budget, January, 19___		
		Total Amounts, by Account	*Number of Units*	*Actual Cost per Unit*	*Total Amounts, by Account*	*Number of Units*	*Standard Cost per Unit*
Putting goods into stock							
Labor	Product units received	$ 168.00	14,000	$.012	$ 153.00	15,300	$.01
Picking							
Labor	Product units picked	348.00	14,500	.024	304.00	15,200	.02
Packing							
Labor		260.00			240.00		
Printed forms		108.00			150.00		
Shipping supplies		200.00			210.00		
Total	Product units packed	$ 568.00	14,200	.04	$ 600.00	15,000	.04
Packing cases	Orders packed	$ 750.00	3,000	.25	$ 540.00	2,700	.20
Warehouse equipment maintenance							
Repairs and operation							
Labor		100.00			100.00		
Repairs and repair parts		30.00			30.00		
Electric power		15.00			22.00		
Total	Product units picked	$ 145.00	14,500	.01	$ 152.00	15,200	.01
Shipping dept. clerical							
Labor		260.00			280.00		
Printed forms		130.00			44.00		
Total	Orders packed	$ 390.00	3,000	.13	$ 324.00	2,700	.12
Capacity costs							
Supervisory labor		350.00			375.00		
Depreciation		166.67			166.67		
Insurance		168.33			168.33		
Taxes		200.00			200.00		
Rent		312.50			312.50		
Total	None	$1,197.50			$1,222.50		
Total warehousing and shipping		$3,566.50			$3,295.50		

RECAP (Budget)
Variable warehouse cost per product unit... $.08
Variable warehouse cost per order shipped... .32
Capacity cost per product unit picked:

$$\frac{\text{Capacity cost}}{\text{Units picked}} = \frac{\$1,222.50}{15,200} = \$.0804$$

Figure 22-8

549

Budgeted capacity costs are segregated from operating costs.   Capacity costs include:

Supervision
Insurance and taxes on inventory
Fixed charges on equipment
Rent

The costs are period costs, rather than product or operation costs.   The budget amounts are decided upon through consideration of (a) changes in prices and wage rates and (b) expected changes in capacity of the warehouse and shipping room.

Expense control: Delivery expense.   The company uses the following standard functional unit costs for the control of garage and delivery department expense:

Function	Work Unit
Loading and unloading trucks	Loading and unloading hours
Truck operation:	
Wages	Operating hours
Gas and oil	Miles
Truck repairs	Miles

Note that separate sets of unit costs might be calculated for trucks of different sizes and trucks in different kinds of service (pick-up and delivery, line-haul).   The budget and standard functional unit costs are shown on page 549.   They are based upon the actual costs shown on the same sheet, adjusted for price and rate changes, volume of work, and the obvious efficiency factors.

The capacity costs for the delivery department and garage are segregated at the bottom of the budget:

Supervision
Fixed charges: garage equipment
Fixed charges: trucks
Garage rent

These costs are based upon the number of trucks the company expects to operate during the coming period.   (This is an illustration of a situation where capacity cost can change relatively frequently.)

Summary: Elements of distribution cost control.   This chapter emphasizes that manufacturing cost may not be all of the cost which can and should be put under cost accounting control or even the larger part of a company's cost which should be so controlled.   The application of the principles of cost control to the field of distribution has developed relatively recently but rapidly and cost accounting is now a valuable tool of the marketing executive.

For cost accounting control purposes, the distribution function of a busi-

BENSON & WEST MANUFACTURING COMPANY
Budget of Delivery Costs and Standard Functional Unit Costs

(Period: One Month)

Accounts	Description of Functional Unit	Actual, December, 19___			Budget, January, 19___		
		Total Amounts, by Account	Number of Units	Actual Cost per Unit	Total Amounts, by Account	Number of Units	Standard Cost per Unit
Loading and unloading	Loading and unloading hours						
Labor............		$ 292.50	90	$3.25	$ 280.00	80	$3.50
Truck operation							
Labor............	Operating hours	747.50	230	3.25	840.00	240	3.50
Gas and oil........	Miles	576.00	4,800	.12	700.00	5,000	.14
Truck repairs							
Labor...........		250.00			280.00		
Garage supplies........		20.00			25.00		
Repair parts—trucks........		110.00			120.00		
Repairs—garage equipment........		100.00			25.00		
Total........	Miles	$ 480.00	4,800	.10	$ 450.00	5,000	.09
Capacity cost							
Supervision........		$ 450.00			$ 500.00		
Trucks							
Depreciation........		125.00			125.00		
Insurance........		33.34			33.34		
Taxes (and licenses)........		40.00			40.00		
Garage equipment							
Depreciation........		41.67			41.67		
Insurance........		8.33			8.33		
Taxes........		12.00			12.00		
Rent—garage........		125.00			125.00		
Total........	None	$ 835.34			$ 885.34		
Total delivery expense........		$2,931.34			$3,155.34		

Figure 22-9

ness may be divided into (a) direct selling and promotion, (b) order department and cash collecting, (c) warehousing, and (d) delivery. Cost standards based upon work units can be of considerable use in control of the last three functions where work flow can be measured. The use of work units in these cases is somewhat comparable to their use in manufacturing operations. Cost standards based upon work units are likely to have relatively limited use in the direct selling and promotion function. In this function, the budget becomes a tool for planning what will be required in the way of people and facilities to accomplish a contemplated program. Once a budget is adopted, a credit variance between actual expense and budget expense might be questioned as a failure to make a cost commitment necessary to carry out the agreed program.

This chapter describes the technique of analyzing distribution costs and determining actual costs per work unit, and also the development of budgets and standard unit costs for use in control and planning. Each of the budgets is set up in two sections: the variable or functional account section, in which projection of costs per work unit is particularly useful, and the capacity cost section which embraces the fixed expense accounts for organization and plant.

QUESTIONS

22-1. Discuss the function of distribution and name the departments of the business which are directly involved in that function.

22-2. (a) Describe an object classification that might be used for the departments named in your answer to Question 22-1.

(b) State the uses and limitations of the object classification in distribution department expense reports.

22-3. In which of the departments (in Question 22-1) are work units or functional units and unit costs likely to be most useful? Why are they likely to be more useful in some departments than in others?

22-4. (a) Name functional accounts and appropriate related work units for each of the departments involved in the distribution function.

(b) Are there alternate work units to any you have named in your answer to (a)?

22-5. Describe the methods by which the direct selling and promotion expense budget is set up.

22-6. Describe the methods by which the warehouse expense budget is set up.

22-7. Describe the methods by which the delivery expense budget is set up.

EXERCISE

22-1. Complete Forms 1 through 6 in the Workbook, using the following additional data:

Form 1—No additional information necessary.

Form 2

Distribute labor as follows:

Putting goods into stock....................	$ 120.00
Picking.................................	225.00
Packing................................	200.00
Warehouse equipment maintenance, repairs, and operation........................	60.00
Shipping dept. clerical....................	175.00
Supervisory labor.......................	200.00
Total.............................	$ 980.00

Distribute printed forms as follows:

Packing................................	$ 75.00
Shipping dept. clerical....................	65.00
Total.............................	$ 140.00

Form 3

Distribute labor as follows:

Loading and unloading....................	$ 175.00
Truck operation.........................	700.00
Truck repairs...........................	175.00
Supervision............................	250.00
Total.............................	$1,300.00

Forms 4, 5 and 6

Actual data for December, 19— is forwarded from Forms 1, 2 and 3.

Form 4—No additional data necessary.

Form 5—Budget volume and variable costs (functional account totals) are to be 20% greater than December, 19—.

Form 6—Budget volume is to be 20% greater than December, 19—.

Budget variable costs (functional account totals) are to be 10% greater than December, 19—.

PROBLEMS

22-1. Assume that some time ago you were assigned the task of studying the warehousing and shipping costs with the purpose of setting some kind of standards. After studying the various functions performed and the costs incurred over a test period, you have prepared:

(1) Budget expenses by object per month, below.

(2) A functional classification of accounts, together with the work units which measure such functions, and a budget of such work units per month, page 554.

(3) An analysis of the labor and supplies accounts according to the functional accounts served, page 555. Labor costs were segregated by analyzing the payroll records and, where necessary, by requiring employees performing two or more functions to keep a record of their time by operations. Supplies were segregated by identifying the items purchased and adjusting for opening and closing supplies inventories.

Required:

Allocate the budgeted costs by object to the functional account classifications and compute the standard cost per functional work unit. Set up the worksheet and compute budget functional costs per month, and standard functional unit costs.

Schedule I
Budget Warehouse and Shipping Costs by Object

(Period: One Month)

Labor..............................	$1,700.00
Supplies...........................	840.00
Repairs and repair parts............	40.00
Electricity........................	60.00
Depreciation......................	200.00
Insurance....	200.00
Taxes.............................	300.00
Rent..............................	500.00
Total........................	$3,840.00

Schedule II
Warehouse and Shipping
Functional Classification of Accounts
and Budget of Work Units per Month

Functional Classification of Accounts	Work Units	Budget: Number of Units per Month
Putting goods into stock—labor	Product units received	20,000
Picking—labor	Product units picked	20,000
Packing	Product units packed	20,000
Labor		
Supplies—printed forms		
Supplies—shipping materials		
Packing cases	Orders packed	2,000
Warehouse equipment: maintenance, repairs, and operation	Product units picked	20,000
Labor		
Repairs and repair parts		
Electricity		
Shipping dept. clerical	Orders packed	2,000
Labor		
Printed forms		
Capacity costs	None	None
Supervisory labor		
Depreciation		
Insurance		
Taxes		
Rent		

Schedule III
Warehouse and Shipping
Analysis of Budget Labor and Supplies by Functions

(Period—One Month)

Functional Account	Labor	Supplies
Putting goods into stock...............................	$ 200.00	$
Picking..	400.00	
Packing..	400.00	
Printed forms....................................		100.00
Shipping materials...............................		300.00
Packing cases....................................		400.00
Warehouse equipment: maintenance, repairs, and operation	100.00	
Shipping dept. clerical............................	200.00	
Printed forms....................................		40.00
Capacity costs....................................	400.00	
Totals.......................................	$1,700.00	$840.00

22-2. An Analysis of Actual Warehouse and Shipping Cost, by Object and Function for January, 19__ for the Benson & West Manufacturing Company is presented on page 556. Using this analysis and the Budget which appears in Figure 22-8, prepare an analysis of variances between actual expense and budget expense. Analyze functional account totals into (a) variances due to quantity of work units and (b) variances due to prices of work units.

Design your own worksheet form.

22-3. An Analysis of Actual Delivery Cost, by Object and Function for January, 19__ for the Benson & West Manufacturing Company is presented on page 557. Using this analysis and the Budget which appears in Figure 22-9, prepare an analysis of variances between actual expense and budget expense. Analyze functional account totals into (a) variances due to quantity of work units and (b) variances due to prices of work units.

Design your own worksheet form.

BENSON & WEST MANUFACTURING COMPANY

Analysis of Actual Warehouse and Shipping Cost, by Object and Function for the Month of January, 19___

Object Classification

Accounts	Amount
Labor......................	$1,423.60
Supplies	
Printed forms.............	218.00
Shipping supplies.........	200.00
Packing cases.............	588.00
Total.................	$1,006.00
Repairs and repair parts....	$ 30.00
Electric light and power....	16.00
Fixed charges	
Depreciation..............	166.67
Insurance.................	168.33
Taxes.....................	200.00
Rent......................	312.50
Total.................	$ 847.50
Total warehousing and shipping.....	$3,323.10

Functional Classification

Accounts	Amount	Description of Unit	Number of Units	Actual Cost per Unit
Putting goods into stock				
Labor.................	$ 165.00	Product units received	15,000	$.011
Picking				
Labor.................	306.60	Product units picked	14,600	.021
Packing				
Labor.................	262.00			
Printed forms.........	110.00			
Shipping supplies.....	200.00			
Total.............	$ 572.00	Product units packed	14,300	.04
Packing cases	588.00	Orders packed	2,800	.21
Warehouse equipment maintenance, repairs, operation				
Labor.................	100.00			
Repairs and repair parts...	30.00			
Electric power........	16.00			
Total.............	$ 146.00	Product units picked	14,600	.01
Shipping dept. clerical				
Labor.................	200.00			
Printed forms.........	108.00			
Total.............	$ 308.00	Orders packed	2,800	.11
Capacity cost				
Supervisory labor.....	390.00			
Depreciation..........	166.67			
Insurance.............	168.33			
Taxes.................	200.00			
Rent..................	312.50			
Total.............	$1,237.50	None		
Total warehousing and shipping.....	$3,323.10			

BENSON & WEST MANUFACTURING COMPANY
Analysis of Actual Delivery Costs, by Object and Function
for the Month of January, 19___

Object Classification

Accounts	Amount
Labor	$1,840.50
Supplies	
Gas	300.00
Oil	239.00
Garage supplies	20.00
Total	$ 559.00
Repairs and repair parts	
Trucks	110.00
Garage equipment	100.00
Total	$ 210.00
Fixed charges	
Depreciation	
Delivery trucks	125.00
Garage equipment	41.67
Insurance	
Delivery trucks	33.34
Garage equipment	8.33
Taxes (and licenses)	
Delivery trucks	40.00
Garage equipment	12.00
Rent—garage	125.00
Total	$ 385.34
Total delivery expenses	$2,994.84

Functional Classification

Accounts	Amount	Description of Unit	Number of Units	Actual Cost per Unit
Loading and unloading				
Labor	$ 313.50	Loading and unloading hours	95	$3.30
Truck operation				
Labor	792.00	Operating hours	240	3.30
Gas and oil	539.00	Miles	4,900	.11
Truck repairs				
Labor	260.00			
Garage supplies	20.00			
Repair parts—trucks	110.00			
Repairs—garage equipment	100.00			
Total	$ 490.00	Miles	4,900	.10
Capacity cost				
Supervision	$ 475.00			
Trucks				
Depreciation	125.00			
Insurance	33.34			
Taxes (and licenses)	40.00			
Garage equipment				
Depreciation	41.67			
Insurance	8.33			
Taxes	12.00			
Rent—garage	125.00			
Total	$ 860.34	None		
Total delivery expenses	$2,994.84			

557

Part Three

COSTS FOR USE IN BUSINESS PLANNING

SHIPMENTS, PRODUCTION, AND PROCUREMENT
BUDGETS

The budget as a planning tool in business. A budget (in its complete form) is a plan of operations, integrated and coordinated, comprising all phases of business activities and summarized to show the financial results of carrying out the plan. It involves distribution, production and procurement, and finance. It covers an advance period of say a month, a quarter of a year, or longer, and it is a formal attempt to make the best use of the men, materials, and facilities available for the period.

The budget is a useful tool in the planning stages of business operations because it is the means of evaluating the several courses of action that might be possible and finally crystallizing decisions into a complete plan. If one set of plans will not produce the desired results, the initial budgets will disclose that fact while there is still time for the management to consider alternate plans. The budget is also useful in the measurement of performance after the budget has been adopted by the management. Acceptance of a budget by a supervisor is a commitment to perform. Actual results are compared with the budget to determine the extent of differences between actual performance and expected performance.

The budget of the Benson & West Manufacturing Company was developed over a period of years. At first, there was no complete integration of the standard cost system and the budgets. The budgets were an informal projection of shipments and costs intended to show how the company would "come out." Now the budget system embraces the complete general ledger classification, with the cost statements and the budget statements integrated into a single structure.

Groups of budgets that comprise the complete plan. Groups of budgets which comprise the complete plan are:

(1) Shipments, production, and procurement budgets (this chapter)
(2) Facilities and expense budgets (chapter 24)
(3) Financial budgets (chapter 25)

Organization; General procedure. The controller of the Benson & West Manufacturing Company acts as the budget officer. The original

BENSON & WEST MANUFACTURING COMPANY
Budget Statement of Profits
by Months, January–July, 19___

	January	February	March	April	May	June	Total (six months)
Sales	$68,540.00	$81,030.00	$150,220.00	$212,050.00	$234,260.00	$83,470.00	$829,570.00
Cost of goods sold (@ Standard)	45,961.25	53,216.25	99,702.50	141,837.50	156,165.00	53,491.25	550,373.75
Gross margin	$22,578.75	$27,813.75	$50,517.50	$70,212.50	$78,095.00	$29,978.75	$279,196.25
Distribution and administrative expense:							
Distribution expense	$16,106.67	$17,491.55	$27,865.49	$37,137.89	$40,473.98	$17,843.37	$156,918.95
Administrative expense	5,215.66	5,215.66	5,215.66	5,215.66	5,215.66	5,215.66	31,293.96
Totals	$21,322.33	$22,707.21	$33,081.15	$42,353.55	$45,689.64	$23,059.03	$188,212.91
Operating net profit	$ 1,256.42	$ 5,106.54	$ 17,436.35	$ 27,858.95	$ 32,405.36	$ 6,919.72	$ 90,983.34
Financial expense (Net)	1,042.52	964.12	1,277.64	2,595.16	3,854.12	4,574.32	14,307.88
Net income	$ 213.90	$ 4,142.42	$ 16,158.71	$ 25,263.79	$ 28,551.24	$ 2,345.40	$ 76,675.46

BENSON & WEST MANUFACTURING COMPANY
Budget Schedule of Financial Expense and Income
by Months, January–July, 19___

	January	February	March	April	May	June	Total (six months)
Financial expense and income							
Sales discount	$ 1,294.80	$ 1,365.32	$ 1,614.12	$ 2,992.40	$ 4,224.20	$ 4,666.60	$ 16,157.44
Interest expense	500.00	500.00	500.00	500.00	500.00	500.00	3,000.00
	$ 1,794.80	$ 1,865.32	$ 2,114.12	$ 3,492.40	$ 4,724.20	$ 5,166.60	$ 19,157.44
Purchase discounts	752.28*	901.20*	836.48*	897.24*	870.08*	592.28*	4,849.56*
Financial expense (Net)	$ 1,042.52	$ 964.12	$ 1,277.64	$ 2,595.16	$ 3,854.12	$ 4,574.32	$ 14,307.88

* Red

Figure 23-1

budget is put together under his direction.   The comparisons of actual performance with budget performance, although prepared by the general ledger clerk and the cost accountant, are reviewed by the controller before they are released.

All the top management people participate in formulating the new budget.   This is to be expected since the budget is the coordinating mechanism used in planning.   The shipments, production, and purchase budgets are worked out through joint efforts of the sales manager, the production manager, and the purchasing agent.   The sales manager submits the estimate of shipment quantities for each product for each month.   The controller's office makes up the production, labor, and purchases budgets from the shipments budget.   (The method of working back from shipments to input is explained later in this chapter.)   The production manager reviews the production budget to determine whether he can meet it.   Likewise, the purchasing agent examines the purchases budget to determine whether it is possible to obtain all the materials in the quantities and dates indicated.

The industrial engineer makes proposals on additions, retirements, and changes in machinery and equipment for the factory, necessary to carry out the production plan.   He estimates the cost of additions and changes. The cost accountant sets the factory expense budgets, working with the industrial engineer and the production manager, and he sets the distribution cost budget, working with the sales manager.   The controller sets the administrative expense budget, getting decisions on salaries and certain other items from the president.

The controller consolidates the individual budgets, setting up a budget profit and loss by months.   He formulates a plan of financing the proposed operations and prepares a schedule of cash receipts and disbursements month by month for the period.

During the preparation of the individual budgets, there are numerous conferences among the executives directly interested, many of them called by the controller.   As the budget work reaches points of top decision, the controller notifies the president, who calls meetings and presides.   He makes the series of decisions affecting several departments jointly, necessary to keep the formulation of the complete budget moving.   All the individual budgets must dovetail, of course, and a number of revisions are made during the planning period to make them dovetail.

The final budget is reviewed by the president with all his major executives, and when it is approved, it becomes the plan of operations for the coming period.

Major budget summaries illustrated.   The major budget summaries are described below, and illustrated in this chapter.   Each summary shows totals for each of the six months and the total for six months.

Budget Statement of Profits (page 562).   This statement shows sales, cost of sales (at standard), gross margin, distribution expense, administrative

BENSON & WEST MANUFACTURING COMPANY
Budget Schedule of Cash Receipts and Disbursements
Six Months Ending June 30, 19___

Particulars	January	February	March	April	May	June	Six Months
Balance, beginning of month	$ 40,000.00	$102,951.55	$ 61,328.07	$ 19,227.86	$ 22,804.06	$ 85,480.12	$ 40,000.00
Add—Expected receipts							
Collections on accounts receivable	$ 63,445.20	$ 66,900.68	$ 79,091.88	$146,627.60	$206,985.80	$228,663.40	$791,714.56
Received from loan	97,000.00						97,000.00
Totals	$160,445.20	$ 66,900.68	$ 79,091.88	$146,627.60	$206,985.80	$228,663.40	$888,714.56
Available for disbursements	$200,445.20	$169,852.23	$140,419.95	$165,855.46	$229,789.86	$314,143.52	$928,714.56
Subtract—Expected disbursements							
Premiums paid							
Workmen's insurance	$	$	$	$ 1,000.00	$	$	$ 1,000.00
Property insurance							
Materials and supplies	36,861.72	44,158.80	40,987.52	43,964.76	42,633.92	29,021.72	237,628.44
Labor	42,775.38	45,103.48	55,929.34	62,086.05	63,052.42	47,280.15	316,226.82
Salaries and commissions	9,500.00	10,126.54	10,614.54	13,306.00	15,714.27	16,576.84	75,838.19
F.I.C.A. tax				3,057.54			3,057.54
Vacation pay						6,414.90	6,414.90
Purchased services	8,356.55	9,135.34	13,660.69	19,637.05	22,909.13	14,144.31	87,843.07
Notes payable—plant						20,000.00	20,000.00
Repayment of loan						100,000.00	100,000.00
Totals	$ 97,493.65	$108,524.16	$121,192.09	$143,051.40	$144,309.74	$233,437.92	$848,008.96
Balances, End of months	102,951.55	61,328.07	19,227.86	22,804.06	85,480.12	80,705.60	80,705.60

Figure 23-2

expense, and net profit. The statement is purely a summary, showing one figure for each of the items named.

Note that in a seasonal business, such as the one at hand, it is very useful to top management to have a complete six months' plan before them. Without a complete plan, management is likely to take it for granted that certain months are likely to be "bad" without realizing (a) what is an acceptable performance in those months and (b) what has to be done in the "good" months to make the six months' period show a profit.

Budget Statement of Cash Receipts and Disbursements (page 564). This statement shows the totals of expected cash receipts from each source and the total of cash disbursements for each class of liability. This schedule is a formal plan for the payment of liabilities which become due in varying amounts and frequencies. It shows whether the proposed plans can be financed properly. The company finances inventories partly by borrowing from the bank at the beginning of the season and re-paying the loans at the end of the season. The cash forecast shows when it will be necessary to borrow, the amount of the loans, and when they can be paid back.

Budget Balance Sheet (pages 566 and 567). This statement shows the expected financial position of the company at the end of each month of the six months' period. Appended (page 568) is a cumulative statement of underabsorbed expense, showing how the factory expense is expected to balance out over the period of six months. Note that there is underabsorbed expense in the months of low production (January, February, and June) and overabsorbed expense in the months of high production (March, April, and May). The expense account balances to zero over the budget period of six months.

Classification of accounts. The budget system described in this chapter was built within the framework of the classification of accounts used by the standard cost system. The budget shipments, goods produced, materials, and direct labor schedules follow the same format as the inventory accounts. Note the list of inventory accounts in the Budget Balance Sheet (page 566):

Finished Goods account is charged for standard cost of goods completed and credited for standard cost of goods sold.

Materials—Raw and In process account is charged for the standard cost of materials *bought* and credited for the standard cost of materials in goods completed. (This is a combination of the old Materials account and the old Materials in Process account.)

Labor in Process account is charged for standard hours in operations completed × standard labor rate per hour and credited for standard cost of labor in product units completed.

Factory Expense in Process account is charged for standard hours in operations completed × standard factory expense rate per hour and credited for standard factory expense in product units completed.

BENSON & WEST MANUFACTURING COMPANY
Budget Balance Sheets, by Months
Six Months Ending June 30, 19__

ASSETS

Account	January 1	January 31	February 28	March 31	April 30	May 31	June 30	Average Investment in Assets
Current Assets and Prepaid Expenses:								
Cash	$ 40,000.00	$102,951.55	$ 61,328.07	$ 19,227.86	$ 22,804.06	$ 85,480.12	$ 80,705.60	$ 62,082.87
Accounts receivable	65,000.00	68,540.00	81,030.00	150,220.00	212,050.00	234,260.00	83,470.00	138,261.66
Less—Reserve for bad debts	1,875.00*	1,930.05*	2,028.65*	2,394.65*	2,768.65*	3,004.64*	2,458.01*	2,430.77*
Materials: Raw and in process		24,970.00	38,250.00	32,770.00	28,450.00	13,460.00	3,150.00	23,508.32
Labor in process		12,427.50	19,487.50	16,312.50	14,712.50	5,625.00	1,387.50	11,658.00
Factory expense in process		5,798.75	8,523.75	6,882.50	6,062.50	2,560.00	693.75	5,086.50
Finished goods		15,385.00	24,655.00	45,038.75	24,881.25	7,097.50	36,725.00	25,630.40
Prepaid workmen's insurance	1,000.00	757.20	539.72	236.20	919.26	600.32	392.24	574.14
Prepaid property insurance	6,602.28	5,501.90	4,401.52	3,301.14	2,200.76	1,100.38		2,750.95
Supplies inventory	6,000.00	3,656.69	7,264.21	3,564.95	2,860.13	1,791.72	1,511.66	3,441.56
Prepaid interest expense		2,500.00	2,000.00	1,500.00	1,000.00	500.00		1,250.00
Total current assets and prepaid expenses	$116,727.28	$240,558.54	$245,451.12	$276,659.25	$313,171.81	$349,470.40	$205,577.74	$271,813.63
Underabsorbed Factory Expense (Figure 23-3c)	$	$ 238.58	$ 1,941.62	$ 824.46	$ 836.33*	$ 2,749.97*	$	$
Fixed Assets:								
Land	$100,000.00	$100,000.00	$100,000.00	$100,000.00	$100,000.00	$100,000.00	$100,000.00	$100,000.00
Building	200,000.00	200,000.00	200,000.00	200,000.00	200,000.00	200,000.00	200,000.00	200,000.00
Office furniture and equipment	21,000.00	21,000.00	21,000.00	21,000.00	21,000.00	21,000.00	21,000.00	21,000.00
Display fixtures	4,000.00	4,000.00	4,000.00	4,000.00	4,000.00	4,000.00	4,000.00	4,000.00
Autos	18,000.00	18,000.00	18,000.00	18,000.00	18,000.00	18,000.00	18,000.00	18,000.00
Delivery trucks	6,000.00	6,000.00	6,000.00	6,000.00	6,000.00	6,000.00	6,000.00	6,000.00
Machinery and equipment	60,000.00	80,000.00	80,000.00	80,000.00	80,000.00	80,000.00	80,000.00	80,000.00
Less—Reserve for depreciation	31,000.00*	33,074.97*	35,149.94*	37,224.91*	39,299.88*	41,374.85*	43,449.82*	38,262.39*
Total fixed assets	$378,000.00	$395,925.03	$393,850.06	$391,775.09	$389,700.12	$387,625.15	$385,550.18	$390,737.61
Total assets	$494,727.28	$636,722.15	$641,242.80	$669,258.80	$702,035.60	$734,345.58	$591,127.92	$662,551.24

* Red.

Figure 23-3a

BENSON & WEST MANUFACTURING COMPANY
Budget Balance Sheets, by Months
Six Months Ending June 30, 19___

LIABILITIES

Account	January 1	January 31	February 28	March 31	April 30	May 31	June 30
Current Liabilities:							
Accounts payable—Materials and supplies	$ 5,000.00	$ 16,306.00	$ 14,376.00	$ 13,722.00	$ 15,570.00	$ 13,966.00	$ 7,822.00
Accrued labor	6,000.00	12,258.46	10,948.27	14,993.73	15,697.48	15,786.00	10,498.09
Accrued salaries and commissions	9,500.00	10,126.54	10,614.54	13,306.00	15,714.27	16,576.84	10,705.81
Accrued F.I.C.A. tax		980.66	1,858.06	3,057.54	1,254.74	2,517.54	3,357.36
Reserve for vacation pay		980.66	1,858.06	3,057.54	4,312.28	5,575.08	
Accrued expense (purchased service)	2,500.00	2,928.28	3,103.53	5,278.57	7,179.25	7,864.93	3,139.70
Accrued property tax		1,200.37	2,400.74	3,601.11	4,801.48	6,001.85	7,202.22
Notes payable—Plant		20,000.00	20,000.00	20,000.00	20,000.00	20,000.00	
Bank loan		100,000.00	100,000.00	100,000.00	100,000.00	100,000.00	
Total current liabilities	$ 23,000.00	$164,780.97	$165,159.20	$177,016.49	$184,529.50	$188,288.24	$ 42,725.18
Net Worth:							
Capital stock	$400,000.00	$400,000.00	$400,000.00	$400,000.00	$400,000.00	$400,000.00	$400,000.00
Surplus—							
Balance, beginning of month	71,727.28	71,727.28	71,941.18	76,083.60	92,242.31	117,506.10	146,057.34
Profits—Month		213.90	4,142.42	16,158.71	25,263.79	28,551.24	2,345.40
Balance, end of month	$ 71,727.28	$ 71,941.18	$ 76,083.60	$ 92,242.31	$117,506.10	$146,057.34	$148,402.74
Total net worth	$471,727.28	$471,941.18	$476,083.60	$492,242.31	$517,506.10	$546,057.34	$548,402.74
Total liabilities and net worth	$494,727.28	$636,722.15	$641,242.80	$669,258.80	$702,035.60	$734,345.58	$591,127.92

Figure 23-3b

BENSON & WEST MANUFACTURING COMPANY
Schedule of Underabsorbed Factory Expense, by Months
Six Months Ending June 30, 19___

Particulars	January	February	March	April	May	June	Total (Six Months)
Expense incurred	$17,091.08	$16,096.79	$18,260.34	$18,951.71	$19,132.61	$15,917.47	$105,450.00
Expense absorbed: Production	16,032.50	13,573.75	18,557.50	19,792.50	20,226.25	12,347.50	100,530.00
Charged to distribution and administration	820.00	820.00	820.00	820.00	820.00	820.00	4,920.00
Total absorbed	$16,852.50	$14,393.75	$19,377.50	$20,612.50	$21,046.25	$13,167.50	$105,450.00
Underabsorbed: Month	238.58	1,703.04	1,117.16*	1,660.79*	1,913.64*	2,749.97	
Underabsorbed: Cumulative (Figure 23-3a)	238.58	1,941.62	824.46	836.33*	2,749.97*		

* Credit

Figure 23-3c

The standard costs on which the budget is based are what are described as attainable standard costs. They are not so tight that supervisors are not likely to meet them month after month and not so loose that supervisors are likely to beat them and show large credit variances. It follows that the budgeted debits to the Materials account and the Labor in Process account respectively are expected to be very nearly the same as the cash to be paid for materials and labor, respectively. If the standard costs charged to the inventory accounts are attainable, as in this case, they can be used to make up the cash budget. If they are not attainable, a correction percentage (called a "realization factor") has to be applied to the standard costs to adjust them to a cash figure.

Budgets in the shipments, production, and procurement group. This group of budgets includes:

(1) Budget shipments, goods produced, and finished goods inventories, by months.

(2) Budget materials in goods produced, materials receipts, and materials inventories, by months.

(3) Budget labor in goods produced, labor input, and labor in process inventories, by months.

(4) Budget factory expense in goods produced, factory expense applied, and factory expense in process inventories, by months.

In general, the shipments, production, and procurement budgets are a formal plan for setting out the estimates of shipments for a number of months in the future and working back to determine (a) what direct labor will have to be provided month by month and (b) what materials will have to be received month by month to meet the production and shipments plans.

Need for shipments, production, and procurement budgets. The need for formal shipments, production, and procurement budgets is described in the following paragraphs:

A good shipment and production budget is the tool for deciding how much finished goods inventory to build up. Finished goods inventories must be built up in the early part of the season to take care of shipments in the later part. Normally, over half of the shipments of the first six months will be made during the months of April and May. It is not possible simply to produce goods as the customers' orders come in.

A good shipment and production plan makes it possible to schedule the labor load with a minimum of laying off and calling back. Ideally, the direct labor load should be scheduled (a) evenly week by week during the six months or, (b) on the basis of three- or four-day work weeks in "slack" periods and five-day work weeks in "busy" periods. It is not feasible to lay off large numbers of employees at one time and attempt to get them back again several months later. Laid-off employees would find employment elsewhere and newly hired employees would have to be put through expensive training. The Benson & West Manufacturing Company has found that it is feasible to vary the number of days in the work week to keep the work force reasonably intact and at the same time avoid some of the risk of building up finished goods inventories against sales estimates.

Note in this connection that the labor budget is a primary formal method of controlling training costs. (The training period is from two to three weeks for the simpler operations to three months for the more complicated operations.) The labor budget operates in the direction of keeping down to a minimum the number of new employees who will have to be hired.

The shipments and production plan operates to keep the in process inventories in balance. These inventories cannot be allowed to get too large because of lack of storage space and because of the obvious need for conserving working capital. On the other hand, the in process work banks must always contain several days' work to allow for differences in speed among individual employees, local stoppage of work due to absenteeism and machine breakdowns, and similar nonpredictable factors.

The plan makes it possible to get the best prices for materials. To do this, purchase contracts must be made at the beginning of the season, and these contracts must be based upon estimated sales of finished goods and planned production.

Note that the Materials Purchases Budget is the primary method of controlling materials prices used by Benson & West. After the materials quantities required are determined in the budget procedure, the purchasing agent obtains prices for quantity lots from various suppliers. The prices accepted by Benson & West become the standard prices used in the cost system.

The Production and Shipments Budget keeps raw materials inventory under control. When the Benson & West Manufacturing Company completes its own production schedules, it notifies suppliers of the dates when materials will be required. The company aims to keep a certain number of days' supply of materials on hand. The number varies from material to material depending upon the length of time required to obtain delivery after the materials are "called up."

Purchase requirements shown by the budget of sales, production, and purchases are the basis for planning when to borrow, how much to borrow, and when to repay loans. The company finances purchases of materials with bank loans, borrowing to pay for materials as bills come due and repaying the loans after the accounts receivable are collected. The budget provides a control over interest cost in somewhat the same way it provides a control over other costs. Under the budget plan, the amounts and periods of the loans are carefully planned in direct relationship to the amounts and discount periods of suppliers' bills. The interest cost is consequently kept down to a practical minimum.

BUDGET PROCEDURE

Budget of shipments, production, and finished goods inventories illustrated.   To illustrate the principles of (1) calculating the required output of finished goods by months to meet the shipments budget and (2) the required purchases of materials and input of labor, assume the expected shipments and desired closing finished goods inventories shown below.

Expected Shipments and Inventory Data, by Months

January–June, 19__

Month	(1) Expected Shipments (Month)	(2) Desired Finished Goods Inventory (Closing)	(3) Minimum Work in Process (Standard Hours)	(4) Desired Working Days per Week*	(5) Desired Days Supply Materials
January..............	1,000	200	500	3	3
February............	2,000	400	500	4	4
March..............	3,000	800	500	5	5
April................	3,000	800	500	5	5
May................	4,000	400	500	5	4
June................	2,000				

* Assume 5 weeks even per month to simplify this illustration.
  Standard hours produced per working day = 250
  Product units produced per working day = 125
  There are no inventories January 1.

Standard Cost Card
Standard Cost per Unit

Product 101

(Physical standards only are shown)

Materials—
  2 yards @ $....................... $
Labor—
  2 hours @ $.......................
Factory expense—
  2 hours @..........................
  _____

Total cost per unit.................... $
  ========

Expected selling price per unit.......... $
  ========

Figure 23-4

The Budget of Shipments, Production, and Finished Goods Inventories for six months that would be evolved from the data is illustrated on page 572. This exhibit shows budget shipments, month and cumulative, on lines 1 and 2, desired finished goods inventories as of the end of each month

Budget Shipments, Production, and Finished Goods Inventories
January–June, 19___

Line	Particulars	January Product Units	January Total Sales Value	January Total Cost	February Product Units	February Total Sales Value	February Total Cost	March Product Units	March Total Sales Value	March Total Cost
	Shipments:									
1.	Month [units: Fig. 23-6(1)]........	1,000	$ 12,000.00	$ 9,000.00	2,000	$ 24,000.00	$ 18,000.00	3,000	$ 36,000.00	$ 27,000.00
2.	Cumulative*.................	1,000	12,000.00	9,000.00	3,000	36,000.00	27,000.00	6,000	72,000.00	54,000.00
	Units produced:									
3.	Month [units: Fig. 23-6(6)]........	1,200		10,800.00	2,200		19,800.00	3,400		30,600.00
4.	Cumulative*.................	1,200		10,800.00	3,400		30,600.00	6,800		61,200.00
	Finished goods:									
5.	End of month (line 4 − line 2)......	200		1,800.00	400		3,600.00	800		7,200.00
6.	Unit amounts from Figure 23-11......		$12/unit	$9/unit						

Line	Particulars	April Product Units	April Total Sales Value	April Total Cost	May Product Units	May Total Sales Value	May Total Cost	June Product Units	June Total Sales Value	June Total Cost
	Shipments:									
1.	Month...............	3,000	$ 36,000.00	$27,000.00	4,000	$ 48,000.00	$ 36,000.00	2,000	$ 24,000.00	$ 18,000.00
2.	Cumulative*............	9,000	108,000.00	81,000.00	13,000	156,000.00	117,000.00	15,000	180,000.00	135,000.00
	Units produced:									
3.	Month...............	3,000		27,000.00	3,600		32,400.00	1,600		14,400.00
4.	Cumulative*............	9,800		88,200.00	13,400		120,600.00	15,000		135,000.00
	Finished goods:									
5.	End of month............	800		7,200.00	400		3,600.00	800		

* *Calculate* cumulative units on this worksheet from the *month* units posted from the schedule, Figure 23-6. *Compare* cumulative units on schedules for proof.

Figure 23-5

on line 6, and required units produced to provide for shipments and inventory on lines 3 and 4.

The product units figures for the whole six months are calculated on a worksheet, as explained in the next section, from which they are posted to the budget. The product units in the budget are extended into dollars (sales value and cost) after the standard cost card for the product has been worked out and the selling price set. It is, of course, logical to set up the quantities (product units, standard hours on the labor budget, and standard yards on the materials budget) all the way through to test them for operating feasibility before extending them into dollar amounts.

Calculating required production of finished goods.   The required production of finished goods is calculated by working back from the budget cumulative sales figures (in product units), taking into consideration the desired inventories of finished goods month by month through the season. Cumulative production would, of course, be the same as cumulative shipments if there were no inventories. If a finished goods inventory is desired at the end of a month, cumulative production would equal cumulative shipments plus the desired closing inventory. The rules, then, for calculating required production by months are:

Cumulative production through the end of any month is the cumulative expected shipments through that month plus the desired finished goods inventory at the end of the month.

Required production *for any month* is the difference between the cumulative production at the end of the month and the cumulative production at the beginning of the month.

The calculation of required production by months for a six months' period is illustrated in the table below. Note that the required production

Required Production of Finished Goods, by Months

(For an Illustrative Six Months' Period)

	(1)	(2)	(3) Desired Finished	(4)	(5)	(6)
			Goods	Required Production (Cumulative)		Required Output
	Expected Shipments	Expected Shipments	Inventory	Product	Standard	Month
Month	(Month)	Cumulative	(Closing)	Units	Hours	(Units)
January	1,000	1,000	200	1,200	2,400	1,200
February	2,000	3,000	400	3,400	6,800	2,200
March	3,000	6,000	800	6,800	13,600	3,400
April	3,000	9,000	800	9,800	19,600	3,000
May	4,000	13,000	400	13,400	26,800	3,600
June	2,000	15,000		15,000	30,000	1,600
	15,000					15,000
Source:	23-4 (1)		23-4 (2)		(4) × 2 hrs.	

Figure 23-6

in both product units and standard hours is calculated. Required production in standard hours (cumulative, column 5) is used as explained in the next two sections to determine how much direct labor will be needed. The standard hours figures represent standard hours in finished goods output.

Budget of labor in goods produced, labor input, and labor in process inventories illustrated. The Budget of Labor in Goods Produced, Labor Input, and Labor in Process Inventories is illustrated on page 575. The format is the same as for the finished goods budget (page 572). The labor budget shows required labor in goods produced, month and cumulative, on lines 1 and 2, desired labor in process inventories on line 6, and the input required to obtain output and work in process inventory on lines 3 and 4.

The standard hours input figures for the six months are calculated as illustrated in the worksheet in the following section. Standard *amounts* (Standard hours × Standard rate per hour) are spread on the budget after the standard cost card has been completed.

Calculating required labor input. Required labor input is determined by working back from required production (standard hours in product completed), taking into consideration the desired work in process month by month through the season. The required input thus determined may then be rounded off to fit a work schedule of three days a week, or four days, or five days, as appropriate.

The first step is to use the formula: Cumulative finished goods output (in standard hours) + Minimum work in process at end of month = *Cumulative required labor input* in standard hours. This calculation is illustrated in Figure 23-8.

After determining the required labor input (Column [3]), the next step is to determine how many work days a week will have to be scheduled to meet the required input. This scheduling is shown in Columns (4) and (5). Three days per week are scheduled for January, 4 days for February, 5 days per week for March, April, and May, and 10 for the month of June. Note that this step in practice might require some experimental calculation to arrive at the proper number of days' work. Column (7) work schedule must not be less than Column (3) required input. Expected actual process inventory is calculated in Column (9) as a check upon the previous calculations, to determine that the in process inventory is neither too large nor too small.

Column 8, "Equivalent Product Units Started," is inserted in Figure 23-8 to build up materials input requirements, in the following section. Only one product is manufactured; therefore, standard hours may be converted readily into equivalent product units started.

Budget of materials in goods produced, materials received, and materials inventories illustrated. The Budget of Materials in Goods

Budget Labor in Goods Produced, Labor Input, and Labor in Process Inventories
January–June, 19__

Line	Particulars	January Product Units	January Standard Hours	January Standard Amount	February Product Units	February Standard Hours	February Standard Amount	March Product Units	March Standard Hours	March Standard Amount
	Labor in goods produced:									
1.	Month [units: Fig. 23-6(6)]........	1,200	2,400	$ 3,600.00	2,200	4,400	$ 6,600.00	3,400	6,800	$10,200.00
2.	Cumulative................	1,200	2,400	3,600.00	3,400	6,800	10,200.00	6,800	13,600	20,400.00
	Labor input:									
3.	Month [hours: Fig. 23-8(6)]........		3,750	5,625.00		5,000	7,500.00		6,250	9,375.00
4.	Cumulative................		3,750	5,625.00		8,750	13,125.00		15,000	22,500.00
	Labor in process inventory:									
5.	End of month (line 4 − line 2)......		1,350	2,025.00		1,950	2,925.00		1,400	2,100.00
6.	Hours/unit and $/hour (Fig. 23-11)....	2 hrs./unit		$1.50/hour						

Line	Particulars	April Product Units	April Standard Hours	April Standard Amount	May Product Units	May Standard Hours	May Standard Amount	June Product Units	June Standard Hours	June Standard Amount
	Labor in goods produced:									
1.	Month................	3,000	6,000	$ 9,000.00	3,600	7,200	$10,800.00	1,600	3,200	$ 4,800.00
2.	Cumulative................	9,800	19,600	29,400.00	13,400	26,800	40,200.00	15,000	30,000	45,000.00
	Labor input:									
3.	Month................		6,250	9,375.00		6,250	9,375.00		2,500	3,750.00
4.	Cumulative................		21,250	31,875.00		27,500	41,250.00		30,000	45,000.00
	Labor in process inventory:									
5.	End of month:................		1,650	2,475.00		700	1,050.00			

Figure 23-7

Required Labor Input, by Months

(For an Illustrative Six Months' Period)

Month	(1) Required Finished Goods Output—Cumulative (Standard Hours)	(2) Minimum Work in Process (Standard Hours)	(3) Required Input—Cumulative (Standard Hours)	(4) Days Per Week	(5) Work Schedule to Meet Required Input (Full Days) Days Per Month*	(6) Standard Hours Per Month	(7) Standard Hours Cumulative	(8) Equivalent Product Units Started (Cumulative)	(9) Expected Actual Process Inventory (Hours)
January	2,400	500	2,900	3	15	3,750	3,750	1,875	1,350
February	6,800	500	7,300	4	20	5,000	8,750	4,375	1,950
March	13,600	500	14,100	5	25	6,250	15,000	7,500	1,400
April	19,600	500	20,100	5	25	6,250	21,250	10,625	1,650
May	26,800	500	27,300	5	25	6,250	27,500	13,750	700
June	30,000		30,000		10	2,500	30,000	15,000	0
Source:	23-6 (5)	23-4 (3)	(1) + (2)			(5) × 250		(7) ÷ 2 hrs.	(7) — (1)

* Five weeks even per month are assumed to simplify the illustration.

Figure 23-8

Budget Materials in Goods Produced, Materials Received, and Materials Inventories

January–June, 19___

Line	Particulars	January Product Units	January Standard Yards	January Standard Amount	February Product Units	February Standard Yards	February Standard Amount	March Product Units	March Standard Yards	March Standard Amount
	Materials in goods produced:									
1.	Month [units: Fig. 23-6(6)]	1,200	2,400	$ 4,800.00	2,200	4,400	$ 8,800.00	3,400	6,800	$13,600.00
2.	Cumulative	1,200	2,400	4,800.00	3,400	6,800	13,600.00	6,800	13,600	27,200.00
	Materials received:									
3.	Month [yards: Fig. 23-10(7)]		4,500	9,000.00		5,250	10,500.00		6,500	13,000.00
4.	Cumulative		4,500	9,000.00		9,750	19,500.00		16,250	32,500.00
	Materials, raw and process:									
5.	End of month		2,100	4,200.00		2,950	5,900.00		2,650	5,300.00
6.	Yards/unit and $/yard from Fig. 23-11		2 yds./unit	$2/yd.						

Line	Particulars	April Product Units	April Standard Yards	April Standard Amount	May Product Units	May Standard Yards	May Standard Amount	June Product Units	June Standard Yards	June Standard Amount
	Materials in goods produced:									
1.	Month	3,000	6,000	$12,000.00	3,600	7,200	$14,400.00	1,600	3,200	$ 6,400.00
2.	Cumulative	9,800	19,600	39,200.00	13,400	26,800	53,600.00	15,000	30,000	60,000.00
	Materials received:									
3.	Month		6,250	12,500.00		6,000	12,000.00		1,500	3,000.00
4.	Cumulative		22,500	45,000.00		28,500	57,000.00		30,000	60,000.00
	Materials, raw and process:									
5.	End of month		2,900	5,800.00		1,700	3,400.00			

Figure 23-9

577

Produced, Materials Received, and Materials Inventories is illustrated on page 577. It is in the same format as the Labor Budget (page 575) except that the former is in standard yards whereas the latter is in standard hours. The standard yards for this budget are calculated as explained in the following section.

Materials requirements and materials receipts. As was indicated previously in this chapter, it is necessary to determine how many yards of materials are required for the product units to be started into production, and also the number of yards of materials to be received each month of the season. Required materials receipts is determined by working back from equivalent product units started, taking into consideration the desired materials inventory month by month through the season. Note that the Materials Budget is set up *after* the Labor Budget has been completed. Any rounding out of the Labor Budget to level the work force must be reflected in the Materials Budget.

Stated in mathematical terms: Cumulative input units (product units started into production) + Desired raw materials inventory (in terms of product units) = *Cumulative required receipts.* Required receipts (still in terms of product units) *for a month* = Cumulative required receipts at the end of the month − Comparable figure at the beginning of the month. These calculations are illustrated in the following table:

Required Materials Receipts, by Months

(For an Illustrative Six Months' Period)

Month	(1) Equivalent Product Units Started— Cumulative	(2) Days Require- ments	(3) Product Units per Day	(4) Total Product Units	(5) Required Receipts— Cumulative	(6) Product Units	(7) Yards
		Raw Materials Inventory				Required Receipts by Months	
January	1,875	3	125	375	2,250	2,250	4,500
February	4,375	4	125	500	4,875	2,625	5,250
March	7,500	5	125	625	8,125	3,250	6,500
April	10,625	5	125	625	11,250	3,125	6,250
May	13,750	4	125	500	14,250	3,000	6,000
June	15,000				15,000	750	1,500
						15,000	30,000
Source:	23-8 (8)	23-4 (5)		(2) × (3)	(1) + (4)		(6) × 2 yds

Figure 23-10

Required receipts *in yards* = Required receipts in product units × Standard yards per product unit.

Standard cost cards. After quantities have been spread on the budgets, as explained in the previous sections, the standard prices and factory expense rates are set (not illustrated) and the standard cost cards extended:

Standard Cost Card
Standard Cost per Unit

Product 101

Materials—
    2 yards @ $2.00.................... $ 4.00
Labor—
    2 hours @ $1.50.................... 3.00
Factory expense—
    2 hours @ $1.00.................... 2.00

Total cost per unit.................. $ 9.00

Expected selling price per unit.......... $12.00

Figure 23-11

Finally, the budget worksheets are extended into dollars, using standard product costs and selling prices per unit, standard materials prices per yard, and standard labor rates per hour.

Budget worksheet for Benson & West Manufacturing Company. Budget worksheets for the Benson & West Manufacturing Company are illustrated on pages 580 (one month only illustrated) and in the Appendix, pages 764 to 795 (six months). The format illustrated above is used in the Benson & West budget, except that it is expanded to provide for four products, and for a cutting department and two assembly departments.

Summary: Preparing the shipments, production, and procurement budgets. The steps in preparing the shipments, production, and procurement budgets are:

(1) Estimate the expected shipments by month and the desired finished goods inventories as of the end of each month in product units, the desired minimum work in process inventory in standard hours, the desired working days per week through the manufacturing season, and the desired days supply of materials in inventory at the end of each month.

(2) Determine the standard yards per unit of product and the standard hours per unit of product. (This information would be available on the standard cost cards.)

(3) Set up the product unit quantities on the budget of shipments, production, and finished goods, for the months of the budget period, using the formulas:

> Cumulative production through the end of any month is the cumulative expected shipments through that month plus the desired finished goods inventory at the end of the month.
>
> Required production *for any month* is the difference between the cumulative production at the end of the month and the cumulative production at the beginning of the month.

BENSON & WEST MANUFACTURING COMPANY
Budget Shipments, Goods Produced,
and Finished Goods Inventories, by Months

Six Months Ending June 30, 19__

(One month illustrated)

		January	
Products	Units	Total Sales	Total Cost
MONTH			

Goods shipped:

A	1,000	$ 7,100.00	$ 3,962.50
B	600	4,740.00	2,767.50
C	500	4,200.00	2,506.25
D	5,000	52,500.00	36,725.00
Total all products	7,100	$68,540.00	$45,961.25

CUMULATIVE

A	1,000	$ 7,100.00	$ 3,962.50
B	600	4,740.00	2,767.50
C	500	4,200.00	2,506.25
D	5,000	52,500.00	36,725.00
Total all products	7,100	$68,540.00	$45,961.25

MONTH

Goods produced:

A	1,500		$ 5,943.75
B	900		4,151.25
C	700		3,508.75
D	6,500		47,742.50
Total all products	9,600		$61,346.25

CUMULATIVE

A	1,500		$ 5,943.75
B	900		4,151.25
C	700		3,508.75
D	6,500		47,742.50
Total all products	9,600		$61,346.25

Month—end finished goods inventories:

A	500		$ 1,981.25
B	300		1,383.75
C	200		1,002.50
D	1,500		11,017.50
Total all products	2,500		$15,385.00

Figure 23-12

(4) Set up the product units and standard labor hours on the budget of labor in goods produced, labor input, and labor in process inventories by working back from the required production (standard hours in product completed), taking into consideration the desired work in process month by month through the season.   The desired input thus determined may then be rounded off to fit a work schedule of three days a week, or four days, or five days, as appropriate.

(5) Set up the product units and standard yards on the budget of materials in goods produced, materials received, and materials inventories. Work back from equivalent product units started in process through the desired raw materials inventory to the required purchases of materials.

(6) Set standard prices for materials and standard rates for labor and factory expense.   Enter them on the standard cost cards and extend them to determine standard product costs.

(7) Using standard product costs, standard materials prices, labor rates, and factory expense rates, extend the budgets described above into dollars.

Budgets relating to factory expense are illustrated and described in the following chapter.

REVIEW QUESTIONS

23-1. The vice president in charge of marketing of the Shipman Manufacturing Company desires an expansion of the product line, saying that "we should make what the customers want or someone else will."   The vice president in charge of manufacturing wants to retain or even curtail the present product line, saying that only through production of large orders of a small number of products can he achieve reasonable production costs.

The chief engineer maintains substantially the same view as the vice president in charge of manufacturing.   He adds that if changes are to be made in the product line, he must know about them some time before the production season starts, because "you can't change a production line overnight."   The treasurer doesn't take sides, but he says he wants to know what the other men are going to do so that he can arrange his financing.   He points out that changing over a production line frequently involves purchase of some new machinery, and furthermore, the business is seasonal, and the company has always financed the manufacturing period by borrowing on inventories.

The president of the company asks you to outline a plan for getting the top executives together in planning for a new season.   State (a) the general nature of the plan, (b) the nature of the participation by each executive, and (c) the steps in the plan.

23-2. Name the major budget summaries and state the use of each summary.

23-3. The budget system of the Benson & West Manufacturing Company was built within the framework of the classification of accounts used by the standard cost system.   The budget shipments, goods produced, materials, and direct labor schedules follow the same format as the inventory accounts.

Make a list of the inventory accounts and describe typical debit and credits to each account.

23-4. Name the budgets included in the shipments, production, and procurement group.

23-5. Discuss the need for shipments, production, and procurement budgets.

DISCUSSION QUESTION

23-6. In working back from the sales budget (which is set up by months of expected shipments) to the procurement budget (which is set up by months of required input), what are some of the factors to be considered in determining
(a) the desired finished goods inventory at the end of each month?
(b) the desired work in process inventory at the end of each month?
(c) the desired materials inventory at the end of each month?

PROBLEMS

23-1.

Standard Cost Card
Standard Cost per Unit

Product X

Materials:	
2 yards A @ $1.50	$ 3.00
Labor:	
3 hours @ $1.25	3.75
Factory expense:	
3 hours @ $1.00	3.00
Total cost per unit	$ 9.75
Expected selling price per unit	$12.50

Expected Shipments and Related Data, by Months

Month	Expected Shipments in Units (Month)	Desired Finished Goods Inventory in Units (Closing)	Minimum Work in Process (Standard Hours)	Desired Working Days for Week*	Desired Days Supply Materials
January	500	100	1,200	4	6
February	800	200	2,250	5	6
March	1,200	300	2,100	5	10
April	1,600	400	750	5	10
May	1,200	200	750	4	8
June	500	0	600	1	6

* To simplify calculations, assume 5 weeks even per month.
  Standard hours produced per working day = 150
  Product units per day = 50

Given the above information, set up the following schedules:

(1) Production requirements and work load, in product units and standard hours. (See Figure 23-6 and Figure 23-8 for illustrated forms.)
(2) Materials requirements and materials receipts (Figure 23-10).

(3) Budget shipments, production, and finished goods inventories (Figure 23-5).
(4) Budget labor in goods produced, labor input, and labor in process inventories (Figure 23-7).
(5) Budget materials in goods produced, materials received, in materials inventories—raw and processed (Figure 23-9).

23-2.

Expected Shipments and Inventory Date. by Months

January–June, 19___

	(1)	(2)	(3)	(4)	(5)
		Desired	*Minimum*		
		Finished	*Work in*	*Desired*	*Desired*
	Expected	*Goods*	*Process*	*Working*	*Days*
	Shipments	*Inventory*	*(Standard*	*Days per*	*Supply*
Month	*(Months)*	*(Closing)*	*Hours)*	*Week**	*Materials*
January............	1,000	300	200	4	5
February...........	1,500	400	200	4	8
March.............	2,000	500	200	5	10
April..............	2,000	500	200	5	10
May..............	1,500	400	200	4	8
June..............	1,000	300	100	2	5

* Assume 5 weeks even per month to simplify this problem.
Standard hours produced per working day = 160
Product units produced per working day = 80
There are no inventories January 1.

Standard Cost Card
Standard Cost per Unit

Product T

Materials	
3 yards @ $2.00	$ 6.00
Labor	
2 hours @ $1.50........................	3.00
Factory expense	
2 hours @ $1.00........................	2.00
Total cost per unit.......................	$11.00
Expected selling price per unit.............	$15.00

Required:

Using the above information, set up the schedules listed under (1) through (5) in Problem 23-1.

Chapter 24

THE FACILITIES BUDGET; EXPENSE BUDGETS

Uses of the facilities and expense budgets. This chapter describes the facilities budgets and the expense budgets. These budgets are the pathway from the shipments, production, and procurements budgets (Chapter 23) to the budget statement of profit. The former is the basic operating plan for the coming period; the latter is the final profit evaluation of the operating plan. After the shipments, production, and procurement budgets have been set up, the facilities budgets are drafted to show what will be required in the way of production and distribution facilities to carry out the proposed operating plan and also what those facilities will mean in fixed expenses.

After the facilities budgets have been completed, the factory expense budgets are laid out to show the expected expense of operating the factory, including the fixed expense calculated in the facilities budget. Likewise, the distribution expense budgets are drafted to show the expected cost of getting the goods to market, and the administrative expense budget to show the cost of top administration.

The sales and cost of sales amounts from the shipments budget and the expense amounts from the distribution expense budget and the administrative expense budget are summarized on the budget statement of profits. The budget statement of profits is the capstone of the whole process of planning which is crystallized in the budget.

The facilities budget. The facilities budget is concerned with the planning of capital assets necessary to carry out the manufacturing and distribution plans of the business. It is related to the shipments and production budgets in that it shows any addition to capital assets which must be made to implement the shipments and production plan. It may also show additions for expected future business.

In the broad sense, operation of the facilities budget involves (1) the approval of new capital assets projects (and likewise the approval of retirements), (2) the formulation of a plan of financing new capital assets (to be incorporated in the financial budget), and (3) the calculation of such fixed charges as depreciation, insurance, and taxes on capital assets (to be taken up in the expense budgets). As indicated above, the facilities

584

budget includes both manufacturing facilities and distribution facilities.

In the Benson & West Manufacturing Company, facilities projects for manufacturing are usually initiated by the industrial engineer and projects for distribution by the vice president in charge of marketing.   There is a regular procedure for estimating the return on investment in proposed additions (described in Chapter 27) and for the executive review and screening of proposals.   Projects approved for a particular period are included in the facilities budget for that period.

Capital asset budgeting in a large company.   The system for preparing and following up capital asset budgets in the Bigelow-Sanford Company is diagrammed in the chart on page (586), which is reproduced from "The Competitive Demand System of Capital Budget Preparation" by Elliott I. Peterson.*   The over-all approach is described by Mr. Peterson:

Clearly, the Bigelow-Sanford Company must approach the preparation of its capital budget with a keen eye on the competitive situation, as well as the quirks and turns of consumer demand.   Capital equipment must be purchased, not necessarily because it replaces worn-out equipment or because it can do the same job a little better, but purely on the basis that it will produce what the customer wants at a cost which will be competitive.

Consequently, ideas form the prime basis on which our capital budget program is founded.   Ideas may come from many sources: sales experience, trends in home decoration, consumer complaints about present fabrics, new equipment on the market, new methods devised by industrial engineers, or even new raw materials developed by the constantly expanding chemical industry.   All such ideas must be evaluated with a view to possible incorporation into projects for exploration and development by research groups.

In preparation of our capital budget, therefore, the company maintains three research groups:

1. *Product Research and Development*, which is constantly at work developing new products, new styles, and new textures and searching out new materials.
2. *Industrial Engineering*, which is constantly devising new plant layouts, plans for work simplification, productivity, improvements, etc.
3. *Manufacturing Engineering*, which is constantly investigating new equipment offered in the market, as well as developing improved machinery for arriving at the desired end result.

The activities of these three research groups are closely watched and evaluated by the very highest level of management.   This is done by means of the Engineering Program Committee, which consists of the president, the executive vice president, and the vice presidents for finance, manufacturing, and products, as well as the managers of the research groups.   Once a year, this key committee considers all ideas presented from any source whatsoever and steers the activity of the research groups into channels which are in conformance with the demands of the consumer or the competitive situation.

Obviously, certain priorities must be established: (1) the requirements of the product and (2) improvements in the fields of both cost and quality.   The size

* Elliott I. Peterson, "The Competitive-Demand System of Capital Budget Preparation," *Tested Approaches to Capital Equipment Replacement*, pp. 54-76.New York: American Management Association, 1954.

of the capital budget, moreover, is limited by the availability of funds, which in turn is dependent upon our best judgment concerning the general business outlook. Considerable thought must therefore be used in considering a capital expenditure from its inclusion in the budget itself to the actual approval of the appropriation. Once the appropriation is approved, the expenditures must be controlled; and, finally, an evaluation must be made to determine whether the objective which was sought has been obtained.   There is not a step along the line which must not be subject to judgment and decision.

Budget of fixed assets and fixed charges: Benson & West Manufacturing Company.   The Budget of Fixed Assets and Fixed Charges of the Benson & West Manufacturing Company appears on page 587. This budget shows a grouping of fixed assets of various types by function (administration, distribution, and manufacturing) and by department.   It also shows estimated depreciation, insurance, and tax charges for one month.   This budget includes $20,000 of new machinery and equipment which are to go into service at the beginning of the budget period.

Bigelow-Sanford Carpet Company, Inc.
Steps in Preparation of Capital Budget

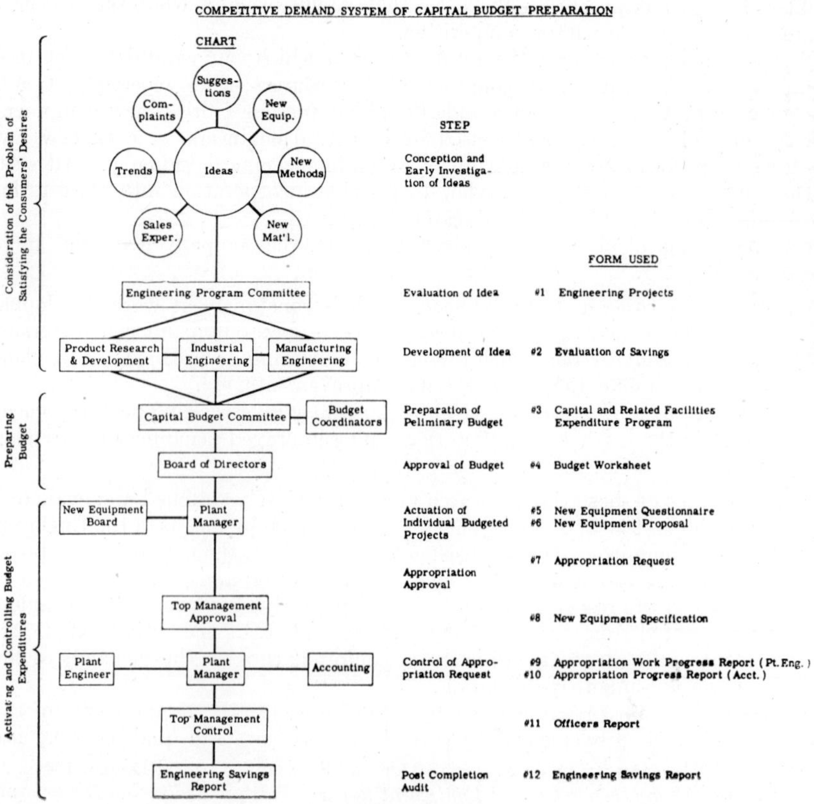

Figure 24-1

BENSON & WEST MANUFACTURING COMPANY
Budget of Fixed Assets, and Fixed Charges
(Six Months' Period: January–June 19-8)

	Totals	General Administration	Sales Department	Order Department and Cash Collecting	Finished Goods Warehouse	Garage and Delivery Department	Building	General Factory	Repair Shop	Raw Material Storage	Cutting Department	Assembly Department No. 1	Assembly Department No. 2
Fixed assets:													
Land	$100,000.00	$	$	$	$	$	$100,000.00	$	$	$	$	$	$
Building	200,000.00						200,000.00	1,000.00					
Office furniture and equipment	21,000.00	4,000.00	4,000.00	12,000.00									
Display fixtures	4,000.00		4,000.00										
Autos	18,000.00		18,000.00										
Delivery trucks	6,000.00					6,000.00							
Machinery and equipment	80,000.00				20,000.00	5,000.00			3,000.00	2,000.00	10,000.00	20,000.00	20,000.00
Total fixed assets	$429,000.00	$4,000.00	$26,000.00	$12,000.00	$20,000.00	$11,000.00	$300,000.00	$1,000.00	$3,000.00	$2,000.00	$10,000.00	$20,000.00	$20,000.00
Depreciation:													
Building	$800.00	$	$	$	$	$	$800.00	$25.00	$	$	$	$	$
Office furniture and equipment	178.33	33.33	20.00	100.00									
Display fixtures	21.66		21.66										
Autos	300.00		300.00										
Delivery trucks	166.67				166.67	166.67						166.66	166.66
Machinery and equipment	608.31								8.33	19.99	80.00		
Total depreciation	$2,074.97	$33.33	$341.66	$100.00	$166.67	$166.67	$800.00	$25.00	$8.33	$19.99	$80.00	$166.66	$166.66
Insurance:													
Building	$400.00	$	$	$	$	$	$400.00	$5.00	$	$	$	$	$
Office furniture and equipment	50.66	8.33	4.00	33.33									
Display fixtures	4.33		4.33										
Autos	100.00		100.00										
Delivery trucks	41.69				168.33	41.69						131.16	131.16
Machinery and equipment	503.72								3.33	9.74	60.00		
Total insurance	$1,100.40	$8.33	$108.33	$33.33	$168.33	$41.69	$400.00	$5.00	$3.33	$9.74	$60.00	$131.16	$131.16
Taxes:													
Building	$342.39	$	$	$	$	$	$342.39	$10.00	$	$	$	$	$
Office furniture and equipment	71.00	10.00	1.00	50.00									
Display fixtures	2.83		2.83										
Autos	70.00		70.00										
Delivery trucks	52.00				200.00	52.00						179.33	179.33
Machinery and equipment	662.15								5.50	17.99	80.00		
Total taxes	$1,200.37	$10.00	$73.83	$50.00	$200.00	$52.00	$342.39	$10.00	$5.50	$17.99	$80.00	$179.33	$179.33

Figure 24-2

The depreciation, insurance, and tax charges are taken up in the expense budgets later in this chapter. The financing of the purchase is covered in the financing budgets described in the next chapter.

Uses of factory expense budgets. The factory expense budgets of the Benson & West Manufacturing Company are prepared from (a) the standard hours produced as budgeted by months for the six months and (b) flexible expense budget tabulations by level (similar to the ones in Chapter 19). The six months' budgets are used to:

(1) Determine standard factory expense rates. These rates are used for the application of expense to the standard cost cards, which are in turn used to determine budget cost of goods produced and cost of goods sold. (Note that the calculation of expense rates which was formerly a part of the standard cost system, Chapter 19, is now a part of the budget procedure. Incidentally, whereas the rates in Chapter 19 were calculated on a straight 80 per cent of capacity, the rates under the budget procedure are calculated on the basis of expected average production for the six months.)

(2) Set up credits to accrued expense and certain other accounts as a basic step in preparing the cash budget and the budget balance sheet.

Budget Factory Expense Incurred: Building Maintenance and Fixed Charges

Month and Cumulative—Six Months Ending June 30, 19-8

(Two months illustrated)

MONTH

Object	January	February
Labor	$1,600.00	$1,600.00
F.I.C.A. tax	32.00	32.00
Workmen's insurance	8.00	8.00
Provision for vacation pay	32.00	32.00
Supplies and repair parts	230.00	230.00
Purchased services and unclassified	576.68	576.68
Depreciation	800.00	800.00
Insurance	400.00	400.00
Taxes	342.39	342.39
Totals	$4,021.07	$4,021.07

CUMULATIVE

Object	January	February
Labor	$1,600.00	$3,200.00
F.I.C.A. tax	32.00	64.00
Workmen's insurance	8.00	16.00
Provision for vacation pay	32.00	64.00
Supplies and repair parts	230.00	460.00
Purchased services and unclassified	576.68	1,153.36
Depreciation	800.00	1,600.00
Insurance	400.00	800.00
Taxes	342.39	684.78
Totals	$4,021.07	$8,042.14

Figure 24-3

The flexible budgets of the type described in Chapter 19 are still used for measuring spending performance month by month, since actual volume of work produced may be different from the volume set up in the six months' budget.

Building maintenance and fixed charges budget. The Building Maintenance and Fixed Charges Budget is a fixed budget (in this illustration), and the same amounts are used each month of the period. In some cases, part of building maintenance might be budgeted on a project basis.

General factory administration expense budget. The budget allowances for variable and semivariable expenses in the General Factory Administration Expense Budget are based upon total budget standard hours for all departments (excluding Building Maintenance). They are accordingly determined for the six months after the direct labor budgets have been set up.

Budget Factory Expense Incurred: General Factory Administration

Month and Cumulative—Six Months Ending June 30, 19-8

(Two months illustrated)

MONTH Object		January	February
Standard hours produced........		30,310	26,565
Labor............................	S-V	$4,350.00	$ 4,350.00
F.I.C.A. tax......................	S-V	87.00	87.00
Workmen's insurance..............	S-V	19.88	19.88
Provision for vacation pay..........	S-V	87.00	87.00
Supplies and repair parts...........	V	215.84	189.17
Purchased services and unclassified...	V	263.52	230.96
Depreciation......................	F	33.33	33.33
Insurance........................	F	8.33	8.33
Taxes............................	F	15.50	15.50
Totals......................		$5,080.40	$ 5,021.17

CUMULATIVE Standard hours produced........	January	February
	30,310	56,875
Labor............................	$4,350.00	$ 8,700.00
F.I.C.A. tax......................	87.00	174.00
Workmen's insurance..............	19.88	39.76
Provision for vacation pay..........	87.00	174.00
Supplies and repair parts...........	215.84	405.01
Purchased services and unclassified...	263.52	494.48
Depreciation......................	33.33	66.66
Insurance........................	8.33	16.66
Taxes............................	15.50	31.00
Totals......................	$5,080.40	$10,101.57

Figure 24-4

The fixed expenses (F) are picked up from the flexible budget and entered unchanged in the monthly budgets.

Each variable expense (V) is based upon an allowance per standard labor hour, computed when the flexible budget was set up for the standard cost system. Thus, the allowances for January would be 30,310 × the standard allowance per hour and the allowances for February would be 26,565 × the standard allowances per hour.

Semivariable labor (S-V) is picked up from the flexible budget which shows the labor allowances for each of several tabulated levels.

F.I.C.A. tax, workmen's insurance, and provision for vacation pay are each based upon a standard percentage of the labor amount.

Cutting department expense budget. The Cutting Department Expense Budget is a flexible budget. The budget allowances for variable and semivariable expenses are based upon budget standard hours for the cutting department shown by the direct labor budget, pages 766–769.

Budget Factory Expense Incurred: Cutting Department

Month and Cumulative—Six Months Ending June 30, 19-8

(Two months illustrated)

	MONTH		
Object		*January*	*February*
Standard hours produced.........		6,810	6,565
Labor............................	S-V	$1,363.84	$1,305.79
F.I.C.A. tax......................	S-V	231.56	224.60
Workmen's insurance...............	S-V	57.89	56.15
Provision for vacation pay..........	S-V	231.56	224.60
Supplies and repair parts...........	V	419.20	404.01
Purchased services and unclassified....	V	291.80	281.20
Depreciation......................	F	99.99	99.99
Insurance........................	F	69.74	69.74
Taxes............................	F	97.99	97.99
Totals......................		$2,863.57	$2,764.07

	CUMULATIVE	
Standard hours produced.........	6,810	13,375
Labor............................	$1,363.84	$2,669.63
F.I.C.A. tax......................	231.56	456.16
Workmen's insurance...............	57.89	114.04
Provision for vacation pay..........	231.56	456.16
Supplies and repair parts...........	419.20	823.20
Purchased services and unclassified....	291.80	573.01
Depreciation......................	99.99	199.98
Insurance........................	69.74	139.48
Taxes............................	97.99	195.98
Totals	$2,863.57	$5,627.64

Figure 24-5

In this case, each of the variable expense accounts is calculated as: January—6,810 hours × the appropriate standard rate per hour; February —6,565 hours × the appropriate standard rate per hour. The fixed (F) and semivariable (S-V) expenses are determined by months as explained above for General Factory Administration Expense.

Assembly department expense budget.   The Assembly Department Expense Budgets are set up in the same way as the Cutting Department Budget, above.   The budgets for Assembly Department No. 1 and Assembly Department No. 2 are illustrated herewith.

Budget Factory Expense Incurred: Assembly Department No. 1

Month and Cumulative—Six Months Ending June 30, 19-8

(Two months illustrated)

MONTH

Object		January	February
Standard hours produced.........		8,500	5,000
Labor.............................	S-V	$1,360.00	$ 920.00
F.I.C.A. tax.......................	S-V	239.70	143.40
Workmen's insurance................	S-V	59.43	35.85
Provision for vacation pay...........	S-V	239.70	143.40
Supplies and repair parts............	V	244.80	144.00
Purchased services and unclassified....	V	190.83	112.25
Depreciation.......................	F	166.66	166.66
Insurance.........................	F	131.16	131.16
Taxes.............................	F	179.33	179.33
Totals........................		$2,811.61	$1,976.05

CUMULATIVE

	January	February
Standard hours produced.........	8,500	13,500
Labor.............................	$1,360.00	$2,280.00
F.I.C.A. tax.......................	239.70	383.10
Workmen's insurance................	59.43	95.28
Provision for vacation pay...........	239.70	383.10
Supplies and repair parts............	244.80	388.80
Purchased services and unclassified....	190.83	303.08
Depreciation.......................	166.66	333.32
Insurance.........................	131.16	262.32
Taxes.............................	179.33	358.66
Totals........................	$2,811.61	$4,787.66

Figure 24-6

Budget Factory Expense Incurred: Assembly Department No. 2

Month and Cumulative—Six Months Ending June 30, 19-8

(Two months illustrated)

MONTH

Object	January	February
Standard hours produced...............	15,000	15,000
Labor....................................	$ 770.00	$ 770.00
F.I.C.A. tax.............................	390.40	390.40
Workmen's insurance.....................	97.60	97.60
Provision for vacation pay..............	390.40	390.40
Supplies and repair parts...............	112.50	112.50
Purchased services and unclassified..........	76.38	76.38
Depreciation............................	166.66	166.66
Insurance...............................	131.16	131.16
Taxes...................................	179.33	179.33
Totals.............................	$2,314.43	$2,314.43

CUMULATIVE

Standard hours produced...............	15,000	30,000
Labor....................................	$ 770.00	$1,540.00
F.I.C.A. tax.............................	390.40	780.80
Workmen's insurance.....................	97.60	195.20
Provision for vacation pay..............	390.40	780.80
Supplies and repair parts...............	112.50	225.00
Purchased services and unclassified..........	76.38	152.76
Depreciation............................	166.66	333.32
Insurance...............................	131.16	262.32
Taxes...................................	179.33	358.66
Totals.............................	$2,314.43	$4,628.86

Figure 24-7

Factory expense budget summary. The Factory Expense Budget Summary is a summary of the expense totals by object account for all departments. It is a record of the supporting departmental budgets (illustrated above). It provides the grand total debit to Factory Expense and credits to prepaid expense, accrued expense accounts, and certain other accounts.

Budget Factory Expense Incurred: All Departments

Month and Cumulative—Six Months Ending June 30, 19-8

(Two months illustrated)

MONTH

Object	January	February
Labor	$ 9,443.84	$ 8,945.79
F.I.C.A. tax	980.66	877.40
Workmen's insurance	242.80	217.48
Provision for vacation pay	980.66	877.40
Supplies and repair parts	1,222.34	1,079.67
Purchased services and unclassified	1,399.21	1,277.48
Depreciation	1,266.64	1,266.64
Insurance	740.39	740.39
Taxes	814.54	814.54
Totals	$17,091.08	$16,096.79

CUMULATIVE

Object	January	February
Labor	$ 9,443.84	$18,389.63
F.I.C.A. tax	980.66	1,858.06
Workmen's insurance	242.80	460.28
Provision for vacation pay	980.66	1,858.06
Supplies and repair parts	1,222.34	2,302.01
Purchased services and unclassified	1,399.21	2,676.69
Depreciation	1,266.64	2,533.28
Insurance	740.39	1,480.78
Taxes	814.54	1,629.08
Totals	$17,091.08	$33,187.87

CREDITS TO PREPAID EXPENSE AND ACCRUED EXPENSE ACCOUNTS

Accounts Credited		
Accrued factory indirect labor	$ 9,443.84	$ 8,945.79
Accrued F.I.C.A. tax	980.66	877.40
Prepaid workmen's insurance	242.80	217.48
Reserve for vacation pay	980.66	877.40
Supplies inventory	1,222.34	1,079.67
Accrued expense (purchased services)	1,399.21	1,277.48
Reserve for depreciation	1,266.64	1,266.64
Prepaid property insurance	740.39	740.39
Accrued property tax	814.54	814.54
	$17,091.08	$16,096.79

Figure 24-8

The Factory Expense Budget Summary for January, if reduced to journal entry form would be:

Dr. Factory expense...............	$17,091.08	
Cr. Accrued factory indirect labor...		$9,443.84
Accrued F.I.C.A. tax...........		980.66
Prepaid workmen's insurance....		242.80
Reserve for vacation pay........		980.66
Supplies inventory.............		1,222.34
Accrued expense...............		1,399.21
Reserve for depreciation........		1,266.64
Prepaid property insurance......		740.39
Accrued property tax...........		814.54

Figure 24-9

The debit to Factory Expense is absorbed into Factory Expense in Process by a later entry. The various credits (except Reserve for Depreciation) are used to set up the cash forecast as explained in Chapter 25.

Standard expense rates based upon expected average production volume. The rate schedule in Figure 24-10 illustrates how departmental factory expense rates are calculated after the departmental expense budgets for six months (above) have been set out. The standard hours and dollars for the various departments shown in the rate schedule are averages for the six months' budget period. In the schedule, building maintenance and fixed charges and general factory administration are allocated to the three producing departments. The rates are then determined by dividing total departmental expense by standard hours produced.

The rates per standard hours are:

Cutting department.............	$.75
Assembly No. 1.................	.65
Assembly No. 2.................	.36

These rates are used on standard product costs schedules to determine standard costs per unit for each product (next section). They are also used for setting up the budget factory expense in goods completed, factory expense applied, and factory expense in process schedules (pages 773-774).

The rates would also be used at the end of each month to record factory expense applied in the general ledger (in the operation of the standard cost system).

Standard product costs per unit. The standard product costs per unit of product for the four products manufactured by Benson & West are shown in Figure 24-11. The standard product costs are used as a factor in setting selling prices (which are also shown in the table). Standard product costs and selling prices are then used to extend the product quantities in the budget shipments, goods produced, and finished goods inventories schedules (Chapter 23, page 580).

Figure 24-10

Line	Particulars	Building Maintenance and Fixed Charges	General Factory Administrations	Cutting	Assembly No. 1	Assembly No. 2	Selling and Administrative	Totals
1	Standard hours produced		33,700†	6,500	7,200	20,000		$17,575.00
2	Total direct departmental expenses	$4,021.07	$5,293.30	$2,881.38	$2,469.82	$2,909.43	$ 820.00	
3	Building maintenance and fixed charges allocated	4,021.07*	400.00	895.51	993.81	911.75		
4	Total general factory administration		$5,693.30					
5	General factory administration expense allocated: (Rate per standard hour = $5,693.30 ÷ 33,700 = $.1689+)—		5,693.30*	1,098.11	1,216.37	3,378.82		
6	Total departmental expense			$4,875.00	$4,680.00	$7,200.00	$820.00	$17,575.00
7	Rates per standard hour			$ .75	$ .65	$ .36		

Department	Standard Hours	Amount Allocated
Cutting	6,500	$1,098.11
Assembly department No. 1	7,200	1,216.37
Assembly department No. 2	20,000	3,378.82
Totals	33,700	$5,693.30

* Red.
† Total.

Figure 24-10

Standard Product Costs per Unit and Standard Selling Prices per Unit Based upon Expected Average Volume for Six Months

Element and Department	Product A Yards or Hours per Unit	Product A Price or Rate	Product A Total Amount per Product Unit	Product B Yards or Hours per Unit	Product B Price or Rate	Product B Total Amount per Product Unit	Product C Yards or Hours per Unit	Product C Price or Rate	Product C Total Amount per Product Unit	Product D Yards or Hours per Unit	Product D Price or Rate	Product D Total Amount per Product Unit
Materials	3 yards	$ .50	$1.50	2 yards	$ .60	$1.20	2 yards	$ .80	$1.60	2 yards	$1.50	$ 3.00
Labor:												
Cutting department	.25 hour	1.50	.375	.25 hour	1.50	.375	.25 hour	1.50	.375	.5 hour	1.50	.75
Assembly department No. 1	1.0 hour	1.25	1.25	1.5 hours	1.25	1.875	1.5 hours	1.25	1.875	2.0 hours	1.25	2.50
Assembly department No. 2												
Factory expense:												
Cutting department	.25 hour	.75	.1875	.25 hour	.75	.1875	.25 hour	.75	.1875	.5 hour	.75	.375
Assembly department No. 1	1.0 hour	.65	.65	1.5 hours	.65	.975	1.5 hours	.65	.975			
Assembly department No. 2										2.0 hours	.36	.72
Totals per product unit			$3.9625			$4.6125			$5.0125			$ 7.345
Standard (desired average) selling prices per unit			$7.10			$7.90			$8.40			$10.50

Figure 24-11

595

The standard product costs would also be used at the end of each month to record cost of goods manufactured @ standard and cost of goods sold @ standard (in the operation of the standard cost system).

Uses of distribution expense budgets. The distribution expense budgets of the Benson & West Manufacturing Company are used:

(1) like the factory expense budgets described above, to set up (a) expenses which will have to be paid in cash ("out of pocket" expenses) and (b) expenses which will not have to be paid in cash during the budget period. This is a step in the preparation of the cash budget.

(2) to provide distribution expense totals for the budget profit and loss statement.

Selling and promotion expense budget. The Selling and Promotion Expense Budget is set up on the basis of what expense is considered necessary, after careful planning, to obtain the sales which have been budgeted. In practice, the sales budget and the selling and promotion expense budget are considered together. The sales executives study the sales statements and the expense statements for the past period, illustrated on pages 744-746 (sales and expense by products, by territories, by class of customer), and

Selling and Promotion Expense Budget

Month and Cumulative—Six Months Ending June 30, 19-8

(Two months illustrated)

MONTH

		January	February
Salaries.........................	S-V	$1,880.00	$ 1,880.00
Commissions.....................	S-V	789.66	933.93
Supplies........................	S-V	114.15	135.00
Purchased services and unclassified...	S-V	5,847.22	6,915.24
Depreciation....................	F	341.66	341.66
Insurance......................	F	108.33	108.33
Taxes..........................	F	73.83	73.83
Rent...........................	F	164.00	164.00
Totals......................		$9,318.85	$10,551.99

CUMULATIVE

	January	February
Salaries.........................	$1,880.00	$ 3,760.00
Commissions.....................	789.66	1,723.59
Supplies........................	114.15	249.15
Purchased services and unclassified...	5,847.22	12,762.46
Depreciation....................	341.66	683.32
Insurance......................	108.33	216.66
Taxes..........................	73.83	147.66
Rent...........................	164.00	328.00
Totals......................	$9,318.85	$19,870.84

Figure 24-12

they consider any new products, territories, classes of customers, and methods of sale. And finally, they decide what expense budget will be necessary to get the sales they are planning to get. They may say, for instance, that to get a certain increase in sales, it will be necessary to add three men in a certain territory, and spend a certain amount for advertising. The distribution expense budget represents the crystallization of a set of plans and not merely an expense control. Once the budget is set, the management would be as likely to analyze an underspending as an overspending. The former situation might mean that the plans originally set up for getting the sales have not been carried out in full.

Order department and cash collection; Warehouse and delivery expense budgets. In preparing these budgets for six months, the fixed charges and the salaries were posted from the monthly worksheets. Theoretically, it would have been possible to spread the variable expenses on the six months' worksheets by (a) estimating the number of work units to be required for each function each month and (b) multiplying by standard functional unit costs to determine the standard budget allowance for the

Budget Order Department: Expense Incurred

Month and Cumulative—Six Months Ending June 30, 19-8

(Two months illustrated)

MONTH

	January	February
Supervisory salaries	$ 400.00	$ 400.00
Other labor	750.88	888.03
Supplies	174.75	206.55
Purchased services and unclassified	322.59	381.51
Bad debts	315.05	372.60
Depreciation	100.00	100.00
Insurance	33.33	33.33
Taxes	50.00	50.00
Rent	54.50	54.50
Totals	$2,201.10	$2,486.52

CUMULATIVE

	January	February
Supervisory salaries	$ 400.00	$ 800.00
Other labor	750.88	1,638.91
Supplies	174.75	381.30
Purchased services and unclassified	322.59	704.10
Bad debts	315.05	687.65
Depreciation	100.00	200.00
Insurance	33.33	66.66
Taxes	50.00	100.00
Rent	54.50	109.00
Totals	$2,201.10	$4,687.62

Figure 24-13

Warehouse Expense Budget
Month and Cumulative—Six Months Ending June 30, 19-8
(*Two months illustrated*)

MONTH

	January	February
Supervisory labor	$ 375.00	$ 375.00
Other labor	491.76	581.58
Supplies	431.03	509.76
Purchased services and unclassified	23.74	28.06
Depreciation	166.67	166.67
Insurance	168.33	168.33
Taxes	200.00	200.00
Rent	312.50	312.50
Totals	$2,169.03	$2,341.90

CUMULATIVE

	January	February
Supervisory labor	$ 375.00	$ 750.00
Other labor	491.76	1,073.34
Supplies	431.03	940.79
Purchased services and unclassified	23.74	51.80
Depreciation	166.67	333.34
Insurance	168.33	336.66
Taxes	200.00	400.00
Rent	312.50	625.00
Totals	$2,169.03	$4,510.93

Figure 24-14

Delivery Department Expense Budget
Month and Cumulative—Six Months Ending June 30, 19-8
(*Two months illustrated*)

MONTH

	January	February
Supervisory labor	$ 500.00	$ 500.00
Other labor	639.24	756.00
Supplies	331.04	391.50
Purchased services and unclassified	562.07	78.30
Depreciation	166.67	166.67
Insurance	41.67	41.67
Taxes	52.00	52.00
Rent	125.00	125.00
Totals	$2,417.69	$2,111.14

CUMULATIVE

	January	February
Supervisory salaries	$ 500.00	$1,000.00
Other labor	639.24	1,395.24
Supplies	331.04	722.54
Purchased services and unclassified	562.07	640.37
Depreciation	166.67	333.34
Insurance	41.67	83.34
Taxes	52.00	104.00
Rent	125.00	250.00
Totals	$2,417.69	$4,528.83

Figure 24-15

month.   This method would provide the same expense control for long-run performance as is used on short-run performance in the standard cost system (Chapter 21).

To keep the illustration simple, an allocation of variable expenses on the basis of budget sales was used, with no recommendation for this method over the more accurate one mentioned above.   The fixed expenses and salaries were posted repetitively for all six months.

Budget Summary of Distribution Expense:
Selling, Order, Warehouse, and Delivery

Month and Cumulative—Six Months Ending June 30, 19-8

(Two months illustrated)

MONTH	January	February
Salaries.............................	$ 3,155.00	$ 3,155.00
Commissions.........................	789.66	933.93
Other labor..........................	1,881.88	2,225.61
Supplies.............................	1,050.97	1,242.81
Purchased services and unclassified.......	6,755.62	7,403.11
Bad debts...........................	315.05	372.60
Depreciation.........................	775.00	775.00
Insurance...........................	351.66	351.66
Taxes...............................	375.83	375.83
Rent................................	656.00	656.00
Totals..........................	$16,106.67	$17,491.55

CUMULATIVE		
Salaries.............................	$ 3,155.00	$ 6,310.00
Commissions.........................	789.66	1,723.59
Other labor..........................	1,881.88	4,107.49
Supplies.............................	1,050.97	2,293.78
Purchased services and unclassified.......	6,755.62	14,158.73
Bad debts...........................	315.05	687.65
Depreciation.........................	775.00	1,550.00
Insurance...........................	351.66	703.32
Taxes...............................	375.83	751.66
Rent................................	656.00	1,312.00
Totals..........................	$16,106.67	$33,598.22

CREDITS TO PREPAID EXPENSE AND ACCRUED EXPENSE ACCOUNTS

Accounts Credited		
Accrued salaries and commissions.........	$ 5,826.54	$ 6,314.54
Supplies inventory......................	1,050.97	1,242.81
Accrued expense (purchased service)......	6,755.62	7,403.11
Reserve for bad debts...................	315.05	372.60
Reserve for depreciation.................	775.00	775.00
Prepaid property insurance..............	351.66	351.66
Accrued property taxes.................	375.83	375.83
Factory expense (building maintenance)...	656.00	656.00
	$16,106.67	$17,491.55

Figure 24-16

Administrative Expense Budget

Month and Cumulative—Six Months Ending June 30, 19-8

MONTH

	January	February
Salaries.............................	$4,300.00	$ 4,300.00
Supplies..............................	70.00	70.00
Purchased services and unclassified........	630.00	630.00
Depreciation...........................	33.33	33.33
Insurance.............................	8.33	8.33
Taxes.................................	10.00	10.00
Rent..................................	164.00	164.00
Totals............................	$5,215.66	$ 5,215.66

CUMULATIVE

Salaries.............................	$4,300.00	$ 8,600.00
Supplies..............................	70.00	140.00
Purchased services and unclassified........	630.00	1,260.00
Depreciation...........................	33.33	66.66
Insurance.............................	8.33	16.66
Taxes.................................	10.00	20.00
Rent..................................	164.00	328.00
Totals............................	$5,215.66	$10,431.32

CREDITS TO PREPAID EXPENSE AND ACCRUED EXPENSE ACCOUNT

Accounts Credited

Accrued salaries.........................	$4,300.00	$ 4,300.00
Supplies inventory.......................	70.00	70.00
Accrued expense (purchased services)......	630.00	630.00
Reserve for depreciation..................	33.33	33.33
Prepaid property insurance...............	8.33	8.33
Accrued property taxes...................	10.00	10.00
Factory expense (building maintenance)....	164.00	164.00
Totals............................	$5,215.66	$ 5,215.66

Figure 24-17

Budget summary of distribution expense. The Budget Summary of Distribution Expense is prepared by recapping month by month all accounts on the supporting four budgets.

A summary of credits to prepaid expense, accrued expense, and other accounts appears at the bottom of the Summary of Distribution Cost. This summary of credits is used to draft the standard journal entries for the cash forecast. The standard journal entry for January (for instance) would be:

Dr. Distribution expense.....................	$16,106.67	
Cr. Accrued salaries and commissions........		$5,862.54
Supplies inventories...................		1,050.97
Accrued expenses (purchased services)....		6,755.62
Reserve for bad debts.................		315.05

Reserve for depreciation...............	775.00
Prepaid property insurance.............	351.66
Accrued property taxes................	375.83
Factory expense absorbed..............	656.00

Note that the credit to Factory Expense Absorbed ($656) represents the amount transferred from the factory expense accounts to the distribution expense accounts to cover rent of the sales department space. Total building maintenance and fixed charges are compiled initially in the factory expense accounts, and the portion chargeable to Distribution is transferred out by this entry.

Administrative expense budget. The Administrative Expense Budget for six months appears below. Since this budget is considered a fixed budget, the same amounts are entered in each of the "Month" columns. Credits to prepaid expense, accrued expense accounts, and other accounts are shown at the bottom of the budget. Most of these credit amounts are used to prepare the cash forecast.

Budget profit and loss statement. The Budget Profit and Loss Statement shown below is prepared from the following budgets previously illustrated:

Shipments, Goods Produced, and Finished Goods
(which provides the sales and cost of sales amounts)
Distribution Expense
Administrative Expense

BENSON & WEST MANUFACTURING COMPANY
Budget Statement of Profits

by Months, January–July, 19-8

(Two months illustrated)

	January	February
Sales.................................	$68,540.00	$81,030.00
Cost of goods sold (@ standard).........	45,961.25	53,216.25
Gross margin........................	$22,578.75	$27,813.75
Distribution and administrative expense:		
Distribution expense.................	$16,106.67	$17,491.55
Administrative expense...............	5,215.66	5,215.66
Totals.......................	$21,322.33	$22,707.21
Net profit...........................	$ 1,256.42	$ 5,106.54

Figure 24-18

Summary. Chapter 23 and this chapter have described a budget system which was developed from a standard cost system. The standards which were used for control of materials and labor cost in the standard cost system became, together with the sales forecast, the basis for the Shipments, Production, and Procurement Budget. The Flexible Expense Budget which was the basis for control of factory expense in the standard cost system became the foundation of the Factory Expense Budget in the complete budget system. Likewise, the budgets and standards developed for the cost control of distribution activities were integrated into the master plan of the new budget.

In the new budget plan, the Shipments Budget, the Distribution Expense Budget, and the Administrative Expense Budget finally came together in the Budget Statement of Profits, which is the focal point of management thinking in the whole planning process. At this point, the management decides whether to adopt the operating plan as set out in the budget or to work on the plan further to see if it can be improved profitwise. Once the budget is accepted by the management, it becomes a commitment to perform.

One further step, and a fundamental one, remains in constructing the *master* budget. That step is the formulation of a plan of current financing for the proposed operating plan and the drafting of a financial budget. That final phase of the budgeting program is described in Chapter 25.

QUESTIONS

24-1. (a) What do you consider the most important reasons for operating facilities budgets?

(b) What are some of the factors to be considered in setting up and approving new facilities projects?

24-2. (a) Explain the uses of the six months' factory expense budgets in a complete budget system.

(b) Explain the uses of the six months' distribution expense budgets in a complete budget system.

24-3. Set up an object classification of expense accounts for use in a budget system, grouping the object accounts in such manner as to facilitate obtaining the credits to prepaid expense, accounts payable, and accrued expense accounts. Show the names of the latter accounts as well as the names of the expense accounts.

24-4. In practice, what is the essential difference between the budgeting of selling and promotion expense and the budgeting of order department and cash collecting expenses?

24-5. Assume that, after setting up the shipments, production and procurement budgets as illustrated in Chapter 23 and the expense budgets as illustrated in Chapter 24, the profit picture is not satisfactory. Does this prove that the time spent in budgeting was wasted?

PROBLEM

24-1. Given the following budget data for the Franklin Corporation, and the appropriate sections of the classification of accounts on pages 605-606, set up budget schedules for:

(1) Factory Expense, by Months. Use Figure 24-8 as a model of form. Since no cumulative budget statements are required in this series of problems, the cumulative section may be omitted. Show calculation of standard factory expense rate for the six months' budget period at bottom of this schedule.

(2) Budget Schedule of Factory Expense in Goods Produced, Factory Expense Charge to Work in Process, and Factory Expense in Process Inventories, by Months. Adapt Figure 23-7.

(3) Budget Schedule of Cumulative Underabsorbed (Overabsorbed) Factory Expense, by Months. Adapt Figure 23-3c.

(4) Administrative and Selling Expense, by Months. Use Figure 24-16 as a model of form. Cumulative section may be omitted.

(5) Budget Statement of Profits (Before Financial Income and Expense), by Months.

Sales, Cost of Sales, and Standard Direct Labor Hours

Month	Budget Sales, in Dollars	Budget Cost of Sales	Budget Standard Direct Labor Hours Input
January	$ 6,250.00	$ 4,875.00	3,000
February	10,000.00	7,800.00	3,750
March	15,000.00	11,700.00	3,750
April	20,000.00	15,600.00	3,750
May	15,000.00	11,700.00	3,000
June	6,250.00	4,875.00	750
Total, six months	$72,500.00	$56,550.00	18,000

Standard direct labor rate = $1.25 per hour
Source: Budget Worksheet,
Solution to Problem............ 23-1(3)   23-1(3)   23-1(4)

Variable Expense Data

Factory expense:

Indirect labor, $.20 per standard direct labor hour
F.I.C.A. tax, 2 per cent of direct labor plus indirect labor
Supplies, $.15 per standard direct labor hour
Power, $.05 per standard direct labor hour

Administrative and selling expense:

Salaries, $600 per month
Commissions: 4 per cent of sales
F.I.C.A. tax: 2 per cent of salaries plus commissions
Advertising pieces: 3 per cent of sales
Bad debts: $\frac{1}{2}$ of 1 per cent of sales

Fixed allowances:

Depreciation, insurance and taxes as shown on the Budget of Fixed Assets and Fixed Charges (page 604)
Administrative and selling salaries, $600 per month

FRANKLIN CORPORATION
Budget of Fixed Assets and Fixed Charges

Fixed Assets as of January 1, 19___ and Additions During January 19, 19___

Cost and Book Value	Land	Building	Machinery	Furniture and Fixtures	Automobiles and Trucks	Total
Cost of assets in use, January 1, 19___	$20,000.00	$96,000.00	$36,000.00	$6,000.00	$6,000.00	$164,000.00
Budget additions, January, 19___			(1) 4,000.00			4,000.00
Accumulated depreciation as of January 1, 19___		4,800.00*	3,600.00*	600.00*	600.00*	9,600.00*
	$20,000.00	$91,200.00	$36,400.00	$5,400.00	$5,400.00	$158,400.00
Monthly fixed charges on assets including budget additions:						
Depreciation		$ 400.00	$ 300.00	$ 50.00	$ 50.00	$ 800.00
Insurance		350.00	250.00	30.00†	24.16†	654.16
Taxes		213.00‡	200.00	25.00	20.00	458.00
Total fixed charges		$ 963.00	$ 750.00	$ 105.00	$ 94.16	$ 1,912.16
Debit fixed charges to		———Factory Expense———		———Administrative and Selling Expense———		

(1) To simplify calculations, it is assumed that the additions for January are recorded as of January 1.

* Credit.

† Round out these two items to $325 for six months.

‡ Taxes on land and building.

FRANKLIN CORPORATION
Classification of Accounts

ASSETS

110 *Current Assets*

111 Cash
112 Accounts Receivable
112R Reserve for Bad Debts
113 Materials: Raw and Process
114 Labor in Process
115 Factory Expense in Process
116 Finished Goods

120 *Prepaid Expenses*

121 Prepaid Insurance
122 Prepaid Interest Expense
123 Factory Supplies
124 Advertising Supplies Inventory
125 Factory Expense Underabsorbed (Overabsorbed)

130 *Fixed Assets*

131 Land
132 Building
133 Machinery
134 Furniture and Fixtures
135 Automobiles and Trucks
130R Reserve for Depreciation

LIABILITIES

140 *Current Liabilities*

141 Accounts Payable—Materials and Supplies
142 Accrued Expenses—Purchased Services (Power)
143 Accrued Factory Wages
144 Accrued Salaries and Commissions
145 Accrued F.I.C.A. Tax
146 Notes Payable—Machinery
147 Accrued Taxes
148 Bank Loan

NET WORTH

151 Common Stock
152 Surplus
153 Profit and Loss

INCOME AND EXPENSE ACCOUNTS

160 *Sales and Cost of Sales*

161 Sales
162 Cost of Sales

Variances from Standard Cost
(The variance accounts are not used in this problem.
All budget figures are expected actual.)

Direct Labor

(Direct labor is charged directly to Account 114)

Operating Expenses
170   *Factory Expense*

171   Indirect Labor
173   F.I.C.A. Tax
174   Supplies
175   Power
177   Depreciation
178   Insurance
179   Taxes

180   *Administrative and Selling Expense*

181   Salaries
182   Commissions
183   F.I.C.A. Tax
184   Advertising Pieces
186   Bad Debts
187   Depreciation
188   Insurance
189   Taxes

Financial Income and Expense
191   Purchases Discounts
192   Sales Discounts
193   Interest Expense

Loss on Retirement of Fixed Assets
199   Loss on Retirement of Fixed Assets

THE FINANCIAL BUDGET

Purpose of the financial budget; Statements. The financial budget
is a formal plan for financing the operations of a coming period. It is
based upon (1) the sales, production, and procurement budgets, (2) the
plant budgets, and (3) the income and expense budgets. It shows the
amount of funds expected to be received from each of the various sources
(including borrowing, if necessary) and the disposition of those funds (including the repayment of funds borrowed). The Benson & West Manufacturing Company uses its financial budget mainly for formulating plans
to finance inventories. The business is seasonal, and the company regularly borrows cash at the beginning of the season when manufacturing
begins and pays off the loans at the end of the season after the goods have
been sold and the cash begins to come in from accounts receivable.

The main statements produced from the financial budget of the Benson &
West Manufacturing Company are:

(1) The Cash Forecast, by months (page 608), which shows the expected
cash receipts from each source, the expected cash disbursements for each
category of account, and the expected month-end cash balances.

(2) Budget Balance Sheets, monthly for six months (pages 609-610). This
statement shows the estimated financial position of the business for each
of the six months covered by the budget. In this case, the working capital
position is satisfactory at the end of each month, and in fact the working
capital is larger at the end of the period than at the beginning. The net
worth likewise increases during the period.

The Cash Forecast is prepared from certain current asset and current
liability worksheets, as explained in the following sections.

Collections on accounts receivable. In this illustration, it is assumed that terms to customers are 2% e.o.m. (2% discount if paid within
ten days after the end of the month in which the sale was made. This is
the same as ten days after the first of the month following sale). The
collections of any month are accordingly calculated on the basis of the
expected accounts receivable as of the first of the month. The expected
cash collections for the month would be the opening balance less write-offs

BENSON & WEST MANUFACTURING COMPANY

Cash Forecast, by Months

Six Months Ending June 30, 19-8

	Reference Page	Line	January	February	March	April	May	June	Six Months
Cash account before loan operation:									
1. Actual cash balance, January 1			$ 40,000.00						$ 40,000.00
2. Estimated cash balances, before loans (beginning)				$ 5,951.55	$ 35,671.93*	$ 77,772.14*	$ 74,195.94*	$ 11,519.88*	
Add—Expected receipts:									
3. Collections on accounts receivable	611	6	$ 63,445.20	$ 66,900.68	$ 79,091.88	$146,627.60	$206,985.80	$228,663.40	$791,714.56
4. Others									
5. Totals			$ 63,445.20	$ 66,900.68	$ 79,091.88	$146,627.60	$206,985.80	$228,663.40	$791,714.56
6. Available for disbursements (Line 1 or Line 2 Less Line 5)			$103,445.20	$ 72,852.23	$ 43,419.95	$ 68,855.46	$132,789.86	$217,143.52	$831,714.56
Subtract expected disbursements:									
Premiums paid—									
7. Workmen's insurance	612	15	$	$	$	$ 1,000.00	$	$	$ 1,000.00
8. Property insurance	612	19							
9. Materials and supplies	613	11	36,861.72	44,158.80	40,987.52	43,964.76	42,633.92	29,021.72	237,628.44
10. Labor	615	18	42,775.38	45,103.48	55,929.34	62,086.05	63,052.42	47,280.15	316,226.82
11. Salaries and commissions	615	24	9,500.00	10,126.54	10,614.54	13,306.00	15,714.27	16,576.84	75,838.19
12. F.I.C.A. tax	615	28				3,057.54			3,037.54
13. Vacation pay	615	32						6,414.90	6,414.90
14. Purchased services	616	41	8,356.55	9,135.34	13,660.69	19,637.05	22,909.13	14,144.31	87,843.07
15. Notes payable—Plant	616	51						20,000.00	20,000.00
16. Totals			$ 97,493.65	$108,524.16	$121,192.09	$143,051.40	$144,309.74	$133,437.92	$748,008.96
17. Estimated cash balances, before loans (ending)			$ 5,951.55	$ 35,671.93*	$ 77,772.14*	$ 74,195.94*	$ 11,519.88*	$ 83,705.60	$ 83,705.60
Cash account with loan projected									
18. Balance, beginning of month			$ 40,000.00	$102,951.55	$ 61,328.07	$ 19,227.86	$ 22,804.06	$ 85,480.12	$ 40,000.00
19. Add—Expected receipts (Line 5)	618	2	$ 63,445.20	$ 66,900.68	$ 79,091.88	$146,627.60	$206,985.80	$228,663.40	$791,714.56
20. Received from loan			97,000.00						97,000.00
21. Totals			$160,445.20	$ 66,900.68	$ 79,091.88	$146,627.60	$206,985.80	$228,663.40	$888,714.56
22. Available for disbursements			$200,445.20	$169,852.23	$140,419.95	$165,855.46	$229,789.86	$314,143.52	$928,714.56
23. Subtract—Expected disbursements (Line 16)	618	6	$ 97,493.65	$108,524.16	$121,192.09	$143,051.40	$144,309.74	$133,437.92	$748,008.96
24. Repayment of loan								100,000.00	100,000.00
25. Totals			$ 97,493.65	$108,524.16	$121,192.09	$143,051.40	$144,309.74	$233,437.92	$848,008.96
26. Balances, end of month			$102,951.55	$ 61,328.07	$ 19,227.86	$ 22,804.06	$ 85,480.12	$ 80,705.60	$ 80,705.60

* Red.

Figure 25-1a

BENSON & WEST MANUFACTURING COMPANY
Budget Balance Sheets, by Months
Six Months Ending June 30, 19-8

ASSETS

Account	January 1	January 31	February 28	March 31	April 30	May 31	June 30	Average Investment in Assets
Current Assets and Prepaid Expenses:								
Cash	$ 40,000.00	$102,951.55	$ 61,328.07	$ 19,227.86	$ 22,804.06	$ 85,480.12	$ 80,705.60	$ 62,082.87
Accounts receivable	65,000.00	68,540.00	81,030.00	150,220.00	212,050.00	234,260.00	83,470.00	138,261.66
Less—Reserve for bad debts	1,875.00*	1,930.05*	2,028.65*	2,394.65*	2,768.65*	3,004.64*	2,458.10*	2,430.77*
Materials: Raw and in process		24,970.00	38,250.00	32,770.00	28,450.00	13,460.00	3,150.00	23,508.32
Labor in process		12,427.50	19,487.50	16,312.50	14,712.50	5,625.00	1,387.50	11,658.00
Factory expense in process		5,798.75	8,523.75	6,882.50	6,062.50	2,560.00	693.75	5,086.50
Finished goods		15,385.00	24,655.00	45,038.75	24,881.25	7,097.50	36,725.00	25,630.40
Prepaid workmen's insurance	1,000.00	757.20	539.72	236.20	919.26	600.32	392.24	574.14
Prepaid property insurance	6,602.28	5,501.90	4,401.52	3,301.14	2,200.76	1,100.38		2,750.95
Supplies inventory	6,000.00	3,656.69	7,264.21	3,564.95	2,860.13	1,791.72	1,511.66	3,441.56
Prepaid interest expense		2,500.00	2,000.00	1,500.00	1,000.00	500.00		1,250.00
Total current assets and prepaid expenses	$116,727.28	$240,558.54	$245,451.12	$276,659.25	$313,171.81	$349,470.40	$205,577.74	$271,813.63
Underabsorbed Factory Expense (Figure 23-3c)	$	$ 238.58	$ 1,941.62	$ 824.46	$ 836.33*	$ 2,749.97*	$	$
Fixed Assets:								
Land	$100,000.00	$100,000.00	$100,000.00	$100,000.00	$100,000.00	$100,000.00	$100,000.00	$100,000.00
Building	200,000.00	200,000.00	200,000.00	200,000.00	200,000.00	200,000.00	200,000.00	200,000.00
Office furniture and equipment	21,000.00	21,000.00	21,000.00	21,000.00	21,000.00	21,000.00	21,000.00	21,000.00
Display fixtures	4,000.00	4,000.00	4,000.00	4,000.00	4,000.00	4,000.00	4,000.00	4,000.00
Autos	18,000.00	18,000.00	18,000.00	18,000.00	18,000.00	18,000.00	18,000.00	18,000.00
Delivery trucks	6,000.00	6,000.00	6,000.00	6,000.00	6,000.00	6,000.00	6,000.00	6,000.00
Machinery and equipment	60,000.00	80,000.00	80,000.00	80,000.00	80,000.00	80,000.00	80,000.00	80,000.00
Less—Reserve for depreciation	31,000.00*	33,074.97*	35,149.94*	37,224.91*	39,299.88*	41,374.85*	43,449.82*	38,262.39*
Total fixed assets	$378,000.00	$395,925.03	$393,850.06	$391,775.09	$389,700.12	$387,625.15	$385,550.18	$390,737.61
Total assets	$494,727.28	$636,722.15	$641,242.80	$669,258.80	$702,035.60	$734,345.58	$591,127.92	$662,551.24

* Red.

Figure 25-1b

BENSON & WEST MANUFACTURING COMPANY
Budget Balance Sheets, by Months
Six Months Ending June 30, 19-8

LIABILITIES

Account	January 1	January 31	February 28	March 31	April 30	May 31	June 30
Current Liabilities:							
Accounts payable—Materials and supplies	$ 5,000.00	$ 16,306.00	$ 14,376.00	$ 13,722.00	$ 15,570.00	$ 13,966.00	$ 7,822.00
Accrued labor	6,000.00	12,258.46	10,948.27	14,993.73	15,697.48	15,786.00	10,498.09
Accrued salaries and commissions	9,500.00	10,126.54	10,614.54	13,306.00	15,714.27	16,576.84	10,705.81
Accrued F.I.C.A. tax		980.66	1,858.06	3,057.54	1,254.74	2,517.54	3,357.36
Reserve for vacation pay		980.66	1,858.06	3,057.54	4,312.28	5,575.08	
Accrued expense (purchased service)	-2,500.00	2,928.28	3,103.53	5,278.57	7,179.25	7,864.93	3,139.70
Accrued property tax		1,200.37	2,400.74	3,601.11	4,801.48	6,001.85	7,202.22
Notes payable—Plant		20,000.00	20,000.00	20,000.00	20,000.00	20,000.00	
Bank loan		100,000.00	100,000.00	100,000.00	100,000.00	100,000.00	
Total current liabilities	$ 23,000.00	$164,780.97	$165,159.20	$177,016.49	$184,529.50	$188,288.24	$ 42,725.18
Net Worth:							
Capital stock	$400,000.00	$400,000.00	$400,000.00	$400,000.00	$400,000.00	$400,000.00	$400,000.00
Surplus—							
Balance, beginning of month	71,727.28	71,727.28	71,941.18	76,083.60	92,242.31	117,506.10	146,057.34
Profits—Month		213.90	4,142.42	16,158.71	25,263.79	28,551.24	2,345.40
Balance, end of month	$ 71,727.28	$ 71,941.18	$ 76,083.60	$ 92,242.31	$117,506.10	$146,057.34	$148,402.74
Total net worth	$471,727.28	$471,941.18	$476,083.60	$492,242.31	$517,506.10	$546,057.34	$548,402.74
Total liabilities and net worth	$494,727.28	$636,722.15	$641,242.80	$669,258.80	$702,035.60	$734,345.58	$591,127.92

Figure 25-1c

610

based upon the experience percentage (this would give gross accounts collected) less sales discounts. This calculation is illustrated in the following exhibit:

Account	January
Accounts receivable:	
1. Balance, beginning of the month..........	$ 65,000.00
Debit—	
2. Sales on account (per shipments budget, page 580).........................	68,540.00
Total debits....................	$133,540.00
Credits—	
3. Write-offs............................	$ 260.00
4. Gross accounts collected (opening balance less write offs)......................	64,740.00
	$ 65,000.00
5. Sales discounts (2% of gross cash receipts)	$ 1,294.80
6. Cash receipts (Gross cash receipt less discounts).........................	63,445.20
7. Balance, end of month (total debits less credits, 3 and 4)....................	$ 68,540.00
Sales discounts:	
8. Month (same as line 5).................	$ 1,294.80
9. Cumulative...........................	1,294.80
Reserve for bad debts:	
10. Balance, beginning of month.............	$ 1,875.00
Debit—	
11. Bad debts charged off (same as line 3)...	260.00
	$ 1,615.00
Credit—	
12. Provision for bad debts (per distribution expense budget, page 599)............	315.05
13. Balance, end of month..................	$ 1,930.05

Figure 25-2

Cash collections on account, $63,445.20, are shown on line 6.

The Sales Discount account and the Reserve for Bad Debts account are both set out on the same budget worksheet as the Accounts Receivable account. Sales discount calculated in the Accounts Receivable section (line 5) is carried down to the Sales Discounts section (line 8). Write-offs calculated on line 3 are carried down to line 11.

The *provision* for bad debts credit to Reserve for Bad Debts, $315.05, is picked up from the Distribution Expense Budget (page 599).

Disbursements charged to prepaid expenses and supplies inven-

tories accounts. Cash payments which are to be charged to prepaid expense accounts usually represent contractual payments (as in the case of insurance policies) or purchases of supplies necessary to maintain an inventory. The budget worksheets for prepaid expenses below illustrate how these two types of cash disbursement are recorded. For insurance,

Account	January	February
Prepaid workmens' insurance:		
14. Balance, beginning of month.........	$1,000.00	$ 757.20
Debit—		
15. Premiums paid.................		
	$1,000.00	$ 757.20
Credit—		
16. Charged to expense (per factory expense budget, page 593).........	242.80	217.48
17. Balance, end of month..............	$ 757.20	$ 539.72
Prepaid property insurance:		
18. Balance, beginning of month.........	$6,602.28	$5,501.90
Debit—		
19. Premiums paid.................		
	$6,602.28	$5,501.90
Credits—		
20. Charged to expense (per expense budgets).....................	$	$
21. Factory (page 593)..............	740.39	740.39
22. Distribution (page 599)...........	351.66	351.66
23. Administration (page 600)........	8.33	8.33
	$1,100.38	$1,100.38
24. Balance, end of month..............	$5,501.90	$4,401.52
Supplies inventory:		
25. Balance, beginning of month.........	$6,000.00	$3,656.69
Debit—		
26. Purchases vouchered.............		6,000.00
	$6,000.00	$9,656.69
Credits—		
27. Charged to expense (per expense budgets).....................	$	$
28. Factory (page 593)..............	1,222.34	1,079.67
29. Distribution (page 599)...........	1,050.97	1,242.81
30. Administration (page 600)........	70.00	70.00
	$2,343.31	$2,392.48
31. Balance, end of month............	$3,656.69	$7,264.21

Figure 25-3

the balance at the beginning of the month is the unexpired portion of the policies. *Premiums to be paid* are entered as debits in the appropriate months. (Credits for insurance expired are picked up from the expense budgets.)

For supplies inventories, the purchases are calculated as the amounts necessary to maintain inventory levels. In setting up the Supplies Inventory Budget, balance at the beginning of the month is entered on the first line. The *credits* are estimated amounts used, posted from the expense budget worksheets (Chapter 24). The debits for purchases to be vouchered are the amounts necessary to build up the inventories to predetermined levels.

Disbursements for materials and supplies. In this illustration, it is assumed that materials and supplies invoices are paid on the 1st, 10th, and 20th days of the month, and that a 2 per cent discount is taken. Thus the gross debits to Accounts Payable in any month would be (a) the opening balance for that month plus (b) 2/3 of the month's purchases. The 2 per cent discount would be taken from the total of the gross debits to arrive at net cash disbursed. The calculation of cash paid during January is illustrated in the budget worksheet below.

Account	*January*
Accounts payable—Materials and supplies:	
1. Balance, beginning of month..............	$ 5,000.00
Credits—	
2. Purchases—Materials (per materials budget, pages 771-772)......................	$48,920.00
3. Purchases—Supplies (per supplies budget, page 612)..........................	
4. Total purchases...................	$48,920.00
5. Total credits........................	$53,920.00
Debit—	
6. Payments on account:	
7. Balance at beginning................	$ 5,000.00
8. ⅔ of month's purchases (approx.)......	32,614.00
9. Total gross payments..............	$37,614.00
10. Purchase discounts (2%).............	$ 752.28
11. Net payments.....................	36,861.72
12. Balance, end of month (line 5 less line 9)...	16,306.00
Purchase discounts:	
13. Month.................................	$ 752.28
14. Cumulative...........................	752.28

Figure 25-4a

The purchases of materials, $48,920, is picked up from the Materials Budget on page 771 and the purchases of supplies from the Supplies Budget on page 612. The calculations described above are made directly in the Accounts Payable Budget worksheet as illustrated above. Gross amount to be paid is $37,614, purchase discount is $752.28, and net cash to be paid is $36,861.72.

The purchase discounts amount is also entered in the Purchase Discounts schedule shown below the Accounts Payable schedule.

Disbursements for labor, salaries and commissions, F.I.C.A. tax, and vacation pay. Factory payrolls (labor) are paid weekly, but the labor budget in Chapter 23 is set up on the basis of the amount of labor accrued each month. To convert the accrued labor for a month to a cash paid for labor for that month, the formula is:

$$\begin{array}{c} \text{Accrued labor,} \\ \text{beginning of month} \end{array} + \begin{array}{c} \text{Accrued during} \\ \text{this month} \end{array} - \begin{array}{c} \text{Accrued labor,} \\ \text{end of month} \end{array} = \begin{array}{c} \text{Cash paid} \\ \text{during the month} \end{array}$$

To use this formula, it is necessary to estimate the accrued as of the end of each month. Assuming that the pay week closes on Saturday, some months will have an accrual of one day's pay (when the month ends on Monday), some an accrual of two day's pay (when the month ends on Tuesday), and so forth. The calculation of cash paid for labor is illustrated in the budget worksheet for Accrued Labor, following.

Salaries and commissions are paid the first of each month, and the amount paid is the amount which was accrued during the past month (that is, the accrued balance at the beginning of this month). (See the following illustration.)

Accrued F.I.C.A. tax is paid quarterly. The amount of each quarterly installment is built up month by month in the budget schedule for that account. Vacation pay is paid in June. The amount of each annual payment is built up month by month in the budget schedule for Reserve for Vacation Pay.

Disbursements for purchased services; Property taxes; Notes payable plant. In this illustration, bills for services (like bills for materials) are paid on the 1st, 10th, and 20th of the month. Accordingly, the payment during any month will be the unpaid bills as of the first of the month plus 2/3 of the bills during the month. The calculation is illustrated in the Accrued Expense (Purchased Service) schedule following. The *credits* for amounts accrued are picked up from the various expense budgets.

Accrued property taxes are paid once a year. Estimated monthly amounts are credited to the Accrued Property Tax schedule (below) and the accumulated credit is extinguished by a cash payment at the end of the year.

January

Accrued labor:
15. Accrual, beginning of month............... $ 6,000.00
    Credits—
16.   Direct labor accrued (per labor budget,
       page 767)......................... 39,590.00
17.   Indirect labor accrued (per factory expense
       budget, page 593)................... 9,443.84

                                    $55,033.84
18. Debit—Cash paid (balance)............... 42,775.38

19. Accrual, end of month (estimated)......... $12,258.46

Accrued salaries and commissions:
20. Balance, beginning of month.............. $ 9,500.00
21. Credits accrued:
22.   Distribution (per distribution expense bud-
       get, page 599)...................... 5,826.54
23.   Administration (per administrative expense
       budget, page 600)................... 4,300.00

                                    $19,626.54
24. Debit: Payments of balances, end of previous
        month............................. 9,500.00

25. Balance, end of month................... $10,126.54

Accrued F.I.C.A. tax:
26. Balance, beginning of month............. $
27. Credits: Accrued this month (per expense
       budget)............................ 980.66

                                    $ 980.66
28. Debit: Cash paid.......................

29. Balance, end of month................... $ 980.66

Reserve for vacation pay:
30. Balance, beginning of month.............. $
31. Credits: accrued this month (per expense
       budget)............................ 980.66

                                    $ 980.66
32. Debit: Cash paid.......................

33. Balance, end of month................... $ 980.66

Figure 25-4b

Notes payable covering purchases of plant are set up in a Notes Payable-Plant schedule (page 616). Credits are set up as of the month(s) when it is expected notes will be signed and debits as of month(s) when it is expected notes will be paid.

January

Accrued expense (purchased services):
34. Balance, beginning of month.............. $ 2,500.00

Credits: Expense bills vouchered—
35.   Factory (per factory expense budget,
     page 593)..........................   1,399.21
36.   Distribution (per distribution expense
     budget, page 599)...................   6,755.62
37.   Administrative (per administrative expense
     budget, page 600)...................   630.00

38.   Total bills vouchered.............. $ 8,784.83

    Total credits........................... $11,284.83

Debit: Cash paid—
39.   Balance at beginning.................. $ 2,500.00
40.   ⅔ of month's purchases..............   5,856.55

41.   Total cash paid................... $ 8,356.55

42. Balance, end of month................... $ 2,928.28

Accrued property tax:
43. Balance, beginning of month.............. $
Credits: Accrued this month—
44.   Factory (per factory expense budget,
     page 593)..........................   814.54
45.   Distribution (per distribution expense
     budget, page 599)...................   375.83
46.   Administrative (per administrative expense
     budget, page 600)...................   10.00

                              $ 1,200.37
47. Debit: Cash paid..........................

48. Balance, end of month................... $ 1,200.37

Notes payable—Plant:
49. Balance, beginning of month.............. $
50. Credit: Notes issued.....................   20,000.00

                              $
51. Debit: Notes paid.......................

52. Balance, end of month................... $20,000.00

Figure 25-4c

Estimated cash balances, before loans. At this point in the budget procedure, estimated cash balances before loans are calculated to determine when bank loans will be required, how large a loan will be needed, and when it can be paid off. A schedule similar to the following one is set up, and the various receipts and payments (from the previous worksheets in this chapter) are entered.

	January	February	March
Cash account before loan operation:			
1. Actual cash balance, January 1....	$ 40,000.00	$	$
2. Estimated cash balances, before loans (beginning)............		5,951.55	35,671.93*'
Add—Expected receipts:			
3. Collections on accounts receivable (page 611).................	$ 63,445.20	$ 66,900.68	$ 79,091.88
4. Others........................			
5. Totals...................	$ 63,445.20	$ 66,900.68	$ 79,091.88
6. Available for disbursements (Line 1 or Line 2 less Line 5)........	$103,445.20	$ 72,852.23	$ 43,419.95
Subtract expected disbursements:			
Premiums paid—			
7. Workmen's insurance (page 612)	$	$	$
8. Property insurance (page 612)..			
9. Materials and supplies (page 613)	36,861.72	44,158.80	40,987.52
10. Labor (page 615)...............	42,775.38	45,103.48	55,929.34
11. Salaries and commissions (page 615)	9,500.00	10,126.54	10,614.54
12. F.I.C.A. tax (page 615)..........			
13. Vacation pay (page 615).........			
14. Purchased services (page 616).....	8,356.55	9,135.34	13,660.69
15. Notes payable—Plant (page 616)..			
Totals...................	$ 97,493.65	$108,524.16	$121,192.09
17. Estimated cash balances, before loans (ending)..............	$ 5,951.55	$ 35,671.93*	$ 77,772.14*

* Credit.

Figure 25-5

The cash balance is negative in February and reaches a negative balance of $77,772.14 in March. A schedule projected through June shows that this is the maximum deficit, and that the cash account is positive in June. The management of the company decides to borrow $100,000 in January and repay it in June.

Cash received from bank loan; Cash paid on bank loan. Assuming that the loan is discounted, the cash received is the gross amount or face value of the loan, less the discount. This calculation is shown in the following schedule.

The Bank Loan schedule indicates that the face amount of the loan is $100,000. Interest prepaid (deducted) is $3,000, and the net cash received $97,000.

The interest prepaid is set up as a debit in the Prepaid Interest Expense schedule, and it is charged off to Interest Expense at the rate of $500 per month.

Cash account with loan projected. The cash account with loan projected is shown on page 619.

Account	*January*
Bank loan:	
1. Balance, beginning of month.............	$
Credit: Loans discounted—	
2. Net cash received...................	97,000.00
3. Interest deducted...................	3,000.00
4. Gross amount..................	$100,000.00
5. Opening balance plus gross loans..........	$100,000.00
6. Debit: Loan paid......................	
7. Balance, end of month..................	$100,000.00
Prepaid interest expense:	
8. Balance, beginning of month.............	$
9. Debit: Interest prepaid (line 3)..........	3,000.00
	$ 3,000.00
10. Credit: Interest charged to expense........	500.00
11. Balance, end of month..................	$ 2,500.00
Interest expense:	
12. Month (line 10).......................	$ 500.00
13. Cumulative...........................	500.00

Figure 25-6

The top part of the schedule "Cash Account Before Loan Operation" (lines 1-17) is the one on page 617, repeated here for the reader's convenience. The summary on lines 18-26 shows the effect of the loan on the cash balance. In the critical month of March, there would be a positive balance of $19,227.86. The complete Cash Forecast for six months appears at the beginning of this chapter (page 608). The complete set of working capital schedules (six months) appears in Appendix II.

Budget balance sheets. The Budget Balance sheets for six months appear on pages 609 and 610. These balance sheets were prepared from the closing balances shown by the working capital account schedules in the appendix and in addition the Plant and Net Worth schedules.

The final test of the budget; Return on investment. After the budget has been set up, the final test is to determine whether the return on the investment is satisfactory. If the return is not satisfactory in the long run, it will be either (a) undesirable or (b) impossible to continue the business. Some of the financial indices which are applied to *actual* balance sheets and operating statements at the end of the operating period should be applied to the *budget* balance sheet and operating statement before the operating period begins. The reason is that if the current planning as reflected in the budget statement is really not satisfactory, the fact should

	January	February	March
Cash account before loan operation:			
1. Actual cash balance, January 1....	$ 40,000.00	$	$
2. Estimated cash balances, before loan (beginning).............		5,951.55	35,671.93*
Add—Expected receipts:			
3. Collections on accounts receivable	$ 63,445.20	$ 66,900.68	$ 79,091.88
4. Others.......................			
5. Totals...................	$ 63,445.20	$ 66,900.68	$ 79,091.88
6. Available for disbursements (Line 1 or Line 2 plus Line 5)........	$103,445.20	$ 72,852.23	$ 43,419.95
Subtract expected disbursements:			
Premiums paid—			
7. Workmen's insurance..........	$	$	$
8. Property insurance............			
9. Materials and supplies...........	36,861.72	44,158.80	40,987.52
10. Labor.......................	42,775.38	45,103.48	55,929.34
11. Salaries and commissions........	9,500.00	10,126.54	10,614.54
12. F.I.C.A. tax....................			
13. Vacation pay...................			
14. Purchased service...............	8,356.55	9,135.34	13,660.69
15. Notes payable—Plant...........			
16. Totals...................	$ 97,493.65	$108,524.16	$121,192.09
17. Estimated cash balances, before loans (ending)..............	$ 5,951.55	$ 35,671.93*	$ 77,772.14*
Cash account with loan projected:			
18. Balance, beginning of month......	$ 40,000.00	$102,951.55	$ 61,328.07
19. Add—Expected receipts (Line 5)...	$ 63,445.20	$ 66,900.68	$ 79,091.88
20. Received from loan (page 618)...	97,000.00		
21. Totals...................	$160,445.20	$ 66,900.68	$ 79,091.88
22. Available for disbursements.......	$200,445.20	$169,852.23	$140,419.95
23. Subtract—Expected disbursements (Line 16)..................	$ 97,493.65	$108,524.16	$121,192.09
24. Repayment of loan............			
25. Totals...................	$ 97,493.65	$108,524.16	$121,192.09
26. Balances, end of months.........	$102,951.55	$ 61,328.07	$ 19,227.86

* Credit.

Figure 25-7

be found out before the operating period starts. It may still be possible to change the plans and improve the situation.

Budget financial and operating statistics for the Benson & West Manufacturing Company for six months illustrate types of information which it is desirable to have (the data are, of course, hypothetical):

% Gross profit to net sales....................	33.65%
% Operating net profit to sales...............	10.96%
% Surplus net profit to sales.................	9.24%
Inventory turnover.........................	8.3 times
% Operating net profit to investment in assets...	13.58%
% Surplus net profit to investment in assets.....	11.57%
% Surplus net profit to average net worth.......	15.03%

QUESTIONS

25-1. What are the purposes of the financial budget?

25-2. (a) Set up a pro-forma budget worksheet for Accounts Receivable, Sales Discounts, and Reserve for Bad Debts. Number the lines, and indicate the source of each item on the worksheet.

(b) Why are these three accounts put on the same worksheet?

25-3. Set up a pro-forma budget worksheet for Prepaid Workmen's Insurance, Prepaid Property Insurance, and Supplies Inventories. Number the lines, and indicate the source of each item on the worksheet.

25-4. (a) Set up a pro-forma budget worksheet for Accounts Payable—Materials and Supplies and Purchase Discounts. Number the lines and indicate the source of each item on the worksheet.

(b) Why are these two accounts put on the same worksheet?

25-5. Set up a pro-forma budget worksheet for Accrued Labor, Accrued Salaries and Commissions, Accrued F.I.C.A. Tax, and Reserve for Vacation Pay. Number the lines, and indicate the source of each item on the worksheet.

25-6. Set up a pro-forma budget worksheet for Accrued Expense (Purchased Service), Accrued Property Tax and Notes Payable—Plant. Number the lines and indicate the source of each item on the worksheet.

25-7. Set up a pro-forma budget worksheet for estimated cash balances, before loans. Number the lines, and indicate the source of each item on the worksheet.

25-8. (a) Set up a pro-forma budget worksheet for Bank Loan, Prepaid Interest Expense, and Interest Expense. Number the lines and indicate the source of each item on the worksheet.

(b) Why are these three accounts put on the same worksheet?

25-9. Set up a pro-forma Cash Account with Loan Projected section to be added to the worksheet in Question 25-7, after the worksheet in Question 25-8 has been completed.

25-10. Name the ratios that might be calculated from the information in the completed budget as the final test of the budget plans. Give the formula for each ratio.

EXERCISES (PROBLEMS) FOR LABORATORY OR HOMEWORK

The Franklin Corporation

This assignment consists in setting up the financial budget for the Franklin Corporation. It is a continuation of Problems 23-1 and 24-1. For certain data, the student will need to refer to his solutions to those problems.

This assignment may be solved as *exercises*, using blanks provided in the Workbook, or as *problems* if the blanks in the Workbook are not used. In the latter case, worksheet forms may be set up from the models in Chapter 25.

Data are provided for a six months' budget cycle. If laboratory time or homework time is available, the full six months' cycle should be assigned. Less than the full six months' cycle may be assigned to the student if only a survey acquaintance with budget procedure is desired. The complete assignment comprises 12 exercises. The exercises are presented in the order in which the worksheets of the financial budget would normally be prepared.

The following trial balance is the starting point of the exercises in this chapter:

FRANKLIN CORPORATION

Trial Balance, January 1, 19__

No.	Accounts	Debits	Credits
111	Cash..	$ 14,000.00	
112	Accounts receivable.........................	8,000.00	
112R	Reserve for bad debts........................		100.00
113	Materials: Raw and process..................		
114	Labor in process............................		
115	Factory expense in process..................		
116	Finished goods..............................		
121	Prepaid insurance...........................		
122	Prepaid interest expense.....................		
123	Factory supplies inventory...................	500.00	
124	Advertising supplies inventory................		
125	Factory expense underabsorbed...............		
130	Fixed assets................................	164,000.00	
130R	Reserve for depreciation.....................		9,600.00
141	Accounts payable—Materials and supplies.......		4,800.00
142	Accrued expense—Purchased power............		60.00
143	Accrued factory wages.......................		
144	Accrued salaries and commissions.............		700.00
145	Accrued F.I.C.A. tax........................		14.00
146	Notes payable—Machinery....................		
147	Accrued taxes...............................		
148	Bank loan..................................		
151	Common stock..............................		140,000.00
152	Surplus....................................		31,226.00
		$186,500.00	$186,500.00

25-1. Prepare Budget of 112 Accounts Receivable, 112R Reserve for Bad Debts, and Sales Discounts, by Months. (See Figure 25-2, for form of worksheet.) Terms of sale: 2/10 e.o.m. Deduct write-offs from opening balances of accounts receivable to arrive at gross accounts collected. Apply the discount percentage to gross accounts collected to determine cash receipts on account.

	Sales on Account	Write-Offs	Provision for Bad Debts
Source: Problem..............	23-1(3)	New data	24-1(4)
January....................	$ 6,250.00	$ 40.00	$ 31.25
February...................	10,000.00	31.25	50.00
March.....................	15,000.00	50.00	75.00
April......................	20,000.00	75.00	100.00
May.......................	15,000.00	100.00	75.00
June......................	6,250.00	75.00	31.25
	$72,500.00	$371.25	$362.50

25-2. Prepare Recaps of Budgets of 113 Materials (Raw and in Process), 114 Labor in Process, 115 Factory Expense in Process, and 116 Finished Goods Inventories, by Months.

> *Sources:*
>
> | | |
> |---|---|
> | Materials | Solution to Problem 23-1(5) |
> | Labor | Solution to Problem 23-1(4) |
> | Factory expense | Solution to Problem 24-1(2) |
> | Finished goods | Solution to Problem 23-1(3) |
>
> Form (for each account) Example: Materials

> *Materials: Raw and in process*
> Balance, beginning of month
> Debit—Materials purchased
>   Total debits
> Credit—Materials in goods completed
> Balance, end of month

25-3. Prepare Budget of Prepaid Expenses and Supplies Inventories, by Months for Accounts 121 Prepaid Insurance, 123 Factory Supplies Inventory, 124 Advertising Supplies Inventory, and 125 Factory Expense Underabsorbed (Overabsorbed). See Figure 25-3 and Figure 23-3c for form of worksheets.

Data for charges to these accounts:

	A/c 121 Insurance Premiums Paid	A/c 123 Factory Supplies Purchases Vouchered	A/c 124 Advertising Supplies Purchases Vouchered	A/c 125 Total Factory Expense Incurred
Source: Problem..............				24-1(3)
January....................	$7,850.00	$ 562.50	$ 435.00	$ 3,000.00
February...................		562.50	435.00	3,321.75
March.....................		562.50	435.00	3,321.75
April......................		450.00	435.00	3,321.75
May.......................		112.50	435.00	3,000.00
June......................		450.00		2,034.75
	$7,850.00	$2,700.00	$2,175.00	$18,000.00

Sources of credits:

Credit A/c	Particulars	Solution to Problem	
121	Insurance expired	Problem 24-1 (1)	Problem 24-1 (4)
123	Supplies used	Problem 24-1 (1)	
124	Supplies charged off		Problem 24-1 (4)
125	Factory expense absorbed	Exercise 25-2 Factory expense in Process A/c	

As indicated above, A/c 125 will be debited for total factory expense incurred and credited for total factory expense absorbed.

25-4. Prepare Recap Budget of 130 Fixed Assets, 130R Reserve for Depreciation, and Loss on Retirement of Fixed Assets. Data for this exercise are in Problem 24-1 (page 602). Note that no assets were retired; machinery additions occur only in January.

Form:

[130] Fixed assets:

1 Balance, beginning of month
2 Debit—Additions
3   Total debits
4 Credits—Retirements
5 Balance, end of month

[130R] Reserve for depreciation

6 Balance, beginning of month
   Credit—Provision for depreciation
7   Factory expense budget
8   Administrative and selling budget
9   Total credits
10 Debit—Write-offs of assets retired
11 Balance, end of month

[199] Loss on retirement of fixed assets

12 Loss—Month (line 4 less line 10)

25-5. Prepare Budget of 141 Accounts Payable, 191 Purchase Discounts, and 142 Accrued Expenses—Purchased Services (Power), by Months. See Figure 25-4a and 25-4c. Purchase terms, accounts payable: 2/10. Each month pay balance as of beginning of month and 2/3 of invoices received during month. *Sources of credits to A/c 141:*

Materials purchases (Solution to Exercise 25-2, A/c 113)
Factory supplies purchases (Solution to Exercise 25-3, A/c 123)
Advertising supplies purchases (Solution to Exercise 25-3, A/c 124)

Pay power bill accrued during the month at the beginning of next month. Power bills accrued, see Solution to Problem 24-1(1).

25-6. Prepare Budget of 143 Accrued Factory Wages, 144 Accrued Salaries and Commissions, and 145 Accrued F.I.C.A. Tax, by Months. See Figure 25-4b for form. *Sources of credits:*

To A/c 143, Direct labor, Solution to Exercise 25-2, A/c 114
           Indirect labor, Solution to Problem 24-1(1)

To A/c 144, Salaries
            Commissions } Solution to Problem 24-1(4)

To A/c 145, F.I.C.A. tax accrued, factory, Solution to Problem 24-1(1)
       F.I.C.A. tax accrued, administrative and selling, Solution to
       Problem 24-1(4).

End of the month accruals:

Month	Accrued Factory Wages	Accrued Salaries and Commissions	Accrued F.I.C.A. Tax
January	$217.50	$ 850.00	$118.00
February	282.75	1,000.00	246.75
March	952.00	1,200.00	379.50
April	–	1,400.00	136.75
May	394.00	1,200.00	247.75
June	272.00	850.00	286.50

25-7. Prepare Budget of 146 Notes Payable—Machinery and 147 Accrued Taxes, by Months. See Figure 25-4c for form. It is expected that a note payable (noninterest-bearing) for $4,000 will be issued in January and paid in June.

Accrued property taxes, both factory and administrative and selling for the six months will be paid in June. See Solution to Problem 24-1 for property tax accruals.

25-8. Prepare a schedule of Estimated Cash Balances, before Loans, and with Loan Projected, by Months, using receipts and payments information from the previous exercises in this chapter. See Figure 25-7 for form.

It is decided to borrow $10,000 at 6% the first of February and repay the loan the first of June. The loan will be discounted at the bank at a cost of $200 interest.

25-9. Prepare Budget of 148 Bank Loan, 122 Prepaid Interest, and 193 Interest Expense, using appropriate information from Exercise 25-8.

25-10. Prepare Budget Statement of Profits, by Months. The required information can all be obtained from the budget worksheets prepared in Exercises 25-1 to 25-9.

25-11. Prepare Budget 151 Common Stock and 152 Surplus, by Months. No change in common stock is expected during the six months and no dividends are expected to be declared.

25-12. Prepare Budget Balance Sheet, by Months. The required information can all be obtained from the budget worksheets prepared in Exercises 25-1 to 25-11.

Chapter 26

COST-VOLUME-PROFIT RELATIONSHIPS;
DIRECT COSTING

What the management wants to know about cost-volume-profit relationships. The budget discussed in Chapters 23-25 is based upon a specific set of volume, cost, and selling price factors. Often the management wants to know what would happen if one of the factors, or some combination of factors, should change. The questions arise in the attempt to ascertain what combination of volume, cost, and price factors will produce the most satisfactory profit. They are likely to be asked from time to time because the volume, cost, or price picture changes.

Suppose, for instance, that actual volume should turn out to be 10 per cent less than the budget volume, what would be the effect upon profits? If all costs were variable, it would be correct to say that if actual volume were 10 per cent less than budget volume, actual profit would be 10 per cent less than budget profit, other factors remaining constant. All costs are not variable, however, and consequently the calculation must take into consideration a certain amount of fixed expenses.

Or suppose selling prices had to be reduced 10 per cent. What would be the effect upon profits? Or suppose the sales manager asks for an increase in the advertising budget of say $100,000 to increase the sales volume in a certain territory. What increase in volume will be required to justify this increase in variable expense?

Assume, finally, that an increase in fixed charges is being considered. What effect would this increase have upon profits? The increase might be incurred for facilities intended to improve service to customers, with only incidental prospect of short-run increase in sales. Or it might be incurred for facilities intended to increase the volume of goods for sale and at the same time decrease variable expenses.

The answers to these questions can conceivably be worked out by recasting the budget, or appropriate parts of it, or by setting up an alternate budget. Several facts may stand in the way of such a solution. In the first place, a great deal of work might be involved in this procedure. In the second place, the question may be an exploratory one and it may not necessarily *require* a change in the budget. Only a reasonably accurate

625

answer to the question may be required. In the exploratory stages of business planning, rough calculations may be quite sufficient to eliminate certain propositions from further consideration, and point up other propositions for more refined treatment. Sometimes, formulas are used for setting out cost-volume-profit relationships. Sometimes, graphic projections of costs and revenues through a range of volumes, known as breakeven charts, are used to show the relationships.

A Committee on Research of the National Association of Cost Accountants made a field study of 50 companies which prepare cost-volume-profit analyses. The committee report states that over half of the companies (31) prepare cost-volume-profit analyses regularly as a part of the budget program[1]:

> Thirty-one of the fifty companies seen in the field study prepare a cost-volume-profit analysis regularly as part of the general process of preparing their budgets. Of these thirty-one companies, twenty-eight also prepare breakeven charts to portray the cost-volume-profit relationships which underlie their budgets. Nineteen companies prepare cost-volume-profit analyses from time to time as special studies, but these companies do not consider these analyses to be a regular part of their budgeting procedure.

The use of formulas and charts for the analysis of cost-volume-profit relationships is explained in the following sections. Interpretation of results is also discussed. It should be stated that the body of concepts and terminology introduced in this chapter is the foundation for the chapters immediately following: Problems of Alternative Choice (Chapter 27) and Distribution Costs (Chapters 28 and 29).

Separation of variable and fixed expense; Marginal balance. A fundamental necessity in cost-volume-profit analysis is the separation of variable from fixed expenses for all functions of the business. The budget statement of profits for May, 19—, on page 627, prepared from the budget of Benson & West Manufacturing Company, illustrates the separation.

Note that the Variable Expense section includes direct material, direct labor, and variable expense in goods shipped, and variable distribution expense. Factory Expense Variance ($919.59) is variance between budgeted variable expense and absorbed variable expense for the month. It arises because so-called variable expenses are not perfectly variable with volume of operations.

The Fixed Expense section includes fixed factory expense, fixed distribution expense, and total administrative expense (all of which is considered fixed in this case). Fixed factory expense is *total* fixed factory expense for the month. The only factory expense charge to cost of goods shipped is the variable expense charge ($19,506.52).

The *Marginal Balance* ($47,827.58) is the difference between Sales

---

[1] "The Analysis of Cost-Volume-Profit Relationships," N.A.C.A. Research Series No. 17, Dec., 1949, p. 526.

BENSON & WEST MANUFACTURING COMPANY
Budget Statement of Profits Showing Marginal Balance

Month of May, 19-8

	Amount		% to Sales
Sales.....................................		$234,260.00	100.00
Less—Variable expense			
Direct materials.......................	$59,880.00		
Direct labor..........................	69,650.00		
Variable factory expense in goods shipped, @ standard rates....................	19,506.52		
Factory expense variance...............	919.59*		
Variable distribution expense...........	38,315.49		
Total variable expense.............		186,432.42	79.58
Marginal balance........................		$ 47,827.58	20.42
Fixed expense			
Factory expense.......................	$ 4,480.25		
Distribution expense..................	2,158.49		
Administrative expense................	5,215.66		
Total fixed expense.................		11,854.40	
Operating profit.........................		$ 35,973.18	

* Credit.

Figure 26-1

($234,260.00) and total Variable Expense ($186,432.32). (The term "contribution margin" is also used to describe this difference. "Contribution" in this connection means "contribution to fixed expenses and profit"). The *Operating Profit* ($35,973.18) is Marginal Balance ($47,827.58) less Fixed Expenses ($11,854.40). Note that the operating profit per this statement is not the same as net profit per the "conventional" statement ($34,319) shown on page 640. The reason is that, in the latter, a portion of fixed factory expense is allocated to inventories, whereas in the statement illustrated in this chapter, fixed factory expense is charged off month by month to the Profit and Loss account.

The *Marginal Balance* percentage is Marginal Balance ($47,827.58) ÷ Sales ($234,260), or 20.42%. The marginal balance percentage provides an index of the increase in net profit (or decrease in net loss) that would accompany an increase in sales. Thus, if the sales volume in the budget is sufficient to cover fixed expenses and leave a profit, an additional $1,000 of sales would produce 20.42% of $1,000 or $204.20 of net profit, all other factors remaining unchanged.

The marginal balance and the marginal balance percentage are likely to be significant in sales planning and pricing. A company having a large marginal balance percentage, for instance, can increase the operating profit comparatively rapidly with small increases in sales. It can likewise decrease the operating profit comparatively rapidly through small decreases in sales.

The management of such a company would likely approve a large sales promotion budget if it believed that the marginal balance on increased sales would justify such a budget.

Breakeven point; Margin of safety. Breakeven point in dollars is the point in volume of sales where marginal balance equals fixed expense: there is no profit and no loss. The managers of a business are interested in knowing the breakeven point because of the effect some of their decisions might have on it. (As will be seen, an increase in fixed expenses, for example, raises the breakeven point, other factors remaining constant.)

The managers are likewise interested in the breakeven point as a measuring standard which can indicate the need for re-appraisal of plans, or for action. If, when the budget is made up, the expected sales volume is close to breakeven point, the management can review the plans to see whether it is possible to improve them. After the budget has been approved, knowledge of the position of the breakeven point may impress the managers with the need for meeting their commitments under the budget. The *margin of safety* is the dollar excess of budget (or actual) sales over breakeven volume of sales. The amount of this excess is an indication of how much sales may decrease before the company will suffer a loss. Obviously, the greater the margin of safety, the better the operating picture for the company in the near future.

Calculations illustrated. Assume:

B = Breakeven point
MB = Marginal balance %
F = Fixed expense

The formula for breakeven point is:

$$B = \frac{100}{MB} \times F$$

For the Benson & West Manufacturing Company (using values shown by the budget statement of profits for May):

$$\frac{100}{20} \times \$11,854.40 = \$59,272$$

This calculation of breakeven point is based upon the assumption that variable expenses do vary with sales and that fixed expenses are in fact fixed for all levels. While these assumptions are too pat for complete reality, the calculation of breakeven point, even on a rough basis, is likely to be useful to the businessman. Particularly where fixed charges are significant does the businessman think in terms of the volume of sales necessary to "cover fixed charges."

Breakeven point percentage is breakeven point in dollars ($59,272)

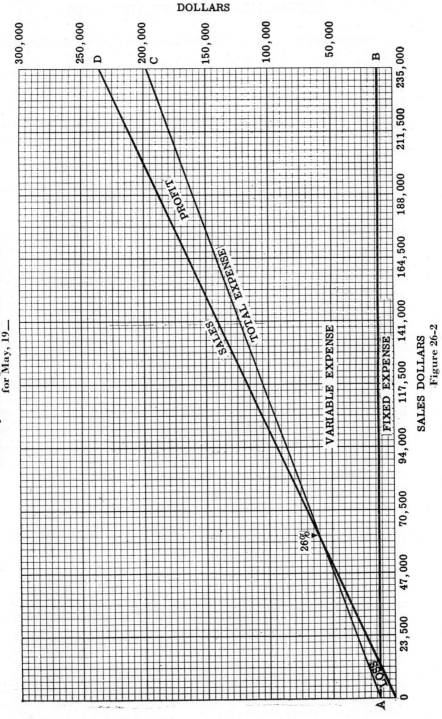

BENSON & WEST MANUFACTURING COMPANY
Breakeven Chart
Based Upon Budget Statement of Profits
for May, 19__

DOLLARS

300,000

250,000   D

200,000   C

150,000

100,000

50,000

B

PROFIT

TOTAL EXPENSE

SALES

VARIABLE EXPENSE

26%

FIXED EXPENSE

LOSS

A

0   23,500   47,000   70,500   94,000   117,500   141,000   164,500   188,000   211,500   235,000

SALES DOLLARS
Figure 26-2

629

÷ capacity sales used as a basis for breakeven calculation ($235,000) = 25.2%.

Margin of safety is Sales ($235,000) — Breakeven point ($59,272) = $175,728. Note that at the Benson & West Manufacturing Company, fixed expenses and breakeven point are low, and the margin of safety is large. When fixed expenses are high and the breakeven point is high, it might not be easy for a company to maintain a comfortable margin of safety.

Breakeven chart. A breakeven chart is a means of projecting graphically the increase in profits as sales increase above the breakeven point and the losses as sales decrease below that point. The chart on page 629 was prepared with sales dollars as the base, scaled in $23,500 steps from zero to $235,000. The charted lines are

> AB—Fixed expenses, $11,854.40
> AC—Total expense: fixed expense only ($11,854.40) at zero level; fixed
>   expense plus $186,432.42 (variable expense) at $235,000 sales level
> OD—Sales

The breakeven percentage (26 per cent) is the point where the sales level (OD) intersects the total expense line (AC). The breakeven point in dollars on the chart would read about $61,000, which is reasonably close to the formula calculation.

The vertical reading between sales and total expense at any selected volume of sales is the profit for that volume of sales (if the volume is above breakeven point) or loss (if the volume is below breakeven point). The chart indicates that fixed expense of the Benson & West Manufacturing Company is relatively small and the breakeven point is low. The company can begin to make a profit on a relatively small volume of sales. On the other hand, the rate of profit does not increase rapidly as sales increases above the breakeven point.

Note that the breakeven chart is based upon certain assumptions with reference to the pattern of selling prices, cost prices, and product mix. It is assumed, for instance, that variable expenses vary directly with sales through all levels. It is also assumed that the mix of products among high profit items and low profit items will remain in the same proportions through successive levels. It should be repeated that breakeven charts are not a substitute for budgets prepared for several sets of conditions, but are a means of visualizing the effect of particular factors upon profits.

On this point, the N.A.C.A. Research bulletin on cost-volume-profit relationships states:

A given break-even chart is based upon a given set of conditions which are expected or assumed to exist for the time the chart is to be used. As stated above, the budget is usually the source of data from which the break-even chart is prepared and hence the chart represents the conditions forecasted or planned when the budget was set up. As such, a break-even chart is a basis toward which to

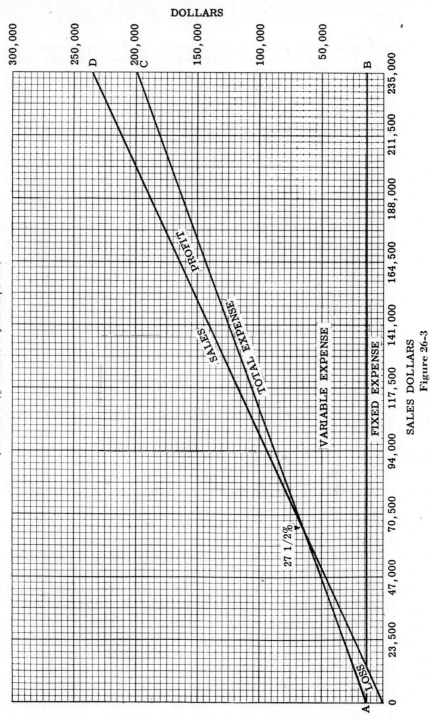

BENSON & WEST MANUFACTURING COMPANY

Breakeven Chart

Based Upon Budget Statement of Profits for May, 19___

(Assume 10% increase in fixed expenses)

SALES DOLLARS

Figure 26-3

631

work rather than a picture of the company's actual profit structure at any one time. In actual circumstances, the underlying non-volume factors are seldom stable for long and it is therefore necessary to revise the figures derived from previous analyses of cost-volume-profit relationships and to draw new break-even charts. The field study indicated that most companies do this for each budget period or whenever the budget is revised.

Under conditions of particularly rapid change break-even charts may become obsolete too soon to justify their preparation. . . .[2]

The chart illustrated uses sales as the base for projecting sales and expenses. Where inventory of finished goods is significant and fluctuating widely in amount, sales value of goods *completed* may be used as the base, instead of sales value of goods shipped.

Effect of increase in fixed expenses. An increase of 10 per cent in fixed expenses would not change the marginal balance percentage but would decrease the budget profits for May to $34,787.74, as follows:

Particulars	*Amount*	*% to Sales*
Sales..............................	$234,260.00	100.00%
Variable expense.....................	186,432.42	79.58
Marginal balance.................	47,827.58	20.42%
Fixed expense (110% of $11,854.40).....	13,039.84	
Operating profit...................	$ 34,787.74	

The breakeven point would increase to $63,858.17, calculated by the formula:

$$B = \frac{100}{MB} \times F$$

Using values shown on the condensed statement of profits above:

$$\frac{100}{20.42} \times \$13,039.84 = \$63,858.17$$

A breakeven chart based upon the budgeted profit and loss statement for May, with fixed expenses increased 10 per cent, appears on page 631. On the chart, the fixed expense line (AB) is plotted at $13,039.84, and total expense at any level is increased by the same amount as fixed expense was increased. The breakeven point, as shown on the chart, is $27\frac{1}{2}$ per cent.

Effect of increase in selling price. In business planning, it is sometimes desirable to calculate the effect of an increase (or decrease) in selling price upon profits and the breakeven point. Assume an increase in selling price of 10 per cent. Calculated on the basis of $234,260 of sales shown in the Budget Statement of Profits for May, the marginal balance per-

[2] "The Analysis of Cost-Volume-Profit Relationships," N.A.C.A. Research Series No. 17, Dec., 1949, p. 541.

centage would increase to 27.65 per cent and the profit would increase to $59,399.28:

Particulars	Amount	% to Sales
Sales (110% of $234,260).............	$257,686.00	100.00%
Variable expense....................	186,432.32	72.35
Marginal balance..................	$ 71,253.68	27.65%
Fixed expense.......................	11,854.40	
Operating profit...................	$ 59,399.28	

The breakeven point in dollars would decrease to $42,945.46, calculated as follows:

$$B = \frac{100}{MB} \times F$$

Using values shown in the condensed Statement of Profits above:

$$\frac{100}{27.65} \times \$11,854.40 = \$42,873.05$$

Effect of increase in variable expenses. An increase of 10 per cent in variable expense would decrease the marginal balance percentage to 12.46 per cent and decrease the budget profits for May to $7,330.40, calculated as follows:

Particulars	Amount	% to Sales
Sales................................	$234,260.00	100.00%
Variable expense (110% of $186,432)....	205,075.20	87.54
Marginal balance..................	$ 29,184.80	12.46%
Fixed expense.......................	11,854.40	
Operating profit...................	$ 7,330.40	

The breakeven point would increase to $95,139.64, calculated by the formula:

$$B = \frac{100}{MB} \times F$$

Using the values shown on the condensed Statement of Profits above:

$$\frac{100}{12.46} \times \$11,854.40 = \$95,139.64$$

Product mix; Marginal balances of product groups. In the previous sections of this chapter, various cost-volume-profit calculations have been made for the business as a whole. They were based upon the budget for May, 19-8 and consequently reflected the expected product mix for that month and the expected total variable expense and total fixed expense for that month. It was recognized that a different product mix and a different division of expense would likely produce different results.

In some cases, product mix and the use of productive capacity for various product groups are important factors in business planning. An interesting example occurs in the steel industry:

Generalizations about the specialty steel producers, then, come hard precisely because the product mixes of specific companies can assume radically different patterns and run off on strange tangents. To show the complexity of the specialty business, a comparison of the two big companies in the alloy field, Crucible and Allegheny-Ludlum, is instructive. . . . (Crucible is No. 14 among U.S. companies; Allegheny is No. 16.). . . . The companies will never react in quite the same way, not only for financial reasons, but also because their businesses are really quite different.

The Crucible "mix" includes practically everything in the book of the specials: cobalt alloys that sell for $5 a pound, or $10,000 a ton (ordinary carbon steels sell for $82 a ton); a light-weight, high-strength alloy called Hytuf that is used for airplane landing gears; stainless steel for chemical vats, breweries, pulp and paper plants, dairy pipe and architectural trim; three ply steels with pliable "soft-centers" for plows; magnets made of an aluminum, nickel and cobalt alloy; razor steels; office equipment steels; precision equipment steels; precision castings; drill steels for mining; and a host of other products. But only 30% of Crucible's sales is contributed by the costly higher temperature alloys; 70% comes from low-grade automotive and farm equipment alloys—the so-called "constructural" alloys. This means that Crucible is vulnerable to the current agricultural depression and to the recent erratic buying habits of Detroit.

Allegheny, on the other hand, has little volume in the low grade alloys that are currently in a slump. It does have a big special steel that is doing particularly well in its own right. That "special" special is high-grade silicon steel, used in transformers and generators. The demand for this stuff keeps well ahead of the company's ability to produce it, and the only ponderable competitor in this field is Armco. Of Allegheny's dollar volume, 20% comes from steels made for the electrical and electronics industry. And *all* of Allegheny's predominantly electric furnace products sell in the high price range.[3]

It is often useful to prepare an analysis of marginal balances of product groups to show the effect of volume and margin upon profits. Such an analysis for the Benson & West Manufacturing Company is presented on page 635. This statement is based upon the budget for the month of May, 19-8, as are the previous illustrations in this chapter.

The statement on page 635 shows that there is a considerable disparity in margin among the four products:

	Product A	Product B	Product C	Product D
Selling price per unit..............	$7.10	$7.90	$8.40	$10.50
Total variable cost per unit........	4.86	5.53	6.01	8.80
Marginal balance.................	$2.24	$2.37	$2.39	$ 1.70

[3] John Chamberlain, "State of Steel," *Barrons*, June 14, 1954, pp. 15-16.

BENSON & WEST MANUFACTURING COMPANY
Analysis of Volume, Costs, and Margin, by Product Group
Based upon the Budget for May, 19-8

	(1)	(2)	(3)	(4)	(5)	(6)	(7)	(8)	(9)	(10)	(11)
		Sales		Variable Cost Manufacturing		Variable Cost: Distribution	Variable Cost: Total	Total Variable Cost Per Unit	Escapable Capacity Costs: Product Groups	Total Escapable Costs	Marginal Balances of Product Groups
Department and Product	Product Units	Per Unit	Total Amount	Per Unit	Total Amount						
Department 1											
A	2,000	$7.10	$ 14,200.00	$3.69650	$ 7,393.00	$ 2,322.54	$ 9,715.54	$4.86			
B	3,400	7.90	26,860.00	4.23736	14,407.70	4,393.21	18,800.91	5.53			
C	3,000	8.40	25,200.00	4.63756	13,912.62	4,121.70	18,034.32	6.01			
Total	8,400		$ 66,260.00		$ 35,713.32	$10,837.45	$ 46,550.77		$477.15	$ 47,027.92	$19,232.08
Department 2											
D	16,000	10.50	168,000.00	7.08270	113,323.20	27,478.04	140,801.24	8.80	477.15	141,278.39	26,721.61
	24,400		$234,260.00		$149,036.52	$38,315.49	$187,352.01		$954.30	$188,306.31	$45,953.69

Marginal balances of product groups (column 11) $45,953.69
Less—Fixed expenses not identified with product groups
Factory expenses .... $ 3,525.95
Distribution expense 2,158.49
Administrative expense .... 5,215.66 .... 10,900.10

Operating profit $35,053.59

Figure 26-4

Product A contributes about ⅓ more margin per unit for fixed expenses and profit than Product D. Sales *in units* of Product D is almost twice (16,000) the total sales of the other products (8,400), however, and Product D contributes a marginal balance of $26,721.61 as compared with a total marginal balance of $19,232.08 for the other products. A change in product mix could make a significant change in the profit picture.

Note that in this analysis of margin by product groups, escapable capacity costs identified with product groups are charged to those groups (Column 9). In this illustration, it is assumed that these capacity costs could be eliminated if the product group were discontinued. Ordinarily, capacity cost would be considered fixed, although if the possibility of eliminating a product group is being considered, some of the capacity cost may be variable.

DIRECT COSTING

Definition. The subject of direct costing, so-called, should be considered in connection with the study of cost-volume-profit relationships (presented in this chapter) and problems of alternative choice (presented in the following chapter). Jonathan Harris, who is usually credited with developing the idea of direct costing in this country, used the term in an article published in 1936.[4] In 1951, W. W. Neikirk, then an associate of Mr. Harris, defined direct costing as follows:

Direct costing should be defined as a segregation of manufacturing costs between those which are fixed and those which vary with volume. Only the prime costs plus variable overhead costs are used to value inventory and cost of sales. The remaining factory expenses are charged off currently to profit and loss. However, the point to be emphasized is that direct costing is primarily a segregation of expenses and only secondarily a method of inventory valuation. By this approach, full attention can be devoted to the effect which direct costing has on the profit and loss statement and supplementary reports.[5]

Statement of profits. A Statement of Profits prepared under the principles of direct costing appears on page 637. This statement is prepared for Benson & West Manufacturing Company for the budget of May, 19-8, in the form presented in Mr. Neikirk's article. The article describes the statement as follows:

A further refinement is that all of the cost and expense items are arranged in descending order of variability. The first item deducted from gross sales is the direct cost of sales which includes only the directly variable costs of manufacturing. Then the sales deductions for returns, allowances, freight, and so forth are deducted. These items are likewise directly variable with sales volume. Selling expenses are deducted next. Although some portion of selling expenses is of a fixed nature, a large amount of these expenses should vary with sales volume and should be

[4] Jonathan Harris, "What Did We Earn Last Month?" *N.A.C.A. Bulletin*, Jan. 15, 1936, pp. 501-26.

[5] W. W. Neikirk, "How Direct Costing Can Work for Management," *N.A.C.A. Bulletin*, Jan., 1951, p. 525.

measured in terms of sales volume. The net amount remaining after deduction of the above items we call "merchandising margin."

The expense classifications after merchandising margin are almost entirely fixed. A quick analysis of the break-even point can be made by simply dividing those overhead expenses by the percentage that merchandising margin is of gross sales.[6]

BENSON & WEST MANUFACTURING COMPANY
Budget Statement of Profits—Direct Costing

Month of May, 19-8

Gross sales..............................	$234,260.00
Standard direct cost of sales..............	149,036.52
Gross margin above direct cost.........	$ 85,223.48
Deductions for returns, allowances, etc......	
Net gross margin....................	$ 85,223.48
Distribution expense....................	38,315.49
Merchandising margin................	$ 46,907.99
Fixed expenses (and adjustments)	
Factory expense........................	$ 4,480.25
Distribution expense....................	2,158.49
Administrative expense.................	5,215.66
Factory variances and adjustments.......	919.59*
Total fixed expenses................	$ 10,934.81
Operating margin.....................	$ 35,973.18
Other income or charges, net..............	
Profit before taxes....................	$ 35,973.18
Allowance for taxes (calculation omitted)....	
Net profit...........................	$ 35,973.18

* Credit.

Figure 26-5

The merchandising margin ($46,907.99) is the excess of sales over variable expenses (not including factory expense variances of $919.59*); the excess represents the "contribution" of revenues toward fixed costs and profit. (The term "merchandising margin" as used by Neikirk is virtually a synonym for "marginal balance" as used by the present author and "contribution margin" as used by others.) It will be noted that the principle on which a direct costing statement of profits is based is fundamentally different from the principle on which a conventional statement of profits is based. Under direct costing, it is assumed that there is no profit during a period unless the income minus the costs identified with that income (the variable cost) exceeds the fixed expense. The fixed expense is regarded as a *period* cost: in the matching of income with cost, the entire fixed expenses of a period are assessed against the income of the period.

[6] Op. cit., p. 527.

Under the conventional basis illustrated in Chapters 23-25, it is assumed that fixed factory expenses are a cost of production and that in the matching of income units with cost units, fixed factory expense must be included in the cost units.

One advantage claimed for the statement of profits prepared by the direct costing method is that it is possible to make a rough calculation of breakeven point and to determine roughly the effect of increases (or decreases) in sales from such a statement. Neither of these rough calculations is possible using conventional statements, unless supplementary data are also used. Another advantage claimed for the direct costing statement of profits is that it sets out results from operations along the lines of responsibility. It shows, for instance, the effects of short-run merchandising activities separately from the costs of the longer-run decisions having to do with capacity.

Comparison of profits under direct costing with profits under conventional costing. When direct costing is applied to the budget of the entire period, the Budget Statement of Profits, by Months appears as shown on page 639. This statement was prepared for the Benson & West Manufacturing Company for the same six months as the conventional statements illustrated in Chapters 23-25.

A comparison of the operating profits under direct costing compared with the operating profits under conventional costing appears on page 640. For the month of January, there was a profit of $1,017.84 under the conventional method (after charging off the month's underabsorbed expense). For the same month, there was a loss of $1,400.52 under direct costing. The difference in profits is due to the fact that all the fixed expenses are charged off to profit and loss under the direct costing method, whereas part of the fixed factory expense resides in work in process and finished goods inventories under conventional costing.

The difference in profits for January is considerable because there were no opening inventories of work in process and finished goods. The inventories which were building up during the month absorbed a relatively large amount of fixed expense under the conventional method. For the six months' period, the difference in profits equals the amount of fixed factory expense in the closing inventories. (The amount is $1,489.62, and the method of determining it will be explained later in this chapter.)

It should be pointed out that although the difference in profits as between the two methods is not dramatic in this illustration, under certain operating conditions it can be dramatic. As some authors on direct costing point out, it is possible to show a decrease in profits with an increase in sales under conventional costing, where production has dropped and where the underabsorbed expense is charged against the current month. The proponents of direct costing maintain that the picture presented by conventional costing in such a situation is a confusing one, and that the

BENSON & WEST MANUFACTURING COMPANY
Budget Statement of Profits, by Months—Direct Costing
Six Months Ending June 30, 19-8

	January	February	March	April	May	June
Sales	$68,540.00	$81,030.00	$150,220.00	$212,050.00	$234,260.00	$83,470.00
Less—Variable expenses:						
Materials	$18,020.00	$20,290.00	$38,360.00	$55,150.00	$59,880.00	$19,450.00
Labor	20,350.00	23,637.50	44,300.00	62,937.50	69,650.00	23,987.50
Variable factory expense in goods shipped						
@ standard rates	5,601.29	6,753.35	12,462.68	17,463.20	19,506.52	7,180.77
(1) Factory expense variance	166.65	821.41	759.83*	889.50*	919.59*	1,582.41
Variable distribution expense	13,948.18	15,333.06	25,707.00	34,979.40	38,315.49	15,684.89
Marginal balance	$58,086.12	$66,835.32	$120,069.85	$169,640.60	$186,432.42	$67,885.57
	$10,453.88	$14,194.68	$30,150.15	$43,409.40	$47,827.58	$15,554.43
Per cent to sales	15%	17%	20%	20%	20%	19%
Fixed expenses:						
Factory expense	$ 4,480.25	$ 4,480.25	$ 4,480.25	$ 4,480.25	$ 4,480.25	$ 4,480.25
Distribution expense	2,158.49	2,158.49	2,158.49	2,158.49	2,158.49	2,158.49
Administrative expense	5,215.66	5,215.66	5,215.66	5,215.66	5,215.66	5,215.66
Total direct expenses	$11,854.40	$11,854.40	$11,854.40	$11,854.40	$11,854.40	$11,854.40
Operating profit (loss*)	$ 1,400.52*	$ 2,340.28	$ 18,295.75	$ 30,555.00	$ 35,973.18	$ 3,730.03
Financial expense	1,042.52	964.12	1,277.64	2,595.16	3,854.12	4,574.32
Net profit (loss*)	$ 2,443.04*	$ 1,376.16	$ 17,018.11	$ 27,959.84	$ 32,119.06	$ 844.29*
(1) *Factory expense variance*						
Expected actual factory expense	$17,091.08	$16,096.79	$18,260.34	$18,951.71	$19,132.61	$15,917.47
Charged to work in process	$11,624.18	$ 9,975.13	$13,719.92	$14,540.96	$14,751.95	$ 9,034.81
Fixed expense charged to profit & loss, as above	4,480.25	4,480.25	4,480.25	4,480.25	4,480.25	4,480.25
Rent charged to administration and distribution	820.00	820.00	820.00	820.00	820.00	820.00
	$16,924.43	$15,275.38	$19,020.17	$19,841.21	$20,052.20	$14,335.06
Expense variance	$ 166.65	$ 821.41	$ 759.83*	$ 889.50*	$ 919.59*	$ 1,582.41

* Red.

Figure 26-6

BENSON & WEST MANUFACTURING COMPANY
Comparison of Budget Profits—Conventional Costing: Direct Costing, by Months
January–June, 19-8

	January	February	March	April	May	June	Six Months
Sales...................	$68,540.00	$81,030.00	$150,220.00	$212,050.00	$234,260.00	$83,470.00	$829,570.00
Operating profit (loss*) Conventional costing (Figure 23-1)							
Operating profits.........	$ 1,256.42	$ 5,106.54	$ 17,436.35	$ 27,858.95	$ 32,405.36	$ 6,919.72	$ 90,983.34
Unabsorbed factory expense.....	238.58	1,703.04	1,117.16*	1,660.79*	1,913.64 *	2,749.97	
Operating profits (net)........	$ 1,017.84	$ 3,403.50	$ 18,553.51	$ 29,519.74	$ 34,319.00	$ 4,169.75	$ 90,983.34
Direct costing: Operating profits (Figure 26-6)............	$ 1,400.52*	$ 2,340.28	$ 18,295.75	$ 30,555.00	$ 35,973.18	$ 3,730.03	$ 89,493.72
Difference in profits............							$ 1,489.62

* Red.

Figure 26-7

640

results shown by direct costing would be clearer to the management.

Direct costing used in connection with actual costs. Although the direct costing Statement of Profits illustrated on page 637 was prepared from standard costs (that is, the standard cost data of Benson & West Manufacturing Company used previously in this text), in some cases, direct cost statements are prepared from actual costs. The N.A.C.A. Research Bulletin on direct costing states:

However, standard costs do not necessarily accompany direct costing and two companies interviewed make no use of standard costs in accounting. In both of these companies historical costing systems are operated, the inventories being costed at actual direct cost. Historical actual costs are also used by these companies in cost-volume-profit studies such as break-even charts and marginal income data.[7]

Other uses of direct costing techniques. In addition to their use in making cost-volume-profit calculations and breakeven charts, direct costing techniques facilitate the solution of problems of alternative choice —such as problems involved in the determination of which products to push to use available production capacity, whether to use a new method of performing a certain operation or to continue the old method, whether to replace a machine with a newer one, and whether to make a certain part or buy it outside. Solution of these problems requires a separation of variable and fixed expenses. The problems are discussed in Chapter 27.

Although the solution of problems of alternative choice is possible under direct costing, it is also possible under conventional flexible budget procedure described in Chapters 23-25. In either case, the classification of expenses along the lines of variability can be extended into the area of the problem.

Direct costing as a means of measuring profit. Numerous articles have been written on direct costing, some of them favorable to the idea and some of them unfavorable. One of the main points of contention is whether direct costing has validity and merit as a means of measuring profit. Some accountants (and the N.A.C.A. Research Committee which issued the bulletin on direct costing) state that experience is not yet complete enough to justify a stand.

Some contend that the statement of profits prepared on the conventional basis can be confusing to a management, and that the direct costing form of statement is clearer. The N.A.C.A. Research Bulletin on the subject says:

In evaluating the effect which changes in sales volume have on profits when using absorption costing, management must consider the two influences, production volume and sales volume, which may work together or in opposition. Full understanding of the situation calls for knowledge of highly technical accounting procedures which few executives possess. The field study provided a substantial amount of evidence to the effect that management is often confused, or at best fails to

[7] "Direct Costing," N.A.C.A. Research Series No. 23, April, 1953, p. 1093.

understand fully, when changes in the fixed cost component of inventory obscure relationships between sales volume and profits which would be readily evident under direct costing.[8]

Charles R. Chambers says:

The consideration of direct costs as an avenue to better accounting methods was caused by several factors. Due to the relatively high overhead rate, the comparability of profits to sales volume in different periods was heavily influenced by the level of factory activity. In the post war period, when materials had become available, the factory was engaged in a program to rebuild the supply of parts and to manufacture new parts for new product lines. The large amount of overhead absorbed in the inventory increase resulted in unusual profits. The comparison of sales volume and profits of this period to later periods did not make sense to operating management. Had the inventory decreased substantially in succeeding periods, comparisons would have been even more disproportionate, since cost of sales in this later period would have included fixed expenses of the previous period carried forward as inventory, in addition to fixed expenses of the later period of lower volume, charged off as unabsorbed overhead.[9]

On the other hand, J. A. Mauriello says:

It is said that fixed costs are costs of capacity to produce and not costs of production. Therefore, they should be considered as period costs rather than product costs. This contention is erroneous. Fixed costs contribute to production to the extent that the capacity to produce is utilized. Under conventional costing, the fixed costs relating to capacity unutilized constitute the volume variance. The remainder of the fixed costs contribute to production and, therefore, are properly treated as product costs.[10]

Although there is marked lack of agreement on the point discussed above, there seems to be considerable support for the use of direct costs for cost control and for aiding in the solution of problems of alternative choice.

Some writers question whether it is possible to separate expenses into variable and fixed totals for a manufacturing business as a whole, assuming that the variable expenses vary with sales (or production valued at sales prices) and that the fixed expenses remain fixed. These writers point out that there are numerous factors of variability for expenses in the various producing and service departments of a business and that it is not necessarily true that a 10 per cent drop in production means a 10 per cent drop in variable expense across the board.

Inventories under direct costing. As was indicated above, under direct costing the process and finished goods inventories would include direct materials, direct labor, and variable factory expense. On the Budget Balance Sheets appearing on page 643, note the following inventory accounts:

[8] "Direct Costing," N.A.C.A. Research Series No. 23, April, 1953, p. 1111.
[9] Charles R. Chambers, "A Conversion to Direct Costs," N.A.C.A. Bulletin, March, 1952, p. 792.
[10] J. A. Mauriello, "Convertibility of Direct and Conventional Costing," N.A.C.A. Bulletin, March, 1954, p. 892.

BENSON & WEST MANUFACTURING COMPANY
Budget Balance Sheets, by Months—Direct Costing
Six Months Ending June 30, 19___

Assets

	January 1	January 30	February 28	March 31	April 30	May 31	June 30
Current assets:							
Cash	$ 40,000.00	$102,951.55	$ 61,328.07	$ 19,227.86	$ 22,804.06	$ 85,480.12	$ 80,705.60
Accounts receivable	65,000.00	68,540.00	81,030.00	150,220.00	212,050.00	234,260.00	83,470.00
Reserve for bad debts	1,875.00*	1,930.05	2,028.65*	2,394.65*	2,768.65*	3,004.64*	2,458.01[2]
Materials—Raw, process, and finished goods		30,900.00	47,740.00	50,550.00	38,110.00	16,130.00	18,150.00
Labor in process and finished goods		19,240.00	30,450.00	36,212.50	25,712.50	8,737.50	17,637.50
Factory expense in process and finished goods —Variable		6,022.89	9,244.67	10,501.91	7,579.67	2,825.10	4,679.13
Factory expense in process and finished goods —Fixed							
Total current assets	$103,125.00	$225,724.39	$227,764.09	$264,317.62	$303,487.58	$344,428.08	$202,184.22
Prepaid expenses and supplies	13,602.28	12,415.79	14,205.45	8,602.29	6,980.15	3,992.42	1,903.90
Fixed assets	378,000.00	395,925.03	393,850.06	391,775.09	389,700.12	387,625.15	385,550.18
Total assets	$494,727.28	$634,065.21	$635,819.60	$664,695.00	$700,167.85	$736,045.65	$589,638.30

Liabilities and Net Worth

	January 1	January 30	February 28	March 31	April 30	May 31	June 30
Current liabilities	$ 23,000.00	$164,780.97	$165,159.20	$177,016.49	$184,529.50	$188,288.24	$ 42,725.18
Capital stock	400,000.00	400,000.00	400,000.00	400,000.00	400,000.00	400,000.00	400,000.00
Surplus:							
Balance, beginning of month	$ 71,727.28	$ 71,727.28	$ 69,284.24	$ 70,660.40	$ 87,678.51	$115,638.34	$147,757.41
Profits—Month		2,443.04*	1,376.16	17,018.11	27,959.84	32,119.06	844.29[d]
Balance, end of month	$ 69,284.24	$ 69,284.24	$ 70,660.40	$ 87,678.51	$115,638.34	$147,757.41	$146,913.12
Total net worth	$471,727.28	$469,284.24	$470,660.40	$487,678.51	$515,638.35	$547,757.41	$546,913.12
Total liabilities and net worth	$494,727.28	$634,065.21	$635,819.60	$664,695.00	$700,157.85	$736,045.65	$589,638.30

* Red.

Figure 26-8

BENSON & WEST MANUFACTURING COMPANY
Budget Factory Expense Rates per Standard Hour: Variable and Fixed

(Period: One Month)

	Building Maintenance and Fixed Charges	General Factory Administration — Variable Expense	General Factory Administration — Rent and Fixed Charges	Cutting — Variable Expense	Cutting — Rent and Fixed Charges	Assembly No. 1 — Variable Expense	Assembly No. 1 — Rent and Fixed Charges	Assembly No. 2 — Variable Expense	Assembly No. 2 — Rent and Fixed Charges	Rent: Selling and Administrative Expense	Totals — Variable Expense	Totals — Rent and Fixed Charges
Standard hours produced..........		33,700		6,500		7,200		20,000				
Total direct departmental expense..	$4,021.07	$5,236.14		$2,613.66	$ 267.72	$1,992.67	$ 477.15	$2,432.28	$ 477.15	$	$12,274.75	$5,300.25
Building maintenance and fixed charges allocated (rent)..........	4,021.07*		400.00		895.51		993.81		911.75	820.00		
Variable general factory administrative expense allocated (Rate per standard hour: $5,236.14 ÷ 33,700 = $.1553+)..		5,236.14*	$457.16	1,009.94		1,118.70		3,107.50				
Fixed general factory administrative expense allocated (Rate per standard hour: $457.16 ÷ 33,700 = $.0135655)..			457.16*		88.18		97.67		271.31			
				$3,623.60	$1,251.41	$3,111.37	$1,568.63	$5,539.78	$1,660.21	$820.00	$12,274.75	$5,300.25
Variable expense rates per standard hour..................				$ .55747		$ .43213		$ .27698				
Fixed expense rates per standard hour..................					$ .19248		$ .21788		$ .08301			

Figure 26-9

644

Materials—Raw, Process, and Finished Goods
Labor in Process and Finished Goods
Factory Expense in Process and Finished Goods

The latter account would be charged monthly for Standard hours in goods completed × Variable factory expense rates computed as shown on the table on page 644:

Variable Expense Rates Per Standard Hour

Cutting room	.55747
Assembly No. 1	.43213
Assembly No. 2	.27698

If it is desired to produce a "conventional" balance sheet (say at the end of six months), the Factory Expense in Process and Finished Goods—Fixed account could be set up by debiting it and crediting Profit and Loss. The amount would be standard hours in inventories × the appropriate fixed expense rates:

Factory expense in process and finished goods—Fixed......... $1,489.49
    profit and loss..................................... $1,489.49
To charge closing inventories with fixed factory expense allocable thereto on the basis of standard hours in the inventories:

	Cutting Room	Assembly No. 2	Total*
Standard hours in inventories	3,425	10,000	
Fixed expense rate	$.19248+	$.08301	
Amount	$659.39	$830.10	$1,489.49

* Difference from Figure 26-7 due to fractions, $.13.

The hours shown in this entry would come from a schedule of standard hours in inventories for June. The entry would be reversed at the beginning of the next period.

REVIEW QUESTIONS

26-1. Define (a) direct costing; (b) marginal balance; (c) conventional costing.

26-2. Which use or uses of cost accounting are served by marginal cost techniques?

26-3. What is the relationship between marginal cost techniques and breakeven point techniques?

26-4. What are the uses and limitations of breakeven charts?

26-5. Compare the basic theory of conventional costing with that of direct costing. On what essential point are the two methods of costing diametrically opposed?

26-6. If direct costing methods are operated in the general ledger, how are inventories valued? Is it feasible to adjust the inventories to reflect some other basis of valuation?

26-7. Explain the merits and defects of (a) conventional costing and (b) direct costing.

EXERCISES

Data for Exercises 26-1 through 26-4:

THE FRANKLIN CORPORATION
Budget Statement of Profits—Direct Costing, by Months
January–July, 19__

Particulars	January	February	March	April	May	June	Six Months
Product units sales	500	800	1,200	1,600	1,200	500	5,800
Sales............................	$6,250.00	$10,000.00	$15,000.00	$20,000.00	$15,000.00	$6,250.00	$72,500.00
Less—Variable cost							
Factory cost (@ $8.037 per unit)							
(Schedule 3)...............	$4,018.50	$ 6,429.60	$ 9,644.40	$12,859.20	$ 9,644.40	$4,018.50	$46,614.60
Administrative and selling expense....	473.75	758.00	1,137.00	1,516.00	1,137.00	473.75	5,495.50
Total variable cost........	$4,492.25	$ 7,187.60	$10,781.40	$14,375.20	$10,781.40	$4,492.25	$52,110.10
Marginal balance...........	$1,757.75	$ 2,812.40	$ 4,218.60	$ 5,624.80	$ 4,218.60	$1,757.75	$20,389.90
Less—Fixed cost							
Factory expense...........	$1,713.00	$ 1,713.00	$ 1,713.00	$ 1,713.00	$ 1,713.00	$1,713.00	$10,278.00
Administrative and selling expense....	811.16	811.16	811.17	811.17	811.17	811.17	4,867.00
Total fixed cost...........	$2,524.16	$ 2,524.16	$ 2,524.17	$ 2,524.17	$ 2,524.17	$2,524.17	$15,145.00
Operating net profit (loss*)........	$ 766.41*	$ 288.24	$ 1,694.43	$ 3,100.63	$ 1,694.43	$ 766.42*	$ 5,244.90
Less—Financial expense (net)........	2.10*	78.43	146.05	251.05	373.80	264.85	1,112.08
Surplus net profit (loss)........	$ 764.31*	$ 209.81	$ 1,548.38	$ 2,849.58	$ 1,320.63	$1,031.27*	$ 4,132.82

* Credit.

646

Data for Exercises 26-1 through 26-4 (*Continued*)

FACTORY EXPENSE BUDGET   Schedule 2

Variable		*Six Months* *18,000* *Std. Hrs.*	*Rate/Hour*
Indirect labor..............		$ 3,600.00	.20
F.I.C.A. tax...............		522.00	.029
Supplies...................		2,700.00	.15
Power.....................		900.00	.05
Total..................		$ 7,722.00	.429

Fixed	*Per Month*		
Depreciation...............	$ 700.00	$ 4,200.00	
Insurance..................	600.00	3,600.00	
Taxes......................	413.00	2,478.00	
Total..................	$1,713.00	$10,278.00	.571
Total expense..............		$18,000.00	$1.000

STANDARD COST CARD   Schedule 3

Variable cost per unit: Product X
Materials:
    2 yards A @ $1.50................. $3.00
Labor
    3 hours @ $1.25.................... 3.75
Variable factory expense
    3 hours @ $.429................... 1.287

    Total variable cost................... $8.037

Reconciliation: Profits for Six Months—(1) Direct Costing and
                (2) Absorption Basis

Budget profits for six months per direct costing (Schedule 1)......		$4,132.82
Credit P & L to record fixed charges in closing inventory		
Standard labor hours in in process inventory (per solution		
to Problem 23-1 [4])....................................	600	
× Fixed factory expense per hour (per Schedule 2)	$.571	342.60
Budget profits per absorption basis (per solution to Exercise 25-10)		$4,475.42

26-1.* Using the budget figures for April in the Budget Statement of Profits—Direct Costing (page 646):

(1) Calculate the breakeven point in sales dollars, using the formula given in Chapter 26. (Do not consider financial expense in any of the exercises in this chapter.)

(2) Make a breakeven chart, based upon the budget for April. (Graph paper for this exercise is included in the Workbook.)

  * Graph paper is the only special "form" required for solution of the exercises in this chapter. Students who are not provided with the Workbook may use arithmetic graph paper.

(3) Within what range of sales does the breakeven point appear in the Budget Statement of Profits—Direct Costing for the Franklin Corporation?

26-2. (1) Calculate the effect upon the breakeven point (in sales dollars) of an increase in sales prices of 10 per cent. Use the Franklin Corporation Statement of Profits for April as the base for the calculations.

(2) Make a breakeven chart to show graphically the situation indicated in (1).

26-3. (1) Calculate the effect upon the breakeven point (in sales dollars) of an increase in fixed expense of 10 per cent. Use the Franklin Corporation Statement of Profits for April as the base for calculation.

(2) Make a breakeven chart to show graphically the situation indicated in (1).

26-4. (1) Calculate the effect upon the breakeven point (in sales dollars) of an increase in variable expenses of 10 per cent. Use the Franklin Corporation Statement of Profits for April as the base for calculation.

(2) Make a breakeven chart to show graphically the situation indicated in (1).

PROBLEMS

26-1. The Ingram Company uses a standard cost system. The standard cost card for *one* unit of Product M and the factory expense budget for a month based upon 1,000 units of production are shown on page 649:

It was estimated that fixed selling and administrative expenses would be $60,000 a month, and that variable selling and administrative expenses would be 20 per cent of dollar sales. The sales price was $250 per unit.

Required:

Arthur B. Ingram, the sole owner, has asked you to make a forecast of profits at different levels of production. He would like to know expected total net income and expected net income per unit of sales at the following levels of volume:

(a) at the breakeven point (wherever that may be)
(b) 800 units of Product M
(c) 1,000 units of Product M
(d) 1,200 units of Product M

Prepare a pro forma income statement showing the income and expense at each of the suggested levels of volume. Use the type of statement illustrated in Figure 26-1. (There will be no factory expense variance in your solution.)

26-2. The Ingram Company (Problem 26-1) operates a standard cost system of the type described on pages 413-421, except that all fixed costs are charged off to Profit and Loss monthly.

The following inventory, cost of sales, and variance accounts are operated:

Materials
Materials in Process and Finished Goods
Labor in Process and Finished Goods
Variable Factory Expense in Process and Finished Goods
Cost of Goods Sold: Materials
Cost of Goods Sold: Labor
Cost of Goods Sold: Variable Factory Expense
Materials Price Variance
Materials Quantity Variance
Labor Variance
Factory Expense Spending Variance (Variable Expense)

Standard Cost
One Unit of Product M

(Estimated production: 1,000 units)

	Dept. 1		Dept. 2		Dept. 3		Total
Materials	200 lbs. of "A" @ .20	$40.00	100 lbs. of "B" @ .10	$10.00			$ 50.00
Labor	3 hrs. @ $2.00	6.00	5 hrs. @ $1.80	9.00	2 hrs. @ $2.50	$ 5.00	20.00
Expense variable	3 hrs. @ .40	1.20	5 hrs. @ 2.00	10.00	2 hrs. @ 4.40	8.80	
Expense fixed	3 hrs. @ .60	1.80	5 hrs. @ 1.00	5.00	2 hrs. @ 1.60	3.20	30.00
		3.00		15.00		$12.00	
		$49.00		$34.00		$17.00	$100.00

Monthly Factory Expense Budget

(Estimated Production: 1,000 Units)

	Dept. 1	Dept. 2	Dept. 3	Total
Variable costs				
Indirect labor	$ 600.00	$ 6,000.00	$ 2,400.00	$ 9,000.00
Supplies	400.00	3,000.00	4,600.00	8,000.00
Heat, light & power	200.00	1,000.00	1,800.00	3,000.00
	$1,200.00	$10,000.00	$ 8,800.00	$20,000.00
Fixed costs				
Rent	$ 500.00	$ 900.00	$ 600.00	$ 2,000.00
Maintenance	500.00	800.00	1,200.00	2,500.00
Depreciation	400.00	2,000.00	600.00	3,000.00
Miscellaneous	400.00	1,300.00	800.00	2,500.00
	$1,800.00	$ 5,000.00	$ 3,200.00	$10,000.00
	$3,000.00	$15,000.00	$12,000.00	$30,000.00

The latter account is the difference between actual variable expense incurred and standard variable expense absorbed into work in process (Standard hours in operations completed × Standard variable expense rate).

During the month of June, 1,200 units were completed. Of these 1,000 were sold @ $250 each. There were no work in process inventories at the end of June. The following costs were incurred during June:

Materials purchases:
"A" 245,000 lbs. @ $.21... $51,450.00
"B" 145,000 lbs. @ $.09... $13,050.00
Material requisitioned:
"A" 236,000 lbs. @ $.21... $49,560.00
"B" 135,000 lbs. @ $.09... $12,150.00
Labor used:
Dept. 1 3,500 hrs. @ $2.00.. $ 7,000.00
Dept. 2 6,200 hrs. @ 1.80.. $11,160.00
Dept. 3 2,000 hrs. @ 2.50.. $ 5,000.00

Factory Expense:	Dept. 1	Dept. 2	Dept. 3	Total
Variable costs				
Indirect labor...........	$ 900.00	$ 5,800.00	$ 2,100.00	$ 8,800.00
Supplies...............	400.00	3,500.00	5,000.00	8,900.00
Heat, light & power.....	300.00	1,500.00	2,000.00	3,800.00
	$1,600.00	$10,800.00	$ 9,100.00	$21,500.00

Fixed costs	Dept. 1	Dept. 2	Dept. 3	Total
Rent...................	$ 500.00	$ 900.00	$ 600.00	$ 2,000.00
Maintenance...........	600.00	800.00	1,600.00	3,000.00
Depreciation...........	400.00	2,000.00	600.00	3,000.00
Miscellaneous..........	500.00	1,200.00	800.00	2,500.00
	$2,000.00	$ 4,900.00	$ 3,600.00	$10,500.00
	$3,600.00	$15,700.00	$12,700.00	$32,000.00

Selling and administrative expenses:
Fixed costs.. $58,000.00
Variable costs... 63,000.00

Required:

(1) Draft journal entries to record the transactions for June.
(2) Post the entries to T accounts.
(3) Prepare Statement of Profits using form in Figure 26-1.

26-3. Referring to Problems 26-1 and 26-2, prepare a Factory Expense Variance report for each of the three departments.

26-4. Referring to Problems 26-1 and 26-2, prepare a Comparative Statement of Profits, comparing the expected results for 1,000 units (Problem 26-1) with the actual results (Problem 26-2).

Explain the differences.

26-5. This problem is related to Problems 26-1 and 26-2. From current wage negotiations it appears that 10 per cent increase in direct labor wage rates will be allowed. Mr. Ingram is concerned about the possible action he should take in order to continue to operate at the same level of net income experienced in June. Some of the alternatives are:

(a) Increase sales volume to 1,500 units a month. Mr. Ingram believes that variable selling and administrative expenses must be increased by 10 per cent more than the current estimate in order to increase sales beyond 1,200 units.

(b) Increase the price of the product. Mr. Ingram does not believe sales price could be increased without reducing sales volume. He estimates that with any increase in price the sales volume would fall to 800 units.

(c) Close department 1 and purchase a semi-finished product ready for processing in departments 2 and 3. The cost of such a product would be $48 per unit of Product M.

Required:

Submit your recommendation to Mr. Ingram. Support your recommendation with any supporting schedules you believe to be necessary. Make any assumption that may be required.

26-6. The Metal Products Co. manufactures three different models of a single product. From the following data, you are to prepare a schedule, supported by computations, showing the sales quantity and sales dollar figure for each model necessary to enable the company to cover its nonvariable costs.

	Annual Sales Budget (Units)	Budgeted Unit Sales Price	Budgeted Sales Allowances for a Year
100	30,000	$15.00	$1,260.00
200	16,000	18.00	480.00
300	10,000	25.00	410.00

1952 Estimates

	Quantity Budgeted for Production	Over-all Estimated Cost per Unit Total	Variable Cost	Non-variable Cost
100	30,500	$15.072	$ 9.871	$5.201
200	15,000	17.335	10.250	7.085
300	10,000	23.756	15.436	8.320

(*AICPA*)

PROBLEMS OF ALTERNATIVE CHOICE;
COSTS FOR SPECIAL PURPOSES

Some problems stated. The managements of most manufacturing companies have a number of problems for which special cost information is desired. For instance, what book cost is available for consideration in quoting prices for special orders? The question is asked in reference to orders which would be manufactured in "extra" capacity, that is, capacity above the volume on which the present budgets and standard costs are based. Where the amount of machine capacity is limited and the company can push any of several products that can be made on the same machine, which product should the company push?

A perennial problem in some businesses is whether the company should continue to make certain parts or buy them outside. Likewise, the problem of machine replacement is a frequent one. Should the company buy automatic machines to do the operation now done manually?

This chapter discusses cost information which is useful to management in making decisions on these and related problems.

Uses of marginal product costs: Regular products; Slack season. Marginal cost is the increase or decrease in total cost which occurs with a small variation in output, hence, *incremental* or differential cost. It does not include any element of fixed costs. . . . Fixed costs of facilities will continue whether or not the facilities are put to use; it may, therefore, be profitable to solicit new business at lower prices even if fixed costs are not covered. . . .[1]

Although the catalog prices or list prices are based upon fully allocated costs for a normal period (that is, include both variable and fixed costs), it may be desirable to offer special prices on certain products during slack seasons when there is unused manufacturing capacity. In the summer, a cookie baking company, for instance, may not be able to sell all its products at prices which cover fully allocated costs, because of the competitive price situation. The company may have to offer reduced prices, possibly on the whole line, but more likely on certain product items which then become

[1] Eric L. Kohler, *A Dictionary for Accountants*, 2nd Ed. (Englewood Cliffs, N. J.: Prentice-Hall, Inc., 1957).

BENSON & WEST MANUFACTURING COMPANY
Standard Product Costs (Variable Costs Only)
Six Months Ending June 30, 19__

Element and Department	Product A — Yards or Hours per Unit	Price or Rate	Total Amount per Product Unit	Product B — Yards or Hours per Unit	Price or Rate	Total Amount per Product Unit	Product C — Yards or Hours per Unit	Price or Rate	Total Amount per Product Unit	Product D — Yards or Hours per Unit	Price or Rate	Total Amount per Product Unit
Materials	3 yards	$ .50	$1.50	2 yards	$ .60	$1.20	2 yards	$ .80	$1.60	2 yards	$1.50	$ 3.00
Labor:												
Cutting department	.25 hour	1.50	.375	.25 hour	1.50	.375	.25 hour	1.50	.375	.5 hour	1.50	.75
Assembly department No. 1	1.0 hour	1.25	1.25	1.5 hours	1.25	1.875	1.5 hours	1.25	1.875			
Assembly department No. 2										2.0 hour	1.25	2.50
Variable factory expense (Rates from Figure 26-9)												
Cutting department	.25 hour	.55747	.13937	.25 hour	.55747	.13937	.25 hour	.55747	.13937	.5 hour	.55747	.27874
Assembly department No. 1	1.0 hour	.43213	.43213	1.5 hours	.43213	.64819	1.5 hours	.43213	.64819			
Assembly department No. 2										2.0 hours	.27698	.55396
Total variable manufacturing cost per unit			$3.69650			$4.23756			$4.63756			$ 7.08270
Variable distribution expense (@ 17.35% of selling price*)			$1.23			$1.37			$1.46			$ 1.82
Standard (desired average) selling prices per unit			$7.10			$7.90			$8.40			$10.50
Marginal balance			$2.17			$2.29			$2.30			$ 1.60
Margin per hour (Assembly department No. 1)			$1.74			$1.31			$1.31			

* The variable distribution expenses per product unit in this illustration (six months) differ slightly from those for May, on which Figure 26-4 is based. The difference is due to the imperfect variability of this expense group month by month in relationship to sales.

Figure 27-1

what is popularly but loosely known as "loss leaders." In the latter case, the hope is to sell other products to each customer along with the loss leader and to secure more marginal income from the output of an oven than would be secured without the loss leader. In any case, the price-setter should know the marginal cost of each product so that he does not set prices which would actually result in out-of-pocket losses. The aim in this case is that each product cover its own variable expenses and make some contribution to fixed expenses.

A rough calculation of marginal costs and marginal balances for separate products at budget volume may be computed by (1) calculating factory expense rates for fixed and variable expense separately, as shown on page 653, and (2) setting up standard product costs for the various products in the usual manner, but charging each product with *variable* expense rates instead of the conventional rate comprising both variable and fixed factory expense. The marginal cost and marginal balance for each of the four products shown on page 653 is:

| Product | Variable | | Total Marginal Cost | Selling Price | Marginal Balance per Product Unit | Average Manufac- turing Cost per Unit at Average Capacity |
	Manu- facturing	Distri- bution				
A	$3.70	$1.23	$4.93	$ 7.10	$2.17	$3.96
B	4.24	1.37	5.61	7.90	2.29	4.61
C	4.64	1.46	6.10	8.40	2.30	5.01
D	7.08	1.82	8.90	10.50	1.60	7.35

The selling prices shown are list prices at the beginning of the season on the basis of average sales capacity. The marginal cost for each product would be the minimum selling price which would cover the out-of-pocket costs of the product.

The marginal costs shown above are computed on the basis of average sales capacity. It is assumed that the variable costs per product unit are the costs of producing additional units *at that level*. In a specific case, this assumption would have to be examined. The variability which is assumed to exist within say 5 per cent of average sales capacity may not exist beyond that point. In the manufacture of pig iron, for instance, an increase in production beyond a certain point may be accomplished only at a *higher* variable cost per ton because standby facilities of sub-standard efficiency may have to be put into use. In practice, marginal costs may have to be calculated at each of a series of volume steps. This calculation would reveal the optimum level of production.

The *average* manufacturing cost per unit at average sales capacity is included in the above table for the sake of comparison. Average cost per unit is the *total* cost including fixed expenses of a certain aggregate quantity produced divided by the number of units produced. The amounts shown come from the standard cost cards on page 595.

Closely related to the problem of costing and pricing in slack seasons is the problem of what to do with the product which is a perennial loser. Assume that the product line includes a product which always shows a loss, when cost is calculated on a fully allocated cost basis. The question of dropping the product is of course a marketing management question, but a marginal cost should be calculated to assist the management. The management needs to know whether the selling price that can be obtained covers the marginal cost—the cost that can be saved by dropping the product. On this point, Greer says:

> When it comes to dropping or subordinating low-margin items, an even more difficult task presents itself. These unsatisfactory items may be by-products, companion items, "fill-ins," high turnover staples, etc. The same is true of customers. Small volume buyers may be adjacent to large ones and thus servable at low incremental cost. Any revenue is welcome from a freight car that would otherwise move empty.
>
> All this is not to decry the value of full exposition of the margin contribution from each item of product and each class of trade, but merely to point out that the whole problem of selective selling is immensely complicated, and not to be quickly solved, even with the best of cost-price analysis.[2]

Special orders of regular product. Assume that the company has an opportunity to sell a special order of its regular product under a special brand name and through channels other than its regular distribution channels. Manufacturing capacity is available. The question is how much would it cost to produce an additional 1,000 units of the product, above the budget volume already set for the regular business. The *marginal cost* would be set for the benefit of the price-setter. It would be hoped that the price would cover the marginal costs and leave a marginal balance. The marginal balance would be profit since the fixed expenses would have been covered by the regular business.

On the question of "price at which to refuse an order," the N.A.C.A. Bulletin "Product Costs for Pricing Purposes," says:

> The marginal analysis is perhaps most widely used for ascertaining when an order should be refused because current out-of-pocket cost of filling the order exceeds the price offered. Many examples are found in situations such as deciding whether or not to meet competitors' price reductions, bidding for special orders which can be obtained only at a low price, etc.
>
> In such problems it may be desirable to distinguish between sunk fixed costs (e.g., depreciation) and fixed costs which require current cash outlays (e.g., salaries). To illustrate, a company developed a product and special purpose machines for manufacturing it. This product was quite profitable in the beginning, but now has been widely copied by competitors and the selling price has been reduced until

---

[2] Howard C. Greer, "Alternatives to Direct Costing," *N.A.C.A. Bulletin*, March, 1954, p. 885.

the full cost of the product is no longer recoverable. The company has decided to continue the product as long as marginal income from it covers direct fixed costs which require current cash outlays such as property taxes on equipment, salaries, and insurance. These costs can be saved by abandoning the product, but such costs as depreciation cannot now be saved.[3]

Regular products when manufacturing capacity is limited. If productive capacity on a particular manufacturing unit is limited, the management may want to know which product to push. The answer would be to push the product which carries the largest marginal balance, stated in terms of the quantitative factor which limits production. Thus, in the manufacture of a line of cookies all of which are produced in the same band oven, oven time would be the limiting factor. The sales department should push the products which earn the largest marginal balance per oven hour.

In the Benson & West Manufacturing Company, this question arises with reference to Products A, B, and C, all of which are produced in assembly department No. 1. To aid in the decision, it may be desirable to compute a marginal balance per hour of manufacturing time for each product, as shown in the last three columns:

Product	Normal Selling Price per Unit	Budget Gross Profit (Per Cent)	Marginal Balance	Hours of Mfg. Time	Margin per Hour
A	7.10	44.6	$2.17	1.25	$1.74
B	7.90	42.2	2.29	1.75	1.31
C	8.40	40.8	2.30	1.75	1.31

Note that the highest priced product (Product C) is not the best performer. It carries the lowest gross profit percentage (40.8 per cent) and (with Product B) makes the lowest margin contribution per hour of manufacturing time ($1.31). Although the company will accept orders for any of the three products when it has the manufacturing capacity to handle them, it should push Product A when there is a question of available manufacturing capacity. If there were a question of selling manufacturing capacity with Product A or Product B or Product C, it would be more profitable to fill the available hours of capacity with Product A (which would contribute $1.74 per hour to fixed charges and profit) rather than with either Product B or C (either of which would contribute $1.31 per hour).

Custom products: Variable order quantities. In this case, the manufacturer is asked to quote selling prices for a specified quantity or for a range of quantities. In addition to the costs which would be expected to vary with the quantity of product produced on the order (such as power for machinery), there are costs to which the manufacturer commits himself when he accepts the order, but which do not vary with units produced.

[3] Research Series No. 24, August, 1953, pp. 1726-27.

Obvious examples of the latter are make-ready time in a printing plant (the time required to put the printing plates in the press and get the press ready to print the job) and "order costs" (costs of paper work necessary to get the job onto the production floors).

In principle, there might be a minimum order quantity, below which quantity the manufacturer would not accept the order. The selling price for this quantity might be based upon a cost which would cover the production costs (variable plus an allocation of fixed expense), the variable costs incurred upon acceptance of the order. To quote a price on additional thousands of units, the price-setter should know the cost per thousand for production, as distinguished from the costs incurred upon acceptance of the order.

On the cost of tools, dies, and set-ups, the N.A.C.A. Bulletin "Product Costs for Pricing Purposes" states:

> Several companies stated that they compute separate product costs for each of a series of volume figures. . . . A variation in this practice is found in a company which separates the cost estimate for each order into a "flat cost" and a "running cost." The former, which includes time and materials used in preparation and set-up, does not vary in total with the length of the run, but decreases on a unit basis as the number of units ordered increases. The running cost varies with the quantity ordered by the customer, but is a constant amount per unit of product. With these costs available, management then knows what price it must obtain to recover costs on an order of any given size.
>
> When repeat orders may or may not be received in the future, it seems common practice to charge the full cost of tools and dies to the first order to insure recovery of their cost in the event additional orders are not forthcoming.[4]

Regular products: Additional processing. In some industries, products are processed through a succession of departments or stages, and it is possible to market some of the products as they come out of an intermediate department or to process those products further in the next department and then sell them. In meat packing plants, for instance, there are many examples of products which can be sold at one stage of manufacture or processed further and sold in a different form.

The question on which the cost accountant can aid the management is whether the additional marginal balance arising after the extra processing justifies the extra processing. Assume that Product X can be processed further to yield Product Y. The cost of additional processing to obtain Product Y is justified if the selling price of Product Y will be greater than the selling price of Product X plus the cost of the extra processing. To illustrate[5]:

---

[4] *Ibid.*, pp. 1713-14.

[5] The formulas for marginal income for additional processing used in this section are quoted from William J. Vatter, "Tailor-Making Cost Data for Specific Uses," *N.A.C.A. Bulletin*, August, 1954, p. 1704.

Fixed manufacturing cost—Product X and Product Y	$ 4,000.00
Variable cost—Product X	2,000.00
Sales value—Product X	8,000.00
Variable cost—Product Y	1,000.00
Sales value—Product Y	14,000.00

The cost of additional processing to obtain Product Y is justified because the sales value of Product Y ($14,000) is greater than the sales value of Product X ($8,000) plus the cost of extra processing of Product Y ($1,000) by $5,000.

The same result is obtained if, instead of making marginal cost and income calculations as above, total cost calculations are made:

Product X is produced and sold			Product X is processed further and sold as Product Y		
Sales—Product X		$8,000.00	Sales—Product Y		$14,000.00
Less—			Less—		
Fixed cost	$4,000.00		Fixed cost	$4,000.00	
Variable cost	2,000.00	6,000.00	Variable cost—X	2,000.00	
			Variable cost—Y	1,000.00	7,000.00
Profit—Product X		$2,000.00	Profit—Product Y		$ 7,000.00

Additional profit on further processing: $7,000 − $2,000 = $5,000

Make or buy parts. In many companies which manufacture an assembly product, the problem of whether to make or buy parts is an important one. In some companies, cost analysis for the solution of make-or-buy problems is a major activity:

A few large companies have fairly elaborate machinery for decision making. The General Electric Company has a "value analysis department" scrutinizing each part cost for full value, whether made or bought. The specialists in this department study designs and materials and methods of making. They measure outside costs against inside costs; they compare the cost of making the part in their different divisions; they bring together all pertinent information. At the International Business Machines Corporation, the tool engineering department examines available facilities and decides whether to make or buy, usually without conducting substantial cost studies outside the plant.[6]

Marginal costs may be useful in arriving at make-or-buy decisions. Assume that it is possible to buy parts ready for assembly. The price for such parts per product unit would be $.48 (plus the cost of materials, which Benson & West would cover). If the offer were accepted, the Benson & West Manufacturing Company cutting department would be eliminated, so far as Product A is concerned. (The cutting department would continue to handle Product B and Product C.) Should the offer be accepted?

[6] Carter C. Higgins, "Make-or-Buy Re-examined," *Harvard Business Review*, March-April, 1955, p. 111.

Benson & West present cost of parts for one unit of Product A is:

Direct cutting department labor................	$.375
Variable cutting department expense............	.13937
Fixed cutting department expense (.25 of $.19248).............................	.04812
Parts cost per unit of product................	$.56249

From an out-of-pocket cost standpoint, the Benson & West Manufacturing Company should accept the offer. The company is now paying $.51437 variable (out-of-pocket) cost to produce parts for Product A, and it would therefore save $.03437 per unit by having the parts made outside.

Suppose the parts were quoted at $.53 per product unit, which is less than Benson & West total parts cost per unit. The Benson & West Manufacturing Company should reject the offer. To accept it would increase the variable or out-of-pocket cost by $.53 minus $.51437 or $.01563 per product unit. The fixed expense would still have to be covered by Benson & West.

Note that the *fixed* cutting department expense of $.04812 per unit is not a factor in the decision. The fixed costs are a *sunk* cost.

It should be noted that there are obviously factors other than cost which must and will be considered by the management in making decisions on the problems outlined in this chapter. In cases of make or buy, Carter C. Higgins lists the following factors:

Reasons for Making

1. Cost studies indicate it is cheaper for you to make than to buy.
2. Making fits your know-how, your equipment, and your tradition.
3. Idle capacity is available to absorb overhead.
4. What you are considering is unusual or complex; direct supervision is needed to assure control.
5. Making will facilitate your control of parts changes, inventories, and deliveries.
6. The part is hard to transport.
7. The design of the part or its processing is confidential.
8. You do not wish to depend on a single outside source of supply.

Reasons for Buying

1. Cost studies indicate it is cheaper for you to buy than to make.
2. Space, equipment, time and/or skill are not available for you to develop the necessary production operations.
3. Because of small volume or because of other capital needs, the investment in making is not attractive.
4. You wish someone else to face seasonal, cyclical, or risky market demands.
5. The need for special techniques, or equipment, makes buying more logical. Your supplier will help you produce a better engineered end product.
6. You think it is best for your executives to concentrate on *your* specialty.
7. You want to check on your own operations.
8. Patents or customer-supplier relationships favor going outside.[7]

[7] *Ibid.*, pp. 118-19.

EQUIPMENT REPLACEMENT

"Accounting" cost study; Economy study. The problem of equipment in manufacturing concerns is a more or less constant one, and decision by the management frequently requires economy studies to show whether investment in proposed new equipment is justified. This section of the chapter presents an assumed situation, first, in the form of an "accounting" cost study to show how the data would appear in conventional cost accounting form and, second, in the form of an economy study. It will be noted that there are fundamental differences between the "accounting study" and the economy study.

The comparative cost study—"accounting" costs (pages 661–662) involves a comparison of the estimated cost of producing and assembling Product A by automatic machines costing $7,500 each with the present cost of bench assembly. It is based upon the original capacity of 6,000 product units per month, which was the approximate operating level of the department under bench assembly methods. It was set up on the account classification used to calculate factory expense rates (page 218).

It was estimated that a machine could turn out a product unit in .125 hours and that 750 machine hours would be required to produce 6,000 product units a month. It was decided to provide four machines which would have a theoretical one-shift capacity of 800 hours a month. Estimated down time of 50 hours for maintenance and repairs would leave a practical capacity of 750 hours, which would meet the output requirement. The machines require 2 operators, and consequently 1,500 man hours would be needed.

The comparative cost summary is supported by the following schedules:

  Figure 27-2a Indirect Labor and Related Accounts
  Figure 27-2b Supplies and Services
  Figure 27-2c Fixed Charges (Except Labor)

In setting up the comparison, it is assumed that the entire production of 6,000 units per month will be done by hand or by machine, and not partly by hand and partly by machine. The entire floor space of the assembly department is charged to Hand Assembly in the one case and to Machine Production in the other case, although machines would not require all the floor space. It is assumed that no profitable alternative for the use of the excess space is available. In this "accounting" study, depreciation on the old machinery and equipment is calculated on cost, and it is assumed that the old machinery and equipment has a life of ten years.

The change in method from hand to machine involves a decrease in direct labor and increases in such machine costs as power, repairs, and depreciation, insurance, and taxes. In machine production, a full-time set-up man to adjust the machines is included.

("Accounting" Costs)
Comparative Costs—Bench Production and Machine Production
Direct Labor and Factory Expense

One-Month Period—6,000 Units Product A

	Accounts	Reference: Figure	Benches	Automatic Machine	Increase or Decrease*
510	Indirect labor..................	27-2a	$ 968.00	$1,368.00	$ 400.00
530	Payroll taxes and workmen's insurance................	27-2a	346.76	113.46	233.30*
540	Supplies and indirect materials.....	27-2b	330.00	545.00	215.00
560	Purchased service..............	27-2b	30.00	450.00	420.00
580	Unclassified....................	27-2b	115.80	115.80	
590	Fixed charges (except labor).......	27-2c	675.65	1,369.00	693.35
500	Total factory expense............		$ 2,466.21	$3,961.26	$1,495.05
	Direct labor...................	27-2a	8,320.00	1,875.00	6,445.00*
	Total direct labor and factory expense (6,000 units Product A)........		$10,786.21	$5,836.26	$4,949.95*
	Direct labor and factory expense per product unit.................		$ 1.80	$ .97	$ .83*

Figure 27-2

("Accounting" Costs)
Comparative Costs—Bench Production and Machine Production
Indirect Labor and Related Accounts

One-Month Period

		Particulars	Benches	Automatic Machine	Increase or Decrease*
		Labor statistics (basis: 6,000 units Product A)			
		Normal machine hours.................		750	
		Normal labor hours...................	6,000	1,500	
(a)		Normal labor dollars.................	$8,320.00	$1,875.00	$6,445.00*
		Indirect labor			
	511	Foreman—Assembly..............	$ 500.00	$ 500.00	
	513	Shop porter—Moving materials.......	150.00	150.00	
	514	Factory storekeeper and clerical......	150.00	150.00	
	515	Other indirect labor................	168.00	168.00	
	516	Set up man.......................		400.00	$ 400.00
(b)	510	Total indirect labor................	$ 968.00	$1,368.00	$ 400.00
(c)		Total labor (a&b).......................	$9,288.00	$3,243.00	$6,045.00*
		Payroll taxes and workmen's insurance			
	531	F.I.C.A. tax (2% of total labor—line [c]).......	$ 185.76	$ 64.86	$ 120.90*
	532	Workmen's insurance (various rates)..	161.00	48.60	112.40*
	530	Total payroll taxes and workmen's insurance.....................	$ 346.76	$ 113.46	$ 233.30*

Figure 27-2a

The comparative cost summary shows that the cost to produce 6,000 units of Product A by automatic machine would be $.97, whereas the cost to produce them by the present hand method is $1.80.

("Accounting" Costs)
Comparative Costs—Bench Production and Machine Production
Supplies and Services

One-Month Period

Particulars	Benches	Automatic Machines	Increase
Kilowatt hour statistics (light and power).......	750	11,250	
Supplies and services accounts			
540 Supplies and indirect materials			
541 Factory operating supplies (estimate)	$ 20.00	$ 20.00	
542 Indirect materials (estimate).......	300.00	300.00	
543 Repairs and repair parts (estimate)	10.00	225.00	$215.00
540 Total supplies and indirect materials	$330.00	$545.00	$215.00
560 Purchased services			
561 Heat, light, and power			
(@ $.04 per kw. hr.)............	$ 30.00	$450.00	$420.00
580 Unclassified (basis: average per month last year).............................	$115.80	$115.80	

Figure 27-2b

("Accounting" Costs)
Comparative Costs—Bench Production and Machine Production
Fixed Charges—Manufacturing (except Labor)

One-Month Period

Particulars	Benches	Automatic Machines	Increase
Plant statistics			
Floor space—square feet..................	6,290	6,290	
Value of machinery and equipment.........	$2,000.00	$30,000.00	
Fixed charges (except labor) accounts			
591 Depreciation—Machinery and equipment	$ 16.66	$ 250.00	$233.34
592 Insurance—Machinery and equipment..	13.33	240.00	226.67
593 Taxes—Machinery and equipment......	16.66	250.00	233.34
599 Rent on building (@ $.10 per square foot)	629.00	629.00	
590 Total fixed charges (except labor)......	$ 675.65	$ 1,369.00	$693.35

Figure 27-2c

Note that it is possible to arrive at the same result as the one shown in Figure 27-2 by considering the effect of only the cost items which would be different under the proposed change in method. Under this plan of calculation, the "no-change" items (certain indirect labor, supplies, indirect materials, and floor space) would not be listed. The *changes* in the other items would be listed. The effect would appear as indicated in the "Increase or Decrease" columns of Figure 27-2, which shows a total saving of $4,949.95, or $.83 per product unit, for the machine method over the bench method.

The "accounting" cost shown in Figure 27-2 would be the basis for some of the uses of cost accounting. For instance, if the entire 6,000 units were made by bench methods, the cost basis for inventory value would be $1.80 per unit. On the other hand, if the entire 6,000 units were made by automatic machine, the cost basis would be $.97 per unit.

For the decision on whether to *replace* benches with automatic equipment, however, the "accounting" costs shown in Figure 27-2 would have to be adjusted. The management would be interested in the cash picture over the remaining life of the assets with reference to the alternatives of (a) keeping the benches or (b) disposing of them and buying automatic equipment. For the purposes of this decision, the benches would be valued at *current* or trade-in value (which we will assume is $1,000). The remaining life of the benches and the estimated life of the automatic machines are each assumed to be 10 years.

A comparison on the basis of "economic" costs is shown in Figure 27-3.

("Economic" Costs)

**Comparative Costs—Bench Production and Machine Production
Annual Costs (Ten-Year Life)**

	(a) Benches	(b) Automatic Equipment	(c) Increase or Decrease*
1. Total direct labor and factory expense..	$ 10,786.21	$ 5,836.26	
2. Less, Book depreciation.............	16.66	250.00	
3. Operating costs (cash outlays)........	$ 10,769.55	$ 5,586.26	
4. Add, Cash cost of equipment........	†8.33+	250.00	
5. Total cost—one month.............	$ 10,777.88	$ 5,836.26	$ 4,941.62*
6. Direct labor and factory expense per unit.........................	1.79	.97	.82*
7. Annual operating costs (cash outlays) (Line 3 × 12)...................	$129,234.60	$67,035.12	
8. Total annual cost (Line 5 × 12)...................	129,334.60	70,035.12	
9. Annual saving using new equipment (8a-8b).......................			59,229.48*

† Current value = $1,000; estimate life 10 years

Figure 27-3

Lines 1-7 are a re-casting of the results shown in Figure 27-2 with adjustment for the cash investment in equipment. Book depreciation is deducted on line 2 and cash cost allocated (based upon current value) is shown on line 4. In this case, the advantage of trading in the benches is slightly less than would appear from the accounting costs. This is because the trade-in value of the benches is less than the book value. The net investment in new equipment is greater in Figure 27-3 than it is in Figure 27-2. Regarding this valuation, Leland says:

> The current value of the old equipment is used, not the book value. The latter is likely to be higher by the difference between actual and book depreciation in past years. It is a sunk cost which has lost significance in an economy study except as it is a factor in a tax saving. The accounting loss arising from the write-off of existing book value of the old asset, after credit for sales proceeds or scrap, is a factor for consideration along with the economy study. It is not a part of the economy study.[8]

Pay-back period. On the basis of saving in production cost, how long will it take the new equipment to pay for itself? A formula is:

$$\text{Pay-back period} = \frac{\text{Cost of new equipment} - \text{Current value of old equipment}}{\left\{\begin{array}{l}\text{Operating cost present}\\ \text{method, excluding de-}\\ \text{preciation}\end{array}\right\} - \left\{\begin{array}{l}\text{Operating cost proposed}\\ \text{method, excluding de-}\\ \text{preciation}\end{array}\right\}}$$

Substituting values from Figure 27-3 and supporting schedules:

$$\frac{\$30,000 - \$1,000}{\$129,234.60 - \$67,035.12} = .46 + \text{years}$$

It should be noted that pay-back period indicates how soon the company may expect to get its money back, but it does not properly evaluate investments in replacements that may be expected to last longer than the pay-back period.

Return on investment. A calculation intended to evaluate the proposed change in terms of return on investment follows:

$$\% \text{ Return} = \frac{\left\{\begin{array}{l}\text{Operating cost—Old equip-}\\ \text{ment including depreciation}\\ \text{on current value}\end{array}\right\} - \left\{\begin{array}{l}\text{Operating cost—New}\\ \text{equipment including}\\ \text{depreciation on cost}\end{array}\right\}}{\text{Cost of new equipment} - \text{Current value of old equipment}}$$

This formula (or others serving the same purpose) may be used where pay-back period does not give a conclusive answer.

[8] T. W. Leland, "Economy Studies in Replacement Decisions," *N.A.C.A. Bulletin,* April, 1951, p. 936. The formulas for cash savings, and for pay-back period and return on investment in the following sections are quoted from the same bulletin.

COSTS FOR SPECIAL PURPOSES

665

QUESTIONS

27-1. (a) In general what is meant by marginal cost? average cost?

(b) In calculating marginal manufacturing cost, is it satisfactory to combine direct materials, direct labor, and variable factory expense cost per unit to arrive at marginal product cost per unit?

(c) Under what conditions might you calculate marginal costs per product unit for the sales department?

27-2. What is meant by "sunk cost"? What consideration is given sunk cost in connection with equipment replacement problems?

27-3. (a) What is meant by "pay-back periods"?

(b) What is meant by "percentage return on investment" in connection with capital equipment replacement?

EXERCISE

27-1. (1) The Lathrop Company is considering machine production in place of the present bench production of Product X. The blank forms in the Workbook provide all data needed for setting up a comparison of costs by the two methods. Required: To fill in all missing calculations on the blank forms.

(2) Assume that the Lathrop Company plans to buy machines and substitute machine production for bench production. Using your solution to Exercise 27-1(1), calculate (a) pay-back period and (b) percentage return on investment. Use the formulas in Chapter 27.

PROBLEMS

27-1. The Chicago Bakery Company manufactures cookies, using a band oven through which the cookies pass at a carefully regulated speed. Both the temperature of the oven and the speed of movement through the oven vary among types of cookie.

In the middle of the winter the company can obtain orders enough to operate the ovens to capacity, and can, to some extent, sell the products which it considers most profitable. In the summer demand is slack, and the company must trim selling prices, at least on certain items.

The treasurer maintains that the company should push the products with the greatest gross profit percentage in winter.

Required:

(1) Using the following information, state whether the treasurer's position is sound. Support your answer with complete calculations. Set up a comparative statement of profits showing gross profit and net profit for each product, and a statement of profit by any other method that would be useful.

(2) The treasurer also maintains that gross profit percentage is a suitable index to use in trimming selling prices in summer. He says that the products with the larger gross profit percentages can be cut, and the products with the lower gross profit cannot be cut. Do you agree? Explain, supporting your answers with calculations.

	Product A	Product B
Pounds per hour	1,000	2,000
Selling price per pound	$.30	$ .21
Variable manufacturing cost per pound	$.15	$ .12
Per cent variable selling cost to sales	10%	10%
Fixed manufacturing cost per month (200 oven hours)		$10,000.00
Fixed selling cost per month		$ 5,000.00

Inventories may be ignored in this problem.

27-2. The Verner Company manufactures a product which is processed first in department A and then in department B. The output of department A is salable as it comes from that department. The management has never sold the product in that form, however, preferring to process it through department B.

The manager asks you whether it would be more profitable to sell the product as it comes from department A, or to do the additional processing in department B.

The following information is available:

Variable cost	
Department A..........................	$ 6,000.00
Department B..........................	3,000.00
Fixed cost	
Department A..........................	3,000.00
Department B..........................	2,000.00
Sales value of production	
As it comes from Department A...........	12,000.00
As it comes from Department B...........	17,000.00

Required:

Write your answer, showing complete calculations.

27-3. Benson & West Manufacturing Company is considering buying a quantity of cut materials for Product D, ready for use in assembly department No. 2. The company has an offer of $3.90 per unit from a contractor. Considering the costs shown in Figure 27-1, should Benson & West accept the offer? Explain.

27-4. The Taylor Company is considering buying a machine to produce Product A. The company produces 8,000 units of product per month by bench methods, using 2,000 direct labor hours @ $1.50 per hour. With one machine, operating 200 hours a month, the company could produce the same number using 800 direct labor hours at the same wage rate. The machine would cost $25,000 and would have an estimated life of 10 years, with insignificant scrap value.

The present indirect labor force includes:

	Per Month
Foreman...........................	$400.00
Shop porter........................	$300.00
Factory storekeeper and clerical........	$300.00
Other indirect labor..................	$250.00

The machine method would require one set-up man (@ $300 per month) in addition to the present indirect labor force. F.I.C.A. tax is 2 per cent and workmen's insurance expense, ½ of 1 per cent.

The present method requires the following (estimated) supplies and services per month:

Factory operating supplies............	$ 80.00
Indirect materials....................	100.00
Repairs and repair parts..............	20.00
Heat, light, and power,	
1,000 kw. hrs. @ $.05..............	50.00
Unclassified.......................	120.00

The proposed machine method would require the same items except that repairs and repair parts would be $200, and heat, light, and power, 5,000 kw. hrs.

The department in which the product is produced occupies 3,000 square feet, and no space will be saved in changing methods. Rent is calculated at $.15 per square foot per month. The benches have a book value of $5,000 and a current value, if disposed of, of $4,000. The benches could be used for 10 years from this date with insignificant scrap value. Insurance and taxes are calculated at 2 per cent and 3 per cent, respectively, of current value of the present equipment and the same rate would apply to the new equipment.

Required:

Set up tables similar to those in Figure 27-2 to show comparative costs of producing Product A. In the summary, show total cost and unit cost for each method, together with increases and decreases.

27-5. Using appropriate information from your solution to Problem 27-4, set out a table showing the marginal costs and savings in machine production over bench production for 8,000 units of Product A, eliminating the "no change" items.

27-6. Using the appropriate information from your solution to Problem 27-4, calculate (a) pay-back period and (b) percentage return on investment. Use the formulas in Chapter 27.

COMPARATIVE COSTS: DISTRIBUTION

Organization of the sales department; Features of the distribution plan. The sales organization of the Benson & West Manufacturing Company consists of the sales manager, who exercises general supervision of the sales department; the assistant sales manager, who handles chain store company accounts; a house salesman, city salesmen, and traveling salesmen; and a sales department clerk, who keeps sales department records. The organization sells three lines of work garments—overalls, coats, and coveralls—and a line of slacks. The slacks are sold exclusively to chain store companies. The work garments are sold to wholesalers and retailers. Coveralls are sold to industrial customers who do not market them, but who supply them to their employees to wear at work. Retail store customers usually buy in smaller quantities than do the other classes of customers, and the prices quoted to retail customers are higher than the prices quoted to the other classes.

The company operates in three territories: the home territory, in which the factory, warehouse, and sales office are located; the eastern territory; and the western territory. Deliveries are made to customers in the home territory by company trucks. A small quantity of the product sold by house sale is accepted at the company warehouse by the customer. Deliveries are made to customers in the other territories by public transport. These deliveries are made F.O.B. the company warehouse.

All goods sold are packed for shipment in the shipping room, except for house sales taken by the customer.

In addition to direct selling by salesmen, the company also sells by direct mail promotion. Goods sold by direct mail promotion are priced at the retail customer selling prices.

Managerial information.[1] The sales manager of the Benson & West Manufacturing Company requires monthly statements on sales, costs, and margins for the following sales categories:

(1) Product lines
(2) Territories

[1] Appendix III is an annotated bibliography of many excellent articles on distribution costs.

(3) Classes of customer (channels of distribution)

(4) Method of sale

The sales manager desires to compare sales, costs, and margins of one product line with another, one territory with another, one channel of distribution with another, and one method of sale with another. Note that the sales manager has more options in his planning than the production manager has. In the factory, once the production lines are set up, it is not easy to change them. In the sales department, if one method of sale is not yielding satisfactory results, the sales manager can consider some other method. If one class of customer or one territory is not showing a satisfactory margin, he can consider switching attention to some other class of customer or territory. Within certain limits, he can do selective selling, applying attention, time, and cost where it will yield the greatest net margin. In any case, the management wants to know whether any product line, or territory, or class of customer, or method of sale is failing to carry its own direct costs.

Note that in the comparative statements, the sales manager compares the *net margin* of one product line or territory, or whatever, with another. Net margin may be described as sales of a category minus all costs (manufacturing and distribution) which can be allocated to the category on some reasonable basis. (Costs for which no reasonable basis of allocation can be found are put at the bottom of a report as "unallocated costs.") Note that the "net margins" shown on these statements are not strictly "marginal balances" as defined in Chapter 26. These statements show a portion of fixed factory and warehouse expense in cost of goods shipped (although they show all other fixed expenses as period costs).

It is useful for the sales manager to consider the factors which make up net margin because it is sometimes possible for him to take action in regard to selling prices and quantities (since different price lists are used for retail customers and for wholesale customers) and also costs. In regard to costs, he can *plan* the efforts to be expended, increasing or decreasing the budget or expected costs, and he can *control* the costs according to the plan, by comparing actual costs with the budget.

Periodic (regular) statements prepared in the four categories of sales and expense named above are illustrated and explained in the following pages. Other distribution cost statements, prepared on a nonperiodic basis are illustrated in Chapter 29.

Statement of profits by product lines; Direct, semidirect, and indirect costs. The management is interested in knowing the net margin by product line to get a clue as to whether the selling prices of various lines are high enough to cover manufacturing cost and direct selling cost, and to make a contribution to fixed charges and profit. Although all the statements listed in the previous section show the effect of selling price policy, this statement focuses attention particularly upon the product groups for which price lists are set up.

The statements related to product lines are:

Statement of Profits by Product Lines, page 671.[2]

Schedule of Sales and Cost of Goods Shipped by Product Lines, page 672.

Allocation of Direct Selling and Promotion Expense to Product Lines, page 673.

Allocation of Order Department and Cash Collecting Expense to Product Lines, page 674.

The Statement of Profits shows that dollar sales of slacks ($105,000) is nearly three times as great as dollar sales of work garments ($38,717); also that there is a net margin on slacks, after allocated expenses, of 25.32%, whereas there is a negative net margin on work garments. Sales of work garments do not carry their own allocated costs.

The total net margin for all products ($21,753.77) is large enough to cover the expenses not allocated to product lines $9,227.65 and leave a net profit on the combined business of $12,526.12.

Following is an explanation of the items charged against sales by product lines:

Factory cost of goods shipped is determined on Figure 28-1a as Quantity shipped × Standard factory cost per unit. Part of warehouse cost is allocated to product lines on the basis of units shipped and part on the basis of orders shipped. Warehouse and shipping cost is determined on Figure 28-1a as Quantity shipped × Unit product cost + Number of orders shipped × Warehouse cost per order. Note that the number of *orders* for slacks can be determined because slacks exclusively are sold to chain store companies.

Direct selling and promotion expense is allocated to product lines in Figure 28-1b. For allocation purposes, the object accounts are classified:

Direct charges to product lines: Those which can be identified with the product line at the point of use or accrual. *Examples:* salary of the assistant sales manager who spends full time on slacks; commissions of the salesmen who spend full time on work garments.

Semidirect charges: Those which cannot be identified with the product at the point of use or accrual, but which can be allocated to product lines on a period basis by some quantitative unit which expresses *use by,* or *benefit received by,* the product lines. *Examples:* sales office salaries, stationery and forms, and other supplies, allocated to product lines on the basis of orders. At the end of the month, a unit cost is computed for each semidirect expense account by the formula: Total cost for the period ÷ Allocation units for the month. Each product line is charged for the object as Units received × Unit cost.

Note that the unit costs for *allocating* selling and promotion expense to product lines may or may not be the same as the functional unit costs used for *controlling* expense (Chapter 22). In this case, they are not the same.

---

[2] All amounts in this and the following statements are fictitious, and they are not based upon any actual company's operating situation.

Statement of Profits, by Product Lines

Particulars	Totals		Work Garments		Slacks	
	Amount	% of Sales	Amount	% of Sales	Amount	% of Sales
Sales..................	$143,717.00	100.00	$38,717.00	100.00	$105,000.00	100.00
Less—Cost of goods shipped:						
Manufacturing............	$ 96,238.00	66.96	$22,738.00	58.73	$ 73,500.00	70.00
Warehousing and shipping..........	3,573.10	2.49	1,533.43	3.96	2,039.67	1.94
Totals..........	$ 99,811.10	69.45	$24,271.43	62.69	$ 75,539.67	71.94
Gross margin..........	$ 43,905.90	30.55	$14,445.57	37.31	$ 29,460.33	28.06
Less—Expenses allocated to product lines:						
Salesmen's salaries and commissions..........	$ 2,294.45	1.60	$ 1,594.45	4.12	$ 700.00	.67
Selling and promotion expense..........	13,695.50	9.53	12,723.50	32.86	972.00	.92
Order department and cash collecting expense	3,682.18	2.56	2,470.83	6.38	1,211.35	1.15
Delivery expense..........	2,480.00	1.72	2,480.00	6.41		
Totals..........	$ 22,152.13	15.41	$19,268.78	49.77	$ 2,883.35	2.74
Net margin..........	$ 21,753.77	15.14	$ 4,823.21*	12.46*	$ 26,576.98	25.32
Less—Expenses not allocated:						
Warehouse expense..........	$ 1,226.50	.85				
Selling and promotion expense..........	1,255.32	.88				
Order department and cash collecting expense	637.83	.44				
Delivery expense..........	885.34	.62				
Administrative expense..........	5,222.66	3.63				
Total..........	$ 9,227.65	6.42				
Net profit..........	$ 12,526.12	8.72				

* Credit.

Figure 28-1

Schedule of Sales and Cost of Goods Shipped, by Product Lines

Particulars	Work Garments				Slacks	Totals All Lines
	Overalls	Coats	Coveralls	Total		
Sales @ retail prices:						
Quantity	700	380	300		10,000	
Selling price per unit	$ 8.00	$ 9.20	$ 10.00		$ 10.50	
Totals	$5,600.00	$3,496.00	$ 3,000.00	$12,096.00	$105,000.00	$143,717.00
Sales @ wholesale prices:						
Quantity	1,020	1,010	1,590			
Selling price per unit	$ 6.40	$ 7.30	$ 8.00			
Totals	$6,528.00	$7,373.00	$12,720.00	26,621.00		
Total sales				$38,717.00	$105,000.00	$143,717.00
Less—Cost of goods shipped:						
Manufacturing—						
Quantity	1,720	1,390	1,890	5,000	10,000	15,000
Unit cost	$ 3.97	$ 4.62	$ 5.02	$	$ 7.35	$
Total cost	$6,828.40	$6,421.80	$ 9,487.80	$22,738.00	$ 73,500.00	$ 96,238.00
Warehousing and shipping—						
Warehousing and packing @ $.176766 per product unit				$ 883.83	$ 1,767.67	$ 2,651.50
Packing cases and clerical cost @ $.32 per order shipped:						
Orders				2,030	850	2,880
Amount				$ 649.60	$ 272.06	$ 921.60
Total warehousing and shipping				$ 1,533.43	$ 2,039.67	$ 3,573.10
Total cost of goods shipped				$24,271.43	$ 75,539.67	$ 99,811.10
Gross margin				$14,445.57	$ 29,460.33	$ 43,905.90

Figure 28-1a

672

Allocation of Direct Selling and Promotion Expenses
to Product Lines

Function	Total Amount	Direct or Semidirect	Description of Unit	Unit Costs for Allocation (Semidirect Expenses)		Work Garments		Slacks	
				Units	Amount per Unit	Units	Amount	Units	Amount
Salesmen's salaries and commissions:									
Salesmen's salaries	$ 700.00	direct			$		$		$700.00
Commissions	1,594.45	direct					1,594.45		
Totals	$ 2,294.45						$ 1,594.45		$700.00
Other direct and semidirect:									
Sales office salaries	$ 300.00	semidirect	Orders	3,000	.10	2,150	$ 215.00	850	$ 85.00
Stationery and forms	150.00	semidirect	Orders	3,000	.05	2,150	107.50	850	42.50
Other supplies	120.00	semidirect	Orders	3,000	.04	2,150	86.00	850	34.00
Telephone	480.00	direct					440.00		40.00
Catalogs	2,181.00	direct		3,635	.60	3,600	2,160.00	35	21.00
Direct mail pieces	2,000.00	direct					2,000.00		
Newspaper advertising	3,600.00	direct					3,600.00		
Sales training manuals	240.00	semidirect	Salesmen	12	20.00	11	220.00	1	20.00
Automobile variable expense	1,032.00	direct					960.00		72.00
Depreciation—Autos	275.00	direct					250.00		25.00
Insurance—Autos	91.67	direct					83.33		8.34
Travel—Autos	45.83	direct					41.67		4.16
Travel—Public transport	300.00	direct							300.00
Subsistence	1,800.00	direct					1,600.00		200.00
Entertainment	1,080.00	direct					960.00		120.00
Total other direct and semidirect	$13,695.50						$12,723.50		$972.00
Indirect:									
Sales manager's salary	$ 1,000.00								
Depreciation—									
Furniture	33.33								
Display fixtures	33.33								
Insurance—									
Furniture	8.33								
Display fixtures	8.33								
Taxes—									
Furniture	4.00								
Display fixtures	4.00								
Rent—Sales office	164.00								
Total indirect	$ 1,255.32								
Total function	$17,245.27								

Figure 28-1b

Note: Slacks are sold only to chain stores. The assistant sales manager handles chain stores. This accounts for the large number of direct costs against slacks.

Allocation of Order Department and Cash Collecting Expense, by Product Lines

Unit Costs for Allocation
(Semidirect Expenses)

Function	Total Amount	Description of Unit	Units	Amount per Unit	Work Garments		Slacks	
					Units	Amount	Units	Amount
Semidirect:								
Credit investigation—Prospective customer...	$ 584.00	Investigations	146	$4.00	145	$ 580.00	1	$ 4.00
Passing on orders for credit....	269.00	Charge orders	2,690	.10	1,840	184.00	850	85.00
Editing orders....	864.00	Orders shipped	2,880	.30	2,030	609.00	850	255.00
Typing shipping orders....	432.00	Orders shipped	2,880	.15	2,030	304.50	850	127.50
Order register and follow-up....	144.00	Orders shipped	2,880	.05	2,030	101.50	850	42.50
Invoicing:								
Headings....	414.40	Invoices	2,960	.14	2,020	282.80	940	131.60
Line items....	42.60	Line items	4,260	.01	3,320	33.20	940	9.40
Charging customers' accounts....	88.80	Invoices	2,960	.03	2,020	60.60	940	28.20
Customers' monthly statements....	95.10	Statements mailed	1,585	.06	1,550	93.00	35	2.10
Recording cash:								
Recording cash sales....	9.30	Cash orders	310	.03	310	9.30		
Crediting customers' accounts....	44.70	Receipts	1,490	.03	1,455	43.65	35	1.05
Bad debts provision....	694.28	½% of charge sales				169.28		525.00
Total semidirect....	$3,682.18					$2,470.83		$1,211.35
Indirect:								
Supervision and general....	$ 400.00							
Fixed charges on furniture and equipment....	183.33							
Rent....	54.50							
Total indirect....	$ 637.83							
Total function....	$4,320.01							

Figure 28-1c

For example, automobile variable expense is a *direct charge* to *product lines* (Figure 28-1b) because the salesman who uses the automobile specializes by product line. For expense control, however, automobile variable expense is reduced to a function-unit cost (a cost per mile).

Indirect expenses (as regards product lines) are expenses which cannot be identified with product lines at the point of use or accrual and furthermore cannot be allocated to product lines on a period basis on any reasonable basis. *Examples* in Figure 28-1b: sales manager's salary, depreciation, insurance, taxes, and rent of sales office. These expenses are shown in the total column at the bottom of the schedule. So that they will not be lost sight of, they are shown on the statement even though they cannot be allocated on any reasonable basis. Total net margin must cover the expenses not allocated if there is to be a profit.

Order department and cash collecting expense is allocated to product lines in Figure 28-1c. Note that in this department there are no expenses which are *direct* as regard product lines. In this case, all the functional unit costs used for the control of expense are also used for allocation of expense to product lines (Figure 28-1c). One additional allocation is made on this statement. Bad debts provision is allocated on the basis of sales.

The whole of delivery variable expense ($2,480.00) is a direct charge to work garments, since all slacks are shipped by public transport on large contracts.

In the above illustration of allocation of distribution costs to product lines, a significant part of the total cost is direct or semidirect cost of the two product lines. Salesmen specialize by product lines, and salesmen cost is therefore direct cost. Orders received call for one product line or the other exclusively, and therefore order department costs which can be allocated to the order are at the same time allocated to product classes.

The extent of direct charging of distribution costs to product lines varies considerably among cases. In some cases very little of the distribution cost except warehouse cost can be charged to the product. Selling, order department, and delivery cost are all joint costs of the whole product list. In any case, the validity of product costs depends upon the extent to which direct costing and semidirect costing *is* possible.

Statement of profits by territory. The management is interested in the net margin by territories statement because it aids in decisions regarding expansion of sales coverage geographically. It shows whether the gross margin of a territory is covering the direct and semidirect costs of the territory. In the case of a new territory, the statement aids in deciding whether to continue putting sales efforts into the territory, and if so, how much effort. In some companies, it also opens the way for review of the effect of territorial selling prices (where different selling prices are charged in different territories) and of the cost of transportation to territories (where the company pays it).

The statements relating to territories are:

Statement of Profits by Territories, page 677.

Schedule of Sales and Cost of Goods Shipped by Territories, pages 678-679.

Allocation of Direct Selling and Promotion Expense to Territories, page 680.

Allocation of Order Department and Cash Collecting Expense to Territories, page 681.

The statement of profits shows that the western territory is the most profitable. It produces over 50 per cent of the total net margin as against 11 per cent for the home territory and 36 per cent for the eastern territory. Also the direct cost of selling is a smaller per cent of sales in the western territory than it is in the other two territories (11 per cent in the western territory as against 25 per cent in the home territory and 13 per cent in the eastern territory). The gross margin percentage does not vary considerably among territories.

In regard to the allocation of distribution costs to territories:

(1) Warehouse and shipping department costs are allocated to territories on the basis of product units shipped (for certain functions) and orders shipped (for other functions). See Figure 28-2a.

(2) Selling and promotion costs provide the opportunity for a great deal of direct charging to territories, since each salesman operates entirely within one territory and since sales promotions are largely newspaper advertising and direct mail pieces, which are likewise identified with specific territories. Of the total selling and promotion cost of $17,245.27, over $12,000 is direct and semidirect cost of the territories. Only $1,255.32 is indirect (unallocated). The semidirect cost of approximately $4,000 is all allocated on bases which would seem to be reasonable for the object to which they apply (orders, catalogs, salesmen).

(3) Order department and cash collecting semidirect expense is allocated (Figure 28-2c) by means of the same functional cost units that are used for control (as illustrated on page 515). Over $3,600 of the total expense of $4,320.01 is so allocated. The remaining $637.83 is indirect (unallocated).

Statement of profits by class of customer. The term "class of customer" refers to the position of the customer as a distributor or user of the company's products. There are three classes of customers who distribute the company's products (retail store companies, wholesale companies, and chain store companies), and one class who uses it (industrial companies). Analysis of costs and profits by class of customer is likely to be revealing to the management because:

(1) Different selling prices may be offered to different classes of customers.

(2) Selling and promotion cost may vary considerably among classes of customers. There may be almost no sales promotion, as such, aimed at chain store company customers. In the case of industrial customers to whom technical products are sold, a great deal of specialized selling effort might be expended to answer the customer's questions and help him solve problems. It is sometimes necessary to know a great deal about the technical aspects of the customer's business.

Statement of Profits by Territories

Particulars	Totals Amount	% to Sales	Home Territory Amount	% to Sales	Eastern Territory Amount	% to Sales	Western Territory Amount	% to Sales
Sales	$143,717.00	100.00	$34,515.00	100.00	$46,096.00	100.00	$63,106.00	100.00
Less—Cost of goods manufactured and shipped:								
Manufacturing	$ 96,238.00	66.96	$22,513.60	65.23	$30,667.50	66.53	$43,056.90	68.23
Warehousing and shipping	3,573.10	2.49	868.10	2.51	1,147.00	2.49	1,558.00	2.47
Totals	$ 99,811.10	69.45	$23,381.70	67.74	$31,814.50	69.02	$44,614.90	70.70
Gross margin	$ 43,905.90	30.55	$11,133.30	32.26	$14,281.50	30.98	$18,491.10	29.30
Less—Expenses allocated to territories:								
Salesmen's salaries and commissions	$ 2,294.45	1.60	$ 815.75	2.36	$ 873.80	1.90	$ 604.90	.96
Selling and promotion expense	13,695.50	9.53	4,442.50	12.87	4,398.50	9.54	4,854.50	7.69
Order department and cash collecting expense	3,682.18	2.56	958.05	2.78	1,127.98	2.44	1,596.15	2.53
Delivery expense	2,480.00	1.72	2,480.00	7.19				
Totals	$ 22,152.13	15.41	$ 8,696.30	25.20	$ 6,400.28	13.88	$ 7,055.55	11.18
Net margin	$ 21,753.77	15.14	$ 2,437.00	7.06	$ 7,881.22	17.10	$11,435.55	18.12
Less—Expenses not allocated:								
Warehouse expense	$ 1,226.50	.85						
Selling and promotion expense	1,255.32	.88						
Order department and cash collecting expense	637.83	.44						
Delivery expense	885.34	.62						
Administrative expense	5,222.66	3.63						
Totals	$ 9,227.65	6.42						
Net profit	$ 12,526.12	8.72						

Figure 28-2

677

Schedule of Sales and Cost of Goods Shipped by Territories and Product Lines

Particulars	Home Territory					Eastern Territory				
	Overalls	Coats	Coveralls	Slacks	Totals	Overalls	Coats	Coveralls	Slacks	Totals
Sales @ retail prices:										
Quantity	140	190	240		570	400	100			500
Selling price per unit	$ 8.00	$ 9.20	$ 10.00	$	$	$ 8.00	$ 9.20	$	$	$
Total retail sales	$1,120.00	$1,748.00	$2,400.00	$	$ 5,268.00	$3,200.00	$ 920.00	$	$	$ 4,120.00
Sales @ wholesale prices:										
Quantity	260	310	540	2,000	3,110	510	440	500	3,000	4,450
Selling price per unit	$ 6.40	$ 7.30	$ 8.00	$ 10.50	$	$ 6.40	$ 7.30	$ 8.00	$ 10.50	$
Total wholesale sales	$1,664.00	$2,263.00	$4,320.00	$21,000.00	$29,247.00	$3,264.00	$3,212.00	$4,000.00	$31,500.00	$41,976.00
Total sales					$34,515.00					$46,096.00
Less—Cost of goods shipped:										
Manufacturing—										
Quantity	400	500	780	2,000	3,680	910	540	500	3,000	4,950
Unit cost	$ 3.97	$ 4.62	$ 5.02	$ 7.35	$	$ 3.97	$ 4.62	$ 5.02	$ 7.35	$
Total cost	$1,588.00	$2,310.00	$3,915.60	$14,700.00	$22,513.60	$3,612.70	$2,494.80	$2,510.00	$22,050.00	$30,667.50
Warehousing and shipping—										
Warehousing and packing @ $.176766 per product unit					$ 650.50					$ 875.00
Packing cases and clerical cost @ $.32 per order shipped—										
Orders					680					850
Amount					$ 217.60					$ 272.00
Total warehousing and shipping					$ 868.10					$ 1,147.00
Total cost of goods shipped					$23,381.70					$31,814.50
Gross margin					$11,133.30					$14,281.50

Figure 28-2a

678

Schedule of Sales and Cost of Goods Shipped by Territories and Product Lines

Particulars	Overalls	Coats	Coveralls	Slacks	Totals	Totals All Territories
			Western Territory			
Retail sales:						
Quantity	160	90	60		310	1,380
Selling price per unit	$ 8.00	$ 9.20	$ 10.00	$	$	$
Total retail sales	$1,280.00	$ 828.00	$ 600.00	$	$ 2,708.00	$ 12,096.00
Wholesale sales:						
Quantity	250	260	550	5,000	6,060	13,620
Selling price per unit	$ 6.40	$ 7.30	$ 8.00	$ 10.50	$	$
• Total wholesale sales	$1,600.00	$1,898.00	$4,400.00	$52,500.00	$60,398.00	$131,621.00
Total sales					$63,106.00	$143,717.00
Less—Cost of goods manufactured and shipped:						
Manufacturing—						
Quantity	410	350	610	5,000	6,370	
Unit cost	$ 3.97	$ 4.62	$ 5.02	$ 7.35	$	
Total cost	$1,627.70	$1,617.00	$3,062.20	$36,750.00	$43,056.90	$ 96,238.00
Warehousing and shipping—						
Warehousing and packing @ $.176766 per product unit					$ 1,126.00	$ 2,651.50
Packing cases and clerical cost @ $.32 per order shipped:						
Orders					1,350	2,880
Amount					$ 432.00	$ 921.60
Total warehousing and shipping					$ 1,558.00	$ 3,573.10
Total cost of goods shipped					$44,614.90	$ 99,811.10
Gross margin					$18,491.10	$ 43,905.90

Figure 28-2a (*Continued*)

679

Allocation of Direct Selling and Promotion Expense to Territories

Functions	Total Amount	Direct or Semidirect	Description of Unit	Unit Costs for Allocation (Semidirect Expenses) — Units	Amount per Unit	Home Territory — Units	Home Territory — Amount	Eastern Territory — Units	Eastern Territory — Amount	Western Territory — Units	Western Territory — Amount
Salesmen's salaries and commissions:											
Salesmen's salary	$ 700.00	direct					$ 140.00		$ 350.00		$ 210.00
Commissions	1,594.45	direct	Basis: sales of slacks (5% of sales, except slacks)				675.75		523.80		394.90
Totals	$ 2,294.45						$ 815.75		$ 873.80		$ 604.90
Other direct and semidirect expense:											
Sales office salaries	$ 300.00	semidirect	Orders	3,000	$ .10	800	$ 80.00	850	$ 85.00	1,350	$ 135.00
Stationery and forms	150.00	semidirect	Orders	3,000	.05	800	40.00	850	42.50	1,350	67.50
Other supplies	120.00	semidirect	Orders	3,000	.04	800	32.00	850	34.00	1,350	54.00
Telephone	480.00	direct					80.00		200.00		200.00
Catalogs	2,181.00	semidirect	Catalogs	3,635	.60	1,110	666.00	1,205	723.00	1,320	792.00
Direct mail pieces	2,000.00	direct					2,000.00				
Newspaper advertising	3,600.00	direct					1,000.00		1,200.00		1,400.00
Sales training manuals	240.00	semidirect	Salesmen	12	20.00	4	80.00	4	80.00	4	80.00
Automobile variable	1,032.00	direct					272.00		424.00		336.00
Depreciation—Autos	275.00	direct					75.00		100.00		100.00
Insurance—Autos	91.67	direct					25.00		33.34		33.33
Licenses and taxes—Autos	45.83	direct					12.50		16.66		16.67
Travel—Public transport	300.00	direct							100.00		200.00
Subsistence	1,800.00	direct					50.00		850.00		900.00
Entertainment	1,080.00	direct					30.00		510.00		540.00
Total direct and semidirect	$13,695.50						$4,442.50		$4,398.50		$4,854.50
Indirect:											
Sales manager's salary	$ 1,000.00										
Depreciation—											
Furniture	33.33										
Display fixtures	33.33										
Insurance—											
Furniture	8.33										
Display fixtures	8.33										
Taxes—											
Furniture	4.00										
Display fixtures	4.00										
Rent—Sales office	164.00										
Total indirect	$ 1,255.32										
Total function	$17,245.27										

Figure 28-2b

Allocation of Order Department and Cash Collecting Expense to Territories

Unit Costs for Allocation
(Semidirect Expense)

Function	Total Amount	Description of Unit	Units	Amount per Unit	Home Territory Units	Home Territory Amount	Eastern Territory Units	Eastern Territory Amount	Western Territory Units	Western Territory Amount
Semidirect:										
Credit investigation—Prospective customers....	$ 584.00	Investigations	146	$4.00	50	$200.00	50	$ 200.00	46	$ 184.00
Passing orders for credit.........	269.00	Charge orders	2,690	.10	690	69.00	750	75.00	1,250	125.00
Editing orders..........	864.00	Orders shipped	2,880	.30	680	204.00	850	255.00	1,350	405.00
Typing shipping orders.......	432.00	Orders shipped	2,880	.15	680	102.00	850	127.50	1,350	202.50
Order register and follow-up.....	144.00	Orders shipped	2,880	.05	680	34.00	850	42.50	1,350	67.50
Invoicing—										
Headings.........	414.40	Invoices	2,960	.14	760	106.40	850	119.00	1,350	189.00
Line items........	42.60	Line items	4,260	.01	1,170	11.70	1,300	13.00	1,790	17.90
Charging customers' accounts.....	88.80	Invoices	2,960	.03	760	22.80	850	25.50	1,350	40.50
Customers' monthly statements.....	95.10	Statements mailed	1,585	.06	480	28.80	505	30.30	600	36.00
Recording cash—										
Recording cash sales.......	9.30	Cash orders	310	.03	110	3.30	100	3.00	100	3.00
Crediting customers' accounts.....	44.70	Receipts	1,490	.03	440	13.20	490	14.70	560	16.80
Bad debts provision......	694.28	% of charge sales				162.85		222.48		308.95
Totals........	$3,682.18					$958.05		$1,127.98		$1,596.15
Indirect:										
Supervision and general.....	$ 400.00									
Fixed charges on furniture and equipment.....	183.33									
Rent........	54.50									
Total indirect......	$ 637.83									
Total function.......	$4,320.01									

Figure 28-2c

(3) Order department, warehousing, and delivery cost may likewise vary considerably among classes of customers. Orders from retail store customers may be numerous and small, whereas orders from wholesalers may be relatively few in number and relatively large in quantity of product. Orders from chain store companies are likely to be large, but they are likely to involve numerous drop shipments to the stores of the customer company. Finished goods warehousing may be done largely for the benefit of retail store customers, who expect immediate delivery on small orders. Delivery may also be provided largely or exclusively for certain classes of customers.

The statements related to classes of customer are:

Statement of Profits by Class of Customer, page 683.
Schedule of Sales and Cost of Goods Shipped by Class of Customer, and by Product Lines (not illustrated).
Allocation of Direct Selling and Promotion Expense to Class of Customer, page 684.
Allocation of Order Department and Cash Collecting Expense to Class of Customer, page 685.

The statement of profits shows that the larger part of the dollar sales volume and the larger part of the total net margin (97 per cent) comes from chain store company customers. Gross margin percentage varies considerably among classes of customer, partly because of the differing price lists. Gross margin percentage is 46 per cent for retail store customers, 33 per cent for wholesale customers, and 28 per cent for chain store company customers. The net margin for chain stores is highest (25 per cent) for all classes, due to the low service costs. Sales to industrial customers did not cover their direct costs, due to the high cost of selling.

The allocations of warehousing and shipping, direct selling and promotion (Figure 28-3a), and order department and cash collecting (Figure 28-3b) are similar in principle to those made in connection with the previous cost analyses in this chapter. Salesman costs (salary, commissions, subsistence, and travel) are direct costs because there is specialization by class of customer. On the other hand, newspaper advertising is indirect because it is expended upon all classes of customers jointly, and it is not considered feasible to allocate it among classes of customer. No satisfactory basis appears to be available.

The only order department and cash collecting cost which is direct is recording cash sales. This account is charged to retail store customers, since the only cash sales are made to customers in that class. Note the relatively small charge to chain stores for credit investigations of prospective customers. The reason is that the number of chain store customers is small (only 35).

Statement of profits by method of sale. The Benson & West

Statement of Profits by Class of Customer

Particulars	Totals Amount	% to Sales	Retail Stores Amount	% to Sales	Wholesalers Amount	% to Sales	Chain Stores Amount	% to Sales	Industrial Amount	% to Sales
Sales	$143,717.00	100.00	$12,096.00	100.00	$23,981.00	100.00	$105,000.00	100.00	$2,640.00	100.00
Less—Cost of goods manufactured and shipped:										
Manufacturing	$ 96,238.00	66.96	$ 6,040.60	49.94	$15,040.80	62.72	$ 73,500.00	70.00	$1,656.60	62.75
Warehousing and shipping	3,573.10	2.49	419.94	3.47	978.36	4.08	2,039.67	1.94	135.13	5.12
Totals	$ 99,811.10	69.45	$ 6,460.54	53.41	$16,019.16	66.80	$ 75,539.67	71.94	$1,791.73	67.87
Gross margin	$ 43,905.90	30.55	$ 5,635.46	46.59	$ 7,961.84	33.20	$ 29,460.33	28.06	$ 848.27	32.13
Less—Expenses allocated to classes of customers:										
Salesmen's salaries and commissions	$ 2,294.45	1.60	$ 263.40	2.18	$ 1,199.05	5.00	$ 700.00	.67	$ 132.00	5.00
Selling and promotion expense	8,095.50	5.63	717.30	5.93	4,945.60	20.62	914.50	.87	1,518.10	57.50
Order department and cash collecting expense	3,682.18	2.56	550.03	4.55	1,613.90	6.73	1,211.35	1.15	306.90	11.63
Delivery expense	2,480.00	1.73	2,480.00	20.50						
Totals	$ 16,552.13	11.52	$ 4,010.73	33.16	$ 7,758.55	32.35	$ 2,825.85	2.69	$1,957.00	74.13
Net margin	$ 27,353.77	19.03	$ 1,624.73	13.43	$ 203.29	.85	$ 26,634.48	25.37	$1,108.73*	42.00*
Less—Expenses not allocated:										
Warehouse expense	$ 1,226.50	.85								
Selling and promotion expense	6,855.32	4.77								
Order department and cash collecting expense	637.83	.44								
Delivery expense	885.34	.62								
Administrative expense	5,222.66	3.63								
Total	$ 14,827.65	10.31								
Net profit	$ 12,526.12	8.72								

Figure 28-3

Allocation of Direct Selling and Promotion Expense to Class of Customer

Function	Total Amount	Direct or Semidirect	Description of Unit	Units	Amount per Unit	Retail Customers Units	Retail Customers Amount	Wholesale Customers Units	Wholesale Customers Amount	Chain Stores Units	Chain Stores Amount	Industrial Units	Industrial Amount
					Unit Costs for Allocation (Semidirect Expense)								
Salesmen's salaries and commissions:													
Salesmen's salaries	$ 700.00	direct			$						$700.00		
Commissions	1,594.45	direct					263.40		1,199.05				$ 132.00
Totals	$ 2,294.45						$263.40		$1,199.05		$700.00		$ 132.00
Other direct and semidirect expense:													
Sales office salaries	$ 300.00	semidirect	Orders	3,000	.10	670	$ 67.00	1,240	$ 124.00	850	$ 85.00	240	$ 24.00
Stationery and forms	150.00	semidirect	Orders	3,000	.05	670	33.50	1,240	62.00	850	42.50	240	12.00
Other supplies	120.00	semidirect	Orders	3,000	.04	670	26.80	1,240	49.60	850	34.00	240	9.60
Telephone	480.00	direct*					30.00		290.00		40.00		120.00
Catalogs	2,181.00	semidirect	Catalogs	3,635	.60	900	540.00	2,200	1,320.00	35	21.00	500	300.00
Sales training manuals	240.00	semidirect	Salesmen	12	20.00	1	20.00	8	160.00			3	60.00
Automobile—Variable	1,032.00	direct							720.00		72.00		240.00
Depreciation—Autos	275.00	direct							200.00				75.00
Insurance—Autos	91.67	direct							66.67				25.00
Licenses and taxes—Autos	45.83	direct							33.33				12.50
Travel—Public transport	300.00	direct									300.00		
Subsistence	1,800.00	direct							1,200.00		200.00		400.00
Entertainment	1,080.00	direct							720.00		120.00		240.00
Total other direct and semidirect	$ 8,095.50						$ 717.30		$4,945.60		$914.50		$1,518.10
Indirect:													
Sales manager's salary	$ 1,000.00												
Direct mail advertising	2,000.00												
Newspaper advertising	3,600.00												
Depreciation—													
Furniture	33.33												
Display fixtures	33.33												
Insurance—													
Furniture	8.33												
Display fixtures	8.33												
Taxes—													
Furniture	4.00												
Display fixtures	4.00												
Rent—Sales office	164.00												
Total indirect	$ 6,855.32												
Total function	$17,245.27												

* Record kept by salesman placing the call. Salesmen specialize by class of customers.

Figure 28-3a

Allocation of Order Department and Cash Collecting Expense to Class of Customer

			Unit Costs for Allocation (Semidirect Expenses)			Retail Customers		Wholesale Customers		Chain Stores		Industrial	
Function	Total Amount	Direct (x)	Description of Unit	Units	Amount per Unit	Units	Amount	Units	Amount	Units	Amount	Units	Amount
Direct and semidirect:													
Credit investigation—													
Prospective customers.......	$ 584.00		Investigations	146	$4.00	25	$100.00	100	$ 400.00	1	$ 4.00	20	$ 80.00
Passing orders for credit...	269.00		Charge orders	2,690	.10	360	36.00	1,240	124.00	850	85.00	240	24.00
Editing orders........	864.00		Orders shipped	2,880	.30	550	165.00	1,240	372.00	850	255.00	240	72.00
Typing shipping orders.......	432.00		Orders shipped	2,880	.15	550	82.50	1,240	186.00	850	127.50	240	36.00
Order register and follow-up...	144.00		Orders shipped	2,880	.05	550	27.50	1,240	62.00	850	42.50	240	12.00
Invoicing—													
Headings...........	414.40		Invoices	2,960	.14	410	57.40	1,340	187.60	940	131.60	270	37.80
Line items.........	42.60		Line items	4,260	.01	480	4.80	2,500	25.00	940	9.40	340	3.40
Charging customers' accounts..	88.80		Invoices	2,960	.03	410	12.30	1,340	40.20	940	28.20	270	8.10
Customers' monthly statements	95.10		Statements mailed	1,585	.06	220	13.20	1,100	66.00	35	2.10	230	13.80
Recording cash—													
Recording cash sales........	9.30		Cash order			195	9.30						
Crediting customers' accounts	44.70		Receipts	1,490	.03	195	5.85	1,040	31.20	35	1.05	220	6.60
½% of charge sales..........	694.28		½% of charge sales	25,041		4,060	36.18	12,380	119.90	6,291	525.00	2,310	13.20
Total direct and semidirect	$3,682.18						$550.03		$1,613.90		$1,211.35		$306.90
Indirect:													
Supervision and general.......	$ 400.00												
Fixed charges on furniture and equipment......	183.33												
Rent..................	54.40												
Total indirect...........	$ 637.83												
Total function........	$4,320.01												

Figure 28-3b

685

Manufacturing Company sells by direct mail and by three classes of salesmen (house salesman, city salesmen, and traveling salesmen). There are differences in selling prices among the methods of sale. Selling prices of direct mail and house sales are higher than selling prices of goods sold by traveling salesmen.

The cost of selling by each method is of interest to the sales manager because it is possible to shift major emphasis to some extent from one method to another. The *nature* of the costs varies considerably among methods. For direct mail selling, there is no salesman's salary or commission, but there is a substantial direct mail advertising cost. For the various classes of salesmen selling, there are important differences in cost. The house salesman has a salary or commission cost; the city salesmen have salary or commission and automobile; and the traveling salesmen have salary or commission, automobile, and subsistence.

There are also cost differences among methods of sales in order department and cash collecting, and warehousing and shipping. Some of the orders that come in from direct mail promotions and the house salesman are cash orders and some are charge sales (which, of course, require accounts receivable bookkeeping). Some of the house sales are taken by the customer unpacked and others are packed and shipped to him, whereas all orders received through other methods of sale are packed and shipped.

The statements related to method of sale are:

Statement of Profits by Method of Sale, page 687.
Schedule of Sales and Cost of Goods Shipped by Method of Sale and by Product Lines (not illustrated).
Allocation of Direct Selling and Promotion Expense to Method of Sale, page 688.
Allocation of Order Department and Cash Collecting Expense to Method of Sale, page 689.

The statement of profits shows that 88 per cent of the total net margin comes from traveling salesmen. The percentage of net margin to sales for each method of sale is house salesman, 36 per cent; traveling salesmen, 19 per cent; city salesmen, 16 per cent; and direct mail promotions, 2.5 per cent. Direct mail selling made a poor showing in sales ($6,828) for the cost of the direct mail pieces ($2,000).

The principles upon which the allocations are made are the same as for the previous projects in this chapter. The following particular points may be noted:

On the statement of profits, Figure 28-4, the entire variable delivery expense of $3,365.34 is included in the Expenses Not Allocated group. Delivery expense does not apply to direct mail sales promotions or to sales by traveling salesmen. It should actually be borne by House Salesmen and City Salesmen (and the margin percentages reduced accordingly), but no basis for allocating the cost between the two methods of sale has been decided upon.

Statement of Profits by Method of Sale

Particulars	Totals Amount	% to Sales	Direct Mail Promotions Amount	% to Sales	House Salesmen Amount	% to Sales	City Salesmen Amount	% to Sales	Traveling Salesmen Amount	% to Sales
Sales	$143,717.00	100.00	$6,828.00	100.00	$5,268.00	100.00	$7,287.00	100.00	$124,334.00	100.00
Less—Cost of goods manufactured and shipped:										
Manufacturing	$ 96,238.00	66.96	$3,402.20	49.83	$2,638.40	50.09	$4,572.80	62.75	$ 85,624.60	68.87
Warehousing and shipping	3,573.10	2.49	271.18	3.97	148.76	2.82	280.60	3.85	2,872.56	2.31
Totals	$ 99,811.10	69.45	$3,673.38	53.80	$2,787.16	52.91	$4,853.40	66.60	$ 88,497.16	71.18
Gross margin	$ 43,905.90	30.55	$3,154.62	46.20	$2,480.84	47.09	$2,433.60	33.40	$ 35,836.84	28.82
Less—Expenses allocated to methods of sale:										
Salesmen's salaries and commissions	$ 2,294.45	1.60	$		$ 263.40	5.00	$ 364.35	5.00	$ 1,666.70	1.34
Selling and promotion expense	10,095.50	7.02	2,616.00	38.31	101.30	1.92	387.70	5.32	6,990.50	5.62
Order department and cash collecting expense	3,682.18	2.56	363.21	5.32	186.82	3.55	449.03	6.16	2,683.12	2.16
Totals	$ 16,072.13	11.18	$2,979.21	43.63	$ 551.52	10.47	$1,201.08	16.48	$ 11,340.32	9.12
Net margin	$ 27,833.77	19.37	$ 175.41	2.57	$1,929.32	36.62	$1,232.52	16.92	$ 24,496.52	19.70
Less—Expenses not allocated:										
Warehouse expense	$ 1,226.50	.85								
Selling and promotion expense	4,855.32	3.39								
Order department and cash collecting expense	637.83	.44								
Delivery expense	3,365.34	2.34								
Administrative expense	5,222.66	3.63								
Total	$ 15,307.65	10.65								
Net profit	$ 12,526.12	8.72								

Figure 28-4

Allocation of Direct Selling and Promotion Expense to Method of Sale

Function	Total Amount	Direct or Semidirect	Description of Unit	Units	Amount per Unit	Direct Mail Promotions Units	Amount	House Sales Units	Amount	City Salesmen Units	Amount	Traveling Salesmen Units	Amount
			Unit Costs for Allocation (Semidirect Expenses)										
Salesmen's salaries and commissions:													
Salesmen's salaries	$ 700.00	direct					$		$		$		$ 700.00
Commissions	1,594.45	direct							263.40		364.35		966.70
Totals	$ 2,294.45						$		$263.40		$364.35		$1,666.70
Other direct and semidirect expense:													
Sales office salaries	$ 300.00	semidirect	Orders	3,000	$ .10	400	$ 40.00	270	$ 27.00	330	$ 33.00	2,000	$ 200.00
Stationery and forms	150.00	semidirect	Orders	3,000	.05	400	20.00	270	13.50	330	16.50	2,000	100.00
Other supplies	120.00	semidirect	Orders	3,000	.04	400	16.00	270	10.80	330	13.20	2,000	80.00
Telephone	480.00	direct							30.00		50.00		400.00
Catalogs	2,181.00	direct	Catalogs mailed	3,635	.60	900	540.00					2,735	1,641.00
Direct mail pieces	2,000.00	direct					2,000.00						
Sales training manuals	240.00	semidirect	Salesmen	12	20.00			1	20.00	2	40.00	9	180.00
Automobile—Variable	1,032.00	direct									160.00		872.00
Depreciation—Autos	275.00	direct									50.00		225.00
Insurance—Autos	91.67	direct									16.67		75.00
Licenses and taxes—Autos	45.83	direct									8.33		37.50
Travel—Public transport	300.00	direct											300.00
Subsistence	1,800.00	direct											1,800.00
Entertainment	1,080.00	direct											1,080.00
Total direct and semidirect	$10,095.50						$2,616.00		$101.30		$387.70		$6,990.50
Indirect:													
Sales manager's salary	$ 1,000.00												
Newspaper advertising	3,600.00												
Depreciation—													
Furniture	33.33												
Display fixtures	33.33												
Insurance—													
Furniture	8.33												
Display fixtures	8.33												
Taxes—													
Furniture	4.00												
Display fixtures	4.00												
Rent—Sales office	164.00												
Total indirect	$ 4,855.32												
Total function	$17,245.27												

Figure 28-4a

Allocation of Order Department and Cash Collecting Expense to Method of Sale

Unit Costs for Allocation (Semidirect Expenses)

Function	Description of Unit	Total Amount	Units	Amount per Unit	Direct Mail Promotions Units	Amount	House Sales Units	Amount	City Salesmen Units	Amount	Traveling Salesmen Units	Amount
Semidirect:												
Credit investigation—Prospective customers	Investigations	$ 584.00	146	$4.00	15	$ 60.00	10	$ 40.00	30	120.00	91	$ 364.00
Passing orders for credit	Charge orders	269.00	2,690	.10	200	20.00	160	16.00	330	33.00	2,000	200.00
Editing orders	Orders shipped	864.00	2,880	.30	400	120.00	150	45.00	330	99.00	2,000	600.00
Typing shipping orders	Orders shipped	432.00	2,880	.15	400	60.00	150	22.50	330	49.50	2,000	300.00
Order register and follow-up	Orders shipped	144.00	2,880	.05	400	20.00	150	7.50	330	16.50	2,000	100.00
Invoicing—												
Headings	Invoices	414.40	2,960	.14	250	35.00	160	22.40	360	50.40	2,190	306.60
Line items	Line items	42.60	4,260	.01	300	3.00	180	1.80	700	7.00	3,080	30.80
Charging customers' accounts	Invoices	88.80	2,960	.03	250	7.50	160	4.80	360	10.80	2,190	65.70
Customers' monthly statements	Statements mailed	95.10	1,585	.06	140	8.40	80	4.80	300	18.00	1,065	63.90
Recording cash—												
Recording cash sales	Cash orders	9.30	310	.03	200	6.00	110	3.30	280	8.40	1,015	30.45
Crediting customers' accounts	Receipts on account	44.70	1,490	.03	125	3.75	70	2.10				
Bad debts provision	% of charge sales	694.28				19.56		16.62		36.43		621.67
Total semidirect		$3,682.18				$363.21		$186.82		$449.03		$2,683.12
Indirect:												
Supervision and general		$ 400.00										
Fixed charges on furniture and equipment		183.33										
Rent		54.50										
Total indirect		$ 637.83										
Total function		$4,320.01										

Figure 28-4b

In Figure 28-4a, direct mail pieces is a direct cost of Direct Mail Promotions and salaries and commissions are direct costs of selling by salesmen.

In Figure 28-4b, the office cost of handling cash orders is compiled in its own account to separate it from the very considerable cost of handling charge sales. Cost of handling cash sales is allocated to Direct Mail Promotions and House Sales on the basis of the number of cash orders.

Procedure: Analysis of sales and cost of sales. It would appear from a study of the statements in this chapter that a great amount of detail is necessary to get them together. Actually, the greater part of the clerical work is identified with the *analysis of sales*, which the sales manager would require in any event for its own usefulness. He should be provided with an analysis of sales and cost of sales by product, territory, by class of customer, and by method of sale, even though no distribution *cost* reports were to be provided. For a complete explanation of manual and machine methods of sales analysis, see the author's *Accounting Systems: Procedures and Methods* (Prentice-Hall).

Partially allocated costs and fully allocated costs. The statements in this chapter are all examples of partially allocated costs in that they reflect the thinking by the cost accountant that reasonable bases can be found for allocating only part of the distribution cost to the cost unit (product, territory, class of customer, or method of sale). Statements reflecting fully allocated costs are those on which *all* costs have been allocated. The inference is either that good bases of allocation were actually found for all costs, or that some of them were allocated on arbitrary bases. In some cases, it is considered necessary to allocate all costs, even if it means using certain arbitrary bases. A cost accountant will contend, for instance, that where costs are to be a factor in setting selling prices, it is necessary to "get everything into them." On the other hand, where costs are used for the measurement of performance or for short-run planning as discussed in this chapter, it is questionable whether any arbitrary bases should be used. It should be kept in mind that if the cost accountant cannot defend his bases, the users of the reports reflecting those losses are likely to lose confidence in the reports.

REVIEW QUESTIONS

28-1. The sales manager of the Benson & West Manufacturing Company receives monthly statements of sales, costs, and margins for the following sales categories:

(1) Product lines
(2) Territories
(3) Classes of customer (channel of distribution)
(4) Methods of sale

Give examples of product lines, classes of customer, methods of sale.

28-2. The monthly statements mentioned in Question 28-1 are all set up on the same format:

Sales
Less—Cost of goods sold
Gross margin
Less—Direct costs and semidirect costs (itemized)
Net margin
Less—Indirect costs
Net profit

(a) Define direct cost, semidirect cost, and indirect cost.
(b) Would the same costs be direct under each of the four categories or projects named in Question 28-1? Explain and illustrate.

28-3. With reference to the statements mentioned in Question 28-1, what do you think is meant by the "contribution theory"?

28-4. What is meant by fully allocated costs? partially allocated costs?

28-5. What is meant by selective selling? Explain the general usefulness of the statements listed in Question 28-1 in respect to selective selling.

28-6. What is meant by the term "comparative costs" in connection with the statements listed in Question 28-1? Why are comparative costs useful to the sales manager?

DISCUSSION QUESTIONS

28-7. Discuss the operating conditions which might cause differences in (a) gross margin and (b) net margin among product lines. Assume that there has been a significant change in margins. What do you think might have caused it?

28-8. Discuss the operating conditions which would cause differences in gross margin and net margin among territories.

28-9. Discuss the operating conditions which might cause differences in gross margin and net margin among classes of customer.

28-10. Discuss the operating conditions which might cause differences in gross margin and net margin among methods of sale.

PROBLEMS

Data for problems **28-1** to **28-3.** Analyses of actual distribution costs by object and function for the Charles Manufacturing Company for May, 19— appear on pages 692-694. The analyses by function include functional unit costs which are used for purposes of control.

28-1. Prepare Statement of Profits by Territory, setting up the statements as illustrated on pages 695-697. These illustrations include allocation data for this problem. Note that in some cases the structure of functional unit costs used for allocation is not the same as the structure used for control.

28-2. Prepare Statement of Profits by Class of Customer, per statements illustrated on pages 698-700.

28-3. Prepare Statement of Profits by Method of Sale, per statements illustrated on pages 701-703.

Data for problems **28-1** to **28-3** (*Continued*)

CHARLES MANUFACTURING COMPANY
Analysis of Actual Direct Selling and Promotional Expense
by Object and Function
for Month of May, 19___

By Object

Account	Amount
Payroll	
Supervisory salaries	$ 1,000.00
Salesman's salary	900.00
Salesmen's commissions	3,200.00
Sales office clerical salaries	300.00
Supplies	
Sales order and report forms	80.00
Sales training and advertising	
Sales training literature	104.00
Catalogs	460.00
Newspaper advertising	2,300.00
Direct mail pieces	240.00
Subsistence and travel	
Salesman's subsistence	2,750.00
Automobile expense—Variable	1,612.00
Travel—Public transport	600.00
Fixed charges	
Fixed charges on office equipment	80.00
Fixed charges on automobiles	330.00
Office rent	600.00
Total direct selling	$14,556.00

By Function

Controllable	Amount	Quantity	Amount per Unit	Description of Functional Units
			Functional Unit Costs for Control	
Direct selling compensation				
Salesman's salary	$ 900.00			
Salesmen's commissions	3,200.00			% to sales
Sales office clerical				
Sales office clerical salaries	300.00			
Sales order and report form	80.00			
Total	$ 380.00	1,900	$ .20	Orders booked
Sales training literature	104.00			Project basis
Catalogs	460.00			Project basis
Newspaper advertising	2,300.00			Project basis
Direct mail pieces	240.00			Project basis
Salesmen's subsistence	2,750.00	275	10.00	Days subsistence
Automobile expense—Variable	1,612.00	20,150	.08	Miles traveled
Travel—Public transport	600.00			
Total controllable	$12,546.00			
Capacity Cost				
Supervisory salaries	$ 1,000.00			
Fixed charges—				
Office equipment	80.00			
Automobiles	330.00			
Office rent	600.00			
Total capacity cost	$ 2,010.00			
Total direct selling	$14,556.00			

Data for problems 28-1 to 28-3 (*Continued*)

CHARLES MANUFACTURING COMPANY
Analysis of Actual Order Department and Cash Collecting Expense
by Object and Function
for Month of May, 19____

By Object

Account	Amount
Payroll	
Supervision.................	$ 400.00
Other.......................	1,861.80
Supplies and service	
Order forms.................	60.00
Billing forms...............	78.80
Office supplies.............	20.00
Postage.....................	75.60
Noncash charges	
Bad debts...................	400.00
Fixed charges on equipment..	90.00
Office rent.................	500.00
Total order department......	$3,486.20

By Function

Controllable	Amount	Quantity	Amount per Unit	Description of Functional Units
Passing orders for credit				
Labor....................	$ 285.00	1,900	$.15	Orders
Order editing				
Labor....................	380.00	1,900	.20	Orders
Order writing				
Labor....................	300.00			
Order forms..............	60.00			
Office supplies..........	20.00			
Total....................	$ 380.00	1,900	.20	Orders
Order register and follow-up				
Labor....................	$ 285.00	1,900	.15	Orders
Invoicing				
Labor....................	400.00			
Billing forms...........	78.80			
Postage.................	75.60			
Total...................	$ 554.40	2,520	.22	Invoices
Charging accounts receivable				
Labor...................	$ 100.80	2,520	.04	Invoices
Receiving cash and crediting accounts receivable				
Labor...................	111.00	2,220	.05	Cash receipts (Credit manager's estimate)
Bad debts...............	400.00			
Total controllable expense.....	$2,496.20			

Capacity Cost

	Amount
Supervisory salary.........	$ 400.00
Fixed charges on equipment.	90.00
Office rent................	500.00
Total capacity cost........	$ 990.00
Total order department.....	$3,486.20

Data for problems **28-1** to **28-3** (*Concluded*)

CHARLES MANUFACTURING COMPANY
Analysis of Actual Delivery Expense
by Object and Function
for Month of May, 19___

By Object

Account	Amount
Payroll	
Supervisory	$ 400.00
Other	1,680.00
Supplies	
Gas and oil	96.00
Repair parts	20.00
Purchased services	
Repair service—Outside	20.00
Fixed charges	
Fixed charges on trucks	165.00
Fixed charges on garage	40.00
Total delivery expense	$2,421.00

By Function

Controllable	Amount	Functional Unit Costs for Control		
		Quantity	Amount per Unit	Description of Functional Units
Loading and unloading				
Labor	$ 400.00	200	$2.00	Labor hours
Truck operation				
Labor	1,200.00	600	2.00	Labor hours
Gas and oil	96.00	1,200	.08	Miles
Truck repairs				
Labor	80.00			
Repair parts	20.00			
Repair service—Outside	20.00			
Total	$ 120.00	1,200	.10	Miles
Total controllable	$1,816.00			

Capacity Cost

Supervisory labor	$ 400.00
Fixed charges	
Trucks	165.00
Garage	40.00
Total capacity cost	$ 605.00
Total delivery expense	$2,421.00

28-1 *(Continued)*

CHARLES MANUFACTURING COMPANY
Statement of Profits by Territory

Month of May, 19—

Particulars	Total	Home Territory	Eastern Territory	Western Territory
Sales...........................	$80,000.00	$32,000.00	$24,000.00	$24,000.00
Less—Cost of goods shipped				
Manufacturing.................	$40,000.00	$16,000.00	$12,000.00	$12,000.00
Warehousing and shipping.......	10,000.00	4,000.00	3,000.00	3,000.00
Totals....................	$50,000.00	$20,000.00	$15,000.00	$15,000.00
Gross margin...................	$30,000.00	$12,000.00	$ 9,000.00	$ 9,000.00
Less—Expenses allocated to territories				
Salesmen's salaries and commissions.......................	$	$	$	$
Selling and promotion expense...				
Order department and cash collecting.....................				
Delivery expense..............				
Totals....................	$	$	$	$
Net margin.....................	$	$	$	$
Less—Expenses not allocated				
Selling and promotion expense...	$			
Order department and cash collecting.....................				
Administrative expense........	2,400.00			
Total....................	$			
Net profit......................	$			

Note: Charge total delivery expense to Home Territory.

28-1 (*Continued*)

CHARLES MANUFACTURING COMPANY
Allocations of Actual Direct Selling and Promotion Costs to Territories
Month of May, 19___

Functions	Total Amount	Direct or Semidirect	Unit Costs for Allocation (Semidirect Expenses)			Home Territory		Eastern Territory		Western Territory	
			Description of Unit	Units	Amount per Unit	Units	Amount	Units	Amount	Units	Amount
Salesmen's salaries and commissions											
Salesmen's salaries	$ 900.00	Semidirect	Chain store customers	60	$15.00	20	$ 300.00	10	$ 150.00	30	$ 450.00
Commissions	3,200.00	Direct					1,280.00		960.00		960.00
Totals	$ 4,100.00						$1,580.00		$1,110.00		$1,410.00
Other direct and semidirect expenses											
Sales office clerical	$	Semidirect	Orders	1,900		650	$	530	$	720	$
Sales training literature		Semidirect	Salesmen	13		5		4		4	
Catalogs		Semidirect	Customers	1,150		430		320		400	
Newspaper advertising		Direct					800.00		600.00		900.00
Direct mail pieces		Semidirect	Pieces	2,000		800		400		800	
Salesman's subsistence		Semidirect	Days subsisted	275		75		110		90	
Automobile expense—Variable		Semidirect	Miles traveled	20,150		4,500		7,500		8,150	
Travel—Public transport		Semidirect	Salesman's estimate				100.00		200.00		300.00
Fixed charges—Autos		Direct	Traveling salesmen	11	30.00		90.00		120.00		120.00
Totals	$						$		$		$
Total direct and semidirect expenses	$						$		$		$
Indirect expense											
Supervisory salary	$										
Fixed charges—Office											
Office rent											
Total	$										
Total direct selling and promotion	$										

28-1 (*Concluded*)

CHARLES MANUFACTURING COMPANY
Allocation of Actual Order Department and Cash Collecting Expense to Territories
Month of May, 19___

Functions	Total Amount	Unit Costs for Allocation (Semidirect Expenses) Description of Unit	Units	Amount per Unit	Home Territory Units	Amount	Eastern Territory Units	Amount	Western Territory Units	Amount
Semidirect Expenses	$					$		$		$
Passing orders for credit..........		Orders	1,900		650		530		720	
Order editing....................		Orders	1,900		650		530		720	
Order writing....................		Orders	1,900		650		530		720	
Order register and follow-up.....		Orders	1,900		650		530		720	
Invoicing........................		Invoices	2,520		900		670		950	
Charging accounts receivable.....		Invoices	2,520		900		670		950	
Receiving cash and crediting accounts		Cash receipts	2,220		805		585		830	
Bad debts provision...............		Credit manager's estimate				160.00		120.00		120.00
Totals..................	$					$		$		$
Indirect expenses										
Supervisory salary................	$									
Fixed charges on equipment.......										
Office rent.......................										
Total........................	$									
Total order department and cash collecting	$									

697

CHARLES MANUFACTURING COMPANY
Statement of Profits by Class of Customer

Month of May, 19__

Particulars	Total	Retail Stores	Wholesale Companies	Chain Store Companies
Sales..........................	$80,000.00	$32,000.00	$28,000.00	$20,000.00
Less—Cost of goods shipped				
Manufacturing...............	$40,000.00	$16,000.00	$14,000.00	$10,000.00
Warehousing and shipping.......	10,000.00	4,000.00	3,500.00	2,500.00
Totals..................	$50,000.00	$20,000.00	$17,500.00	$12,500.00
Gross margin....................	$30,000.00	$12,000.00	$10,500.00	$ 7,500.00
Less—Expenses allocated to class of customers				
Salesmen's salaries and commissions.....................	$	$	$	$
Selling and promotion expense...				
Order department and cash collecting.....................				
Delivery expense..............				
Totals....................	$	$	$	$
Net margin....................	$	$	$	$
Less—Expenses not allocated				
Selling and promotion expense...	$			
Order department and cash collecting.....................				
Administrative expense........	2,400.00			
Total....................	$			
Net profit......................	$			

Note: Charge total delivery expense to Retail Stores.

CHARLES MANUFACTURING COMPANY

Allocation of Actual Direct Selling and Promotion Costs to Class of Customers

Month of May, 19___

Functions	Total Amount	Direct or Semidirect	Description of Unit	Unit Costs for Allocation (Semidirect Expenses) Units	Amount per Unit	Retail Stores Units	Retail Stores Amount	Wholesale Companies Units	Wholesale Companies Amount	Chain Store Companies Units	Chain Store Companies Amount
Salesmen's salaries and commissions											
Salesmen's salaries	$ 900.00	Direct					$1,280.00		$1,120.00		$ 900.00
Commissions	3,200.00	Direct									800.00
Total	$ 4,100.00						$1,280.00		$1,120.00		$1,700.00
Other direct and semidirect expenses											
Sales office clerical	$		Orders	1,900		1,750	$	90	$	60	$
Sales training literature			Salesmen	13		10		3			
Catalogs			Customers	1,150		1,050	240.00	65		35	
Direct mail pieces			Direct	275		200		75			
Salesmen's subsistence			Days subsisted	20,150		14,500		5,650			
Automobile expense—Variable			Miles								
Travel—Public transport			Salesman's estimate	11	$30.00	8	240.00	3	90.00		
Fixed charges—Autos			Traveling salesmen								
Totals	$						$		$		$
Total direct and semidirect expense	$						$		$		$
Indirect expense											
Newspaper advertising	$										
Supervisory salary											
Fixed charges—Office											
Office rent											
Total	$										
Total direct selling and promotion	$										

CHARLES MANUFACTURING COMPANY

Allocation of Actual Order Department and Cash Collecting Expense to Class of Customer

Month of May, 19___

Functions	Total Amount	Unit Costs for Allocation (Semidirect Expenses)			Retail Stores		Wholesale Companies		Chain Store Companies	
		Description of Unit	Units	Amount per Unit	Units	Amount	Units	Amount	Units	Amount
Semidirect expenses										
Passing orders for credit..........	$	Orders	1,900	$	1,750	$	90	$	60	$
Order editing.............		Orders	1,900		1,750		90		60	
Order writing.............		Orders	1,900		1,750		90		60	
Order register and follow-up......		Orders	1,900		1,750		90		60	
Invoicing.............		Invoices	2,520		2,200		130		190	
Charging account receivable.......		Invoices	2,520		2,200		130		190	
Receiving cash and crediting accounts		Cash receipts	2,220		2,050		110		60	
Bad debts provision.............		Credit manager's estimate				160.00		140.00		100.00
Totals........	$					$		$		$
Indirect expenses										
Supervisory salary............	$									
Fixed charges on equipment........										
Office rent............										
Total.......	$					$		$		$
Total order department and cash collecting............	$					$		$		$

28-3 (*Continued*)

CHARLES MANUFACTURING COMPANY
Statement of Profits by Method of Sale

Month of May, 19—

Particulars	Totals	Direct Mail	House Salesmen	Traveling Salesmen
Sales..........................	$80,000.00	$1,840.00	$6,000.00	$72,160.00
Less—Cost of goods shipped				
Manufacturing.................	$40,000.00	$ 920.00	$3,000.00	$36,080.00
Warehousing and shipping.......	10,000.00	230.00	750.00	9,020.00
Totals....................	$50,000.00	$1,150.00	$3,750.00	$45,100.00
Gross margin....................	$30,000.00	$ 690.00	$2,250.00	$27,060.00
Less—Expenses allocated to method of sale				
Salesmen's salaries and commissions........................	$	$	$	$
Selling and promotion expense...				
Order department and cash collecting.....................				
Totals....................	$	$	$	$
Net margin.....................	$	$	$	$
Less—Expenses not allocated				
Selling and promotion expense...	$			
Order department and cash collecting.....................				
Delivery expense..............				
Administrative expense.........	2,400.00			
Totals....................	$			
Net profit......................	$			

Note: Charge total delivery expense to Expenses Not Allocated.

CHARLES MANUFACTURING COMPANY
Allocation of Actual Direct Selling and Promotion Costs to Method of Sale
Month of May, 19__

Functions	Total Amount	Direct or Semidirect	Unit Costs for Allocation (Semidirect Expenses)			Direct Mail		House Salesmen		Traveling Salesmen	
			Description of Unit	Units	Amount per Unit	Units	Amount	Units	Amount	Units	Amount
Salesmen's salaries and commissions											
Salaries............	$ 900.00										$ 900.00
Commissions........	3,200.00				$		$		$240.00		2,960.00
Other direct and semidirect expense	4,100.00								$240.00		$3,860.00
Sales office clerical......		Semidirect	Orders	1,900		230	$	200		1,470	
Sales training literature.........		Semidirect	Salesmen	13				2		11	
Direct mail pieces........		Direct									2,750.00
Salesmen's subsistence......		Direct									1,612.00
Automobile expense—Variable....		Direct									600.00
Travel—Public transport......		Direct									330.00
Fixed charges—Autos.........		Direct									
Totals.........	$					$		$		$	
Total direct and semidirect expense	$					$		$		$	
Indirect expense											
Catalogs..........	$										
Newspaper advertising.......											
Supervisory salary.........											
Fixed charges—Office......											
Office rent........											
Total.........	$										
Total direct selling and promotion..	$										

28-3 (Concluded)

CHARLES MANUFACTURING COMPANY

Allocation of Actual Order Department and Cash Collecting Expense to Method of Sale

Month of May, 19____

Functions	Total Amount	Description of Unit	Unit Costs for Allocation (Semidirect Expenses) Units	Amount per Unit	Direct Mail Units	Amount	House Salesmen Units	Amount	Traveling Salesmen Units	Amount
Semidirect expenses	$			$		$		$		$
Passing orders for credit..........		Orders	1,900		230		200		1,470	
Order editing................		Orders	1,900		230		200		1,470	
Order writing...............		Orders	1,900		230		200		1,470	
Order register and follow-up......		Orders	1,900		230		200		1,470	
Invoicing..................		Invoices	2,520		230		300		1,990	
Charging accounts receivable......		Invoices	2,520		230		300		1,990	
Receiving cash and crediting accounts.....		Cash receipts	2,220		230		300		1,690	
Bad debts provision.............		Credit manager's estimate						30.00		370.00
Totals........	$					$		$		
Indirect expenses										
Supervisory salary.............	$									
Fixed charges on equipment.......										
Office rent.................										
Total............	$									
Total order department and cost collecting.....	$									

COMPARATIVE COSTS—DISTRIBUTION (CONCLUDED): SPECIAL ANALYSES

The analyses discussed in this chapter are an extension or subdivision of the analyses presented in Chapter 28, as indicated in the following tabulation:

CHAPTER 28 Costs by:	CHAPTER 29 Costs by:
Territory	City, salesman's route, delivery route.
Class of customer	Order, order by size; customer, customer by volume.
Method of sale	Individual salesman; individual direct mail project.
Product line	Individual product.

If the sales manager is receiving reports on sales and costs by territories, he may occasionally desire further analyses by city and salesman's routes. If he is receiving reports by class of customer (retail, wholesale, industrial, and so forth) he may desire information on what customers or what volume groups are profitable, and further what size of order is profitable. Along the line of methods of sale (by salesmen of various types, and by direct mail), he may want to know whether certain individual salesmen and mail order promotions are profitable. And finally he may desire, to supplement the product line analysis, an analysis of costs by individual products.

I. TERRITORY COST ANALYSES

Statement of net margin by city and salesmen's routes. All the sales in the eastern territory are made by salesmen. The principal cities are Aldora City, in which John Wilson spends full time, and Belmont City, in which Wells North spends full time. Four other cities, constituting what is called Route No. 1, are covered by George Anderson who travels the route once a month. A like number of cities, comprising Route No. 2, are canvassed monthly by Fred Shields.

The Statement of Net Margin by Cities and Salesmen's Routes (page 705) has been set up to show the extent to which the gross margin (sales less cost of sales including warehousing and shipping cost) for each city and route covers allocated distribution cost. Although the eastern territory as a whole is profitable (as shown by the Statement of Profits by Territory, page 677), the sales manager suspects that certain parts of the coverage are not as profitable as other parts. The Statement of Net Margin confirms this suspicion. It shows that the two main cities and Route No. 1 are relatively profitable, showing net margins of 20 per cent, 18 per cent, and 15 per cent of sales, respectively, but that Route No. 2 is relatively unprofitable (3 per cent of sales). Also the more profitable cities make up the larger part of the net margin for the whole territory. Aldora City, for instance, contributes almost half of the net margin of the territory. The sales manager would have to decide whether it is possible to make the routes more profitable, or whether the routes should be reconstructed or covered less frequently by salesmen, or whether they should be covered by direct mail promotion or otherwise and the salesmen shifted to more profitable areas.

Statement of Net Margin by Cities and Salesmen's Routes

Eastern Territory

Particulars	Totals Eastern Territory	Aldora City (Wilson, Salesman)	Belmont City (North, Salesman)	Route No. 1 (Anderson, Salesman)	Route No. 2 (Shields, Salesman)
Sales	$46,096.00	$18,438.40	$13,828.80	$9,219.20	$4,609.60
Less—Cost of sales (including warehousing)	31,814.50	12,725.80	9,544.35	6,362.90	3,181.45
Gross margin	$14,281.50	$ 5,712.60	$ 4,284.45	$2,856.30	$1,428.15
Less—Direct selling and promotion costs					
Salesmen's salaries and commission	$ 873.80	$ 409.52	$ 307.14	$ 104.76	$ 52.38
Selling and promotion expense	4,398.50	1,089.09	1,085.94	1,113.81	1,109.66
Total	$ 5,272.30	$ 1,498.61	$ 1,393.08	$1,218.57	$1,162.04
Trading margin	9,009.20	4,213.99	2,891.37	1,637.73	266.11
Less—Order department and cash collecting expense	1,127.98	427.24	337.99	228.55	134.20
Net margin	$ 7,881.22	$ 3,786.75	$ 2,553.38	$1,409.18	$ 131.91

Figure 29-1

To answer the questions as to what expenses are allocated to the cities and routes, two supporting schedules are presented with the Statement of Net Margin. They are:

Allocation of Direct Selling and Promotion Costs to Cities and Salesmen's Routes (page 706).
Allocation of Order Department and Cash Collecting Costs to Cities and Salesmen's Routes (page 707).

The former statement shows that a large part of the direct selling and promotion cost of the territory is chargeable directly to the cities and

Allocation of Direct Selling and Promotion Costs to Cities and Salesmen's Routes

Eastern Territory

Functions	Total Amounts for Eastern Territory	Direct or Semidirect	Unit Costs for Allocation (Semidirect Expenses)			Aldora City John Wilson, Salesman		Belmont City Wells North, Salesman		Route No. 1 George Anderson, Salesman		Route No. 2 Fred Shields, Salesman	
			Description of Unit	Units	Amount per Unit	Units	Amount	Units	Amount	Units	Amount	Units	Amount
Salesmen's salaries and commissions													
Salaries	$ 350.00	Direct					$ 200.00		$ 150.00		$		$
Commissions	523.80						209.52		157.14		104.76		52.38
Totals	$ 873.80						$ 409.52		$ 307.14		$ 104.76		$ 52.38
Other direct and semidirect expenses													
Sales office salaries	$ 85.00	Semidirect	Orders	850	$ .10	340	$ 34.00	255	$ 25.50	170	$ 17.00	85	$ 8.50
Stationery and forms	42.50	Semidirect	Orders	850	.05	340	17.00	255	12.75	170	8.50	85	4.25
Other supplies	34.00	Semidirect	Orders	850	.04	340	13.60	255	10.20	170	6.80	85	3.40
Telephone	200.00	Direct					40.00		30.00		60.00		70.00
Catalogs	723.00	Semidirect	Catalog	1,205	.60	485	291.00	360	216.00	240	144.00	120	72.00
Newspaper advertising	1,200.00	Direct					300.00		350.00		250.00		300.00
Sales training manuals	80.00	Semidirect	Salesmen	4	20.00	1	20.00	1	20.00	1	20.00	1	20.00
Automobile—Variable	424.00	Direct				700	56.00	800	64.00	2,000	160.00	1,800	144.00
Depreciation—Autos	100.00	Direct					25.00		25.00		25.00		25.00
Insurance—Autos	33.34	Direct					8.33		8.33		8.34		8.34
Licenses and taxes—Autos	16.66	Direct					4.16		4.16		4.17		4.17
Travel—Public transport	100.00	Direct											100.00
Subsistence	850.00	Direct				20	200.00	20	200.00	25	250.00	20	200.00
Entertainment	510.00	Direct					80.00		120.00		160.00		150.00
	$4,398.50						$1,089.09		$1,085.94		$1,113.81		$1,109.66

Figure 29-1a

706

Allocation of Order Department and Cash Collecting Costs to Cities and Salesmen's Routes

Eastern Territory

Functions	Amounts for Eastern Territory	Unit Costs for Allocation (Semidirect Expenses)			Aldora City John Wilson, Salesman		Belmont City Wells North, Salesman		Route No. 1 George Anderson Salesman		Route No. 2 Fred Shields, Salesman	
		Description of Unit	Units	Amount per Unit	Units	Amount	Units	Amount	Units	Amount	Units	Amount
Semidirect:												
Credit investigations—Prospective customers	$ 200.00	Investigations	50	$4.00	15	$ 60.00	15	$ 60.00	10	$ 40.00	10	$ 40.00
Passing orders for credit	75.00	Charge orders	750	.10	290	29.00	205	20.50	170	17.00	85	8.50
Editing orders	255.00	Orders shipped	850	.30	340	102.00	255	76.50	170	51.00	85	25.50
Typing shipping orders	127.50	Orders shipped	850	.15	340	51.00	255	38.25	170	25.50	85	12.75
Order register and follow-up	42.50	Orders shipped	850	.05	340	17.00	255	12.75	170	8.50	85	4.25
Invoicing—												
Headings	119.00	Invoices	850	.14	340	47.60	255	35.70	170	23.80	85	11.90
Line items	13.00	Line items	1,300	.01	525	5.25	400	4.00	250	2.50	125	1.25
Charging customers' accounts	25.50	Invoices	850	.03	340	10.20	255	7.65	170	5.10	85	2.55
Customers' monthly statements	30.30	Statements mailed	505	.06	165	9.90	160	9.60	120	7.20	60	3.60
Recording cash—												
Recording cash sales	3.00	Cash orders	100	.03	50	1.50	50	1.50				
Crediting customers' accounts	14.70	Receipts	490	.03	160	4.80	160	4.80	115	3.45	55	1.65
Bad debts provision	222.48	% of charge sales				88.99		66.74		44.50		22.25
	$1,127.98					$427.24		$337.99		$228.55		$134.20

Figure 29-1b

routes.   Since each salesman is identified with a city or a route, his entire compensation, travel, subsistence, and entertainment can be charged to his city or route.   Newspaper advertising can likewise be charged to the city or route.   Certain other (semidirect) expenses are allocated on the basis of orders, catalogs distributed, or salesmen.   On this statement, no headquarters capacity cost is allocated to cities.

The Allocation of Order Department and Cash Collecting Costs (page 707) shows that all the costs in this department (except capacity cost) are semidirect as regards cities and routes.   The same unit costs for allocation (orders, invoices, line items, statements, and so forth) are used on this schedule as were used to allocate costs to the territories.

Net margin on the cities in a salesman's route.   Where a salesman covers a route (instead of serving one city exclusively), it may be desirable to determine the net margin on each city in the route, as well as the trading margin for the entire route.   If one or more of the cities in a route do not cover their own costs, it may be possible to change the route to include other cities which can be expected to make the route more profitable.

A Statement of Sales, Cost of Sales, and Direct Selling and Promotion Costs by Cities for Salesman's Route No. 1 appears on page 709.   This statement is an analysis of the $1,637.73 trading margin for the route shown on the Statement of Margin by Cities and Routes, page 705.   It provides a column for each city in the route showing sales, cost of sales, gross margin, direct costs, and net margin of the city.   All the cities in the route except Falls City cover their own direct costs.   Falls City fails to cover its direct costs by $18.48.

Note that travel and subsistence within the city are charged to the city, but that intercity travel is not charged to the city.   Note that the salesman does not go to one city and return immediately to his base, thus permitting charging the city with the entire trip.   Instead, he travels from one city in the route to the next, finally completing the circle at the base from which he started.   Intercity travel and subsistence is accordingly a joint cost of all the cities in the route.   It is shown at the bottom of the statement.   In the case illustrated, 300 miles of travel were required to move from base to Calumet City, 150 miles from Calumet City to Dalton City, and so on; 150 miles of travel were required to get from Falls City back to the base.   The entire cost of intercity travel ($146) is deducted from net margin by cities in the Total Route column, along with certain other costs not allocated to individual cities.

Delivery route costs.   If a delivery truck route were set up to serve Route No. 1, the costs could be allocated in a manner similar to direct selling costs, illustrated in the previous section.   Each city would be charged with its own intracity truck costs.   Gas and oil would be charged on a per-mile basis, as would truck repairs.   Truck driver and helper would be charged on a per-hour basis.   Intercity costs would be charged to the

Sales, Cost of Sales, and Direct Selling and Promotion Costs, by Cities for Salesman's Route No. 1

George Anderson, Salesman

Functions	Total Route No. 1		Calumet City		Dalton City		Everett City		Falls City		To Base	
	Units	Amount	Units	Amount	Units	Amount	Units	Amount	Units	Amount	Units	Amount
Sales		$9,219.20		$3,687.68		$2,765.76		$1,843.84		$921.92		
Cost of sales (including warehousing)		6,362.90		2,545.16		1,908.87		1,232.58		676.29		
Gross margin, by cities		$2,856.30		$1,142.52		$ 856.89		$ 611.26		$245.63		
Costs allocated to cities:												
Commission		$ 104.76		$ 41.90		$ 31.43		$ 20.95		$ 10.48		
In city												
Travel (@ $.08 per mile)	800	64.00	240	19.20	200	16.00	160	12.80	200	16.00		
Subsistence (@ $10 per day)	20	200.00	6	60.00	5	50.00	4	40.00	5	50.00		
Newspaper advertising		250.00		50.00		40.00		70.00		90.00		
Entertainment		160.00		40.00		20.00		20.00		80.00		
Order costs (@ $.19 per order)	170	32.30	68	12.92	51	9.69	34	6.46	17	3.23		
Customer costs (@ $.60 per customer)	240	144.00	96	57.60	72	43.20	48	28.80	24	14.40		
Total allocated costs		$ 955.06		$ 281.62		$ 210.32		$ 199.01		$264.11		
Net margin, by cities		$1,901.24		$ 860.90		$ 646.57		$ 412.25		$ 18.48*		
Costs not allocated to cities:												
Intercity												
Travel (@ $.08 per mile)	1,200	$ 96.00	300	$ 24.00	150	$ 12.00	300	$ 24.00	300	$ 24.00	150	$12.00
Subsistence (@ $10 per day)	5	50.00	1	10.00	½	5.00	1	10.00	1½	15.00	1	10.00
Total		$ 146.00		$ 34.00		$ 17.00		$ 34.00		$ 39.00		$22.00
Telephone		60.00										
Sales training manual		20.00										
Depreciation—Auto		25.00										
Insurance—Auto		8.34										
License and tax—Auto		4.17										
Total cost not allocated		$ 263.51										
Trading margin for route		$1,637.73										

Figure 29-2

route, as would the fixed charges on the truck assuming that the truck was used exclusively on the one route.

Intraterritory warehouse costs. In all the previous illustrations it has been assumed that all goods are shipped out of the central warehouse located at the factory. If a warehouse were located in one of the territories, for the benefit of that territory, it would be charged with the cost of transporting goods from the factory to the territory. Functional unit costs would be computed for the territory warehouse as was done for the main warehouse, on the basis of say product units and orders, and these would be applied to shipments out of the territory warehouse.

II. CUSTOMER COST ANALYSES

Individual customers and customers classified by volume; Functional unit costs. As was indicated in the first section of this chapter, the *class of customer* costs illustrated in Chapter 28 may be analyzed further into costs for (a) individual customers and for customers classified by monthly volume and (b) individual orders and orders classified by size. Such analyses would likely be made on a test basis to determine what customers and customer volumes do cover their own direct costs and likewise what orders and sizes of orders cover their own direct costs.

The principles are the same as for the allocation of distribution costs to cities or salesmen's routes, illustrated above. Direct costs of the customers or orders are identified and charged to them. Semidirect costs are likewise identified and work units or allocation units selected for charging those costs to customers or orders. The remaining costs, the indirect costs, are allocated on some arbitrary basis or not allocated at all. In making allocations to customers, all the departments (selling, order department and cash collecting, warehouse, and delivery) may be represented among the direct and semidirect costs. In making the allocations to orders, sometimes only the *house* costs (order department and warehouse) are included, since they comprise the major direct and semidirect costs of orders.

The first tabulation, Figure 29-3, is an assembly of the functional unit costs for Order Department and Warehousing which are used to make the allocations to customers and orders. It was prepared from an analysis of Actual Order Department and Cash Collecting Costs by Function and an analysis of Actual Warehouse Costs by Function. This tabulation provides a column for each of four different types of order:

Cash "take" orders: The customer comes to the warehouse, is served by the house salesman, pays cash, and takes the goods with him.

Cash "send" orders: The customer comes to the warehouse or sends a mail order, pays cash, and instructs that the goods be sent to him.

Charge "take" orders: The customer comes to the warehouse, is served by the house salesman, takes the goods with him, and has the amount charged to his account.

Charge "send" orders: The customer (a) comes to the warehouse and is served by the house salesman or (b) sends in a mail order, or (c) is called on by a city salesman or a traveling salesman who sends the order in. The goods are shipped and billed the customer.

The tabulation was set up on the basis of a one product unit order representing the only sale to the customer during one month. Note that, as might be expected, a cash "take" order represents the least house cost ($.075 per order). As indicated in Figure 29-3, such order involves only the house operations of recording cash sales in Order Department and Cash Collecting, and putting goods into stock, order picking, and equipment maintenance, repairs, and operation in the warehouse. A charge "send,"

Functional Unit Costs for Allocation of Certain House Costs to Orders of Various Types

Department and Function	Cost Unit	Cash "Take"		Cash "Send"		Charge "Take"		Charge "Send"	
Order department and cash collecting									
Credit investigation— Prospective customers	Not allocated								
Passing orders for credit	Charge orders					(a)	.10	(a)	.10
Editing orders	Orders shipped			(a)	.30			(a)	.30
Typing shipping orders	Orders shipped			(a)	.15			(a)	.15
Order register and follow-up	Orders shipped			(a)	.05			(a)	.05
Invoicing—									
Headings	Invoices					*		(a)	.14
Line items	Line items					*		(b)	.01
Charging customers' accounts	Invoices					(a)	.03	(a)	.03
Customers' monthly statements	Statements					(c)	.06	(c)	.06
Recording cash sales	Cash orders	(a)	.03	(a)	.03				
Crediting customers' accounts	Receipts					(c)	.03	(c)	.03
Bad debts	Not allocated								
Warehousing									
Putting goods into stock	Product units	(d)	.015	(d)	.015	(d)	.015	(d)	.015
Order picking	Product units	(d)	.02	(d)	.02	(d)	.02	(d)	.02
Packing labor and expense	Product units packed			(d)	.05			(d)	.05
Packing cases	Packing case			(e)	.10			(e)	.10
Equipment maintenance, repairs, and operation	Product units packed	(d)	.01	(d)	.01	(d)	.01	(d)	.01
Shipping department clerical	Orders packed			(a)	.12			(a)	.12
Total house cost for a 1-product unit order			$.075		$.845		$.265		$1.185
Recap by cost unit									
Per order (assuming 1 invoice for each order)		(a)	.03	(a)	.65	(a)	.13	(a)	.89
Per line item								(b)	.01
Per customer month						(c)	.09	(c)	.09
Per product unit		(d)	.045	(d)	.095	(d)	.045	(d)	.095
Packing case				(e)	.10			(e)	.10

Credit investigations (not allocated to orders)
Bad debts (not allocated to orders)

* No invoices are typed for "Charge Takes." The customer's account is charged from the sales order written by the salesman.

Figure 29-3

as might likewise be expected, represents the greatest house cost ($1.185 per order). An order of this type involves all the operations of passing for credit, order writing and billing, accounts receivable, and cash collecting in Order Department and Cash Collecting, and of course all the operations in Warehouse and Shipping, including packing the product in a packing case. As Figure 29-3 shows, 15 operations in the two house departments are required to process a charge "send" order.

A Recap by Cost Unit section is included at the bottom of Figure 29-3. In this recap, all the "per order" costs are combined, all the "per product unit" costs, etc. By this recapping, the 15 functional unit costs shown in detail in the main table at the top of the figure are reduced to the following five functional unit costs:

Example:
Charge "send"

Per order...............	$.89
Per line item...........	.01
Per customer month.....	.09
Per product unit........	.095
Packing case...........	.10 (for a single product item)

Use of these recapped functional unit costs for allocation purposes saves clerical work.   It is obviously simpler to apply five unit costs to a customer or order than to apply the 15 detailed functional unit costs.

Illustrations: Individual customer; Customers classified by volume. An analysis of Distribution Costs and Margins for a particular customer (Fred Norton) appears on page 713.   This analysis is made of a particular customer's account to determine whether gross profit on the account covers the direct and semidirect costs of distribution.   The analysis covers a period of time (one month in this case).   Direct and semidirect costs of all departments (selling, order department and cash collecting, and delivery) are included.

The cost analysis illustrated is based upon the following quantitative data collected for each account:

Number of orders
Number of line items
Number of customer months
Number of product units
Packing cases used, and the actual cost of each

In the analysis illustrated, it is shown that gross profit on sales to Fred Norton did not cover the direct and semidirect costs of distribution.   The gross profit was $1.59, the total allocated distribution cost, $2.77, and the net margin, $1.18 (loss).   The company actually sustains an out-of-pocket loss of $1.18, which could have been avoided by not accepting the order.   It is possible that the sales manager might consider placing a higher limit on the size of order that will be accepted, or offer quantity

Distribution Costs and Margins, by Customer

Customer: Fred Norton   *Month:* January, 19___

Particulars	Quantity	Amount per Unit	Total Amount
Sales.....................................	3 dungarees	$4.50	$13.50
Factory cost............................		3.97	11.91
Gross profit.......................		$ .53	$ 1.59

Selling expense

Commission..........................	5%		.68
Sales office clerical....................	1 order	.35	.35

House costs

Cost Unit

Description	Quantity	Amount per Unit	
Order..............................	1	.89	.89
Line item............................	1	.01	.01
Customer month.....................	1	.09	.09
Product unit........................	3	.095	.28
Packing case........................	1	.10	:10
Credit investigation and bad debts provision			
Credit investigations..................			
Bad debts provision...................	½ of 1%		.07
Parcel post allowance..................			.30
Total allocated distribution cost.....			$ 2.77
Net margin...........................			$ 1.18*

* Loss.

Figure 29-4

discounts.   The purpose of the quantity discounts would be to encourage customers to buy such a volume of goods as would yield a net margin to the company.

Analysis of the costs of handling customers' accounts raises the question "What volume of sales to a customer is necessary to cover direct and semi-direct cost of distribution?"   An analysis of Distribution Costs and Margins, by Customer, for Certain Monthly Volumes appears on page 714. It shows margins and costs for 6 separate volumes: 5, 10, 15, 20, 25, and 30 units during one month.   It will be seen that the point where gross margin just covers direct and semidirect distribution costs is between 15 units and 20 units, say 17.   This analysis is based upon a single order per month.   It should be noted that if the customer sends in more than one order during the month, a larger total quantity than 17 units will be necessary to cover the increased handling costs.   Test analyses similar to the one illustrated could be made to show the effect upon costs of handling one, or two, or three orders during the month.

House costs for orders of various sizes.   An analysis of House Costs for Orders of Various Sizes appears on page 714.   (House cost is Order

Department and Warehouse Cost.) The analysis is based upon four assumed sizes of order (in terms of a particular product): 1 unit, 5 units, 10 units, and 20 units. Note that the cost per unit of product drops sharply as the number of product units increases:

1 unit...............	$1.185 per unit
5 units.............	.313 per unit
10 units.............	.209 per unit
20 units.............	.154 per unit

Distribution Costs and Margins, by Customers, for Certain Monthly Volumes

	Purchases per Month					
Particulars	5 Product Units	10 Product Units	15 Product Units	20 Product Units	25 Product Units	30 Product Units
Sales...................	$22.50	$45.00	$67.50	$90.00	$112.50	$135.00
Factory cost..........................	19.85	39.70	59.55	79.40	99.25	119.10
Gross margin (11.77% of sales)......	$ 2.65	$ 5.30	$ 7.95	$10.60	$ 13.25	$ 15.90
Selling expense						
Commission (5% of sales)..............	$ 1.125	$ 2.25	$ 3.375	$ 4.50	$ 5.63	$ 6.75
Sales office clerical (@ $.35 per order)....	.35	.35	.35	.35	.35	.35
House cost						
Per order (one order)...................	.89	.89	.89	.89	.89	.89
Per line item (one line item)...........	.01	.01	.01	.01	.01	.01
Per customer month (one customer month)	.09	.09	.09	.09	.09	.09
Per product unit (@ $.095 per unit).....	.475	.95	1.425	1.90	2.375	2.85
Packing case (actual)	.12	.15	.18	.20	.22	.25
Bad debts provision (½ of 1% of sales)....	.11	.225	.34	.45	.56	.675
Parcel post allowance (@ $.10 per unit)....	.50	1.00	1...0	2.00	2.50	3.00
Total allocated distribution cost.....	$ 3.67	$ 5.915	$ 8.16	$10.39	$ 12.625	$ 14.865
Net margin...........................	$ 1.02*	$ .615*	$ .21*	$ .21	$ .625	$ 1.035

* Loss.
Note: The above tabulation is based on one order per month. If the customer placed more than one order during the month, the monthly quantity required to show a positive net margin would be greater than the approximately 17 shown above.

Figure 29-5

House Costs for Orders of Various Sizes

(Basis: One "charge send" order of one line item from the customer during the month)

House Cost	1 Product Unit	5 Product Units	10 Product Units	20 Product Units
Per order (one order)...........	$ .89	$ .89	$ .89	$ .89
Per line item (one line item).....	.01	.01	.01	.01
Per customer month (one customer month)...............	.09	.09	.09	.09
Per product unit (@ $.095 per unit).....................	.095	.475	.95	1.90
Packing case (actual)..........	.10	.12	.15	.20
Total house cost..........	$1.185	$1.585	$2.09	$3.09
House cost per product unit	$1.185	$ .317	$ .209	$ .154

Figure 29-6

III. METHOD OF SALE ANALYSES

Analyses described. The Benson & West Manufacturing Company sells by direct mail promotion, by house salesman, by city salesman, and by traveling salesman. The Monthly Statement of Profits by Method of Sale (page 687) shows the net margin earned during the month by each method. It indicates that direct mail promotions for the month were less profitable than salesman promotion, and that city salesmen were less profitable than house salesmen or traveling salesmen.

Study of the Monthly Statement of Net Margin by Method of Sale would raise the question as to what individual direct mail promotions do not cover their own direct and semidirect costs, and likewise what salesmen do not cover their own direct and semidirect costs. Figure 29-7 is a statement of sales, gross margin, and direct salesman costs for two sales-

**Sales, Gross Margin, and Direct Salesmen Costs
by Salesman**

Period: Month of ____

Particulars	Anderson Amount	% to Sales	Shields Amount	% to Sales
Sales..........................	$9,219.20		$4,609.60	
Less—Cost of sales (including warehousing)...............	6,362.90		3,181.45	
Gross margin.............	$2,856.30	31%	$1,428.15	31%
Less—Direct salesman costs				
Commission..................	$ 104.76		$ 52.38	
Telephone..................	60.00		70.00	
Automobile—variable expense..	160.00		144.00	
Subsistence.................	250.00		200.00	
Entertainment..............	160.00		150.00	
Total..................	$ 734.76	8%	$ 616.38	13%
Net margin....................	$2,121.54	23%	$ 811.77	18%

Figure 29-7

men, selected for purposes of illustration. Note that Shields contributes slightly over ⅓ as much net margin ($811.77) as does Anderson ($2,121.54). Both salesmen cover their costs comfortably but Shields consumes a larger portion (13 per cent) of his sales for salesman costs than does Anderson (8 per cent). Note also that both salesmen sell equally profitable goods in terms of gross margin (31 per cent).

IV. PRODUCT COST ANALYSES

Analyses described; Difficulty of allocation. The Statement of Profits illustrated on page 671 is a statement by product *lines*. The two lines are work garments (including overalls, coats, and coveralls) and slacks. As far as slacks are concerned, the statement shows a product cost. It does not show the product costs for overalls or coats or coveralls. It would be desirable to obtain product costs for the three products in the work garment line, if it were feasible to do so. Such costs would be useful to the sales manager when he is setting up his price lists. Examination of the Statement of Profits by Product Lines shows, however, that probably only salesmen's commissions are direct selling costs of the products in the work garment line. Furthermore, it is doubtful whether any of the other costs could be set up as semidirect costs of products, with sound bases of allocation. The reason is that the work garment salesmen do not specialize by type of garment. Since a customer may buy any of the work garments, the salesman expends his efforts on the customer as a customer. He may spend as much effort on a product which a customer does not buy as on the ones which he does buy.

QUESTIONS

29-1. What special analyses might be prepared as a subdivision of territory costs? class of customer costs? method of sale costs? product line costs?

29-2. What is meant by the statement that the intercity cost of a salesman's route is a joint cost of the cities?

29-3. What might the sales manager do if a certain city in the middle of a route consistently fails to cover its direct costs?

29-4. What is meant by "house costs"? Why would house costs per order probably be different for the following: cash take orders, cash send orders, charge take orders, and charge send orders?

29-5. What might the sales manager do about small orders which do not cover their cost? Customers whose volume does not cover the cost of handling?

29-6. Why are costs by method of sale particularly important to the sales manager?

29-7. (a) What is meant by the statement that the validity of a distribution cost (territory, class of customer, method of sale, product line) depends upon the amount of direct charging which is possible?

(b) What is meant by a distribution according to customer characteristics? according to product characteristics?

(c) Why is it frequently impossible to get a good allocation of distribution costs to products?

PROBLEMS

29-1. Prepare a statement of net margin by cities and salesmen's routes for month of May, 19__, setting up the forms as illustrated on pages 718-720. These illustrations include allocation data for this problem.

29-2. Prepare a statement of sales, cost of sales, and direct selling and order department costs by cities for salesman's route No. 1 for May, 19—, setting up the form as illustrated on page 721.

29-3. Using the functional unit costs on page 720, set up a table of house costs for an order of 1 product unit, 5 product units, 10 product units, and 20 product units. Show total house cost and cost per product unit for each size order. Include bad debts.

Assume a sales value per product unit of $8 and the cost of a packing case for each order size as follows:

1 product unit..................	$.40
5 product units................	.45
10 product units...............	.60
20 product units...............	.80

Also assume one invoice for each order size.

29-4. Using the data on functional unit costs on page 720 and additional data given in this problem, set up a table of distribution costs and margins for customers having monthly volumes of 1, 2, 5, and 10 product units (in a single monthly order).

Assume a sales volume of $8 per unit, a factory cost of $4 per unit, sales commission of 4 per cent of sales, and sales office clerical cost of $.20 per order.

Packing cases and parcel post allowances:

	Packing Case	Parcel Post
1 product unit...............	$.45	$.40
2 product units..............	.60	.50
5 product units..............	.70	.60
10 product units.............	.80	.80

29-5. Set up an analysis of distribution costs and margins for customer William Brown for May, 19—, using the functional unit costs shown on page 720, and the following information:

Sales...............................	$80.00
Factory cost.........................	40.00
Commission (4% of sales value)	
Sales office clerical, 2 orders @.........	$ .20
Orders..............................	2
Invoices............................	2
Product units........................	10
Packing cases, 2 @...................	$ .70
Credit investigations.................	None
Bad debts provision, ½ of 1% of sales value	
Parcel post allowance, 2 @............	$ .50

Allocation of Direct Selling and Promotion Costs to Cities and Salesmen's Routes
Month of May, 19___

Function	Direct or Semidirect	Totals—Territory	Units for Allocation (Semidirect Expenses) Description of Unit	Units	Amount per Unit	Alameda (Jones, Salesman) Units	Amount	Borden City (Smith, Salesman) Units	Amount	Route No. 1 (Williams, Salesman) Units	Amount	Route No. 2 (Sills, Salesman) Units	Amount
Salesmen's commissions		$ 820.00					$210.00		$260.00		$200.00		$150.00
Selling and promotion expense													
Sales office clerical	Semidirect	$ 128.00	Orders	640		160		200		160		120	
Sales training literature	Semidirect	32.00	Salesmen	4		1		1		1		1	
Catalogs	Semidirect	160.00	Customers	400		100		120		100		80	
Newspaper advertising	Direct	900.00					500.00		400.00				
Salesmen's subsistence	Direct	900.00	(Days)	90	10.00	22	220.00	20	200.00	24	240.00	24	240.00
Automobile expense—Variable	Direct	652.00	(Miles)	8,150	.08	1,800	144.00	1,600	128.00	2,550	204.00	2,200	176.00
Automobile expense—Fixed	Direct	120.00					30.00		30.00		30.00		30.00
Totals		$2,892.00					$		$		$		$
Total direct and semidirect expense		$3,712.00					$		$		$		$

29-1 (*Concluded*)

Allocation of Order Department and Cash Collecting Costs to Cities and Salesmen's Routes
Month of May, 19__

Function	Totals—Territory	Description of Unit	Units	Amount per Unit	Alameda (Jones, Salesman) Units	Amount	Borden City (Smith, Salesman) Units	Amount	Route No. 1 (Williams, Salesman) Units	Amount	Route No. 2 (Sills, Salesman) Units	Amount
Passing orders for credit	$ 96.00	Orders	640		160	$	200	$	160	$	120	$
Order editing	128.00	Orders	640									
Order writing	128.00	Orders	640									
Order register and follow-up	96.00	Orders	640									
Invoicing	191.40	Invoices	870		210		260		220		180	
Charging accounts receivable	34.80	Invoices	870									
Receiving cash and crediting accounts receivable	37.50	Receipts	750		180		230		190		150	
Bad debts	205.00	Estimate				52.50		65.00		50.00		37.50
Totals	$916.70					$		$		$		$

719

29-1 (*Continued*)

Statement of Net Margin by Cities and Salesmen's Routes

Month of May, 19___

Particulars	Totals for Territory	Alameda (Jones)	Borden City (Smith)	Route No. 1 (Williams)	Route No. 2 (Sills)
Sales..	$20,500.00	$5,250.00	$6,500.00	$5,000.00	$3,750.00
Less—Cost of sales (including warehousing)..	12,812.50	3,281.25	4,062.50	3,125.00	2,343.75
Gross margin......................	$ 7,687.50	$1,968.75	$2,437.50	$1,875.00	$1,406.25
Less—Direct selling and promotion costs					
Salesmen's commission..................					
Selling and promotion expense...........					
Total.............................	$	$	$	$	$
Trading margin....................					
Less—Order department and cash collecting expense............................					
Net margin.............................	$	$	$	$	$

Data for problems **29-3** to **29-5**

Functional Unit Costs for Allocation of Certain House Costs to Orders of Various Sizes

Department and Function	Cost Unit Description	Amount
Order department and cash collecting		
Passing orders for credit......................	Order	$.15
Order editing..............................	Order	.20
Order writing..............................	Order	.20
Order register and follow-up..................	Order	.15
Invoicing..................................	Invoice	.22
Charging accounts receivable..................	Invoice	.04
Receiving cash and crediting accounts receivable..	Invoice	.05
Bad debts.................................	½ of 1% of sales	
Warehousing		
Putting goods into bins......................	Product unit	$.20
Maintenance of storage space.................	Product unit	.04
Getting goods out of bins....................	Product unit	.30
Packing goods (labor and packing materials)....	Product unit	.15
Packing cases.............................	Actual cost per case	
Equipment operation........................	Product unit	.03
Warehouse clerical.........................	Order	.19
Total house cost for a 1-product unit order:		
Recap by cost unit		
Per order.................................		$.89
Per invoice...............................		.31
Per product unit..........................		.72
Packing case.............................		actual
Bad debts.................................	½ of 1% of sales	

29-6. The Johnson Meat Packing Company desires to study its distribution costs (selling, administrative, and general expenses) which in the aggregate constitute 65 per cent of the total cost of doing business. From the information following, prepare an exhibit showing the allocation of total distribution cost per cwt.

Sales, Cost of Sales, and Direct Selling and Order Department Costs, by Cities

Salesman's Route No. 1   Williams, Salesman

Month of May, 19__

Particulars	Total Route No. 1 Units	Amount	Anaconda City Units	Amount	Blackmer City Units	Amount	Canton City Units	Amount	Dunn City Units	Amount	To Base Units	Amount
Sales (including warehousing)....		$5,000.00		$1,000.00		$1,250.00		$1,250.00		$1,500.00		
Cost of sales (including warehousing)....		3,125.00		625.00		781.25		781.25		937.50		
Gross margin, by cities.........		$1,875.00		$ 375.00		$ 468.75		$ 468.75		$ 562.50		
Cost allocated to cities												
Commission		$ 200.00		$ 40.00		$ 50.00		$ 50.00		$ 60.00		
In city												
Travel (@ $.08 per mile)....	1,150		200		300		250		400			
Subsistence (@ $10 per day)....	20		4		5		5		6			
Order costs (@ $1.63 per order*)....	160		30		35		40		55			
Customer costs (@ $.40 per customer)....	100		20		25		25		30			
Total allocated costs....		$		$		$		$		$		
Net margin, by cities....		$		$		$		$		$		
Costs not allocated to cities												
Intercity												
Travel (@ $.08 per mile)....	1,400	$	300	$	200	$	400	$	300	$	200	$
Subsistence (@ $10 per day)....	4		1		½		1		1		½	
Total....		$		$		$		$		$		$
Sales training manual....		8.00										
Fixed charges on automobile....		30.00										
Total cost not allocated....		$										
Net trading margin for route....		$										

* Average cost per order for Route No. 1:

Total order department and cash collecting costs charged to Route No. 1 (Solution to Problem 29-1)........	$228.70
÷ Number of orders for Route No. 1....	160
Average cost per order....	1.43 (−)
+ Average cost per order for sales office clerical....	.20
Total average cost....	1.63

† This is the cost per catalog, per Solution to Problem 29-1.

of meat products for each size—class of order (expressed in pounds per order). Carry out unit costs to hundredths of a cent.

An analysis to determine basic causes of cost variation in selling, administrative, and general expense items discloses that each element of expense varies according to one of the following three bases: (1) number of orders; (2) number of items or invoice lines per order; and (3) weight of order expressed in cwt. Expenses varying according to these three factors account for the total distribution cost of a given order.

The analysis of each class of distribution expense discloses that expenses are attributable to each of these three factors as follows:

	Expenses Based on			
Distribution Cost Controls	Number of Orders	Number of Items	Number of Cwt.	Total
Selling expense control...............	$2,310.00	$1,080.00	$ 210.00	$3,600.00
Packing and delivery expense control...	260.00	320.00	620.00	1,200.00
Administrative & general expense control	1,170.00	580.00	340.00	2,090.00
Total distribution cost...............	$3,740.00	$1,980.00	$1,170.00	$6,890.00

Data by order-size classes follow:

Order-size Class	Number of Orders	Total Number of Items	Total Cwt.
Under 50 pounds.....................	2,800	4,090	700
50-199 pounds....................	2,900	8,410	2,610
200-499 pounds....................	600	2,280	1,860
500-999 pounds....................	400	2,400	2,800
1,000 pounds and over..............	100	820	1,030
All orders........................	6,800	18,000	9,000

(AICPA)

Part Four

COST PLANNING

Chapter 30

COST PLANNING

Meaning of the term "cost planning"; Typical projects. Cost planning usually involves planning cost accounting procedures and making recommendations on cost accounting policies. It combines the management aspect and the creative aspect of cost accounting. It involves ascertaining on the one hand the problems of the management and the cost reports that will be useful to the management in making decisions on those problems, and on the other hand, how to get those reports. The cost planner must be thoroughly familiar with cost accounting, cost controls, and the uses of costs in business planning, and he must have a good knowledge of accounting procedures and methods.

Cost planning may be done by the supervising cost accountant or by a staff man for a private company, or it may be done by a consultant for a client. It is interesting to note that in professional accounting and industrial engineering circles, cost planning is often done by what is known as the "management services" division of the firm. The name of the division indicates the broad nature of the service which the cost planner performs.

Some cost planning assignments appear to be fundamentally systems design and installation assignments and others appear to be advice or policy assignments. Thus, a cost planner or "cost systems man" may be called upon to design and install a cost system complete from the general ledger down to the job tickets and requisitions. Such an assignment may come, for instance, from a growing company which has had only financial accounting and whose management now requires a comprehensive system of cost accounting and control. The company may have grown from a one-man management to a multiple-echelon management in which supervision and decision require records and reports. In such a company, it is no longer possible for the top supervisors to function by first-hand observation of performance.

Similarly, a cost planner may be asked to design a budget system including the production and procurement, plant and expense, and financial budgets. Such a system might be complete from the forecast balance sheet and statement of profits down to the basic papers. In cases of this kind, the company may have many of the pieces of a budget system, but no system which will crystallize and integrate the planning activities of the business and show whether the plans can be expected to produce a profit.

A cost planning project may be concerned with designing *part* of a complete system, such as labor classification and controls. An assignment of this kind frequently involves not only designing the labor classifications and the reports for the management, but sometimes also the timekeeping, payroll, and payroll analysis procedures. This is particularly true where an incentive wage payment plan is involved in the controls. A new incentive wage payment plan often calls for some new payroll analysis procedures.

Advice or policy assignments are described by such questions as the following: "Our sales department claims that selling prices based upon our present costs would price us out of the market. It is possible that our expense allocation plan is not sound. Analyze our costs and give us your opinion." "Certain members of our top management believe the company should change from conventional cost accounting to direct costing. Give us your opinion." "Does the costing which we propose to set up for our government contracts conform with government regulations?" And, of course, many others.

Designing a complete cost system often includes giving opinions on policy. Any cost system is designed with direct reference to the major use(s) to be made of the costs, and this fact usually calls for policy opinion on methods of pricing materials, volume of production upon which to base factory expense rates, and so forth.

Cost surveys are sometimes done by professional cost men, and these surveys are closely related to cost planning. Setting up product costs for a client is an example. This involves not only determining how costs should be calculated, but also doing the calculating and taking the responsibility for the mechanical work of assembling the costs.

COMPLETE COST SYSTEM PLANNING ASSIGNMENT

Initial conference. A cost system planning assignment usually starts with the executives who use (or will use) cost accounting data and reports. They call in the cost systems man and state their problems; he in turn explains what is generally involved in designing a system that will provide the information required. Often it is necessary for the cost systems man to make a preliminary survey of the client's products, plant, and records to enable him to determine the scope of a detailed survey program and the general type of solution that can be expected.

Assume that the manufacturer of a large assembly product states that he needs a cost system which will show what the various products cost and which will provide a basis for "pricing the product." In the preliminary conference, the cost planner is likely to ask to see some of the products and to be conducted on a tour through the factory. As to products, he may ask such questions as how many end-product models there are, whether they are assembled for stock or to customer's order, approximately how many parts go into the products, and of these, how many are manufactured by the client and how many are bought outside.

In the factory proper, the cost system man will be interested in the departmental arrangement as between service departments and producing departments, and within the latter, whether the work appears to be done on a job-shop basis (with production orders issued from the sales orders) or on an assembly-line basis (with blanket production orders issued, say, month by month). In some factories, of course, certain products are made on a job-shop basis and certain products on an assembly-line basis. This fact obviously has a fundamental bearing upon the *type* of cost system that can be installed.

The cost planner will also observe what appear to be work centers within departments, such as welding, machining (drill press, lathe, planer, etc.), painting, assembly, and packing. These centers may become factory expense centers in the new system. The basic theory is that each product should bear the factory expense cost of the facilities used in making the product. It will be observed whether different products require the use of different machines and other facilities, and also whether the machines are large enough to represent significant fixed charges, maintenance and repairs, and power.

The completeness of the product specifications, bills of materials and operations lists are immediately important in a proposed cost system project of this kind. The client concern may have an engineering department turning out drawings and blueprints supported by bills of materials (lists of parts and materials which go into each product). The first question is whether the bills of materials are absolutely complete. Since it is impossible to control materials costs without knowing exactly what goes into the product, incomplete bills of materials will have to be made complete. Control may be established either by releasing materials from stores on standard bills of materials (for the number of product units in the order) and excess piece requisitions as required, or by releasing materials on requisitions which would be checked against master bills of materials by the cost clerk. This is necessary to determine whether an operator has spoiled a piece of material and simply got another piece of material out of the storeroom and started again.

The second question is whether the materials and parts have been classified and numbered on some logical scheme. This is important since cost records would be set up according to such a plan.

The completeness of operations lists is important in a similar way. The operations list is supposed to show the direct labor operations (cutting, grinding, welding, etc.) that must be performed on a part and also operations performed outside the plant (such as heat treating, plating, etc.), if there are any. The existence and use of complete operations lists facilitates analysis of labor costs on the cost sheets to explain differences among orders.

The cost systems man is interested in the type and extent of standards in use in the factory. Are there quantity standards for materials, indicating, for instance, the raw size of a specified steel stock to be allowed for a certain part? Are there time standards per piece for each labor operation? Are direct labor people paid on an incentive basis? The answers to these questions have a bearing on the feasibility of using standard costs.

Certain questions are asked relating to the volume of the factory operation. How many units of product are made each month? How many employees are there in the factory? in the office?

These are some of the questions that a cost systems man may ask in the initial trip through the plant. He also asks questions about how the product is marketed. These questions may relate to the channels of distribution used, whether the company has its own salesmen and what geographic area is covered, and what methods of selling are used.

At the end of the initial conference, the experienced cost systems man will know what detailed information he needs to gather, and approximately how much time will be required for detailed survey, design, and installation.

The detail survey. The detail survey is made from "the top down" or "from the general to the detailed," for the accumulation of the maximum amount of necessary basic information with the minimum of inconvenience to the interviewees.

The cost systems man usually assembles:

(1) An organization chart showing the executives at the various levels and also the lines of responsibility for the various functions of the business (general administration, selling, manufacturing, finance, etc.). For the accounting, cost accounting, and related record work activities, it is usually useful to set out the chart down to the lowest rank of supervisor and indicate the number of people under each supervisor.

(2) A set of accounting and cost accounting classifications and reports, with complete information on (a) the frequency of each report and (b) names of the executives who receive each report. The analyst can get a great deal of information about the existing system by studying the classifications and reports, asking questions about the features which are not clear to him. Also, a study of these items will reveal information which is lacking, which the executives *should be* receiving for the performance of their duties.

It is usually desirable to obtain a set of production reports, since the consultant will have the problem of deciding whether the present system of quantity control is satisfactory as the basis of a cost system.

(3) Information about the product structure. The analyst must obviously find out what the company makes. The amount of engineering detail the analyst must ask for depends upon the nature of the product, the size of the business, and the nature of the cost accounting assignment. Where goods are made for stock and sold from stock, the analyst can begin by asking for catalogs and price lists. There may also be products and parts classifications that can be made available to the consultant for examination. Likewise, the engineering or sales department may have formal product specifications which will be useful to the analyst.

(4) A chart of plant layout and flow of production. The plant layout chart is drawn to scale and it shows machines and work places, storage areas (raw, process, and finished goods), salesrooms and offices. In some cases, lines may be drawn to show the flow of production from raw materials storage through the various work places and in process banks, and finally to finished goods.

(5) Lists of people and job descriptions (or groups of people and job descriptions which apply to the groups).

In addition to the above view from the top, the analyst will usually prepare flow charts, tracing the flow of accounting paper work. Flow charts are forms for gathering all the details that are *needed*, controlling against the inadvertent omission of needed details on the one hand and the accumulation of too many details on the other hand. In the detail survey for a complete cost system, it is usually necessary to cover the following paper work procedures:

(1) Materials purchase and payment, receiving, storing, and issuing.
(2) Labor timekeeping, payroll (with detail study of wage payment plans), and labor distribution.
(3) Expense accounting.
(4) Sales order, production order, shipping order and billing.

Some basic factors in the design of a cost system. Some of the basic factors in the design of a cost system are considered in the following questions and comments:

Are the present quantity controls suitable for the determination of unit costs in a cost system? The quantity controls relate to materials, work in process, and finished goods, and they are intended to tie the reported quantities from the point where the goods are ordered to the point where the goods are shipped and billed. The analyst answers this question by a study of (a) the plant layout and flow of production chart, (b) the materials purchasing, receiving, storing, and issuing chart, and (c) the sales order, production order, shipping order, and billing chart. If the present quantity controls are not satisfactory, the analyst will have to make the fact known, either as a special recommendation for company action or by designing the necessary controls into the new system.

What is the proper organization of cost centers for the allocation of costs to product and what work units should be used as:

(a) statistical measures of work done
(b) cost units (after dollars have been applied) for putting product costs together.

The selection of cost centers and work units is done by study of the plant and flow of production chart and also the production reports in use in the factory.

Does the established labor accounting provide proper control of quantities paid in a piece-rate wage payment or other incentive plan? Study the timekeeping, payroll, and labor distribution chart.

Are the labor timekeeping and labor distribution procedures in operation suitable for the new classification of labor accounts which the analyst contemplates for the new system?

Is the materials distribution procedure in operation suitable for handling the new classification of materials charges which the analyst contemplates for the new system? Study the materials purchasing, storing, and issuing charts.

Can the expense accounting procedure be readily adapted to the classification of expense accounts that the analyst is developing for the new system?

Are the current product specifications and manufacturing standards actually reflected in product costs being computed? Is it possible that the specifications and standards developed by the engineering department are not reflected completely and accurately in the predetermined product costs?

Can the present clerical staff in the client company handle the load of operating the new system, or will additional employees be required? In some cases, a new cost system can be handled with fewer people than were required for the old system. In other cases, more people will be required. The cost planner must be able to state the number of people needed.

Are the people who will have to make the new system work cooperative? In this matter, a great deal depends upon the consideration and tact with which the cost planner made his survey. It is a foregone conclusion that the new system will not work without the cooperation of the people who are supposed to operate it.

Preliminary report. In some assignments, it is desirable or necessary for the cost systems man to present a preliminary report to the client after he has determined what can be done and how many days consulting time will be required. The client may have requested such a report when he originally authorized the assignment, or the cost systems man may make the suggestion himself. In the former case, the client may want to know what the consultant thinks of the possibilities of the program after he has had an opportunity to make a preliminary examination of the plant, organization, records, and reports. In the latter case, the consultant may desire to put into writing just what the assignment is supposed to cover and what will be the probable result, to eliminate possible misunderstanding. Very frequently, client executives express the thought that certain features of the old accounting system ought to be changed by the consultant without realizing that the scope of the original assignment would be increased significantly by including those features.

Just how much of the detail survey work should be done before the preliminary report is written depends upon the nature of the assignment (that is, what the client is asking for in the first place) and the size and complexity of the client's organization. In some cases, the cost systems man can present such a report after a two weeks' survey.

The first section usually states the assignment as given by the client and describes the preliminary survey which has just been completed. "This is what you have asked for, and this is what we have done."

The next section might be headed, "What Was Found." It would be in effect a report on the diagnosis of the client's old system. This section would list the features of the old system which should be corrected or the operating conditions which have special significance in regard to the operation of a new system. It is often useful for the cost systems man to explain what he found to provide information that the client himself may not have and also to give the client the means for determining that the consultant has actually located all the factors that require attention.

The "What Was Found" section lays the groundwork for the next section which is "Recommendations." In designing a new cost system, the consultant keeps those features of the present system that fit into the proposed new system and work properly, changes those features which have a logical place but which are not working properly, designs new features to fill in the missing parts, and integrates the whole into one system. The recommendations would cover all these phases of the proposed work.

The final section is "Implementing the Recommendations." Under this heading are explained (a) the parts of the program that the client's own personnel can do, (b) the parts that the client's personnel and the consultant should do jointly, and (c) the parts that the consultant should do independently.

Rough classifications and statements. At some time near the end of the survey, after the cost planner has formulated the new system, he will draw up rough classifications and statements and present them to the client management. In conference, he will explain them in detail and receive comments and suggestions that the executives may have. Actually, this is the first step in the design of the new system. The executives who are going to use the reports must be given an opportunity to state what they want and do not want. The cost planner's recommendations will be expertly drawn, but often executives will want additional accounts for functions and activities with which they are directly concerned. Since cost reports are tools, they must be designed to fit the needs of the users. The cost planner must of course come up with a classification that is flexible and a basic plan that will work, and at reasonable clerical cost.

Designing the system. Like the detailed survey, the design work is done from the top down. The cost man starts with the classifications of accounts and the statements (balance sheet, statement of profits, etc.) and works down to the papers which will be used to record transactions. Thus, after the rough classifications and statements have been presented and discussed, the cost planner will:

(1) Design smooth statements and classifications.
(2) Design standard journal entries. These entries constitute the master plan of journals together with the general journal accruals and deferrals necessary to operate the accounts.
(3) Design the journals, using the standard journal entries as the basis for design.
(4) Design the account forms and the accounting papers for recording transactions.
(5) Prepare a rough draft of the manual of instructions for operating the system.

Installation. The man who designs the system (or an assistant) helps the line accounting people install the system. In a typical situation, he may be present in the cost department through the whole first month of operation of the new system, explaining the new details to the people who are assigned to operate or supervise the system. Numerous questions will come up, and the cost man will answer them. In the early part of the month, he will spend all his time instructing and answering questions. During the latter part of the month, he may finish writing the manual. At that time, of course, he is in a position to include in the manual those points which came to light during the installation which were not covered in the rough draft of the manual.

At the end of the month, the cost man assists in preparing the statements and presents them to the management, explaining them in detail. If points come to light which indicate the need for giving further instruction or advice, the cost man covers the necessary points.

COST ACCOUNTING UNDER GOVERNMENT CONTRACTS

Allowable costs and nonallowable costs. The cost planner may be consulted on cost accounting for the manufacturer who supplies goods to the United States Government or its agencies under cost reimbursement contracts. In these cases, the cost planner is concerned not only (or even primarily) with the mechanical aspects of recording costs under the contract but also with questions of what costs are allowable and what costs are not allowable under the contract. A statement of contract cost principles under the Armed Services Procurement Regulation, with examples of allowable and nonallowable costs, follows*:

SECTION XV

Contract Cost Principles

15-000 *Scope of Section.* This section sets forth, in general, standards for the determination and allowance of costs in connection with the performance of cost-reimbursement type contracts.

15-001 *Effective Date of Section.* This section shall be complied with on and after 1 March 1949, although compliance is authorized from the date of its issuance (but see Part 6 as to effective dates of Cost Interpretations set forth therein).

PART 1—APPLICABILITY

15-101 *Types of Contracts.* Subject to the requirements of paragraph 15-102, the provisions of Part 2, Part 3, or Part 4 of this section (whichever part is applicable) shall be followed in connection with all cost-reimbursement type contracts (including cost-reimbursement subcontracts thereunder), except that in the case of such contracts having negotiated overhead rates the applicable provisions of this section shall be used only as a basis for negotiating such rates but shall be followed for all other items of cost. The provisions of Part 2 shall be followed for all cost-reimbursement type contracts other than those covered in Parts 3 and 4, the provisions of Part 3 shall normally be followed for all research and development cost or cost-sharing contracts with educational or other nonprofit institutions, and the provisions of Part 4 shall normally be followed for all construction contracts (as defined in said Part 4) and for all contracts for architect-engineer services related to construction; however, when deemed by the head of the procuring activity concerned to be more suitable for a particular contract, Part 2 may be followed in place of Part 3 or Part 4. The term "cost-reimbursement type contract," as used throughout this section, includes cost or cost-sharing contracts, cost-plus-a-fixed-fee contracts, and the cost-reimbursement portion of time-and-materials contracts.

15-102 *Contract Provisions.* In order for the principles for determination of costs outlined in Part 2, Part 3, or Part 4 of this section to be binding upon the Government and upon a contractor, the applicable principles must be (a) set forth in the contract or appended thereto, or (b) specifically incorporated by reference in the contract. The cost principles outlined in Part 2, Part 3, or Part 4 of this section (whichever is applicable) shall be made a part of every contract of the type referred to in paragraph 15-101 executed as of a date on or after March 1949, except that any such contract (i), may, to the extent necessary in a particular case, expressly provide for the allowability of any of the kinds of costs referred to in Part 5 of this section unless any such kind of costs is expressly excluded under Part 2, Part 3, or Part 4 (whichever is applicable), and (ii) may exclude any item of allowable cost set forth in Part 2, Part 3, or Part 4.

* Section 15, Armed Services Procurement Regulation, 1955 edition, revised May 28, 1956, pp. 1501-1505.

15-200 *Scope of Part.* This part sets forth principles for the determination of costs in connection with cost-reimbursement type contracts (which term, as used in this part, includes cost-reimbursement subcontracts thereunder) other than (i) research and development cost or cost-sharing contracts with educational or other nonprofit institutions, and (ii) construction contracts for architect-engineer services related to construction.

15-201 *General Basis for Determination of Costs.* The total cost of a cost-reimbursement type contract is the sum of the allowable direct costs incident to the performance of the contract, plus the properly allocable portion of allowable indirect costs, less applicable income and other credits. The tests used in determining the allowability of costs also include (i) reasonableness, (ii) application of generally accepted accounting principles and practices, and (iii) any limitations as to types or amounts of cost items set forth in this Part 2 of Section XV or otherwise included in the contract. Failure to mention any item of cost in this part is not intended to imply that it is either allowable or not allowable. The use of normal or standard costs (with appropriate adjustments for variances, unallowable costs and the other provisions of this part) is acceptable in determining amounts of provisional or interim payments, but final allowable costs must represent actual costs. Income and other credits arising out of operations under the contract, where the related cost was reimbursed or accepted as an allowable cost, will be credited to the Government.

15-202 *Allowable Direct Costs.*

15-202.1 *Materials.* The cost of materials includes the cost of all items purchased, supplied, manufactured or fabricated, which enter directly into the end product or which are used or consumed directly in connection with furnishing such product. In computing material costs, consideration will be given to reasonable overruns, spoilage, and defective work. Withdrawals from a contractor's stock will be charged in accordance with the pricing system used by the contractor, *provided* such system is in accordance with sound accounting practice and is consistently followed. Reasonable charges arising from differences between periodic physical inventory quantities and related material-control records will be included in arriving at the cost of materials, provided that such charges (i) do not include "write-downs" of values, and (ii) relate to the period of performance of the contract. All credits arising from differences between periodic physical inventory quantities and related material-control records shall be taken into account. In calculating the cost of materials, there shall be deducted all cash discounts, trade discounts, rebates, and other allowances and credits taken by the contractor, including (a) credit for any materials returned to stock or to vendors, and (b) credit for the value of scrap resulting from performance of the contract, whether or not such scrap is sold. Such discounts, rebates, allowances and credits may be applied directly to the charges for materials involved or may be apportioned through credits to indirect costs.

15-202.2 *Labor.* Direct labor cost consists of salaries and wages properly chargeable directly to the performance of the contract. Generally such salaries and wages will be charged at the actual rates paid by the contractor. However, if it is the contractor's consistent accounting practice to make such charges on the basis of average rates, this practice will be acceptable if it is demonstrated by the contractor that the Government will not be prejudiced thereby.

15-203.3 *Other Direct Costs.* There are numerous items of cost which are generally classified as indirect costs but which may, in particular cases, properly be chargeable directly to the contract, where the contractor demonstrates that such costs are specifically related to the contract.

15-203 *Allowable Indirect Costs.* For accounting purposes indirect costs usually fall into the following three categories, although for purposes of allowability any such costs are subject to the limitations of this part:

(a) manufacturing and production expenses, which are the indirect costs incurred in the operation of production departments;

(b) selling and distribution expenses, which are costs incurred in connection with the marketing of the contractor's products;

(c) general and administrative expenses, which are costs incurred in the general management, supervision and conduct of the business as a whole.

In establishing a method of equitably apportioning the indirect costs, consideration should be given to such factors as charges of subcontractors, fixed asset improvement programs, and any unusual circumstances involved in the contractor's operation; and such factors should be carefully reviewed from time to time, particularly when there is a change in the nature or volume of production, to determine whether the method of apportionment continues to be equitable. Whenever items ordinarily chargeable as indirect costs are charged to a Government contract as direct costs, the cost of similar items applicable to other work of the contractor must be eliminated from indirect costs apportioned to the contract.

15-204 *Examples of Items of Allowable Costs.* Subject to the requirements of paragraph 15-201 with respect to the general basis of determining allowability of costs, and irrespective of whether the particular costs are treated by the contractor as direct or indirect, the following items of costs are considered allowable within the limitations indicated:

(a) Advertising in trade and technical journals, *provided* such advertising does not offer specific products for sale but is placed for the purpose of offering financial support to journals which are valuable for the dissemination of technical information within the contractor's industry (but see paragraph 15-205 (a)).

(b) Bonds and insurance, including self-insurance (but see paragraph 15-205 (p)).

(c) Compensation of corporate officers, executives and department heads. (The term "compensation" includes all amounts paid or set aside, such as pension and retirement benefits in accordance with the interpretation set forth in paragraph 15-601, salaries, royalties, license fees, bonuses, and deferred compensation benefits. The total compensation of an individual may be questioned and the amount allowed may be limited; and in connection therewith, consideration will be given to the relation of the total compensation to the services rendered).

(d) Depreciation and depletion, based on cost of acquisition (but see paragraph 15-205 (b) and (o)).

(e) Directors and executive committee fees and expenses; the expenses of stockholders meetings, annual reports, and reports and returns prepared for governmental authorities; and registry and transfer charges resulting from changes in ownership of securities issued by the contractor.

(f) Freight, transportation, and material handling.

(g) Improvement of working conditions, employer-employee relations, and standards of performance.

(h) Jigs, dies, fixtures, patterns, drawings and special tools.

(i) Legal, accounting, and consulting services and related expenses (but see paragraph 15-205 (d) and (l)).

(j) Manufacturing and production engineering, that is, engineering related immediately to manufacturing and production as distinguished from research, experimentation, and development.

(k) Materials and supplies.

(l) Memberships in trade, business and professional organizations.

(m) Miscellaneous office and administrative services and supplies, including communication expenses.

(n) Overtime compensation for direct or indirect labor, to the extent expressly provided for elsewhere in the contract or otherwise authorized by the Government.

(o) Patents, purchased designs, and royalty payments, to the extent expressly provided for elsewhere in the contract or otherwise authorized by the Government.

(p) Pension and retirement plans in accordance with the interpretation set forth in paragraph 15-601 and group health, accident and life insurance plans (but see paragraph 15-205 (p)).

(q) Plant maintenance and protection.

(r) Recruiting (including "help wanted" advertising) and training of personnel.

(s) Research and development specifically applicable to the supplies or services covered by the contract.

(t) Salaries and wages, direct and indirect (but see paragraph 15-204 (c)).

(u) Subcontracts and purchase orders.

(v) Taxes (but see paragraph 15-205 (i) and (r)).

(w) Traveling expenses.

(x) Vacation, holiday and severance pay, sick leave and military leave, to the extent required by law, by employer-employee agreement or by the contractor's established policy.

15-205 *Examples of Items of Unallowable Costs.* Irrespective of whether the particular costs are treated by the contractor as direct or indirect, the following items of cost are considered unallowable, except as indicated:

(a) Advertising, except "help wanted" advertising, and advertising in trade and technical journals (see paragraph 15-204 (a) and (r)).

(b) Amortization or depreciation of (i) unrealized appreciation of values of assets, or (ii) assets fully amortized or depreciated on the contractor's books of account.

(c) Bad debts (including expenses of collection) and reserves for such debts.

(d) Commissions and bonuses (under whatever name) in connection with obtaining or negotiating for a Government contract.

(e) Contingency reserves.

(f) Contributions and donations.

(g) Dividend payments.

(h) Entertainment.

(i) Federal taxes on income and excess profits.

(j) General research, unless specifically provided for elsewhere in the contract.

(k) Interest on borrowings (however represented), bond discount and expenses, and financing charges.

(l) Legal, accounting and consulting services and related expenses incurred in connection with organization or reorganization, prosecution or patent infringement litigation, defense of anti-trust suits, and the prosecution of claims against the United States.

(m) Losses from sales or exchanges of capital assets, including investments.

(n) Losses on other contracts.

(o) Maintenance, depreciation and other costs incidental to excess facilities (including machinery and equipment) other than reasonable standby facilities.

(p) Premiums for insurance on the lives of directors, officers, proprietors or other persons, where the contractor is the beneficiary directly or indirectly.

(q) Selling and distribution activities not related to the contract products.

(r) Taxes and expenses in connection with financing, refinancing, or refunding operations, including the listing of securities on exchanges.

QUESTIONS

30-1. (a) What is meant by cost planning?

(b) Give several examples of cost planning assignments.

30-2. Outline the steps in a typical cost planning assignment from the initial conference to the final report.

30-3. In a general assignment (a complete cost system from the general ledger down), what types of survey information are collected in the detail survey? What methods or techniques are used for assembling the various types of information?

30-4. Name some of the basic factors that the systems man will have to consider before designing a complete cost system, which will have a direct bearing on the design of the system. What parcels of survey information (Question 30-3) will be used in considering each factor?

30-5. Name the steps in *designing* a complete cost system.

30-6. Discuss the work to be done by the cost systems man during the installation of a new cost system.

30-7. Name some allowable costs and some nonallowable costs under a cost reimbursement contract, under the Armed Services Procurement Regulation.

APPENDICES

A COMPLETE SET OF COST CONTROL REPORTS

Control reports listed. The following control reports illustrated in this appendix are prepared monthly for the Benson & West Manufacturing Company:

Profits:
Statement of Profits: Budget and Actual

Sales and Gross Profit:
Sales and Gross Profit by Product: Budget and Actual
Sales and Gross Profit, Class of Customer by Product
Sales and Gross Profit, Territories by Product

Warehouse and Shipping:
Warehouse and Shipping Variance Report

Materials:
Materials Price Variance, by Class of Materials
Materials Quantity Variance, by Class of Materials

Labor:
Labor Variance Report, Department by Product

Factory Expense:
Factory Expense Variances: Department totals
Factory Expense Variance Report: Building Maintenance and Fixed Charges
Factory Expense Variance Report: General Factory Administration
Factory Expense Variance Report: Cutting Department
Factory Expense Variance Report: Assembly Department No. 1
Factory Expense Variance Report: Assembly Department No. 2

Distribution Cost:
Variance Report: Direct Selling and Promotion
Variance Report: Order Department and Cash Collecting
Variance Report: Delivery Expense

Administrative Expense:
Administrative Expense: Budget and Actual

With these reports, it is possible to control every function and activity of the business. The reports are so set up that the over-all picture can be obtained quickly from the Statement of Profits and details can be obtained from the supporting reports. Thus, if gross margin per the Statement of Profits is less than budget (which it is), the reader of the reports can study the supporting sales and gross profit reports to see what products or classes of customers or territories account for the decrease. It is useful to study these reports to see how much gross profit each of the products is contributing and to see how much volume is coming from each class of customers (since selling prices and costs of selling differ for retail store customers, wholesalers, and chain store customers).

It is also useful to study them to determine how much gross profit each territory is contributing, to determine how far it seems to be worth while to send the salesmen.

If the materials price variance or the materials quantity variance is significant, it is possible to determine in what classes of materials the variances occur by referring to the supporting schedules of variances. Labor variance, in a similar way, is analyzed by department on a report which supports the Statement of Profits.

If the net factory expense variance per the Statement of Profits is significant, the reader can study the supporting factory expense reports to determine what supervisor ran over his budget and for what object of expense.

And similarly, if the variable distribution expenses per the Statement of Profits appear to be out of line with sales, or if the capacity costs of distribution have increased or decreased significantly, the reader can examine the supporting reports to pin-point the area of change.

The statements are illustrated and discussed in the following sections of this chapter.

Statement of profits. The Statement of Profits (page 743) provides a comparison of actual results for one month (March) with budget. It shows that actual profits ($10,751.06) were less than budget profit ($15,836.85) by $5,085.79. This is a large decrease. What caused it? Factors which the reader would pick up immediately from the statement are:

(1) Actual sales ($143,717) were less than budget sales ($145,590) by $1,873. The expected gross profit on lost sales was $1,019.05.

(2) Variances from standard cost on manufacturing and warehousing operations totaled $3,699.11. These variances constitute a direct loss of expected gross margin. The expected gross margin for the actual volume of sales was $44,603.45, and the actual gross margin (after charging off the variances) was $40,904.34. The company could have had $3,699.11 more profit if all standards had been met.

(3) Among the selling and general expense accounts the actual variable expense totals for order department and delivery department are *greater* than the budget totals, although the sales volume is *less* than budget. Although it is not expected that variable distribution costs will vary di-

BENSON & WEST MANUFACTURING COMPANY
Statement of Profits: Budget and Actual
Month of March, 19___

Particulars	Budget Amount	Budget % to Sales	Actual Amount	Actual % to Sales	Increase or Decrease* Amount	Increase or Decrease* % to Budget	Reference Figure No.
Sales.........................	$145,590.00	100.0	$143,717.00	100.0	$1,873.00*	1.3*	I-2
Less—Cost to make and ship:							
Manufacturing (@ standard)......	$ 96,672.00	66.4	$ 95,805.20	66.7	$ 866.80*	.9*	I-5
Warehousing and shipping........	3,295.50	2.3	3,308.35	2.3	12.85	.4	I-6
Total cost to make and ship....	$ 99,967.50	68.7	$ 99,113.55	69.0	$ 853.95*	.9*	
Expected gross margin...........	$ 45,622.50	31.3	$ 44,603.45	31.0	$1,019.05*	2.2*	
Less—Variances from standard cost:							
Materials price variance........	$		$ 420.00	.3	$ 420.00		I-5
Materials quantity variance.....			350.00	.2	350.00		I-6
Labor variance..................			970.25	.7	970.25		I-7
Factory expense variances.......			1,694.11	1.2	1,694.11		I-8
Warehouse and shipping variances.			264.75	.1	264.75		I-14
Net variances...................	$		$ 3,699.11	2.5	$3,699.11		
Gross margin....................	$ 45,622.50	31.3	$ 40,904.34	28.5	$4,718.16*	10.3*	
Less—Selling and general expense:							
Selling and promotion variable expense..	$ 15,765.50	10.8	$ 15,577.45	10.8	$ 188.05*	1.2*	I-15
Selling and promotion capacity cost..	1,587.82	1.1	1,667.82	1.2	80.00	5.0	I-15
Order department and cash collecting variable expense...	3,423.50	2.4	3,682.18	2.6	258.68	7.6	I-16
Order department and cash collecting capacity cost..	637.83	.4	637.83	.5			I-16
Delivery variable expense.......	2,270.00	1.6	2,480.00	1.7	210.00	9.3	I-17
Delivery capacity cost..........	885.34	.6	885.34	.6			I-17
Administrative expense..........	5,215.66	3.6	5,222.66	3.6	7.00	.1	I-18
Total selling and general expense..	$ 29,785.65	20.5	$ 30,153.28	21.0	$ 367.63	1.2	
Net profit......................	$ 15,836.85	10.8	$ 10,751.06	7.5	$5,085.79*	32.1*	

* Red.

Figure 1-1

rectly with volume of sales, it is necessary to find out why they were greater than budget when the sales volume is less than budget.

(4) Actual selling and promotion expense capacity cost ($1,667.82) is greater than budget ($1,587.82) by $80, and actual administrative expense is slightly greater ($7) than budget.

Sales and gross profit reports. These reports show:

(1) sales and gross profit contribution of each product (below)

(2) sales and gross profit contribution of each class of customer (retail

BENSON & WEST MANUFACTURING COMPANY
Sales and Gross Profit by Product: Budget and Actual

Month of March, 19—

Particulars	Budget	Actual	Increase or Decrease*
Product A:			
Quantity.....................	1,800	1,720	80*
Sales value....................	$12,780.00	$12,128.00	$ 652.00*
Gross profit....................	5,706.00	5,368.40	337.60*
% Gross profit to sales...........	44.6%	44.3%	.3%*
Product B:			
Quantity.....................	1,500	1,390	110*
Sales value....................	$11,850.00	$10,869.00	$ 981.00*
Gross profit....................	4,995.00	4,516.70	478.30*
% Gross profit to sales...........	42.2%	41.6%	.6%
Product C:			
Quantity.....................	1,900	1,890	10*
Sales value....................	$15,960.00	$15,720.00	$ 240.00*
Gross profit....................	6,517.00	6,326.70	190.30*
% Gross profit to sales...........	40.8%	40.2%	6%*
Product D:			
Quantity.....................	10,000	10,000	
Sales value....................	$105,000.00	$105,000.00	
Gross profit....................	31,700.00	31,700.00	
% Gross profit to sales...........	30.2%	30.2%	
All products:			
Quantity.....................	15,200	15,000	200*
Sales value....................	$145,590.00	$143,717.00	$1,873.00*
Gross profit....................	48,918.00	47,911.80	1,006.20*
% Gross profit to sales...........	33.6%	33.3%	.3%*
Warehousing and shipping expense:			
Variable........................	$ 2,073.00	$ 2,112.00	$ 39.00
Fixed..........................	1,222.50	1,196.35	26.15
Totals......................	$ 3,295.50	$ 3,308.35	$ 65.15
Gross margin (Figure I-1)..........	$45,622.50	$44,603.45	

* Red.

Figure I-2

store customers, wholesale customers, chain store customers, and industrial users) (below)

(3) sales and gross profit contribution of each territory (page 746)

In the product statement, page 744, it will be seen that sales and gross profits of Products A, B, and C were all less than budgeted. Actual sales and gross profit of Product D were same as budget (in this illustration). That product accounts for ⅔ of the total sales, but the gross profit percentage on Product D is less than the percentage on any of the other products.

Note also that the actual gross profit percentages of Products A, B, and C are slightly less than budget percentages. This means that the average selling prices per unit reflected in the budget were not actually achieved. Possible causes are listed on page 746.

BENSON & WEST MANUFACTURING COMPANY
Sales and Gross Profit, Class of Customer by Product

Month of March, 19___

Particulars	Total All Classes	Retail Stores	Whole- sales	Chain Stores	Indus- trials
Product A:					
Quantity.........	1,720	700	1,020		
Sales value.......	$ 12,128.00	$ 5,600.00	$ 6,528.00		
Gross profit.......	5,368.40	2,849.00	2,519.40		
% Gross profit to sales........	44.3%	50.9%	38.6%		
Product B:					
Quantity.........	1,390	380	1,010		
Sales value.......	$ 10,869.00	$ 3,496.00	$ 7,373.00		
Gross profit......	4,516.70	1,759.40	2,757.30		
% Gross profit to sales........	41.6%	50.3%	37.4%		
Product C:					
Quantity.........	1,890	300	1,260		330
Sales value.......	$ 15,720.00	$ 3,000.00	$10,080.00		$2,640.00
Gross profit.......	6,326.70	1,509.00	3,817.80		999.90
% Gross profit to sales........	40.2%	50.3%	37.9%		37.9%
Product D:					
Quantity.........	10,000			10,000	
Sales value.......	$105,000.00			$105,000.00	
Gross profit.......	31,700.00			31,700.00	
% Gross profit to sales........	30.2%			30.2%	
All products:					
Quantity.........	15,000	1,380	3,290	10,000	330
Sales value.......	$143,717.00	$12,096.00	$23,981.00	$105,000.00	$2,640.00
Gross profit......	47,911.80	6,117.40	9,094.50	31,700.00	999.90
% Gross profit to sales........	33.3%	50.6%	37.9%	30.2%	37.9%

Figure I-3

(1) The product mix between sales to retail customers and sales to wholesalers contemplated in the budget was not actually maintained. (Selling prices to wholesalers are less than prices to retailers, and an mcrease in volume of sales to wholesalers tends to decrease the gross profit percentage.)

From data in the class of customer statement, page 745, it can be determined that chain store customers contribute 73 per cent of the sales volume (in dollars) and 65 per cent of the gross profit. Gross profit percentage on sales to chain stores is 30.2 per cent, whereas the gross profit percentage on sales to retail store customers is 50.6 per cent and to wholesaler customers, 37.9 per cent.

(2) In the territory statement, below, it is seen that the western territory produces more sales and more gross profit than either of the other two territories.

Note that only the product statement shows a comparison of actual sales and gross profit with *budget*. Sales are budgeted by product, but no formal attempt is made to budget sales by class of customer or by territory.

BENSON & WEST MANUFACTURING COMPANY
Sales and Gross Profit, Territories by Product

Month of March, 19—

Particulars	Total All Territories	Home Territory	Eastern Territory	Western Territory
Product A:				
Quantity	1,720	400	910	410
Sales value	$12,128.00	$ 2,784.00	$ 6,464.00	$ 2,880.00
Gross profit	5,368.40	1,212.00	2,887.70	1,268.70
% Gross profit to sales	44.3%	43.5%	44.7%	44.1%
Product B:				
Quantity	1,390	500	540	350
Sales value	$ 10,869.00	$ 4,011.00	$ 4,132.00	$ 2,726.00
Gross profit	4,516.70	1,726.00	1,664.20	1,126.50
% Gross profit to sales	41.6%	43.0%	40.3%	41.3%
Product C:				
Quantity	1,890	780	500	610
Sales value	$ 15,720.00	$ 6,720.00	$ 4,000.00	$ 5,000.00
Gross profit	6,326.70	2,843.40	1,515.00	1,968.30
% Gross profit to sales	40.2%	42.3%	37.9%	39.4%
Product D:				
Quantity	10,000	2,000	3,000	5,000
Sales value	$105,000.00	$21,000.00	$31,500.00	$52,500.00
Gross profit	31,700.00	6,340.00	9,510.00	15,850.00
% Gross profit to sales	30.2%	30.2%	30.2%	30.2%
All products:				
Quantity	15,000	3,680	4,950	6,370
Sales value	$143,717.00	$34,515.00	$46,096.00	$63,106.00
Gross profit	47,911.80	12,121.40	15,576.90	20,213.50
% Gross profit to sales	33.3%	35.1%	33.8%	32.0%

Figure I-4

Sales by class of customer and by territory are studied carefully, however, when sales by product are budgeted since trends in those two areas will be reflected in product sales.

Variance reports for materials and direct labor.   Under this heading are the following reports:

(1) Materials price variance, by class of materials (page 748)
(2) Materials quantity variance, by class of materials (page 748)

These reports are important at the Benson & West Manufacturing Company because materials cost is a significant part of total product cost. The former report shows the profit or loss to the company arising from the difference between standard materials prices on which selling prices are based and actual prices paid.   The latter report shows the loss due to the cutting department cutting more materials for the product units produced than was allowed in the standards.

(3) Labor variance, department by product (page 749)

This report provides a comparison of the standard value of labor operations completed in each department (standard hours produced @ standard rate per hour) and actual wages paid.   It will be noted that of the total variance shown by the Statement of Profits ($970.25), $507 occurred in department No. 2, where approximately ⅔ of the standard labor hours were produced.

Variance reports for factory expense.   A summary which shows departmental totals is shown on page 750.   It is supported in turn by a report for each department:

Building Maintenance and Fixed Charges (page 751)
General Factory Administration (page 752).
Cutting Department (page 753).
Assembly Department No. 1 (page 754).
Assembly Department No. 2 (page 755).

Each of these reports sets out the complete list of accounts for the department and provides a comparison of actual expenses with budget expenses.   The Building Maintenance and Fixed Charges report is based upon a fixed budget.   Each of the other reports incorporates the flexible budget principle.   Actual expenses are compared with a budget which has been adjusted to reflect current volume of operations.

The complete set of reports is given to the president of the company and the general superintendent.   The report for each department is also given to the foreman of that department.   Each foreman is responsible for the expenses of his department, and he is so held by the general superintendent.

The accounting aspects of preparing the expense reports are explained in Chapter 19.

BENSON & WEST MANUFACTURING COMPANY
Materials Price Variance, by Class of Materials

Month of March, 19—

Actual Quantities

Material	@ Standard Prices	@ Actual Prices	Price Variances
a	$ 2,500.00	$ 2,600.00	$100.00
b	1,500.00	1,450.00	50.00*
c	2,800.00	2,870.00	70.00
d	22,500.00	22,800.00	300.00
Totals (Figure I-1)	$29,300.00	$29,720.00	$420.00

Figure I-5

* Credit

BENSON & WEST MANUFACTURING COMPANY
Materials Quantity Variance, by Class of Materials

Month of March, 19—

@ Standard Prices

Material	Standard Quantities Allowed	Excess Quantities Used	Total Quantities
a	$ 2,550.00	$100.00	$ 2,650.00
b	1,560.00	60.00	1,620.00
c	2,560.00	40.00	2,600.00
d	24,000.00	150.00	24,150.00
Totals (Figure I-1)	$30,670.00	$350.00	$31,020.00

Figure I-6

Variance statement—warehouse and shipping. This report is basically a comparison of actual expenses with budget adjusted to current volume. In the report illustrated, the controllable variance (difference between actual expense and budget adjusted to current volume) is $243.80. The variance report (page 756) shows the following information:

Column (1)—Original budget (page 549)

Column (2)—Charge Cost of Shipments

This charge is Number of units shipped × Standard warehouse and shipping cost per unit as shown by the Budget and Standard Functional Unit Costs report (page 549).

Column (3)—Budget adjusted to level

The actual units are posted to this report from an analysis of actual costs. The standard functional unit costs are posted from the Budget and Standard Functional Unit Costs report.

Column (4)—Actual expense

BENSON & WEST MANUFACTURING COMPANY
Labor Variance Report, Department by Product

Month of March, 19___

Product	(a) Standard Hours Produced	(b) Standard Rate	(c) Standard Value (Charge Labor in Process) (a × b)	(d) Actual Hours	(e) Actual Rate	(f) Actual Value (Credit Accrued Payroll) (d × l)	(g) Labor Variances (c − f)
Cutting department:							
A..........	425	$1.50	$ 637.50	430	$1.52	$ 653.60	$ 16.10
B..........	325	1.50	487.50	330	1.52	501.60	14.10
C..........	400	1.50	600.00	420	1.52	638.40	38.40
D..........	4,000	1.50	6,000.00	4,100	1.52	6,232.00	232.00
Totals...	5,150	1.50	$ 7,725.00	5,280	1.52	$ 8,025.60	$300.60
Assembly department No. 2:							
D..........	19,000	$1.25	$23,750.00	19,100	$1.27	$24,257.00	$507.00
Assembly department No. 1:							
A..........	1,760	$1.25	$ 2,200.00	1,780	$1.27	$ 2,260.60	$ 60.60
B..........	2,017.5	1.25	2,521.87	2,020	1.27	2,565.40	43.53
C..........	2,767.5	1.25	3,459.38	2,770	1.27	3,517.90	58.52
Totals...	6,545.0	1.25	$ 8,181.25	6,570	1.27	$ 8,343.90	$162.65
Plant......	30,695.0		$39,656.25	30,950		$40,626.50	$970.25
Reference........							Figure I-1

Figure I-7

749

BENSON & WEST MANUFACTURING COMPANY
Factory Expense Variances: Department Totals

Month of March, 19___

Line	Particulars	Detail Schedule	(a) Original Budget	(b) Absorbed	(c) Admin. & Selling Expense	(d) Budget Adjusted to Level	(e) Actual Expense	(f) Net	(g) Spending	(h) Volume
									Variances	
								Net	Spending	Volume
	Service departments:									
1	Building maintenance and fixed charges....	I-9	$ 4,021.07	$ 3,201.07		$ 4,021.07	$ 4,156.25	$ 135.18	$135.18	$
2	General factory administration....	I-10	5,873.20	5,120.37	$820.00	5,501.15	5,559.16	438.79	58.01	380.78
3	Total service....		$ 9,894.27	$ 8,321.44	$820.00	$ 9,522.22	$ 9,715.41	573.97	$193.19	$380.78
	Producing departments:									
4	Cutting....	I-11	$ 5,339.42	$ 3,636.50		$ 4,313.02	$ 4,381.23	724.73	$ 68.21	$656.52
5	Assembly No. 1....	I-12	5,023.67	4,123.35		4,403.21	4,511.20	387.85	107.99	279.86
6	Assembly No. 2....	I-13	7,112.61	6,840.00		6,768.91	6,847.56	7.56	78.65	71.09*
7	Total producing....		$17,475.70	$14,619.85		$15,485.14	$15,739.99	$1,120.14	$254.85	$865.29
8	Total plant, including Interdepartment charges....		$27,369.97	$22,941.29		$25,007.36	$25,455.40			
9	Eliminate total Interdepartment charges (Line 3, Column (b))....			8,321.44			8,321.44			
10	Net charges to work in process....			$14,619.85	$820.00					
11	Net total actual factory expense....						$17,133.96	$1,694.11		

* Red.

Figure I-8

Column (5)-(7) Variances, computed according to the formulas shown at the head of the columns

Variance report: Selling and promotion expense. The Variance Report: Direct Selling and Promotion (page 757) is a formal comparison of this month's actual expenses with the *original budget* for the month. It shows dollar variances; also actual functional units and actual functional unit costs.

It is sometimes necessary to study the number of work units and the unit costs to get the complete story of a variance. For subsistence, to cite an example in Figure I-15, there is a net saving over the budget of $100. Analysis shows, however, that the salesmen spent more per day than the standard ($10 against $9.50) and that the apparent saving over the budget was due to the quantity factor. The salesmen were on the road a fewer number of days than had been planned (180 days against 200 days planned). A similar situation occurs in automobile variable. Although a net variance may appear to be satisfactory, an analysis into price and quantity factors may disclose some conditions that should be investigated.

BENSON & WEST MANUFACTURING COMPANY
Factory Expense Variance Report

	Department	Building Maintenance and Fixed Charges	
	Month of	March	19__

Particulars	(1). Original Budget	(2) Actual Expense	(3) Spending Variance (2) — (1)
Direct department expense:			
Supervisor......................	$ 500.00	$ 500.00	$
Janitor, firemen, and watchmen.......	1,100.00	1,150.00	50.00
F.I.C.A. tax.....................	32.00	33.00	1.00
Workmen's insurance...............	8.00	8.25	.25
Provision for vacation pay...........	32.00	33.00	1.00
Janitor's supplies..................	40.00	42.00	2.00
Coal............................	190.00	195.00	5.00
Repairs to building.................	300.00	280.00	20.00*
Electric light and power.............	200.00	210.00	10.00
Unclassified......................	119.07	205.00	85.93
Depreciation on building.............	800.00	800.00	
Insurance on building...............	400.00	400.00	
Taxes on building..................	300.00	300.00	
Total direct departmental expense...	$4,021.07	$4,156.25	$135.18
Expense charged to other departments....			
	4,021.07*	4,021.07*	
Spending variance (Figure I-8).........		$ 135.18	

* Red.

Figure I-9

BENSON & WEST MANUFACTURING COMPANY
Factory Expense Variance Report

Department __General Factory Administration__

Particulars	Variability	(1) Budget Rate/Hour: Variable	(2) Budget for Normal Volume	Month — (3) Budget Adjusted to Current Volume	March — (4) Actual Expense	19— (5) Spending Variance (3) − (2)
Budget hours			35,500	30,950		
Actual hours						
Direct departmental expense:						
Supervisory labor	F		$3,200.00	$3,200.00	$3,200.00	$
Clerical and production control labor	S-V		950.00	825.00	850.00	25.00
Machinists	S-V		500.00	325.00	350.00	25.00
F.I.C.A. tax	S-V		93.00	87.00	88.00	1.00
Unemployment insurance	S-V		23.25	21.75	22.00	.25
Provision for vacation pay	S-V		93.00	87.00	88.00	1.00
Printed forms and office supplies	V	.005	177.50	154.75	156.00	1.25
Electric light and power	V	.003	106.50	92.85	95.00	2.15
Telephone and telegraph	V	.002	71.00	61.90	63.00	1.10
Professional engineers' fees	V		100.00	100.00	100.00	
Unclassified	F	.0028673	101.79	88.74	90.00	1.26
Depreciation on office furniture and fixtures	F		9.16	9.16	9.16	
Depreciation on machinery and equipment	F		25.00	25.00	25.00	
Insurance on office furniture and fixtures	F		2.00	2.00	2.00	
Insurance on machinery and equipment	F		6.00	6.00	6.00	
Taxes on office furniture and fixtures	F		3.00	3.00	3.00	
Taxes on machinery and equipment	F		12.00	12.00	12.00	
Total direct departmental expense			$5,473.20	$5,101.15	$5,159.16	$58.01
Rent: 4,000 square feet @ $.10 per square foot			400.00	400.00	400.00	
Total departmental expense			$5,873.20	$5,501.15	$5,559.16	$58.01
General factory administration expense charged to other departments		.16544	5,873.20*	5,120.37	5,120.37	$58.01*
Spending variance (Actual expense − Budget adjusted to current level)				$ 380.78		
Volume variance (Budget adjusted to current level − Charges to other departments)						
Net variance (Actual expense − Charges to other departments)					$ 438.79	

* Red.

Figure I-10

BABSON & WEST MANUFACTURING COMPANY

Factory Expense Variance Report

Department ____ Cutting

Particulars	Variability	(1) Budget Rate/Hour: Variable	(2) Budget for Normal Volume	(3) Month Budget Adjusted to Current Volume	(4) March, 19__ Actual Expense	(5) Cutting Spending Variance (3) − (2)
Budget hours			7,500	5,150	5,280	
Standard hours produced						
Actual hours						
Direct labor cost (Standard rate, $1.50; Actual rate, $1.60)			$11,250.00	$7,725.00	$8,184.00	$459.00
Total indirect labor (as below)			1,575.00	1,351.50	1,360.00	8.50
						Spending Variance
Direct departmental expense:						
Supervision	S-V		$ 800.00	$ 700.00	$ 700.00	$
Clerical	S-V		700.00	600.00	600.00	
Other indirect labor	V	.01	75.00	51.50	60.00	8.50
F.I.C.A. tax	S-V		256.50	181.53	190.88	9.35
Workmen's insurance	S-V		64.12	45.38	47.72	2.34
Provision for vacation pay	S-V		256.50	181.53	190.88	9.35
Factory operating supplies	V	.04	300.00	206.00	210.00	4.00
Repairs and repair parts	V	.03	225.00	154.50	160.00	5.50
Electric light and power	V	.02	150.00	103.00	110.00	7.00
Unclassified	V	.0144338	108.25	74.33	75.00	.67
Depreciation on machinery and equipment	F		100.00	100.00	100.00	
Insurance on inventory	F		44.72	44.72	44.72	
Insurance on machinery and equipment	F		25.00	25.00	25.00	
Taxes on inventory	F		48.00	48.00	48.00	
Taxes on machinery and equipment	F		50.00	50.00	48.00	
Total direct departmental expense			$ 3,203.09	$2,565.49	$2,612.20	$ 46.71
Service charges:						
Rent: 8,955 square feet @ $.10+ per square foot	F		895.51	895.51	895.51	
General factory administration:	V		1,240.82			
Original budget: 7,500 standard hours @ $.16544	V		1,240.82			
Adjusted budget: 5,150 standard hours @ $.16544				852.02		
Actual: 5,280 actual hours @ $.16544					873.52	21.50
Total department expense			$ 5,339.42	$4,313.02	$4,381.23	$ 68.21
Cutting department expense charged to work in process:						
5,150 standard hours produced @ $.71				3,656.50	3,656.50	
Spending variance (Actual expense − Budget adjusted to current volume)						$ 68.21
Volume variance (Budget adjusted to current volume − Charge to work in process)				$ 656.52		
Net variance (Actual expense − Charge work in process)					$ 724.73	

Figure I-11

753

BENSON & WEST MANUFACTURING COMPANY
Factory Expense Variance Report

Department .... Assembly No. 1

Month of .... March .... 19__

Particulars	Variability	Budget Rate/Hour: Variable	(1) Budget for Normal Volume	(2) Budget Adjusted to Current Volume	(3) Actual Expense	(4) Spending Variance (3) − (2)
Budget hours			8,000	6,545	6,570	
Standard hours produced						
Actual hours						
Total direct labor (Standard rate, $1.25; Actual rate, $1.30)			$10,000.00	$8,181.25	$8,541.00	$359.75
Total indirect labor, as shown below			1,230.00	1,030.90	1,110.00	79.10
Total labor			$11,230.00	$9,212.15	$9,651.00	$438.85
Direct departmental expense:						
Supervision	S-V		$ 700.00	$ 600.00	$ 650.00	$ 50.00
Shop porters	S-V		370.00	300.00	325.00	25.00
Other indirect labor	V	.020	160.00	130.90	135.00	4.10
F.I.C.A. tax	S-V		184.24	184.24	193.02	8.78
Workmen's insurance	S-V		56.15	46.06	48.26	2.20
Provision for vacation pay	S-V		224.60	184.24	193.02	8.78
Factory operating supplies	V	.015	120.00	98.18	100.00	1.82
Repairs and repair parts	V	.020	160.00	130.90	132.00	1.10
Electric light and power	V	.010	80.00	65.45	67.00	1.55
Unclassified	V	.016728	133.82	109.48	110.00	.52
Depreciation on machinery and equipment	F		170.00	170.00	170.00	
Insurance on inventory	F		89.50	89.50	89.50	
Insurance on machinery and equipment	F		40.00	40.00	40.00	
Taxes on inventory	F		96.00	96.00	96.00	
Taxes on machinery and equipment	F		81.65	81.65	81.65	
Total direct departmental expense			$ 2,706.32	$2,326.60	$2,430.45	$103.85
Service charges:						
Rent: 9,938+ square feet @ $.10 per square foot			993.81	993.81	993.81	
General factory administration:						
Original budget: 8,000 standard hours @ $.16544			1,323.54			
Adjusted budget: 6,545 standard hours @ .16544				1,082.80		
Actual: 6,570 actual hours @ .16544					1,086.94	4.14
Total departmental expense			$ 5,023.67	$4,403.21	$4,511.20	$107.99
Assembly department No. 1 expense charged to work in process:						
6,545 standard hours produced @ standard rate, $.63				4,123.35	4,123.35	
Spending variance (Actual expense − Budget adjusted to current volume)						$107.99
Volume variance (Budget adjusted to current volume − Charge work in process)				$ 279.86		
Net variance (Actual expense − Charges work in process)					$ 387.85	

Figure L-12

Factory Expense Variance Report

Department _____ Assembly No. 2

Month of March, 19__

Particulars	Varia-bility	Budget Rate/Hour: Variable	(1) Budget for Normal Volume	(2) Budget Adjusted to Current Volume	(3) Actual Expenses	(4) Variance (3) − (2) Spending Variance
Budget hours produced..........			20,000			
Standard hours produced........				19,000		
Actual hours...................					19,100	
Total direct labor (Standard rate, $1.25; actual rate, $1.30).....			$25,000.00	$23,750.00	$24,830.00	$1,080.00
Total indirect labor (as shown below).....			1,020.00	914.00	920.00	6.00
Total labor.....			$26,020.00	$24,664.00	$25,750.00	$1,086.00
						Spending Variance
Direct departmental expense:						$
Supervision.................	S-V		$ 600.00	$ 500.00	$ 500.00	
Shop porters.................	S-V		300.00	300.00	300.00	
Other indirect labor.........	S-V	.006	120.00	114.00	120.00	6.00
F.I.C.A. tax.................	S-V		520.40	493.28	515.00	21.72
Workmen's insurance..........	S-V		130.10	123.32	128.75	5.43
Provision for vacation pay...	S-V		520.40	493.28	515.00	21.72
Factory operating supplies...	V	.004	80.00	76.00	78.00	2.00
Repairs and repair parts.....	V	.002	40.00	38.00	39.00	1.00
Electric light and power.....	V	.004	80.00	76.00	78.00	2.00
Unclassified.................	V	.0011985	23.97	22.77	25.00	2.23
Depreciation on machinery and equipment...	F		170.00	170.00	170.00	
Insurance on inventory.......	F		89.50	89.50	89.50	
Insurance on machinery and equipment...	F		40.00	40.00	40.00	
Taxes on inventory...........	F		96.00	96.00	96.00	
Taxes on machinery and equipment...	F		81.65	81.65	81.65	
Total direct departmental expense......			$ 2,892.02	$ 2,713.80	$ 2,775.90	$ 62.10
Service charges:						
Rent: 9,117.5 square feet @ $.10 per square foot.....			911.75	911.75	911.75	
General factory administration: Original budget: 20,000 standard hours @ $.16544... Adjusted budget: 19,000 standard hours @ .16544... Actual: 19,100 actual hours @ .16544...			3,308.84	3,143.36	3,159.91	16.55
Total departmental expense......			$ 7,112.61	$ 6,768.91	$ 6,847.56	$ 78.65
Assembly department No. 2 expense charged to work in process: Standard hours produced @ $.36...				6,840.00	6,840.00	
Spending variance (Actual expense − Budget adjusted to current volume)........						$ 78.65
Volume variance (Budget adjusted to current volume − Charge work in process)......				$ 71.09*		
Net variance (Actual expense − Charge work in process)........					$ 7.56	

* Red.

Figure I-13

755

BENSON & WEST MANUFACTURING COMPANY
Warehouse and Shipping Variance Report
Month of March, 19___

| | (1) | (2) | Budget Adjusted to Level | | | | (4) | (5) | Variances | |
| | | | (3) | | | | | | (6) | (7) |
Function	Original Budget	Charge Cost of Shipments†	Description of Units	Actual Units	Per Unit	Amount	Actual Expense	Net (4 − 2)	Controllable (4 − 3)	Volume (3 − 2)
Formula		$						$	$	$
Putting goods into stock	$ 153.00		Product units received	14,000	$.01	$ 140.00	$ 210.00		$ 70.00	
Order picking	304.00		Product units picked	15,000	.02	300.00	300.00			
Packing	600.00		Product units packed	14,880	.04	595.20	744.00		148.80	
Packing cases	540.00		Orders packed	2,880	.20	576.00	576.00			
Warehouse equipment—Maintenance, repair, and operation	152.00						150.00			
Shipping department clerical	324.00		Product units picked	15,000	.01	150.00	150.00			
			Orders packed	2,880	.12	345.60	345.60			
Totals	$2,073.00	2,112.00				$2,106.80	$2,325.60	$213.60	$218.80	$ 5.20*
Capacity cost:										
Supervision	$ 375.00					$ 375.00	$ 400.00			
Insurance and taxes on inventory	285.00					285.00	285.00			
Fixed charges on equipment	250.00					250.00	250.00			
Rent—Warehouse	312.50					312.50	312.50			
Totals	$1,222.50	1,196.35				$1,222.50	$1,247.50	51.15	25.00	26.15
Total function	$3,295.50	$3,308.35				$3,329.30	$3,573.10	$264.75	$243.80	$20.95
		I-1								

Reference, Figures

† Charge cost of shipments:

Variable—
14,880 units shipped @ $.08 .... $1,190.40
2,880 orders shipped @ $.32 .... 921.60

Total $2,112.00

Fixed—
14,880 units shipped @ $.0804 .... 1,196.35

Total charge $3,308.35

Figure I-14

*Credit

BENSON & WEST MANUFACTURING COMPANY
Variance Report: Direct Selling and Promotion
for Month of March, 19___

Function	Description of Functional Unit	Budget			Actual Expense			Variance
		Units	Per Unit	Amount	Units	Per Unit	Amount	
Direct selling by salesmen:								
Salaries..............			$	$ 700.00		$	$ 700.00	$
Commissions............	5% of sales			1,729.50			1,594.45	135.05*
Subsistence.............	Days subsisted	200	9.50	1,900.00	180	10.00	1,800.00	100.00*
Travel:								
Automobile—Variable expense.....	Miles traveled	13,000	.07	910.00	12,900	.08	1,032.00	122.00
Public transport........				500.00			300.00	200.00*
Sales promotion........				9,000.00			9,101.00	101.00
Sales office clerical activities......	Orders received	2,850	.36	1,026.00	3,000	.35	1,050.00	24.00
Totals (Figure I-1).........				$15,765.50			$15,577.45	$188.05*
Capacity cost:								
Supervision........				$ 900.00			$ 1,000.00	$100.00
Fixed charges........				523.82			503.82	20.00*
Sales office rent........				164.00			164.00	
Total capacity cost (Figure I-1)..				$ 1,587.82			$ 1,667.82	$ 80.00
Total function........				$17,353.32			$17,245.27	$108.05*

* Credit.

Figure I-15

757

BENSON & WEST MANUFACTURING COMPANY
Variance Report: Order Department and Cash Collecting
for Month of March, 19___

Function	Description of Functional Unit	Budget Units	Budget Per Unit	Budget Amount	Actual Units	Actual Per Unit	Actual Amount	Variance
Credit investigation—Prospective customers	Investigations	140	$4.00	$ 560.00	146	$4.00	$ 584.00	$ 24.00
Passing orders for credit	Charge orders	2,600	.09	234.00	2,690	.10	269.00	35.00
Editing orders	Orders shipped	2,700	.28	756.00	2,880	.30	864.00	108.00
Typing shipping orders	Orders shipped	2,700	.15	405.00	2,880	.15	432.00	27.00
Order register and follow-up	Orders shipped	2,700	.05	135.00	2,880	.05	144.00	9.00
Invoicing:								
Headings	Invoices	2,800	.15	420.00	2,960	.14	414.40	5.60*
Line items	Line items	4,000	.01	40.00	4,260	.01	42.60	2.60
Charging customers' accounts	Invoices	2,800	.02	56.00	2,960	.03	88.80	32.80
Customers' monthly statements	Statements mailed	1,400	.06	84.00	1,585	.06	95.10	11.10
Recording cash sales	Cash orders	250	.03	7.50	310	.03	9.30	1.80
Crediting customers' accounts	Receipts	1,200	.03	36.00	1,490	.03	44.70	8.70
Bad debts provision	½% of charge sales			690.00			694.28	4.28
Totals (Figure I-1)				$3,423.50			$3,682.18	$258.68
Capacity costs:								
Supervision and general				$ 400.00			$ 400.00	$
Fixed charges on furniture and equipment				183.33			183.33	
Rent				54.50			54.50	
Total capacity cost (Figure I-1)				$ 637.83			$ 637.83	
Total function				$4,061.33			$4,320.01	$258.68

* Credit.

Figure I-16

BENSON & WEST MANUFACTURING COMPANY
Variance Report: Delivery Expense
for Month of March, 19___

Function	Description of Functional Unit	Budget			Actual Expense			Variance
		Units	Per Unit	Amount	Units	Per Unit	Amount	
Loading and unloading............	Loading and un-loading hours	80	$3.50	$ 280.00	80	$ 4.00	$ 320.00	$ 40.00
Trucks operation:								
Wages................	Operating hours	240	3.50	840.00	240	4.00	960.00	120.00
Gas and oil.............	Miles	5,000	.14	700.00	4,800	.15	720.00	20.00
Truck repairs............	Miles	5,000	.09	450.00	4,800	.10	480.00	30.00
Totals (Figure I-1)...........				$2,270.00			$2,480.00	$210.00
Capacity cost:								
Supervision.................				$ 500.00			$ 500.00	$
Fixed charges:								
Garage equipment..........				62.00			62.00	
Trucks...................				198.34			198.34	
Garage rent.................				125.00			125.00	
Total capacity cost (Figure I-1)......				$ 885.34			$ 885.34	$
Total function.........				$3,155.34			$3,365.34	$210.00

Figure I-17

BENSON & WEST MANUFACTURING COMPANY
Administrative Expense: Budget and Actual

for Month of March, 19__

	Budget	Actual	Increase or Decrease*
Salaries:			
Executive salaries—			
President...................	$1,800.00	$1,800.00	$
Controller and treasurer..............	1,000.00	1,000.00	
Cost accountant....................	700.00	700.00	
Head bookkeeper..................	500.00	500.00	
Totals.....................	$4,000.00	$4,000.00	$
Office salaries—			
Receptionist......................	300.00	325.00	25.00
Total salaries.................	$4,300.00	$4,325.00	$25.00
Supplies:			
Printed forms....................	$ 40.00	$ 50.00	$10.00
Office supplies...................	30.00	35.00	5.00
Total supplies.................	$ 70.00	$ 85.00	$15.00
Purchased services:			
Electric light and power...............	$ 20.00	$ 22.00	$ 2.00
Telephone and telegraph..............	60.00	70.00	10.00
Legal and accounting fees..............	200.00	180.00	20.00*
Dues and subscription................	50.00	50.00	
Donations.......................	60.00	50.00	10.00*
Total purchased services..........	$ 390.00	$ 372.00	$18.00*
Travel.............................	$ 200.00	$ 180.00	$20.00*
Unclassified.......................	$ 40.00	$ 45.00	$ 5.00
Noncash charges:			
Depreciation—Furniture and equipment...	$ 33.33	$ 33.33	$
Insurance—Furniture and equipment......	8.33	8.33	
Taxes—Furniture and equipment........	10.00	10.00	
Rent.............................	164.00	164.00	
Total noncash charges............	$ 215.66	$ 215.66	$
Total department (Figure I-1).............	$5,215.66	$5,222.66	$ 7.00

* Red.

Figure I-18

Note also that the sales promotion budget was exceeded, and that the budget for capacity cost was exceeded, either by an addition to supervisory staff time or by a raise in salary.

Variance statement: Order department and cash collecting. The variance statement for Order Department and Cash Collecting (page 758) is the same in form and method of preparation as the variance report for Selling and Promotion. Note that total actual expense exceeded total budget by $258.65. This is caused partly by increased unit costs and partly by increased work load. (The amount of the excess spending attributable to each cause can be "analyzed out" if desired.)

Variance statement: Delivery. This report is similar in structure and use to the analysis reports and variance reports prepared for the Selling Department and the Order Department, illustrated and explained earlier in this chapter. Note that the unit costs of labor are considerably above standard.

Administrative expense: Budget and actual. This report is a simple comparison of actual expense with the original budget, account by account. The $7 net increase in spending over the budget is the difference between several increases and several decreases over the budget.

Journal entries. Following are the journal entries upon which the Statement of Profits on page 743 is based:

(1)

Materials inventory..........................	$29,300.00	
Materials price variance....................	420.00	
Accounts payable.......................		$29,720.00

To record purchases of materials for month of March, as follows:

Actual Quantities

Material	@ Standard Prices	@ Actual Prices	Price Variance
a............	$ 2,500.00	$ 2,600.00	$100.00
b............	1,500.00	1,450.00	50.00*
c............	2,800.00	2,870.00	70.00
d............	22,500.00	22,800.00	300.00
	$29,300.00	$29,720.00	$420.00

* Credit

(2)

Materials in process inventory...............	$30,670.00	
Materials quantity variance.................	350.00	
Materials inventory....................		$31,020.00

To record materials used for month of March, as follows:

(@ Standard Prices)

Material	Standard Quantities Allowed	Excess Quantities Used	Total Quantities
a............	$ 2,550.00	$100.00	$ 2,650.00
b............	1,560.00	60.00	1,620.00
c............	2,560.00	40.00	2,600.00
d............	24,000.00	150.00	24,150.00
	$30,670.00	$350.00	$31,020.00

(3)

Labor in process inventory.................	$39,656.25	
Labor variance............................	970.25	
Accrued payroll........................		$40,626.50

To record standard labor produced and actual
labor accrued for month, per Summary of
Labor Costs, page 749.

(4)

Factory expense control account..............	$17,133.96	
Accounts payable and other credits.......		$17,133.96

To record actual factory expense including actual building maintenance and fixed charges

(5)

Factory expense in process inventory.........	$14,619.85	
Administrative and selling expense...........	820.00	
Factory expense variance...................	1,694.11	
Factory expense control.................		$17,133.96

To record (a) standard factory expense absorbed per Summary of Standard Factory Expense Applied (Figure I-8) and (b) standard
rent charge to administrative and distribution
departments, to close actual factory expense,
and to record expense variance

(6)

Finished goods inventory....................	$88,277.20	
Materials in process inventory...........		$34,292.00
Labor in process inventory..............		39,300.00
Factory expense in process inventory.....		14,585.20

To record standard cost of goods manufactured for month, per Summary of Standard
Cost of Goods Manufactured, Figure I-19

(7)

Cost of goods sold.........................	$95,805.20	
Finished goods inventory...............		$95,805.20

To record cost of goods sold for month, as
follows:

		Standard Cost	
Product	Quantity	Each	Total
A.................	1,720	$3.93	$ 6,759.60
B.................	1,390	4.57	6,352.30
C.................	1,890	4.97	9,393.30
D................	10,000	7.33	73,300.00
	15,000		$95,805.20

(Standard product costs used in this entry and in the gross profit schedules, Figures
I-2 to I-4, are rounded to the nearest cent.)

BENSON & WEST MANUFACTURING COMPANY
Cost of Goods Produced, by Element

Month of March, 19__

Product	Quantity	Materials		Labor		Factory Expense		Total	
		Each	Total	Each	Total	Each	Total	Each	Total
A......	1,920	$1.50	$ 2,880.00	$1.625	$ 3,120.00	$ .808	$ 1,551.36	$3.933	$ 7,551.36
B......	1,290	1.20	1,548.00	2.25	2,902.50	1.123	1,348.67	4.573	5,899.17
C......	1,790	1.60	2,864.00	2.25	4,027.50	1.123	2,010.17	4.973	8,901.67
D......	9,000	3.00	27,000.00	3.25	29,250.00	1.075	9,675.00	7.325	65,925.00
Totals....	14,000		$34,292.00		$39,300.00		$14,585.20		$88,277.20

Figure I-19

Appendix II ~~~~~~

COMPLETE BUDGET FOR BENSON & WEST
MANUFACTURING COMPANY
(a hypothetical company)

Six Months Ending June 30, 19__

For the following budget statements, see the text chapters:

Figure 23-1   Budget Statement of Profits (page 562)
Figure 23-2   Budget Schedule of Cash Receipts and Disbursements (page 564)
Figure 23-3   Budget Balance Sheets (pages 566-567)

Figure numbers. The illustrations of budget worksheets in Chapters 23-25 each cover two or three months. They are all taken from the six months' illustrations in this Appendix. As far as applicable, the same series of figure numbers is used in Appendix II as in Chapters 23-25.

BENSON & WEST MANUFACTURING COMPANY
Budget Shipments, Goods Produced, and Finished Goods Inventories, by Months
Six Months Ending June 30, 19___

Product	January Units	January Total Sales	January Total Cost	February Units	February Total Sales	February Total Cost	March Units	March Total Sales	March Total Cost
Goods shipped									
A	1,000	$ 7,100.00	$ 3,962.50	1,500	$ 10,650.00	$ 5,943.75	2,000	$ 14,200.00	$ 7,925.00
B	600	4,740.00	2,767.50	1,200	9,480.00	5,535.00	1,800	14,220.00	8,302.50
C	500	4,200.00	2,506.25	1,000	8,400.00	5,012.50	2,000	16,800.00	10,025.00
D	5,000	52,500.00	36,725.00	5,000	52,500.00	36,725.00	10,000	105,000.00	73,450.00
Total all products	7,100	$68,540.00	$45,961.25	8,700	$ 81,030.00	$ 53,216.25	15,800	$150,220.00	$ 99,702.50
CUMULATIVE									
A	1,000	$ 7,100.00	$ 3,962.50	2,500	$ 17,750.00	$ 9,906.25	4,500	$ 31,950.00	$ 17,831.25
B	600	4,740.00	2,767.50	1,800	14,220.00	8,302.50	3,600	28,440.00	16,605.00
C	500	4,200.00	2,506.25	1,500	12,600.00	7,518.75	3,500	29,400.00	17,543.75
D	5,000	52,500.00	36,725.00	10,000	105,000.00	73,450.00	20,000	210,000.00	146,900.00
Total all products	7,100	$68,540.00	$45,961.25	15,800	$149,570.00	$ 99,177.50	31,600	$299,790.00	$198,880.00
Goods produced — *MONTH*									
A	1,500		$ 5,943.75	1,500		$ 5,943.75	2,500		$ 9,906.25
B	900		4,151.25	1,400		6,457.50	1,700		7,841.25
C	700		3,508.75	1,200		6,015.00	2,100		10,526.25
D	6,500		47,742.50	6,000		44,070.00	12,500		91,812.50
Total all products	9,600		$61,346.25	10,100		$ 62,486.25	18,800		$120,086.25
CUMULATIVE									
A	1,500		$ 5,943.75	3,000		$ 11,887.50	5,500		$ 21,793.75
B	900		4,151.25	2,300		10,608.75	4,000		18,450.00
C	700		3,508.75	1,900		9,523.75	4,000		20,050.00
D	6,500		47,742.50	12,500		91,812.50	25,000		183,625.00
Total all products	9,600		$61,346.25	19,700		$123,832.50	38,500		$243,918.75
Month-end finished goods inventories									
A	500		$ 1,981.25	500		$ 1,981.25	1,000		$ 3,962.50
B	300		1,383.75	500		2,306.25	400		1,845.00
C	200		1,002.50	400		2,005.00	500		2,506.25
D	1,500		11,017.50	2,500		18,362.50	5,000		36,725.00
Total all products	2,500		$15,385.00	3,900		$ 24,655.00	6,900		$ 45,038.75

(*Figure 23-12b will be found on page 770*)

Figure 23-12a

BENSON & WEST MANUFACTURING COMPANY
Budget Labor in Goods Produced, Labor Input, and Labor in Process Inventories, by Months
Six Months Ending June 30, 19___

MONTH

	January				February				March			
		Standard Hours: Dollars				*Standard Hours: Dollars*				*Standard Hours: Dollars*		
	Product Units	Cutting Department	Assembly No. 1	Assembly No. 2	Product Units	Cutting Department	Assembly No. 1	Assembly No. 2	Product Units	Cutting Department	Assembly No. 1	Assembly No. 2
Labor in goods produced												
A...........	1,500	375	1,500		1,500	375	1,500		2,500	625	2,500	
B...........	900	225	1,350		1,400	350	2,100		1,700	425	2,550	
C...........	700	175	1,050		1,200	300	1,800		2,100	525	3,150	
D...........	6,500	3,250		13,000	6,000	3,000		12,000	12,500	6,250		25,000
Total units, standard hours.......	9,600	4,025	3,900	13,000	10,100	4,025	5,400	12,000	18,800	7,825	8,200	25,000
Total standard dollars, by department		$ 6,037.50	$ 4,875.00	$16,250.00		$ 6,037.50	$ 6,750.00	$15,000.00		$11,737.50	$10,250.00	$ 31,250.00
Grand total, standard dollars.........				$27,162.50				$27,787.50				$ 57,237.50

CUMULATIVE

	January				February				March			
		Standard Hours: Dollars				*Standard Hours: Dollars*				*Standard Hours: Dollars*		
	Product Units	Cutting Department	Assembly No. 1	Assembly No. 2	Product Units	Cutting Department	Assembly No. 1	Assembly No. 2	Product Units	Cutting Department	Assembly No. 1	Assembly No. 2
A...........	1,500	375	1,500		3,000	750	3,000		5,500	1,375	5,500	
B...........	900	225	1,350		2,300	575	3,450		4,000	1,000	6,000	
C...........	700	175	1,050		1,900	475	2,850		4,000	1,000	6,000	
D...........	6,500	3,250		13,000	12,500	6,250		25,000	25,000	12,500		50,000
Total units, standard hours.......	9,600	4,025	3,900	13,000	19,700	8,050	9,300	25,000	38,500	15,875	17,500	50,000
Total standard dollars, by department		$ 6,037.50	$ 4,875.00	$16,250.00		$12,075.00	$11,625.00	$31,250.00		$23,812.50	$21,875.00	$ 62,500.00
Grand total, standard dollars.........				$27,162.50				$54,950.00				$108,187.50

MONTH — Labor charged to process

A	625	4,000		500	1,000		500	1,000	
B	625	2,500		500	2,000		1,250	2,050	
C	560	2,000		565	2,000		750	3,000	
D	5,000		15,000	5,000		15,000	5,000		25,000
Total standard hours	6,810	8,500	15,000	6,565	5,000	15,000	7,500	6,050	25,000
Total standard dollars, by department	$10,215.00	$10,625.00	$18,750.00	$9,847.50	$6,250.00	$18,750.00	$11,250.00	$7,562.50	$31,250.00
Grand total, standard dollars	$39,590.00			$34,847.50			$50,062.50		

CUMULATIVE

A	625	4,000		1,125	5,000		1,625	6,000	
B	625	2,500		1,125	4,500		2,375	6,550	
C	560	2,000		1,125	4,000		1,875	7,000	
D	5,000		15,000	10,000		30,000	15,000		55,000
Total standard hours	6,810	8,500	15,000	13,375	13,500	30,000	20,875	19,550	55,000
Total standard dollars, by department	$10,215.00	$10,625.00	$18,750.00	$20,062.50	$16,875.00	$36,250.00	$31,312.50	$24,437.50	$68,750.00
Grand total, standard dollars	$39,590.00			$74,437.50			$124,500.00		

Month-end labor in process inventories

A	250	2,500		375	2,000		250	500	
B	400	1,150		550	1,050		1,375	550	
C	385	950		650	1,150		875	1,000	
D	1,750		2,000	3,750		5,000	2,500		5,000
Total standard hours	2,785	4,600	2,000	5,325	4,200	5,000	5,000	2,050	5,000
Total standard dollars, by department	$4,177.50	$5,750.00	$2,300.00	$7,987.50	$5,250.00	$6,250.00	$7,500.00	$2,562.50	$6,250.00
Grand total, standard dollars	$12,427.50			$19,487.50			$16,312.50		

Figure 23-13a

BENSON & WEST MANUFACTURING COMPANY
Budget Labor in Goods Produced, Labor Input, and Labor in Process Inventories, by Months
Six Months Ending June 30, 19___

	April				May				June				Average Month
	Standard Hours: Dollars				*Standard Hours: Dollars*				*Standard Hours: Dollars*				
	Product Units	Cutting Department	Assembly No. 1	Assembly No. 2	Product Units	Cutting Department	Assembly No. 1	Assembly No. 2	Product Units	Cutting Department	Assembly No. 1	Assembly No. 2	
MONTH													
Labor in goods produced													
A	2,300	575	2,300		1,700	425	1,700		1,000	250	1,000		
B	2,000	500	3,000		3,150	787.5	4,725		2,050	512.5	3,075		
C	2,300	575	3,450		2,850	712.5	4,275		1,450	362.5	2,175		
D	12,500	6,250		25,000	14,000	7,000		28,000	8,500	4,250		17,000	
Total units, standard hours....	19,100	7,900	8,750	25,000	21,700	8,925	10,700	28,000	13,000	5,375	6,250	17,000	
Total standard dollars, by department		$11,850.00	$10,937.50	$31,250.00		$13,387.50	$15,375.00	$35,000.00		$8,062.50	$7,812.50	$21,250.00	
Grand total, standard dollars...				$54,037.50				$61,762.50				$37,125.00	
CUMULATIVE													
A	7,800	1,950	7,800		9,500	2,375	9,500		10,500	2,625	10,500		
B	6,000	1,500	9,000		9,150	2,287.5	13,725		11,200	2,800	16,800		
C	6,300	1,575	9,450		9,150	2,287.5	13,725		10,600	2,650	15,900		
D	37,500	18,750		75,000	51,500	25,750		103,000	60,000	30,000		120,000	
Total units, standard hours....	57,600	23,775	26,250	75,000	79,300	32,700	36,950	103,000	92,300	38,075	43,200	120,000	
Total standard dollars, by department		$35,662.50	$32,812.50	$93,750.00		$49,050.00	$46,187.50	$128,750.00		$57,112.50	$54,000.00	$150,000.00	
Grand total, standard dollars...				$162,225.00				$223,987.50				$261,112.50	
MONTH													
Labor charged to process													
A		625	2,500			250	1,500			125	500		
B		125	2,450			300	4,725			433	3,075		
C		750	3,000			275	3,725			242	2,175		
D		6,000		25,000		6,000		24,000		3,000		16,000	
Total standard hours		7,500	7,950	25,000		6,825	9,950	24,000		3,800	5,750	16,000	

768

					CUMULATIVE				
Total standard dollars, by department	$11,250.00	$9,937.50	$31,250.00	$10,237.50	$12,437.50	$30,000.00	$5,700.00	$7,187.50	$20,000.00
Grand total, standard dollars...		$52,437.50	$52,437.50		$52,675.00			$32,887.50	
A...............	2,250	8,500		2,500	10,000		2,625	10,500	
B...............	2,500	9,000		2,800	13,725		3,233	16,800	
C...............	2,625	10,000		2,900	13,725		3,142	15,900	
D...............	21,000		80,000	27,000		104,000	30,000		120,000
Total standard hours	28,375	27,500	80,000	35,200	37,450	104,000	39,000	43,200	120,000
Total standard dollars, by department	$42,562.50	$34,375.00	$100,000.00	$52,800.00	$46,812.50	$130,000.00	$58,500.00	$54,000.00	$150,000.00
Grand total, standard dollars...		$176,937.50			$229,612.50			$262,500.00	
Month-end labor in process inventories									
A...............	300	700		125	500		433		
B...............	1,000	550		512.5			492		
C...............	1,050			612.5					
D...............	2,250		5,000	1,250		1,000			
Total standard hours	4,600	1,250	5,000	2,500	500	1,000			
Total standard dollars, by department	$6,700.00	$1,562.50	$6,250.00	$3,750.00	$625.00	$1,250.00	$1,387.50	$1,387.50	$11,658.00
Grand total, standard dollars...		$14,712.50			$5,625.00				

Average Budget Labor in Process Inventories

Product	Cutting Department	Assembly No. 1	Assembly No. 2	Total
A............	$ 325.50	$1,292.50	$	$ 1,618.00
B............	1,067.40	572.50		1,639.90
C............	1,016.10	760.00		1,776.10
D............	2,874.00		3,750.00	6,624.00
Totals........	$5,283.00	$2,625.00	$3,750.00	$11,658.00

Figure 23-13b

BENSON & WEST MANUFACTURING COMPANY

Budget Shipments, Goods Produced, and Finished Goods Inventories, by Months

Six Months Ending June 30, 19___

	April			May			June			
	Product Units	Total Sales	Total Cost	Product Units	Total Sales	Total Cost	Product Units	Total Sales	Total Cost	Average Inventory
Goods shipped — MONTH										
A	2,500	$17,750.00	$9,906.25	2,000	$14,200.00	$7,925.00	1,500	$10,650.00	$5,943.75	
B	2,000	15,800.00	9,225.00	3,400	26,860.00	15,682.50	2,200	17,380.00	10,147.50	
C	2,500	21,000.00	12,531.25	3,000	25,200.00	15,037.50	1,600	13,440.00	8,020.00	
D	15,000	157,500.00	110,175.00	16,000	168,000.00	117,520.00	4,000	42,000.00	29,380.00	
Total all products	22,000	$212,050.00	$141,837.50	24,400	$234,260.00	$156,165.00	9,300	$83,470.00	$53,491.25	
CUMULATIVE										
A	7,000	49,700.00	27,737.50	9,000	63,900.00	35,662.50	10,500	74,550.00	41,606.25	
B	5,600	44,240.00	25,830.00	9,000	71,100.00	41,512.50	11,200	88,480.00	51,660.00	
C	6,000	50,400.00	30,075.00	9,000	75,600.00	45,112.50	10,600	89,040.00	53,132.50	
D	35,000	367,500.00	257,075.00	51,000	535,500.00	374,595.00	55,000	577,500.00	403,975.00	
Total all products	53,600	$511,840.00	$340,717.50	78,000	$746,100.00	$496,882.50	87,300	$829,570.00	$550,373.75	
Goods produced — MONTH										
A	2,300		9,113.75	1,700		6,736.25	1,000		3,962.50	
B	2,000		9,225.00	3,150		14,529.38	2,050		9,455.62	
C	2,300		11,528.75	2,850		14,285.62	1,450		7,268.13	
D	12,500		91,812.50	14,000		102,830.00	8,500		62,432.50	
Total all products	19,100		$121,680.00	21,700		$138,381.25	13,000		$83,118.75	
CUMULATIVE										
A	7,800		30,907.50	9,500		37,643.75	10,500		41,606.25	
B	6,000		27,675.00	9,150		42,204.38	11,200		51,660.00	
C	6,300		31,578.75	9,150		45,864.37	10,600		53,132.50	
D	37,500		275,437.50	51,500		378,267.50	60,000		440,700.00	
Total all products	57,600		$365,598.75	79,300		$503,980.00	92,300		$587,098.75	
Month-end finished goods inventories										
A	800		3,170.00	500		1,981.25				$ 2,179.37
B	400		1,845.00	150		691.88				1,345.31
C	300		1,503.75	150		751.87				1,294.89
D	2,500		18,362.50	500		3,672.50	5,000		36,725.00	20,810.83
Total all products	4,000		$24,881.25	1,300		$7,097.50	5,000		$36,725.00	$25,630.40

Figure 23-12b

770

BENSON & WEST MANUFACTURING COMPANY

Budget Materials in Goods Produced, Materials Receipts, and Materials Inventories, by Months

Six Months Ending June 30, 19___

	January			February			March		
	Product Units	Standard Yards	Standard Dollars	Product Units	Standard Yards	Standard Dollars	Product Units	Standard Yards	Standard Dollars
Materials in goods produced									
MONTH									
A (3 yards unit)	1,500	4,500	$ 2,250.00	1,500	4,500	$ 2,250.00	2,500	7,500	$ 3,750.00
B (2 yards unit)	900	1,800	1,080.00	1,400	2,800	1,680.00	1,700	3,400	2,040.00
C (2 yards unit)	700	1,400	1,120.00	1,200	2,400	1,920.00	2,100	4,200	3,360.00
D (2 yards unit)	6,500	13,000	19,500.00	6,000	12,000	18,000.00	12,500	25,000	37,500.00
Totals	9,600	20,700	$23,950.00	10,100	21,700	$23,850.00	18,800	40,100	$ 46,650.00
CUMULATIVE									
A	1,500	4,500	$ 2,250.00	3,000	9,000	$ 4,500.00	5,500	16,500	$ 8,250.00
B	900	1,800	1,080.00	2,300	4,600	2,760.00	4,000	8,000	4,800.00
C	700	1,400	1,120.00	1,900	3,800	3,040.00	4,000	8,000	6,400.00
D	6,500	13,000	19,500.00	12,500	25,000	37,500.00	25,000	50,000	75,000.00
Totals	9,600	20,700	$23,950.00	19,500	42,400	$47,800.00	38,500	82,500	$ 94,450.00
Materials receipts									
MONTH									
A ($ .50/yard)		9,000	$ 4,500.00		4,500	$ 2,250.00		7,500	$ 3,750.00
B ($ .60/yard)		5,400	3,240.00		3,200	1,920.00		6,100	3,660.00
C ($ .80/yard)		4,600	3,680.00		3,700	2,960.00		4,700	3,760.00
D ($1.50/yard)		25,000	37,500.00		20,000	30,000.00		20,000	30,000.00
Totals		44,000	$48,920.00		31,400	$37,130.00		38,300	$ 41,170.00
CUMULATIVE									
A		9,000	$ 4,500.00		13,500	$ 6,750.00		21,000	$ 10,500.00
B		5,400	3,240.00		8,600	5,160.00		14,700	8,820.00
C		4,600	3,680.00		8,300	6,640.00		13,000	10,400.00
D		25,000	37,500.00		45,000	67,500.00		65,000	97,500.00
Totals		44,000	$48,920.00		75,400	$86,050.00		113,700	$127,220.00
Month-end inventories: raw and process									
A ($ .50/yard)		4,500	$ 2,250.00		4,500	$ 2,250.00		4,500	$ 2,250.00
B ($ .60/yard)		3,600	2,160.00		4,000	2,400.00		6,700	4,020.00
C ($ .80/yard)		3,200	2,560.00		4,500	3,600.00		5,000	4,000.00
D ($1.50/yard)		12,000	18,000.00		20,000	30,000.00		15,000	22,500.00
Totals		23,300	$24,970.00		33,000	$38,250.00		31,200	$ 32,770.00

Figure 23-14a

BENSON & WEST MANUFACTURING COMPANY

Budget Materials in Goods Produced, Materials Receipts, and Materials Inventories, by Months

Six Months Ending June 30, 19___

	April			May			June			Average Inventory
	Product Units	Standard Yards	Standard Dollars	Product Units	Standard Yards	Standard Dollars	Product Units	Standard Yards	Standard Dollars	
Materials in goods produced										
MONTH										
A	2,300	6,900	$ 3,450.00	1,700	5,100	$ 3,450.00	1,000	3,000	$ 1,500.00	
B	2,000	4,000	2,400.00	3,150	6,300	2,400.00	2,050	4,100	2,460.00	
C	2,300	4,600	3,680.00	2,850	5,700	3,680.00	1,450	2,900	2,320.00	
D	12,500	25,000	37,500.00	14,000	28,000	37,500.00	8,500	17,000	25,500.00	
Totals	19,100	40,500	$ 47,030.00	21,700	45,100	$ 47,030.00	13,000	27,000	$ 31,780.00	
CUMULATIVE										
A	7,800	23,400	$ 11,700.00	9,500	28,500	$ 11,700.00	10,500	31,500	$ 15,750.00	
B	6,000	12,000	7,200.00	9,150	18,300	7,200.00	11,200	22,400	13,440.00	
C	6,300	12,600	10,080.00	9,150	18,300	10,080.00	10,600	21,200	16,960.00	
D	37,500	75,000	112,500.00	51,500	103,000	112,500.00	60,000	120,000	180,000.00	
Totals	57,600	123,000	$141,480.00	78,000	168,100	$141,480.00	92,300	195,100	$226,150.00	
Materials receipts										
MONTH										
A		6,900	$ 3,450.00		2,800	$ 1,400.00		1,500	$ 750.00	
B		1,800	1,080.00		6,400	3,840.00		1,500	900.00	
C		4,600	3,680.00		5,200	4,160.00		400	320.00	
D		23,000	34,500.00		19,000	28,500.00		13,000	19,500.00	
Totals		36,300	$ 42,710.00		33,400	$ 37,900.00		16,400	$ 21,470.00	
CUMULATIVE										
A		27,900	$ 13,950.00		30,700	$ 15,350.00		32,200	$ 16,100.00	
B		16,500	9,900.00		22,900	13,740.00		24,400	14,640.00	
C		17,600	14,080.00		22,800	18,240.00		23,200	18,560.00	
D		88,000	132,000.00		107,000	160,500.00		120,000	180,000.00	
Totals		150,000	$169,930.00		183,400	$207,830.00		199,800	$229,300.00	
Month-end inventories: raw and process										
A		4,500	$ 2,250.00		2,200	$ 1,100.00		700	$ 350.00	$ 1,741.66
B		4,500	2,700.00		4,600	2,760.00		2,000	1,200.00	2,540.00
C		5,000	4,000.00		4,500	3,600.00		2,000	1,600.00	3,226.66
D		13,000	19,500.00		4,000	6,000.00				1,600.00
Totals		27,000	$ 28,450.00		15,300	$ 13,460.00		4,700	$ 3,150.00	$23,508.32

Figure 23-14b

772

BENSON & WEST MANUFACTURING COMPANY
Budget Factory Expense in Goods Produced, Factory Expense Applied, and Factory Expense in Process Inventories, by Months
Six Months Ending June 30, 19___

	January			February			March		
	Cutting Department	Assembly No. 1	Assembly No. 2	Cutting Department	Assembly No. 1	Assembly No. 2	Cutting Department	Assembly No. 1	Assembly No. 2
Factory expense in goods produced									
Standard hours (Figure 23-13)	4,025	3,900	13,000	4,025	5,400	12,000	7,825	8,200	25,000
Expense rate per hour (Figure 24-10)	$ .75	$ .65	$ .36	$ .75	$ .65	$ .36	$ .75	$ .65	$ .36
Standard dollars, by department	$3,018.75	$2,535.00	$ 4,680.00	$ 3,018.75	$ 3,510.00	$ 4,320.00	$ 5,868.75	$ 5,330.00	$ 9,000.00
Standard dollars, all departments			$10,233.75			$10,848.75			$20,198.75
MONTH									
Standard hours	4,025	3,900	13,000	8,050	9,300	25,000	15,875	17,500	50,000
Standard dollars, by department	$2,535.00	$4,680.00	$ 3,018.75	$ 6,037.50	$ 6,045.00	$ 9,000.00	$11,906.25	$11,375.00	$18,000.00
Standard dollars, all departments			$10,233.75			$21,082.50			$41,281.25
CUMULATIVE									
Factory expense charged to work in process									
Standard hours	6,810	8,500	15,000	6,565	5,000	15,000	7,500	6,050	25,000
Standard dollars, by department	$5,107.50	$5,525.00	$ 5,400.00	$ 4,923.75	$ 3,250.00	$ 5,400.00	$ 5,625.00	$ 3,932.50	$ 9,000.00
Standard dollars, all departments			$16,032.50			$13,573.75			$18,557.50
MONTH									
Standard hours	6,810	8,500	15,000	13,375	13,500	30,000	20,875	19,550	55,000
Standard dollars, by department	$5,107.50	$5,525.00	$ 5,400.00	$10,031.25	$ 8,775.00	$10,800.00	$15,656.25	$12,707.50	$19,800.00
Standard dollars, all departments			$16,032.50			$29,606.25			$48,163.75
CUMULATIVE									
Month-end factory expense in process inventories									
Standard hours	2,785	4,600	2,000	5,325	4,200	5,000	5,000	2,050	5,000
Standard dollars, by department	$2,088.75	$2,990.00	$ 720.00	$ 3,993.75	$ 2,730.00	$ 1,800.00	$ 3,750.00	$ 1,332.50	$ 1,800.00
Standard dollars, all departments			$ 5,798.75			$ 8,523.75			$ 6,882.50

Figure 23-15a

BENSON & WEST MANUFACTURING COMPANY

Budget Factory Expense in Goods Produced, Factory Expense Applied, and Factory Expense in Process Inventories, by Months

Six Months Ending June 30, 19___

	April			May			June			Average Month
	Cutting Department	Assembly No. 1	Assembly No. 2	Cutting Department	Assembly No. 1	Assembly No. 2	Cutting Department	Assembly No. 1	Assembly No. 2	
Factory expense in goods produced										
Standard hours (Figure 23-13)	7,900	8,750	25,000	8,925	10,700	28,000	5,375	6,250	17,000	
Expense rate per hour (Figure 24-10)	$ .75	$ .65	$ .36	$ .75	$ .65	$ .36	$ .75	$ .65	$ .36	
Standard dollars, by department	$ 5,925.00	$ 5,687.50	$ 9,000.00	$ 6,693.75	$ 6,955.00	$ 10,080.00	$ 4,031.25	$ 4,062.50	$ 6,120.00	
Standard dollars, all departments			$20,612.50			$23,728.75			$ 14,213.75	
				CUMULATIVE						
Standard hours	23,775	26,250	75,000	32,700	36,950	103,000	38,075	43,200	120,000	
Standard dollars, by department	$17,831.25	$17,062.50	$27,000.00	$24,525.00	$24,017.50	$37,080.00	$28,556.25	$29,080.00	$ 43,200.00	
Standard dollars, all departments			$61,893.75			$85,622.50			$ 99,836.25	
Factory expense charged to work in process				*MONTH*						
Standard hours	7,500	7,950	25,000	6,825	9,950	24,000	3,800	5,750	16,000	
Standard dollars, by department	$ 5,625.00	$ 5,167.50	$ 9,000.00	$ 5,118.75	$ 6,467.50	$ 8,640.00	$ 2,850.00	$ 3,737.50	$ 5,760.00	
Standard dollars, all departments			$19,792.50			$20,226.25			$ 12,347.50	
				CUMULATIVE						
Standard hours	28,375	27,500	80,000	35,200	37,450	104,000	30,000	43,200	120,000	
Standard dollars, by department	$21,281.25	$17,875.00	$28,800.00	$26,400.00	$24,342.50	$37,440.00	$29,250.00	$28,080.00	$ 43,200.00	
Standard dollars, all departments			$67,956.25			$88,182.50			$100,530.00	
Month-end factory expense in process inventories										
Standard hours	4,600	1,250	5,000	2,500	500	1,000	925			
Standard dollars, by department	$ 3,450.00	$ 812.50	$ 1,800.00	$ 1,875.00	$ 325.00	$ 360.00	$ 693.75	$		
Standard dollars, all departments			$ 6,062.50			$ 2,560.00				$5,086.87

Average Factory Expense in Process Inventories

Product	Cutting Department	Assembly No. 1	Assembly No. 2	Total
A	$ 162.50	$ 672.10		$ 834.85
B	533.70	297.70		831.40
C	508.05	395.20		903.25
D	1,437.00		1,080.00	2,517.00
Totals	$2,641.50	$1,365.00	$1,080.00	$5,086.50

Figure 23-15b

BENSON & WEST MANUFACTURING COMPANY
Budget of Fixed Assets and Fixed Charges (Abbreviated)
(Six-Month Period: January–June, 19__)

	Totals	General Administration	Sales Department	Order Department and Cash Collecting	Finished Goods Warehouse	Garage and Delivery Department	Building	General Factory	Repair Shop	Raw Material Storage	Cutting Department	Assembly Department No. 1	Assembly Department No. 2
Fixed assets:	$	$	$	$	$	$	$	$	$	$	$	$	$
Land..................	$100,000.00						$100,000.00						
Building..............	200,000.00						200,000.00						
Office furniture and equipment	21,000.00	4,000.00	4,000.00	12,000.00				1,000.00					
Display fixtures......	4,000.00		4,000.00										
Autos.................	18,000.00		18,000.00										
Delivery trucks.......	6,000.00					6,000.00							
Machinery and equipment...	80,000.00				20,000.00	5,000.00			3,000.00	2,000.00	10,000.00	20,000.00	20,000.00
Total fixed assets......	$429,000.00	$4,000.00	$26,000.00	$12,000.00	$20,000.00	$11,000.00	$300,000.00	$1,000.00	$3,000.00	$2,000.00	$10,000.00	$20,000.00	$20,000.00
Depreciation:	$	$	$	$	$	$	$	$	$	$	$	$	$
Building..............	800.00						800.00						
Office furniture and equipment	178.33	33.33	20.00	100.00				25.00					
Display fixtures......	21.66		21.66										
Autos.................	300.00		300.00										
Delivery trucks.......	166.67					166.67							
Machinery and equipment...	608.31				166.67				8.33	19.99	80.00	166.66	166.66
Total depreciation....	$ 2,074.97	$ 33.33	$ 341.66	$ 100.00	$ 166.67	$ 166.67	$ 800.00	$ 25.00	$ 8.33	$ 19.99	$ 80.00	$ 166.66	$ 166.66
Insurance:	$	$	$	$	$	$	$	$	$	$	$	$	$
Building..............	400.00						400.00						
Office furniture and equipment	50.66	8.33	4.00	33.33				5.00					
Display fixtures......	4.33		4.33										
Autos.................	100.00		100.00										
Delivery trucks.......	41.69					41.69							
Machinery and equipment...	503.72				168.33				3.33	9.74	60.00	131.16	131.16
Total insurance.......	$ 1,100.40	$ 8.33	$ 108.33	$ 33.33	$ 168.33	$ 41.69	$ 400.00	$ 5.00	$ 3.33	$ 9.74	$ 60.00	$ 131.16	$ 131.16
Taxes:	$	$	$	$	$	$	$	$	$	$	$	$	$
Building..............	342.39						342.39						
Office furniture and equipment	71.00	10.00	1.00	50.00				10.00					
Display fixtures......	2.83		2.83										
Autos.................	70.00		70.00										
Delivery trucks.......	52.00					52.00							
Machinery and equipment...	662.15				200.00				5.50	17.99	80.00	179.33	179.33
Total taxes...........	$ 1,200.37	$ 10.00	$ 73.83	$ 50.00	$ 200.00	$ 52.00	$ 342.39	$ 10.00	$ 5.50	$ 17.99	$ 80.00	$ 179.33	$ 179.33

Figure 24-2

BENSON & WEST MANUFACTURING COMPANY
Budget Factory Expense Incurred: Building Maintenance and Fixed Charges
Month and Cumulative—Six Months Ending June 30, 19__

MONTH

Object	January	February	March	April	May	June	Average Month
Labor	$ 1,600.00	$ 1,600.00	$ 1,600.00	$ 1,600.00	$ 1,600.00	$ 1,600.00	$ 1,600.00
F.I.C.A. tax	32.00	32.00	32.00	32.00	32.00	32.00	32.00
Workmen's insurance	8.00	8.00	8.00	8.00	8.00	8.00	8.00
Provision for vacation pay	32.00	32.00	32.00	32.00	32.00	32.00	32.00
Supplies and repair parts	230.00	230.00	230.00	230.00	230.00	230.00	230.00
Purchased services and unclassified	576.68	576.68	576.68	576.68	576.68	576.68	576.68
Depreciation	800.00	800.00	800.00	800.00	800.00	800.00	800.00
Insurance	400.00	400.00	400.00	400.00	400.00	400.00	400.00
Taxes	342.39	342.39	342.39	342.39	342.39	342.39	342.39
Totals	$ 4,021.07	$ 4,021.07	$ 4,021.07	$ 4,021.07	$ 4,021.07	$ 4,021.07	$ 4,021.07

CUMULATIVE

Object	January	February	March	April	May	June
Labor	$ 1,600.00	$ 3,200.00	$ 4,800.00	$ 6,400.00	$ 8,000.00	$ 9,600.00
F.I.C.A. tax	32.00	64.00	96.00	128.00	160.00	192.00
Workmen's insurance	8.00	16.00	24.00	32.00	40.00	48.00
Provision for vacation pay	32.00	64.00	96.00	128.00	160.00	192.00
Supplies and repair parts	230.00	460.00	690.00	920.00	1,150.00	1,380.00
Purchased services and unclassified	576.68	1,153.36	1,730.04	2,306.72	2,883.40	3,460.08
Depreciation	800.00	1,600.00	2,400.00	3,200.00	4,000.00	4,800.00
Insurance	400.00	800.00	1,200.00	1,600.00	2,000.00	2,400.00
Taxes	342.39	684.78	1,027.17	1,369.56	1,711.95	2,054.34
Totals	$ 4,021.07	$ 8,042.14	$12,063.21	$16,084.28	$20,105.35	$24,126.42

Figure 24-3

BENSON & WEST MANUFACTURING COMPANY
Budget Factory Expense Incurred: General Factory Administration
Month and Cumulative—Six Months Ending June 30, 19___

MONTH

Object	January	February	March	April	May	June	Normal Month
Standard hours produced	30,310	26,565	38,550	40,450	40,775	25,550	33,700
Labor	$ 4,350.00	$ 4,350.00	$ 4,650.00	$ 4,650.00	$ 4,650.00	$ 4,350.00	$ 4,500.00
F.I.C.A. tax	87.00	87.00	87.00	93.00	93.00	87.00	90.00
Workmen's insurance	19.88	19.88	26.50	26.50	26.50	19.88	23.19
Provision for vacation pay	87.00	87.00	93.00	93.00	93.00	87.00	90.00
Supplies and repair parts	215.84	189.17	274.50	288.04	290.36	181.94	239.98
Purchased services and unclassified	263.52	230.95	335.15	351.67	354.40	222.13	292.97
Depreciation	33.33	33.33	33.33	33.33	33.33	33.33	33.33
Insurance	8.33	8.33	8.33	8.33	8.33	8.33	8.33
Taxes	15.50	15.50	15.50	15.50	15.50	15.50	15.50
Totals	$ 5,080.40	$ 5,021.17	$ 5,529.31	$ 5,559.37	$ 5,564.42	$ 5,005.11	$ 5,293.30

CUMULATIVE

Object	January	February	March	April	May	June
Standard hours produced	30,310	56,875	95,425	135,875	176,650	202,200
Labor	$ 4,350.00	$ 8,700.00	$13,350.00	$18,000.00	$22,650.00	$27,000.00
F.I.C.A. tax	87.00	174.00	267.00	360.00	453.00	540.00
Workmen's insurance	19.88	39.76	66.26	92.76	119.26	139.14
Provision for vacation pay	87.00	174.00	267.00	360.00	453.00	540.00
Supplies and repair parts	215.84	405.01	679.51	967.55	1,257.91	1,439.85
Purchased services and unclassified	263.52	494.48	829.63	1,181.30	1,535.70	1,757.83
Depreciation	33.33	66.66	99.99	133.32	166.65	199.98
Insurance	8.33	16.66	24.99	33.32	41.65	49.98
Taxes	15.50	31.00	46.50	62.00	77.50	93.00
Totals	$ 5,080.40	$10,101.57	$15,630.88	$21,190.25	$26,754.67	$31,739.78

Figure 24-4

BENSON & WEST MANUFACTURING COMPANY
Budget Factory Expense Incurred: Cutting Department
Month and Cumulative—Six Months Ending June 30, 19___

MONTH

Object	January	February	March	April	May	June	Normal Month
Standard hours produced	6,810	6,565	7,500	7,500	6,825	3,800	6,500
Labor	$ 1,363.84	$ 1,305.79	$ 1,492.30	$ 1,492.30	$ 1,483.94	$ 1,446.74	$ 1,430.82
F.I.C.A. tax	231.56	224.60	254.84	254.84	234.42	142.92	223.87
Workmen's insurance	57.89	56.15	63.71	63.71	8.60	35.73	55.96
Provision for vacation pay	231.56	224.60	254.84	254.84	234.42	142.92	223.86
Supplies and repair parts	419.20	404.00	461.52	461.52	422..2	233.81	400.43
Purchased services and unclassified	291.80	281.20	321.25	321.25	294.10	162.75	278.72
Depreciation	99.99	99.99	99.99	99.99	99.99	99.99	99.99
Insurance	69.74	69.74	69.74	69.74	69.74	69.74	69.74
Taxes	97.99	97.99	97.99	97.99	97.99	97.99	97.99
Totals	$ 2,863.57	$ 2,764.07	$ 3,116.18	$ 3,116.18	$ 2,995.72	$ 2,432.59	$ 2,881.38

CUMULATIVE

Object	January	February	March	April	May	June
Standard hours produced	6,810	13,375	20,875	28,375	35,200	39,000
Labor	$ 1,363.84	$ 2,669.63	$ 4,161.93	$ 5,654.23	$ 7,138.17	$ 8,584.91
F.I.C.A. tax	231.56	456.16	711.00	965.84	1,200.26	1,343.18
Workmen's insurance	57.89	114.04	177.75	241.46	300.06	335.79
Provision for vacation pay	231.56	456.16	711.00	965.84	1,200.26	1,343.18
Supplies and repair parts	419.20	823.20	1,284.72	1,746.24	2,168.76	2,402.57
Purchased and unclassified	291.80	573.01	894.26	1,215.51	1,509.61	1,672.36
Depreciation	99.99	199.98	279.97	399.96	499.95	599.94
Insurance	69.74	139.48	209.22	278.96	348.70	418.44
Taxes	97.99	195.98	293.97	391.96	489.95	587.94
Totals	$ 2,863.57	$ 5,627.64	$ 8,743.82	$11,860.00	$14,855.72	$17,288.31

Figure 24-5

BENSON & WEST MANUFACTURING COMPANY
Budget Factory Expense Incurred: Assembly Department No. 1
Month and Cumulative—Six Months Ending June 30, 19___

MONTH

Object	January	February	March	April	May	June	Normal Month
Standard hours produced	8,500	5,000	6,050	7,950	9,950	5,750	7,200
Labor	$ 1,360.00	$ 920.00	$ 920.00	$ 1,360.00	$ 1,500.00	$ 920.00	$ 1,163.34
F.I.C.A. tax	239.70	143.40	169.64	224.90	278.74	162.14	203.09
Workmen's insurance	59.43	35.85	42.81	56.23	69.68	40.53	50.75
Provision for vacation pay	239.70	143.40	169.64	224.90	278.74	162.14	203.09
Supplies and repair parts	244.80	144.00	174.24	228.96	286.56	165.60	207.36
Purchased services and unclassified	190.83	112.25	135.83	178.48	243.78	129.09	165.04
Depreciation	166.66	166.66	166.66	166.66	166.66	166.66	165.04
Insurance	131.16	131.16	131.16	131.16	131.16	131.16	131.16
Taxes	179.33	179.33	179.33	179.33	179.33	179.33	179.33
Totals	$ 2,811.61	$ 1,976.05	$ 2,089.31	$ 2,750.62	$ 3,134.65	$ 2,056.65	$ 2,469.82

CUMULATIVE

Object	January	February	March	April	May	June	Normal Month
Standard hours produced	8,500	13,500	19,550	27,500	37,450	43,200	7,200
Labor	$ 1,360.00	$ 2,280.00	$ 3,200.00	$ 4,560.00	$ 6,060.00	$ 6,980.00	$ 1,163.34
F.I.C.A. tax	239.70	383.10	552.74	777.64	1,056.38	1,218.52	203.09
Workmen's insurance	59.43	95.28	138.09	194.32	264.00	304.53	50.75
Provision for vacation pay	239.70	383.10	552.74	777.64	1,056.38	1,218.52	203.09
Supplies and repair parts	244.80	388.80	563.04	792.00	1,078.56	1,244.16	207.36
Purchased services and unclassified	190.83	303.08	438.91	617.39	861.17	990.26	165.04
Depreciation	166.66	333.32	499.98	666.64	833.30	999.96	166.66
Insurance	131.16	262.32	393.48	524.64	655.80	786.96	131.16
Taxes	179.33	358.66	537.99	717.32	896.65	1,075.98	179.33
Totals	$ 2,811.61	$ 4,787.66	$ 6,876.97	$ 9,627.59	$12,762.24	$14,818.89	$ 2,469.82

Figure 24-6

BENSON & WEST MANUFACTURING COMPANY
Budget Factory Expense Incurred: Assembly Department No. 2
Month and Cumulative—Six Months Ending June 30, 19___

MONTH

Object	January	February	March	April	May	June	Normal Month
Standard hours produced	15,000	15,000	25,000	25,000	24,000	16,000	20,000
Labor	$ 770.00	$ 770.00	$ 1,250.00	$ 1,250.00	$ 1,232.00	$ 788.00	$ 1,010.00
F.I.C.A. tax	390.40	390.40	650.00	650.00	624.64	415.76	520.20
Workmen's insurance	97.60	97.60	162.50	162.50	156.16	103.94	130.05
Provision for vacation pay	390.40	390.40	650.00	650.00	624.64	415.76	520.20
Supplies and repair parts	112.50	112.50	187.50	187.50	180.00	120.00	150.00
Purchased services and unclassified	76.38	76.38	127.32	127.32	122.16	81.44	101.83
Depreciation	166.66	166.66	166.66	166.66	166.66	166.66	166.66
Insurance	131.16	131.16	131.16	131.16	131.16	131.16	131.16
Taxes	179.33	179.33	179.33	179.33	179.33	179.33	179.33
Totals	$ 2,314.43	$ 2,314.43	$ 3,504.47	$ 3,504.47	$ 3,416.75	$ 2,402.05	$ 2,909.43

CUMULATIVE

Object	January	February	March	April	May	June	Normal Month
Standard hours produced	15,000	30,000	55,000	80,000	104,000	120,000	20,000
Labor	$ 770.00	$ 1,540.00	$ 2,790.00	$ 4,040.00	$ 5,272.00	$ 6,060.00	$ 1,010.00
F.I.C.A. tax	390.40	780.80	1,430.80	2,080.80	2,705.44	3,121.20	520.20
Workmen's insurance	97.60	195.20	357.70	520.20	676.36	780.30	130.05
Provision for vacation pay	390.40	780.80	1,430.80	2,080.80	2,705.44	3,121.20	520.20
Supplies and repair parts	112.50	225.00	412.50	600.00	780.00	900.00	150.00
Purchased services and unclassified	76.38	152.76	280.08	407.40	529.56	611.00	101.83
Depreciation	166.66	333.32	499.98	666.64	833.30	999.96	166.66
Insurance	131.16	262.32	393.48	524.64	655.80	786.96	131.16
Taxes	179.33	358.66	537.99	717.32	896.65	1,075.98	179.33
Totals	$ 2,314.43	$ 4,628.86	$ 8,133.33	$11,637.80	$15,054.55	$17,456.60	$ 2,909.43

Figure 24-7

BENSON & WEST MANUFACTURING COMPANY
Budget Factory Expense Incurred: All Departments
Month and Cumulative—Six Months Ending June 30, 19__

MONTH

Object	January	February	March	April	May	June	Normal Month
Standard hours produced............							
Labor...........................	$ 9,443.84	$ 8,945.79	$ 9,912.30	$10,352.30	$10,465.94	$ 9,104.74	$ 9,704.16
F.I.C.A. tax....................	980.66	877.40	1,199.48	1,254.74	1,262.80	839.82	1,069.16
Workmen's insurance.............	242.80	217.48	303.52	316.94	318.94	208.08	267.95
Provision for vacation pay.......	980.66	877.40	1,199.48	1,254.74	1,262.80	839.82	1,069.15
Supplies and repair parts........	1,222.34	1,079.67	1,327.76	1,396.02	1,409.44	931.35	1,227.77
Purchased services and unclassified.	1,399.21	1,277.48	1,496.23	1,555.40	1,591.12	1,172.09	1,415.24
Depreciation....................	1,266.64	1,266.64	1,266.64	1,266.64	1,266.64	1,266.64	1,266.64
Insurance.......................	740.39	740.39	740.39	740.39	740.39	740.39	740.39
Taxes...........................	814.54	814.54	814.54	814.54	814.54	814.54	814.54
Totals......................	$17,091.08	$16,096.79	$18,260.34	$18,951.71	$19,132.61	$ 15,917.47	$17,575.00

CUMULATIVE

Object	January	February	March	April	May	June	Normal Month
Standard hours produced............							
Labor...........................	$ 9,443.84	$18,389.63	$28,301.93	$38,654.23	$49,120.17	$ 58,224.91	
F.I.C.A. tax....................	980.66	1,858.06	3,057.54	4,312.28	5,575.08	6,414.90	
Workmen's insurance.............	242.80	460.28	763.80	1,080.74	1,399.68	1,607.76	
Provision for vacation pay.......	980.66	1,858.06	3,057.54	4,312.28	5,575.08	6,414.90	
Supplies and repair parts........	1,222.34	2,302.01	3,629.77	5,025.79	6,435.23	7,366.58	
Purchased services and unclassified.	1,399.21	2,676.69	4,172.92	5,728.32	7,319.44	8,491.53	
Depreciation....................	1,266.64	2,533.28	3,799.92	5,066.56	6,333.20	7,599.84	
Insurance.......................	740.39	1,480.78	2,221.17	2,961.56	3,701.95	4,442.34	
Taxes...........................	814.54	1,629.08	2,443.62	3,258.16	4,072.70	4,887.24	
Totals......................	$17,091.08	$33,187.87	$51,448.21	$70,399.92	$89,532.53	$105,450.00	

CREDITS TO PREPAID EXPENSE AND ACCRUED EXPENSE ACCOUNTS

Accounts Credited	January	February	March	April	May	June	
Accrued factory indirect labor...	$ 9,443.84	$ 8,945.79	$ 9,912.30	$10,352.30	$10,465.94	$ 9,104.74	
Accrued F.I.C.A. tax.............	980.66	877.40	1,199.48	1,254.74	1,262.80	839.82	
Prepaid workmen's insurance......	242.80	217.48	303.52	316.94	318.94	208.08	
Reserve for vacation pay.........	980.66	877.40	1,199.48	1,254.74	1,262.80	839.82	
Supplies inventory..............	1,222.34	1,079.67	1,327.76	1,396.02	1,409.44	931.35	
Accrued expense (purchased services)	1,399.21	1,277.48	1,496.23	1,555.40	1,591.12	1,172.09	
Reserve for depreciation.........	1,266.64	1,266.64	1,266.64	1,266.64	1,266.64	1,266.64	
Prepaid property insurance.......	740.39	740.39	740.39	740.39	740.39	740.39	
Accrued property tax.............	814.54	814.54	814.54	814.54	814.54	814.54	
Totals......................	$17,091.08	$16,096.79	$18,260.34	$18,951.71	$19,132.61	$ 15,917.47	

Dr. Factory Expense, J/E No. 7

Figure 24-8

BENSON & WEST MANUFACTURING COMPANY
Standard Expense Rate—Based upon Expected Average Production Volume

Line	Particulars	Building Maintenance and Fixed Charges	General Factory Administrations	Cutting	Assembly No. 1	Assembly No. 2	Selling and Administrative	Totals
1	Standard hours produced		33,700‡	6,500	7,200	20,000		
2	Total direct departmental expenses	$4,021.07	$5,293.30	$2,881.38	$2,469.82	$2,909.43	$	$17,575.00
3	Building maintenance and fixed charges allocated	4,021.07*	400.00	895.51	993.81	911.75	820.00	
4	Total general factory administration		5,693.30‡					
5	General factory administration expense allocated: (Rate per standard hour = $5,693.30 ÷ 33,700 = $.1689+)		5,693.30*	1,098.11	1,216.37	3,378.82		
6	Total departmental expense			$4,875.00	$4,680.00	$7,200.00	$820.00	$17,575.00
7	Rates per standard hour			$ .75	$ .65	$ .36		

Department	Standard Hours	Amount Allocated
Cutting	6,500	$1,098.11
Assembly department No. 1	7,200	1,216.37
Assembly department No. 2	20,000	3,378.82
Totals	33,700	$5,693.30

* Red
‡ Total

Figure 24-10

BENSON & WEST MANUFACTURING COMPANY
Standard Product Costs per Unit and Standard Selling Prices per Unit
Based upon Expected Average Volume for Six Months

Element and Department	Product A Yards or Hours per Unit	Product A Price or Rate	Product A Total Amount per Product Unit	Product B Yards or Hours per Unit	Product B Price or Rate	Product B Total Amount per Product Unit	Product C Yards or Hours per Unit	Product C Price or Rate	Product C Total Amount per Product Unit	Product D Yards or Hours per Unit	Product D Price or Rate	Product D Total Amount per Product Unit
Materials	3 yards	$ .50	$1.50	2 yards	$ .60	$1.20	2 yards	$ .80	$1.60	2 yards	$1.50	$ 3.00
Labor:												
Cutting department	.25 hour	1.50	.375	.25 hour	1.50	.375	.25 hour	1.50	.375	.5 hour	1.50	.75
Assembly department No. 1	1.0 hour	1.25	1.25	1.5 hours	1.25	1.875	1.5 hours	1.25	1.875	2.0 hours	1.25	2.50
Assembly department No. 2												
Factory expense:												
Cutting department	.25 hour	.75	.1875	.25 hour	.75	.1875	.25 hour	.75	.1875	.5 hour	.75	.375
Assembly department No. 1	1.0 hour	.65	.65	1.5 hours	.65	.975	1.5 hours	.65	.975	2.0 hours	.36	.72
Assembly department No. 2												
Totals per product unit			$3.9625			$4.6125			$5.0125			$ 7.345
Standard (desired average) selling prices per unit			$7.10			$7.90			$8.40			$10.50

Budget Order Department; Selling and Promotion Expense Incurred

Month and Cumulative—Six Months Ended June 30, 19__

Selling and Promotion	January	February	March	April	May	June
			MONTH			
Salaries....................	$1,880.00	$ 1,880.00	$ 1,880.00	$ 1,880.00	$ 1,880.00	$ 1,880.00
Commissions...............	789.66	933.93	1,729.50	2,441.36	2,694.78	960.91
Supplies...................	114.15	135.00	250.00	352.90	389.85	138.90
Purchased services and						
unclassified..............	5,847.22	6,915.24	12,806.00	18,076.95	19,969.68	7,115.01
Depreciation...............	341.66	341.66	341.66	341.66	341.66	341.66
Insurance..................	108.33	108.33	108.33	108.33	108.33	108.33
Taxes.....................	73.83	73.83	73.83	73.83	73.83	73.83
Rent......................	164.00	164.00	164.00	164.00	164.00	164.00
Totals................	$9,318.85	$10,551.99	$17,353.32	$23,439.03	$25,622.13	$10,782.64
			CUMULATIVE			
Salaries....................	$1,880.00	$ 3,760.00	$ 5,640.00	$ 7,520.00	$ 9,400.00	$11,280.00
Commissions...............	789.66	1,723.59	3,453.09	5,894.45	8,589.23	9,550.14
Supplies...................	114.15	249.15	499.15	852.05	1,241.90	1,380.80
Purchased services and						
unclassified..............	5,847.22	12,762.46	25,568.46	43,645.41	63,615.09	70,730.10
Depreciation...............	341.66	683.32	1,024.98	1,366.64	1,708.30	2,049.96
Insurance..................	108.33	216.66	324.99	433.32	541.65	649.98
Taxes.....................	73.83	147.66	221.49	295.32	369.15	442.98
Rent......................	164.00	328.00	492.00	656.00	820.00	984.00
Totals................	$9,318.85	$19,870.84	$37,224.16	$60,663.19	$86,285.32	$97,067.96

Figure 24-12

Order Department	January	February	March	April	May	June
			MONTH			
Supervisory salaries.........	$ 400.00	$ 400.00	$ 400.00	$ 400.00	$ 400.00	$ 400.00
Other labor................	750.88	888.03	1,644.50	2,321.38	2,546.43	913.68
Supplies.................	174.75	206.55	382.50	539.94	596.47	212.52
Purchased services and						
unclassified..............	322.59	381.51	706.50	997.30	1,096.82	392.53
Bad debts.................	315.05	372.60	690.00	974.00	1,075.99	383.37
Depreciation...............	100.00	100.00	100.00	100.00	100.00	100.00
Insurance..................	33.33	33.33	33.33	33.33	33.33	33.33
Taxes.....................	50.00	50.00	50.00	50.00	50.00	50.00
Rent......................	54.50	54.50	54.50	54.50	54.50	54.50
Totals................	$2,201.10	$ 2,486.52	$ 4,061.33	$ 5,470.45	$ 5,971.54	$ 2,539.93
			CUMULATIVE			
Supervisory salaries.........	$ 400.00	$ 800.00	$ 1,200.00	$ 1,600.00	$ 2,000.00	$ 2,400.00
Other labor................	750.88	1,638.91	3,283.41	5,604.79	8,169.22	9,082.90
Supplies..................	174.75	381.30	763.80	1,303.74	1,900.21	2,112.73
Purchased services and						
unclassified..............	322.59	704.10	1,410.60	2,407.90	3,504.72	3,897.25
Bad debts.................	315.05	687.65	1,377.65	2,351.65	3,427.64	3,811.01
Depreciation...............	100.00	200.00	300.00	400.00	500.00	600.00
Insurance..................	33.33	66.66	99.99	133.32	166.65	199.98
Taxes.....................	50.00	100.00	150.00	200.00	250.00	300.00
Rent......................	54.50	109.00	163.50	218.00	272.50	327.00
Totals................	$2,201.10	$ 4,687.62	$ 8,748.95	$14,219.40	$20,190.94	$22,730.87

Figure 24-13

BENSON & WEST MANUFACTURING COMPANY
Budget Warehouse Expense Incurred

Month and Cumulative—Six Months Ending June 30, 19__

Warehouse Expense Incurred	January	February	March	April	May	June
			MONTH			
Supervisory labor	$ 375.00	$ 375.00	$ 375.00	$ 375.00	$ 375.00	$ 375.00
Other labor	491.76	581.58	1,077.00	1,520.29	1,679.47	598.38
Supplies	431.03	509.76	944.00	1,322.55	1,472.08	524.48
Purchased services and classified	23.74	28.06	52.00	73.40	81.08	28.89
Depreciation	166.67	166.67	166.67	166.67	166.67	166.67
Insurance	168.33	168.33	168.33	168.33	168.33	168.33
Taxes	200.00	200.00	200.00	200.00	200.00	200.00
Rent	312.50	312.50	312.50	312.50	312.50	312.50
Totals	$ 2,169.03	$ 2,341.90	$ 3,295.50	$ 4,138.74	$ 4,455.13	$ 2,374.25
			CUMULATIVE			
Supervisory labor	$ 375.00	$ 750.00	$ 1,125.00	$ 1,500.00	$ 1,875.00	$ 2,250.00
Other labor	491.76	1,073.34	2,150.34	3,670.63	5,350.11	5,948.48
Supplies	431.03	940.79	1,884.79	3,207.34	4,679.42	5,203.90
Purchased services and classified	23.74	51.80	103.80	177.20	258.28	287.17
Depreciation	166.67	333.34	500.01	666.68	833.35	1,000.02
Insurance	168.33	336.66	504.99	673.32	841.65	1,009.98
Taxes	200.00	400.00	600.00	800.00	1,000.00	1,200.00
Rent	312.50	625.00	937.50	1,250.00	1,562.50	1,875.00
Totals	$ 2,169.03	$ 4,510.93	$ 7,806.43	$11,945.17	$16,400.30	$18,774.55

Figure 24-14

BENSON & WEST MANUFACTURING COMPANY
Budget Delivery Department Expense Incurred

Month and Cumulative—Six Months Ending June 30, 19__

Delivery Department	January	February	March	April	May	June
			MONTH			
Supervisory salaries	$ 500.00	$ 500.00	$ 500.00	$ 500.00	$ 500.00	$ 500.00
Other labor	639.24	756.00	1,400.00	1,976.24	2,183.16	777.84
Supplies	331.04	391.50	725.00	1,023.41	1,130.57	402.81
Purchased services and unclassified	562.07	78.30	145.00	204.68	226.11	80.56
Depreciation	166.67	166.67	166.67	166.67	166.67	166.67
Insurance	41.67	41.67	41.67	41.67	41.67	41.67
Taxes	52.00	52.00	52.00	52.00	52.00	52.00
Rent	125.00	125.00	125.00	125.00	125.00	125.00
Totals	$ 2,417.69	$ 2,111.14	$ 3,155.34	$ 4,089.67	$ 4,425.18	$ 2,146.55
			CUMULATIVE			
Supervisory salaries	$ 500.00	$ 1,000.00	$ 1,500.00	$ 2,000.00	$ 2,500.00	$ 3,000.00
Other labor	639.24	1,395.24	2,795.24	4,771.48	6,954.64	7,732.48
Supplies	331.04	722.54	1,447.54	2,470.95	3,601.52	4,004.33
Purchased services and unclassified	562.07	640.37	785.37	990.05	1,216.16	1,296.72
Depreciation	166.67	333.34	500.01	666.68	833.35	1,000.02
Insurance	41.67	83.34	125.01	166.68	208.35	250.02
Taxes	52.00	104.00	156.00	208.00	260.00	312.00
Rent	125.00	250.00	375.00	500.00	625.00	750.00
Totals	$ 2,417.69	$ 4,528.83	$ 7,684.17	$11,773.84	$16,199.02	$18,345.57

Figure 24-15

BENSON & WEST MANUFACTURING COMPANY
Budget Summary of Distribution Cost Incurred:
Warehouse, Order, Selling, and Delivery

Month and Cumulative—Six Months Ending June 30, 19__

	January	February	March	April	May	June
			MONTH			
Salaries................	$ 3,155.00	$ 3,155.00	$ 3,155.00	$ 3,155.00	$ 3,155.00	$ 3,155.00
Commissions............	789.66	933.93	1,729.50	2,441.36	2,694.78	960.91
Other labor.............	1,881.88	2,225.61	4,121.50	5,817.91	6,427.06	2,289.90
Supplies................	1,050.97	1,242.81	2,310.50	3,238.80	3,588.97	1,278.71
Purchased services and unclassified............	6,755.62	7,403.11	13,709.50	19,352.33	21,373.69	7,616.99
Bad debts...............	315.05	372.60	690.00	974.00	1,075.99	383.37
Depreciation............	775.00	775.00	775.00	775.00	775.00	775.00
Insurance...............	351.66	351.66	351.66	351.66	351.66	351.66
Taxes...................	375.83	375.83	375.83	375.83	375.83	375.83
Rent....................	656.00	656.00	656.00	656.00	656.00	656.00
Totals.............	$16,106.67	$17,491.55	$27,865.49	$37,137.89	$ 40,473.98	$ 17,843.37
			CUMULATIVE			
Salaries................	$ 3,155.00	$ 6,310.00	$ 9,465.00	$12,620.00	$ 15,775.00	$ 18,930.00
Commissions............	789.66	1,723.59	3,453.09	5,894.45	8,589.23	9,550.14
Other labor.............	1,881.88	4,107.49	8,228.99	14,046.90	20,473.96	22,763.86
Supplies................	1,050.97	2,293.78	4,595.28	7,834.08	11,423.05	12,701.76
Purchased services and unclassified............	6,755.62	14,158.73	27,868.23	47,220.56	68,594.25	76,211.24
Bad debts...............	315.05	687.65	1,377.65	2,351.65	3,427.64	3,811.01
Depreciation............	775.00	1,550.00	2,325.00	3,100.00	3,875.00	4,650.00
Insurance...............	351.66	703.32	1,054.98	1,406.64	1,758.30	2,109.96
Taxes...................	375.83	751.66	1,127.49	1,503.32	1,879.15	2,254.98
Rent....................	656.00	1,312.00	1,968.00	2,624.00	3,280.00	3,936.00
Totals.............	$16,106.67	$33,598.22	$61,463.71	$98,601.60	$139,075.58	$156,918.95

CREDITS TO PREPAID EXPENSE AND ACCRUED EXPENSE ACCOUNTS

Accounts Credited						
Accrued salaries and commissions...............	$ 5,826.54	$ 6,314.54	$ 9,006.00	$11,414.27	$ 12,276.84	$ 6,405.81
Supplies inventory........	1,050.97	1,242.81	2,301.50	3,238.80	3,588.97	1,278.71
Accrued expense (purchased service).....	6,755.62	7,403.11	13,709.50	19,352.33	21,373.69	7,616.99
Reserve for bad debts.....	315.05	372.60	690.00	974.00	1,075.99	383.37
Reserve for depreciation...	775.00	775.00	775.00	775.00	775.00	775.00
Prepaid property insurance	351.66	351.66	351.66	351.66	351.66	351.66
Accrued property taxes....	375.83	375.83	375.83	375.83	375.83	375.83
Factory expense (building maintenance)..........	656.00	656.00	656.00	656.00	656.00	656.00
Totals.............	$16,106.67	$17,491.55	$27,865.49	$37,137.89	$ 40,473.98	$ 17,843.37

Dr. Distribution Expense, J/E No. 8

Figure 24-16

BENSON & WEST MANUFACTURING COMPANY
Budget Administrative Expense Incurred

Month and Cumulative—Six Months Ending June 30, 19—

	January	February	March	April	May	June
			MONTH			
Salaries...............	$ 4,300.00	$ 4,300.00	$ 4,300.00	$ 4,300.00	$ 4,300.00	$ 4,300.00
Supplies...............	70.00	70.00	70.00	70.00	70.00	70.00
Purchased services and						
unclassified..........	630.00	630.00	630.00	630.00	630.00	630.00
Depreciation...........	33.33	33.33	33.33	33.33	33.33	33.33
Insurance..............	8.33	8.33	8.33	8.33	8.33	8.33
Taxes..................	10.00	10.00	10.00	10.00	10.00	10.00
Rent...................	164.00	164.00	164.00	164.00	164.00	164.00
Totals.............	$ 5,215.66	$ 5,215.66	$ 5,215.66	$ 5,215.66	$ 5,215.66	$ 5,215.66
			CUMULATIVE			
Salaries...............	$ 4,300.00	$ 8,600.00	$12,900.00	$17,200.00	$21,500.00	$25,800.00
Supplies...............	70.00	140.00	210.00	280.00	350.00	420.00
Purchased services and						
unclassified..........	630.00	1,260.00	1,890.00	2,520.00	3,150.00	3,780.00
Depreciation...........	33.33	66.66	99.99	133.32	166.65	199.98
Insurance..............	8.33	16.66	24.99	33.32	41.65	49.98
Taxes..................	10.00	20.00	30.00	40.00	50.00	60.00
Rent...................	164.00	328.00	492.00	656.00	820.00	984.00
Totals.............	$ 5,215.66	$10,431.32	$15,646.98	$20,862.64	$26,078.30	$31,293.96

CREDITS TO PREPAID EXPENSE AND ACCRUED EXPENSE ACCOUNT

Accounts Credited						
Accrued salaries...........	$ 4,300.00	$ 4,300.00	$ 4,300.00	$ 4,300.00	$ 4,300.00	$ 4,300.00
Supplies inventory..........	70.00	70.00	70.00	70.00	70.00	70.00
Accrued expense (purchased						
services)...............	630.00	630.00	630.00	630.00	630.00	630.00
Reserve for depreciation.....	33.33	33.33	33.33	33.33	33.33	33.33
Prepaid property insurance..	8.33	8.33	8.33	8.33	8.33	8.33
Accrued property taxes.....	10.00	10.00	10.00	10.00	10.00	10.00
Factory expense (building						
maintenance)...........	164.00	164.00	164.00	164.00	164.00	164.00
Totals.............	$ 5,215.66	$ 5,215.66	$ 5,215.66	$ 5,215.66	$ 5,215.66	$ 5,215.66

Dr. Administrative Expense, J/E No. 9

Figure 24-17

BENSON & WEST MANUFACTURING COMPANY
Cash Forecast, by Months
Six Months Ending June 30, 19___

	January	February	March	April	May	June	Six Months	Ref. Figure	Ref. Line
Cash account before loan operation:									
1. Actual cash balance, January 1	$ 40,000.00						$ 40,000.00		
2. Estimated cash balances, before loans (beginning)		5,951.55	35,671.93*	77,772.14*	74,195.94*	11,519.88*			
Add—Expected receipts:									
3. Collections on accounts receivable	$ 63,445.20	$ 66,900.68	$ 79,091.88	$ 146,627.60	$ 206,985.80	$ 228,663.40	$ 791,714.56	25-2	6
4. Others									
5. Totals	$ 63,445.20	$ 66,900.68	$ 79,091.88	$ 146,627.60	$ 206,985.80	$ 228,663.40	$ 791,714.56		
6. Available for disbursements (Line 1 or Line 2 Less Line 5)	$ 103,445.20	$ 72,852.23	$ 43,419.95	$ 68,855.46	$ 132,789.86	$ 217,143.52	$ 831,714.56		
Subtract—Expected disbursements:									
Premiums paid—									
7. Workmen's insurance				$ 1,000.00			$ 1,000.00	25-3	15
8. Property insurance								25-3	19
9. Materials and supplies	36,861.72	44,158.80	40,987.52	43,964.76	42,633.92	29,021.72	237,628.44	25-4	11
10. Labor	42,775.38	45,103.48	55,929.34	62,086.05	63,052.42	47,280.15	316,226.82	25-4	18
11. Salaries and commissions	9,500.00	10,126.54	10,614.54	13,306.00	15,714.27	16,576.84	75,888.19	25-4	24
12. F.I.C.A. tax				3,057.54			3,057.54	25-4	28
13. Vacation pay					6,414.90	6,414.90	6,414.90	25-4	32
14. Purchased services	8,356.55	9,135.34	13,660.69	19,637.05	22,909.13	14,144.31	87,843.07	25-4	41
15. Notes payable—Plant						20,000.00	20,000.00	25-4	51
16. Totals	$ 97,493.65	$ 108,524.16	$ 121,192.09	$ 143,051.40	$ 144,309.74	$ 133,437.92	$ 748,008.96		
17. Estimated cash balances, before loans (ending)	$ 5,951.55	$ 35,671.93*	$ 77,772.14*	$ 74,195.94*	$ 11,519.88*	$ 83,705.60*	$ 83,705.60*		
Cash account with loan projected									
18. Balance, beginning of month	$ 40,000.00	$ 102,951.55	$ 61,328.07	$ 19,227.86	$ 22,804.06	$ 85,480.12	$ 40,000.00	25-6	2
19. Add—Expected receipts (Line 5)	63,445.20	$ 66,900.68	$ 79,091.88	$ 146,627.60	$ 206,985.80	$ 228,663.40	$ 791,714.56		
20. Received from loan	97,000.00						97,000.00	25-6	6
21. Totals	$ 160,445.20						$ 888,714.56		
22. Available for disbursements	$ 200,445.20	$ 169,852.23	$ 140,419.95	$ 165,855.46	$ 229,789.86	$ 314,143.52	$ 928,714.56		
23. Subtract—Expected disbursements (Line 16)	$ 97,493.65	$ 108,524.16	$ 121,192.09	$ 143,051.40	$ 144,309.74	$ 133,437.92	$ 748,008.96		
24. Re-payment of loan						100,000.00	100,000.00		
25. Totals	$ 97,493.65	$ 108,524.16	$ 121,192.09	$ 143,051.40	$ 144,309.74	$ 233,437.92	$ 848,008.96		
26. Balances, end of months	$ 102,951.55	$ 61,328.07	$ 19,227.86	$ 22,804.06	$ 85,480.12	$ 80,705.60	$ 80,705.60		

* Red

Figure 25-1

BENSON & WEST MANUFACTURING COMPANY

Budget: Accounts Receivable, Sales Discounts, and Reserve for Bad Debts, by Months

Six Months Ending June 30, 19___

Account	J/E	January	February	March	April	May	June	Six Months
Accounts receivable:								
1. Balance, beginning of month		$ 65,000.00	$ 68,540.00	$ 81,030.00	$150,220.00	$212,050.00	$234,260.00	$ 65,000.00
Debit—								
2. Sales on account	1	68,540.00	81,030.00	150,220.00	212,050.00	234,260.00	83,470.00	829,570.00
		$133,540.00	$149,570.00	$231,250.00	$362,270.00	$446,310.00	$317,730.00	$894,570.00
Credits—								
3. Writeoffs	2	$ 260.00	$ 274.00	$ 324.00	$ 600.00	$ 840.00	$ 930.00	$ 3,228.00
4. Cash receipts, gross		64,740.00	68,266.00	80,706.00	149,620.00	211,210.00	233,330.00	807,872.00
		$ 65,000.00	$ 68,540.00	$ 81,030.00	$150,220.00	$212,050.00	$234,260.00	$811,100.00
5. Sales discounts (2%)	3	$ 1,294.80	$ 1,365.32	$ 1,614.12	$ 2,992.40	$ 4,224.20	$ 4,666.60	$ 16,157.44
6. Cash receipts, net		63,445.20	66,900.68	79,091.88	146,627.60	206,985.80	228,663.40	791,714.56
7. Balance, end of month		$ 68,540.00	$ 81,030.00	$150,220.00	$212,050.00	$234,260.00	$ 83,470.00	$ 83,470.00
Sales discounts:								
8. Month	3	$ 1,294.80	$ 1,365.32	$ 1,614.12	$ 2,992.40	$ 4,224.20	$ 4,666.60	$
9. Cumulative		1,294.80	2,660.12	4,274.24	7,266.64	11,490.84	16,157.44	
Reserve for bad debts:								
10. Balance, beginning of month		$ 1,875.00	$ 1,930.05	$ 2,028.65	$ 2,394.65	$ 2,768.65	$ 3,004.64	1,875.00
Debit—								
11. Bad debts charged off	2	260.00	274.00	324.00	600.00	840.00	930.00	3,228.00
		$ 1,615.00	$ 1,656.05	$ 1,704.65	$ 1,794.65	$ 1,928.65	$ 2,074.64	$ 1,353.00*
Credit—								
12. Provision for bad debts	7	315.05	372.60	690.00	974.00	1,075.99	383.37	3,811.01
13. Balance; end of month		$ 1,930.05	$ 2,028.65	$ 2,394.65	$ 2,768.65	$ 3,004.64	$ 2,458.01	$ 2,458.01

* Red

Figure 25-2

BENSON & WEST MANUFACTURING COMPANY
Budget: Prepaid Expenses, by Months
Six Months Ending June 30, 19___

Account	J/E	January	February	March	April	May	June	Six Months
Prepaid workmen's insurance:								
14. Balance, beginning of month		$1,000.00	$757.20	$539.72	$236.20	$919.26	$600.32	$1,000.00
Debit—								
15. Premiums paid					1,000.00			1,000.00
		$1,000.00	$757.20	$539.72	$1,236.20	$919.26	$600.32	$2,000.00
Credit—								
16. Charged to expense	6	242.80	217.48	303.52	316.94	318.94	208.08	1,607.76
17. Balance, end of month		$757.20	$539.72	$236.20	$919.26	$600.32	$392.24	$392.24
Prepaid property insurance:								
18. Balance, beginning of month		$6,602.28	$5,501.90	$4,401.52	$3,301.14	$2,200.76	$1,100.38	$6,602.28
Debit—								
19. Premiums paid								
		$6,602.28	$5,501.90	$4,401.52	$3,301.14	$2,200.76	$1,100.38	$6,602.28
Credits—								
20. Charged to expense	6							
21. Factory	7	740.39	740.39	740.39	740.39	740.39	740.39	4,442.34
22. Distribution	8	351.66	351.66	351.66	351.66	351.66	351.66	2,109.96
23. Administration		8.33	8.33	8.33	8.33	8.33	8.33	49.98
		$1,100.38	$1,100.38	$1,100.38	$1,100.38	$1,100.38	$1,100.38	$6,602.28
24. Balance, end of month		$5,501.90	$4,401.52	$3,301.14	$2,200.76	$1,100.38	$ —	$ —
Supplies inventory:								
25. Balance, beginning of month		$6,000.00	$3,656.69	$7,264.21	$3,564.95	$2,860.13	$1,791.72	$6,000.00
Debit—								
26. Purchases vouchered*			6,000.00		4,000.00	4,000.00	2,000.00	16,000.00
		$6,000.00	$9,656.69	$7,264.21	$7,564.95	$6,860.13	$3,791.72	$22,000.00
Credits—								
27. Charged to expense	6							
28. Factory	7	1,222.34	1,079.67	1,327.76	1,396.02	1,409.44	931.35	7,366.58
29. Distribution	8	1,050.97	1,242.81	2,301.50	3,238.80	3,588.97	1,278.71	12,701.76
30. Administration		70.00	70.00	70.00	70.00	70.00	70.00	420.00
		$2,343.31	$2,392.48	$3,699.26	$4,704.82	$5,068.41	$2,280.06	$20,488.34
31. Balance, end of month		$3,656.69	$7,264.21	$3,564.95	$2,860.13	$1,791.72	$1,511.66	$1,511.66

* The credits representing estimated usage are entered on this schedule before the purchases vouchered amounts are calculated. The purchases are calculated as the amounts necessary to maintain inventory levels.

Figure 25-3

BENSON & WEST MANUFACTURING COMPANY

Budget: Current Liabilities (Except Bank Loans) and Purchase Discounts, by Months

Six Months Ending June 30, 19___

Account	J/E	January	February	March	April	May	June	Six Months
Accounts payable—Materials and supplies:								
1. Balance, beginning of month		$ 5,000.00	$16,306.00	$14,376.00	$13,722.00	$15,570.00	$13,966.00	$ 5,000.00
Credits—								
2. Purchases—Materials	4	$48,920.00	$37,130.00	$41,170.00	$42,710.00	$37,900.00	$21,470.00	$229,300.00
3. Purchases—Supplies	9		6,000.00		4,000.00	4,000.00	2,000.00	16,000.00
4. Total purchases		$48,920.00	$43,130.00	$41,170.00	$46,710.00	$41,900.00	$23,470.00	$245,300.00
5. Total credits		$53,920.00	$59,436.00	$55,546.00	$60,432.00	$57,470.00	$37,436.00	$250,300.00
Debit—								
Payments on account:								
6.								
7. Balance at beginning		$ 5,000.00	$16,306.00	$14,376.00	$13,722.00	$15,570.00	$13,966.00	$ 78,940.00
8. ⅔ of month's purchases		32,614.00	28,754.00	27,448.00	31,140.00	27,934.00	15,648.00	163,538.00
9. Total gross payments		$37,614.00	$45,060.00	$41,824.00	$44,862.00	$43,504.00	$29,614.00	$242,478.00
10. Purchase discounts (2%)	10	$ 752.28	$ 901.20	$ 836.48	$ 897.24	$ 870.08	$ 592.28	$ 4,849.56
11. Net payments		36,861.72	44,158.80	40,987.52	43,964.76	42,633.92	29,021.72	237,628.44
12. Balance, end of month		16,306.00	14,376.00	13,722.00	15,570.00	13,966.00	7,822.00	7,822.00
Purchase discounts:								
13. Month	10	$ 752.28	$ 901.20	$ 836.48	$ 897.24	$ 870.08	$ 592.28	$
14. Cumulative		752.28	1,653.48	2,489.96	3,387.20	4,257.28	4,849.56	4,849.56
Accrued labor:								
15. Accrual, beginning of month		$ 6,000.00	$12,258.46	$10,948.27	$14,993.73	$15,697.48	$15,786.00	$ 6,000.00
Credits—								
16. Direct labor accrued	5	39,590.00	34,847.50	50,062.50	52,437.50	52,675.00	32,887.50	262,500.00
17. Indirect labor accrued	6	9,443.84	8,945.79	9,912.30	10,352.30	10,465.94	9,104.74	58,224.91
18. Debit—Cash paid (balance)		$55,033.84 / 42,775.38	$56,051.75 / 45,103.48	$70,923.07 / 55,929.34	$77,783.53 / 62,086.05	$78,838.42 / 63,052.42	$57,778.24 / 47,280.15	$326,724.91 / 316,226.82
19. Accrual, end of month (estimated)		$12,258.46	$10,948.27	$14,993.73	$15,697.48	$15,786.00	$10,498.09	$ 10,498.09
Accrued salaries and commissions:								
20. Balance, beginning of month		$ 9,500.00	$10,126.54	$10,614.54	$13,306.00	$15,714.27	$16,576.84	$ 9,500.00
Credits accrued:								
21.								
22. Distribution	7	5,826.54	6,314.54	9,006.00	11,414.27	12,276.84	6,405.81	51,244.00
23. Administrative	8	4,300.00	4,300.00	4,300.00	4,300.00	4,300.00	4,300.00	25,800.00
24. Debit: Payments of balance, end of previous month		$19,626.54 / 9,500.00	$20,741.08 / 10,126.54	$23,920.54 / 10,614.54	$29,020.27 / 13,306.00	$32,291.11 / 15,714.27	$28,282.65 / 16,576.84	$86,544.00 / 75,838.19
25. Balance, end of month		$10,126.54	$10,614.54	$13,306.00	$15,714.27	$16,576.84	$10,705.81	$ 10,705.81

Figure 25-4

BENSON & WEST MANUFACTURING COMPANY
Budget: Current Liabilities (Except Bank Loans) and Purchase Discounts, by Months
Six Months Ending June 30, 19___

Account	J/E	January	February	March	April	May	June	Six Months
Accrued F.I.C.A. tax:								
26. Balance, beginning of month		$	$ 980.66	$ 1,858.06	$ 3,057.54	$ 1,254.74	$ 2,517.54	$
27. Credits: Accrued this month	6	980.66	877.40	1,199.48	1,254.74	1,262.80	839.82	6,414.90
		$ 980.66	$ 1,858.06	$ 3,057.54	$ 4,312.28	$ 2,517.54	$ 3,357.36	$ 6,414.90
28. Debit: Cash paid					3,057.54			3,057.54
29. Balance, end of month		$ 980.66	$ 1,858.06	$ 3,057.54	$ 1,254.74	$ 2,517.54	$ 3,357.36	$ 3,357.36
Reserve for vacation pay:								
30. Balance, beginning of month		$	$ 980.66	$ 1,858.06	$ 3,057.54	$ 4,312.28	$ 5,575.08	$
31. Credits: Accrued this month	6	980.66	877.40	1,199.48	1,254.74	1,262.80	839.82	6,414.90
		$ 980.66	$ 1,858.06	$ 3,057.54	$ 4,312.28	$ 5,575.08	$ 6,414.90	$ 6,414.90
32. Debit: Cash paid							6,414.90	6,414.90
33. Balance, end of month		$ 980.66	$ 1,858.06	$ 3,057.54	$ 4,312.28	$ 5,575.08	$	$
Accrued expense (purchased services):								
34. Balance, beginning of month		$ 2,500.00	$ 2,928.28	$ 3,103.53	$ 5,278.57	$ 7,179.25	$ 7,864.93	$ 2,500.00
Credits: Expense bills vouchered—								
35. Factory	6	$ 1,399.21	$ 1,277.48	$ 1,496.23	$ 1,555.40	$ 1,591.12	$ 1,172.09	$ 8,491.53
36. Distribution	7	6,755.62	7,403.11	13,709.50	19,352.33	21,373.69	7,616.99	76,211.24
37. Administrative	8	630.00	630.00	630.00	630.00	630.00	630.00	3,780.00
38. Total bills		$ 8,784.83	$ 9,310.59	$ 15,835.73	$ 21,537.73	$ 23,594.81	$ 9,419.08	$ 88,482.77
Total credits		$ 11,284.83	$ 12,238.87	$ 18,939.26	$ 26,816.30	$ 30,774.06	$ 17,284.01	$ 90,982.77
Debit: Cash paid—								
39. Balance at beginning		$ 2,500.00	$ 2,928.28	$ 3,103.53	$ 5,278.57	$ 7,179.25	$ 7,864.93	$ 28,854.56
40. ⅔ of month's purchases		5,856.55	6,207.06	10,557.16	14,358.48	15,729.88	6,279.38	58,988.51
41. Total cash paid		$ 8,356.55	$ 9,135.34	$ 13,660.69	$ 19,637.05	$ 22,909.13	$ 14,144.31	$ 87,843.07
42. Balance, end of month		$ 2,928.28	$ 3,103.53	$ 5,278.57	$ 7,179.25	$ 7,864.93	$ 3,139.70	$ 3,139.70
Accrued property tax:								
43. Balance, beginning of month		$	$ 1,200.37	$ 2,400.74	$ 3,601.11	$ 4,801.48	$ 6,001.85	$
Credits: Accrued this month—								
44. Factory	6	814.54	814.54	814.54	814.54	814.54	814.54	4,887.24
45. Distribution	7	375.83	375.83	375.83	375.83	375.83	375.83	2,254.98
46. Administrative	8	10.00	10.00	10.00	10.00	10.00	10.00	60.00
		$ 1,200.37	$ 2,400.74	$ 3,601.11	$ 4,801.48	$ 6,001.85	$ 7,202.22	$ 7,202.22
47. Debit: Cash paid								
48. Balance, end of month		$ 1,200.37	$ 2,400.74	$ 3,601.11	$ 4,801.48	$ 6,001.85	$ 7,202.22	$ 7,202.22
Notes payable—Plant:								
49. Balance, beginning of month		$	$20,000.00	$20,000.00	$20,000.00	$20,000.00	$20,000.00	$
50. Credit: Notes issued	11	20,000.00						20,000.00
		$20,000.00	$20,000.00	$20,000.00	$20,000.00	$20,000.00	$20,000.00	$20,000.00
51. Debit: Notes paid								
52. Balance, end of month		$20,000.00	$20,000.00	$20,000.00	$20,000.00	$20,000.00	$20,000.00	20,000.00

Figure 25-4 (*Continued*)

BENSON & WEST MANUFACTURING COMPANY
Budget: Bank Loan, Prepaid Interest Expense and Interest Expense, by Months
Six Months Ending June 30, 19___

Account	January	February	March	April	May	June	Six Months
Bank loan:							
1. Balance, beginning of month	$	$100,000.00	$100,000.00	$100,000.00	$100,000.00	$100,000.00	$
Credit: Loans discounted—							
2. Net cash received	97,000.00						
3. Interest deducted	3,000.00						
4. Gross amount	$100,000.00	$	$	$	$	$	$100,000.00
5. Opening balance plus gross loans	$100,000.00	$100,000.00	$100,000.00	$100,000.00	$100,000.00	$100,000.00	$100,000.00
6. Debit: Loan paid						100,000.00	100,000.00
7. Balance, end of month	$100,000.00	$100,000.00	$100,000.00	$100,000.00	$100,000.00	$	$
Prepaid interest expense:							
8. Balance, beginning of month	$ 3,000.00	$ 2,500.00	$ 2,000.00	$ 1,500.00	$ 1,000.00	$ 500.00	$
9. Debit: Interest prepaid							3,000.00
	$ 3,000.00	$ 2,500.00	$ 2,000.00	$ 1,500.00	$ 1,000.00	500.00	3,000.00
10. Credit: Interest charged to expense	500.00	500.00	500.00	500.00	500.00	500.00	3,000.00
11. Balance, end of month	$ 2,500.00	$ 2,000.00	$ 1,500.00	$ 1,000.00	$ 500.00	$	$
Interest expense:							
12. Month	$ 500.00	$ 500.00	$ 500.00	$ 500.00	$ 500.00	$ 500.00	$
13. Cumulative	500.00	1,000.00	1,500.00	2,000.00	2,500.00	3,000.00	

Figure 25-6

MODEL JOURNAL ENTRIES

The following model journal entries are presented to illustrate the debit and credit relationship between (a) Shipments, Production, and Procurement Schedules and (b) Expense Schedules to (c) Working Capital Schedules.

J/E No. 1—Sales. The debits to the Budget Accounts Receivable schedule are picked up from the Budget *Shipments*, Production, and Procurement schedule (Figure 23-12).

Accounts receivable...................................	$68,540.00	
Sales (per Budget Shipments Schedule)...............		$68,540.00

Post sales on account per Budget Shipments Schedule (Figure 23-12) to Budget Accounts Receivable Schedule (Figure 25-2)

J/E No. 2—Accounts receivable written-off.

Reserve for bad debts.................................	$ 260.00	
Accounts receivable................................		$ 260.00

Calculate write-offs on basis of experience percentage and enter as credits on Budget Accounts Receivable Schedule (Figure 25-2). Enter same amounts as debits on Budget Reserve for Bad Debts Schedule (Figure 25-2).

J/E No. 3—Sales discounts.

Sales discounts.......................................	$ 1,294.80	
Accounts receivable................................		$ 1,294.80

Calculate sales discounts (2% of [opening balance of accounts receivable less write-offs]) and enter as credits on Budget Accounts Receivable Schedule (Figure 25-2). Enter same amounts as debits on Budget Sales Discounts Schedule (Figure 25-2).

(On the Budget Accounts Receivable Schedule, calculate and enter net cash receipts. Opening balance less write-offs equal gross cash receipts. Gross cash receipts less discounts equal net cash receipts. Net cash receipts amounts will be used on the Cash Forecast.)

J/E No. 4—Materials purchased. The credits to the Budget Accounts Payable—Materials and Supplies Schedule are picked up from the Budget Materials in Goods Produced, Materials *Received*, and Materials Inventory Schedule (Figure 23-14).

Materials: Raw and in process (per Budget Materials Schedule)......................................	$48,920.00	
Accounts payable—Materials and supplies............		$48,920.00

Post materials purchases per Budget Materials Schedule (Figure 23-14) to Budget Accounts Payable Schedule (Figure 25-4).

J/E No. 5—Direct labor input. The credits to the Budget Accrued Labor Schedule are picked up from the Budget Labor in Goods Produced, Labor *Input*, and Labor in Inventory Schedule (Figure 23-13).

Labor in process (per Budget Labor Schedule)............ $39,590.00
    Accrued labor.................................... $39,590.00
Post direct labor input per the Budget Labor Schedule (Figure 23-13) to Budget Accrued Labor Schedule (Figure 25-4).

J/E No. 6—Factory expense incurred.

The credits to various budget asset and liability schedules for factory expense items incurred are picked up from the Budget Factory Expense Schedule (Figure 24-8).

Factory expense (per Budget Factory Expense Schedule).... $17,091.08
    Accrued labor (Figure 25-4)............................ $ 9,443.84
    Accrued F.I.C.A. tax (Figure 25-4)....................   980.66
    Prepaid workmen's insurance (Figure 25-3)............   242.80
    Reserve for vacation pay (Figure 25-4)...............   980.66
    Supplies inventory (Figure 25-3)......................   1,222.34
    Accrued expense (Purchased services) (Figure 25-4).....   1,399.21
    Reserve for depreciation (not illlustrated)............   1,266.64
    Prepaid property insurance (Figure 25-3).............   740.39
    Accrued property tax (Figure 25-4)....................   814.54
Post credits to budget asset and liability schedules from Budget Factory Expense Schedule (Figure 24-8)

J/E No. 7—Distribution expense incurred.

The credits to various budget asset and liability schedules for distribution expense incurred are picked up from the Budget Distribution Expense Schedule (Figure 24-16).

Distribution expense (per Budget Distribution Schedule).... $16,106.67
    Accrued salaries and commissions (Figure 25-4)........ $ 5,826.54
    Supplies inventory (Figure 25-3)......................   1,050.97
    Accrued expense (purchased services) (Figure 25-4).....   6,755.62
    Reserve for bad debts (Figure 25-2)...................   315.05
    Reserve for depreciation (Figure 24-2)................   775.00
    Prepaid property insurance (Figure 25-3)..............   351.66
    Accrued property taxes (Figure 25-4)..................   375.83
    Factory expense absorbed (Building Maintenance) (Figure 23-3c)....................................   656.00
Post credits to budget asset and liability schedules from Budget Distribution Expense Schedule (Figure 24-16)

J/E No. 8—Administrative expense incurred.

The credits to various budget asset and liability schedules for administrative expense incurred are picked up from the Budget Administrative Expense Schedule (Figure 24-17).

Administrative expense (per Budget Administrative Expense Schedule)..................................... $ 5,215.66
    Accrued salaries and commissions (Figure 25-4)........ $ 4,300.00
    Supplies inventory (Figure 25-3)......................   70.00
    Accrued expense (purchased services) (Figure 25-4).....   630.00
    Reserve for depreciation (not illustrated)............   33.33
    Prepaid property insurance (Figure 25-3)..............   8.33
    Accrued property taxes (Figure 25-4)..................   10.00
    Factory expense (Building Maintenance) (Figure 23-3c)   164.00
Post credit to budget assets and liability schedules from Budget Distribution Expense Schedule (Figure 24-17)

J/E No. 9—Purchase supplies.

Purchases of supplies is calculated directly from the Budget Supplies Inventory Schedule (Figure 25-3) after the credits for supplies used have been posted (Journal Entries #6, #7 and #8).

Supplies inventory......................................	$ xxx.xx	
Accounts payable—Materials and supplies............		$ xxx.xx

Working from the Budget Supplies Inventory Schedule, calculate purchases necessary to maintain inventory level. Enter debit on Supplies Inventory Schedule and credit on Accounts Payable Schedule.

J/E No. 10—Purchase discounts.

Accounts payable......................................	$ 752.28	
Purchase discounts................................		$ 752.28

Working from the Budget Accounts Payable Schedule (Figure 25-4), calculate purchase discounts as illustrated on that schedule.   Enter debit on Budget Accounts Payable Schedule and credit on Budget Purchase Discounts Schedule (Figure 25-4)

J/E No. 11—Notes payable—Plant. The credit to Budget Notes Payable—Plant Schedule for notes issued is picked up from the Plant Budget (Chapter 24).

Plant..	$20,000.00	
Notes payable—Plant.............................		$20,000.00

Appendix III

ANNOTATED BIBLIOGRAPHY—DISTRIBUTION COSTS

BOOKS

Clewett, Richard M. (editor), *Marketing Channels for Manufactured Products.* Homewood, Illinois: Richard D. Irwin, Inc., 1954.

This is an excellent background book for the study of distribution costs. Note especially Chapter 18, "Analytical Approach to Channel Policies—Sales Analysis," and Chapter 19, "Analytical Approach to Channel Policies—Marketing Cost Analysis."

Heckert, J. Brooks, and Robert B. Miner, *Distribution Costs*, 380 pp. New York: The Ronald Press Company, 1953.

Longman, Donald R., and Michael Schiff, *Practical Distribution Cost Analysis*, 443 pp. Homewood, Illinois: Richard D. Irwin, Inc., 1955.

PUBLICATIONS OF THE NATIONAL ASSOCIATION OF COST ACCOUNTANTS

Control of Direct Selling Expense; Control of Other Distribution Costs

Allyn, S. C. (Treasurer, National Cash Register Co.), "Sales Records," *N.A.C.A. Yearbook* (1929), pp. 124-133.

Quota system used by the company, and records for operation.

"Cost Control for Marketing Operations—General Considerations," *N.A.C.A. Bulletin* (April, 1954), Research Series No. 25.

Required reading.

"Cost Control for Marketing Operations—Order Getting," *N.A.C.A. Bulletin* (June, 1954), Research Series No. 26.

Required reading.

Crockett, Horace G. (Scovell, Wellington & Co.), "Analysis of Selling Costs and Proper Basis of Salesmen's Compensation," *N.A.C.A. Bulletin*, Vol. VII, No. 7 (December 1, 1926), pp. 228-249.

"I have chosen as the subject of my talk, 'Analysis of Selling Costs and Proper Basis of Salesmen's Compensation." It seems to me that these problems are very closely allied and that it is almost impossible to consider one without giving some thought to the other. . . ."

"It is very important to establish normal selling costs based on a budget and sales quota, even if you are going to do nothing but distribute selling costs to the product in order to have a complete final cost of each article sold, passing over for the time any thought of changing the basis of salesmen's compensation.   If you start to distribute certain selling expenses that are practically fixed, either to territories or to products, on the basis of sales volume—which sometimes seems to be the only possible base—you are immediately impressed with the very evident injustice of that plan if it is based upon actual or past sales.   You soon realize that a fair normal or quota is the only fair basis.   That is exactly the same problem that you encounter when you try to distribute certain fixed expenses to the departments in a factory, and there, as you know, you always use normal."

Dick, R. H., "Reorganization of the Distribution Department," *N.A.C.A. Yearbook* (1931), pp. 136-148.

> How the sales department of a hypothetical company was reorganized.   The entire program is outlined, and facts and figures typical of an actual company are presented.
> "Briefly, the steps we took in evolving the budget were:
> (1) Making the market analysis by analyzing past performance and calculating the potentials.
> (2) Laying out the territories.
> (3) Setting up the quotas for each territory.
> (4) Establishing the total company budget.
> (5) Setting up control records for the administration of the budget."

Frost, A. G. (The Wahl Company), "How to Reduce the Cost of Selling," *N.A.C.A. Bulletin*, Vol. VII, No. 7 (December 1, 1925), pp. 239-263.

> Control of direct selling costs.   Description of a complete plan with forms and reports.

Hedges, Elihu (Sales Research and Statistics, Bausch & Lomb Optical Co.), "Profits Through Controlled Distribution," *N.A.C.A. Bulletin*, Vol. XIV, No. 16 (April 15, 1933), pp. 1159-1186.

> Sales research and statistics used at Bausch & Lomb.   The term "controlled distribution" is the keynote of this article.

McNiece, Thomas M. (market analyst), "Problems in the Development of Standards for a Small Business Selling to Producers," *N.A.C.A. Yearbook* (1933), pp. 266-283.

> Technical.   Read this for ideas on approach.

Perry, William E. (Controller, Scranton Lace Co.), "Distribution Costs and Methods," *N.A.C.A. Bulletin*, Vol. XXVIII, No. 12 (February 15, 1947), pp. 731-746.

> Required reading.   Description of controls on direct selling costs at Scranton Lace Co.   Market survey, sales units and quotas, the sales call, preplanned coverage, territories, salesmen's reports, standard distribution costs.   Definition of sales call as a cost unit is particularly significant:
> "The next essential step in sales planning is also entirely a problem of sales management and not accounting, viz., setting up a job standard for the salesman's call on the customer.   It is, of course, realized that when two human beings come into such a contact they are not going to follow completely any standard pattern of behavior.   Nevertheless, it is important that the salesman understand what ground he is expected to cover on a salesman's call.   This involved. . . ."

Reitell, Charles (Stevenson, Jordan, & Harrison), "Standard Costs in the Field of Distribution," *N.A.C.A. Bulletin*, Vol. XX, No. 3 (October 1, 1938), pp. 159-164.

> Profit realization by product.   Sales compensation plan based upon *net* profit realization.
> "At this time is introduced the most difficult factor in getting satisfactory distribution costs, namely, that the time and expense needed to break down *actual* merchandising costs by products, by territories, by salesman, and by type of selling

outlets, are so great that the ends seldom justify the expenditure. That is why *standard* costs bring more satisfactory results. . . ."

Net profit realization. "Typical salesmen are interested in selling volume. More enlightened sales management, however, is pushing their salesmen to sell the more profitable items. Unfortunately, up to this time the more profitable items have been segregated from the less profitable ones on the gross margin rather than on the net operating profit. Therefore, the burden now falls on cost accounting to analyze the net profit realization that is made by each salesman. This can be accomplished by a system of weighting wherein no profit information is broadcast through the selling force. . . ."

Robnett, Ronald H. (Assistant Professor of Accounting, Massachusetts Institute of Technology), and Herbert E. Tucker (Partner, Charles Rittenhouse & Co.), "Planning and Controlling Salesmen's Costs in Quali-Kumfort Shoe Company" (fictitious name), *N.A.C.A. Bulletin*, Vol. XIX, No. 15 (April 1, 1936), pp. 873-895.

Description of an actual professional assignment in which the consultants set for themselves the following objectives:

(1) Evaluation of the various sections of the country to get what they termed "disclosure of buying power. . . ."

(2) Realignment of territories in terms of potential sales outlets, distance to be covered between cities, etc. . . .

(3) Planning routes within territories. . . .

(4) Determination of differences between territories in travel costs. . . .

(5) Development of a salesman payment plan based upon the principle of salary plus bonus.

Shaw, C. E. (Dennison Manufacturing Co.), "Reduction of Cost of Sales," *N.A.C.A. Bulletin*, Vol. V, No. 13 (March 15, 1924), pp. 7-10.

Control of direct selling costs. "The first step along these lines was to analyze the cost of the canvass itself. On the basis of time studies taken on several salesmen late in the fall of 1920 and the spring of 1921, we determined that the actual time spent by the average salesman in the presence of the customer was about 15 per cent of his total working time. . . . A start was made in 1921 along experimental lines to determine to what degree non-selling work could be reduced and actual selling time increased. . . ."

Sweetster, Frank L. (General Manager, Dutchess Manufacturing Co.), "Fundamentals of Business Management—Sales," *N.A.C.A. Bulletin*, Vol. V, No. 13 (March 15, 1924), pp. 3-7.

Training of salesmen, sales territories and valuation, sales budget (quotas), sales expenses. "The analysis of product and a monthly report of gross margins, distribution costs and net profits or losses by grades and varieties of products, as well as by territories, is accomplished by use of punched card tabulating machines."

Distribution Cost Standards: Warehouse Costs; Order Filling and Cash Collecting

"Cost Control for Marketing Operations—Order Filling," *N.A.C.A. Bulletin*, (August, 1954), Research Series No. 27.

Required reading.

Lang, J. J. (J. J. Lang Company), "How Should Freight and Handling Charges on Finished Goods in Branch Warehouse Be Handled?" *N.A.C.A. Yearbook* (1930), pp. 71-79.

Marguiles, William (Certified Public Accountant), "Controlling the Costs of a Credit and Collection Department," *N.A.C.A. Bulletin*, Vol. XXIII, No. 2 (September 15, 1941), pp. 67-85.

Comparing (a) probable loss on credit sales with (b) probable loss on unabsorbed expense which would result if the sale were refused.

Naumann, Frank J. (Accountant, Dennison Manufacturing Co.), "The Development of Standard Order—Handling and Order Filling Cost Rates," *N.A.C.A. Bulletin*, Vol. XIV, No. 2 (January 15, 1933), pp. 777-787.

"We were somewhat appalled when we first came to learn that (our warehouse costs) amounted approximately to $1,350,000 compared with a cost for factory operations of some $8,500,000 and an average yearly sales of some $17,000,000." Development of standard functional unit costs on such factors as invoices, stock items, customer-months, units or packages, cubic inch, dollars of total expense. Application to products for selling price purposes. Accounting procedure: absorbing at standard; order filling cost variance account.

Control of Transportation Expense

Dickson, J. Frank, Jr. (Vice President, H. B. Church Truck Service Co.), "The Determination of Trucking Costs," *N.A.C.A. Bulletin*, Vol. XXVIII, No. 16 (April 15, 1947), pp. 1018-1030.

Required reading. Procedures used by trucking companies which may be adapted to use by companies which operate their own fleets. Linehaul costs, pick up and delivery costs, and terminal costs.

Rasmussen, C. F. (City Sales Manager, Premier Pabst Corporation, Milwaukee), "What Is the Cost of Operating a Truck?" *N.A.C.A. Bulletin*, Vol. XVIII, No. 18 (May 15, 1937), pp. 1028-1033.

The significance of various unit costs of operating trucks in city delivery.

Distribution Cost Budget

Christie, George N. (General Sales Manager, Gifford-Wood Co.), "Budgetary Control in Elevating and Conveying Machinery Distribution," *N.A.C.A. Yearbook* (1931), pp. 150-157.

Actual experience described.

Frey, Albert W. (Assistant Dean, Amos Tuck School of Administration and Finance, Dartmouth College), "The Control of Marketing Costs Through the Use of Standards," *N.A.C.A. Bulletin*, Vol. XVII, No. 2 (September 15, 1935), pp. 55-73.

Susceptibility of control of various marketing functions. Functions which are not susceptible of control. Functions which can be controlled as functions. Functions which can be controlled and for which cost standards and budgets are effective instruments. Importance of establishing controls over functions before instituting cost standards and budgetary controls. How standards are set. An illustration of budgeting (i.e., measurement of performance). "Also, it should be noted that the figures are for control purposes only and cannot be used for costing in such a way that profit by products, territories, etc., can be determined . . ." (page 69).

Greer, Howard C. (General Manager, Kingan & Co.), "Standards for Selling Activities in a Meat Packing Company," *N.A.C.A. Yearbook* (1929), pp. 175-185.

Description of an actual case. "With these three measures—margin, tonnage, and expense—we think we shall have a very good check on the productivity and value of each man and each territory. . . ."

———, "Development of Standards for the Control of Selling Activities," *N.A.C.A. Bulletin*, Vol. XIII, No. 14 (March 15, 1932), pp. 943-961.

Required reading. Functional unit costs and their use in setting up budgets for the control of selling activities. Analysis of variances between actual and budget. Short but complete illustration of (1) classification of distribution expenses, actual, (2) analysis of distribution expense according to units of functional service, and (3) comparison of budget and actual for year, with explanation of variances.

Heckert, J. Brooks (Ohio State University), "Budgetary Control of Manufacturing and Commercial Expense," *N.A.C.A. Bulletin*, Vol. XXVIII, No. 14 (March 15, 1947), pp. 869-880.

Use of the budget as a coordinating tool in management. Classification of expense into fixed and variable groups, and significance of such classification. Analysis of expense by nature of items. Analysis by functional operations: direct, semi-direct, and indirect expenses.

Howell, Harry E. (Auditor, Grinnell Company, Inc.), "The Accounting Mechanics of Budgetary Control for Small Companies," *N.A.C.A. Yearbook* (1933), pp. 210-250.

An excellent article on how the budget is put together. Complete set of worksheets illustrated.

Knowland, R. G. (Vice President and General Manager, Bigelow-Sanford Carpet Co.), "The Use of Costs in Selling in the Carpet Industry," *N.A.C.A. Yearbook* (1931), pp. 158-167.

Actual experience described. Note particularly the discussion of the planning and control of inventories in an industry in which the style factor and the control of inventories are important.

Neilsen, A. C. (President, A. C. Neilsen Co.), "Continuous Marketing Research— A Vital Factor in Controlling Distribution Costs," *N.A.C.A. Yearbook* (1936), pp. 220-255.

A description of certain phases of the work done by the Neilsen organization.

Reitell, Charles (Stevenson, Jordan, & Harrison), "Applying Standard Costs and Budgets to Distribution," *N.A.C.A. Yearbook* (1937), pp. 228-250.

Required reading. A complete standard cost and budget system applied to the distribution activities of a brewery. Presents "in considerable detail, definite standards and budgets covering the whole gamut of the distribution field. By that, I mean standards and budgets for delivery, advertising, selling—and even standards for opening new territories." All parts of the system are illustrated, up to the Profit and Loss Statement which shows variances for selling, advertising, administrative, and delivery.

Schoenfeldt, Lee (Acting Manager, Commercial Research Division, General Electric Co.), "Controlling Distribution Costs," *N.A.C.A. Yearbook* (1936), pp. 256-277.

A description of methods used by General Electric Co.

Willard, J. A. (Bigelow, Kent, Willard & Co.), "Setting of Sales Standards," *N.A.C.A. Yearbook* (1929), pp. 146-175.

Outline of methods and description of published sources of statistical material. Sales forecasting by the "analogy" method and by the "analysis" method. Very good introduction of breakeven charts to students of distribution costs. Illustration of sometimes overlooked fact that the cost of getting an increased volume of sales may exceed the profit on those sales. Classified list of salesmen's compensation plans.

Accounting for Distribution Costs; Distribution Cost Reports

Cameron, A. T. (Partner, Edward P. Moxey and Company) and Cheffey, W. H. (Auditor, Union Switch and Signal Co.), "Should Any Part of Selling and Distribution Costs Be Treated as Deferred Charges to a Later Financial Period? If So, Under What Conditions and to What Extent?" *N.A.C.A. Yearbook* (1930), pp. 80-84.

Koehler, Walter C. (Controller's Staff, Westinghouse Electric and Manufacturing Company), "Capital Investment in Pricing," *N.A.C.A. Yearbook* (1939), pp. 334-351.

> "We have felt that, in control of profits, too much emphasis has been given to the rate of profit based upon sales billed, as reported for each major line of product. . . . The favorable ratio does not mean anything unless it, plus volume, gives a fair return on the capital invested. . . .
> "Through studies of this type, in which return on investment is given a prominent position, we provide business management with an additional measuring stick on operating performance.   We bring together in the rate of return—in one figure, the activity of the business, as measured by volume; the rate of profit on the selling price of the goods sold; and the investment which made possible the entire activity, and which makes possible its continuation.
> ". . . we set up a total investment value, by major lines of product, under the following five major classifications:
> (1) Operating Cash
> (2) Accounts and Notes Receivable
> (3) Inventories
> (4) Land and Buildings
> (5) Machine Tools, Fixtures and Trucks"
> The bulletin discusses value of return on investment information to various executives in an organization.

Patterson, Thomas H. (General Supervisor of Cost Accounting, Armstrong Cork Company), "The Commodity Profit and Loss Report," *N.A.C.A. Bulletin*, Vol. XXVI, No. 22 (July 15, 1945), pp. 1040-1054.

> The commodity profit and loss report developed down to the point of per cent return on investment in facilities used in manufacturing and distributing.

Analysis of Distribution Costs

Arenson, Herman I. (University of Colorado), "Methods of Distribution Cost Analysis," *N.A.C.A. Bulletin*, Vol. XXIX, No. 1 (September 1, 1947), pp. 13-24.

> Required reading.   A clear statement of the problems and elements of solutions. Discussion of analysis by territories.

Barrett, James H. (Assistant to Vice President and Treasurer, Kellogg Company), "The Analysis and Distribution of Sales Distribution Costs," *N.A.C.A. Bulletin*, Vol. IX, No. 12 (February 15, 1928), pp. 655-670.

> Distribution of advertising, sampling special trade promotion plans, catalogs, etc., to product class.

Bigelow, Carle M. (M.E., Carle M. Bigelow & Co.), "Controlling Distribution Costs," *N.A.C.A. Bulletin*, Vol. XVI, No. 1 (September 1, 1934), pp. 16-29.

> Some elemental problems described.   Approach to distribution costs.

Buckley, Homer J. (President, Buckley, Dement & Co.), "Relation Between Sales Promotion and Accounting," *N.A.C.A. Bulletin*, Vol. IX, No. 16 (April 15, 1928), pp. 925-940.

> The need for cost accounting in the direction of sales efforts.

Dennison, Henry S. (President, Dennison Manufacturing Co.), "Sales Cost Accounting," *N.A.C.A. Bulletin*, Vol. X, No. 5 (November 1, 1928), pp. 241-249.
The need for cost accounting in the direction of sales effort. Beginnings of the distribution cost program at Dennison Manufacturing Co.

Farrell, A. C. (Head of Department of Sales Accounting, Dennison Manufacturing Company), "When Should Selling and Distribution Costs Be Apportioned to Sales Districts? What Items Should Be So Apportioned?" *N.A.C.A. Yearbook* (1930), pp. 67-70.

Freeman, E. Steward (Chief Statistician, Dennison Manufacturing Co.), "The Manufacturer's Marketing Cost," *N.A.C.A. Bulletin*, Vol. XI, No. 6 (November 15, 1929), pp. 331-353.
Required reading. Note particularly the sections:
How joint and indirect costs affect the problem
Need for new technique of marginal and relative costs
Method of accounting for order filling and money collecting
Method of analyzing earnings by towns
Relation of marketing costs to selling prices.

Groves, A. E., "The Cost of Distribution," *N.A.C.A. Bulletin*, Vol. VII, No. 3 (October 1, 1925), pp. 69-81.
Classification of accounts—manufacturing and distribution.

Knapp, C. Howard (Vice President and Controller, Waitt & Bond, Inc.), "Problems in the Development of Standards for a Small Business Selling to Consumers," *N.A.C.A. Yearbook* (1933), pp. 292-311.
Interesting discussion of classification of accounts based upon a classification used by Association of National Advertisers in a questionnaire circulated among its members.

Lowles, D. C. (Auditor, Perfection Stove Company), "Setting Up Records to Fit the Sales and General Departments," *N.A.C.A. Yearbook* (1929), pp. 102-118.
Good explanation and illustrations of records:
County card (statistical information)
Prospect record
Inventory record
Shipments records
Record of unfilled orders
Territorial sales quota and bonus record (by salesmen)
Salesman's record of sales
Remittance register
Cash disbursements record
District sales and operating expense report
Operating or trading report

Riddle, Lester P. (Supervisor of Tabulating, R. G. Le Tourneau, Inc.), "Analytical and Accounting Control of Sales and Gross Profit by Punched Cards," *N.A.C.A. Bulletin*, Vol. XXIX, No. 6 (November 15, 1947), pp. 323-334.
An answer to the question of how some of the information required for distribution costing can be obtained and summarized. A semitechnical discussion requiring some knowledge of machine tabulating.

Rose, Albert A. (Sales Cost Accountant, Beech-Nut Packing Co.), "New Technique in Selling and Administrative Cost Accounting," *N.A.C.A. Bulletin*, Vol. X, No. 3 (October 3, 1928), pp. 107-124.
Distribution of actual selling and administrative costs to territories and products. Reports to management.

Rosseter, Lewis E. (Staff Member, Price, Waterhouse & Co.), "Unit Functional Analysis of Distribution," *N.A.C.A. Bulletin*, Vol. XXII, No. 10 (January 15, 1941), pp. 533-556.

> Good discussion of theory. Illustrative Problem: distribution to (a) territories, (b) products within territories.

Waymire, J. O. (Distribution Cost Accountant, Eli Lilly Company), "Distribution Costs," *N.A.C.A. Yearbook* (1939), pp. 317-333.

> Distribution of costs to product groups and territories.

Analysis of Distribution Costs by Organization and Operating Divisions

Everleigh, C. F., and J. O. Wagmire (Eli Lilly Company), "Distribution Cost Accounting," *N.A.C.A. Bulletin*, Vol. XIII, No. 1 (September 1, 1931), pp. 1-15.

> Distribution to product class on basis of item frequency.

Gidney, Col. H. A. (Controller, Gulf Oil Corporation of Pennsylvania), "What Items Should Be Included in Selling and Distribution Costs and Should All Such Items Be Allocated to Lines or Products Sold?" *N.A.C.A. Yearbook* (1930), pp. 50-56.

Greer, Howard C. (General Manager, Kingan & Co., meat packers), "Distribution Cost Analysis—Methods and Examples," *N.A.C.A. Bulletin*, Vol. XI, No. 19 (June 1, 1930), pp. 1305-1320.

> The approach to distribution cost analysis. Examples:
> (1) Analysis of distribution expenses by territories
> (2) Analysis of distribution expense by customer according to order and account size.
> (3) Analysis of distribution expenses by commodities
> (4) Analysis of distribution expenses by types of order.
> Distribution to product classes on basis of item frequency.

Johnson, O'Neal M. (in charge of the Statistical and Accounting Bureau, International Association of Ice Cream Manufacturers), "Distribution Costs in the Ice Cream Industry," *N.A.C.A. Yearbook* (1937), pp. 203-221.

> Actual case. Distribution of costs to salesmen—drivers routes.

Kleinhaus, H. I. (General Manager, Controllers Congress, National Retail Dry Goods Association), "Uniform Accounting Procedure As an Aid in Reducing Retail Operating Costs," *N.A.C.A. Bulletin*, Vol. XIX, No. 9 (January 1, 1938), pp. 519-533.

> Development of a uniform method of accounting by the Controllers Congress. Classification of expenses. Direct application to departments followed as far as possible. The "contribution" of a sales department to the total store's undistributed expense and profit.

Knapp, C. Howard (Vice President, Waitt and Bond, Inc.), "When Should Consideration Be Given to Selling and Distribution Costs for Different Sizes or Order?" *N.A.C.A. Yearbook* (1930), pp. 90-94.

———, "Allocation of Selling and Administrative Costs to the Article of Sale," *N.A.C.A. Bulletin*, Vol. XII, No. 4 (October 15, 1930), pp. 289-304.

> Distribution of costs to product classes (cigars).

———, "How to Determine Costs on Pre-Determined Sales Forecasts," *N.A.C.A. Bulletin*, Vol. XIV, No. 12 (February 15, 1933), pp. 901-930.

> Distribution of costs to product classes (cigars).

Magor, D. M. (Controller, York Ice Machinery Corporation), "Distributor Accounting Procedure for Planned Profit Control," *N.A.C.A. Bulletin*, Vol. XXI, No. 10 (January 15, 1940), pp. 621-636.

Description of an excellent system developed by York Ice Machinery Corporation for its distributors. Forms illustrated. Classification of expenses into variable and fixed groups. Budgeting. Determining the breakeven point.

McNiece, Thomas M. (Market Analyst), "Under What Circumstances Should Selling and Distribution Costs Be Allocated to Specific Lines or Products and on What Basis?" *N.A.C.A. Yearbook* (1930), pp. 57-67.

Regnes, L. G. (Controller, Briggs and Stratton Corporation), "When Is It Necessary to Apportion Selling and Distribution Cost to Different Classes of Customers and How Should That Be Done?" *N.A.C.A. Yearbook* (1930), pp. 85-90.

Titus, Walter F. (Vice President in Charge of Manufacturing, International Business Machines Co.), "Analysis of Selling and Distributing Costs," *N.A.C.A. Yearbook* (1937), pp. 222-228.

Distribution Costs and Pricing Policy

Freeman, E. S. (Chief Statistician, Dennison Manufacturing Co.), "Distribution Cost Analysis and Its Influence on Pricing Policy," *N.A.C.A. Bulletin*, Vol. XV, No. 1 (September 1, 1933), pp. 3-37.

The construction of costs intended to be used as a factor in selling price policy. Computing the cost by products. Price-cost relation as guide to policy. What calls are worth making. What products are worth selling. When to refuse an order. Staple products vs. specialty products.

Greer, Howard C. (Vice President, Kingan & Co., meat packers), "Distribution Costs as Factors in Pricing Policy," *N.A.C.A. Bulletin*, Vol. XVIX, No. 15 (November 1, 1937), pp. 263-280.

Sawyer, Albert E. (Market Research Staff, Dennison Manufacturing Co.), "Cost Accounting as Evidence in Cases Arising under the Robinson-Patman Act," *N.A.C.A. Bulletin*, Vol. XIX, No. 2 (February 15, 1938), pp. 681-696.

Taggart, Herbert F. (Professor of Accounting, University of Michigan), "The Standard Brands Case," *N.A.C.A. Bulletin*, Vol. XXI, No. 4 (October 15, 1939), pp. 195-262.

INDEX

INDEX

A

Account classification (*See* Classification of accounts)

Account manual for allocating expense, 102

Account numbers, means of setting up four-place numbers, 280

Accounts (*only selected separate accounts are indexed*):
  account manual, 102
  Administrative Expense, 27
  allocation, classification for, 209-10
  book inventory method for expense, 34-6
  Change of Standards Variance, 487
  classification of, for small manufacturer, 25
  control (*See* Control accounts)
  Cost of Goods Sold, 25
  Direct Labor, 25
  Expense account numbers, 21
  Factory Expense, 25, 57
  factory expense account classification, 177
  Factory Expense Applied, 198-200
  Finished Goods, 25, 244
  flexible budget departmental expense, 461-2
  for estimate costs, 379
  for maintenance supplies and repair parts, 102
  for process costs, 319
    by-product method, 358
    joint-product method, 361-2
  job order cost system accounts, 72-3
  Materials Inventory, 24
  physical inventory method for expense, 31-3
  Purchases of Materials, 25
  Selling and Shipping Expense, 27
  Spoiled Work, 106
  Work in Process, 24, 106

Accounts payable:
  use of voucher to eliminate ledger, 48
  voucher, 74

Accounts receivable, use of cash forecast in preparing, 607, 611

Actual basis for applying factory expense, 189-91

Actual factory expense, 180

Administrative Expense account, 27

Administrative and selling payroll, 145

Allocation:
  classification of accounts for, 209-10
  definition, 208
  direct labor cost rate, 212-3
  direct labor hour rate, 211-2
  factory expense, 187-200
  factory expense centers, 215-21
  factory expense to products, 208-21
  machine rate, 215-21
  primary processes as bases for, 363
  prime cost rate, 213-5
  product unit rate, 211

Allocation and control figures, differences between, 670, 675

Alternative choice problems:
  direct costing and, 641
  dropping items that show perennial losses, 655
  examples, 652
  goods processed in different degrees, 657-8
  make or buy parts, 658-9
  marginal product costs, 652
  pricing below total expenses, 652, 654
  product policy when capacity is limited, 656
  special orders of regular product, 655-6
  sunk fixed costs in pricing, 655-6
  variable expense as a base for pricing, 653-4
  variable order sizes of custom goods, 656-7

Assembly cost, 14

Attendance time card, 131-2

Attendance time card postings, 136-7

B

Balance sheet:
  description, 27-8
  preparation from trial balance, **37**

Betterment orders, 20

Bid orders, 234-5

Bill of lading, 75

Process costs, by-product method (*Cont.*)
statement of gross profits, 358
transfer entries, 359
accounts for, 361-2, 365
accounts illustrated:
no inventories, 364-5
with inventories, 369-70
allocation bases, primary processing, 363
cost of goods sold, with inventories, 368
description, 361
gross profits statement:
no inventories, 361
with inventories, 363
inventory and cost statistics, with inventory, 366
journal entries and accounts:
no inventories, 362
with inventories, 365
process cost worksheet, 371
scrap credits, 367
Producing departments, 274
Product:
cost formula, 4-5
unit cost, 5
Product engineering and cost accounting, 110-1
Product lines, profit statements by, 670-5, 716
Production control and cost accounting, 110-1
Production orders, 21
Profits:
comparative statements by different pricing methods, 118
effect of materials pricing method on, 115-6
statements by various pricing methods, 118
Profits statement, 27, 29
Purchase invoices:
in standard costs, 420
materials price variance report, use in preparing, 488
Purchase order form, 73, 75
Purchase requisition form, 73, 74
Purchased services expense, 176
Purchases of Materials account, 25

Q

Quantity control:
definition, 109
finished goods, 229
forms, job order cost system, 109
multiple-stage process costing, 321
need for in process cost system, 312
piece-rate wage payment plan, 169
process cost system, 311-2
protection points, 110
single-stage process costing, 311-2
spoilage, 106

Questions, 11-2, 21, 39-41, 62, 91-2, 121-3, 148-9, 173-4, 201-2, 222, 254-5, 299-300, 330, 349, 372, 393, 421, 442-3, 475, 503, 521, 526, 552, 581-2, 602, 620, 645, 665, 690-1, 716, 737

R

Raw materials inventory account, 39
Realization factor, 569
Receiving record form, 74
Receiving report form, 75
Repair labor time, 165
Repair orders, 20-1
Replacement prices for materials, 114-5
Reports:
actual factory expense rates on a seasonal basis, 192
balance sheet, 28
cost of goods completed, 231
cost of goods manufactured and sold, 29
cost of goods sold, 230
cost of pig iron produced, single-stage process costing, 309-11
cost and profit on custom orders, 235, 236
expected cumulative under- and over-applied factory expense, 200
factory expense and factory expense applied, 199
factory expense rate by level of production, 193
factory expense statement, 179
gross profit by product class, 235, 237
labor report, weekly, 165
profits statement, 29
sales and inventory position, 237-8
unit costs on production orders, 233
Requisition journal:
factory expense, use in establishing, 182
materials, use in accounting for, 80, 83
Requisitions:
bills of materials in lieu of, 75
definition of, 75
in cost accounting cycle, 55-6
form for, 82
pricing of, 82-3
pricing of, forms for, 113
purchase, 73-5

S

Sales:
invoice, 240
profitable products vs. others, 235, 238
Sales journal:
description of, 52, 54
goods sold, use of, in recording, 246

Voucher (*Cont.*)
  purpose of, 46-7
  system, 46-51
    entries for, 49
  uses of copies, 48
Voucher register:
  description of, 49-51
  distribution cost, use in finding, 543, 545
  expense account procedure, use of in, 280, 282
  factory expense, use in establishing, 180-2
  function of, 46
  labor, use of in accounting for, 142
  larger manufacturing business, 280-1
  materials, use in accounting for, 76

W

Waiting time, 161, 165, 433
Waste, 72, 104, 106-7
Weighted average price, 112, 114
Work, measured and unmeasured, 521
Work orders, 20-1
Work in Process account, 24, 106
Work in Process Control account, 55, 60
Work in Process Inventory account, 39
Work in Process ledger, 55
Work loading, office and clerical, 517-9, 523-6
Workmen's insurance entry, 163